WHAT
THE
BIBLE
TEACHES

Contributors

JACK HUNTER
Jack Hunter is a native of Scotland, who for many years served the Lord extensively in Great Britain, while engaged in secular employment. Since 1970 he has devoted himself to full-time public service with the widening of his field of service to include U.S.A. and Canada.

ALBERT LECKIE
Albert Leckie was born in Airdrie, Scotland. Since he was a young man he has devoted his life to serving the Lord. He conducts a number of series of Bible Readings throughout Great Britain and has visited various continents in the ministry of the Word.

SYDNEY MAXWELL
Although born in Ulster, Sydney Maxwell's service took him to the Prairies of Canada. He is a member of the editorial board of the magazine Truth and Tidings, in which he answers Bible questions month by month. He is now resident in Vancouver.

THOMAS BENTLEY
Although born in Belfast, Thomas Bentley's field of service has been Malaysia for the last twenty seven years. He has travelled extensively preaching the gospel and teaching the Word of God.

ALBERT McSHANE
Albert McShane, a native of Northern Ireland, has been in full-time service since 1944. He has been associated closely with the Lurgan Bible Readings for several years and has ministered the Word in Canada, U.S.A., Australia and New Zealand. His published ministry includes commentaries on James and 1 Samuel.

WHAT THE BIBLE TEACHES

with
Authorised Version
of
The Bible

IN NINE VOLUMES
COVERING THE NEW TESTAMENT

VOLUME 1

JOHN RITCHIE LTD
KILMARNOCK, SCOTLAND

ISBN-13: 978 1 904064 38 1
ISBN-10: 1 904064 38 8

WHAT THE BIBLE TEACHES
Copyright © 2000 by John Ritchie Ltd.
40 Beansburn, Kilmarnock, Scotland

www.ritchiechristianmedia.co.uk

Re-typeset and printed 2007

Typeset at John Ritchie Ltd., 40 Beansburn, Kilmarnock.
Printed by Bell and Bain, Glasgow.

CONTENTS

ABBREVIATIONS

AV	Authorised Version of King James Version 1611
JND	New Translation by J.N. Darby 1939
LXX	Septuagint Version of Old Testament
Mft	New Translation by James Moffat 1922
NASB	New American Standard Bible 1960
NEB	New English Bible 1961
Nestle	Nestle (ed.) Novum Testamentum Graece
NIV	New International Version 1973
NT	New Testament
OT	Old Testament
Phps	New Testament in Modern English by J.B. Philips 1962
RSV	Revised Standard Version 1952
RV	Revised Version 1881
TR	Textus Receptus or Received Text
Wey	New Testament in Modern Speech by R.E. Weymouth 1929

PREFACE

They follow the noblest example who seek to open the Scriptures to others, for our Lord Himself did so for those two dejected disciples of Emmaus (Luke 24:32). Whether it is the evangelist "opening and alleging that Christ must needs have suffered and risen from the dead" (Acts 17:3) or the pastor-teacher "expounding ... in all the scriptures the things concerning himself" (Luke 24:27) or stimulating our hope "through the patience and comfort of the scriptures" (Rom 15:4), he serves well in thus giving attendance to the reading of the Scriptures (1 Tim 4:13).

It is of course of equal moment to recognise in the exercise of able men, the continued faithfulness of the risen Head in giving gifts to the Church, in spite of her unfaithfulness. How good to recognise that "the perfecting of the saints ... the work of the ministry...the edifying of the body of Christ" need not be neglected. Every provision has been made to ensure the well-being of the people of God. And every opportunity should be taken by the minister of Christ and those to whom he ministers to ensure that the saints "grow up into him in all things which is the head, even Christ" (Eph 4:15).

At various times in the post-apostolic period, certain teachers have come to prominence, sometimes because they succumbed to error, sometimes because in faithfulness they paid the ultimate price for the truth they had bought and would not sell. Some generations had Calvin and Luther, others Darby and Kelly, but in every generation God's voice is heard. It is important that we hear His voice today and recognise that He does speak through His servants. The contributors to this series of commentaries are all highly-respected expositors among the churches of God. They labour in the Word in the English-speaking world and have been of blessing to many throughout their years of service.

The doctrinal standpoint of the commentaries is based upon the acceptance of the verbal and plenary inspiration of the Scriptures so that their inerrant and infallible teachings are the only rule of conscience. The impeccability of Christ, His virgin birth, vicarious death and bodily resurrection are indeed precious truths worthy of the Christian's defence, and throughout the volumes of this series will be defended. Equally the Rapture will be presented as the hope of the Church. Before the great Tribulation she will be raptured and God's prophetic programme will continue with Jacob's trouble, the public manifestation of Christ and the Millennium of blessing to a restored Israel and the innumerable Gentile multitude in a creation released from the bondage of corruption.

May the sound teaching of these commentaries be used by our God to the blessing of His people. May the searching of the Scriptures characterise all who read them.

The diligence of Mr. K. Stapley in proof-reading and his valuable comments on the authors' MSS are gratefully acknowledged. Without such co-operation, the production of this commentary would not have been expedited so readily.

T. WILSON

GALATIANS
J. Hunter

GALATIANS
Introduction

1. **Authorship**
2. **Churches of Galatia**
3. **Date of Writing**
4. **Purpose of Writing**
5. **Bibliography**
6. **Outline**

1. Authorship

Paul is stated in 1:1 to be the author and 5:2 mentions his name again. No case of any real merit has been brought forward to the contrary and few books of Paul have been so unquestionably accepted as genuine. Many of the Early Fathers make mention of it and quote it. Furthermore the historical data and personal history of chapters 1 and 2 authenticate its Pauline authorship.

2. The Churches of Galatia

Long and protracted arguments have been put forward as to their identity and probably we shall never know with certainty. Two suggestions have been made as to these people, one based on the geographical/racial use of the word Galatia, the other on its political usage to describe the Roman province including Southern Galatia.

1. The Northern Galatian Theory

Those who propound this theory believe that Paul was writing to the Gauls who inhabited the northern plateau known as Galatia and that reference to Paul's work among them is mentioned in Acts 16:6; 18:23. This was the view of the early Church and is vigorously set forth by J.B. Lightfoot in his commentary. Hoary with tradition, it allowed for the two visits to Galatia recorded in the Acts and implied in the epistle (see 4:13). The known fickleness of the Gauls seemed to be seen in their change of attitude to Paul (see 4:16). The towns where the churches were established were reckoned to be *Pessinus, Ancyra, Tavium,* leading cities in Northern Galatia or Galatia proper.

2. The Southern Galatian Theory

This theory was first propounded in Europe toward the close of the 18th century but has been made popular in the English speaking world by W.M.

Ramsay in his commentary on Galatians and other works. He demonstrated that the Province of Galatia extended southward to include the towns of Antioch (in Pisidia), Iconium, Lystra and Derbe. He argues that there is no record of churches in the North but we do have of churches in the South. Certainly it would seem strange that Luke should tell us so much about the churches in the South (Acts 13 and 14) and that Paul should never mention them.

However, the identity of the Galatians does not affect the teaching of the epistle. Whoever these people were, they were in grave danger through the presence and influence of false teachers preaching another gospel.

3. Date of Writing

The date of the Epistle has been the subject of much controversy, and no doubt many saints will feel that the time of writing is unimportant, and what really matters is the teaching. However the following viewpoints may be noted:-

1. Those who accept the North Galatian Theory must place the date *after* the events recorded in Acts 18:23, and so Lightfoot suggests it was written around AD 57 or 58.

2. Those who hold to the South Galatian Theory obviously see it as written much earlier. Here again there are differences of opinion depending on the identification of Paul's visit to Jerusalem mentioned in Gal 2:1-10 (as will be discussed later). Those who connect the visit of Gal 2 with the famine-relief visit of Acts 11:30 maintain it was written *before* the Jerusalem council of Acts 15 and suggest AD 48 or 49.

3. Those who see the visit to Jerusalem in Gal 2 to be the same as that of Acts 15 place the date *after* the council. Again opinions differ, some holding it was written during the second missionary journey around AD 52; others maintain it was probably during the third missionary journey, thus making the date around AD 55 or 56.

We must now give ourselves to a consideration of the visits made by Paul to Jerusalem. The problem is as follows. Luke in Acts reports three visits by Paul. (1) Acts 9:26-29; (2) Acts 11:30-12:25; (3) Acts 15:1-29. However, in Galatians Paul mentioned only two visits (see 1:18-2:1).

There is little doubt that Acts 9:26-29 and Gal 1:18 refer to the same occasion. The question now arises: does Paul's *second* visit in Galatians equate with the one in Acts 11 or 15? Is it the same as the famine-relief visit of Acts 11 or the meeting with the council in Acts 15? As so many scholars and commentators have differed radically it does not become one to be dogmatic.

Thesis 1:
Galatians 2 is same as Acts 11

Those who maintain the above connection maintain it is the most straightforward and natural way to look at the incidents, removing any suggestion of Paul omitting to mention his going to Jerusalem on the famine visit when he outlines his movements in Galatians.

It is pointed out that if the council took place before Galatians was written all Paul needed to do was to refer them to the decrees which had been publicised. It is also noted that Galatians indicates a private meeting whereas Acts points to a *public* meeting. Likewise attention is drawn to the fact that Titus is mentioned in Galatians but not in the Acts account, emphasising that the word "again" in Gal 2:1 means "the second time" and must refer to the famine visit. The omission could have played into the hands of his enemies, who could have charged him with misrepresenting the facts. If he had been more often in Jerusalem than he had stated then his contact with Jerusalem was more than he was willing to admit.

Thesis 2:
Galatians 2 is same as Acts 15

As indicated earlier the difference of judgment among eminent scholars points to the fact that one cannot be dogmatic, but the writer feels that the weight of evidence lies with this identification. Lightfoot in his commentary indicates from the geography, the timing, the persons involved, the subject of dispute, the character and results confirmed that there is no correspondence between Galatians 2 and the famine visit of Acts 11.

Going back to the points raised in the previous thesis (to the identification of Gal 2 and Acts 11) let us now deal briefly with them.

Paul does not mention the famine visit because it had nothing to do with the point at issue. It was a mission of mercy, there being nothing in the references (Acts 11:30; 12:25) to indicate that it had in view anything other than handing over the collection to the elders. Note too there is no mention of the apostles. Being a time of persecution, James having been murdered, Peter having been imprisoned; maybe the rest of the Twelve were keeping a low profile.

Paul had given the Galatians the decrees issued at Jerusalem (see Acts 16:4,6), but obviously the false teachers have so undermined Paul's authority that they had lost confidence in him. These teachers, claiming to have come from headquarters (Jerusalem) and obviously representing an element in the church that rebelled against the decree, were able to sway the Galatian converts.

Gal 2:2 would seem to allow for both a public meeting (2a) and a private meeting (2b).

It is true that Titus is not mentioned by name in Acts 15, but it would seem the expression in Acts 15:2, "and certain other of them" would make room for him as well as others.

Scholars observe that the word "again" (*palin*) is the usual word so translated and is more indefinite than the word translated "second" in the NT.

Note also that Gal 2:2 indicates Paul made known to the apostles the gospel he preached to the Gentiles, and his work was confirmed by them (see vv.7-10). This he could not have done during the famine visit of Acts 11 before his first missionary journey.

A number of other matters should now be noted that identify Gal 2 and Acts 15:

1. *Circumcision*: See Acts 15:1 and Gal 2:3;
2. *Speakers*: Paul, Barnabas, Peter and James being mentioned in each account;
3. *Declaration*: How God had worked among the Gentiles (Acts 15:12; Gal 2:2,8,9);
4. *Agreement*: See Acts 15:22; Gal 2:9, noting too the agreement of Peter (Acts 15:10) and James (Acts 15:19)
5. *Special Pleading*: Judaizers in each case contending for circumcision; see Acts 15:5; Gal 2:4-5.

Finally as to chronology, if the famine visit of Acts 11 is the same as recorded in Gal 2, it must have taken place around the time of the death of Herod Agrippa I (AD 44). If this was 14 years after Paul's conversion (Gal 2:1), that places his conversion in AD 30, during the life of the Lord. Obviously this cannot be. It should be noted that many believe the 14 years should be added to the 3 years of Gal 1:18, making 17 years in all. Some however say Herod's death was not until AD 46, and using the old inclusive reckoning would make Paul's conversion AD 33. This very neat reckoning is based on the assumption that the 14 years are dated from Paul's conversion, but is ruled out entirely if the 14 years are additional to the 3 years of Gal 1:18.

4. Purpose of Writing

As the gospel began to be preached in Gentile territory and Gentiles began to profess faith in the Lord Jesus, so the problems began to increase. These problems were raised by Jews. What was the relationship of the Gentiles to the Law of Moses? Were they to be allowed to ignore it completely? Had it not a place seeing it was of divine origin? And what about the rite of circumcision? If the Gentiles were to be among the people of the Covenant (as they would say) should they not carry in their bodies the mark and seal of the covenant?

Wider issues arose from such questions: was the Church only to be an extension of Judaism? If salvation was for all, was faith in Christ sufficient? Were law-works needed to complete justification? And what about table fellowship? Could Jew and Gentile eat together and eat the same food?

Clearly Paul had preached a pure gospel. Law-keeping did not enter into it: salvation was in Christ alone. The Law condemned but on the cross Christ had borne its curse.

Then word came through that the Galatians were turning back to the Law. False teachers had come from Jerusalem, claiming to be from James and having his support. They proclaimed that faith in Christ was insufficient, that the converts must be circumcised and keep the Law and that Paul's doctrine of the gospel was wrong.

Paul was deeply moved. The teaching destroyed the foundations of the gospel. Christianity would finish as a sect of Judaism, an extension of the Jews' religion.

The attack on Paul was threefold:

1. They attacked Paul's claim to be an apostle. If they could undermine his authority they could destroy his teaching. He was not one of the original Twelve called and sent forth by Christ: he was apart from them. Well-meaning in his preaching, nevertheless he was on his own. All must look to Jerusalem and the Twelve for the true gospel. Paul answers this challenge in chapters 1 and 2.

2. The gospel preached by Paul was good but insufficient. It did not go far enough for it left out the Law and no-one ever knew God among His people without observing it. Christ had honoured it, and the apostles too. Who was Paul to set all this aside? Paul answers such teaching in chapters 3 and 4.

3. Not only so, but the Law was necessary for good living. Its precepts were to help all to live a good life. Life for God without Law must inevitably lead to lawlessness and immorality and every kind of excess. Paul answers these arguments in chapters 5 and 6 as he sets before them a Spirit-filled life.

It is important to note that although the Galatian problem was a first-century problem, the emphasis of modern charismatic teaching on Christ-plus-experience has the same root.

5. Bibliography

Cole, R.A. *Galatians*. London: T.N.T.C., 1965.
Hendriksen, W. *Galatians*. London: Banner of Truth Trust, 1968.
Hogg and Vine. *The Epistle to the Galatians*. London: Pickering and Inglis.
Kelly, W. *Lectures on Galatians*. London: Morrish.
Lightfoot, J.B. *Galatians*. London: Macmillan and Co., 1880.
Ridderbos, H.N. *The Epistle of Paul to the Churches of Galatia (N.I.C.N.T.)*. Grand Rapids, 1953.
Stott, J.R.W. *The Message of Galatians*. London: Inter-Varsity Press, 1968.
Trew, W. *Galatians*. Precious Seed Publications.
Vine W.E. *Expository Dictionary of New Testament Words*. London: Oliphant, 1940.
Wuest, K.S. *Galatians in the Greek New Testament*. Grand Rapids: W.B. Eerdmans Publishing Company, 1944.
Ritchie, J. *Notes on Galatians*. John Ritchie: Kilmarnock.

6. Outline

Chapters 1 and 2 - Historical

The Origins of the Gospel

I. *The Authority of Paul*	1:1-5
1. The Declaration of Apostleship	1:1-2
2. The Death of Christ	1:3-5
II. *The Amazement of Paul*	1:6-10
1. Defection of the Galatians	1:6
2. Perverters of the Gospel	1:7
3. Protest of Paul	1:8-10
III. *The Defence of Paul*	1:11-24
1. Preaching by Revelation	1:11-12
2. Before Conversion	1:13-14
3. At Conversion	1:15-16
4. After Conversion	1:17-24
IV. *The Same Gospel*	2:1-10
1. Movement by Revelation	2:1-2
2. Titus and Circumcision	2:3-5
3. Fellowship Established	2:6-10
V. *Paul and Peter in Conflict*	2:11-21
1. The Incident at Antioch	2:11-14
2. Teaching Arising from Incident	2:15-21

Chapters 3 and 4 - Doctrinal

The Vindication of the Gospel

I. *Law or Faith*	3:1-14
1. The Experience of the Galatians	3:15
2. The Experience of Abraham	3:6-9
3. Curse and Blessing	3:10-14
II. *Law and Promise*	3:15-22
1. Priority of the Promise	3:15-18
2. Purpose of the Law	3:19-22
III. *Sons of God*	3:23-29
1. Condition under Law	3:23-25
2. Blessings in Christ	3:26-29
IV. *Heirs of God*	4:1-11
1. Slaves to Sons	4:1-7
2. Paul's Passionate Plea	4:8-11

Chapters 5 and 6 - Practical

The Power of the Gospel

Text and Exposition

CHAPTERS 1 AND 2 - HISTORICAL
THE ORIGINS OF THE GOSPEL

1. The Authority of Paul (1:1-5)

1. *The Declaration of Apostleship*
   1:1-2

> v.1 "Paul, an apostle, (not of men, neither by man, but by Jesus Christ, and God
> the Father, who raised him from the dead;)
> v.2 And all the brethren which are with me, unto the churches of Galatia:"

It is interesting to observe what is absent and present in these first five verses. There is no "I thank my God for you" or "praying always for you" nor is there praise for these churches, for Paul's heart is heavy. He does stress matters that will be prominent in the epistle; his own authority as an apostle and the basis of the gospel - the substitutionary death of the Lord Jesus to rescue us, and all according to the will of God the Father. No place here for law-keeping or circumcision! He is anxious to get to the very heart of the matter, and deal with the problems that were taking them away from the true gospel.

1   Paul immediately states he is an apostle, but does not follow it with, "by the will of God" (as in 1 Cor, 2 Cor, Eph, Col, 2 Tim) but states that it is not *from* men as to its *source*, nor *by* man as to its *agency*. He was not appointed by a body of *men*, nor did a particular *man* commission him as their representative. His apostleship came directly from divine Persons, Jesus Christ and God the Father. He thus lifts the whole matter Completely outside the realm of human appointment and agency. If the Twelve had been commissioned by the Lord Jesus on earth, the same Person had commissioned him from heaven. No doubt his opponents would be asserting that he did not know the Lord Jesus here on earth, had never seen Him, and so was never sent by Him. He did not fulfil the qualifications set forth in Acts 1:21-22. In stating his apostleship in this way the question of his *authority* is settled. There is a *uniqueness* attached to the Twelve and Paul when the word "apostle" is applied to them. They formed a *unique* company, and had no successors. To obey apostolic teaching is to be in the true apostolic succession. By uniting Jesus Christ with God the Father Paul indicates that they are one in their appointment of him as their representative. To reject him as an apostle was to reject the Father and the Son who commissioned him. The mention of the Resurrection of Christ is to establish that it was as the Risen One that Christ sent him and that it was serious to be found opposing the one who so honoured Christ. Thus Paul declares that he is independent of the original Twelve and everybody else.

It is essential to note again the *unique* authority vested in the apostles. It has not been passed on to others. There is no scriptural authority for a body of men to "ordain" other men; nor is there room for the teaching of the Roman Catholic Church that the church alone has the authority to interpret Scripture; nor is there place for the modernist who, denying inspiration, would substitute his own interpretation. We must bow completely to the authority of the apostles.

2   Since we are not told who the brethren are who are with Paul, it is fruitless to hazard a guess. Usually Paul would name them, but here would mention them to show that he was not alone in his stand for the gospel. It is as well to note here that these others are *brethren* and stand in contrast to him as an *apostle*. All Christians are *brethren*; only a few were apostles.

Mention of the *churches* of Galatia indicates the fruit of the gospel, leading to the setting up of local churches as the unit of testimony in each locality to bear witness to Christ. Paul does not write to the *church* of Galatia but to the *churches* thus recognising the autonomy of each such church. Note too that nothing is added to commend them. Paul is restrained because of the seriousness of conditions among them: the denial of the true gospel, the setting aside of his authority as an apostle, the turning again to the weak and beggarly elements. Their doctrinal error, or their being influenced by such, weighed heavily upon his heart.

2.   *The Death of Christ*
    1:3-5

> v.3   "Grace be to you and peace from God the Father, and from our Lord Jesus Christ,
> v.4   Who gave himself for our sins, that he might deliver us from this present evil world, according to the will of God and our Father:
> v.5   To whom be glory for ever and ever. Amen."

3   Two words in these early verses are stressed: firstly *"apostle"* and then *"grace"*. Paul would desire that they should continue to enjoy the grace and peace that had come to them, but grace tells them that the source of their salvation is God's favour and undeserved kindness. Grace indicates what God has done, thereby eliminating anything that men can do. This struck at the foundation of the new teaching. It was from this grace they were in danger of falling. Peace was the result: peace with God, knowing the blessedness of being reconciled to Him, all sins forgiven, and going on to enjoy the peace of God. Such a blessing could never come through law-keeping. Note here as in v.1 that the Lord Jesus is mentioned along with God the Father, thus indicating His Deity. It draws attention to the oneness, equality, unity, distinctiveness of His Personality. Inspired writers would never confound the Persons nor divide the essence.

4   Paul now makes known the very heart of the gospel. "Who gave himself" - the *Fact*: "for our sins" - the *Reason*: "deliver us from this present evil age" - the *Purpose*: "according to the will of our God and Father" - the *Testimony*. Again, "who gave himself" - *History*: "for our sins" - *Doctrine*: "deliver us from this present evil age" - *Revelation*: "the will of our God and Father" - *Eternal Counsel*.

Ponder such words. "He gave himself" - in all the greatness of His Person, in all the dignity of His excellence, in all the majesty of His worth, in all the glory of His power. And it was for our sins; He offered Himself in a vicarious and sacrificial sense, bearing the judgment due to them, standing there as our Substitute. If this is so, there is no need for it to be supplemented by law-keeping of any kind. If He died for our sins, God is satisfied. It is erroneous to try to add to it. The objective was to deliver us, to rescue us out of this present evil world. W.E. Vine in his Expository Dictionary draws attention to the fact that the verb "deliver" is in the middle voice, indicating the interest of the one who does so, telling of the delight and pleasure of God in our deliverance.

We are delivered from this present evil *age* (not world): God's objective was not to take us out of this world, but to leave us here to live for Him. No doubt one day He will remove us completely at the Rapture. There is the possibility that the "present evil age" is in contrast with "the age to come". The "Present evil age" indicates the world as an evil System controlled by the Evil One, Satan, with its many corrupting principles and practices. God has rescued us out of it that we might be free to serve Him. We therefore are looked upon as clear not only Of its moral and political corruption, but also of its religious corruption so evident in Galatia.

All this is in harmony with the will of our God and Father. How one loves the *possessive* character of *our*. He is *ours* (how wonderful!) because He has made us His. Salvation in its fulness is traced back to the divine will, not to our will. Note too how the Father and Son are both involved in this great work. To reject the work of the Son is to reject the will of the Father.

5   Paul now bursts into praise, lost in wonder, magnifying the God who has done so great a work. Let this glory go on for ever, unto the ages of ages. Let us too bow in worship and add our Amen - so let it be.

Notes

1 Paul's accurate use of prepositions has often been noticed. *OF (apo)* means *from* and has reference to *source*. *BY (dia)* denotes *agency*. Lightfoot comments: "The first preposition denotes the fountain-head whence the apostle's authority springs, the second the channel through which it is conveyed. Thus in the first clause he distinguishes himself from the false apostles, who did not derive their commission from God at all; in the second he ranks himself with the Twelve, who were commissioned directly from God".

3 Note the order of divine Persons is different here from v.1. it may be that the Lord Jesus is put first in v.1 because He commissioned Paul, whereas in v.3, although both Persons are looked upon as the Source of grace and peace, it would be normal for God the Father to be put first. Also as he is going on to speak of the work of the Lord Jesus, He being put second connects Him with that work.

4 On this verse William Trew comments: "That which gives character to this present age, stamping it emphatically as 'evil', is the cross of Christ - the murder by men of God's Son - tremendous emphasis is laid upon the cross of Christ, rather than upon the death of Christ. 'The cross' would focus our thought upon the *manner* of His death rather than upon the fact of it. It was not only that He died, but He died upon the cross, the expression of man's awful hatred not only of Christ and of God, but also of all who are Christ's".

Trench defines "age" (*aiōn*) as follows: "All that floating mass of thoughts, opinions, maxims, speculations, hopes, impulses, aims, aspirations. At any time current in the world, which it may be impossible to seize and accurately define, but which constitutes a most real and effective power, being the moral or immoral atmosphere which at every moment of our lives we inhale, again inevitably to exhale".

Note that Paul speaks of it in Eph 2:2 as "the course of this world". That kind of world stands in contrast to "the age to come" when Christ will be supreme and "man's day" will be over.

II. The Amazement of Paul (1:6-10)

1. *Defection of the Galatians*
   1:6

> v.6 "I marvel that ye are so soon removed from him that called you into the grace of Christ unto another gospel:"

Reference to the opening of other epistles shows that at this point Paul would thank God for the saints, then pray for them, for he did appreciate the grace of God bestowed upon them, but here all this is absent. We find not thankfulness and prayer, but amazement, warning and a pronouncement of judgment upon those who would endeavour to change the gospel and pollute the pure stream of grace. Note how central Christ is to Paul's gospel. He speaks of the grace of Christ, the gospel of Christ, and himself as the servant of Christ.

6 Paul is amazed that they have so quickly and rashly changed their position. W.E. Vine in his treatment of the word "removed" (*metatithēmi*) in his Dictionary observes: "the present tense suggests that the defection of the Galatians from the truth was not yet complete and would continue unless they changed their views. The middle voice indicates that they were themselves responsible for their declension, rather than the Judaizers who had influenced them". Paul however has not given them up. There was still hope that they would be recovered (see 5:10). The seriousness of the movement was that it was away from God, from "him who called you". To give up the pure gospel was to give up God. The call of God in grace pointed them to Christ, and they were the objects of the grace of Christ for grace here is associated with Christ as well as God. Note again the stress on grace. Everything comes to us because of the generosity and love of God, apart from human merit or works. Thus clearly Paul warns of the dangerous position into which they were putting themselves. Turning their backs on God, abandoning the position of grace which had made them the objects of the grace of Christ, they were going back to law-keeping. They were turning to "another" gospel - a gospel without its source in God, a gospel which preached Christ plus Law, a gospel which was not of grace alone. Paul uses the word "gospel" for no doubt his critics called their message "gospel". After all, all false teaching claims to be "gospel", for its teachers never put forward their message as error. It is only seen to be such by those who hold to the gospel of pure grace.

2. *Perverters of the Gospel*
    1:7

> v.7 "Which is not another; but there be some that trouble you, and would pervert the gospel of Christ."

Two different words used in v.6 and v.7 are translated "another". The first means "another of a different kind", the second "another of the same kind". The Galatians were turning to a different gospel which was not the same as Paul preached. It was not that they were placing a different emphasis on certain aspects of the gospel; it was a false gospel, in the words of the NIV, "a different gospel which is really no gospel at all".

Paul now speaks of those who were troubling the churches. The verb *tarassō* means to "trouble, agitate, disturb". The church was in a state of perplexity, excitement, turmoil, doubt and mental confusion. These men were out to pervert, to change the gospel of Christ. Wuest suggests "to pervert" (*metastrephō*) means "to reverse, to change to the opposite, to turn about". They were reversing the gospel, proclaiming a message which was the opposite to what it really was: making it a gospel of works instead of free grace, a gospel of Christ plus Law.

It is interesting to note that troubling the church and perverting the gospel are brought together. The trouble is from inside, not from outside. The gospel and Christ are betrayed from within. All this should speak volumes to us of how active is Satan. How new converts need to be carefully watched so as to be protected in our day from false cults and their teachers.

3. *Protest of Paul*
   1:8-10

> v.8 "But though we, or an angel from heaven, preach any other gospel unto you
> than that which we have preached unto you, let him be accursed.
> v.9 As we said before, so say I now again, If any man preach any other gospel unto
> you than that ye have received, let him be accursed.
> v.10 For do I now persuade men, or God? or do I seek to please men? for if I yet
> pleased men, I should not be the servant of Christ."

8-9 In v.8 Paul is stating a *hypothetical* situation (his reference to an angel from heaven would confirm this) whereas in v.9 he is stating the actual Position. He is stressing that the status of the messengers does not make their message true and valid. It is the content of the message that is important. We must not judge the gospel by the men who preach it; rather we must judge them by the gospel they preach. Those who were perverting the gospel were claiming authority because they came from Jerusalem, the mother church, and were possibly using the name of James without his permission. But Paul had stated his gospel was received from God the Father and from Christ personally, so that every other message must be false, and would bring the preachers under the judgment of God. The credentials (so-called) of the preacher must not be allowed to mislead. The dignity of office in the religious world and the attainments of scholarship are no guarantee that the message is right. If they bring a message different from the apostolic gospel then they must be rejected. The office and learning of a pope give him status, but the many celebrations of the Mass expose him as a purveyor of another gospel. Paul is stating a vital principle, and this rigorous test must be applied to all forms of communication whether preaching, writing or broadcasting. Is it consistent with the true gospel of the NT, the pure grace of God to sinners, or is it marked by an admixture, an addition of any kind? If so, it must be refused. There is a curse upon all those who seek to change the gospel. Paul stresses that the gospel which he preached (v.8) and which they received at conversion (v. 9) is the only true gospel.

10 In holding fast to the pure gospel and pronouncing anathema (judgment) so strongly upon false teachers, Paul now throws out the challenge - am I seeking to find favour with men or God? It would seem that his enemies knew of Paul's attitude declared in 1 Cor 9:22, "I am made all things to all men", and were stating that Paul was not to be trusted: he would preach circumcision to the Jews to get their favour, but among Gentiles he did not insist on law-keeping. No doubt they would point to the circumcision of Timothy as an example of how he changed his position. In taking such a strong hand against false teachers, Paul could hardly be accused of pleasing men by trying to win their favour and esteem. To seek men's favour and approval was inconsistent with being a servant (bondslave) of Christ. Paul was no time-server, no man pleaser. He was quite clear that "no man can serve two masters" (Matt 6:24). His deep devotion to Christ had rendered him gloriously independent of men. In 1 Cor 4:1-5 he declares that as a steward and servant only the judgment of the Lord counted with him. Human judgment meant little to him. He felt that self-evaluation ("I judge not mine own self") was of no account. He would gladly wait for the Lord's estimate at the Judgment Seat of Christ. May such sturdy independence mark us. A strong stand against all forms of error is not popular in a day of compromise. Paul was no religious politician suiting himself to every wind of doctrine. May we be imitators of Paul in this matter.

Notes

6,7 "Another gospel: which is not another": Wuest comments as follows: "Paul uses two Greek words, both of which mean another, but which have a further distinct meaning of their own. The first is *heteros*, the second *allos*. *Heteros* means another of a different kind, *allos*, another of the same kind. *Heteros* denotes qualitative difference, *allos* numerical difference. *Heteros* distinguishes one of two. *Allos* adds one besides - *Heteros* sometimes refers however, not only to difference in kind but also speaks of the fact that the character of the thing is evil or bad. That is, the fact that something differs in kind from something else, makes that thing to be of an evil character. We have the word heterodoxy, made up of *heteros* and the word *doxa* which means opinion. Paul's doctrine of grace is God's truth, and anything that differs in kind from it must necessarily be false doctrine. Heterodoxy is false doctrine."

8,9 Note here that Paul as Christ's representative is pronouncing the curse upon the false teachers, invoking God's wrath upon them. He includes himself and his fellow-preachers and mentions even an angel from heaven (whose message normally would be accepted as from God) as meriting God's judgment if they set forth anything contrary to what Paul had preached. The subtlety of the preaching lay in the fact that the false teachers seemed to believe in Christ with just an extra few things added. But these extra things corrupted the gospel, polluted the pure stream of grace and effectively set aside the all-sufficiency of the work of Christ. *Christ supplemented is Christ supplanted.*

III. The Defence of Paul (1:11-24)

1. *Preaching by Revelation*
     1:11-12

> v.11 "But I certify you, brethren, that the gospel which was preached of me is not after man.
> v.12 For I neither received it of man, neither was I taught it, but by the revelation of Jesus Christ."

1-10 form the introduction and Paul now moves to the defence of his ministry. Savage attacks had been made against him as the truth of his message was denied by his enemies, maintaining his message was incomplete, because no place was given to circumcision and the keeping of the Law.

Paul now presents six arguments to answer his critics.

1. *1:11-12*   The gospel he preached was revealed to him by Christ and was totally independent of man.
2. *1:13-14*   The fact that he excluded circumcision etc., from his message was not due to ignorance of the law for he was steeped in its instruction in his early days.
3. *1:15-17*   After conversion he had no contact with Jerusalem nor with the apostles. Indeed it was three years after his conversion before he met any of the apostles.
4. *1:18-24*   In Jerusalem he met Peter and James during a stay of only fifteen days.
5. *2:1-10*   While there the apostles expressed their full fellowship with the message he preached.
6. *2:11-21*   He had to withstand Peter because of his inconsistency in acting contrary to the truth of the gospel. (Peter may have been recognised by many of the Judaizers as the leader of the apostles.)

11-12 Paul had maintained in vv.6-10 that there was only one true gospel, the one he preached. All others were false. How could this assertion be proved? Only by drawing attention to its source and origin. Paul now denies three sources for his teaching and states the one true source. First of all he says it was not "after man"; that is, it had not man as its origin and source. It had not been devised nor invented by man. This can easily be seen, for Paul's gospel made everything of Christ and the grace of God, and so made nothing of man. It was not a human gospel. No man would devise a message which gave him no place. Secondly, Paul declares he did not receive it "of man"; that is, no human agency was involved. It had not been handed down to him even as a tradition of the fathers. This was a direct hit at the Jews who were corrupting the gospel, for they gloried in the tradition of the fathers. Thirdly, Paul maintains he was not "taught" it; that is, he received no course of instruction to become acquainted with its message. His case was unique. The Galatians had received the message through Paul's preaching, the way most of us have come to know the gospel. We are indebted to others who made it known to us, but not Paul.

Paul now makes known the one true source - the Lord Himself. It was a "revelation", an uncovering of Christ to his soul. Until his experience on the Damascus road, Paul had considered Christ to be an impostor. But now He was revealed to him as the true Messiah, the Son of God. His true glory had been unveiled to him. Christ had crashed into his life in this transforming experience and had commissioned him to make known His name to the Gentiles. He had received the true gospel from the Lord Himself so that all others must be rejected as false, no matter who the preacher was.

Notes

12 *Revelation of Jesus Christ.* Scholars differ as to whether this is an objective or subjective genitive. If objective, Christ is the substance of the revelation, the Person revealed, rather than the Author. Then God would be the source, the One who revealed Christ to Paul was God. Wuest maintains it is a subjective genitive. God did the revealing; He gave the revelation.

The question has been raised whether Paul had knowledge of the gospel before he was converted. Did he know Christ when he was being educated at Jerusalem? It can hardly be substantiated that Paul met Christ before his conversion. Nevertheless he must have been acquainted with the message, or why did he persecute the saints? He also heard Stephen's testimony if not much else. In his bigotry he totally rejected the gospel and the implications of Christ's death, resurrection and ascension and it was not until Christ revealed Himself to him that he was totally convinced as to who He was and the great and amazing transformation took place in his life, with its radical turnabout.

2. *Before Conversion*
   ## 1:13-14

> v.13 "For ye have heard of my conversation in time past in the Jews' religion, how that beyond measure I persecuted the church of God, and wasted it:
> v.14 And profited in the Jews' religion above many my equals in mine own nation, being more exceedingly zealous of the traditions of my fathers."

Paul now begins to speak of his conversion in order to prove that man had no place in it, but that it was solely by the revelation of Jesus Christ. Apart from Luke's account of it in Acts 9, Paul makes at least seven references to it: (1) On the stairs of the castle in Jerusalem (Acts 22); (2) Before Felix the governor (Acts 24); (3) Before King Agrippa (Acts 26; (4) To the Galatians here (Gal 1); (5) To the Corinthians (1 Cor 15); (6) To the Philippians (Phil 3); (7) To Timothy (1 Tim 1). Paul goes on to show that his life *before, at* and *after* his conversion was such that it was impossible for him to have received the gospel from anyone, especially from any of the twelve apostles in Jerusalem.

13   Paul now indicates two things that marked his life before his conversion. In v.13 he draws attention to his hatred of the Christians, and in v.14 to his fanatical zeal as a Jew. "Conversation" or "manner of life" shows that to Paul religion was a way of life to be taken seriously. He does not give details here of the forms his persecution took, only of his determination to wipe out the church of God, to ravage, destroy and ruin it. Elsewhere we are told that he hounded them over a wide area, having authority to enter houses, to arrest both men and women, to put them in prison and to endeavour to get them to blaspheme. He even used his vote to have them put to death (see Acts 8:3; 9:2; 22:4; 26:10).

14   What lay behind Paul's persecuting of the Christians and his terrorist activities is now revealed. It was his fanaticism for the Jewish religion. He tells us he

advanced and outstripped his fellow Jews in his intense passionate zeal to practise
and uphold the traditions of his fathers. The greater his zeal for his religion the
greater his enmity to the christian faith. As far as he was concerned they were
incompatible. They were diametrically opposed. They were at enmity. Even in
his unconverted days Paul realised that Law and Grace could not be mixed and
he stood for a gospel of works and was completely opposed to the gospel of
grace which set aside all works as a means of salvation. Similarly, Paul could not
countenance a crucified Messiah (see 3:13).

Three things have now emerged:

1.   Because of his complete involvement in his religion and his total opposition
     to Christianity; because of his murderous persecution of the Christians and
     the arrogant haughty spirit he developed, no man could have persuaded him
     of the error of his position, not even an apostle. Only Christ could have dealt
     with him, as He did on the Damascus road.

2.   It was impossible for him to introduce law-keeping into his message as even
     in unconverted days he realised how utterly opposed they were.

3.   His gospel of salvation through faith, apart from works, could not be attributed
     to ignorance of the Law. His preaching, opposed as it was to what he practised
     in early days, was contrary to his natural inclinations and religious training.
     All this proved that he had received it from God.

3.   *At Conversion*
       1:15-16

> v.15 "But when it pleased God, who separated me from my mother's womb, and
>   called me by his grace,
> v.16 To reveal his Son in me, that I might preach him among the heathen; immediately
>   I conferred not with flesh and blood:"

We must not isolate Paul's conversion from the context. It is introduced to
show that man had nothing to do with it. It was all accomplished by God.
Afterward he had nothing to do with any man ("flesh and blood") nor with any of
the apostles. Three things are stated as to his conversion, each accomplished by
God.

1. *Separated from birth.* Parallels can be traced in Isa 49:1,5 and Jer 1:5. Here
we have the sovereign act of God in foreordaining Paul to salvation and
apostleship. He was set apart from birth and his life work marked out for him.

2. *Called by grace.* This refers to his experience on the road to Damascus. Not
only does Paul see the root of all as the good pleasure of God, but declares the
call, having nothing to do with his own merit, came to him because of the grace
of God. As Paul seems to make the "calling" and "revelation" distinct, would the

"calling" refer to what was outward, what arrested him, *how* his conversion was accomplished, namely by the light from heaven, the voice of Christ, and the sight of the Lord?

3. *"Reveal his Son in me"*. Some have translated "to me" or "through me", and one translation uses both. It probably refers to inward spiritual illumination as to him was made known the Son of God. It is remarkable that he uses the expression "His Son". It was not "Christ" who was unveiled to him but Jesus, the impostor (as he thought) whom he hated. He was the Son of God and equal with God. Thus there was revealed to him the Deity of the Lord Jesus. This revelation not only saved him, it also transformed him. Possibly the fulness of the revelation was conveyed to him in the days that followed his conversion.

There is now made known the purpose of all this divine activity. It was in order that he might preach Christ as the gospel, as glad tidings to the nations. We must note the connection between salvation and service. The calling of Paul had in view his apostleship to the Gentiles and, while this was unique to him, it should be stressed that the call of the gospel has in view each of us taking our place in the service of God. So Paul has now made it clear that not only his conversion, but also his call to serve among the Gentiles was fully and entirely of God. He had no choice in the matter. Elsewhere, as in Acts 26:15-18, he makes it clear that his commission was from the risen Lord Himself.

Notes

15 The contrast between vv.13-14 and vv.15-16 has often been noted. In the first two verses when Paul is speaking of himself, it is "I"; whereas in the last two verses it is "God". He thus vividly shows that he owes everything to divine intervention. He was completely absorbed in his religion and completely obsessed with persecuting the saints, when *God* arrested him and stopped his mad career. So his salvation and apostleship were due solely to the action of God.

16 It is only fair to note that there are those who feel that "to reveal his Son in me" is to be equated with "called me by his grace", the second phrase being a repetition of the first from a slightly different perspective.

4.   *After Conversion*
     1:17-24

> v.17 "Neither went I up to Jerusalem to them which were apostles before me; but I went into Arabia, and returned again unto Damascus.
> v.18 Then after three years I went up to Jerusalem to see Peter, and abode with him fifteen days.
> v.19 But other of the apostles saw I none, save James the Lord's brother.
> v.20 Now the things which I write unto you, behold, before God, I lie not.
> v.21 Afterwards I came into the regions of Syria and Cilicia;
> v.22 And was unknown by face unto the churches of Judaea which were in Christ:
> v.23 But they had heard only, That he which persecuted us in times past now preacheth the faith which once he destroyed.
> v.24 And they glorified God in me."

Having established that his reception of the gospel and commission to preach were wholly of God, Paul now proceeds to show that after his conversion he did not consult any person, nor did he go to Jerusalem to visit the apostles, but he went firstly to Arabia, secondly to Jerusalem and thirdly to Syria and Cilicia. Because of the lapse of time from his conversion, around three years, and because of the time spend in obscurity, he was not known to the churches in Judaea, but of course the story of his conversion had been circulated, and glory had been given to God.

17 In v.16 Paul tells us of the decision he made not to consult any person. The tremendous, revolutionary experience had taught him two things at least: the Lord Jesus had revealed Himself to him, and He had commissioned him. The deep assurance gripped Paul that this meeting with Christ placed him on equality with the Twelve, with equal status and authority. Just as the risen Christ had commissioned them, even so He had Paul. It was this that gave Paul his sturdy independence. He acknowledged that as to time they were apostles before him, but this did not give them any priority. The same Person had commissioned both. This shattering experience had so altered his thinking, had so demolished all his former training, that with the words of Christ still ringing in his ears, he decided to seek the solitude of Arabia to think through all the implications of the commission he had received. What tremendous courage would be needed to renounce completely all the past, and go out on this great new adventure. It would be at this time he was led to an understanding of "the mysteries" to which he so often refers later in his epistles. Alone with God he was prepared for the years of public service he so valiantly rendered to the cause of Christ, and received the resolve and conviction that would enable him to serve despite such terrible persecution and suffering.

Some have thought that the three years in Arabia were to him the equivalent of the three years the Twelve apostles spent with Christ. However this much is clear, that all true servants of Christ need a time of private dealing with God - a preparation to serve Him. Moses had forty years in the backside of the desert ere he was commissioned at the burning bush. David was taken from the sheepfolds to lead Israel. Elijah was in the hill country of Gilead before his appearing to Ahab. John the Baptist was in the deserts till the day of his showing unto Israel. Even the Lord Jesus had thirty years in private for three in public. How interesting that the ratio of private to public with the Lord should be ten to one. May we all learn this lesson! Sacrifices must be made if we are going to serve the Lord as He deserves. We cannot live the way so many Christians do if we are going to prepare ourselves adequately for our task in life. Time must be given to prayer and Bible study. No indication is given as to how any of the above were prepared. Every servant is different. No rigid curriculum as in Bible School will suffice for this great work. Only personal training by God is sufficient. May God open our eyes to see this and save us from the modern trend of a solely educated ministry.

18   We are now told that after three years he went up to Jerusalem. We are not told whether it was three years after his conversion or after his return to Damascus. Usually assumed to be dated from his conversion, it is the visit mentioned in Acts 9:26. No doubt his opponents would gladly seize on this information, but from it could hardly establish his dependence upon the Jerusalem apostles. After all a long time had elapsed since his conversion. He had vigorously proclaimed Christ in the synagogue at Damascus (Acts 9:20), so much so that the Jews took counsel to kill him (Acts 9:23). He went up "to see" Peter. (W.E. Vine in his Expository Dictionary tells us that the verb *historeō* means "to visit in order to become acquainted with".) Paul is establishing he went on a *private* visit to Peter, not on an *official* visit to receive a mandate to preach. No doubt this visit would give Paul a great insight into the life of Christ.

How eagerly he would listen as Peter told of his time with the Lord Jesus. (How one would have loved to have listened in to the conversation!) Paul would learn of the Person of the Lord while He was here. All this would be important background to his vision of Christ on the Damascus road. Peter on the other hand, would be glad to meet Paul and hear a first-hand account of his meeting with the risen Lord. What a pleasant, informative fifteen days must have been spent! What pleasure those days would give to the Lord as He watched His two apostles!

19   It must be assumed that none of the other apostles, for whatever reasons, were in Jerusalem at that time. Paul mentions James, the Lord's brother. Is he to be looked upon as an apostle in the same sense as the Twelve and Paul? Note the following considerations:

1. That in the progress of the gospel others were included in the apostolic band such as Barnabas (Acts 14:14), Andronicus and Junia (Rom 16:7). James then was an apostle, not in the strict sense of the Twelve but in a general sense, as he did not fulfil the complete qualifications of Acts 1:21-22, not believing on the Lord while He was here (see John 7:5; 1 Cor 15:7). This seems feasible.

2. Hendriksen and others would translate "save" by "only", so that Paul is saying that in addition to Peter he had seen no other apostles, only one other person of importance, James, the Lord's brother.

3. Some again would translate "save" as "unless it were" implying "if he is reckoned to be such". The matter is not all-important, as Paul is indicating his complete freedom from apostolic influence. This visit was brought to an abrupt close by a threat to Paul's life (Acts 9:29-30).

20   This strong, solemn affirmation of truthfulness would seem to have as its background the charge of his accusers that he had more contact with the Twelve than he was prepared to admit, that he had misrepresented the facts. Paul vehemently denies the charge.

21   Going now to these remote areas would indicate the impossibility of contact with the Twelve to be influenced by them. There is now passed over in silence a large part of Paul's life, a period of fourteen years, if the fourteen years of 2:1 are reckoned from this point and not from conversion. If on the other hand the fourteen years are reckoned from conversion then around eleven years are in view. A long time is involved one way or the other! We do know, of course, from the Acts that he spent a year or so at Antioch before going on his first missionary journey with Barnabas. This assumes that Acts 15 and Gal 2 refer to the same event.

22-24   Being so long away meant he was unknown in Judaea although his story was well known. What a difference to our day! How quickly those with outstanding conversions are made celebrities, made famous as they are called upon to give their testimony, or even to write a book! This man, the greatest servant next to the Lord Jesus, spent a long time in obscurity, *"unknown"* yet destined to leave his mark for centuries upon history. How good to be happy and contented to be *"unknown"* until God brings us forward. Little wonder then that they glorified God and not Paul for his wonderful experience. The attitude of the churches in Judaea stands in contrast to the attitude of some Galatians who grudged the rich grace of God to the Gentiles.

Notes

17 *Arabia*. The term Arabia was used vaguely in the ancient world. It may not have been used of present-day Arabia but of an area near Damascus. On the other hand, some references place it near Sinai.

Luke in the Acts omits all mention of this visit. The events between Paul's conversion and his visit to Jerusalem in Acts 9:19-25 are set down as if they all happened without a break of any kind. Yet this Arabian visit must be fitted somewhere in the text. Lightfoot suggests that it took place between vv.19-20 of Acts 9, although the "straightway" of v.20 seems to militate against this view. The only other place the visit can be placed is between vv.22-23, the "after many days" of v.23 allowing for the Arabian visit before Paul is seen again in Damascus. We shall probably never know with certainty the order of events. Neither Paul nor Luke is giving a complete biography. Paul in Galatians mentions events to prove he was not dependent on the Jerusalem apostles, whereas Luke is writing concerning the progress of the gospel. From Luke's silence we would infer that Paul's visit to Arabia was not so much to preach and establish churches (for Luke would have noted that), but to have a time of quietness and meditation after his violent entrance into the apostolic band. He would need time to think through the implications of his commission by the risen Lord. The RV however makes a significant break in the middle of Acts 9:19, and commences a new paragraph with the words "And he was certain days with the disciples". This break is also followed by the RSV and the NIV. It would thus seem they are allowing for the Arabian visit at this point.

IV. The Same Gospel (2:1-10)

1. *Movement by Revelation*
   ### 2:1-2

> v.1 "Then fourteen years after I went up again to Jerusalem with Barnabas, and took Titus with me also.
> v.2 And I went up by revelation, and communicated unto them that gospel which I preach among the Gentiles, but privately to them which were of reputation, lest by any means I should run, or had run, in vain."

In ch. 1 Paul was labouring to show that his apostleship was completely and totally independent of the twelve apostles. Now in ch.2 he reports that, at the historic meeting with them, they were in complete agreement with the gospel he preached, and with his apostleship to the Gentiles. This would come as a big blow to his opponents, and should have shown the Galatians the falseness of the claims of those false teachers. Not only so, but the Church as a whole is for ever indebted to Paul for the courage he displayed in going up to Jerusalem, in having this matter thrashed out, and thus in preserving for us the pure stream of the gospel of God's grace. Paul never compromised the great truths of the gospel. May God give grace to follow in his steps.

1   As has been noted many date the fourteen years here from his conversion, but, as Paul is seeking to show how little he was in touch with Jerusalem after his conversion, it seems more natural to take the fourteen years to refer to the time between his first visit (1:18) and this visit. Paul is stressing not how long after his conversion this visit took place, but the length of time between visits. In computing when this visit took place a great deal depends on the year of the crucifixion. If it took place in AD 33 then Paul was converted in AD 34, thus dating the first visit to Jerusalem three years later as AD 37, and this meeting fourteen years later as AD 51. But all dates must be approximate.

Titus is omitted by name in Luke's account, but mentioned here because he was to become a test-case of Paul's doctrine. Note again Paul's courage and determination to settle this crucial matter. Many a one, less courageous and less sensitive, would have left Titus, an uncircumcised Gentile, at Antioch, lest his presence antagonised the Judaizers. But Paul recognised that his presence would highlight the issue under discussion and Titus not being circumcised was a great victory for Paul and the gospel.

2   Paul now makes known that he went to Jerusalem as a result of a revelation from the Lord. No details are given of the revelation. This was the *divine* side, whereas the *human* side is stated in Acts 15:2, where the delegates were sent by the church in Antioch. Whether the revelation was before or after the church decision is not stated. Here Paul considers the revelation all important in establishing that his movements were dictated by the Lord (see note below on divine and human factors). He tells us that he had a private meeting with the leaders before the public assembly. Paul clearly deemed it wise to set the matter before these leaders and if possible, get their approval of his gospel, so that a "united front could be presented against the Judaizers at the public meeting. In addition it would establish that he had not "run in vain". This does not mean that he was unsure of the gospel he had preached for so many years or wanted apostolic approval, but he was afraid of his enemies winning the day and his whole work being completely spoiled. Intimation of the result is seen in Paul's use of the present tense, "I preach", indicating he was still preaching the same gospel as he had been before the meeting of the council.

Notes

2 In relation to divine and human factors it is to be noted that in Num 13:1-2 it is said that the sending of the spies was by the command of the Lord to Moses, whereas in Deut 1:22 it is stated to be at the request of the people. Again, in Acts 9:29-30 when the threat to kill Paul was known the brethren helped him to escape, whereas in Acts 22:17-21 Paul tells us the Lord told him to leave Jerusalem quickly. In Acts 13:1-4 it is the Holy Spirit that called Barnabas and Paul to a new sphere of service, but the call was conveyed by one of the prophets. Thus through a human channel the mind of God was made known to the servants and the church. Acts 10 provides yet another illustration: the vision and the voice of the Spirit preparing Peter for the visit of the servants from Cornelius.

2   *Titus and Circumcision*
   2:3-5

> v.3   "But neither Titus, who was with me, being a Greek, was compelled to be circumcised:
> v.4   And that because of false brethren unawares brought in, who came in privily to spy out our liberty which we have in Christ Jesus, that they might bring us into bondage:
> v.5   To whom we gave place by subjection, no, not for an hour; that the truth of the gospel might continue with you."

3-4 Titus was an example of the kind of person under consideration. Should he be received uncircumcised, or must he undergo the surgical rite? The demand for him to be circumcised seemed to have arisen from the demands of false brethren, for they were not true Christians, but pseudo-Christians, sham-Christians. It is stated firstly that they were brought in "unawares" that is, "secretly, surreptitiously, under cover." Secondly they came in "privily", that is, they came in "by stealth"; they slipped in; they infiltrated; they were planted; they sneaked in; they were interlopers to do the work of those who were intent on making circumcision compulsory for every convert. Note the contrast in the words "liberty" and "bondage". These words vividly set forth the real issue at stake. It was not so much Jew and Gentile, or circumcision and uncircumcision, but freedom in Christ or bondage to Law. The true gospel had liberated, emancipated, freed men and women from the rules and regulations of the Law and to submit to such demands was to put "free" people into bondage again. Titus exemplified it perfectly, an uncircumcised Gentile, yet truly converted by faith in Christ. Was that not enough? Or must he be circumcised and become a Jew, in order to be saved? That Paul declares would be slavery. As we know Peter came out clearly on Paul's side. "Why tempt ye God, to put a yoke upon the neck of the disciples, which neither our fathers nor we were able to bear?' (Acts 15:10)

5 Paul now declares that he had to take a vigorous stand for the truth of the gospel. From the account in Acts 15 he was joined by the leaders of Jerusalem. It is most refreshing to note that the ground of no compromise was maintained throughout the whole conference, and this unyielding stand preserved the truth of the gospel not only for the Gentiles at that time but for us too. How much we owe to this intrepid warrior of the Cross. How good to see this united stand. Scholars like to talk about "Paul's gospel" and "Peter's gospel", but there is only one gospel today and the apostles are united in their testimony to it. As later noted, Paul and Peter had different spheres of service, but their gospel was the same.

Notes

3 In Acts 16:3 we are told that Paul circumcised Timothy, but here he stoutly refused to circumcise Titus. The Jews would look upon Timothy as a Gentile, being uncircumcised, but the Gentiles would regard him as a Jew because of his upbringing. Paul circumcised him because he felt the Jews would then listen to him. It was a matter of expediency. It meant nothing to Timothy and was not performed as necessary for salvation but for his greater usefulness in the gospel. But when circumcision was demanded as a condition of salvation in the case of Titus Paul refused it completely, because it was an addition to the gospel of grace.

Circumcision was a minor surgical act performed on a male person. In Gen 17 God commanded it as the sign of the covenant between Him and His people. In Abraham's case it was a sign that he had previously trusted in God (Rom 4:11). But the Jews losing sight of its spiritual value placed emphasis on the rite alone, thus rendering it of no value in God's sight. In the NT circumcision is no longer demanded by a gospel alike to Jew and Gentile nor does believers' baptism take its place.

3. *Fellowship Established*
   2:6-10

v.6　"But of these who seemed to be somewhat, (whatsoever they were, it maketh no matter to me: God accepteth no man's person:) for they who seemed to be somewhat in conference added nothing to me:
v.7　But contrariwise, when they saw that the gospel of the uncircumcision was committed unto me, as the gospel of the circumcision was unto Peter;

v.8   (For he that wrought effectually in Peter to the apostleship of the circumcision,
      the same was mighty in me toward the Gentiles:)
v.9   And when James, Cephas, and John, who seemed to be pillars, perceived the
      grace that was given unto me, they gave to me and Barnabas the right hands of
      fellowship; that we should go unto the heathen, and they unto the circumcision.
v.10 Only they would that we should remember the poor; the same which I also was
      forward to do."

Paul now brings before us the results of the conference:

1. The status and independence of Paul's apostleship is recognised and established without an admission of its inferiority to that of the Twelve.

2. Spheres of labour are clearly delineated.

3. Complete and total fellowship between Paul and leaders at Jerusalem is clearly demonstrated.

4. The Judaizers are rejected and Paul fully accepted by the Jerusalem leaders.

5. Above all circumcision and law-keeping are refused as necessary to full salvation.

6 Here Paul indicates that the leaders in Jerusalem "added nothing" did not even add to his gospel such things as circumcision nor find his message defective in any way. They did not add to it or subtract from it. It remained unchanged in every way, being found complete. (Could it be otherwise seeing he had received it by revelation?) They could not communicate any fresh content to his message, nor increase his knowledge of it. It also meant that his status as an apostle was fully recognised and did not need any further confirmation from them.

We must now note how Paul speaks of the leaders in these verses. He refers to them in vv.2,6 (twice) and 9. The AV would seem to obscure the connection in these verses when it is noted that "reputation" (v.2), "seemed" (v.6 twice) and "seemed" (v.9) are from the same Greek word (*dokeō*) (see note below). In v.2 he says they were men of repute, conspicuous leaders. In v.6 they are reputed to be "somewhat"; that is, they held a place of prominence and authority. In v.9 they are reckoned to be "pillars', that is, men who carried the weight of responsibility in the local church. Paul thus acknowledges their position of honour and esteem in the church at Jerusalem, but now says in v.6 that what they once were made no difference to him. The fact that Peter and John had accompanied the Lord on earth, and were reckoned to be part of the privileged three, and that James, the Lord's brother, had been reared alongside Him, gave them no superiority. Such claims could not be accepted as giving status above others. God does not respect persons nor accept them because of outward privilege. Why then should Paul or others accord them a superior place?

All this would seem to indicate that Paul's opponents were stressing that the Jerusalem leaders must be accorded the supreme place because of their association with the Lord Jesus on earth. All this was calculated to discredit Paul in their eyes. In speaking thus of the Jerusalem leaders Paul is not being disrespectful nor trying to discredit them (he would then have been guilty of the same action as his opponents), but is driven to it because of the extravagant claims of the Judaizers in relation to these men. Paul thus acknowledges their *status* but not their *superiority*. His commission and gospel had come from the same source, the Lord Jesus Christ.

7-8   It is not to be inferred from the AV of v.7 that there are two gospels: Paul's gospel to the Gentiles that did not demand circumcision and Peter's gospel to the Jews that included circumcision. What is in view is not a *different content* in the messages preached, but a *different sphere* of labour. Different audiences are in view. The words "of the circumcision" and "of the uncircumcision" are genitives of connection drawing attention to the people addressed, the genitives being objective. V.8 indicates that it was fully accepted that God was using both Peter and Paul in different spheres, with resultant blessing. There was divine recognition of each as an apostle appointed by God to operate in different realms.

9   The scene before us must have delighted the heart of God and Christ as these five men stood and shook hands, thereby pledging themselves unitedly to carry the same gospel to the world of Jew and Gentile. It was an historic moment. Not only was Paul being *accepted* as an equal (as to apostleship), but was being seen to be such by this act. Moreover the gospel of the grace of God was to be heralded forth without addition of any kind. Paul had been fully vindicated, and the Jerusalem leaders shown to be true to the gospel (see note on "right hand").

We must now note the order of the names. In relation to the gospel in vv.7-8 only Peter is mentioned but when the leaders at Jerusalem are noted, the order is James, Cephas (Peter) and John. James would seem to be mentioned first because without doubt he wielded great influence in the church, which influence was felt outside Jerusalem. Being chairman of the conference (Acts 15) pointed to his authority and influence and his name gave special weight to the decision of Gentile freedom from the law. (It would seem from Acts 21:18-26 that James and the elders, although clear as to the fundamentals of the gospel, still observed certain Jewish ritual.) Peter is then mentioned as prominent in taking the gospel to the Jews and then John, who seemed later to have left Jerusalem and is reputed to have taken up residence in Ephesus. He was then banished to the Isle of Patmos. It is interesting to observe that four of the five wrote twenty-one NT books: Paul thirteen; John five; Peter two; James one. (Hebrews is not stated to be written by Paul or anyone else.)

10   The only stipulation made at Jerusalem was that they should continue to remember the poor. Paul, of course, had done (Acts 11) and would continue to do so (Acts 24:17). Paul is thus seen to be an apostle, a preacher and a man of deep compassion. Does such compassion compel us to meet the need of the poor who are always with us and to do good to all men (6:10)?

Notes

6 R.A. Cole in his exposition draws attention to the three times Paul uses the participle hoi dokountes. In each case the expression is slightly fuller and stronger. Thus in v.2 "they" are described as *hoi dokountes*, "the somebodies"; in v.6 they have become *hoi dokountes einai ti*, "those who seemed to have some official position" (although Paul at once bursts out in indignant expostulation that God cares nothing about any such rating). In v.9 they are *hoi dokountes stluloi einai*, "those who are rated as pillars of the church".

9 The giving of the hand would seem to suggest friendship, partnership, agreement. Note the following Scriptures:

1. 2 Kings 10:15 "he gave him his hand"; 2. 1 Chron 29:24 RV margin "gave the hand": NIV "pledged their submission"; 3. Ezra 10:19 "gave their hands"; 4. Ezek 17:18 "he had given his hand"; 5. Lam 5:6 "we have given the hand".

Clearly the giving of the hand suggests a *pledge* given. In Ezek 17:18 it is equated with an oath or a covenant broken after the pledge had been given.

V. Paul and Peter in Conflict (2:11-21)

1.   *The Incident at Antioch*
     2:11-14

> v.11 "But when Peter was come to Antioch, I withstood him to the face, because he was to be blamed.
> v.12 For before that certain came from James, he did eat with the Gentiles: but when they were come, he withdrew and separated himself, fearing them which were of the circumcision.
> v.13 And the other Jews dissembled likewise with him; insomuch that Barnabas also was carried away with their dissimulation.
> v.14 But when I saw that they walked not uprightly according to the truth of the gospel, I said unto Peter before them all, If thou, being a Jew, livest after the manner of Gentiles, and not as do the Jews, why compellest thou the Gentiles to live as do the Jews?"

The situation now before us is both startling and serious. Paul and Peter, those two great apostles, publicly opposed each other, while others watched the titanic struggle. How could such a situation have developed, especially after what has been previously recorded in vv.1-10? Who would have thought that Peter would have acted in this way, to find himself in a position where he must be publicly rebuked before all, and be blamed? And all this after the decision of the council.

The scene has shifted to Antioch. Peter is paying a visit to the church, and is happy to share a meal with the Gentile Christians. No doubt this included the love-feast (*agapē*; see Jude 12 and 1 Cor 11:21) as well as ordinary meals. Peter seems to have overcome his Jewish prejudices and is answering fully to the revelation from the Lord in Acts 10 and in loyalty to his statement before the council of Acts 15. This was the expression of true fellowship and indicated the unity of Jewish and Gentile believers, but it was to be short-lived. Certain brethren came down from the church in Jerusalem, claiming to have come from James, and were astounded to see Peter enjoying social fellowship with the Gentile believers. It would seem from this incident and the other recorded in Acts 21:18-27 that the Jerusalem church was completely Jewish and still held to law-keeping in daily life being "zealous of the law". Because of these conditions they were able to hold to their former Jewish mode of living and were quite insulated in their fellowship and clearly were glad it was this way for it meant no radical change for them. They immediately began to exert pressure on Peter to restrict his fellowship and revert to the former Jewish way of life. This Peter did out of fear. Other believers were affected and followed Peter in his withdrawal. Even Barnabas ultimately associated himself with Peter so that the result was a divided fellowship. Seemingly Paul was absent when this took place, but on his arrival moved quickly to offset this deadly peril. To him Peter's conduct had doctrinal and moral implications. His action was a denial of his doctrine. Left to himself he probably never would have acted in this way. Nevertheless he had involved himself in such a way as to demand quick and effective action from Paul. The Law could not be accepted as a way of life.

11   The opening word "but" indicates a contrast to what went before; despite all that had taken place this is what happened. Paul says that he withstood, opposed, resisted, stood out against Peter at this time. He was resisting an attack upon the gospel, albeit an unwitting attack by Peter.
   We must note certain things at this point:

1. Very often difficulties will arise from the most unlikely source - here from Peter. It was all so unexpected since Peter had received the vision of Acts 10; had defended his admission of Gentiles to the Church (Acts 11:4-17); had declared in Acts 15:7-11 that God had received Gentiles, making no difference between them and Jews. Now he was acting contrary to all these declarations.

2. Difficulties created publicly must be dealt with publicly, especially if doctrine is at stake. Peter's withdrawal had been public and had public repercussions, so must be dealt with in the same way. Sometimes it is wise not to wash dirty linen in public, but on an occasion such as this Paul felt it would be entirely wrong to have private discussion. On this matter confrontation was necessary. How opposed is such an action to the climate of compromise today! Collisions must be avoided at all costs we are told.

3. Paul is seen here to be defending his gospel and his status as an apostle to the Gentiles. The conditions at Antioch being undermined were the result of his teaching. In this respect Paul was fearless. Not even a man like Peter with all his authority and stature could be allowed to act in such a way. As Paul had not yielded to the Judaizers (2:5), so he would not retreat before Peter. What he had fought for at Jerusalem he would uphold, defend and vindicate at Antioch. He was thus demonstrating his complete independence of other apostles.

4. While the issue at Antioch was a question of food and fellowship and not circumcision, Paul saw clearly that a person cannot be saved apart from the Law and then continue to live under the Law. If law-keeping was not essential to salvation then it was not essential for christian living.

Paul says Peter was to be blamed. The RV renders, "he stood condemned:" that is, his own actions outlined in vv.12-14 condemned him fully. Not only so, but his conscience enlightened by the previous vision must have condemned him. And he must have stood condemned by his Gentile brethren for such inconsistent conduct. How deeply perplexing!

12   The arrival of certain brethren from Jerusalem revealed a weakness in Peter's make-up. He was vulnerable to pressure here from a strong appeal to him from exclusive Jewish teaching. No doubt it could not have been easy for Jews to abandon their lifelong habits. Nevertheless God had educated Peter in particular in these things and he should have reacted differently. Had not this weakness been manifest before when he denied knowledge of his Lord to the maid? The imperfect tense of "withdrew" may suggest it was gradual; bit by bit he stopped his association. Vine suggests it is a metaphor for lowering a sail. So Peter is seen to be trimming his sails to what he considered was a more comfortable wind. His withdrawal leads of course to his "separation", this latter word also being in the imperfect tense. Peter, the first man to learn the truth of the Gentile admission to Church fellowship, is now the first to withdraw from it. The reason is now given: he feared the Jews. Was he afraid that a report of his fellowship with the Gentiles would impair his status and authority in the Jerusalem church? Did he want to remain popular even at the expense of setting aside truth? How one dislikes writing thus about such a great man as Peter. How one wishes it had been otherwise. How Paul stands in such vivid contrast. He cared not for favour with the Jews or any man and was willing to pay the price for loyalty to the truth of the gospel. Witness his constant persecution by these men. May we learn the lesson. God save us from instability!

13   The result of Peter's action was catastrophic. The other Jews followed his example. Thus Peter virtually separated the Jewish believers from their Gentile brethren, causing a complete cleavage in the assembly. His action thus destroyed the friendship, harmony, agreement and fellowship that had bound them together. We are now told that Barnabas was led away and joined the separatists. This must have been a big blow to Paul. It was Barnabas who had partnered him in winning the Gentiles to Christ. He had been sent with Paul by the church at Antioch to state the case in Jerusalem. Now he had turned against all this and threw his weight in with Peter and the others. Assuming that Paul was absent at this time (one could hardly think of him standing idly by and watching this development), it shows how quickly things can deteriorate when such godly influence and intelligent understanding are not available. Cole makes an interesting suggestion about Barnabas, "When we attempt to estimate the character of Barnabas, we should not forget this incident. It shows the danger of theological compromise, the besetting sin of loving natures. To Barnabas, no doubt, this was simply a matter of love. He did not want to grieve the brethren from Jerusalem; a brief abstention from fellowship with his Gentile fellow-believers was all that would be necessary. Once the Jerusalem emissaries had departed the old terms could be resumed. Was not this a small sacrifice to make for peace? But to Paul, this was peace at any price and he was not prepared to buy peace on those terms" (p.76).

Note the words "dissemble" and "dissimulation" mean "hypocrisy" or "play-acting". Now a hypocrite is a person who pretends to be what he is not. He is playing a part by covering up his real identity. Here Peter was covering up his real motive, acting as though loyal to the Law whereas the real reason was fear of the Judaizers. Paul here draws aside the veil and reveals the sham of it all. Peter was acting a part, covering up his true feelings and suppressing his true knowledge out of fear. Let us note how the false action of a good man can create a dangerous situation and lead others astray.

14 We must note Paul's motive. He did not oppose Peter because he loved an argument nor because he wanted to score over Peter, and humiliate him. It was because of "the truth of the gospel": the same reason why he refused to bow to the demands of the Judaizers in v.5. Paul says they were not walking "straight" according to the gospel. That is, the gospel had united Jew and Gentile and made them one in Christ, but Peter's action had separated them. The word "uprightly" means "to walk in a *straight* path". Peter and others had deviated from the straight path of the gospel. Again it draws attention to the fact that Peter's attitude was not "straight". It was crooked. He was playing with truth. In v.13 he was not *real*; in v.14 he was not *straight*.

Paul now faces Peter publicly in what seems to have been a church meeting. He is not over-awed by Peter's so-called "infallibility". No private meeting is contemplated. Things had gone too far for that. Quick, decisive, public action was called for at this stage. Paul's action and Paul's teaching are placed before us, but nothing of Peter's feelings or reaction. We can understand how he felt. His shame and discomfiture must have been apparent to all. Paul's argument is clear. If Peter as a Jew, now converted, abandoned Jewish exclusiveness as to eating and drinking and enjoyed fellowship with the Gentile believers, how was it that he had renounced this fellowship and demanded that the Gentiles observe Jewish food laws? In other words, Peter's action had put Gentile believers in a very awkward position. They had either to put themselves under Law to preserve harmony, which was a denial of the truth of the gospel, or accept open division in the church.

Paul saw clearly the issues affected "the truth of the gospel" and his action preserved for the immediate future the unity of the churches and their heavenly calling. Peter's conduct on this occasion contradicted the revelation given to him in Acts 10 and forced the Gentiles in effect to become Jews. If others had seen as clearly the issues we would never have seen the Roman Catholic Church with its mixture of Paganism and Judaism nor Protestant churches with their modernism and ecumenical bias, fast going into apostasy. Rather the primitive simplicity of NT church gatherings would have been preserved down the ages, the authority of the word of God owned, the sovereignty of the Holy Spirit recognised and the Lordship of Christ acknowledged.

2. *Teaching Arising from the Incident*
   2:15-21

v.15 "We who are Jews by nature, and not sinners of the Gentiles,
v.16 Knowing that a man is not justified by the works of the law, but by the faith of Jesus Christ, even we have believed in Jesus Christ, that we might be justified by the faith of Christ, and not by the works of the law: for by the works of the law shall no flesh be justified.
v.17 But if, while we seek to be justified by Christ, we ourselves also are found sinners, is therefore Christ the minister of sin? God forbid.
v.18 For if I build again the things which I destroyed, I make myself a transgressor.
v.19 For I through the law am dead to the law, that I might live unto God.
v.20 I am crucified with Christ: nevertheless I live; yet not I, but Christ liveth in me: and the life which I now live in the flesh I live by the faith of the Son of God, who loved me, and gave himself for me.
v.21 I do not frustrate the grace of God: for if righteousness came by the law, then Christ is dead in vain."

Let us observe that in these verses we have the first occurrence in the epistle of the word "justify". Justification is the basic doctrine of the letter. It is also to be noted too the first mention of "law" and "faith" linked with Christ.

There is a problem as to where Paul's words to Peter end and the teaching begins. From v.15 is Paul addressing Peter or the assembled church? Or is he speaking to the Galatians? In all probability Paul, having rebuked Peter, now includes the whole company in his address, setting plainly before them this basic teaching, for this teaching sums up the whole letter. However it does seem to be mainly directed to the Jewish section of the church as he contrasts justification by works and justification by faith.

This section divides into two parts:
1. vv.15-16: Justification by faith;
2. vv.17-21: The teaching defended.

15-16 Paul is now showing how unsound doctrinally was the position of Peter and the Jews. As Jews they had been born into that favoured race so privileged compared with Gentiles in their gross sins and godless living. Enjoying the only divinely-revealed religion, but realising that observing the Law could never give them a standing before God, they had put their faith in the Lord Jesus, and so had been justified. Obviously that previous decision was contrary to their present action. How salutary this teaching would be to the Galatians who were listening to Judaizers. If in v. 14 he shows their action to be *morally* wrong, here he shows their action to be *doctrinally* wrong. It was contrary to the truth of the gospel.

The word "justified" means to be declared or pronounced *righteous*. It is a legal or forensic term, connected with a law-court. It is the opposite of condemnation. We were sinners guilty and condemned, but God in the wonder of His grace and because of the work of Christ has declared us righteous, cleared us of every charge against us. This new relationship is entered into by us through faith in Christ. No works nor merit on our part could ever have secured it for us. It is all of God's grace. How it humbles man's pride. So Paul presses home to the Jews the utter inadequacy of the Law to give them any standing, "for by the works of the law shall no flesh be justified". What a strong, sweeping statement.

Note that in the phrase "the faith of Jesus Christ", "of Jesus Christ is an objective genitive meaning "faith *in* Jesus Christ". It is not His faith but ours in Him. Note also that he says:

1. "*a man*" is justified by faith in Christ: that is "*any* man";

2. "*we believed*": that is, Paul and the others;

3. "*no flesh*": that is, the *whole* of mankind is shut up to Christ and faith in Him.

17-21 The enemies of Paul were constantly assailing his gospel. They were arguing that to claim that faith alone in Christ could save, the Law must be set aside completely. To their mind this was impossible. God's Law could never be abrogated. It would be sin to do so. Thus Christ was a minister of sin, not the minister of the circumcision (Rom 15:8). To set aside the Law put the Jews in the same position as Gentile sinners, depending entirely on the grace of God, without merit of any kind. This they would not have. So the

Gentiles must be made to obey the Law for salvation. Paul now deals with this argument.

17   This verse is of a highly compressed nature. Paul sees clearly that the teaching is an assault upon the Person of Christ as well as on the gospel and he is anxious to defend his Lord and His honour. He strongly repudiates the slander upon Christ. He declares that seeking justification in Christ alone, apart from the Law did put them in the position of sinners, but that was their true position before God. As such they needed a Saviour and Christ had met that need. He had saved them from their sins and not led them into sin.

It may be that a second interpretation should be stated. It could be that facing Peter and the Jews, Paul declares that if they sought justification in Christ, but must now return to the Law (as Peter and Barnabas and the Jews were doing) they had proved themselves sinners in following Christ, so Christ had led them to sin, He was the minister of sin. How abhorrent to Peter, who really loved the Lord, would be such a conclusion. But it was impossible for Christ to be guilty in this way. It was they who were guilty in turning away from Christ.

A third interpretation has much to commend it, as linking closely with v.18. A paraphrase will bring out the teaching. "But if, while seeking to be justified by Christ, we are judged (by our enemies) to be sinners (because we abandoned the Law), then Christ has led us to sin". Their opponents were claiming that to abandon the Law was sin, therefore Christ was the minister of sin. But this could never be.

A fourth interpretation is held by some. By accepting Christ but refusing the Law as a moral standard, you are making people law-breakers, giving them licence to sin - the heresy of antinomianism. But there is nothing in the preceding or succeeding context to suggest it. Rather Paul deals with this subject in 5:13.

18   Paul now states that sinnership is not in *abandoning* the Law as they claimed, but in *going back* to the Law. To restore and rebuild what one had previously torn down - the Law as a means of justification - is to be a *real law-breaker*. This was what Peter had done by his action in refusing to eat with Gentiles. He had undermined a basic principle of the gospel. He was either wrong in turning solely to Christ from the Law, or he was wrong in turning away from Christ to the Law. The Galatians were in the same danger. To add to Christ in any way is to detract from His sufficiency as Saviour.

19   Paul now goes a step further. He had not only repudiated the Law as a means of salvation, he has died to it, so that he cannot return to it! Looking back he sees his whole experience under Law proved its inadequacy as a means of salvation. It only brought despair and condemnation, making constant demands without giving the power to fulfil them. It could not give life. (Note the contrast between "death" and "life" and between "Law" and "God".) It proved him to be a sinner, and then punished him for being one! So he turned away from it to find life in Christ and to live unto God. This he explains in v.20. Enough to declare that life lived to God and for His pleasure is not in Law-keeping (cf. Rom 7:1-13).

20   Paul now explains how he came to live unto God; how impossible it is to put oneself back under Law. His opening statement, true of all believers, "I am crucified with Christ", is a matter of divine revelation. We would never have known such a thing took place, had God not told us. When we read the Gospels we are reading only what took place *outwardly*. We must go to the epistles for the doctrine of the cross. This is a doctrinal statement to be accepted by the believer. But it must be noted that while this verse is often used in relation to holy living, its primary meaning is that Paul (and the believer too) has *died to the Law* in identification with Christ who bore its penalty. As such it has no more claim upon him, and he has no responsibility to keep it. He is now in a new sphere, living a new life.

We must learn the meaning of *"crucifixion"*. It was a *public, judicial* act. It meant the person's life was terminated in an act of judgment. That life had been brought to a close. What is stressed is not *burial* but an act of *judgment* by God (see note below). Here is something that took place at the cross. When Christ died, He not only died for our sins and bore the curse of the broken Law, but He died to remove *the man* who had committed the sins and broken the Law. Note too that the verb is in the perfect tense, which denotes a past act with present results. It is not a present experience for it is reckoned to have taken place at the cross, "I have been crucified with Christ", but the reality of it lives in his soul. Let us grasp the significance of all this. I am identified with Christ in His death. The cross means an end of *me* as a sinner, as one seeking to earn salvation by my own efforts. It is the end of my old self, the sinful evil "I" has gone.

This does not mean that the believer no longer lives as an individual. He does but it is no longer the old "I" who lives but Christ who lives in him. Life is no longer *self*-centred but *Christ*-centred. The cross has taught him that the old life is finished: he has entered into a new experience in which Christ is living out His life in Him. The "flesh" here refers to the body through which the new life is manifested. But it is a life of faith and not of obedience to an external code. "The faith of Jesus Christ" uses an objective genitive as in v.16 and refers not to His faith but to our faith in Him. Note the thrust of the passage: life lived unto God for His pleasure is not one of striving to keep the Law but a life lived in dependence upon Christ as Son of God. Such a title, "Son of God", would indicate the power of Him whose life was being lived out in Paul's life. His heart is rising in adoration. This glorious Son of God out of love for him personally gave Himself for him. How this brings one down in His presence. The writer remembers an occasion early in christian life when reading this verse and as the wonder of it broke on his soul, he determined that such a glorious Person should have his whole life, without reserve of any kind. If He could give Himself unreservedly for me, I should give myself unreservedly to Him.

It only remains now to note how personal all this is to Paul. In vv.18-20 he uses the personal pronoun "I" nine times. Note too he uses "me" three times in v.20. It has all been very real to him. As he addressed the gathering that day, and expounded the doctrine, his reference to how it was working out in his own life must have made a great impact. This is surely how it should be. Doctrine must be translated into daily living. Paul was living this life on the principle of faith and yet it was Christ who was living in him. Such intimate nearness and fellowship with Christ will not only transform life but will give us to see that the doctrine can be worked out to give us a firmer grasp of the doctrine.

> "Take my life and let it be
> Consecrated, Lord, to Thee."

21 Paul now declares that he cannot set aside nor make null and void the grace of God by going back to Law-keeping. To do so was to declare that works were necessary for justification and was to say in effect that Christ's death was unnecessary. Peter, Barnabas, the Galatians and all today who maintain salvation is by works are setting aside the pure grace of God which offers salvation free to all apart from human effort of any kind, and are declaring that Christ's death was unnecessary. "In vain" (*dōrean*) means "without a cause", "needlessly", "for nothing". It was all a big mistake. The doctrine of the Judaizers struck at and undermined the grace of God and the death of Christ, the two great foundations of the christian faith.

Notes

17 Within the four interpretations "found sinners" has the meanings
(1) finding themselves to be sinners the same as the Gentiles;
(2) finding themselves to be sinners for following Christ, when the Law was necessary for salvation;
(3) judged sinners by their opponents because they abandoned the Law,
(4) finding they are free to sin.
20 Similar language is used in Rom 6:6. "Our old man is crucified with him". This took place at the cross. The "old man" is the person we were before conversion and looks to the *order* of man to which we belonged. That order was *terminated* at the cross under God's judgment. Note the old man is not *buried* but is *crucified*. God is finished with him completely. At baptism the old man is not buried; it is the *believer* who is buried.

CHAPTERS 3 AND 4 - DOCTRINAL
THE VINDICATION OF THE GOSPEL

1. Law or Faith (3:1-14)

1. *The Experience of the Galatians*
    3:1-5

> v.1 "O foolish Galatians, who hath bewitched you, that ye should not obey the truth, before whose eyes Jesus Christ hath been evidently set forth, crucified among you?
> v.2 This only would I learn of you, Received ye the Spirit by the works of the law, or by the hearing of faith?
> v.3 Are ye so foolish? having begun in the Spirit, are ye now made perfect by the flesh?
> v.4 Have ye suffered so many things in vain? if it be yet in vain.
> v.5 He therefore that ministereth to you the Spirit, and worketh miracles among you, doeth he it by the works of the law, or by the hearing of faith?"

In a sense Paul was defending the gospel in the earlier chapters, but there he was asserting his authority as an apostle, and that the gospel he received was directly from Christ. Now he turns from his experience to the Scriptures to defend the gospel. He will first draw the attention of the Galatians to their own experience, that of receiving the Spirit by faith (1-5); then he will go to the experience of Abraham to show that he was justified by faith (6-9); finally, he will show the inability of the law in these realms and declare the triumph of Christ (10-14).

1   Paul cries out: "O foolish Galatians!" The word "foolish" means "senseless", "lacking understanding". They could think but were not using their mental powers to the full. To embrace a doctrine which set aside the grace of God and the death of Christ was foolishness in the extreme, and showed a complete lack of understanding and logical thinking. It was thoughtless, senseless, foolish and lacking spiritual insight. "Who have *bewitched* you, *charmed* you, *fascinated* you by their teaching?" Bruce uses the word "*hypnotised*". They had come under the spell of the false teachers. (Note most critical translations leave out "that ye should not obey the truth".) How could they be so affected when Christ had so publicly been portrayed to them in the preaching? "*Jesus Christ crucified*" had been Paul's theme, and he had made it so clear and plain that he likens it to a public notice board on which was placarded a message in large letters. Vividly, graphically, boldly he had presented Christ as crucified so that he marvelled that even the weakest of them should have been affected by the false teaching. Note in each of these five verses, Paul asks a question that gets to the heart of the matter and shows them the folly of the way they were taking. Every public man, whether evangelist or teacher, should take note of how inspired writers present truth clearly and for the intelligent judgment of readers.

2   Paul now challenges the Galatians, "Answer this question and thus settle the whole matter. Go back to the beginning, to your conversion. How did you receive the Spirit?" That they possessed the Spirit he would not deny, but was He received by keeping the Law or on believing the gospel? There was only one answer. It was by believing, by the hearing of faith. "Hearing" refers to the message they heard and "faith" to the means by which they received this salvation. Note the reception of the Spirit constituted them true Christians (see Rom 8:9). No one ever received the Spirit by keeping the Law. Observe too the contrast between "works" and "hearing" (believing), between "law" and "faith". They are exact opposites and so cannot be mixed as the Galatians were trying to do. It was also obvious that being Gentiles they were not acquainted with the Law in unconverted days and had only become acquainted with it when the false teachers arrived and presented their message. Having cleared this matter, the beginning of their spiritual experience and their reception of the Spirit, Paul has another question for them.

3   He now appeals to them. "How can you be so foolish, so illogical. If you began your Christian life in the Spirit how can it be completed in the flesh? And if you could not obtain salvation by works how can you produce holiness by works after conversion? Cannot you see that if spiritual life is begun by the Spirit, it must be developed by Him?" The whole of this new life is supernatural and so it is impossible for circumcision, or Law-keeping of any kind, to bring it to maturity. Note that if in v.2 the contrast was between Law and faith, in v.3 it is between "the Spirit and "the flesh". Paul is indicating that in the realm of Lawkeeping there is no provision for an indwelling Spirit. It was a retrograde step and not by the leading of the Spirit of God. How illuminating are Paul's arguments! How decisive as he brings before them these alternatives! You would wonder how, with this epistle before them, the folly of law-works had not been clearly seen. Give the Spirit of God His true place in the whole plan of salvation and all is clear and we will be saved from defection of any kind.

4   Yet another question is asked by Paul. It is an excellent Pauline method to bring out the issues involved. In v.2 it was how the Spirit was received: in v.3 how could the flesh perfect the work of the Spirit: in v.4 it is to ask were their sufferings for the gospel to be all in vain? In those early days suffering was the common lot of Christians, but it would all be for nothing if they went on to embrace the Law. Quickly he adds, "if it be yet in vain". Paul still held out hope that they would refuse to capitulate to the false teachers. He encourages them by indicating he expects something better from them. Later in 5:10 he makes known his confidence that they would turn away from such false teaching. Nevertheless it must have been a harrowing experience for Paul as he waited for their response to his appeals and arguments. When we think too of the state of other churches his burden must have been great.

5   Paul is back again to the test question of v.2. In v.2 he dealt with their past reception of the Spirit; now he refers to the present supply of the Spirit's power. Paul is again challenging in question form. It was God who had given them the Spirit; it was God who had performed miracles among them. Paul does not indicate whether the miracles were performed by himself or others, but he does state that the power of God was present among them. He challenges them; did such power arise from their own efforts - the works of the Law - or by the message of the gospel? Clearly the answer is the same as to the other questions. Yet with such irrefutable evidence of the power of God still with them, they were in danger of turning away from the true gospel that had brought them such blessing. Thus he has shown that their own experience has amply proved that all blessing had come through the gospel he had preached to them.

Notes

1 *Prographō* "evidently set forth" (AV), is translated "openly set forth" (RV); "publicly portrayed" (RSV); "clearly portrayed" (NIV); "portrayed" (JND). W.E. Vine in his Expository Dictionary comments: "In Gal 3:1 however, it is probably used in another sense, unexampled in the Scriptures but not uncommon in the language of the day, i.e. *proclaimed, placarded*, as a magistrate proclaimed the fact that an execution had been carried out, placarding his proclamation in a public place." K.S. Wuest explains: "The word is found in early secular documents where a father posted a proclamation that he would no longer be responsible for his son's debts." The large roadside hoardings with their message today would convey the idea. So did Paul in his preaching vividly portray Christ as the crucified One.

Note the recurrence in the epistle of "the cross" and "crucified". Here in Galatians the idea of "the cross" is prominent, whereas in Hebrews "the *blood*" is emphasised and in Romans "the *death*" of Christ. "Crucified" here is in the perfect tense, suggesting a past act with continuing significance.
2 This is the first mention of the Holy Spirit, whose ministry is very prominent later, especially in ch.5.

2.   *The Experience of Abraham*
   3:6-9

v.6   "Even as Abraham believed God, and it was accounted to him for righteousness.
v.7   Know ye therefore that they which are of faith, the same are the children of Abraham.
v.8   And the scripture, foreseeing that God would justify the heathen through faith, preached before the gospel unto Abraham, saying, In thee shall all nations be blessed.
v.9   So then they which be of faith are blessed with faithful Abraham."

Paul now in a masterly way turns the attention of the saints to Abraham. In what circumstances was he justified? Clearly the opponents of Paul, in forcing circumcision upon the Galatians, were bringing forward circumcision as instructed by God in Gen 17 as binding upon all who claimed to be His people. Thus works were necessary. In vv.1-5 Paul had demonstrated that the reception of the Spirit was by faith; so now in these verses he will prove that Abraham was justified by faith and not by works, in this case, not by circumcision. So circumcision was not necessary for salvation. How one admires Paul's clear, masterly handling of the whole situation, taking up the legalists on their own ground as the seed of Abraham. Step by step he is demolishing their doctrine.

6 Consider Abraham now, says Paul, for he came into blessing through faith and not by works. He quotes Gen 15:6 to prove his point, "Abraham believed God". Despite God's promise Abraham was old with no family. When he raised his problem with God, God reiterated His promise and taking him outside drew his attention to the stars and proclaimed, "So shall thy seed be". Abraham immediately responded by believing God, and it was reckoned to him for righteousness. (In Rom 4 Paul shows this took place before he was circumcised.) Clearly Abraham is accepted as righteous in virtue of his faith. It could not be of works for he just believed God's promise. He was not the first man to have faith, nor was he the first righteous man, but he was the first person in whom the principle of being reckoned righteous in virtue of faith is demonstrated.

We must be careful with the little word "*for*". It does not mean that faith is equated with righteousness, nor does it mean "instead of" righteousness. Faith has not this meritorious value. It was not Abraham's faith as faith which gave him a standing with God, but rather his faith in the promise of God in the word of God. He believed what God said. It was that on which his faith rested. So it is today. All who are prepared to believe the message of the gospel, the word that comes from God, are reckoned righteous, declared by God to be so. (In Rom 4 it is faith in God that is stressed.) God does not make the believer *righteous* or sinless in himself for up to the moment of conversion he was in the wrong; he was unrighteous; he was a sinner. God reckons him to be righteous in virtue of his faith in Christ. To *reckon* righteous does not mean to *make* righteous; it refers to *status* not *condition*. We have been brought into right relationship with God.

7 Understand then, says Paul, that, if Abraham was blessed on the principle of faith, all who exercise such faith are the sons (not children) of Abraham. Abraham's true descendants are not those who carry the mark of circumcision in their bodies, but those who are marked by faith. Abraham is thus seen to be the father of all those who have faith and his "sons" take character from him. Not physical descent but spiritual descent is what counts. So Paul is pointing to the folly of adding anything to the faith which the Galatians possessed. The sole condition demanded by God for blessing was fulfilled in their faith in Him.

8 The *Scripture* foreseeing and preaching to Abraham must refer to God. This shows that inspired writers identified the Scriptures with God, so that when "the

Scripture says" it is tantamount to saying, "God says". This looks toward and justifies belief in the inspiration of Scripture. (See Rom 9:17, "The Scripture saith unto Pharaoh".) The Scripture in view here is Gen 12:3. Paul is building on the words "all nations". God had in view the blessing of the Gentiles ("heathen" in AV means "Gentiles"). He would *bless* them by justifying them. The present tense of "would justify" declares the ground upon which God accepts any person at any time: it is on the principle of faith. In the same way as Abraham, the Gentiles would be blessed, whether the Galatians or ourselves.

See how he is pressing home the great truth of justification by faith alone. "The gospel" referred to here is the message of God at that time to Abraham, in which was inherent the principle of justification by faith. The same *principle* is inherent in the gospel today, although the *message* is different. (Those who tell us there is only "one gospel" seem to overlook the fact that the gospel of the grace of God is different in *content* from what was made known to Abraham and from the declaration of John the Baptist.)

9   Paul now reaches his conclusion. Those who are "of faith" in the sense of believing God are one with Abraham. While the principle applies to all, Gentiles particularly are in view here. In believing God before circumcision Abraham was in a sense on Gentile ground. Thus Paul assures the Galatians they were on the right path.

Notes

6 Darby has an interesting footnote on Rom 4:3, which he translates, "it was reckoned to him as righteousness". He says, "I am not quite satisfied with 'as'; but it is the nearest approach to the sense in English. 'For', I object to; because then faith is made of positive worth, having the value of righteousness; whereas the sense is that he was holden for righteous in virtue of faith. The man was held to have righteousness. It is a Hebrew form. See Ps 106:31. Gen 15:6, where there is no preposition, makes the force of the expression plain." It should be observed that Darby translates the close of Gen 15:6 thus: "and he reckoned it to him (as) righteousness".
6-9 In his introduction to this section Wuest observes
"The occasion for his argument is found in the fact that the Judaizers taught that the natural descendants of Abraham were his children, and thus accepted with God. All of which meant that only the circumcised could be saved. Thus, circumcision was a prerequisite of salvation. This teaching was based on a misapprehension of Gen 12 and 17. They argued that no one could participate in the blessings of God's covenant with Abraham and so in the Messianic salvation which was inseparably connected with it, unless he was circumcised. The mistake they made was in failing to distinguish between the purely Jewish and national covenant God made with Abraham, which had to do with the earthly ministry and destiny of the Chosen People as a channel which God would use in bringing salvation to the earth, and that salvation which came through a descendant of Abraham, the Messiah. Circumcision was God's mark of separation upon the Jew, isolating him in the midst of the Gentile nations, in order that He might use the nation Israel for His own purposes. It had nothing to do with the acceptance of salvation by the Jew. Over against

this contention, Paul argues that Abraham was justified by faith, not by circumcision. In Rom 4:9-10 he proves his case conclusively when he shows that Abraham was declared righteous before he was circumcised, which demonstrates that his circumcision had nothing to do with his acceptance of salvation."

3. *Curse and Blessing*
     3:10-14

> v.10 "For as many as are of the works of the law are under the curse: for it is written, Cursed is every one that continueth not in all things which are written in the book of the law to do them.
> v.11 But that no man is justified by the law in the sight of God, it is evident: for, The just shall live by faith.
> v.12 And the law is not of faith: but, The man that doeth them shall live in them.
> v.13 Christ hath redeemed us from the curse of the law, being made a curse for us: for it is written, Cursed is every one that hangeth on a tree:
> v.14 That the blessing of Abraham might come on the Gentiles through Jesus Christ: that we might receive the promise of the Spirit through faith."

Having set out in the previous verses the truth of justification by faith, Paul now begins to show the other side, "No man is justified by the law" (v.11). This section divides into two parts:

1. vv.10-12: The Inability of the Law;
2. vv.13-14: The Triumph of Christ.

In the first section, vv.10-12, he brings forward three OT texts, one in each verse, so from them we can gather the flow of thought. In v. 10 he quotes Deut 27:26 to show that the curse of God rests upon all who do not fully and totally keep the Law. In v.11 he draws attention to Hab 2:4 which declares that the way to life is through faith. Then in v.12 he cites Lev 18:5 to demonstrate the incompatibility of the principles of Law and faith. They cannot be harmonised or brought together.

In the second section vv.13-14, he declares that what we could not do, i.e. deliver ourselves from the curse of the Law , Christ has done for us on the cross. The point has been reached when he can now introduce Christ as the Redeemer and show the results that accrue from such a mighty work. So there is a way that leads to "cursing" (v.10) and a road that leads to "blessing" (v.14). They are completely opposite, one marked by "works" and the other marked by "faith". They can never be merged. You cannot add Law to faith in Christ, as the Galatians were being tempted to do.

10 Paul now goes to the very heart of the problem facing the Galatians, the Law and salvation, and unequivocally declares that to practise the works of the Law was to bring oneself under the curse of God. (It is not tenable to hold that it is the curse of the Law that is in view and not the curse of God. It was, after all, the breaking of God's Law that incurred the wrath of God.) The whole Law must be kept and that continually, not just part of the Law part of the time (see James 2:10-11). But it was impossible for anyone to do so, so the curse falls upon "everyone". The universality of sin is assumed and hence all who held to the works of the Law must ultimately perish. What a terrible burden such men as the Pharisees and now the Judaizers were placing upon themselves and others. And when the principle is extended today, one shudders to think of so many religious people who are staking everything upon a form of baptism as the means of grace to get them to heaven.

11   If in v. 10 Paul shows that to put oneself under Law is to earn a curse, then in v.11 he declares that the Law cannot justify. His thrust is clear. In declaring Abraham to have been justified by faith, his opponents would answer that Abraham lived before the Law, but now that the Law had come it must be taken into account. The Law must be *added* to Abraham's faith. Paul will have none of it. The principle of Law and the principle of faith cannot be fused. They are contradictory. You cannot add Law to Christ. Christ *supplemented* is Christ *supplanted*. The principle is clear, "The just shall live by *faith*". This is a basic principle that should have been a light to all. Such a clear Scripture must be allowed its full value and all other statements must be interpreted in its light. The statement is used here to show that a man is accepted by God on the principle of faith. To endeavour to keep the Law by doing its works has no atoning value. The sinner must look to another, to Christ, who has paid the price.

12   Another equally clear statement from Paul is "the law is not of faith". If in v.11 a man is justified by faith then clearly Law-keeping is cancelled as a means of acceptance with God, for the principle of Law is clear, "The man that *doeth* them shall live in them". It does not call for faith but for obedience. You must do to live, whereas the true principle is you must *believe* (have faith) to live. So with the utmost clarity Paul has exposed the utter bankruptcy of the Law to give a person acceptance with God. The Judaizers had convinced the Galatians that Christ's work was not sufficient, that He had only *partly purchased* them, and so it was necessary for them to add their quota of works for salvation. How this thinking continued through the centuries can be seen in the Roman Catholic dogma of works (penance, confession, etc.), and in the setting aside of the death of Christ as the sole means of salvation by the apostate Protestant churches. Verse 13 will show us the fulness of the redemption wrought for us by Christ.

13   Paul now triumphantly declares that Christ has redeemed us from the curse of the Law. It is the first mention of the Lord since 2:21. Christ has done what the Law could not do. He has brought us out from under the curse the Law had brought upon us. "Redeemed" here has in view the price that was paid to free us. Note firstly *what* Christ has done, He has redeemed us; then *how* He did it, by becoming a curse for us.

What does it mean? He *was made* a curse for us? (Note the similar language in 2 Cor 5:21, "He was made sin for us".) It means here that He stood in the place of those who had broken the Law and bore the penalty due to them. Yet He personally had never broken the Law. (just as in 2 Cor 5:21, He took the sinner's place and bore the sinner's judgment, although He Himself was sinless.) So on the cross God *reckoned* Him to be what He was not. There *He became sacrificially what we were actually*. He took our place, bore our judgment, died our death. Yet He was Himself sinless, pure, holy, righteous. He never became a sinner or a Law-breaker, but He was treated as such by God. And it was all *for us*. What this meant to Him we shall never fully understand but what was ours fell on Him in those dread hours on Calvary. Now we are free! The price has been paid: the Redeemer has died. We have come out from under the curse, delivered for ever. However, many expositors feel that the "us" must be limited to the Jews who were under the Law and not to Gentiles. This being so, the message is clear to the Gentile Galatians. If the Jews under the Law came under the curse of God, what folly it is for Gentiles to follow their example! Then v.14 indicates that the death of Christ is also the basis for blessing to Gentiles and the "we" of v.14 includes both Jew and Gentile, as each receive the Holy Spirit through faith.

Paul now quotes Deut 21:23, "Cursed is everyone that hangeth on a tree". This refers to the Jewish custom of hanging bodies on a tree after stoning. "Tree" is used of the cross by Paul in Acts 13:29, "they took him down from the tree", and by Peter in 1 Pet 2:24, "his own self bore our sins in his own body on the tree". The expression "hanged on a tree" recurs in Acts 5:30 and Acts 10:39.

The message is clear; Christ died under the curse, the judgment of God. This to the Jews was a very real stumbling-block (1 Cor 1:23). How could the Christ, the Messiah, the Anointed of God, ever die under the divine curse? It was "anathema" to them. Probably when "Christ and him crucified" was preached the Jews would respond, "Anathema Jesus", "Jesus is accursed". Yet, says Paul, He had to bear that curse on the tree that we might be blessed.

14 Two blessings are now shown to be the result of the death of Christ. They come to us "in Christ Jesus" because of faith-union in Him; firstly the blessing of Abraham which is justification by faith and secondly the reception of the Holy Spirit through faith. What the Law could not secure is found in Christ.

Notes

10 We must note that there is nothing wrong with the Law in itself. Man came under its curse by seeking to make its observance a way of salvation. Paul says in Rom 7:12 that the law is holy and the commandment holy, just and good. He has been answering the question, "Is the law sin?" He refutes such a suggestion, declaring that it reveals sin. It was originally given to a "redeemed" people but according to 1 Tim 1:8-10 its application was not to righteous people but to Law-breakers. He tells us it is *holy* - because of its source, a holy God, and its standards which are holy. It is *just* - because its claims are righteous and wrong-doing is condemned and to be punished. It is *good* - because its precepts were beneficial and for the good of men.

11 It has been suggested that Paul was extracting a meaning from Hab 2:4 other than the prophet intended. But even if Habakkuk intended "faithfulness", is not that quality the product of "faith"? Here in Galatians, in establishing the truth of justification by faith, Paul *illustrates* from Abraham and establishes the *principle* from Hab 2:4.

13 Five times in vv.10-13 the idea of "curse" is before us. Three things emerge:

1   We were under the curse of the Law because of disobedience.

2   Christ interposed Himself and bore the penalty incurred by us.

3   We have been redeemed, brought out from under the curse to freedom. Note all was accomplished by Christ in His death not by life-obedience.

Hogg and Vine draw attention to three words in relation to the work of Christ.

(1) *Agorazō*, usually translated "buy", draws attention to the price that has been paid, e.g. in 1 Cor 6:20.

(2) *Exagorazō* as here in Galatians means "to purchase *with a view* to freedom". We were redeemed out of the curse of the Law as Darby translates in v.13.

(3) *Lutroō* meaning "to release on receipt of a ransom", the actual deliverance being prominent, the setting at liberty.

II. Law and Promise (3:15-22)

1. *Priority of the Promise*
   3:15-18

v.15 "Brethren, I speak after the manner of men; Though it be but a man's covenant, yet if it be confirmed, no man disannulleth, or addeth thereto.

v.16 Now to Abraham and his seed were the promises made. He saith not, And to seeds, as of many; but as of one, And to thy seed, which is Christ.

v.17 And this I say, that the covenant, that was confirmed before of God in Christ, the law, which was four hundred and thirty years after, cannot disannul, that it should make the promise of none effect.

v.18 For if the inheritance be of the law, it is no more of promise: but God gave it to Abraham by promise."

Paul is at his most masterly here as he anticipates an objection from his opponents. They would argue that it was true that the promise was given to Abraham and he was reckoned righteous because he believed it, but since then the Law was brought in and obviously its introduction must be taken into account. If it did not set aside the promise, it certainly added to it, so that to faith must be added the works of the Law.

15   Paul's language is most conciliatory. He brings forward an illustration, an analogy from human affairs. Once a covenant, agreement or will has been legally ratified, it cannot be set aside or cancelled, nor can one add a clause to it. If this would violate a fundamental principle of honour among men, how much more in relation to God's promise. To add to it, as the Judaizers were seeking to do, was to say that God had gone back on His promise, had altered the terms and so was guilty of a breach of faith. This was unthinkable.

16   This verse is a parenthesis to add force to the argument. If the promises were to be fulfilled in the "seed", i.e. in Christ, then the coming of the Law could not annul the promises, for the Redeemer had not yet come. In addition, Paul argues, the retention of a singular noun (seed) has in view only Christ as the One in whom the promises of God would find ultimate fulfilment (see note below).

17   The words, "in Christ", are omitted by most reliable translators. They lack MS support and obscure the force of Paul's argument. Paul now clinches his argument by drawing attention to the fact that 430 years passed before the Law was given and so could not set aside the promise which was, so to speak, signed and sealed so long ago. The promise rested on the unchanging word of God and could not be set aside by the Law.

18   If the inheritance is to be obtained on the principle of Law-keeping, then the principle of promise is set aside completely. But God gave the inheritance to Abraham on the principle of promise. *Charizomai*, "to give by an act of grace", is translated as "gave" (AV) but as "gave it in grace" (JND). The perfect tense is used to emphasise the *permanence* of the gift. For God to have given it on the principle of Law-keeping would have meant that its fulfilment depended on the obedience of man and all would have been forfeited on that ground. This was what was being presented to the Galatians ultimately to their condemnation. No, all must come from God by *grace* and *promise* and be received by *faith*.

But all this raises another question: why then was the Law given? Has it no place at all in the divine revelation? What use was it? Paul will answer this in the verses that follow.

Notes

16 It has been noted that the word "seed" is a collective noun as Paul well knew, using it in that sense in v.29 of this chapter. It is also used in this way in Gen 15:5; Gen 16:10; Gen 22:17. Again it is used as a singular of one person in Gen 4:25; Gen 21:13. The context then must decide how it is used.

If the reference to "seed" here goes back to Gen 22:18, then the Holy Spirit is enlightening us as to its meaning, therefore otherwise we would probably have never known or expected such a meaning.

(The same is true of the Lord's explanation of Exod 3:6 in Matt 22:32.) Gen 22:17 indicates as noted above its collective sense, as the references to "the stars of the heaven" and "the sand which is upon the seashore".

This verse has been used to prove the inspiration of *words* as Matt 22:32 to prove the inspiration of *tenses* in the Holy Scriptures.

17 Gen 15:13 and Acts 7:6 mention 400 years; Exod 12:40 and Gal 3:17 430 years from the promise to Abraham in Gen 15 to the giving of the Law in Exod 19. So in Gen 15:13 and Acts 7:6 the round number of 400 years must take in the sojourning in Canaan as well as Egypt where they were afflicted. Exod 12:40 would then give "the (whole) sojourning of the children of Israel (who dwelt in Egypt)" as 430 years.

2. *Purpose of the Law*
3:19-22

> v.19 "Wherefore then serveth the law? It was added because of transgressions, till the seed should come to whom the promise was made; and it was ordained by angels in the hand of a mediator.
> v.20 Now a mediator is not a mediator of one, but God is one.
> v.21 Is the law then against the promises of God? God forbid: for if there had been a law given which could have given life, verily righteousness should have been by the law.
> v.22 But the scripture hath concluded all under sin, that the promise by faith of Jesus Christ might be given to them that believe."

The question of the whole purpose of the Law is now raised. Let us see the progress of thought in this chapter. If the Law was unable to bestow the Holy Spirit (vv.1-5) and to justify a person in the sight of God (vv.6-9), if it could bring only a curse and not a blessing (vv.10-14) and had no relation to the promise of God (vv.15-18), what then was its purpose? In fact did it not seem to be opposed to the promises of God? By raising and answering two questions (vv.19-21) Paul will show the true reason for the Law and its relation to the promise.

19 Paul now declares the real point of the Law. Note a number of things:

1. It was an *addition* ("added"). Being supplementary, it was therefore inferior.

2. He now gives a *definition* ("for the sake of transgressions"): the Law revealed sin as transgression.

3. He now observes its *termination* ("till Christ, the Seed, should come"); it was only temporary.

4. He declares now its *administration* ("ordained by angels");

5. Finally its *mediation* is given ("the hand of a mediator" referring to Moses).

Observe here that the introduction of the Law was to show sin in a new light as *transgression*, the violation of a known law, as Rom 4:15 states clearly, "Where no law is, there is no transgression". Rom 5:14 indicates the conditions that obtained before the Law, "Nevertheless death reigned from Adam to Moses, even over them that had not sinned after the similitude of Adam's transgression". Sin was present but not known as transgression but once the Law was promulgated with its "Thou shalt" and "Thou shalt not" then those who broke it were seen to be in rebellion against the authority of God as they stepped over the limitations imposed by God and so violated the rights of others. The knowledge of sin was there before the Law but it was now enhanced in a new way as transgression. So the Law did not bring a sense of *holiness* but of *sin*, of shortcoming, while showing God to be righteous in punishing sin. Therefore the Law did not bring salvation, but showed men their need of it. Yet during all the centuries of Law God saved men by faith as He did before the Law and as He has done since. If the Law brought only the sense of sin to those Jews who were under it, what folly it was for the Galatians who were Gentiles to put themselves under it.

The Law is now declared to be a purely interim measure. It was protempore; it was temporary until the time when Christ arrived who was the true Seed to whom the promise referred, then it would be superseded having served its purpose. Thus for the Galatians or for others to go back to the Law was putting the clock back. The Law was now outdated as the revelation of God proceeded. It had been brought alongside the promise, fulfilled its function and was now set aside in the full revelation of God in Christ.

We are now told the Law was given by angels to Moses. Three times in the NT angels are mentioned in relation to the giving of the Law. In Acts 7:53 as Stephen drives home the guilt of the nation, he draws attention to their privilege in receiving the law in its majestic authority through the ministry of angels. Yet they failed to keep it. In Heb 2:2 it is mentioned in contrast to the gospel, "the word spoken by angels" in contrast to "so great salvation". Here in Gal 3 it is shown to be in contrast with God's direct revelation to Abraham. The mediation is declared to be two-fold: on God's side angels; on man's side, Moses. He is now showing that the Law is inferior because not only was it 430 years later than the promise, but there were also two intermediaries, an angel and Moses, whereas the revelation to Abraham was direct and intimate.

20   It is clear that a mediator at any time does not act for one Party, but is a third party who comes between two other parties. This is the meaning of the phrase, "a mediator is not a mediator of one (party)". So Moses was a mediator because he stood between the people and God. "But God is one" means that when God gave His promise to Abraham, there was no mediator: God assumed all the obligations and responsibilities. God was the *sole contracting party*. Everything depended on God, nothing on man. With the Law there were two contracting parties, leaving man responsible to keep his part, to be obedient, without the power to do so. With the promise to Abraham all was unconditional, for God undertook to do all that was required.

The Law was therefore inferior in dignity to the promise because of the requirement of a mediator. What a difference between Law and grace:

1. Law only condemns and curses, makes sin more heinous, whereas grace gives life;

2. Law was but temporary, a passing phase in God's ways, whereas grace is God's permanent way in dealing with men;

3. Law was mediated with God at a distance, but grace is God coming near to men, taking it upon Himself to bless men;

4. Law laid obligations upon men who were unable to fulfil them, whereas in grace all is undertaken by God Himself.

21 Having proved that the Law could not annul the promise and was really inferior to it, does that mean it was in opposition to the promise? "God forbid," says Paul for both came from the same God. They therefore could not be against each other, for God is not at war with Himself. Representing different expressions of the character of God they cannot conflict with each other.

Now the Law was not designed to give life, otherwise there would have been two ways to obtain it: by Law and by promise or grace. The Law only brought a sense of sin, condemnation, judgment and death. It was never intended to indicate God's attitude to men, always a disposition of grace.

22 But contrary to what is stated in v.21, the Law was never intended to impart life. Righteousness could not be attained thereby so that the fact is the Scripture hath concluded, declared, shut up all under sin. By its declarations the Scripture shows the true position of all men as shut up, locked up, under the power of sin so as to be unable to escape. Possibly such Scriptures as Deut 27:26 and Ps 143:2 are envisaged. See Rom 3:9-20 for other Scriptures to prove all under sin.

The word "all" being neuter, literally means "all things", but the words "under sin" that follow indicate that persons are in view. It is now stated that all were declared to be in such a helpless condition in order that they might be driven to faith in the great Deliverer, Jesus Christ, so that the promised righteousness and life might be given to them. All that man needs is now declared to be in Christ: liberty, freedom, justification, salvation, life. The phrase "faith of Jesus Christ" with its objective genitive indicates that Christ is the Object of faith. Only with faith in Him do righteousness and life come.

Notes

20 The setting forth of Christ as the one Mediator in 1 Tim 2:5 is different from here. There it has to do with the salvation of men. The One who stands between God and men must possess the attributes of Him toward whom He acts (i.e. of God). Yet at the same time He must participate in the nature of those for whom He acts (i.e. of men). The Mediator must therefore be both divine and human, and also be prepared to offer His sinless life in atonement for human sin.

As the Mediator of the new and better covenant (Heb 8:6; 9:15; 12:24) He is the One responsible for its introduction, administration and establishment. Note that *Surety* of the better covenant (Heb 7:22) presents a different thought. Christ as Surety is the personal *Guarantor* of its terms to His people. These terms are made sure to us because He has been accepted by God as our great High Priest after the order of Melchisedec as God has sworn by oath. His Suretyship is based on His Priesthood so that His presence before God guarantees to us the spiritual blessings of the better covenant.

III. Sons of God (3:23-29)

1. *Conditions under Law*
       3:23-25

> v.23 "But before faith came, we were kept under the law, shut up unto the faith which should afterwards be revealed.
> v.24 Wherefore the law was our schoolmaster to bring us unto Christ, that we might be justified by faith.
> v.25 But after that faith is come, we are no longer under a school master."

Paul is now showing that the Law was a parenthesis, fulfilling certain functions until Christ came. He sets forth the Law as a prison or a jailor (v.23) then as a guardian (v.24). But when the age of faith dawned there was through faith in Christ an emergence from these restrictive conditions to the full status of sons of God.

23 The phrase "after faith is come" has in view the present time. It links with v.19 "till the *seed* should come", with v.22 "faith of Jesus Christ" and with v.24 "unto Christ". Faith was always necessary as the link with God before Christ came, but His coming was the summit of revelation and all the doctrines concerning His Person and work fill out that revelation. Before the cross men of God put faith in the Christ of *prophecy*, whereas our faith is in the Christ of *history*. The faith that was exercised in each case is the same but now all is much clearer and fuller since the coming of Christ. "Kept under the law" indicates that some were held in custody probably in protective custody. Thus while the Law held the Jew in custody, bondage because of its strict demands and his inability to meet them, yet it also protected him from the sins and vices of the nations around him. "Shut up" indicates he was "under restraint", "in restrictive confinement", "with no way of escape", hemmed in, awaiting the revelation of the faith in its fulness in Christ, who would lead them out of all their bondage into freedom and liberty.

24   The Law is now declared to be our schoolmaster (AV). "Schoolmaster" is an unfortunate translation and "tutor" is equally unsatisfactory, as both project the idea of teaching, which idea is totally absent from the word *paidagōgos*. The *paidagōgos* was a person responsible for the moral and physical well-being of the child. The NIV renders "put in charge" but possibly J.B. Phillips gets as near as any with "a strict governess". The Law is not viewed here as though it were an elementary form of teaching, leading or preparing for a more advanced form of teaching, namely, the gospel. Rather it is seen as fulfilling certain functions "up to" (JND), that is having (in view) the coming of Christ. "To bring us" (AV) should be omitted. Note the end in view in vv.23-24: in v.23, to the revelation of the faith; in v.24, up to Christ. "The faith" and "Christ" go together, so that we are justified on the principle of faith.

25   Paul now repeats the important statements of the two previous verses. Verse 25a refers to v.23; v.25b to v.24. Now that the new era has dawned we are no longer under the supervision of the Law. It has been set aside, its office ended by the coming of Christ. The revelation of God has moved on; there can be no turning back.

2.   *Blessings in Christ*
   3:26-29

v.26 "For ye are all the children of God by faith in Christ Jesus.
v.27 For as many of you as have been baptized into Christ have put on Christ.
v.28 There is neither Jew nor Greek, there is neither bond nor free, there is neither male nor female: for ye are all one in Christ Jesus.
v.29 And if ye be Christ's, then are ye Abraham's seed, and heirs according to the promise."

Paul is now indicating the blessings that are ours since the era of faith has arrived:

1.   We are the sons of God (v.26);

2.   We are all one (v. 28);

3.   We are Abraham's seed (v.29).

He has dropped the Jewish "we" for "ye" including both Jew and Gentile. We noted in v.13 the first mention of Christ since 2:20; now we note that "after faith is come" (v.25) He is mentioned five times. How true this is, for now everything centres in Christ. He is pre-eminent in this day of faith and by His coming and cross has broken down the division that existed (see Eph 2:13-16).

26   The conjunction "for" connects with the previous verse and indicates that faith having come and the Law being abrogated we have now the status of sons which status frees us from the bondage of Law. The word "children" here should read "sons". Stress is laid on the fact of relationship being ours by *faith*, not by the works of the Law. Note that we become sons by faith *in Christ Jesus*, that is, at the moment of conversion. It is important to observe that every blessing is ours at conversion whether understood or not. We are told that *salvation* is in Christ Jesus (2 Tim 2:10); *redemption* is in Christ Jesus (Rom 3:24); *grace* is in Christ Jesus (2 Tim 2:1). We are never asked to go through an experience to merit a spiritual blessing for we have received them *all* in Christ (Eph 1:13). Note too that it is "in Christ Jesus" not "in Jesus Christ" (see note below).

27   "As many of you" equates with "ye all" of v.26, so that there is no suggestion that some were baptised and others not baptised. The NT does not envisage an unbaptised believer. "Baptized" implies water baptism, for in the NT baptism means water baptism unless it is indicated otherwise. "Baptized into Christ-indicates our union with Christ. This union is by faith in Christ, but is symbolised by baptism, the *rite* standing for the *reality*. "Baptized into Christ" refers back to "faith in Christ" in the previous verse, thus drawing attention to the close connection in the NT between conversion and baptism. The converts were baptised upon their profession of faith. In Mark 16:16 the Lord Jesus said: "He that believeth and is baptized shall be saved". The two acts were never intended to be separated, so that when they were received into the local assembly they were already baptised believers.

"Put on Christ" means that He is their righteousness. The expression equates with "faith in Christ" (v.26) and "baptized into Christ" (v.27), these three expressions having to do with the believer's standing in Christ. No works of Law are necessary to be added to our faith in Him.

28   Paul now declares that in this new standing and relationship all distinctions have disappeared. All are accepted before God in Christ on the same ground, no matter who they are or what they are. "One in Christ Jesus" is connected with *standing*. It has nothing to do with *gathering* or *outward unity*. We are all "one in Christ Jesus" supposing we never gather. Being a Jew did not give one priority before God; being a free man did not give one favour with God; and being a male did not assure privileged treatment from God. No *national* distinctions, Jew or Gentile; nor *social* distinctions, bond or free; nor *sex* distinctions, male or female, were recognised. How wonderful is the grace of God! Every wall, barrier and curtain has been swept away. Borders and frontiers have gone: no racial discrimination, no segregation, no colour bar. It matters not whether capitalist or communist, wealthy, middle class or working class. Being over-privileged or under-privileged or of the Third World makes no difference. In Christ all have equal status - all one in Christ Jesus.

This does not mean that these distinctions have ceased to exist. After conversion a person was still a Jew or a Gentile and this did create problems for which Paul had to legislate (Rom 14; 1 Cor 8). Hence a believer was still a slave or a master (see Eph 6; Col 3,4). And there were still male and female, so instructions had to be given as to the status of each (1 Cor 11; 1 Cor 14; 1 Tim 2). One was surprised to note some time ago Gal 3:28 being quoted as a proof-text for women taking part in church gatherings!

In the phrase "one in Christ Jesus", "one" being masculine, the RV renders, "ye are all one *man* in Christ Jesus", thus connecting the expression with the "one new man" of Eph 2:15. "One" here indicates not only our relationship "in Christ" but also indicates that all who are "in Him" are fused together. It is a similar idea to the truth of the "one body", "one-referring to a corporate personality which has come to light in the ways of God, finding its very existence centred in Christ. It is the Church, a spiritual entity, in its existence and life seen to be far above, superior to, and independent of the sectional interests that mark this world.

29 Paul now reaches a glorious conclusion as he declares that if they be Christ's, then they are spiritually the seed of Abraham. The Judaizers were claiming that the Gentiles must be circumcised and keep the Law in order to become Abraham's seed. Paul has proved that all that was promised to Abraham has been fulfilled in Christ, so that to be united to Christ the true Seed, is to be linked with Abraham and thus to be constituted heirs in association with Christ. The "seed" in v.16 is Christ, but in this verse it refers to Christians because of their union with Him. Logically it follows that if sons then heirs. It is to be observed that in Rom 8:17 heirship is connected with being children, not with being sons.

Notes

26 Christ Jesus: The emphasis falls on the first word. *Jesus* Christ is the One who was here, who is now in the glory. *Christ* Jesus is the One in glory who was once on earth. Paul usually speaks of Him as Christ Jesus for he came to know Him in the glory. Our links, like Paul's, are not with the Lord before the cross, but with Him in glory.

Sons of God: When believers are viewed as children, the emphasis is on *birth*; when viewed as sons, the emphasis is on *dignity* and *character*. The apostle John never speaks of believers as sons, always as children, reserving the word "son" for the Lord Jesus.

IV. Heirs of God (4:1-11)

1. *Slaves to Sons*
4:1-7

v.1 "Now I say, That the heir, as long as he is a child, differeth nothing from a servant, though he be lord of all;

v.2 But is under tutors and governors until the time appointed of the father.

v.3 Even so we, when we were children, were in bondage under the elements of the world:

v.4 But when the fulness of the time was come, God sent forth his Son, made of a woman, made under the law,

v.5 To redeem them that were under the law, that we might receive the adoption of sons.

v.6 And because ye are sons, God hath sent forth the Spirit of his Son into your hearts, crying, Abba, Father.

v.7 Wherefore thou art no more a servant, but a son; and if a son, then an heir of God through Christ."

In ch. 3 Paul contrasted the Law and the promise to show the temporary nature of the Law and the *permanence* of the promise. Here in ch. 4 he contrasts the *position* of the believer under Law and under grace, and moves to the climax in 5:1, declaring that Christ has set us free. So, stand fast in this liberty and do not submit to the yoke of slavery being imposed upon you. In vv.1-3 he shows the position under Law and in vv.4-7 that under grace, and concludes by reminding them of sonship and heirship. Then in vv.8-11 he endeavours to show them the folly of their retrograde action, by reminding them of former days and to expose the impure motives of the Judaizers in vv.12-20. He then reverts in vv.21-31 to the experience of Abraham. If in ch. 3 Abraham and Moses were prominent, now it is Abraham, Sarah and Isaac, Hagar and Ishmael, also Mount Sinai and Jerusalem. The whole import of the allegory is to demonstrate that believers now are born under the system of grace, born of the Spirit of God and therefore that the Galatians must be finished with the Law that genders bondage. "Cast it out", he exhorts as Abraham cast out Hagar and Ishmael. To what lengths the apostle has gone in his love for them to show them their true position in Christ and the result and tragedy of turning again to Law-works.

1-2 Paul now uses an illustration well known to his readers. A child or minor is heir to a large and prosperous estate, but while he is still so young and immature, he is not capable of administering it, so his position is no different from that of a servant or slave. He is continually under orders to do one thing or another. He is under the control of "tutors" or "guardians" who look after his *person*, and "governors" or "stewards" who look after his *property*. He is under care and discipline; everything is done for him, although he owns it all. This will be his status until he reaches his majority, the date of which was stipulated by his father. The title is his, but not the liberty or freedom of a son. Any official business will be done through his legal representative whose signature will be necessary in any contract.

3 By stating "Even so we", it would seem that Paul had Jews in mind. In v.8, however, he will speak of the Gentiles. By drawing the attention of the Galatians to the condition of the Jews under bondage to the Law, he is thereby showing the folly of Gentiles putting themselves under it. He views them as children under "the elements of the world". The word "elements" is variously translated (see note). *Stoicheion*, meaning "elements" or "first principles", was used of the letters of the alphabet, the A B C or elementary teaching. Here it refers to the Jewish religion. "Of the world" would suggest the teaching was of an earthly nature, connected with material things and appealing to the senses. The phrase, "the elements of the world," has in view the Law and its teaching, no doubt including the multitude of rules and regulations added by Jewish teachers down the centuries, the keeping of which brought its adherents into bondage and slavery. Its whole appeal was to the physical and external. Circumcision, for example, was set forth as a means of salvation but only enslaved its followers. This would be in line with the teaching of 3:23. And "worldly rudiments" show man after the flesh trying vainly to work out his salvation by keeping the Law.

4 "But ... God". How wonderful to view divine intervention in the history of mankind! God moves in order to redeem and to bestow the blessing of sonship. We have four things brought before us:

1   The fulness of the time;

2   The sending of the Son of God;

3   Born of a woman;

4   Born under Law.

Let us look at them more closely.

1. "The fulness of the time" speaks of the *end* of an appointed period and the *beginning* of another. This was a new beginning in God's ways. The moment had arrived in God's calendar and in the history of men for a radically new movement. It was a time opportune in every way.

    a   It was the time of *divine* appointment. Daniel's Seventy Weeks were running their course, and the time referred to as "unto the Messiah the Prince" had now arrived (Dan 9:25). Many prophetic Scriptures were now at the point of being fulfilled.

b   *The Law* had fully served its purpose; the inability of man to keep it had been fully demonstrated and sin was now seen to be rebellion against the authority of God. The time in view in the phrase of 3:24 "up to Christ", had arrived.

c   *Morally* we are told the world had sunk to an abysmal low. The old gods had lost their hold over the masses and even pagans were crying out for something real.

d   *Politically* the Roman power was in undisputed command and their road-making would make easy the spread of the gospel.

e   The use of the Greek language would facilitate the onward march of the gospel.

In every way "the time appointed of the father" had come (4:2). The day of liberation, freedom and redemption had arrived. Everything would now centre in the Lord Jesus Christ, the Son of God, for the Seed had come (3:19).

2. The sending of the Son of God. Who would have thought that God would send His own Son to accomplish redemption? Elsewhere we are told "the Father sent the Son" (1 John 4:14) and that "Christ Jesus came into the world" (1 Tim 1:15). The Jews believed the Messiah was to come but not the Son of God. They reject the Lord on that ground. "Therefore the Jews sought the more to kill him, because he not only had broken the sabbath, but said also that God was his Father, making himself equal with God" (John 5:18). Such a relationship within the Godhead was not clearly made known until the Lord was here on earth. This statement indicates the cost to God of our redemption; He would send His own Son. "God sending his own Son" (Rom 8:3); "He that spared not his own Son" (Rom 8:32). How near to the heart of God lay this great matter of our redemption! The work was such that no other could have undertaken it. Only the Son was capable of doing it.

No angel could our place have taken,
Highest of the high though he;
Nailed to the cross, despised, forsaken,
Was One of the Godhead three!

O how vile our low estate,
Since our ransom was so great.

3. "Born of a woman" or "woman-born". This refers to His *humanity*, while "God sent forth his Son" refers to His *deity*. These two expressions bring

before us the uniqueness of the Person of the Lord; He was God and He was Man. In Him there was the union of two perfect and complete natures, the divine and human. And yet He was *one Person*. He was not a dual Personality, but a divine Person in human conditions (see note below). Here Paul is drawing attention more to the fact of the Lord's humanity than to His virgin birth. Yet the expression "born of a woman" is most significant. While it is true we were all "born of a woman", the fact that this statement stands in close proximity to His Sonship and deity, with no mention of a father, makes it most impressive. It is consistent with the record elsewhere of the virgin birth (Luke 1:34-35; Matt 1:18-25), and connects with the statement in Gen 3:15, "the seed of the woman", all combining to show that the Lord Jesus was not conceived by the ordinary processes of generation.

4. "Made under the law" indicates that He was born a Jew. As such he was subject to Jewish Law, so He was circumcised (Luke 2:21) and was required to keep the Law. He was the only person ever to keep the Law perfectly. All others failed. It was necessary for Him to be born while the Law was still recognised so as to redeem them who were under the Law, as the next verse will demonstrate. It is never stated that Christ kept the Law for us. Not His life-obedience but His sin-bearing is vicarious.

5   The purpose of His coming is now stated: He came to redeem, to purchase with a view to freedom. In 3:13 it is stated that He redeemed from the curse of the Law; here that they are brought out from the Law-system with its attempts at salvation by works. This must have been a most revealing statement to the Galatians, showing them that if Law-keepers had to be redeemed, it was so foolish of them to place themselves in that very position.

The two results of God sending His Son are that God redeems and that we receive sonship. How redemption was accomplished is not stated, but we know from 1:4 it was by Christ giving Himself in death, and from 3:13 by His becoming a curse for us. But how do we receive sonship? Notice the expression, "the adoption of sons"; it means son-placing, in God's family as full-grown, adult sons, in contrast to being *born* into the family as children. So we are born into God's family as children, but *placed* there as sons.

Our relationship as children emphasises *birth*, whereas sonship emphasises *dignity* and *status*. Note too the contrast suggested in v.3 and v.5 between children under the Law and sons under grace, there being no suggestion of growth as *Christians* in the passage from children to sons.

Note the contrast between the Lord's Sonship and ours. He is the Son of God. His is a filial relationship, eternal and unoriginated by its very *nature*, whereas ours is by adoption, by an act of God's grace.

6   Paul now indicates that the proof of their sonship is the presence of the Holy Spirit within. Note the four major subjects brought before us.

1   The involvement of the Godhead in salvation.

2   The sovereign action of God in sending the Holy Spirit.

3   The Spirit of His Son.

4   The joyful expression of relationship.

Let us now expand on these four themes.

1. *The Involvement of the Godhead in Salvation*
God sent His Son; God sends the Holy Spirit; the Spirit thus sent is the Spirit of His Son. Divine Persons are seen accomplishing all that is necessary for our blessing while we are merely the recipients of that blessing. The fellowship of Father, Son and Spirit is seen in the great acts of salvation, namely in the incarnation of Christ, in His death upon the cross, in the gift of the Holy Spirit and the gift of sonship. How impressive to every believing heart are the movements of the Godhead in salvation.

2. *The Sovereign Action of God in sending the Holy Spirit*
Because we are sons God gives us the Holy Spirit at conversion. We are never asked to go through an experience to receive the Spirit nor any other blessing. We have every spiritual blessing in Christ (Eph 1:3). God never says, "Do this to be that". Rather He says "you are that, now be that". So the presence of the Holy Spirit within authenticates sonship.

3. *He is the Spirit of the Son*
That we might enjoy and experience the fulness of this relationship we have the Spirit of the Son. This is the only place where the title, the Spirit of the Son, is used. In Rom 8:15 He is called the Spirit of sonship. We have now the Spirit of His Son to correspond to our status as sons. We can now enter into the closeness and intimacy of this relationship, the Spirit helping and strengthening us in our hearts to love, serve, trust and adore. This is native to us now because we have the Spirit of the Son. Natural parents who adopt can give status but cannot give their spirit to their chosen boy or girl. Let us ever wonder and delight that spiritually God can and has given the Spirit.

4. *The Joyful Expression of Relationship*
We cry, "Abba, Father". "Abba" is an Aramaic word, the language spoken in those early days. "Father" is a Greek word *patēr*, the equivalent of "Abba". Note here it

is the Spirit who cries, "Abba, Father", whereas in the parallel passage in Rom 8:15 it is we who cry. The Spirit thus bears witness with our spirit. It is of interest that these are the words the Lord Jesus used in the Garden of Gethsemane (Mark 14:36) in an hour of deepest pressure. The same words, obviously indicating intimacy, nearness, dependence are now upon the lips of the believer. They were the true expression of His Sonship as they are of ours. We are told the word "Abba" is a diminutive used by infants thus suggesting complete trust. Vine suggests in his Expository Dictionary that "Father" is the word of maturity, the intelligent realisation of a relationship, the unreasoning trust of absolute dependence, the love and devotion of a grateful heart.

7 "Wherefore", because God has sent His Son to redeem and the Holy Spirit into our hearts as proof of our sonship, we are no longer slaves but sons. Emancipation, deliverance and relationship are ours as sons and God has also made us heirs. God having accomplished it all, it has nothing to do with works or human action. Note the singular "thou" for this is true of each individual believer. "We" of v.3 would refer to Jews; "we" of v.5 to Jews and Gentiles; "ye" of v.6 to the Galatians in particular; but "thou" here in v.7 to each and every saint.

Notes

3 RSV rendering "slaves to the elemental spirits of the universe" suggests bondage to the tyranny of evil spirits. But this seems foreign to the prevailing Jewish context.

4 The union of two complete natures in one Person is known to the theologians as hypostatic union. We sometimes speak of the Lord Jesus doing certain things as God (e.g. stilling the storm) and certain things as Man (e.g. sleeping in the boat) but we must be very careful not to divide His Person. He is not two Persons but one Person, the Son of God, of one substance with the Father. The Westminster Shorter Catechism says: "The only Redeemer of God's elect is the Lord Jesus Christ, who being the eternal Son of God became man and so was, and continueth to be God and man in two distinct natures and one Person for ever."

2.   Paul's Passionate Plea
4:8-11

v.8   "Howbeit then, when ye knew not God, ye did service unto them which by nature are no gods.
v.9   But now, after that ye have known God, or rather are known of God, how turn ye again to the weak and beggarly elements, whereunto ye desire again to be in bondage?
v.10 Ye observe days, and months, and times, and years.
v.11 I am afraid of you, lest I have bestowed upon you labour in vain."

Paul yet again endeavours to show the Galatians the terrible danger to which they were exposing themselves in turning to Judaism. Having proved to them justification was by faith and not by works; that the Law could only curse; that the Law but proved men to be transgressors and was only temporary until Christ came; that the condition under Law was like a minor hemmed in by restrictions, and that the Godhead had liberated and freed them, granting to them the status of sons and the gift of the Holy Spirit, Paul now seeks by a stark contrast to alert them to the danger of entering into fresh bondage.

8   He brings before them their pre-conversion days when they were in ignorance of the true God and were in bondage ("did service") to idols. Paul recalled the Corinthians' former manner of life in 1 Cor 12:2 and the Thessalonians being Gentiles who knew not God (1 Thess 4:5). Note the connection between ignorance and idolatry. As men gave up the knowledge of God, so they "changed the glory of the incorruptible God into an image made like to corruptible man, and to birds, and to four footed beasts, and creeping things" (Rom 1:21-23). This is seen today in the Roman Catholic community in the worship of Mary, images, etc. To worship and serve the created thing rather than the Creator is the sin of idolatry (Rom 1:25). He speaks here of "them which by nature are no gods", the word "nature" referring to origin or birth. Whether it be the idol or more likely the demon behind the idol, they were created and by the very nature of the case could not be reckoned as gods. They were gods in name only, having been given such status by the worshippers. Paul does not deny the fact of their existence but does deny their deity. The words of Paul to the Corinthians apply here, "the things which the Gentiles sacrifice, they sacrifice to demons and not to God" (1 Cor 10:20, cf. Deut 32:17). Tersely he dismisses them as "no gods". (Read Ps 115:4-8; Isa 46:6-7; cf. Isa 46:3-4; 63:9.)

9   But "*now*" in contrast to "*then*" of v.8, they had come to know God but lest they might consider this was due to their own efforts, he quickly amends his statement to "rather known by God", in order to draw attention to the divine initiative in their salvation. Paul marvels at three things:

1   They were turning away from the revelation of the true God, from the God who redeemed them, from the God who had liberated them, from the God who had so richly blessed them. He had brought them out from the darkness, ignorance and hopelessness of idolatry, had forgiven them, made them sons and heirs. His Spirit indwelt them and His strength empowered them. To turn their back on such a God was to Paul incomprehensible.

2   They were turning to Law-keeping. He describes its teaching as weak and beggarly. "Weak" because of its lack of power to redeem, to justify and liberate; the Law could define sin, convict

of sin, pronounce judgment on sin, but could not deliver from sin. It could diagnose sin but could not cure it. How could they turn from an experience of the power of God to the impotence of Judaism. "*Beggarly*" means poverty-stricken, powerless to enrich. How wonderfully the gospel had enriched them. Fulness of blessing brought to them every spiritual blessing in Christ. It amazed Paul that they should even consider turning to that which had nothing to offer, no riches to give, no blessings to bestow.

3   They were putting themselves in a new bondage, this time to Judaism. It should be noted there are two different words translated "again" in this verse. The first word, *palin*, meaning "repeated action", shows they were in bondage, first to pagan idolatry, now to Judaism. The second word, *anōthen*, should be rendered "anew" as in RV and JND in John 3:3,7. Darby translates the phrase in this verse, "to which ye desire to be again *anew* in bondage". This seems to be correct as the bondage would be the same in effect, to a new master, to the *Law* and not to *idols*.

10 They were observing (*paratēreō* indicating a "careful observance") days, months, times, years. Paul, an ex-Pharisee, well-acquainted with their punctilious observances is alarmed that they were getting involved in this useless, lifeless, ritualism. Days refer to the Sabbaths (Exod 20:8-11); months refer to the New Moons (1 Chron 23:31); times or seasons to the annual Feasts (Lev 23); years to the Sabbatical Year (the seventh year, Lev 25:4) and the year of jubilee (Lev 25:10). They were getting occupied with external things. The danger of observing special days and months and sacred seasons was that men were inclined to think the discharge of these duties left them free at other times to do as they liked. How true this is today of the greater part of Christendom with its religious calendar, festival days and ornate ritual. May the Lord preserve us in the simplicity of the apostolic faith. Thus Paul sought to show them the danger of turning away from the splendour of the grace of God to legalism.

11 Paul is fearfully apprehensive of the outcome. He had expended prodigious effort in bringing the gospel to them. The "labour" or "toiling to the point of exhaustion" had been worth it all to bring them to Christ. Few among us know the joy of thus labouring and planting assemblies. He is now afraid lest it may have been in vain, to no purpose. How it all must have pained him. Can you see the tear-dimmed eye, the bleeding heart? O this care of the churches, this burden, this concern, this anxiety! May God give us more interest in and care for them.

V. The Appeal of Paul (4:12-20)

1.   *The Reception of Paul*
   4:12-15

> v.12 "Brethren, I beseech you, be as I am; for I am as ye are: ye have not injured me
> at all.
> v.13 Ye know how through infirmity of the flesh I preached the gospel unto you at the
> first.
> v.14 And my temptation which was in my flesh ye despised not, nor rejected; but
> received me as an angel of God, even as Christ Jesus.
> v.15 Where is then the blessedness ye spake of? for I bear you record, that, if it had
> been possible, ye would have plucked out your own eyes, and have given them
> to me."

Paul's tone is changing. Note "I beseech you" (v.12) and later, "my little children" (v.19). The heart of the shepherd is coming to the surface. All along it has been Paul the teacher, the theologian; now it is the shepherd, the shepherd-teacher of Eph 4:11, as it should be with love for those we teach. How easy to accept teaching when we know that behind it there is a heart that loves us. Let all who are teachers cultivate this exemplary manner. How Paul loved them will again be seen later as he speaks of "travail", "enduring birth-pangs all over again", that they might be delivered from legalism, that Christ be formed in them.

12   Paul now makes his appeal, beseeching them, "Be as I am", that is, "turn away from the Law as I had to do to find acceptance with God". Liberty and life are only to be found in Christ. To go back to Law-keeping is regression. Paul longed that they might be delivered from the false teaching, and fully enjoy the liberty that was in Christ. "Become like me", as clear from the Law as a means of salvation, having died to it in Christ and stand fast in the liberty that is in Christ. "I am as ye are" means that Paul had become like them in seeking salvation only in Christ as if he were a Gentile (2:15,16). He had come out from its bondage and, finding his need met in Christ, was free entirely from it. What folly for them to put themselves under it.

The expression "ye did me no wrong" (RV) should be connected with vv.13-15, as the aorist tense would confirm, looking back to an occasion in the past. The RV commences a new sentence here and so joins it to the succeeding verses. The strength of Paul's language in the previous verses could have given the impression of personal grievance, but Paul, realising this, hurries to assure them this is not so. Rather the welcome he had received from them put him in their debt. His language was the outcome, not of personal grievance, but of love for them, in his alarm at their turning away from the true gospel. He felt their turning away from him to the false teachers, but this was to their injury, and a blow to the true gospel.

13   In vv.13-15 Paul is vividly recalling to them the circumstances of his first visit. He says he came to them in weakness (infirmity) of body and preached the gospel to them. The nature of this bodily illness is not made known. Clearly the Galatians did not need an explanation, but much conjecture has led to many suggestions. A number of expositors hold that in Pamphylia Paul contracted malaria, which with its accompanying prostrating headache, left him an ill man, and he was forced to leave the lower region of Perga for the highlands of Galatia. Despite his physical condition he preached the gospel on his arrival and many were won for Christ. However in the Acts account Luke makes no mention of any such illness (see note below for other suggestions).

14   The word "temptation" or "trial" seems to equate with "infirmity" in the previous verse. The expression "of the flesh" (v.13) and "in my flesh" would suggest it was physical. The AV says "my trial", suggesting it was a trial to Paul, whereas the RV translates, "a temptation to you", indicating it was a trial to others. Whatever the nature of Paul's illness it produced a loathing or disgust in those who saw it and normally would mean the rejection of the unfortunate sufferer. "Despise" means "to treat with contempt", "to despise utterly". "Reject" is "to loathe", "to spit out". Hogg and Vine remark, "The sentence is elliptical: 'although my disease repelled you, you did not on that account refuse to hear my message' ". They did not judge the messenger or reject the message because of outward appearance. Possibly they were acquainted with the disease and its symptoms and so felt sympathetic to the sufferer, especially when they listened to the message of the gospel from his lips. Despite the repulsive character of his illness they received him as a messenger (angel) of God, as Christ Jesus. Clearly Paul's physical condition was such as to make them want to turn away in disgust. Yet he was so absorbed in his message, so taken up with Christ, the treasure so shining through the earthen vessel that the excellency and exceeding greatness of the power was seen to be of God. The physical was forgotten as Paul declared the glorious message of the gospel, and they received him as a messenger from another world and accorded to him a welcome worthy of the Lord Himself. This was as it should be for he was Christ's representative, carrying His authority, and declaring His message. The words of the Lord Jesus come to mind, "He that heareth you heareth me; and he that despiseth you despiseth me" (Luke 10:16). He does not rebuke them as he did at Lystra, when after healing the cripple, they wanted to pay him divine honour (Acts 14:8-18). Obviously their enthusiastic reception of him was not because of his physical appearance. Rather in spite of it, as they saw Christ living in him, speaking through him, they recognised God's powerful interest in declaring the gospel.

15   Paul now indicates that things had changed. What had happened to the joy they had experienced when he was among them preaching? What a blessing they had received in discovering Christ. How happy had been the fellowship between them as they congratulated themselves in having received such blessing. How satisfied they had been with his company. In those early days of spiritual prosperity they would have plucked out their eyes and given them to him. The fellowship was so deep and intimate that no sacrifice was too great to make for him. Some have thought this refers to serious eye-trouble and link it with 6:11. However it may only be a vivid figure of speech, indicating they would have parted with their most precious possession. Now they were in danger of deserting him, of turning away from him. What was the cause of their defection? How could such a friend, such a messenger have become their enemy?

Notes

13 Many consider that the "infirmity" and "temptation" (v.14) are the same as the "thorn in the flesh" (2 Cor 12:7). All kinds of suggestions have been made in endeavouring to identify it. It has been identified as malaria, ophthalmia (eye-trouble), epilepsy, a speech impediment, physical suffering, carnal desire and spiritual trials. Clearly we do not know the precise nature and the lack of identification has meant that many suffering believers have drawn strength and comfort from this experience. It does seem to have been painful, humiliating and recurring.

14 It is remarkable that despite the repulsive character of Paul's illness they received him warmly and cordially. A servant's appearance should not determine his acceptance. He may or may not be attractive and pleasing. He may be gifted or not so gifted; physically healthy or like Paul at this time, with impaired health. What is all-important is the message he brings to the people. There is a tradition that Paul was ugly; certainly the Corinthians thought his appearance unimpressive and his speech of no account.

2.   The Concern of Paul
   4:16-20

   v.16 "Am I therefore become your enemy, because I tell you the truth?
   v.17 They zealously affect you, but not well; yea, they would exclude you, that ye might affect them.
   v.18 But it is good to be zealously affected always in a good thing, and not only when I am present with you.
   v.19 My little children, of whom I travail in birth again until Christ be formed in you,
   v.20 I desire to be present with you now, and to change my voice; for I stand in doubt of you."

Having drawn attention in the previous verses to the close fellowship they had enjoyed together in early days, Paul now raises the question of their present hostile attitude. He seeks to expose the impure motives of the false teachers and declares his deep exercise that Christ might be formed in them. He longed to be with them. Speaking would be so much easier than writing. How his love for these saints shines out. The less he was loved the more he seemed to love. They may have adopted the attitude of an "enemy" to him, but Paul's affection for them remained the same. Would that we could learn the lesson.

16   Their hostility to Paul lay in the fact that he had told them the truth by drawing their attention to the true nature of this "other gospel" and by rebuking them for turning away from their liberty in Christ to embrace Law-keeping with its resultant bondage. What a contrast between receiving him as a messenger from God, even as Christ Jesus and now treating him as an enemy. The phrase "tell you the truth" is in the present continuous drawing attention not only to what he had said previously but also to the present letter. Paul was following the example of the Lord Jesus "a Man that hath told you the truth". "Faithful are the wounds of a friend" (Prov 27:6).

Paul is drawing attention to their fickleness. When he came to them with such a wonderful message, they treated him as if he were the Lord; now, when what he said was unpalatable, he was treated like an enemy. How true this is today. When Paul's ministry suits, it is a commandment from the Lord, but when it is unacceptable and he teaches that women are to be silent in the churches, then he is considered a woman-hater! Every true servant must be prepared for rejection and hostility when his message cuts across the opinion of the day. Yet when he must declare certain home-truths for the good of his hearers, it must be done as Paul was doing it, with a heart full of love for the saints. Our attitude to those who teach us should be governed by their loyalty to the Scriptures, not by whether they agree with our whims and fancies.

17   Paul now seeks to expose the impure motives of the false teachers. They were zealously and earnestly trying to win the confidence and the affections of the Galatians, but their motives were not honourable. Paul's expression "but not well", means it was not for a good purpose. It was to exclude them, to shut them out, to isolate them, to alienate them, not only from Paul, but from the freedom that was in Christ and the gospel. The reason behind their interest in these converts was that the Galatians might turn to them for assurance of salvation ("affect" meaning "to seek"). If they could persuade them that the gospel preached by Paul was not enough for salvation, then they would turn away from Paul and his gospel and seek further help from them. Thus they would have the Galatians in their clutches. The converts would be depending on them to instruct them as to full salvation. It reminds us of the Dark Ages: when the pure gospel was lost sight of, works were taught to be necessary to salvation, and men were in ecclesiastical bondage. Cole suggests Paul is thinking back to 3:22-23, to the expression, "shut up" (RV). He comments, "The Law deliberately 'herded men together' as sinners so that they might find salvation; these Judaizers are 'bolting men outside' lest they should enjoy salvation. There could be no greater contrast then between the Judaizers and the very Law that they profess to teach".

18   This verse is highly compressed and has been expounded in different ways. Some think Paul is referring to the false teachers, and is saying that their interest would be quite legitimate if it was for the Galatians' blessing. Others feel that he is referring to the Galatians themselves, that having been warm and cordial in their attitude to him when he was with them, he wished it would be the same when he was absent. The present writer feels Paul is referring to himself, and saying, "It is an admirable thing to be sought after, as long as the motives are honourable and pure, as mine are toward you, not only when I am present with you, but also now when I am absent from you". He now explains how deeply he was seeking their good.

19 Very tenderly he addresses them as "my little children". They were his for he had brought them to Christ. He had brought them to birth, so to speak. Paul is deeply moved; his emotions are rising. His expression now goes beyond "brethren": they were his own children. He felt for them as only one can who has brought others to Christ, as he now sees them in very real danger. He says he is travailing in birth-pangs again. The first time was to bring them to Christ; now it was that Christ should be formed in them. The first was to free them from idolatry (v.8): the second to free them from Law-keeping. The first was the agony of the evangelist: the second the agony of the pastor-teacher (Eph 4:11). His ardent desire was to see Christ formed in their lives. This would be the concrete evidence of their salvation. It is true that *morphoō* refers to what is inward, to inner being, the thoughts, aspirations, desires, but surely with reflection in their ordinary, everyday life.

20 Paul longed and fervently wished to be with them. However at the moment this was impossible. Being absent from them he is perplexed about them (RV). If only he could be with them, then he could assess accurately their condition and deal with it accordingly. He recognised the value of personal contact, of face to face dealing. He would then be able to adjust his speech to their state. He could be more tender or more stern as the situation demanded. In either case, with more understanding, he could expound in detail what was necessary to help them in their spiritual crisis. He obviously preferred to speak than to write, for the voice is usually more effective than the pen.

VI. The Two Covenants (4:21-31)

1. *Historical Setting*
4:21-23

v.21 "Tell me, ye that desire to be under the law, do ye not hear the law?
v.22 For it is written, that Abraham had two sons, the one by a bondmaid, the other by a freewoman.
v.23 But he who was of the bondwoman was born after the flesh; but he of the freewoman was by promise."

In vv.21-31 Paul develops a completely new line of argument for the Galatians to ponder. He brings it forward at the close of the doctrinal section in order to drive home to his hearers the utter folly of putting themselves under Law. He takes up certain well-known facts in the life of Abraham and declares in v. 24 that such things are an allegory, illustrating the inevitable antagonism between the gospel and the Law. According to Vine's Expository Dictionary *allēgoreō* signifies "to speak, not according to the primary sense of the word, but so that the facts stated are applied to illustrate principles". Of course such a method does not deny the literal meaning of the passage.

Paul deals firstly with the historical setting (vv.21-23), then with the spiritual teaching (vv.24-27), and finally with the application of the teaching (vv.28-31). In the first section he shows that Abraham had two sons, born of different mothers and in different ways. In the second section he speaks of two covenants, two Jerusalems and of slavery and freedom. In the final section he reveals what has been in his mind all along, that they should "cast out" the false teachers.

21 Paul now challenges the Galatians for they could not deny that they desired to be under law. The word "law" is used in two different senses. The first refers to the principle of the law, keeping the law as a way of life to attain salvation and holiness. The second refers to the books of the Law most probably here the Pentateuch (Genesis to Deuteronomy). He now takes them on their own ground and challenges whether they had seriously considered what the Law taught. He now seeks to prove to them that the Law would point them in the opposite direction to the way they were taking. It would condemn and not justify. His use of the Law here must have surprised and amazed the Galatians and their false teachers. Would that it had the same effect today upon many who are under law, who believe and teach that certain religious duties must be performed in order to obtain salvation. Are not both Protestantism and Roman Catholicism built upon this foundation? To a greater or a lesser degree have they not embraced a great deal of Jewish ceremony? How else can we account for large ornate buildings, imposing ritual, the clergy as a distinct class, the smoke of incense and all the paraphernalia that accompanies such religion? All their order of services based on the temple worship is far removed from the simple gatherings envisaged in the NT. Will not God's judgment be upon the false teachers today who enslave thousands as it was upon those who sought to enslave the Galatians?

22 Paul now reverts to a formula used by the Lord in the wilderness with the Devil, "It is written", thereby drawing attention to the authority of the Scriptures. He reminds them that Abraham had *two* sons from *different* mothers. The boast of the Jew was that he was a son of Abraham. Their physical descent was all important. In John 8 the Lord Jesus sought to show them that although they were physical descendants of Abraham, they were not his spiritual children. Their violent opposition proved that, far from Abraham being their father, it was the Devil. We can see where Paul is leading them.

What if their actions proved them to be morally descended from the *wrong son* and the *wrong mother*? The stress here is laid on the *different* mothers. If physical descent was all that mattered then the Ishmaelites had the same claim as the Jew. But note that while two mothers are stressed, it is clearly stated that one was a bondmaid (Hagar), the other was a free woman (Sarah). There is a double descent from Abraham, but it will prove to be all important who is their mother. The child will take character from the mother - to be a slave or free. He now shows the difference in birth (v.23), in attitude (v.29) and in inheritance (v.30).

23   Paul now noted *how* they were born. Ishmael was born "according to flesh" but Isaac "through the promise" (JND). The history is as follows. Because Abraham was childless he spoke to God about a son and heir (Gen 15). God responded by promising that Abraham himself would be the father (without mentioning at this time who would be the mother). He further promised that Abraham's seed would be as the stars of heaven. Sarah, no doubt aware of the promise of God and seeing she was barren, made the suggestion that Abraham should take Hagar, the slave girl, and have children by her (Gen 16). In due time Ishmael was born. Later God intimated to Abraham that Sarah would be the mother of the heir and that He would establish the covenant with Isaac (Gen 17). Abraham was then 100 years old and Sarah 90 years old. It seemed physically impossible for them to have a child. But the promise was made by God and in the passage of time Isaac was born. So it can now be seen that Ishmael was born according to the flesh, that is, by natural processes in the course of nature. Isaac, however, was born contrary to nature. When the promise was made to Abraham, he considered not his body now dead, nor the deadness of Sarah's womb (Rom 4:19 RV), but believed that what God had *promised* He was able to perform. Sarah received strength to conceive seed (Heb 11:11) and was delivered of a child when she was past age, judging Him faithful who had *promised*. Note too that Isaac born through promise (v.23) is stated in v.29 to be born after the Spirit, that is, by the supernatural power of the Holy Spirit the promise was fulfilled. So Ishmael represents the fruit of the work of nature while Isaac represents the fruit of the promise of God. He was Spirit-born as are all the true children of God. So one represents those who have experienced only the natural birth: the other those who are born of the Spirit.

2.   *Spiritual Teaching*
   4:24-27

   v.24 "Which things are an allegory: for these are the two covenants; the one from the mount Sinai, which gendereth to bondage, which is Agar.
   v.25 For this Agar is mount Sinai in Arabia, and answereth to Jerusalem which now is, and is in bondage with her children.

v.26 But Jerusalem which is above is free, which is the mother of us all.
v.27 For it is written, Rejoice, thou barren that bearest not; break forth and cry, thou
that travailest not: for the desolate hath many more children than she which
hath an husband."

24-25 Paul now indicates that the historical narrative was figurative and taught deep spiritual truths. The two women represent two covenants, clearly the old and the new. Hagar he connects with Mount Sinai where the Law was given. The Law begets ("gendereth") children to slavery, that is, to the same status as their mother. To put oneself under Law as the Galatians were tempted to do (and many today) leads to bondage. In v.25 Paul shows that the old covenant of Law promulgated at Mount Sinai was now centred in Jerusalem. Was not that the origin of the teaching which was enslaving the Galatians? This extension to Jerusalem was brilliant but only too true, for Jerusalem was the true home of Judaism. It was from there that the principle of Law-keeping was being sent forth; that circumcision and the observance of the legal code was necessary to be saved. Both Jew and Gentile were to subscribe to it, although it all sprang from the wrong source, from the wrong mother. Hagar, Mount Sinai, Jerusalem are all in the same line, in the wrong line. How it must have been borne home to the Galatians: that Hagar, Mount Sinai, Arabia, Jerusalem are tantamount to slavery.

26 Paul does not tabulate all that stands in antithesis. It can be stated: Hagar and Sarah; Ishmael and Isaac; Sinai and Zion; earthly Jerusalem and heavenly Jerusalem; Jews and others under Law and the christian believers; bondage and freedom. "Jerusalem above" is the system of grace, for the true gospel comes from heaven, from God. It is "free", since it is not subject to legal ordinances. And it is the mother of all Christians, for that "mother" gave us both origin and formation of character. How true this is! We were born from above. Our citizenship is there. Our names are written there. Our lives are governed and character formed by heaven's standards. Our prayers ascend there, our hope is centred there. One day soon we hope to be there.

27 Paul now quotes Isa 54:1 to set forth that the children of the heavenly Jerusalem will far outnumber those of the earthly Jerusalem. To link it with the previous verses Sarah was the barren and desolate who cried for children and Hagar the woman who had a husband. But in due time the position was reversed. Thus, although the Law had been prominent in the past, grace had now come into prominence and the vast multitude saved through the gospel would far exceed those under the Law. The verse quoted from Isa 54 was firstly a promise to the Jewish nation in a difficult day that the future would be one of blessing and rejoicing, but is here used in a secondary sense to establish the position of grace over Law.

Notes

24 It is most instructive to note Paul's allegorising of this OT passage under the inspiration of the Spirit of God. He sees behind the narrative deep spiritual principles and lessons. This confirms what is stated in Rom 15:4 that things written before were for our instruction and also confirms to the spiritual mind the supreme value of the OT Scriptures. There are two extremes we must avoid:

1   Fanciful interpretations. Paul's appeal to his readers, "Do you not hear the Law?" would suggest they should have noted such things. It should have been apparent. We too must take note of such principles embedded in the Scriptures.

2   Ignoring the OT altogether as many do to their loss. Let us see that our handling of the OT is both intelligent and spiritual.

26 Vine in his *Expository Dictionary* makes an interesting observation of the term "mother": "Of the heavenly and spiritual Jerusalem, Gal 4:26, which is 'free' (not bound by law imposed externally, as under the Law of Moses), 'which is our mother' (RV), i.e. of Christians, the metropolis, mother-city, used allegorically, just as the capital of a country is 'the seat of its government, the centre of its activities and the place where the national characteristics are most fully expressed' ". Thus the heavenly Jerusalem would be the metropolis of Christianity, just as the earthly Jerusalem was the metropolis of Judaism. It would seem too from this and other Scriptures that the "mother" speaks of formation of character. This will be developed fully in the practical section of chs. 5 and 6. For certainty Christianity has produced a new society of saved men and women whose lives have been transformed under the heavenly system of Grace. Theirs is a new life far beyond that which is produced by a system of Law-keeping.

3.   *Application of Teaching*
   4:28-31

> v.28 "Now we, brethren, as Isaac was, are the children of promise.
> v.29 But as then he that was born after the flesh persecuted him that was born after the Spirit, even so it is now.
> v.30 Nevertheless what saith the scripture? Cast out the bondwoman and her son: for the son of the bondwoman shall not be heir with the son of the freewoman.
> v.31 So then, brethren, we are not children of the bondwoman, but of the free."

In applying the teaching Paul now enforces from the allegory that they are the true children (v.28). He warns them that they can expect persecution (v.29) and calls for vigorous action to be finished with the false teaching (v.30). He then sums up in v.31 the meaning of the allegory. It is possible that 5:1 should be connected with ch.4 and yet it also connects with 5:13 so possibly it forms a bridge, summing up what has gone before, while heading the practical section. It seems also to sum up the teaching of the whole epistle.

28   Many translators have "ye" instead of "we". "Ye", which is emphatic, would press home to the Galatians their true status as Abraham's seed (3:29). Like Isaac they were the children of promise. Their birth had been supernaturally brought about by God. If "we" is retained, it suggests that all Christians, Jew and Gentile, were born not of the will of the flesh, nor of the will of man, but of God. So clearly it is not physical descent that counts but the supernatural action of God by His Spirit.

29   Paul now continues the narrative of Hagar with Gen 21, the weaning of Isaac. Ishmael is said to have mocked Isaac. Paul takes this up as indicating deep hostility and says that it has always been true that those born of the flesh have acted in this way towards those born of the Spirit. Paul here plainly declares Isaac's birth to be of the Spirit. This is justified since both Abraham and Sarah were past the age of producing children, so that only the power of God had accomplished the birth. "Even so it is now" indicates that this miracle of new birth continues and that people so born can expect to be persecuted. 1 Chron 5:10,19 and Ps 83:6 show that this hostility continued through the centuries, as the continuous tense of the verb "was persecuting" may reinforce. In the setting here it is those dedicated to a religion of works who persecute the true people of God. How history has proved this to be true: in the deep-seated hostility of the Pharisees and others to the Lord Jesus; in the bitter persecution of Paul by the Judaizers; in the ferocious, murderous onslaught of the Roman Catholic Church against the Huguenots; in the hostility of the nominal Establishment against those who would uphold, preach and practise the true gospel.

The allegory itself draws vivid attention to opposites:

Hagar	Sarah
Ishmael	Isaac
Old Covenant	New Covenant
Sinai	Zion
Earthly Jerusalem	Heavenly Jerusalem
Slavery	Freedom
Flesh	Promise
Flesh	Spirit
Persecuting	Persecuted
Expulsion	Inheritance
Judaism	Christianity

30   The issue of this stormy scene in Abraham's household was that at the request of Sarah (supported by the divine command) Hagar and Ishmael were cast out and disowned. Clearly Paul is calling on the Galatians to adopt the same tactics and be finished with the false teaching of works. Let them take decisive, urgent and permanent action to rid themselves of that which God had disowned.

The inheritance, all the spiritual blessings of the gospel, belong to those who are free-born. The purveyors of the gospel of works have no place in God's order.

Note again the connection between sons and heirs (cf. 4:7). The exclusive nature of sonship and heirship must surely cause us to recognise the differences between saved and unsaved. There can be no fellowship between saved and unsaved. They are incompatible, their natures, tastes and desires being totally opposed. Such a mixture as is seen in Christendom today is unknown in the word of God.

31 In conclusion, Paul shows that we are the *spiritual* descendants of Abraham. This does not mean as some suggest that we inherit the promises of the OT nor that these promises are spiritual and not literal. The earlier teaching was not to show that the Church has taken the place of Israel, but that Abraham was justified by faith, that the works of the Law only brought a curse and that all blessing now is received through faith. The allegory crowns the teaching that Law-keeping enslaves. Thus Paul by his teaching was seeking to free the Galatians from the influence of false teachers, not to set aside Israel. The promises made to Abraham and his seed still stand and God will yet honour His word and fulfil His promises to the nation of Israel. His phrase "not children of the bondwoman" indicates freedom from the Law. The article is omitted before "bondwoman" but is present before "free", for we are not children of any slave or of any system, but are children of "the free". This latter expression indicates that we are under the reign of grace which is not subject to the bondage to Law. Thus Paul ends the doctrinal section by reminding us we are the only "free" people in the world.

CHAPTERS 5 AND 6 - PRACTICAL
THE POWER OF THE GOSPEL

1. Freedom in Christ (5:1-15)

1. *Falling from Grace*
5:1-6

v.1 "Stand fast therefore in the liberty wherewith Christ hath made us free, and be not entangled again with the yoke of bondage.
v.2 Behold, I Paul say unto you, that if ye be circumcised, Christ shall profit you nothing.
v.3 For I testify again to every man that is circumcised, that he is a debtor to do the whole law.
v.4 Christ is become of no effect unto you, whosoever of you are justified by the law; ye are fallen from grace.
v.5 For we through the Spirit wait for the hope of righteousness by faith.
v.6 For in Jesus Christ neither circumcision availeth any thing, nor uncircumcision; but faith which worketh by love."

We now arrive at the practical section of the epistle. In chs. 1 and 2 Paul established that his apostleship was divine in origin, that he was directly commissioned by Christ Himself and thus was independent of the Twelve. In chs. 3 and 4 he proved that a person is justified by faith alone apart from works of the Law which could only bring one under the curse of God and that God had set them in His presence redeemed, possessed of His Spirit and with the dignity of sons and heirs. Now in chs. 5 and 6 he will show that the resultant life for God can be produced only by the power of the Spirit of God. Note "Walk in the Spirit" (5:16); "led of the Spirit" (5:18); "live in the Spirit" (5:25) "soweth to the Spirit" (6:8). In 5:1-5 he warns them of circumcision, declaring that if they submit to it they will have "fallen from grace" (vv.1-6). Then in vv.7-12 he makes known that such doctrine is not of God and the false teachers will pay the penalty for working such havoc. Finally in vv.13-15 he points to the danger of using their freedom wrongly.

1   There is much to be said for v. 1 standing on its own. It is a magnificent statement which clearly and fully declares the message of the whole epistle. Most translations have two sentences as the RV: "With freedom did Christ set us free: stand fast therefore and be not entangled again in a yoke of bondage". The first part of the verse is a statement of fact; the second an appeal. "With freedom" would mean with *complete* freedom, that is, freedom from every kind of slavery in the past. Some render it "for freedom", looking forward to the future life realised and manifested by the power of the Spirit. Note too that it is Christ who set free. It was accomplished by Him on the cross and has nothing to do with human effort. Freedom here is not so much from the penalty and power of sin nor from the wrath of God but "from the Law and its curse" in view of living a life for God by the Spirit. Freedom, liberty, deliverance, emancipation - all was theirs in Christ. How foolish to be freed from one form of slavery to go back into another, into Law-keeping.

He now makes his appeal: in view of what Christ has accomplished, in appreciation of the mighty deliverance and triumph wrought for you in the realisation of your new status, stand fast and hold your grounds. Do not allow yourselves to slip away into bondage as before. "The *yoke of bondage*", here is the works of the Law, possibly particularly circumcision of which he speaks in the following verses. They were in danger of being held by it, of bowing down under it as under a load. In the Jerusalem council which dealt with such an issue, Peter spoke out lest they "put a yoke upon the neck of the disciples, which neither our fathers nor we were able to bear". In contrast to this yoke is the invitation of Christ, "Take my yoke upon you ... for my yoke is easy, and my burden is light" (Matt 11:29-30).

2   "I Paul say unto you", seems to be a throwback to ch.1. He is now asserting his apostleship and authority, pronouncing decisively upon the outcome of their giving way to pressure to be circumcised. (It may also carry the suggestion that he was the very Paul for whom at one time they would have sacrificed so much, 4:15.) He now states that if they get circumcised they are setting aside Christ. Their profession of Christ would have no value, for they had chosen circumcision instead of Christ. The message of the Judaizers was, "Except ye be circumcised ... ye cannot be saved". Under such influences it would seem as if the Galatians were in danger of gradually slipping into Judaism. They were observing days, months and years (4:10) and were being put under pressure to be circumcised. In the Galatian situation circumcision to Paul was not a surgical operation, nor merely a religious observance. It represented a system of salvation by good works. It declared a gospel of human effort apart from divine grace. It was Law supplanting grace; Moses supplanting Christ, for to add to Christ was to take from Christ. *Christ supplemented was Christ supplanted*: Christ is the only Saviour - solitary and exclusive. Circumcision would mean excision from Christ.

3   Paul now solemnly asserts that any person who received circumcision is obligated to keep the whole Law. If a person allows the validity of circumcision he must allow the validity of every other claim of the Law. James in his epistle in declaring the unity of the Law maintained that to keep the whole Law and offend in one point was to be guilty of all (2:10). Paul here states that to keep one point means that the whole must be kept. If anyone takes the position that keeping the Law is the way to acceptance with God and the means of salvation, then the whole Law must be observed. This was to take upon oneself an intolerable burden. Paul is endeavouring to open their eyes to what lay before them. Having been persuaded to keep days etc. (4:10), they now were being encouraged to be circumcised, leading to their keeping the whole Law. It was hardly progress! They would actually become Jews in practice in order to become Christians! How foolish it was! For to continue in that course was to bring themselves under the curse of the Law (see 3:10).

4   This verse has in view those who are trying to be justified by the Law. The same people are in view in vv.2,3 and 4. If circumcised (v.2) then they must keep the whole Law (v.3) and so must seek to be justified by Law (v.4). To be among these people means that "Christ has become of no effect" to them, for they have put themselves in a position where they are deprived of the spiritual blessings found in Christ. "Severed from Christ" (RV), He can have no effect upon them or profit them in any way. To seek righteousness by works was to cut themselves off from the Source of all blessing. Darby renders, "Ye are deprived of all profit from the Christ as separated (from Him)". "Ye are fallen from grace" means that those who seek to be justified by Law or human works or merit of any kind have rejected grace as the principle of getting right with God. It is impossible to have both. There are not two ways of being saved, nor two Saviours. It is either Law or grace. You cannot receive Christ then add your own works. He is the all-sufficient Saviour. To add to Him is to say that the grace of God and the work of Christ are not enough for salvation. In this is condemned much of the religion of today.

However, it must be pointed out that others have interpreted differently. There are those who maintain that it has in view a Christian who has sinned and that "fallen from grace" means the loss of their salvation. This view is known as "the falling-away doctrine". But the passage before us has not Christians in view, but those who must choose between circumcision and Christ. Such a doctrine is contrary to such Scriptures as John 3:16; 6:47; 10:28. And there are those who teach that the verse has in view a person justified before God who has fallen from grace because he seeks holiness by human attainment and not by the power of the Holy Spirit. Wuest, who seems to hold such a viewpoint, says, "because they had lost their hold upon sanctifying grace, does not mean that God's grace had lost its hold upon them in the sphere of justification ... because the process of sanctification is temporarily retarded in a believer's life, does not say that his justification is taken away". However the verse itself seems to be decisive, it speaks of "whosoever of you are justified by Law". Justification not sanctification is in view.

5 "We" here means "we Christians" and stands in contrast to those in v.4 who have "fallen from grace". "Wait" is to "look forward eagerly". "Hope" is "the thing hoped for", the realisation of the hope. "The hope of righteousness" looks forward to the time at the coming of the Lord when God will fulfil all His promises, when what we are in Christ (i.e. righteous) will be fully and completely made manifest when we are conformed to the image of His Son. "Through the Spirit" would mean they are taught and enlightened by the Spirit. "Faith" would show they are on the principle of faith, not of works. Thus they stand in contrast to those who are trusting in circumcision, in a mark in the flesh, and so in the principle of human works. Note the contrast with v.4. In v.4 it is *"by the law"*; here in v.5 it is *"by faith"*. The one principle stands opposed to the other.

6 Paul now plainly declares that being circumcised is no advantage nor is being uncircumcised a disadvantage. To be "in Christ Jesus" is all that matters. To be circumcised before conversion (as Paul was) carried no force and to be uncircumcised (as the Galatians) was likewise of no account. To be accepted before God in Christ and to be united to Christ were complete and final. This union is expressed in faith working through love. So faith is the energy that produces love and love is the fruit of faith. The genuine character of faith is demonstrated in actions of love. This is the first mention of love in the epistle. Note too that vv.5-6 bring together faith, hope and love. This triad of christian graces is brought together in such passages as 1 Cor 13:13; 1 Thess 1:3; Col 1:4-5.

Notes

3 "Debtor" (*opheiletes*) indicates a person who is under obligation, here to keep the Law, an obligation clearly which the Christian is not to take upon himself. He has shown clearly that the believer is justified by faith, not by the Law. He has declared that Christ has borne its curse and judgment. Now he shows the believer is not obliged to keep the Law. There are those who teach that the *ceremonial* law is set aside but that the *moral* law must be kept. That would mean we must observe the seventh day as the Sabbath, for we cannot pick and choose what part of the moral law we want to observe and disregard the rest. We are clear of the Law entirely. Rom 8:4 is clear, "The righteous requirements of the law are fulfilled in us who walk ... after the spirit". Whatever was of permanent value in the moral Law is now included in the teaching of the NT. Obedience is enabled as one walks after the Spirit.

5 It is not always easy to determine whether "spirit" should have a capital "S" or a small "s". The word *pneuma* occurs 18 times in the epistle and the AV uses the capital "S" 16 times and small "s" twice (6:1,18). This order is followed by the RV; RSV; JND; NIV; *Expanded Paraphrase* (Bruce). The context would seem to justify this interpretation.

2. *The Confidence of Paul*
5:7-12

v.7 "Ye did run well; who did hinder you that ye should not obey the truth?
v.8 This persuasion cometh not of him that calleth you.
v.9 A little leaven leaveneth the whole lump.
v.10 I have confidence in you through the Lord, that ye will be none otherwise minded: but he that troubleth you shall bear his judgment, whosoever he be.
v.11 And I, brethren, if I yet preach circumcision, why do I yet suffer persecution? then is the offence of the cross ceased.
v.12 I would they were even cut off which trouble you."

Paul is deeply moved as he speaks of those who were propagating error and indicates the danger of this evil teaching spreading. His concern for their preservation is seen as he speaks of "who did hinder you" (v.7), "he that troubleth you" (v.10); "I would they were cut off which trouble you" (v.12). He indicates a very real danger, "a little leaven leaveneth the whole lump", showing them that the evil teaching, if not rejected fully, will give its character to the whole church. So Paul has before him the teachers and their teaching and makes solemn statements concerning them.

7 Three things are stated of the Galatians: firstly, they had been running well; secondly, they had been obeying the truth; thirdly, someone had hindered them, had stopped them. Paul was fond of using the metaphor of the games (see 1 Cor 9:26; Phil 2:16; 3:14; 2 Tim 4:7). Clearly the Galatians had made an excellent start to the christian life, enjoying to the full their liberty and freedom in Christ. They were "obeying the truth". "The truth" refers to the doctrine; "obeying" to their manner of life. So they combined doctrine with practice: they lived what they believed. Then the false teachers arrived and were hindering them. "Hinder" means "to impede progress by breaking up the road, or placing an obstacle in the path". These teachers had stopped them running and had caused them to leave the path of true obedience. Paul is indicating they were listening to the wrong people, and so disobeying the truth of God. Some think that, since the basic meaning of "hinder" is "to cut into", Paul has in view one runner cutting into another's path and so impeding his progress.

The presentation of a gospel of works had put doubts into their minds and was robbing them of their liberty in Christ. Paul now declares God is not in the new teaching.

8 "Persuasion" refers to the false teaching that circumcision and Lawkeeping were necessary for salvation. The word itself would draw attention either to the act of persuading on the part of the false teachers, or to the fact that Galatians were being persuaded. However the main thrust of the verse is to declare that the origin of the teaching is not of God. "Not of him that calleth you" refers to God. The implication is that the source was hostile to God and so could not be for their spiritual blessing. It was contrary to the gospel of grace and of justification by faith. If the teaching was not of God it could only hinder them and turn them from the path of true blessing. The calling of God had been to freedom and liberty, not to bondage.

9 Paul continues with plain statements to show them the folly of their ways. To embrace this doctrine was to turn away from the truth (v.7), to follow that which was not of God (v.8) and to tolerate evil. "Leaven" here refers to doctrinal error, which gives character to the whole if not judged. It always symbolises what is evil. The children of Israel were to put leaven out of their homes to keep the Feast of Unleavened Bread (Exod 13:6-7). The Lord Jesus spoke of the leaven of the Pharisees and the Sadducees when He referred to their doctrine (Matt 16:6-12). The expression of this verse is found in 1 Cor 5:6 referring to moral evil. It does not mean that a "little" will ultimately corrupt the whole, but that the presence of a "little" gives character to the whole. The character of the whole is tainted by the presence of the "little". Would that all had the clear vision of Paul to see the insidious workings of evil and error. How the Church has been plagued with teachings that are not of God. May God preserve us in simplicity to hold fast the pure gospel.

10 Dark and perilous though the situation seemed to be, nevertheless Paul states his conviction that they will take the view that the message he brought to them was the real gospel and what the Judaizers were setting forth was not of God. His confidence did riot rest in them but in their Lord. Clearly he had come to the conclusion in the presence of the Lord that He would turn them to the right road. He felt sure in this situation that right and truth would triumph.

In the second half of the verse Paul declares that the judgment of God would fall on these troublers. They would bear the judgment as to the confusion and havoc they had caused. In due time they would pay the penalty for their sin, bearing the grievous burden of the judgment of God. "Whoever he be" indicates that there is no respect of persons with God. No matter how exalted or influential the man, or high sounding his claims, in the end he would be dealt with by God. How comforting this should be to us in days of apostasy.

11   It would seem that Paul's opponents were claiming that Paul still advocated circumcision, possibly basing their claim on his having circumcised Timothy. It was true he had circumcised Timothy, a young man of mixed parentage, so that his witness in the gospel among Jews would be more acceptable. But that was not imposing circumcision as necessary to salvation. Paul now refers to this charge questioning why, if it were true, he was still suffering persecution. It would stop immediately. Why would his enemies persecute him if he preached their own doctrine? He now states that if he preached circumcision he would no longer be preaching the cross. The cross was a stumbling-block or offence to the Jews. The preaching of the cross put away everything in which they gloried. It set aside both circumcision and Law-keeping. It took away their monopoly in the spiritual realm. It broke down for ever the wall of separation between Jew and Gentile. It claimed that Christ was the substance and fulfilment of all the types and shadows. This was all completely offensive to them, arousing deep hostility, which was expressed in their persecution of Paul.

Note that circumcision and the cross are set in contrast. To preach circumcision was popular; to preach the cross was to invite persecution, opposition, hatred and malice. To preach circumcision was to tell sinners they could save themselves; to preach the cross was to declare their inability to save themselves, asserting that only Christ could save and that through the cross. The Jew hated to be told that his works were to no avail, that salvation had been provided by God and procured by Christ on the cross, and men still hate this preaching. It was this hatred that cost Stephen his life (Acts 6:13-14; 7:51-60), the first of many martyred in this glorious cause. The preaching of the cross is still a "scandal" (JND) offensive to the natural and religious man, for he hates to be told he is a ruined sinner in rebellion against God, under condemnation and on the road to hell, whom only Christ can save. Ours is a day of compromise. Men do not care to be brought to a place of decision. Yet the true gospel calls upon them to make a choice. It is circumcision or Christ, works or grace, bondage or liberty, slavery or freedom. The choices are mutually exclusive.

12   Paul now uses very strong language. He desires that these false teachers would "cut themselves off" (RV), that they would excommunicate themselves and so leave the Galatians in peace. However it should be noted that other translations render, "mutilate themselves"; "make eunuchs of themselves"; "emasculate themselves". This would suggest a number of things:

1   As a eunuch has lost the power of propagation, so these teachers
        would be rendered impotent in spreading their false doctrine.

2   If circumcision was a help to salvation, why not castrate themselves
        as a greater help to salvation?

3   In mutilating themselves by castration they would show they were
        no better than pagan priests who practised this ritual, and
        therefore not fit to be counted among the people of God. In Phil
        3:2 Paul refers to them as "the concision" or "the mutilators".

Notes

9 This principle has been clearly demonstrated in the sphere of christian profession, that Scriptural
truth has been challenged and then set aside, e.g.

   1   The inspiration of the Scriptures is held now only by evangelicals and even limited by
some of them;

   2   The Person of Christ, His deity, true humanity, sinlessness, atoning death, physical
resurrection, literal coming, millennial reign have all been assailed;

   3   The priesthood of all believers has been long lost as we see the arrogant claims of the R.C.
Church for its priests; the non-conformists upholding the system of clerisy with its
distinction between clergy and laity;

   4   The silence of women in the church is challenged in a clamant demand for women to take
public part and to appear uncovered in the gatherings of the saints;

   5   Spiritual gifts are confused as the rapid progress of the charismatic movement has left
many unable to make a difference between temporary and permanent gifts;

   6   The gospel of the grace of God has been corrupted into a gospel of human attainment,
adding human effort to complete the work of Christ.

10 Some think that an individual is in view here and in v.7. But throughout the epistle Paul refers
to them in the plural (see 1:7; 4:17; 5:12; 6:12,13). On occasion he will refer to both (see 1:7,
"*some*"; 1:19, "*any man*"). Again he refers to both in 5:7, "*who*"; in 5:10, "*he*"; but in v.12, "*they*".

3.   *The Meaning of Freedom*
  5:13-15

   v.13 "For, brethren, ye have been called unto liberty; only use not liberty for an
occasion to the flesh, but by love serve one another.
   v.14 For all the law is fulfilled in one word, even in this; Thou shalt love thy neighbour
as thyself.

v.15 But if ye bite and devour one another, take heed that ye be not consumed one
of another."

"Called to liberty" could be the title to this section; in fact it is the message of
the whole epistle. V.13 connects with v.1, "for freedom Christ set us free", with
v.8, "this persuasion cometh not of him that calleth you ... ye are called unto
liberty" and with v.6, "faith which worketh by love". Paul now shows that this
liberty is expressed in not allowing the flesh to control life (v.13), in loving your
neighbour as yourself (v.14) and in not damaging each other (v.15). It is
summarised in the expression, "by love serve one another". It leads to "be servants
one of another". Love is thus seen to be expressed in servitude and true liberty
is found.

13   Paul reminds them that this divine call was to liberty. But liberty was not
to lead to license, to do what they liked. In the next section he will show it is
expressed in a life lived under the control of the Spirit of God but here he
indicates a danger, that of allowing the flesh to use this liberty as a base of
operations for self-indulgence. The flesh is always on the look-out for a
springboard from which to assert itself. How often the phrase "christian
liberty" has been used as an excuse to attend places of worldly amusement,
to take part in sports of all kinds, to indulge in social drinking and to read
questionable literature. Freedom *from* sin is not freedom to sin. True liberty
is seen in serving each other. Note the connection between *"liberty"* and
"serve". In Exod 21 the Hebrew servant said, "I will not go out free ... he shall
serve him for ever" - a true analogy. In Mark 10:42-45 the Lord observed among
men the desire to exercise lordship, but taught it must be otherwise with His
own. The greatest and chiefest would be servant of all! He set the example,
for He came to serve all. This service is to be "in love". This demands deep
affection, tender care, ready sympathy, willingness to help and sacrificial giving.
Thus we serve each other.

14   Paul now states that complying with the whole law is seen in loving your
neighbour as yourself. This is based on Lev 19:18. The Lord Jesus endorsed this
in Matt 22:39. In Rom 13:8 Paul states, "He that loveth another hath fulfilled the
whole law". In v.9 of that chapter he quotes, "Thou shalt love thy neighbour as
thyself". Between these statements he quotes the commandments: no adultery,
no killing, no stealing, no false witness, no coveting. The practice of these things
violates the law of love toward our neighbour. The parable of the Good Samaritan
defines our neighbour as anyone who comes our way who needs help and
assistance (Luke 10:29-37). To love one another as ourselves is to seek at all
times their highest good and well-being. Note that Paul is not wanting them to
go back to the Law, but is declaring that what the Law demanded without giving
strength to accomplish, true christian liberty is able to produce.

15 Obviously there was internal strife, possibly between those affected by the false teaching and those who were refusing it. "Bite" and "devour" would suggest unrestrained abuse of each other. They were acting more like animals than saints. Paul declares this would destroy the testimony. Let us take the lesson to heart. Continual strife leads to extinction.

II. Life by the Spirit (5:16-26)

1. *The Perpetual Struggle*
   5:16-18

> v. 16 "This I say then, Walk in the Spirit, and ye shall not fulfil the lust of the flesh.
> v.17 For the flesh lusteth against the Spirit, and the Spirit against the flesh: and these are contrary the one to the other: so that ye cannot do the things that ye would.
> v.18 But if ye be led of the Spirit, ye are not under the law."

In the earlier verses he has vividly contrasted liberty and bondage (v.1), then liberty and licence (v.13). Now he is showing that liberty is expressed in life by the Spirit. In this section (vv.16-26) the Holy Spirit is mentioned seven times. Paul now exposes the deadly enmity and hostility between the flesh and the Spirit (vv.16-18). Then he contrasts the works of the flesh and the fruit of the Spirit (vv.19-23). Finally he draws attention to walking by the Spirit (vv.24-26).

16 Paul now maintains that to enjoy true liberty, to experience the power of love and to avoid destroying each other, they must determine to allow the Holy Spirit to control their lives. This is the only way to keep in check the lusts of the flesh. The reception of the Spirit at conversion is no guarantee of a life of victory; this is only assured as we allow Him to take full control. This control is not a crisis-experience but involves submissive obedience to the word of God day by day. (In christian living we cannot separate the Spirit and the Word.) Note here that the Spirit and the flesh are in contrast, whereas in v.18 it is the Spirit and the Law. The desires and cravings of the flesh are ever with us and, if they are not to dominate our lives, we must decide to walk boldly and undeviatingly in the power of the Spirit of God. There is a clear intimation here of conflict between the Spirit and the flesh and so between the new nature and the old, sinful nature of the believer. The next verse draws attention to this being a perpetual conflict. This verse (16) also draws attention to the power of the Spirit of God to enable us to fulfil not our old self, but the new self.

17 If the previous verse showed the *contrast* between the Spirit and the flesh (the absence of the article before each word would stress the contrast), this verse now draws attention to the *antagonism* between them. Clearly there is no such thing as the eradication of the sinful nature. The energies of the flesh and the Spirit are directed against each other as adversaries. There is constant conflict being waged in the believer's life between these two forces, the indwelling Spirit and the corrupt, sinful nature. They are fundamentally opposed.

The last phrase of the AV in this verse seems unfortunate, seemingly indicating that the conflict within nullifies the power to do what is right, as in Rom 7. The RV renders, "that ye may not do the things that ye would". This would seem to suggest that the strength of the indwelling Spirit is available so that there is no need to yield to the evil desires of the flesh, thus preventing us from carrying out its promptings. To anticipate the following verse, power is available to produce not the works of the flesh, but the fruit of the Spirit.

18 Two expressions are used in relation to the believer and the Holy Spirit in this section (vv.16-18). We are to walk in the Spirit and to be led by the Spirit. The Spirit leads and we walk in the path marked out by Him, obviously producing a life to the glory of God, in obedience to His word, with the works of the flesh refused and the fruit of the Spirit cultivated. From such a life will flow out rich blessing to others. "To walk" indicates a purpose of heart, a determination to follow the Spirit's leading. This is necessary because of fleshy energy opposing the work of the Spirit to prevent us from living this new life. The choice is ours to refuse the flesh and to be led of the Spirit. The expression "to be led of the Spirit" is often used in relation to worship, prayer and even to ministry, but primarily it refers to the experience of His control in every sphere of life. If this control and leading is not a daily experience, it is not possible to be led of the Spirit in the gatherings of the saints.

Now we are not under the Law if so guided by the Spirit. Paul is contrasting the Law and the Spirit and indicates that to live life under the Law as the Galatians were in danger of doing was opposed completely to life in the Spirit, a life above and beyond the life of Law-keeping. If they wanted to enjoy this life by the Spirit, then they must repudiate the Law both as a means of justification and as a way of life. It is interesting to note again that in v.17 the Spirit and the flesh are opposed to each other, but in v.18 it is the Spirit and the Law, so that to live a full life in the Spirit both the flesh and the Law must be renounced. Thus placing the flesh and the Law on the same platform shows most strikingly their close alliance and united opposition to life in the Spirit. Paul will now proceed to expand on the life that the flesh produces and the life produced by the Spirit, so that the Galatians can check whether or not their lives are spiritual.

2. *The Flesh and the Spirit*
   5:19-23

v.19 "Now the works of the flesh are manifest, which are these; Adultery, fornication, uncleanness, lasciviousness,

v.20 Idolatry, witchcraft, hatred, variance, emulations, wrath, strife, seditions, heresies,

v.21 Envyings, murders, drunkenness, revellings, and such like: of the which I tell
      you before, as I have also told you in time past, that they which do such things
      shall not inherit the kingdom of God.
v.22 But the fruit of the Spirit is love, joy, peace, longsuffering, gentleness, goodness,
      faith,
v.23 Meekness, temperance: against such there is no law."

19-21   Paul has been encouraging the Galatians to walk in the Spirit, to be
led by the Spirit. He now details the evil the flesh produces and the beautiful
traits the Spirit produces. He plainly declares that those who practise the
first are not born again. It is the utmost folly to maintain that one habitually
indulging in these things is saved but will not inherit the kingdom. The
kingdom is entered by new birth (John 3:5). The truly converted person turns
away from such living to produce the fruit of the Spirit. True, he may be
overtaken (Gal 6:1), but that is contrary to the tenor of his life. Fifteen things
are brought before us as marking the activity of the flesh (see note below).
The first three have to do with the realm of sex, the next two with the
realm of pagan religion, followed by eight linked with social life and finally
two in the realm of strong drink. We shall now indicate the main features
of each.

Fornication (*porneia*), despite much that has been written, is never used in the
NT of simple adultery. It could mean pre-marital sin (the probable meaning of
the exceptional case of Matt 5:19) or marriage entered into under false pretences,
or marriage within forbidden degrees. It is unlawful sexual indulgence.

Uncleanness (*akatharsia*) is that which is impure, unclean, soiled, as opposed
to that purity which can see God (Matt 5:8). It could refer to words, thoughts,
desires, as well as actions. Some suggest it is unnatural vice.

Lasciviousness (*aselgeia*), wantonness, licentiousness or indecency is the sin of
the man who shocks public decency, who knows no restraint, who in his lack of
self-control gives free-play to his sinful desires, caring not what others say or
think. It is the shameless conduct of the person who is ready for any form of
sinful pleasure. Lightfoot says a man may be *akathartos* (unclean) and hide his
sin; he does not become *aselgēs* (lascivious) until he shocks public decency. He
is the man of utter shamelessness, of animal lust, enslaved to sheer
self-indulgence, whose acts are a shocking outrage, defying public opinion and
all forms of decency.
Idolatry (*eidōlolatreia*) is the worship of the creature rather than the Creator,
by bowing down to images their hands have made. Nevertheless it involved
sacrificing to demons, fellowship with evil spirits (1 Cor 10:19-21), and the
worshipper became a slave to the depraved ideas his idol represented (Rom
1:23-25).

Witchcraft (*pharmakeia*), translated "sorcery" in RV (cf. our word "pharmacy"), originally meant the use of drugs, which in pagan religions came to be associated with appeals to occult powers, all calculated to draw attention to the mysterious power of the sorcerer (see Acts 8:9; 13:8-11; 19:19). Here it means traffic with evil spirits, spiritism. Note that in Rev 21:8 fornicators (whoremongers) sorcerers idolaters will suffer the second death.

Hatred (*echthra*), enmities (RV) or hostility, stands in vivid contrast to the christian virtue of love to all men. At enmity means they cannot live at peace with others, but live in mutual animosity, hateful and hating one another (Titus 3:3) as can be seen in the so-called class-struggle, and internationally amongst nations.

Variance (*eris*), strife or discord, is the expression of enmity, or rivalry which has its outcome in strife, contention, fighting, quarrelling and wrangling.

Emulation (*zēlos*), many translate "jealousy", is the desire to have what another possesses. This is an advance upon "variance", as it expresses a strong desire to be equal. Hogg and Vine comment: "Here the meaning is wholly bad; this jealousy arises not out of love but out of enmity, and is an advance upon strife if only because the personal element is more prominent in it".

Wrath (*thumos*) is outburst of anger, fit of rage, or uncontrolled temper. It signifies a blaze of temper which does not last but flares up and then subsides.

Strife (*eritheia*), selfish ambition, self-seeking or rivalry is the spirit which produces "factions" (RV), which well-nigh wrecked the church at Corinth. *Eritheia* came to mean "canvassing for office", so position is the motive, rather than a desire to serve others.

Sedition (*dichostasia*), standing apart (hence division), highlights those who take sides, separating to follow leaders thus dividing the saints rather than uniting them.

Heresy (*hairesis*), from "to choose", is the holding of an opinion so strongly it leads to a "sect" (so translated in Acts 5:17; 15:5; 24:5; 26:5; 28:22). The difference between these last two words is that the former is the beginning of a sect; the latter is division developed and matured. Usually it is seen in an over-emphasis or a perversion of truth.

Envying (*phthonos*) is the feeling of displeasure that grudges what another possesses. It can be as cruel and bitter as the spirit that murdered Abel, sold Joseph, persecuted David and murdered Christ. The distinction between jealousy (*zēlos*) and envy seems to be that *zēlos* desires to have what another possesses, whereas *phthonos* desires to deprive another of his possessions.

Drunkenness (*methē*) is excessive indulgence, the habitual intoxication of an alcoholic. This is a sin, not only a disease. To make it only a disease, as in our society, destroys personal responsibility. In 1 Cor 6:10, such persons are declared never to inherit the kingdom. They are unconverted.

Revellings (*kōmos*) are orgies, carousels, wild parties, the outcome of drunkenness, for alcohol and debauchery go together.

"And such like" indicates the list is not exhaustive. He warns them now as he had when with them, that those who practise such things have never experienced the new life of the Spirit. In Rom 6:1 there were those who claimed that to experience the full grace of God one must continue to sin, which Paul refutes entirely. The believer has died in Christ to sin. He is finished with the old life, here designated "the works of the flesh". What a terrible world man after the flesh has created. With what relief one now turns to consider the fruit of the Spirit.

22-23   The nine-fold fruit of the Spirit is now unfolded. "Fruit" is in contrast to "works". "Works" indicate the energy and activity of man, what he produces. "Fruit" suggests the product of an inward power, here of the Holy Spirit. "Fruit" is in the singular, indicating the unity of the qualities, their connection with each other, so that all can be seen in the life of the Christian. They must not be confused with the spectacular and temporary gifts of the Spirit in 1 Cor 12 given to some believers. "Fruit" here also suggests the spontaneous character of the life produced.

These nine qualities divide into three groups. Firstly, qualities which are Godward are set forth: love, joy, peace; then the qualities that are seen in relation to others: longsuffering, gentleness, goodness; and finally the qualities relating to himself: faith, meekness, temperance. Little wonder Paul concludes, "Against such there is no law". On the contrary these qualities fulfil the Law. Law was given to restrain man's evil nature, to suppress it, even to condemn it. But there is no condemnation of a life given over to producing the fruit of the Spirit. Let us now consider such fruit in detail.

Love (*agapē*) is the word that is used for God's love to men (John 3:16), the love that has been shed abroad in our hearts (Rom 5:5). It suggests that we love others as God loves them. This is very challenging, for the love of God is resolute, flowing out to men no matter what they say about Him, or how they act against Him. This should be our attitude. Did not the Lord teach, "Love your enemies, bless them that curse you, do good to them that hate you, and pray for them which despitefully use you, and persecute you" (Matt 5:44)? But possibly, in view of v.15, *agapē* may have in view love for other Christians, meaning that no matter what they say about us, or how they act toward us, we just keep loving them. We do not develop hard feelings nor become embittered against them. We never refuse to forgive, nor do we seek revenge. We do not meet insult with insult, injury with injury, but despite their unchristian spirit and bitter opposition, we seek only their highest good. As 1 Cor 13 teaches, manifesting this love, we are longsuffering, kind, not easily provoked; we think no evil; we bear all things; we endure all things (vv.4-7), thus silencing the criticism of the world. Too often men have been justified in their assertions that the history of Christianity has been one of bitterness, wrangling and division. Manifesting *agapē* would be true godliness, true God-likeness. It can only be produced by the Spirit of God, and calls for real subjection to His leading. To act like this shows this love to be of the mind and will, as well as of the heart. It demands determination for it is contrary to nature. Let us listen again to the words of the Lord Jesus, "By this shall all men know that ye are my disciples, if ye have love one to another" (John 13:35).

Joy (*chara*) is ours because of our knowledge of and fellowship with God (Rom 5:11) and is associated with the presence of the Holy Spirit (Rom 14:17; 1 Thess 1:6). Because of this link with divine Persons it can be enjoyed at all times and is not dependent on our circumstances. It is a deep contentment and delight in the ways of God, and its possession enables us to welcome different forms of trials (or testing) in life (James 1:2).

Peace (*eirēnē*) is not the peace with God we have as justified, but the peace of God in our hearts. It is that peace, tranquility or contentment which is enjoyed by those who live in harmony with the will of God. The Lord spoke of giving to His disciples "my peace" and "my joy" (John 14:27; 15:11).

Longsuffering (*makrothumia*), translated by some "patience", is patience with regard to people. It is used of God in 1 Pet 3:20. It is self-restraint in the face of provocation; tolerance when others annoy, oppose and sorely try us. We do not lose our temper or seek to retaliate but, turning away from all thoughts of anger and revenge, seek to act toward them in patient forbearance as God did toward us.

Gentleness (*chrēstotēs*) is mostly translated "kindness". It is used of God in Titus 3:4 and of the yoke of Christ in Matt 11:30, where it is translated "easy" of a yoke which does not chafe. We should be marked by a gentle kindness as we go through life, with a compassion for others. Such qualities are sadly missing in a godless world.

Goodness (*agathōsunē*) is similar in meaning to the previous word. Trench in NT Synonyms suggests that chrestotes is the kindlier aspects of goodness, as seen in the Lord's dealings with the penitent woman in Luke 7:36-50. *Agathō sunē* includes the sterner qualities by which doing good to others is not necessarily by gentle means. Trench illustrated it by Christ cleansing the temple (Matt 21:12-13). Lightfoot suggests *chrēstotēs* is a kindly disposition towards one's neighbour; agathosune a kindly activity for the benefit of others. So here is a goodness which is beneficial always to others, but to be so, must on occasions be firm when rebuke and correction are necessary for lasting benefit.

Faith (*pistis*) probably means "faithfulness", "fidelity", "loyalty", "trustworthiness", "reliability". This quality would make us reliable as those taking character from God (1 Cor 1:9) and Christ (Rev 1:5). Hogg and Vine, however, suggest it expresses "trustfulness, the habit of mind which does not doubt that God is working all things together for good and those who love Him ... that seeks to realise the truth of the apostle's word concerning love that it 'believeth all things'. Suspicion of God ... is a work of the flesh, and so is suspicion of those around us; it darkens and embitters the soul, hinders efficiency in service and makes fellowship impossible".

Meekness (*praütēs*) is a quality claimed by the Lord Jesus (Matt 11:29). It is often translated "gentleness". It would seem to be the opposite of self-assertiveness, arrogance and violence and descriptive of one who is gentle and mild. But it is not weakness. If the Lord was meek, then it was the result of submission to the will of God and of a consciousness of inward power. This would suggest that meekness is strength under control. Moses was the meekest man upon the earth, but in the context (Num 12) he was a man who allowed God to vindicate him. A meek man is one who accepts the will of God without resentment, who can afford to be gentle and mild because of inward strength, and who is under the perfect control of God. *Praütēs* is associated with lowliness (Matt 11:29) and wisdom (James 3:13).

Temperance (*enkrateia*) is usually rendered "self control". Temperance today means self-control in relation to drink, whereas here it is self-control in all things. It is used in 1 Cor 7:9 of control of sexual desire and in 1 Cor 9:25 of an athlete's discipline of his body. It indicates the mastery over every desire, impulse, appetite and longing. It enables a person to walk through this world completely in control of himself, so that he triumphs when others around him are falling This quality produced by the Spirit spells victory.

Paul now says, "Against such there is no law". How could there be, seeing they are produced by the Spirit of God? Law, given to restrain and condemn, finds nothing in these excellent qualities to demand such action. On the contrary these virtues fulfil the Law and give pleasure to the Law-giver. They found perfect expression in the life of the Lord Jesus and should be manifest in the life of every Christian. What transformation will be seen as with exercised hearts we seek to produce such fruit.

Notes

19-21 Since most translations omit "adultery" and "murder" we have not dealt with them.

20 Two words in the NT are translated "wrath": *orgē* and *thumos*. Vine in his Expository Dictionary notes: "*thumos* is to be distinguished from *orgē* in this respect, that *thumos* indicates a more agitated condition of the feelings, an outburst of wrath from inward indignation, while *orgē* suggests a more settled or abiding condition of mind, frequently with a view to taking revenge. *Orgē* is less sudden in its rise than *thumos*, but more lasting in its nature. *Thumos* expresses more the inward feeling, *orgē* the more active emotion. *Thumos* may issue in revenge, though it does not necessarily include it. It is characteristic that it quickly blazes up and quickly subsides, though that is not necessarily implied in each case".

3.   *Walking by the Spirit*
   5:24-26

> v.24 "And they that are Christ's have crucified the flesh with the affections and lusts.
> v.25 If we live in the Spirit, let us also walk in the Spirit.
> v.26 Let us not be desirous of vain glory, provoking one another, envying one another."

In this section Paul is summing up. V.24, which links with vv.19-21, shows the believer's position in relation to the flesh, whereas v.25 links with vv.22-23 and indicates that, having received life by the Spirit, we should allow Him to guide our walk.

24 "They that are Christ's", or "are of Christ" encompasses every believer. "Have crucified" is in the aorist tense, referring to a past act, here to conversion. "The flesh" refers to our sinful nature. What is stated here is true of every Christian, that they "have crucified" the flesh (it is not an exhortation to crucify) and so indicates that the believer's *position* is in view. It became true of the believer at conversion when he accepted Christ as his Saviour and so God's verdict on the flesh. Then the break took place to free him to live by the Spirit. Possibly one can do no better than quote John Ritchie " 'And they that are Christ's' - 'of Christ Jesus' (RV) - have crucified the flesh with its 'passions and lusts'. They have accepted God's verdict and condemnation (Rom 8:3) as expressed in the cross and come to reckon of them as He does (Rom 6:11). This is not a slow, painful process, attained by self-denial and mortification, as Romanism would make it, but faith's acceptance of what God has accomplished by Christ's death and acquiescence in it. Its experience is varied; its fact is alike for all. Growth in grace, progress in acquaintance with God, with accompanying distrust of self, will give fuller manifestation of it, in word and deed, but it is there from the beginning in all who are 'of Christ'."

Note the important phrase, "This is not a *slow painful process*". A great deal has been written of the believer nailing the flesh to the cross, and it is a slow painful process as the flesh is left there to die. This is not the teaching. We are credited here with accepting God's judgment of the flesh at the cross. Our decisive acceptance of Christ meant we are finished with that way of life and are now committed to the new life in the Spirit. We must believe, and will find it is comfort to know, that the flesh is judged. It is now ours to live by the Spirit.

"Affections" (*pathēma*, "passions" in many translations) seems to suggest evil promptings and impulses. *Pathēma* is reckoned to be passive, whereas "lust" (*epithumia*) suggests strong desires, which are active in nature. We accept the sentence of death upon the flesh. Wuest says of the above words; "The former... speaking of the innate forces resident in the evil nature; the latter... speaking of these forces reaching out to find expression in the gratification of these desires".

25   "If" here means "since" or "in view of the fact that". Seeing that we have life by the Spirit, then we must allow Him to guide us step by step. The word "walk" here differs from the "walk" in v.16. In the latter verse it is the ordinary word *peripateō* signifying the whole round of activities of the individual, whereas here it is *stoicheō* which signifies "to walk in line", or "to keep in rank" having in view our life in relation to others. We must keep step with each other. We can only do so by submission to the Holy Spirit. If this is so our relations with each other will be harmonious, and the assembly will be marked by unity. If we walk by the Spirit in our private life (v.16) then we will find ourselves, by the same Spirit, keeping in step with our brethren. This life by the spirit is open to each of us and should be our normal experience in life.

26   Note the repetition of "one another". By the power of the Spirit we can keep in step with each other. To live with each other has always been a problem in assembly life and Paul can see dangers. We can become conceited which would be the meaning of *kenodoxos*, rendered here "vain glorious". To have a false opinion of ourselves and our capabilities tends to provoke others, or causes us to become envious of others. "Provoke" (*prokaleō*) means to "challenge another". Self-conceit would cause us to challenge others, to try to demonstrate our supposed superiority. "Envy" (*phthoneō*) indicates displeasure because of the prosperity of another. Conceited persons envy others because of their spiritual gifts or attainments. Let each of us shun these things, and seek by love to serve each other. Let us be "at peace among ourselves" (1 Thess 5:13). Some expositors feel this verse should be connected with ch.6.

III. Doing Good Unto All (6:1-10)

1.   *Bearing Burdens*
6:1-6

v.1   "Brethren, if a man be overtaken in a fault, ye which are spiritual, restore such an one in the spirit of meekness; considering thyself, lest thou also be tempted.

v.2 Bear ye one another's burdens, and so fulfil the law of Christ.
v.3 For if a man think himself to be something, when he is nothing, he deceiveth himself.
v.4 But let every man prove his own work, and then shall he have rejoicing in himself alone, and not in another.
v.5 For every man shall bear his own burden.
v.6 Let him that is taught in the word communicate unto him that teacheth in all good things."

It is interesting to note in approaching this section that Wuest maintains it is an appeal to those who have not been enticed by the wiles of the Judaizers to restore their brethren who have been led astray. Cole adopts the same position. Accordingly, having spoken of those who walk by the Spirit, who do not provoke or envy others, he now indicates that such are available to help others in an hour of need. We must always remember we form part of a fellowship where love and care find expression in helping others to bear burdens.

1   This verse would seem to bring before us one who has failed to "walk by the Spirit". Having come under the power of the flesh, he has been trapped into sinning. "Brethren" indicates the sphere of relationship, and would remind us that in the situation envisaged, we must act toward him as a brother, not as an enemy. Four things are brought before us: firstly, the nature of the sin, "overtaken in some trespass" ("fault" is too mild); secondly, who are to deal with it, "ye which are spiritual"; thirdly, what is to be done, "restore him"; and fourthly, how it is to be accomplished, "in the spirit of meekness". We are immediately impressed with the emphasis on restoration.' It is the responsibility of the 'spiritual' to act quickly to restore the brother to his previous condition. His sorrow and repentance are assumed, because he has sinned.

The word *paraptōma* is a trespass, a falling aside, a deviation from the path of righteousness. "Overtaken" (*prolambanō*) from the root "to anticipate" is used of Mary anointing Christ *before* the usual time. Here it would seem the brother was surprised and so fell into transgression. Taken off his guard, he had fallen before he fully grasped what had taken place. (It should be said there are those who think "overtaken" means one Christian detecting another in the very act of sinning.) What is to be done in such a circumstance? Should one expose him and try to demonstrate one's superior holiness or seek quickly to help him to repair the damage and thus restore him? Such a situation brings to light those who are "spiritual". It is not that any one of us decides he is more spiritual than others and thus is qualified to act toward our brother but the fact that he moves quickly to help the brother proves he is spiritual.

"Restore" (*katartizō*) is "to mend or repair", as in Matt 4:21; Mark 1:19. We are asked to repair the damage done to our brother by his sin, to make him fully operational again. In 1 Cor 1:10 it is rendered -perfectly joined together-, showing us that what has been severed must be re-united. So we can help our fallen brother to get back into fellowship with God and with his brethren. Some think it has a surgical connection and means to set a bone, emphasising the need for spiritual men to act with skill and a tender touch to repair the damage with as little pain as possible and so perfectly to restore the brother. It is interesting to note the word is translated "perfect" in 1 Thess 3:10, "perfect that which is lacking".

We are now told how it is to be done, "in the spirit of meekness". Meekness (*praütēs*) is not weakness but strength. It is not toleration of evil, nor indifference to it, but a recognition of its terrible effects upon the one who has sinned. It indicates, not a fleshly confidence, but a deep dependence on God to help one to help others. Finally we are told that the spiritual man will perform such a service to his brother with due realisation of his own vulnerability to sin. It is not that both were tempted and he got the victory, but one was tempted and fell and the other recognises that "but for the grace of God, there go I". We are disqualified if we feel we could never be tempted and fall, for such do not know the terrible power of the flesh. So each of us should be ambitious to be spiritual, with a manifest desire to help our brethren when ensnared by the Devil. What an excellent service to be able to render to each other. Vine notes that the word "restore" is the continuous present, "suggesting the necessity for patience and perseverance in the process".

2 "To bear" (*bastazō*) means "to carry", "to share", "to support", "to put the shoulder under the burden another is carrying". "Burdens" (*baros*) means "a weight", which weighs us down, such as difficulties, trials, sorrows, infirmities or failures. Possibly we cannot disassociate it from helping our brother to overcome the result of spiritual weakness (v.1). Here the teaching is plain. We all have burdens to bear, and we are not expected to carry them alone. We must not only be prepared to help others with their burdens, which is the thrust of the passage, but we must be humble enough to accept the help of others with our burdens. As our great High Priest, the Lord Jesus is willing and able to help and to give spiritual strength, so that it is ours to "cast our burden upon the Lord" (Ps 55:22) and to "cast our care (anxiety RV) upon him" (1 Pet 5:7). Nevertheless in His wisdom God has ordered it that we should help each other, so that the value of fellowship is realised, for in this way such fellowship is strengthened and is calculated to lighten our burden. To do this is to fulfil the law of Christ, not the law of Moses. Plainly Paul is contrasting Christ and Moses. The law of Moses imposed burdens they were not able to bear (see Acts 15:10): the law of Christ taught them to share burdens. The law of Christ would have in view such Scriptures as John 13:34,35; 15:12. By loving one another as Christ loved us, let us hasten to fulfil this ministry of burden-bearing, by giving support and help. Let us be prepared to receive help and not endeavour to hide our need. So shall we learn fully to value each other as partners in sharing with, and caring for each other.

3   This verse has in view the person who would refuse to help his brother when he has sinned, who is not prepared to bear another's burdens, and is too proud to allow others to help him - Paul says he is self-deceived. He has an exaggerated sense of his own importance. He thinks himself above helping anyone or being helped. There is a vivid contrast between "something" and "nothing". He is so big in his own eyes, that he would never humble himself to help the fallen or share a burden, and will never admit to having any faults nor to needing any help. In reality he is the antithesis of his own opinion of himself, "he is nothing". He deceives no-one but himself. "I say... to every man... not to think of himself more highly than he ought to think" (Rom 12:3).

4   In contrast to the man of v.3 in his self-assumed superiority over others, we are now counselled to prove our own work. Prove (*dokimazō*) means "to prove in order to approve". We are asked to examine ourselves constantly (for the tense is continuous), and this must be in the light of God's word, and of the Lord Jesus' example. (We must never compare ourselves with others. This is most unwise, see 2 Cor 10:12.) Such wise testing of ourselves becomes the true ground of rejoicing or glorying. It is a rejoicing in what God has accomplished in us.

5   Paul now makes known the personal responsibility of each believer. "Burden" (*phortion*) is something light enough to be carried, whereas in v.2 *baros* points to crushing weight, too heavy to be carried. We are responsible to God for the life that we live. We carry our own load of responsibility towards God and men now, and at the Judgment Seat of Christ we shall answer for ourselves and not another. It is the man who has examined himself and his work in the presence of God, and realises his own strength and weakness, who will be anxious to help others to bear their burdens, and will never be guilty of a smug superiority over others.

6   While it is true that each must bear his own burden, this does not absolve us from the responsibility of caring and providing for others. Doing good to all has been shown to mean restoring the brother who has fallen (v.1), helping others to bear their burdens (v.2) and now providing for the needs of those who serve the Lord. The responsibility is placed upon those who receive instruction ("him that is taught in the word") to communicate, to share, to provide for the temporal needs of those who teach them. This principle is fully established in 1 Cor 9 although Paul did not always avail himself of it. Most commentators refer this verse to a congregation supporting a minister or pastor, but the NT knows nothing of one-man ministry, of a man being paid a stipend or salary in return for spiritual services. The long established principle of clerisy and the more modern innovation of paid-pastors in some assemblies are foreign to the word of God. There are those gifted by the Lord to feed the flock and spread the gospel, who have gone forth "taking nothing of the Gentiles". It is our privilege and responsibility to support them.

Notes

1 Boice has an interesting note on this verse. He says "There is a closer connection between the example given in this verse and the preceding injunctions than most English Versions indicate. After 'brothers', the Greek has the introductory concessive clause (*ean kai*) which has (in this case) the effect of stressing the following situation as an exception that is in some sense extreme. The effect is as follows: Having spoken of the need to walk by the Spirit and having encouraged his readers so to walk, Paul now says, in effect 'Nevertheless, if a believer should disregard this injunction and fail so to walk, thereby falling into sin, you who do walk by the Spirit should restore him'. A similar use of *ean kai* occurs in 1 Cor 7:11". "Fault" (*paraptōma*) is rendered "offence" in Rom 4:25; 5:15,16,17,18,20, and translated in the RV as "trespass". It must be rendered as such here, for a definite fall is in view.

2 "Bear" (*bastazō*) occurs four times in the epistle: first in 5:10 referring to the sentence of God upon the Judaizers; next in 6:2 connected with helping other Christians with their burdens; then in 6:5 each bears his own load; and finally in 6:17 in view of his physical sufferings for Christ.

2. *Sowing and Reaping*
6:7-10

> v.7 "Be not deceived; God is not mocked: for whatsoever a man soweth, that shall he also reap.
> v.8 For he that soweth to his flesh shall of the flesh reap corruption; but he that soweth to the Spirit shall of the Spirit reap life everlasting.
> v.9 And let us not be weary in well doing: for in due season we shall reap, if we faint not.
> v.10 As we have therefore opportunity, let us do good unto all men, especially unto them who are of the household of faith."

7 Paul now sets forth a basic, fundamental principle of life, that as a man sows, so shall he reap. We must not allow ourselves to be deceived in this important matter, nor to be under any false illusions. We cannot live as we please without reaping the harvest, for God is not mocked. "Mocked" (*muktērizō*) is "to turn up one's nose at", and so "to treat with contempt", "to sneer at", "to scoff". A strengthened form of the word, (*ekmuktērizō*) is translated "derided" in Luke 16:14, 23:35. We cannot cheat or fool God, while we may deceive men.

This law of sowing and reaping cannot be altered. It is true in the agricultural realm. What we sow, whether cabbage or turnip, we reap. If we sow sparingly, we reap sparingly; if bountifully, we reap bountifully (2 Cor 9:6). We cannot escape the inexorable working of this law. Men like to close their eyes to this law: so do some Christians. Hosea reminds us, "They have sown the wind, they shall reap the whirlwind" (8:7). The principle is clear. The Galatians were in danger of sowing to the flesh in following the false teachers; they must turn away from such and begin to sow to the Spirit. Being deceived they would reap a terrible harvest.

8 The contrast is vivid and startling: "sow - flesh - corruption", or "sow - Spirit - life everlasting". Note that we determine the outcome, for we choose to sow to the flesh or to the Spirit. We are ultimately what we determined to be for character is the outcome of choice of conduct. We can sow to the flesh, indulge our evil nature and produce its works in the grosser sins set forth in 5:19-21, or in the lesser forms by holding a grudge, or nourishing a spite or secretly desiring revenge. When we spend our time in the wrong company, read the wrong literature, listen to the wrong music, we are living only for ourselves and the resultant harvest is "we shall of the flesh reap corruption". Corruption involves deterioration of an originally-better condition. Here merely gratifying our natural desires leads to moral decay and degeneration, moving on from bad to worse, until we ultimately perish for corruption is placed in opposition to eternal life.

He now places before us that we can choose to sow to the Spirit. Earlier he has spoken of "walking in the Spirit", of being "led by the Spirit" and of "living by the Spirit", now of "sowing to the Spirit". This would require setting our mind on things above (Col 3:2); bringing every thought into captivity to the obedience of Christ (2 Cor 10:5); loving the brethren and seeking the good of all; witnessing for Christ; walking with God; giving ourselves to prayer; reading of the Scriptures; attending the stated gatherings of the local assembly; and being involved in its worship and witness. In so doing we shall enjoy eternal life now, and enjoy it in its fulness in eternity. We must go in now for this sowing to the Spirit, refusing resolutely to sow to the flesh.

9   The idea of reaping is associated with perseverance in doing good, here and in v. 10. Paul is encouraging them not to become weary in this good work, for it is so easy to become discouraged when there is little resulting from toil. Had Paul to remind himself of this as he laboured and toiled for the Galatians and seemed to see so little fruit? "In due season" would suggest that in God's time we shall reap, not only here but at the Judgment Seat. We must not be discouraged, nor faint, nor give up, despite the effects upon us of continued effort. This possibly looks back to v.2 and would encourage us to bear each other's burdens.

10   "Opportunity" is the same word (*kairos*) translated "season" in v.9. Let us seize the opportunity presented to us to do good. Darby, in a note on "do good", comments, "This supposes more positive activity of service than 'doing good' in v.9, which is the character of conduct. 'Let us do good' here is the service and labour in which it is shown". We are to be like the Lord Jesus who "went about doing good" (Acts 10:38). There is no limitation placed on who will benefit from such good works. We serve all. While there is no limitation, there is a special sphere which concerns us, "the household of faith". In this we follow God's example, who is the "Saviour of all men, especially of those who believe" (1 Tim 4:10). "The household of faith" includes every Christian and over leaps denominational barriers. All our brothers and sisters have a claim upon our love and consideration and we must fulfil our responsibility to do good to each of them as the opportunity presents itself.

IV. A New Creation (6:11-18)

1. *The Aim of False Teachers*
6:11-13

> v.11 "Ye see how large a letter I have written unto you with mine own hand.
> v.12 As many as desire to make a fair shew in the flesh, they constrain you to be circumcised; only lest they should suffer persecution for the cross of Christ.
> v.13 For neither they themselves who are circumcised keep the law; but desire to have you circumcised, that they may glory in your flesh."

11   There has been much controversy as to whether he wrote the whole epistle in his own hand or just the closing verses (11-18). Usually Paul would dictate his epistles but write by hand the closing words and sign his name (see Rom 16:22; 1 Cor 16:21; Col 4:18; 2 Thess 3:17). (Once a letter had been forged in his name, 2 Thess 2:2.) Some think he wrote the letter himself because of its tremendous importance. It is a technical point that does not affect the truth of the epistle. Again, the reference to "large letters" (RV) has been taken to suggest his eyesight was defective, but this method could have been used for emphasis.

12   Paul now returns to circumcision and the cross, as he speaks of "many", the false teachers, and of "a fair show" ("make a good impression", NIV). They wanted to display their religious zeal by large numbers being circumcised, so they brought pressure upon the converts to conform. It made a big show before men. To please God was far from their mind in influencing the converts. Paul reveals that not only did they want status before men by having a large following but by insisting on circumcision they were avoiding persecution, so inseparable from the preaching of the cross. The cross set aside the wisdom of man, and every form of ritualism as a means of salvation, declaring that man as a sinner was under the righteous judgment of God, his only hope being in Christ and Him crucified. These men were not really interested in the spiritual welfare of the Galatians, but in themselves. Their own prestige and safety were paramount. To insist on circumcision removed the reproach of the cross and saved them from becoming the target of the hatred of their fellow-Jews. Their gospel placed circumcision above the cross, works above faith, the external above the internal, the outward above the inward. This same mistake has been perpetuated down the ages. Christianity without the cross appeals to the natural man, while doing something for salvation ministers to his pride.

13   Paul now draws attention to the hypocrisy of these men, with their blatant insincerity and pride. They did not keep the whole Law, but they were insisting on the Galatians being involved in its keeping. He thus declares the bankruptcy of the Law and exposes the true aim of these men. They wanted to "glory" or boast of the large number of conversions. This would justify them and the means used. It is a weakness of human nature, seen today in the boasting of conversions, and in the counting of beads, as the results of campaigns. Like many today they would be able to quote statistics.

2.   The Aim of the Apostle
   6:14-16

v.14 "But God forbid that I should glory, save in the cross of our Lord Jesus Christ, by whom the world is crucified unto me, and I unto the world.
v.15 For in Christ Jesus neither circumcision availeth any thing, nor uncircumcision, but a new creature.
v.16 And as many as walk according to this rule, peace be on them, and mercy, and upon the Israel of God."

14   The false teachers may glory in the mark of circumcision upon the flesh of their converts; Paul can only glory in the cross. He boasts in it, for through it he had been saved from the penalty due to him as a sinner. He had been delivered from the deadness of Judaism and from this present evil age. It may be a stumbling-block to the Jew and foolishness to the Greek (1 Cor 1:23) but to Paul it was the revelation of God's love and grace and wisdom, and through it he had been brought into living contact with the Man who there died for him. Note the full expression, "the cross of our Lord Jesus Christ". "The cross" speaks of atonement, God's way of dealing with the question of sin, the provision of salvation for sinners under divine judgment. For Paul it held a unique and supreme place. "Lord Jesus Christ" brings before us the fulness of His Person and worth. This One is Lord of all. As Jesus He is the Saviour; as Christ He is the Anointed of God. "Our" is possessive and indicates relationship with Him. Paul now declares that by the cross the world is crucified to him and he to the world. It is a two-fold crucifixion. The world is dead to him, and he to it. He is finished with it for ever. The world in its broadest aspect is the system all around us that is anti-God and anti-Christ, energised by Satan and sustained by the ungodly. For Paul personally it was the religious world with its ceremonies and ritual from which he turned to Christ (see Phil 3:4-9). W. Trew in quoting v.14 says Paul "is content it should be so. Henceforth he is an object of the world's hatred, because he is so much like Christ, to be got rid of by the world at any cost, and after a life of suffering service he would be led out to a martyr's death. And to his heart the great world system was utterly obnoxious to be got rid of whatever the cost; henceforth there would be nothing in the world system capable of attracting his heart. The flesh can produce nothing in the way of religion or culture of any kind in which he can boast. Christ, only Christ, satisfies his heart, holds his love, deserves his homage and service, and is worthy of his supreme endeavour to please and glorify. To be His, only His, exclusively His, he gladly turns his back upon the world, to walk henceforth to the rule of the new creation". F.F. Bruce in his *Expanded Paraphrase* puts it thus: "that the cross forms a permanent barrier between the world and me and between me and the world". In a footnote on the words "permanent barrier" he says, "There seems to be a play on the two senses of Greek *stauroō* here: (a) to erect a fence, (b) to crucify". There is no doubt the cross is the dividing line between the believer and the world. Note that the cross in 3:13 delivers us from the curse of the *Law*; in 5:24 it is applied to the *flesh* and we are seen to have crucified it when Christ was received at conversion; here in 6:14 it is applied to the *world*.

15   Paul now sums up in an important statement. Circumcision, which marked the Jew, and uncircumcision, which marked the Gentile, did not count for anything as to salvation. Circumcision did not help in any way, nor did uncircumcision hinder in any way. What was necessary was the experience of becoming a new creature in Christ. The presence or absence of a mark on the body had no bearing in the matter, but a work of God from within had. Paul sweeps aside in a few words all the teaching of the Judaizers about the need of circumcision and the danger of uncircumcision by showing that God produces a new creation that is in complete contrast to the old. *Kainos* is new in quality, different entirely in character from the old.

16   The "rule" is the principle stated above, that all blessing is in the cross and is realised by those who are new creatures in Christ. "Many" refers to the true Christians who accept the truth of new creation in v.15. For all such Paul desires they may constantly experience that *peace* and tranquility which comes from fellowship with Christ and the *mercy* or succour that comes from the great High Priest (Heb 4:14). The term "Israel of God" has been variously interpreted. Some think that two companies are in view in the verse. The first, "as many as walk according to this rule are the Christians; the second, "the Israel of God" are the nation of Israel. This is untenable, seeing the nation had been set aside as God's people. Others hold that the first company are the believing Gentiles and the second company the believing Jews. But can this be sustained? The "many who walk according to this rule" must mean every Christian, for they stand in contrast to the "many who desire to make a fair show in the flesh" (v.12). Why then should Paul add another company, and divide between Jewish and Gentile believers? It is contrary to his emphasis in this epistle and also in Eph 2:15, "one new man". Earlier he had shown that the blessing of Abraham had rested upon all who "are of faith" (3:9); that all who belong to Christ are the true "seed of Abraham" and "heirs according of the promise" (3:29); that God bestows His blessing on all true believers regardless of nationality (3:28). It is in the light of this that many translators legitimately translate *kai* (and) as "even", hence "even the Israel of God". Thus the third interpretation would seem to be the proper one, that those who "walk according to this rule" are defined as "the Israel of God". He thus declares that the false teachers were entirely wrong in demanding Gentiles to be circumcised, and in claiming that unless they did so they would never be among

God's people (Israel). The true Israel was now composed of both Jew and Gentile whose trust was in Christ alone. It should be added that the acceptance of this last interpretation does not mean that the Church is the continuation of Israel. By the term "the Israel of God" Paul is defining the true people of God. There is still a national future for Israel as distinct from the Church.

3.   *The Benediction*
      6:17-18

> v.17 "From henceforth let no man trouble me: for I bear in my body the marks of the Lord Jesus.
>
> v.18 Brethren, the grace of our Lord Jesus Christ be with your spirit. Amen."

17   Paul now looks to the future, and desires that no one should trouble him. He has in mind the Judaizers who were constantly insisting upon the mark of circumcision, and those activities constantly distressed and distracted him. He indicates the true marks were to be found in *his* body, sustained out of loyalty to Christ. Let no more be heard of their doctrine, marking other people's bodies at no cost to themselves. The "marks" of the Lord Jesus are all the sufferings he bore and endured as he preached the gospel. This did not diminish as time went on as 2 Cor 11:23-27 proves so fully. Because he had borne so much should encourage them to bear a little. How good to know the sufferer will one day be crowned.

18   Paul opened the epistle with "grace" (1:3); he now closes with the mention of "grace". He opened it as an apostle (1:1); he closes it as a brother, saying to them "brethren". We may not have the marks on our bodies, but we can enjoy the grace of our Lord Jesus Christ in our spirits.

EPHESIANS
A. Leckie

EPHESIANS
Introduction

1. **Authorship of the Epistle**
2. **Destination of the Epistle**
3. **Background to the Epistle**
4. **Locality from which the Epistle was written**
5. **Purpose of the Epistle**
6. **Outline of the Epistle**
7. **Theology of the Epistle**
8. **Bibliography**

1. Authorship of the Epistle

There can be little doubt that here we have an epistle written by the apostle Paul. His name is twice mentioned (1:1; 3:1). The reference to his imprisonment (3:1; 4:1; 6:20); his sphere of service (3:8); his revelation of the mystery (3:1-11); his exclusive teaching on the church as the body of Christ (1:23; 3:6; 4:4; 4:15-16; 5:23-33) place the authorship beyond argument. The epistle, too, beautifully completes his teaching: in the epistle to the Romans we "have died with Christ" (6:8); in the epistle to the Colossians we are "risen with Christ" (3:1); in the epistle to the Ephesians we "are seated in Christ in heavenly places" (2:6).

2. Destination of the Epistle

We now enter the realm of controversy. Enough has been written on the "pros and cons" of Ephesus as the destination. The epistles to the Colossians and to Philemon, which were written at about the same time and certainly delivered at the same time as the epistle to the Ephesians, deal with specific problems. There appears to be no particular problem among the Ephesians and because of this the epistle may have been written over a period of time. This may account for the absence of personal greetings. It might well be that the Ephesians were the first recipients but that Ephesus was not necessarily its ultimate destination.

3. Background to the Epistle

Accepting the Ephesians as the initial recipients of the epistle, we can proceed with a few details of its background. Ephesus was the capital of Proconsular Asia; it was well known for its Temple of Diana (or Artemis) and its large Theatre; there was also a Jewish Synagogue (Acts 19:8). It may well be that certain Jews from Ephesus were present in Jerusalem on the day of Pentecost, the birth day of the Church (Acts 2:9).

The apostle Paul had a variety of experiences associated with the work of God at Ephesus:

a)   He was "forbidden of the Holy Ghost to preach the word" there (Acts 16:6).
b)   According to Acts 18:18-21, when he did visit Ephesus, though it was desired that he should tarry, he consented not and with a promise to return if God should will, he left to go to Jerusalem.
c)   On another occasion so as not to be delayed on his way to Jerusalem, he sailed by Ephesus and sent for the Ephesian elders that they might come to him at Miletus (Acts 20:15-17).
d)   He reasoned there with the Jews (Acts 18:19); he spake boldly in the synagogue, disputing and persuading (Acts 19:8); he disputed daily in the school of Tyrannus (Acts 19:9); he testified both to the Jews and also to the Greeks repentance toward God and faith toward our Lord Jesus Christ (Acts 20:21); he testified the gospel of the grace of God (Acts 20:24); he preached the Kingdom (Acts 20:25); he shunned not to declare all the counsel of God (Acts 20:27); and all Asia heard the word of the Lord Jesus and the word of God grew mightily and prevailed (Acts 19:10:20).

It was at Ephesus that Aquila and Priscilla expounded the way of God more perfectly to Apollos who knew only the baptism of John, and Paul taught the need of believing on Christ Jesus to those twelve disciples of John (Acts 18:24-26; 19:1-7). At Ephesus those one-time disciples of John spoke with tongues and prophesied (Acts 19:6); special miracles were wrought by God through the apostle Paul (Acts 19:11-12); an evil spirit testified to knowing both Jesus and Paul and prevailed against the sons of Sceva so that fear fell on all, the name of the Lord Jesus was magnified and many who believed confessed and shewed their deeds (Acts 19:13-20).

The apostle Paul experienced much opposition at Ephesus: in 1 Cor 15:32 he writes of having fought with beasts at Ephesus. There was opposition from the Jews: certain of them were hardened and spoke evil of that way and some lay in wait for him (plotted against him) (Acts 19:9; 20:19). There was also strong opposition from the silversmiths who made silver shrines for the goddess Diana: incited by Demetrius there was no small stir about "that way" so that the silversmiths were full of wrath and the whole city was filled with confusion (Acts 19:21-41). It may well have been that it was at Ephesus during the uproar that Priscilla and Aquila gave to the apostle Paul the shelter of their home and thereby laid down their neck for him (Rom 16:3,4). Onesiphorus too had ministered to Paul when Paul was at Ephesus (2 Tim 1:16).

In his moving address at Miletus to the elders of the church at Ephesus, the apostle Paul reflects on the three years he had been in Ephesus and gives warning and counsel in view of future dangers. Of those three years he reminded the elders not only of his message (already referred to) but of his consistent manner, humility of mind and tears (Acts 20:18-19). Referring to dangerous wolves entering among them and men with a sectarian spirit rising amongst them, he reminded them he had warned them with tears night and day for three years.

The apostle's concern for the saints at Ephesus can be seen in his beseeching Timothy to abide there because of the strange doctrine of law-teachers (1 Tim 1:3-7); and when he desires Timothy to come to him he is careful to send Tychicus to Ephesus (2 Tim 4:9-12).

In a short time, within the space of a generation, the church at Ephesus had left its first love and there was the possibility of "the lampstand being removed out of its place" (Rev 2:1-5).

4. The Locality from which the Epistle was written

The apostle writes this epistle as an ambassador in a chain (6:20). He refers twice to his being a prisoner (3:1; 4:1). This is therefore one of the "Prison Epistles". It should be noted that the word "bond" or "chain" in 6:20 is in the singular, indicating his imprisonment at the time of writing was custodial, and the epistle was written during those two years the apostle dwelt in his own hired house (Acts 28:30).

5. Purpose of the Epistle

Though from the standpoint of Jewish malice the apostle was bound with a chain for the hope of Israel (Acts 28:20), he makes it clear to the Ephesian saints that his imprisonment was related to God's purpose concerning him. He was a prisoner of Christ Jesus for them as Gentiles (3:1), and his tribulations also were for them as Gentiles (3:13). In his epistle to the Colossians he writes concerning his twofold stewardship (1:24-26). Firstly, it was given to him, now that Christ was absent, to "fill up" in His stead the afflictions of Christ for His body's sake which is the church; this involved, for the apostle, sufferings in his flesh for the sake of the Gentiles (Col 1:24). Secondly, he had a stewardship given to him for the Gentiles to "fill up" the word of God, even the mystery, which had been hid from ages and from generations (Col 1:25-26). There was evidently divine intervention in the plans of the apostle Paul. He had planned to visit Jerusalem and then Rome on the way to Spain (Rom 15); he did go to Rome, not as a preacher but as a prisoner, and during his imprisonment he filled up instead of Christ the afflictions of Christ and at the same time he filled up the word of God, "even the mystery". He therefore writes in Eph 6:19,20 and Col 4:3 of "the mystery for which I am bound". In the epistle to the Ephesians the apostle writes concerning "the mystery of his will" (1:9); the revelation and stewardship of the mystery (3:1-12); the greatness of the mystery (5:32); and the mystery of the gospel (6:19). In the epistle to the Colossians he writes concerning the stewardship of the mystery (1:25-26); the mystery of God (2:2) and the mystery of Christ (4:3).

6.Outline of the Epistle

7. Theology of the Epistle

While our blessings in Christ are amply dealt with in the epistle to the Ephesians, it must be seen that God is primarily working for Himself and for His own glory. In ch.1 our blessings in Christ are for "the praise of his glory"; in ch.2 Jew and Gentile are made alive "that in the ages to come he might show (display) the exceeding riches of his grace", and Jew and Gentile are made nigh that there might be in a coming kingdom "an holy temple in the Lord"; in ch. 3 through the church God is now making known to the principalities and powers His manifold wisdom, and throughout all future ages there shall be glory to God in the church by Jesus Christ; in ch. 4 the ultimate of the church is "a perfect man, unto the measure of the stature of the fulness of Christ"; in ch. 5 Christ will yet present to Himself a church all-glorious; and in ch. 6 the armour to stand against the devil is God's provision to be put on and taken.

8. Bibliography

Abbott, T.K. *A Critical and Exegetical Commentary on the Epistles to the Ephesians and to the Colossians* (ICC). Edinburgh: Clark, 1897.

Allan, John A. *The Epistle to the Ephesians*. London: S.C.M., 1959

Barth, Markus. *The Broken Wall: A Study of the Epistle to the Ephesians*. Chicago: Judson, 1959.

Beare, F.W. "The Epistle to the Ephesians". Vol.X. *The Interpreter's Bible*. Ed. G.A. Buttrick. New York: Abingdon, 1953.

Beet, J. Agar. *A Commentary on St. Paul's Epistles to the Ephesians, Philippians, Colossians, and to Philemon*. London: Hodder and Stoughton, 1890.

Bruce, F.F. *The Epistle to the Ephesians*. London: Pickering and Inglis, 1961.

Darby, J.N. *Synopsis of the Bible*. Bible & Gospel Trust, Kingston-upon-Thames.

Ellicott, Charles J. *St. Paul's Epistle to the Ephesians*. London: Longmans, Green, 1855.

Findlay, G.G. *The Epistle to the Ephesians*. London: Hodder and Stoughton, 1904.

Foulkes, Francis. *The Epistle of Paul to the Ephesians*. London: Tyndale, 1963.

Hanson, Stig. *The Unity of the Church in the New Testament, Colossians and Ephesians*. Uppsala: Almquist and Wiksells, 1946.

Hendriksen, William. *Ephesians*. Grand Rapids: Baker, 1967.

Houlden, J.L. *Paul's Letters from Prison: Philippians, Colossians, Philemon and Ephesians*. London: Penguin, 1970.

Johnston, George. *Ephesians, Philippians, Colossians and Philemon*. London: Nelson, 1967.

Kelly, W. *Lectures on Ephesians*. Bible Trust Publishers, Addison, Illinois.

Kirby, J. C. *Ephesians, Baptism and Pentecost*. London: SPCK, 1968.

Lenski, R.C.H. *The Interpretation of St. Paul's Epistles to the Galatians, to the Ephesians and to the Philippians*. Columbus: Wartburg, 1937.

Lock, W. *St. Paul's Epistle to the Ephesians*. London: Methuen, 1929.

Mackay, John A. *God's Order: The Ephesian Letter and This Present Time*. New York: Macmillan, 1953.

Moule, H.C.G. *The Epistle to the Ephesians*. Cambridge: University Press, 1887.

Robinson, J. Armitage. *St Paul's Epistle to the Ephesians*. London: Macmillan, 1903.

Salmond, S.D.F. *Ephesians* (EGT). London: Hodder and Stoughton, 1917.

Scott, E.F. *The Epistles of Paul to the Colossians, to Philemon and to the Ephesians*. London: Hodder and Stoughton, 1930.

Simpson, E.D. and Bruce, F.F. *Commentary on the Epistles to the Ephesians and the Colossians*. London: Marshall, Morgan and Scott, 1957.

Thompson, G.H.P. *The Letters of Paul to the Ephesians, to the Colossians and to Philemon*. Cambridge University Press, 1967.

Zerwick, Max. *The Epistle to the Ephesians*. Eng. T. London: Burns and Oates, 1969.

1. Our Blessings in Christ (1:1-3:21)

The repetition of "in Christ Jesus", "in Christ", "in him" is the key to an understanding of this section of the epistle. What we are and have in Christ is the theme.

1.   *Salutation*
   1:1,2

v.1   "Paul, an apostle of Jesus Christ by the will of God, to the saints which are at
      Ephesus, and to the faithful in Christ Jesus:
v.2   Grace be to you, and peace, from God our Father, and from the Lord Jesus
      Christ."

1   Paul thinks of himself and those to whom he is writing in relation both to
Christ Jesus and to God. For himself he was an apostle of Christ Jesus and
that by the will of God; as for the Ephesians they were saints in relation to
God and also the faithful in Christ Jesus. Paul was not an apostle of the Lamb
chosen by our Lord on the mount of the Beatitudes - those were twelve in
number (Matt 19:28; Rev 21:14). The twelve, though becoming part of the
church, had and will have an important role in connection with the nation of
Israel. When the early saints were scattered abroad after the stoning of
Stephen, the twelve apostles remained at Jerusalem, a link between the church
in its infancy and the rejected nation (Acts 8:1). In the coming millennial age
the same twelve will remain a link between the church in glory and re-gathered
Israel (Rev 21:14). Paul as an apostle of Christ Jesus, the ascended Christ, in
his teaching directs us more particularly to our blessings in the heavenlies.
He was an apostle too by the will of God (see also 1 Cor 1:1; 2 Cor 1:1; Col
1:1; 2 Tim 1:1). His apostleship was by divine call (Rom 1:1), by divine
command (1 Tim 1:1), and by divine will (Eph 1:1); human agency, whether
by appointment or commission, was excluded. Paul's reference to God's will
throughout Eph 1 should be observed, viz v.5 "the good pleasure of his will",
v.9 "the mystery of his will", and v.11 "the counsel of his own will". The
Ephesians were "saints", God's holy ones; they were "the faithful in Christ
Jesus", not so much in terms of fidelity but by their exercise of faith (see 1
Tim 6:2). "In Christ Jesus" refers to the position into which their faith had
placed them.

2   The epistle commences with grace and peace and concludes with peace and
grace (6:23,24). Whereas grace is the divine side of the matter and refers to God's
favour towards us, peace is our side, what we enjoy. It is undoubtedly true that
both relate to God our Father as the source and the Lord Jesus Christ as the
agent, but mentioning both together, as he does so often, Paul is stating our
Lord's equality with God the Father.

2.   *The praise of His Glory*
   1:3-14

v.3   "Blessed be the God and Father of our Lord Jesus Christ, who hath blessed us
      with all spiritual blessings in heavenly places in Christ:

v.4   According as he hath chosen us in him before the foundation of the world, that we should be holy and without blame before him in love:

v.5   Having predestinated us unto the adoption of children by Jesus Christ to himself, according to the good pleasure of his will,

v.6   To the praise of the glory of his grace, wherein he hath made us accepted in the beloved.

v.7   In whom we have redemption through his blood, the forgiveness of sins, according to the riches of his grace;

v.8   Wherein he hath abounded towards us in all wisdom and prudence;

v.9   Having made known unto us the mystery of his will, according to his good pleasure which he hath purposed in himself:

v.10   That in the dispensation of the fulness of times he might gather together in one all things in Christ, both which are in heaven, and which are on earth; even in him:

v.11   In whom also we have obtained an inheritance, being predestinated according to the purpose of him who worketh all things after the counsel of his own will:

v.12   That we should be to the praise of his glory, who first trusted in Christ.

v.13   In whom ye also trusted, after that ye heard the word of truth, the gospel of your salvation: in whom also after that ye believed, ye were sealed with that Holy Spirit of promise.

v.14   Which is the earnest of our inheritance until the redemption of the purchased possession, unto the praise of his glory."

There are three sub-sections in vv.3-14 and each concludes with a note of praise. In vv.3-6 Paul's teaching has to do with *the will of God* as it relates to the saints in the *past* and in the *future*. In regard to the past he refers to their *election* before the foundation of the world; as for their future he refers to their *predestination* unto the adoption of children; and concludes with the note of praise in v.6 "to the praise of the glory of his grace". In vv.7-12 Paul's teaching has to do with the *work of Christ* and again as it relates to the *past* and the *future*. In regard to the past he speaks of their *redemption* through His blood; in regard to the future he speaks of their *inheritance* and concludes once more with a note of praise in v.12 "that we should be to the praise of his glory". In vv.13-14 Paul's teaching has to do with the *witness of the Holy Spirit* as it relates to the *past* and the *future*. With regard to the past he refers to their being *sealed* with the Holy Spirit of promise; as for their future that same Holy Spirit of promise is the *earnest* of their inheritance; and yet again he concludes with a note of praise in v.14 "unto the praise of his glory".

3   This verse is fraught with the thought of blessing. The saints bless God for having blessed them with all spiritual blessings. When we bless God we add nothing to Him, but we ascribe to Him the praise that He is due. When, however, God blesses us He adds everything to us that is worth having, "all spiritual blessings". The Blesser is the God and Father of our Lord Jesus Christ, and the blessings are all spiritual and in the heavenlies in Christ. The Blesser is one whom neither the Patriarchs nor the nation of Israel knew as such - He is the God and Father of our Lord Jesus Christ risen from the dead (John 20:17); the blessings are in keeping with this - they are in Christ now at God's right hand, not seated on the throne of David, and are therefore heavenly and not earthly, spiritual and not temporal. No earthly nor temporal blessing could exceed these. Read *en pasē eulogia*, "with every spiritual blessing", and understand that spiritual blessings in their totality are the endowment of every saint of God. God does not dole out His blessings piecemeal; there are no first, second nor third blessings; they are all ours. The enjoyment of them is another matter.

4   Now Paul enlarges upon the spiritual blessings with special regard to the Blesser. In v.4 a sovereign God makes a choice in Christ before the foundation of the world; in v.5 the Father of our Lord Jesus Christ, according to the good pleasure of His will, predestinates unto sonship. God is seen to be moving for His own glory and the eternal satisfaction of His own heart. In v.4 He would have a people before (*katenōpion*) Him in love; in v.5 He would have a people to (*eis*) Himself as sons. Election as taught in v.4 has to do with a sovereign God, is connected with the past and is related to persons; predestination as taught in v.5 has to do with the Father's good pleasure, is connected with the future and is related to a position marked out for persons (see also Rom 8:29). Israel knew something of election and sonship, but with a difference: their election was as a nation, they were an elect race; their sonship was as a nation, "Israel is my son". The election of this unique day is individual as is also the sonship.

The fact of election is taught in our Bibles whether it be with respect to "angels", "Israel" or "the church", and though there might be much about it we cannot understand, we humbly and worshipfully accept the truth of it. To understand it fully one would require to know as much as God knows. It is man's proud mind that dismisses what it cannot fully understand.

Paul acquaints us with the *sphere, time* and *purpose* of God's choice. The sphere was "in Christ": the choice of the individual was in Christ and not because of anything in the individual. The time was "before the foundation of the world" (see also John 17:24; 1 Pet 1:20): before the world was made and time commenced and man had been introduced or sin had entered. The purpose was "that we should be holy and without blame before him in love". While the thought of "before him" anticipates the future, yet all of this is now true in essence of the saints of God. What the church will be on that great day when Christ presents it to Himself (5:27), so each child of God is in essence now and will be eternally before the face of God. While many take the expression "in love" as introducing the subject of predestination in v.5, the thought appears to be that God's purpose is to have a people before Him, not only suited to His holy nature, "holy and without blemish", but in the enjoyment of His love.

5   Predestination is simply to "mark out beforehand" (see also Acts 4:28; Rom 8:29,30; 1 Cor 2:7). The word occurs twice in this chapter (vv.5,11) and the connection is not only important but precious: in v.5 it is predestination to sonship, in v.11 predestination to an inheritance. "The adoption of children" is but one word (*huiothesia*) and occurs in Rom 8:15,23; Rom 9:4; Gal 4:5; Eph 1:5. It is a compound of two words and means literally "the placing of sons" or "sonship". We have received the sonship (Gal 4:5); we have a spirit of sonship (Rom 8:15); but sonship in its fulness involves physical conformity to God's Son and for this we wait (Rom 8:23), and to this we are predestined (Eph 1:5) (see also Rom 8:29). The Father will have to Himself many sons bearing the image of His own Son and accomplishes this through Jesus Christ (see also Gal 4:4,5). The Father thereby gives expression to the good pleasure of His own will. God's intention to have the good pleasure in men He did not achieve (Luke 2:14) but found in His own Son (Matt 3:17; 17:5; Mark 1:11; Luke 3:22), and will secure in us by marking us out to be like His own Son.

6 "Accepted in the beloved" sums up vv.4,5. The rendering of *charitoō* as "accepted" is perhaps rather restricted. The word occurs elsewhere only in Luke 1:28 and is translated "highly favoured". By his usage of this particular word Paul is referring to the fulness of God's favour bestowed upon us in the matter of our election and predestination. Whereas we were "blessed in Christ" (v.3), "chosen in him" (v.4), now the apostle speaks of being "highly favoured in the beloved". This fulness of divine favour is ours in the One who is beloved of His Father. Not only has divine favour been bestowed upon us in the Beloved, but this is an expression of the glory of God's grace and must become a matter of praise to God now and forever.

7 In vv.7-12 Paul writes of the work of Christ as it relates to the past and the future. Observe the repetition of "in whom" in vv.7,11: "in whom we have redemption through his blood, the forgiveness of sins" (v.7); "in whom also we have obtained an inheritance" (v.11). Paul, in his defence before Agrippa associates forgiveness with an inheritance in Acts 26:18. The will of God regarding us could not be realised apart from the work of Christ; we could not have been so divinely favoured unless our need by reason of our sins had been dealt with. Now Paul makes known that in the same riches of His grace whereby God forgave us our sins, He takes us to Himself and makes known the secrets of His heart. Our sins or trespasses (*paraptōma*) required divine forgiveness or remission (*aphesis*), and this we have as a present possession in Him (the Beloved) and through His blood. All is according to the riches of God's grace. God has met us in our need, not according to our need but according to the riches of His grace. In v.6 Paul refers to the glory of God's grace and in v.7 the riches of God's grace. The glory of His grace is grace that becomes His glory; the riches of His grace is grace that abundantly meets our need.

8 "Wherein he hath abounded toward us" indicates that there is that in the riches of His grace that is over and above the meeting of our need as sinners. In the same riches of His grace whereby God remitted our trespasses, He has abounded toward us in all wisdom and prudence. Wisdom or enlightenment (*sophia*) and prudence or intelligence (*phronēsis*) refer not to the manner in which God has abounded, but rather to what he has bestowed or imparted to enable us to know what is beyond mere flesh and blood - the intelligence to know and all wisdom to admire.

9 In using the aorist tense in the phrase "having made known unto us the mystery of his will", Paul is referring to something already revealed, no doubt in Christ. The revelation is not God's will particularly, but a secret related to it. A mystery in the NT is the revelation of something hitherto unrevealed (Eph 3:3-6,9). V. 10 indicates that this secret associated with God's will concerns the dispensation of the fulness of times. We now have for a second time in this chapter reference to God's good pleasure (see also v.5) and here it is related to what God has purposed in Christ.

10 This and the following verse direct our minds to the secret of God's will in connection with the dispensation of the fulness of times. In v.10 we learn that God will gather together in one all things in Christ; and in v.11 that we have been predestinated, according to divine purpose, to obtain an inheritance in Him. "The fulness of times" (*tou plērōmatos tōn kairōn*) is quite different from "the fulness of time" (*to plērōma tou chronou*) in Gal 4:4. Not only is "time" plural in Eph 1:10 and singular in Gal 4:4, but the words are different. *Chronos* is time in terms of duration or a definite point; *kairos* refers rather to the characteristic circumstances of a period of time. "Fulness" (*plērōma*) signifies complement, full extent or full number. Here in 1:10 Paul projects the mind to a future era when the differing seasons have all been put to the test, have run their course and their complement has been reached. This season will be the coming Kingdom age, commonly spoken of as the millennium. The coming Kingdom will in fact be the seventh age and appropriately it is here spoken of as "the fulness of times". Paul writes of the dispensation (*oikonomia*) of the fulness of times. The primary thought in "dispensation" is not a period of time but rather administration or how matters are dispensed. It is a household word: the owner of the house predetermines the management or stewardship of his house and entrusts this to his chief steward. Paul is therefore writing of the future administration of the coming millennial age and we learn that God's purpose then is to gather together in one all things in Christ, both which are in heaven and which are on earth (see also Acts 3:21; Col 1:20). "To gather together in one" (*anakephalalomai*) occurs only here and in Rom 13:9 and signifies to reduce under one head. All things therefore in heaven and earth will converge on Christ, become subject to Him and take character from Him. The groaning creation will be delivered from its bondage of corruption; Israel's wanderings will cease and her hardness disappear; nations shall gladly serve the restored Nation of Israel; Satan the great deceiver will be bound and banished, and the Church will be triumphant in glory. One objection to this view is that sin shall occur, death as divine judgment for evil shall be meted out, and at the end of the millennial reign of Christ there shall be a dreadful attack on Jerusalem inspired and led by the Devil. It must be observed that Paul does not say that "everything" shall be gathered together in one in Christ but "the all things" (*ta panta*), i.e. all things that come within the circumference of divine purpose. Everything outside divine purpose shall be dealt with and the Son of God shall hand a perfect Kingdom back to His Father (1 Cor 15:24).

11   "In him" at the close of v.10 belongs to this v.11 "In him, in whom also we have obtained an inheritance". The emphasis is upon the person in whom the inheritance has been obtained: in the Beloved we have forgiveness (v.7), and in Christ we have an inheritance (v.11). If the verb *klēroō*, "to obtain an inheritance", is to be taken in its middle sense, then the thought as expressed in the AV is correct; if however it is taken in its passive sense, then the rendering ought to be "in him, in whom we have been made an inheritance". Both the context and the NT teaching on the subject of the inheritance suggest the verb must be understood in its middle sense. In the context of Eph 1 the saints' predestination is spoken of in verses 5 and 11. In v.5 they are predestinated to the position of sons, and in v.11 they are predestinated to an inheritance. Sonship and heirship are linked together, we are heirs because we are sons (Heb 1:2; Gal 4:7; Luke 15:11,12). Furthermore, believers have the seal of the Holy Spirit of promise and this is the earnest of their inheritance (vv.13-14). Israel is spoken of as God's inheritance (Deut 32:9; Is 19:24,25); but the emphasis in the NT is not that the saints are an inheritance but rather have an inheritance (Rom 8:17; Col 1:12; 1 Pet 1:3,4). As is the case in our becoming sons, so also our obtaining an inheritance - we were predestinated from all eternity. Since the predestination to heirship is according to divine purpose, God is seen to be effectively working all things according to the counsel (purpose) of His own will to achieve it.

12   From vv.3-10 the apostle has employed the first person pronoun embracing in it all believers. Now in vv.11-12 it takes on a particular significance and the apostle is identifying himself with believing Jews as distinct from the believing Gentiles of v.13. He is thinking of believing Jews of this day of grace who have hoped in Christ in advance of their own nation (*proelpizō*, "to hope before"). In a somewhat similar way he speaks of himself as a believing Jew born spiritually in advance of his own nation (1 Cor 15:8). Whereas restored Israel in a coming age will be blessed as they become subject to the reign of Christ in His manifested glory, believing Jews of this day of grace will share with Christ in that glory (Col 3:4) and will become the theme of praise by adoring hosts.

13   In this and the following verse the apostle is thinking of believing Gentiles. His use in v.13 of the second person pronoun suggests this. The theme now is the "witness of the Holy Spirit". In v.13 "in whom" occurs twice, and it is essential to notice that the AV has inserted "trusted" after the first - no doubt to give the sense as the translators saw it. It would appear, however, that the first "in whom" is an extension of v.11 "in whom also we have obtained an inheritance". The teaching of v.13 therefore is "in whom ye also obtained an inheritance" and "in whom ye were sealed with that Holy Spirit of promise". Believing Gentiles had also obtained an inheritance after they had heard, or rather having heard the word of truth, the word in which God has revealed divine truth and which was on their part the glad news of their salvation. "In whom, having also believed, ye were sealed" (RV). There is no thought of a time lapse; the tense employed is the aorist, "having believed". Nor is Christ presented as the object of faith; the connection is "in whom ye obtained an inheritance and in whom ye were sealed". Thus sealed these Gentile believers became God's property (2 Tim 2:19). There is involved in the word "seal" the concept of authority (Esth 3:12; 1 Kings 21:8) and what is irreversible (Dan 6:17; Eph 4:30). As a seal of the righteousness of faith Abraham received the external sign of circumcision (Rom. 4:11). Here however the seal of divine ownership is the indwelling Holy Spirit as the Holy Spirit of promise. As the Holy Spirit of promise He is not Himself the promised One (Acts 1:4), but rather connected with the immutable promise of our future blessings.

14   This same Holy Spirit of promise is the earnest (*arrabōn*) of our inheritance. The earnest is the part-price paid as a pledge of ultimate full payment or the engagement ring as a pledge of marriage. The indwelling Holy Spirit of promise is the divine pledge that we shall receive our inheritance and also in the meantime by His gracious ministry He enables us to enjoy what awaits us. The "purchased possession" (*peripoiēsis*) signifies what has been acquired and laid by and refers to what Christ has acquired for Himself (Matt 13:44, "the field"). At His appearing our Lord shall redeem (*apolutrōsis*) by power what He has acquired and then we shall receive our inheritance. In that coming age of glory we shall be to His praise.

3.   *Prayer of the Apostle*
1:15-23

v.15   "Wherefore I also, after I heard of your faith in the Lord Jesus, and love unto all the saints,

v.16   Cease not to give thanks for you, making mention of you in my prayers;

v.17   That the God of our Lord Jesus Christ, the Father of glory, may give unto you the spirit of wisdom and revelation in the knowledge of him:

v.18   The eyes of your understanding being enlightened; that ye may know what is the hope of his calling, and what the riches of the glory of his inheritance in the saints,

v.19   And what is the exceeding greatness of his power to us-ward who believe, according to the working of his mighty power,

> v.20 Which he wrought in Christ, when he raised him from the dead, and set him at his own right hand in the heavenly places,
> v.21 Far above all principality, and power, and might, and dominion, and every name that is named, not only in this world, but also in that which is to come:
> v.22 And hath put all things under his feet, and gave him to be the head over all things to the church,
> v.23 Which is his body, the fulness of him that filleth all in all."

The apostle now gives thanks for the Ephesian saints and prays for their enlightenment on three particular matters, viz. (1) "the hope of his calling" (v.18), (2) "the riches of the glory of his inheritance in the saints" (v.18), and (3) "the exceeding greatness of his power to us-ward who believe" (v.19). "The hope of his calling" has already been considered in vv.3-6, as also "the riches of the glory of his inheritance in the saints" in vv.7-14. "The exceeding greatness of his power to us-ward who believe" has yet to be expounded and this the apostle will do in chapter 2:1-10.

15 Having referred in v.13 to the gospel of their salvation, and to their having believed, which had now been confirmed by a report, the apostle gives thanks not only for their faith in the Lord Jesus but for their love unto all the saints. Some omit "and love", but it appears the weight of authority is in favour of its retention as in Col 1:4. This same apostle reminds the Galatians that "faith worketh by love" (Gal 5:6). Faith in the Lord Jesus must evidence itself by love unto all the saints.

16 "In my prayers" (*epi tōn proseuchōn mou*, at my prayers). In his hired house despite his chain, the apostle had his stated times for prayer when he mentioned the Ephesian saints, possibly by name, and ever gave thanks for them.

17 "The God of our Lord Jesus Christ, the Father of glory" is not only different from v.3 but is quite unique. The God of our Lord Jesus Christ is God in relation to Christ [as a man]: Psalm 22:10 from His birth; Psalm 22:1 in the darkness of Golgotha; John 20:17 as a man risen from the dead; Heb 1:9 [as an] exalted man in heaven. The Father of glory is the source of all glory. In his prayer the apostle, in vv.20-23, states in thrilling language what the Father of glory has done for Christ as man, viz. "raised him from the dead, and set him at his own right hand far above all." As God He was always far above all, but now this is true of Him as man. "The spirit of wisdom and revelation" is the Holy Spirit in that particular character revealing God and His purpose, and capacitating the believer to admire the wonder of it all. They had been sealed with the Holy Spirit of promise upon believing, but now the apostle's prayer is for their enlightenment by the same Spirit, "in the knowledge (*epignōsis*, knowledge that influences) of him". All else by way of enlightenment that is worth while must stem from this.

18 Read "The eyes of your heart" - the weight of authority favours "heart" (*kardia*) and not "understanding" (*dianoia*). The apostle is thinking of something deeper than the faculty of reflection and meditation. He thinks of the core of personal life and of the seat of affection. When enlightenment reaches the heart, conviction is begotten and not just opinions formed. Paul prays "that ye may know what", i.e. know the reality of what they had already apprehended. Whereas in 4:4 it is the "hope of your calling", here in 1:18 it is "the hope of his calling", the hope God has for Himself in the divine call and this is twofold, viz. (v.4) to have us before Him in love, and (v.5) to have us to Him as sons. "What the riches of the glory of his inheritance in the saints": an inheritance in or among the saints does not mean that the saints are God's inheritance. The apostle employs similar language in Acts 20:32; Acts 26:18 "an inheritance among all them which are sanctified". In v.14 the inheritance is ours, yet to be possessed; in v.18 it is God's, yet to be given and in which He shall display the riches of His glory among the recipients. "The riches of his grace" (v.7) is the measure of divine pardon enjoyed now; "the riches of the glory of his inheritance" (v.18) has yet to be displayed among His saints.

19 In this and the following verse, the apostle desires the saints to know that the same mighty power, that raised Christ from the dead and set Him at God's right hand in righteousness, has been exercised toward them in wondrous grace. The exceeding greatness of God's power (*dunamis*, unquestioned ability) toward us was according to the working (*energeia*, efficient operation) of the might (*kratos*, force superior to all opposition) of His strength (*ischus*, inherent vital power). The apostle refers here to the exceeding greatness of God's power; in 2:7 to the exceeding riches of God's grace, in 3:19 to the love of Christ which passeth (exceedeth) knowledge.

20 The working of God's mighty power effectually wrought in Christ in a two-fold way: (1) raising Him from the dead, and (2) setting Him at God's right hand. Our Lord was raised from the dead by the glory of the Father (Rom 6:4), and by the mighty power of God (Eph 1:19-20). The glory of the Father demanded it and the power of God performed it. Nothing that man could do could have kept that sacred body in the sepulchre - neither the stone, nor the seal, nor the soldiers. Each hitherto expression of God's power, even in creation, was eclipsed by a power that in its greatness surpassed them all. From among the dead to a place far above all principality and power was the immeasurable range. God has "set" (caused to sit down) Christ "at his own right hand", in the place of supreme authority. Now as *man* He sits where in fact no angel could ever sit (Heb 1:13). He is "in the heavenly places" (1:3; 2:6; 3:10; 6:12; *ouranios*: heavenlies with *epi* "upon" or "in", i.e. what pertains to or is in the heavenlies). "Heavenly places" is a very comprehensive sphere and must not be confused with heaven itself (*ouranos*), "the third heaven" (Heb 9:24; 2 Cor 12:2). The fact that Christ is there, together with the good principalities and powers (3:10), and spiritual wickedness (6:12), makes clear that the contrast is, in a general way, between what is earthly and what is heavenly (see 1 Cor 15:48).

21 "Far above" (*huperanō*) is used in 4:10; Heb 9:5 in terms of position; here in 1:21 in terms of rank and dignity. In the parallel passage in Col 1:16 reference is made to things in the heavens and things on the earth, visible and invisible. It may therefore be that "every principality and power" refer to supra-mundane invisible angelic beings, and "might and dominion" refers to the corresponding mundane visible authority entrusted to men. "Every name that is named" suggests place or position apportioned (3:15), or approval given (5:3); and this comprehends not only this age (*aiōn*), but the coming one. In His exalted dignified rank our Lord by divine assent is "far above all".

22 "And hath put all things under his feet" is a quotation from Psalm 8:6 (see also Heb 2:8). Not only is our Lord supreme in relation to the varied ranks of administration and government, but all things have already in divine purpose been put under His feet (cf. Heb 2:8, "not yet seen"). In the greatness of His position as the head over all things (see v. 10), He has been given to the church.

23 Paul says of the church, "which is his body". The church as Christ's body mystically is exclusively Pauline teaching - this was the mystery revealed to him. Vital, indivisible, organic union is involved and indicates the unique character of the church. If all things are put under His feet (v.22), this must exclude the church as being His body. The church, His body, is the fulness or complement (*plērōma*) of Christ. As an exalted head Christ would be incomplete without the church His body. Christ mystically is the head in heaven indivisibly united to the church His body. Not only is the church as His body His complement, but through it as head He manifests Himself. He too fills all in all and this anticipates the dispensation of the fulness of times when all things in heaven and earth shall be headed up in Christ (v.10); and as head over all things (v.22) He shall fill all things with Himself (4:10). The supremacy of Christ is thrilling: not only far above every principality and every name, but all things are put under his feet; He is the head over all things and He fills all things.

4. *Jew and Gentile Made Alive*
   ### 2:1-10

> v.1 "And you hath he quickened, who were dead in trespasses and sins;
> v.2 Wherein in time past ye walked according to the course of this world, according to the prince of the power of the air, the spirit that now worketh in the children of disobedience:
> v.3 Among whom also we all had our conversation in times past in the lusts of our flesh, fulfilling the desires of the flesh and of the mind; and were by nature the children of wrath, even as others.

v.4   But God, who is rich in mercy, for his great love wherewith he loved us,
v.5   Even when we were dead in sins, hath quickened us together with Christ, (by
      grace ye are saved;)
v.6   And hath raised us up together, and made us sit together in heavenly places in
      Christ Jesus:
v.7   That in the ages to come he might shew the exceeding riches of his grace in his
      kindness toward us through Christ Jesus.
v.8   For by grace are ye saved through faith; and that not of yourselves: it is the gift
      of God:
v.9   Not of works, lest any man should boast.
v.10 For we are his workmanship, created in Christ Jesus unto good works, which
      God hath before ordained that we should walk in them."

From an introduction in ch. 1 to divine counsel and purpose concerning the church in the manner of election, predestination and inheritance, we now have the dreadful material upon which God had to work. None save God could have done anything with such apparently hopeless material. The apostle's repeated use of the prefix *sun* "together" (vv.5,6,21,22) indicates he has before him particularly the work of God toward Jew and Gentile: vv.1-10, Jew and Gentile morally, both alike dead; vv.11-22, Jew and Gentile dispensationally, the one afar off and the other nigh. So in vv.1-10, the dead are made alive (quickened) (v.5); in vv.11-22, those afar off are made nigh (v.13).

As in ch. 1 the apostle again thinks of past and future: in vv.1-10, in time past how both Jew and Gentile walked and lived (vv.2,3), but as the result of being made alive there will be in them a future display of the exceeding riches of God's grace (v.7). In vv.11-22, in time past as the uncircumcision the Gentiles were apart from Christ, alienated from the covenants, strangers, having no hope and without God; but, having been made nigh, together with believing Jews in a future age they will be seen as a holy temple in the Lord (v.21).

Verses 1-10 are a continuation of 1:19 where the apostle, having referred to the exceeding greatness of God's power to us-ward who believe, digressed to illustrate that power first working in Christ. Now the apostle speaks of that power to us-ward. In righteousness it did two things for Christ: "raised him from the dead, and set him at God's right hand in the heavenly places" (1:20). In grace it has done three things for us who believe: "quickened us, raised us up and made us sit in heavenly places" (2:5,6). The reason for this difference is that the exceeding greatness of God's power toward Christ was in respect of physical death, but in our case moral death was involved. There is of course another obvious difference: whereas Christ has been set *at God's right hand* in heavenly places (1:20), we are made to sit in heavenly places (2:6). God's right hand is reserved for Christ. It becomes evident that the apostle is not thinking of God's resurrection power in our daily living, but in our salvation.

Verses 1-3 are an exposure of what man is by nature and practice. By nature he is dead; by practice he is devil-led and disobedient. Verses 4-6 are an exposition of God's intervention in mercy, love and grace. Verses 7-10 are an explanation of God's purpose for the future and the present: in future ages He will display in those quickened, raised and seated the exceeding riches of His grace; in the meantime by their walk there should be a manifestation of those good works predetermined for them.

1 "And you" refers to the Ephesian Gentiles as distinct from "we" Jews (v. 3). "... hath he quickened" though no doubt implied, is an insertion by the translators. "... who were dead in trespasses and sins": "in trespasses and sins" is the dative without the preposition "in" but must not be interpreted as death to sin as in Rom 6:2. It is the instrumental dative and signifies dead through or in respect of trespasses and sins (see Col 2:13). Trespass (*paraptōma*) and sin (*hamartia*) might sum up the whole occasion of man's moral death: trespass involving disobedience, sin involving ignorance. "Dead" or "being dead" conveys the solemn fact that man by nature is devoid of even one living principle God-ward.

2 "Wherein in time past ye walked" indicates that the spirit or influence that works in the children of disobedience had directed their walk as unregenerate along the road of trespasses and sins. The apostle is really speaking of "sons" and not "children" (see also 5:6): son implies character, and the character here is having no regard for the will of God either by disobedience or wilful unbelief. They had once walked according to the course (*aiōn*) of this world (*kosmos*), i.e. the particular age in which they lived in this world system that had dispensed with God. Like a dead fish carried along by the current, whatever was the order of the day therein they walked "... according to the prince (ruler) of the power (authority) of the air". The ruler is the devil; the authority is the demons, evil spirits viewed collectively as the authority over which the devil rules; and the air is their sphere of operation. "The air" must be interpreted literally, and note the word (*aēr*) refers to the air we breathe. "... the spirit" is not so much the ruler himself nor his authority, but their influence which is as pervasive as the air man breathes.

3 Despite the blessings showered upon the Jew and his place of favour before Jehovah, he was no different from the Gentile. "... also we all" refers to the Jew, and "even as others" to the Gentile. Among those sons of disobedience the Jew also had his manner of life, going to and fro in time past in the lusts of his flesh. "... the lusts of our flesh" - here were the root causes of their disobedience: living to satisfy the desires and passions of a nature depraved by the fall. These desires were manifold and expressed themselves in a twofold way, viz. *poiountes ta thelēmata, doing* the things willed of the flesh (*sarx*) and of the mind (*dianoia*). Doing the things willed of the flesh may refer to the reckless abandon of the depraved nature expressing itself in dissipation and prodigality; doing the things willed of the mind (*dianoia*, faculty of thought) may refer to the deliberate choice of the mind or intellect, however refined, but with total disregard to the will of

God. By natural generation the Jew was no different from others. No matter how a man may be advantaged by environment or favour of any kind, by nature, as belonging to a fallen race, he is exposed to the wrath of God. The elder brother who, despite his claim to many years of faithful service, would not yield to his father's entreaties, was as much a son of disobedience as the "prodigal" when wasting his substance with riotous living in a far country.

4   The natural reaction to a corpse is that of Abraham "to bury out of sight" (Gen 23:4). Here in v.4 we have God's intervention on behalf of those dead in trespasses and sins: in His rich mercy and great love He quickens and by His grace saves those whom He might righteously have buried out of His sight. If Jew and Gentile deserved wrath, God would exercise rich mercy; and if they were corpses on account of their trespasses and sins, He would quicken. The relationship of mercy to love is brought before us here: God's rich compassion is because of the greatness of His love. The great love of God expresses itself in rich compassion toward the undeserving.

5   Now the apostle expatiates upon "the exceeding greatness of his power to us-ward who believe" (1:19). He seems still to have before him the Jew: "(We too being dead in offences) has quickened us with the Christ (ye are saved by grace)" JND. We too, as you Gentiles, were dead in sins (*paraptōma*) but God has quickened us together, both Jew and Gentile, with Christ. By grace ye Gentiles are saved. Since your condition was the same as ours as Jews, your salvation too must be entirely of grace. This quickening, being made alive, took place ideally when God by His mighty power raised Christ from the dead, for "hath quickened" is the aorist tense.

6   Not only has God "quickened" (v.5), but "hath raised us up together, and made us sit together in heavenly places in Christ Jesus". Having been made alive ideally with Christ in His resurrection, there is also sharing ideally in Christ all that was involved in His resurrection and exaltation, save, as we have already seen, in His pre-eminence. The aorist tense again is employed, so that in the purpose of God all has already been accomplished.

7   The exceeding greatness of God's power raised Christ and set Him in the place of supremacy at God's right hand. That same power has quickened the morally dead, raised and seated them in the heavenlies, but with an important difference. Throughout the ages to come God will display in them the surpassing riches of His grace in His kindness toward them; but it was neither grace nor kindness (benevolence) that gave the place of supremacy to Christ - it is His by right. "The ages to come" as distinct from "the age to come" (1:21) suggests that this display shall remain undiminished as long as time shall last.

8   Again reverting to the Ephesians as having been Gentiles, the apostle reminds them it was by God's grace they had been saved and adds to his former statement in v.5 that this salvation is "through faith". Since it is by faith, works are excluded (v.9). Moreover this faith was not of themselves: it was of God. Whatever may precede the exercise of faith, this faith is the gift of God. One objection to this interpretation is that "faith" (*pistis*) is feminine and "that" (*touto*) is neuter. However, it is submitted that the demonstrative pronoun (*touto*) does not qualify (*pistis*) but the preceding statement "through faith" (*dia tēs pisteōs*). To argue that "the gift of God" is explanatory of the statement "for by grace are ye saved through faith" is invalid. If salvation is by grace, it cannot be other than a gift. Paul did not find it necessary in v.5 to add the explanatory statement, "it is the gift of God"; but he does in v.8 only because he adds "through faith". There are other references to faith as a gift: 2 Pet 1:1; Phil 1:29; Acts 3:16.

9   What is of grace excludes works (Rom 11:6), and because it is not of works boasting is excluded.

10   Though works are not a means to salvation, they are a necessary evidence of it. The emphasis is still upon God: we are His workmanship (*poiēma*) (see also Rom 1:20); and it is workmanship with an end in view, to produce a beautiful design. As such we are a new creation in Christ Jesus "unto good works" (*epi ergois agathois*), for or with a view to good works. These good works in which we should walk, not only transcend the Law of Moses but in terms of divine purpose precede it. The Law was introduced incidentally (Rom 5:20; Gal 3:19); and temporarily (Gal 3:19,24). These good works were "before ordained" by God; their importance cannot therefore be over-stressed. It does not necessarily imply that the specific works were detailed in divine foreknowledge, but rather that their character was - they were to be "good works".

5.   *Jew and Gentile Made Nigh*
   ## 2:11-22

v.11 "Wherefore remember, that ye being in time past Gentiles in the flesh, who are called Uncircumcision by that which is called the Circumcision in the flesh made by hands;

v.12 That at that time ye were without Christ, being aliens from the commonwealth of Israel, and strangers from the covenants of promise, having no hope, and without God in the world:

v.13 But now in Christ Jesus ye who sometimes were far off are made nigh by the blood of Christ.

v.14 For he is our peace, who hath made both one, and hath broken down the middle wall of partition between us;

v.15 Having abolished in his flesh the enmity, even the law of commandments contained in ordinances; for to make in himself of twain one new man, so making peace;

v.16 And that he might reconcile both unto God in one body by the cross, having slain the enmity thereby:

v.17 And came and preached peace to you which were afar off, and to them that were nigh.

v.18 For through him we both have access by one Spirit unto the Father.

v.19 Now therefore ye are no more strangers and foreigners, but fellow citizens with the saints, and of the household of God;

v.20 And are built upon the foundation of the apostles and prophets, Jesus Christ himself being the chief corner stone;

v.21 In whom all the building fitly framed together groweth unto an holy temple in the Lord:

v.22 In whom ye also are builded together for an habitation of God through the Spirit."

In vv.1-10 there was no difference morally between Jew and Gentile, both were dead, "we too being dead in offences" (v.5 JND). In vv.11-22 there was however a difference as far as God's dispensational dealings with them as men in the flesh were concerned: the Gentile was far off and without privilege; the Jew was nigh and highly privileged (v.17). Morally, as far as their manner of life had been concerned, there was no difference (v.3); ceremonially there was a difference, because between them there was the middle wall of partition and enmity (vv.14-15).

In vv.11-13 Paul addresses himself to the Ephesians as believers who were formerly Gentiles in the flesh: "ye being in time past Gentiles in the flesh" (v.11), "ye were without Christ" (v.12), "ye who sometimes were far off" (v.13). In vv.14-18 Paul views both Gentile believers and Jewish believers as one (vv.14,15,16). The "you" and "them" of v.17 have become "our" and "we" (vv.14,18). Both are made one (v.14), both are reconciled (v.16), and both have access (v.18). In vv.19-22 Paul reverts to the Ephesian Gentile believers, employing as in vv.11-13 the second person pronoun "ye" (vv.19,22). If they were once outside of the privileges that belonged to the Jewish nation as aliens from that particular commonwealth (*politeia*) (v.12), they now shared a much higher privilege with believing Jews as fellowcitizens (*sumpolitēs*) (v.19); if they once were strangers (*xenos*) from the covenants of promise (v.12), now they were no more strangers (v.19). They had not become fellowcitizens with Old Testament saints, as is sometimes taught, but rather shared equally with all the saints the privileges of this day of grace, as in fact they were also builded together with converted Jews for an habitation of God (v.22). While the reconciliation of v.16 is to God, it should be understood that the enmity of vv. 15,16 was, in the first instance, between Jew and Gentile. The peace spoken of in vv.14,15,17 is also, in the context, between Jew and Gentile.

11 The marvel of divine grace toward us is best understood by considering what we are now in relation to what we once were. They were "Gentiles" or "the nations" as distinct from the favoured nation of Israel. This is what they were "in the flesh" by natural or physical descent. They were called, perhaps contemptuously, "Uncircumcision" by those who were called "Circumcision". Belonging to the nations they did not have the mark of circumcision, the sign of the covenant. This physical mark of circumcision is referred to as "made by hands" to contrast it with the spiritual circumcision of this day of grace (see Col 2:11).

12 Each of the statements of this verse must be understood as comparing Gentile with Jew and not unbeliever with believer. "Without Christ" is not simply apart from Christ as Saviour, but apart from Him as Israel's promised Messiah; "aliens from the commonwealth (*politeia*, Acts 22:28 'freedom') of Israel" is "estranged from the privileges of Israel's theocracy", not for moral reasons but as being of "the nations"; and "strangers from the covenants of promise", for national reasons not beneficiaries of the various covenants of promise, be they Abrahamic, Mosaic, Davidic, etc. (Rom 9:4); "having no hope", having no prospect of a future inheritance nor present joyful anticipation of it (Acts 26:6,7; Heb 11:8-16); and "without God (*atheoi*) in the world", for in a world estranged from God they were without the knowledge of Him as the true and living God.

13 Now those who were once far off from Israel's privileges are made nigh, not merely with the dispensational and ceremonial nearness formerly enjoyed by that nation (see v.17), but by the means of Christ's blood shed sacrificially they were now "in Christ Jesus", vitally united to the risen exalted Saviour. There could be no union without sacrifice.

14 Converted Jew and Gentile look up by faith to Christ Jesus now at God's right hand and exclaim, "He is our peace", thinking not so much of peace between them and God but between each other. He "hath made both one": since "both" and "one" are neuter, the thought seems to be that both converted Jew and Gentile, once in separate and divided positions, have been made one in their relation to God and each other. He "hath broken down the middle wall (*mesotoichon*, partition wall) of partition (*phragmos*, fence or hedge)"; see also Matt 21:33: not only was Israel as a nation formerly made nigh (v.17), but God had hedged them round about (Matt 21:33), thereby separating them from other nations (Deut 23:3,4; Acts 21:28,29). Christ has dismantled the fence that had thus divided.

15 The enmity that existed between Jew and Gentile has, in the sphere of Christianity, been abolished (*katargeō*, nullified). Since the enmity was caused by the separating wall of v.14, then the "law of commandments contained in ordinances" relates to the ceremonial law. Christ abolished the enmity in His flesh. It is not here the question of sin, but rather those ceremonial ordinances given to the nation of Israel termed "carnal ordinances" (Heb 9:10 *dikaiōmasi sarkos*, ordinances of flesh). God not only sent His Son in the likeness of sinful flesh (Rom 8:3), but He sent Him forth, made of a woman and made under the law (Gal 4:4). In the likeness of sinful flesh and as come under the law, He died on the tree and thereby terminated that order of man to whom these ordinances applied (see also Rom 7:4; Col 2:20-22). The glorious result is that corporately in the church there is no longer "the twain", Jew and Gentile, but a new creation in Christ risen and exalted. This new creation is today "one new man": "one" in contrast to "twain"; "new" in the sense of there never having been anything like this before, all Jewish and Gentilish traits are gone; and "man" considered too as a person and in one sense never otherwise than complete. And so, Paul adds, "making peace": now converted Jew and Gentile look back to "the tree" and gratefully acknowledge that there peace between them was made.

16 Not only have both been made one (v.14), but now both have been reconciled in one body to God. The reference to one body is an advance on having been made one: the subject is now reconciliation to God and this has been effected by the cross. "Both", being masculine, relates to persons, Jews and Gentiles. The blood of Christ for guilt makes nigh in Christ Jesus (v.13); His flesh in death annuls the enmity between Jew and Gentile caused by the ceremonial law (vv.14,15); by the cross the enmity between Jew and Gentile has been slain (not annulled) (v.16). Death by crucifixion is neither natural nor accidental: it is judicial. There is involved a sentence passed and a sentence executed. Hence the enmity in v.16 is not abolished (annulled): it is slain. The cross was the end before God of man in the flesh, not simply in terms of termination but a judicial sentence. The divine verdict or sentence on all flesh in Gen 6:13 was carried out at Calvary. There could not be reconciliation between Jew and Gentile now until those distinctions as men in the flesh (v.11) had been slain. The cross effected this: "I am crucified with Christ... not I, but Christ" (Gal 2:20). Not only have both been reconciled to each other so that there is now no impediment to unity, but both are reconciled to a holy God so that amity exists and peace is enjoyed.

17 Christ is our peace (v.14) on the throne; He made peace (v.15) on the cross; He now comes and preaches peace (v.17). He preaches peace not only through His servants, but with them (Acts 10:36; Matt 28:20; Mark 16:20). The glad tidings are announced to the Gentile who was afar off (dispensationally) and the Jew who was nigh (dispensationally).

18 Both have been made one (v.14); both have been reconciled to God (v.16); both have access to the Father (v.18). "Access unto the Father is not confined to prayer (*prosagōgē*, admission or introduction, 3:12; Rom 5:2). Through Christ at God's right hand both converted Jew and Gentile by the one and same Spirit are introduced to the Father in the intimacy of this personal relationship. This admission or access renders communion and prayer in the Spirit a continual privilege.

19 From vv.19-22 Paul seeks to emphasise to the Ephesian saints their blessings conjointly with converted Jews, both now and in the future. They were no more outside the pale of divine favour. If in God's dealings with men anterior to Calvary the Gentile was considered a stranger, outside of the family and a foreigner without any personal rights, now by divine grace they were fellowcitizens with all the saints of this era, having equal rights and privileges as those who belong to the same city (Luke 15:15), or country (Acts 21:39). They were of the same household of God, of the same spiritual family.

20   They were built upon the foundation laid by the apostles and prophets in their teaching, Jesus Christ Himself being the chief corner stone (*akrogōniaios*). The corner stone or corner foundation stone was not the top stone of the building; it was laid at the foundation as a strong angle stone, and not only occupied an honourable position but gave strength and character to the building (see also 1 Pet 2:6). All the living stones in this spiritual building are built in relation to Jesus Christ the corner stone.

21   Paul says they are "in" Jesus Christ, not simply "upon". By reason of vital union all the building fitly framed together groweth or increaseth unto an holy temple in the Lord. The weight of authority omits the article before "building" and a number of translators therefore render "all the building" as "every or each several building". The context favours the AV, "all the building" or "the whole building". The entire chapter is establishing the thought of oneness: "both one" (v.14), "one new man" (v.15), and "one body" (v.16). Observe too the recurrence of "both" (vv.14,16,18). If we accept "together" as consistently referring to Jew and Gentile: "quickened us together" (v.5), "raised us up together" (v.6) and "made us sit together" (v.6), then "fitly framed together" (v.21) must be the same and does not refer to buildings but individual believers being framed together. I judge the same must apply in v.22, "builded together". The apostle is speaking of believing Jews and believing Gentiles being joined together in this whole building that is growing unto an holy temple in the Lord. "An holy temple in the Lord" is the church in its future millennial glory; John sees no temple in that holy city because the whole city is a temple: it is a temple-city (Rev 21:22).

22   Paul is saying, "In whom ye Ephesian Gentile believers are now being builded together with Jewish believers for an habitation of God through or in the Spirit". "Habitation" (*katoikētērion*) is "a permanent dwelling place".

6.   *Revelation and Stewardship of the Mystery*
3:1-13

v.1   "For this cause I Paul, the prisoner of Jesus Christ for you Gentiles,
v.2   If ye have heard of the dispensation of the grace of God which is given me to you-ward:
v.3   How that by revelation he made known unto me the mystery; (as I wrote afore in few words,

v.4   Whereby, when ye read, ye may understand my knowledge in the mystery of
      Christ)
v.5   Which in other ages was not made known unto the sons of men, as it is now
      revealed unto his holy apostles and prophets by the Spirit;
v.6   That the Gentiles should be fellowheirs, and of the same body, and partakers of
      his promise in Christ by the gospel:
v.7   Whereof I was made a minister, according to the gift of the grace of God given
      unto me by the effectual working of his power.
v.8   Unto me, who am less than the least of all saints, is this grace given, that I
      should preach among the Gentiles the unsearchable riches of Christ;
v.9   And to make all men see what is the fellowship of the mystery, which from the
      beginning of the world hath been hid in God, who created all things by Jesus
      Christ:
v.10 To the intent that now unto the principalities and powers in heavenly places
      might be known by the church the manifold wisdom of God,
v.11 According to the eternal purpose which he purposed in Christ Jesus our Lord:
v.12 In whom we have boldness and access with confidence by the faith of him.
v.13 Wherefore I desire that ye faint not at my tribulations for you, which is your
      glory."

The recurrence of "For this cause" in vv.1,14 of ch. 3 indicates the obvious division in the teaching, viz. Revelation and Stewardship of the Mystery (vv.1-13), Prayer of the Apostle (vv.14-19), Doxology (vv.20-21).

The parenthetical nature of ch. 3 must be observed. In ch. 2 the apostle has taught a radical change in God's dealings with Jew and Gentile. Now in chapter 3 he digresses to state his authority for the teaching. A revelation had been received by him and a stewardship committed to him. The revelation was "the mystery of Christ" (v.4), concerning which he had already written "in few words" in 2:11-22. There is in 3:5,9 a simple definition of a mystery, viz. something now revealed that formerly had not been made known or enlightenment concerning a matter hitherto hid. The revelation is explained in v. 6. Acquainting the readers with the wonder of this mystery the apostle follows the pattern of chapters 1 and 2 by sweeping in thought from the past to the future. As for the past, here was a mystery unrevealed in former generations to the sons of men (v.5) and which throughout past ages had been hid in God who created all things (v.9). As for the future, the apostle concludes the chapter in v.21 "unto him be glory in the church by Christ Jesus throughout all ages, world without end. Amen".

In the first instance, the revelation of the mystery was received by the apostle Paul; but there were subsequent revelations by various means. The revelation was first given to the apostle Paul by God (vv.2,3), then to the holy apostles and prophets by the Spirit (v.5). After that there was illumination for all by preaching (vv.8,9), and lastly the revelation was committed to writing that the saints at Ephesus and all saints might read and understand (vv.3,4). A unique stewardship was also committed to the apostle Paul: vv.2,3 "the dispensation (stewardship) of... the mystery", and v.9 "the fellowship (stewardship) of the mystery". In his discharge of this stewardship the apostle served and suffered. In his service he "wrote" (v.3), he "spoke" by the Spirit (v.5) and he "preached" (v.8). His suffering involved imprisonment (v.1) and tribulation (v. 13).

1   For "I Paul", see 2 Cor 10:1; Gal 5:2; Col 1:23; Philemon 19. This declaratory ego by the apostle emphasises the apostolic authority with which he is about to refer to the revelation and stewardship of the mystery given him. "The prisoner of Christ Jesus" RV suggests his imprisonment was somewhat different from what might be the common lot of the children of God in a hostile world. "Christ Jesus" associates his being a prisoner with divine purpose, while "for you Gentiles" defines both the occasion and the purpose of his imprisonment. From the human standpoint his imprisonment could be attributed to Jewish aversion to the apostle's mission to the Gentiles. This particular mission is repeatedly referred to in the NT (see Acts 9:15; 22:21; Rom 1:5; 11:13; Gal 2:2,9). Human aversion to this mission commenced within the circle of Christians (Acts 15:1,2) and reached its climax when his brethren after the flesh lifted up their voice saying "Away with such a fellow... for it is not fit that he should live" (Acts 22:22).

There was, however, the overruling hand of God in the apostle's imprisonment. The apostle John found himself in the isle called Patmos for the word of God: with the result that we have the book of the Revelation. The apostle Paul finds himself in prison and we have those epistles that contain his exposition of the mystery concerning converted Gentiles being brought into blessings on the same plane as converted Jews (Eph 6:19,20; Col 4:3).

2   "If ye have heard" ought not to cast a doubt on the Ephesian saints being the recipients of this letter, nor if Paul had previously communicated this matter to them. It is a rhetorical statement based on what they had heard "... of the dispensation (*oikonomia*) of the grace of God which is given me to you-ward". (For *oikonomia* see notes on 1:10.) Paul was a chosen vessel as the chief steward to whom was committed in the first instance the divine course of action in this day of grace in the bringing in of the Gentiles and incorporating them with converted Jews into the church as the body of Christ. In vv.7,8 the apostle refers to the grace that was given him as an unworthy servant of God to implement his particular service for God; but here in v.2 he seems to be thinking rather of the grace of God reaching out to the Gentiles.

3   "The mystery" here is not simply the gospel in terms of grace reaching out in salvation to the Gentiles - hence the apostle is not referring to his experience on the Damascus road (Acts 9:15; 26:16-18). Nor is the mystery the fact of the church in this day of grace - this was revealed by our Lord in Matt 16:18. The mystery revealed to Paul was the unique character of the church as the body of Christ in which converted Jew and Gentile are co-members. I question if in fact the embryo of this revelation was contained in the words spoken to Paul on the Damascus road "Saul, Saul, why persecutest thou me?" (Acts 9:4). That the Lord feels for

His own on earth is not confined to the church; this will be so in a future day when the church is in heaven (Matt 25:34- 40). We may conjecture as to when this revelation was given, but no-one can be certain. The apostle received abundant revelations (2 Cor 12:7). The point to be recognised is that he was the first recipient, and that since it was a divine revelation it was not conjectured in his own mind nor conjured by his own intellect, great though that was. It is important to note that the apostle Paul is the only writer who refers to the church as a body. It might be questioned if the apostle Peter entered into the wonder of Jew and Gentile being co-members of the same body. "... as I wrote afore in few words" refers to 2:11-22.

4   The importance of reading is stressed in this verse; this is how understanding is acquired now that divine revelation for our day is complete. "My knowledge" (*sunesis*), translated "intelligence" in RV, is not self-approbation. Here was an intelligence by divine revelation that would be discerned by the reader. "The mystery of Christ" (see also Col 4:3) is a mystery related to the person and work of Christ.

5   For "other ages" (*geneai*) see also v.21. The reference is not as in v.9 to time but to generations of mankind in respect of character, interests, etc. "The sons of men" means mankind at large including and extending beyond the Jewish nation. Here was a mystery completely unknown, not merely not understood by former generations but not even revealed.

  Apostles and prophets are mentioned in 2:20; 4:11, but here they are spoken of as holy to emphasise their suitability for revelation and as an authentication of their message. "By the Spirit" or "in Spirit" refers not only to the source of revelation but the necessary condition for reception.

6   Here we have the mystery defined insofar as the writer would at this point develop it. "The Gentiles", referred to as "Gentiles in the flesh" becoming in the ways of God "fellowheirs, and of the same body, and partakers of his promise in Christ by the gospel". This situation is unique to this day of grace: not the Gentiles (nations) blessed through the nation of Israel as was the mind of God for a past day and will in fact be realised in an age to come, but Jew and Gentile sharing equally on the same common plane all the blessings of this day of grace. The blessings here referred to might be thought of like this: "joint heirs of God's inheritance, a joint body of Christ and joint partakers of promise of the Holy Spirit in Christ Jesus by the gospel."

7   Referring to his unique ministry in connection with the mystery, the apostle speaks of himself in a self-abnegating manner. He had become a minister (*diakonos*) involving subordination and this ministry was "according to (*kata*) the gift of the grace of God" given him. As for the discharge of his ministry (*diakonia*), this was "according to (kata)... the effectual working (*energeia*) of his power". His particular service was a gift of grace and therefore, apart from personal merit, his ability to perform was divinely given: in fact it was the same effectual working of God's power that raised our Lord from the dead and set Him at His own right hand.

8   Now the apostle further declares his personal unworthiness as he expatiates upon his ministry and the grace given him. The undoubted contrast is between Paul "less than the least" and "the unsearchable riches of Christ". "Less than the least" (*elachistoteros*) is but one word that is beyond translation into English: it is a combination of comparative and superlative and would require to be rendered "more least". The apostle's comparison is not with other apostles but with all saints. To "preach among the Gentiles" was the apostle's sphere for announcing glad tidings. "The unsearchable (*anexichniastos*) riches of Christ" refers to the untraceable riches of God's grace that centre in Christ now going out to the Gentiles in particular.

9   The weight of authority accepts stewardship or dispensation (*oikonomia*) rather than fellowship (*koinōnia*). The apostle not only announced the glad tidings of the untraceable riches of Christ among the Gentiles (v.8), he made all who received the testimony to see (*phōtizō*, have the knowledge of) the manner of God's working out the mystery hid in His heart and undisclosed throughout the former ages of God's varied dealings with men. "From the beginning of the world" (*apo tōn aiōnōn*) is literally "from the ages". This great plan, the stewardship of which was revealed to the apostle Paul, was "hid in God", not only conceived and kept secret by Him but laid up as a treasure in His heart.
    With "who created all things" omit "by Jesus Christ". Why this mention of creation? Verse 10 will explain the amazing fact that in creation God was erecting a stage upon which He would display the church to angelic beings.

10   "Now" in this present unique era - upon the stage He Himself erected, God is making known (*gnōrizō*, as vv.3,5) unto the principalities (*archai*, rulers) and powers (*exousiai*, authorities) in heavenly places by (*dia*, through) the church His manifold wisdom (*polupoikilos sophia tou theou*, very varied wisdom of God). "Manifold" (*polupoikilos*) occurs only here in the NT and is different from 1 Pet 4:10 "manifold grace" by reason of the added prefix (*polus*, many). Little did these angelic beings realise as they witnessed God's power in creation and in fact sang together (Job 38:7) that God had a secret hid in His heart, that He was erecting a stage upon which in our day He would introduce the church and display in it to these same angelic beings His very varied wisdom. If Jew and Gentile failed God in everything entrusted to them, and the climax of their guilt was seen in their joint condemnation to crucifixion of the Son of God, what an object lesson to angelic beings of the multifarious wisdom of God must be seen in Jew and Gentile joint-heirs, a joint-body and joint-partakers of God's promise. Here is the master-piece of divine wisdom.

11 "According to the eternal purpose" (*kata prothesin tōn aiōnōn*) is literally "according to the purpose of the ages". Not only was the working out of the mystery hidden in God throughout the ages (v.9), but the ages themselves were serving the purpose God made and realised in Christ Jesus our Lord.

12 "In whom" refers to Christ Jesus our Lord by whom there has been realised God's purpose in the ages. "Boldness" (*parrhēsia*, Acts 4:29,31; 2 Cor 7:4; Eph 6:19) is the thought of free unfettered unambiguous speaking; not freedom to be irreverent (see v.14), but to express all that might be in the heart. "Access" (2:18 *prosagōgē*) is admission; "confidence" (*pepoithēsis*) is reliance, trust. In "by the faith of him" the apostle employs here, as often, the objective genitive and we might read "through faith in him" (see also Rom 3:22; Gal 2:16,20). All thought of personal merit or presumption is excluded.

13 "Wherefore", i.e. since a revelation has been vouchsafed to me of a mystery hitherto unrevealed and hid in the heart of God concerning the incorporation of Gentiles into the church, which church is a display of the master-piece of divine wisdom to angelic beings, and since a stewardship has been entrusted to me involving the announcement of the unsearchable riches of Christ among the Gentiles and enlightening all as to the working out of this mystery, and since all is according to the purpose of the ages made in Christ Jesus our Lord, and you with me have freedom of utterance to God and confidence of access into His presence, "... I desire that ye faint not (*ekkakeō*, to relax, to lose spirit, to despond) at my tribulations for you". These tribulations (*thlipsis*, pressure, affliction) of mine are for "... your glory", your incorporation into this ineffable church. See v.1, "I Paul, the prisoner of Christ Jesus for you Gentiles".

7. *Prayer of the Apostle*
3:14-19

> v.14 "For this cause I bow my knees unto the Father of our Lord Jesus Christ,
> v.15 Of whom the whole family in heaven and earth is named,
> v.16 That he would grant you, according to the riches of his glory, to be strengthened with might by his Spirit in the inner man;
> v.17 That Christ may dwell in your hearts by faith; that ye, being rooted and grounded in love,
> v.18 May be able to comprehend with all saints what is the breadth, and length, and depth, and height;
> v.19 And to know the love of Christ, which passeth knowledge, that ye might be filled with all the fulness of God."

Here is the second of the apostle's prayers in this epistle. It was not sufficient that principalities and powers witness the master-piece in divine wisdom in the church; the apostle desires that the saints should apprehend and enjoy it. The manner of approach should be observed "I bow to my knees" (v.14); and also the mode of address "unto the Father ... of whom the whole family in heaven and earth is named" (vv.14,15). The desire of the apostle was twofold: (i) that the saints apprehended God's glory which is immeasurable (v.18) and (ii) that they know the love of Christ which is incomprehensible (v.19). The end in view was that they "might be filled with all the fulness of God" (v.19). To apprehend the immeasurable and know the incomprehensible is not only beyond flesh and blood and human intellect at its highest, it is beyond any of the saints of God who might be weak and vacillating. To be "rooted and grounded in love" (v.17) was a necessary pre-requisite, and this could only be realised as their inner man was strengthened with might by the Spirit of the Father (v.16) and Christ was dwelling in their hearts by faith (v.17). In the prayer of 1:15-23 the apostle has before him that the saints be enlightened as to God's purpose concerning them, hence his reference to "the spirit of wisdom and revelation" in 1:17. In the prayer of 3:14-19 the apostle's desire is that the saints enjoy their unique place in divine love (vv.17,19) and accordingly he thinks of their being strengthened in the inner man by the Spirit of the Father (v. 16).

14 "For this cause" as v.1 refers to their glory already expounded and his desire that they lose not spirit through his tribulations for them (v.13). "I bow my knees" shows a reverent posture that helps in an understanding of the boldness and confidence of v.12. Thus did Solomon (1 Kings 8:54) and Daniel (Dan 6:10) pray, as also our Lord (Luke 22:41), Stephen (Acts 7:60), the apostle Peter (Acts 9:40) and the apostle Paul (Acts 20:36). In truth every knee shall yet bow to God (Rom 14:11) and that will include heavenly, earthly and infernal beings (Phil 2:10). Most authorities seem to agree on the omission of "... of our Lord Jesus Christ".

15 In "of whom the whole family" (*pasa patria*) the omission of the definite article indicates this should read "every family". The apostle is therefore not thinking of one family, some of whom are in heaven and some on earth, but rather of different families. These families are named by the Father, suggesting not only designation but authority, approval and supremacy. Adam exercised his authority when he "gave names to all cattle, and to the fowl of the air, and to every beast of the field" and "whatsoever Adam called every living creature, that was the name thereof" (Gen 2:19-20). Approval is also involved "but fornication, and all uncleanness, or covetousness, let it not be once named among you, as becometh saints" (5:3); and God has declared the supremacy of Jesus by giving Him "a name which is above every name" (Phil 2:9). In 1:21 the apostle refers to "every name that is named, not only in this world, but also in that which is to come"; but here in 3:15 he refers to families in heaven and earth being named not simply by but out of the Father in terms of source. By naming them the

Father not only exercises authority, but sets each family in relation to Himself in varied relationships. The apostle no doubt is thinking of divine purpose in relation to the world to come: his reference to the heavens and earth as in 1:10, "things in the heavens and things upon the earth" JND, suggest this. Families on earth are referred to in Gen 12:3; 28:14; Amos 3:2. Their future blessing is foretold in Gen 12:3, and some of those families might be referred to in Isa 19:23-25. As for families in heaven, there shall be those there and we might think of angels, friends of bridegroom and others. Did not our Lord have this on His mind when He spoke to His disciples of His Father's house and there being many abodes there (John 14:2)? There will, however, be a family in heaven in a unique way associated with the Son and for that reason closer to the heart of the Father, and for them the apostle would now pray.

16   The apostle now reveals the secret of not "fainting", not "losing spirit" (v.13). The Father could strengthen (*krataioō*, cause to acquire strength) and that with power (*dunamei*) in the inner man. This inward strengthening is in the inner man which delights in the law of God (Rom 7:22), can be renewed (2 Cor 4:16), and is by the Spirit of the Father. All that pertains to the flesh and the natural man is excluded; here is a realm beyond their reach. The apostle's prayer was that the Father would not only grant them this, but would do so according to the riches of His glory and thus cause them to anticipate the wealth of divine glory yet to be made known.

17   That Christ is in every believer is true (John 14:20; 2 Cor 13:5), but here it is something in advance of that. It is Christ by a once-for-all act taking up His residence (*katoikēsai* aorist, dwell) in the heart of the believer, in the centre or seat of his affection, and that experience known to and enjoyed by unwavering undistracted faith. As day follows night, "being rooted and grounded in love" is the obvious result of Christ residing in the heart by faith: the believer is rooted as a tree and grounded as a building, i.e. established in divine love.

18   "May be able" (*hina exischusēte*, aorist) is in order that ye may obtain strength. Strengthened by the Spirit in the inner man (v.16), Christ dwelling in the heart by faith and established in divine love (v.17), brings strength "to comprehend" (*katalambanō*, apprehend). To comprehend in the sense of fully understanding is beyond even all the saints, and that despite being divinely strengthened in the inner man. "With all saints" shows that no one saint in isolation can apprehend "... what is the breadth, and length, and depth, and height". By leaving the sentence unfinished the apostle states no object. The object is not "the love of Christ" (v.19) for the simple reason that v.19 is another sentence. It would appear the apostle is thinking of the mystery which in its breadth and length embraces such opposite elements as Jew and Gentile, and in its depth meets the need of both, and its height glorifies God.

These terms of measurement suggest order and this of necessity is characteristic of all God's work. To apprehend breadth, length, depth and height one requires to be in the centre and this appears to be the exercise of the apostle's heart.

19 "The love of Christ" in this epistle is His love to the Church (5:25-27). If breadth, length, depth, and height of v.18 may be apprehended, the love of Christ surpasses knowledge (*huperballousan*, surpassing); yet it is not unknowable.

In "filled with (*eis*, unto) all the fulness of God", two matters must be observed: (a) "filled with" should read "filled unto"; and (b) "the fulness of God" cannot be "the fulness of the Godhead" (Col 2:9) for this is incommunicable. Whatever this fulness might be no-one could contain it. The "fulness of God" must relate to what of God is communicable to the saints: "filled with the knowledge of his will" (Col 1:9); "fill you with all joy and peace in believing" (Rom 15:13); "partakers of the divine nature" (2 Pet 1:4); and "of his fulness have all we received, and grace for grace" (John 1:16).

8. *Doxology*
3:20-21

> v.20 "Now unto him that is able to do exceeding abundantly above all that we ask or think, according to the power that worketh in us,
> v.21 Unto him be glory in the church by Christ Jesus throughout all ages, world without end. Amen."

With an acknowledgment of divine ability (v.20) and an ascription of glory (v.21) the apostle brings to its conclusion the first section of the epistle. Has the apostle been praying that the saints may apprehend God's glory which is immeasurable (v.18) and know the love of Christ which is incomprehensible (v.19)? Now he acknowledges that the Father is abundantly able (v.20). Has he spoken of the manifold wisdom of God seen in the church (v. 10)? Now he ascribes glory in the church by Christ in a future age (v.21). The doxology might be summed up in this way: "unto him that is able" (v.20), "Unto him be glory" (v. 21).

20 "Now (but) unto him that is able to do exceeding abundantly (*huperekperissou*, in over abundance, beyond all measure - see also 1 Thess 3:10; 5:13) above all that we ask or think (*noeō*, conceive in one's mind)", says the apostle. There is no room for idle or empty speculation here; the apostle does not say "above all that we *can* ask or think". He is thinking of petitions and thoughts conceived in the mind by a God-given desire to enter more deeply into the mind and purpose of God. Within that sphere of honest desire God is able, and remarkably the power to know and enjoy the loftiest spiritual truth is resident in each believer, "according to the power that worketh in us".

21   Unto the Father be glory, says the apostle, in the church in or by Christ
Jesus "... throughout all ages, world without end. Amen" (*eis pasas tas geneas
tou aionos tin aionon*, to all generations of the age of ages). If the age of the ages
be the coming millennium, as I judge it to be, then the church in its peculiar and
unique relationship to Christ will be seen by generations to the glory of the
Father. The church on earth today displays to angelic beings in the heavenlies
the multi-varied wisdom of God (v.10). In the age of the ages it shall display from
its place in the heavenlies with Christ Jesus glory to the Father to generations of
men on the earth. Amen.

II. Our responsibility to the Lord (4:1-6:9)

The apostle follows the pattern of his other epistles by calling on his readers
to translate doctrine into practice. As in Rom 12:1 and Col 3:1 there is the
"therefore" of challenge (4:1). "Then" (*oun* Col 3:1) is the "therefore" of Rom
12:1 and Eph 4:1. The appeal of Rom 12:1 is based on the mercies of God
expounded in the previous chapters; in Col 3:1 on the prior teaching of being
risen with Christ; and here in Eph 4:1 on the unfolding of the divine call already
dealt with. The challenge of the christian walk is not one of blind obedience, but
intelligent appraisal: hence in each appeal there is the particle (*oun*) expressing
consequence (4:1,17; 5:1,15). In chapter 2 they had been reminded how they
had walked in time past (v.2), and that now they were a new creation in Christ
Jesus to walk in good works (v.10). These good works in which they should walk
are amplified in 4:1-6:9.

Responsibilities General in their Character (4:1-5:21)

1.   Walk Worthy of the Lord
4:1-16

v.1   "I therefore, the prisoner of the Lord, beseech you that ye walk worthy of the
vocation wherewith ye are called,
v.2   With all lowliness and meekness, with longsuffering, forbearing one another in
love;
v.3   Endeavouring to keep the unity of the Spirit in the bond of peace.
v.4   There is one body, and one Spirit, even as ye are called in one hope of your
calling;
v.5   One Lord, one faith, one baptism,
v.6   One God and Father of ail, who is above all, and through all, and in you all.
v.7   But unto every one of us is given grace according to the measure of the gift of
Christ.
v.8   Wherefore he saith, When he ascended up on high, he led captivity captive,
and gave gifts unto men.
v.9   (Now that he ascended, what is it but that he also descended first into the lower
parts of the earth?
v.10 He that descended is the same also that ascended up far above all heavens,
that he might fill all things.)

v.11 And he gave some, apostles; and some, prophets; and some, evangelists; and some, pastors and teachers;

v.12 For the perfecting of the saints, for the work of the ministry, for the edifying of the body of Christ:

v.13 Till we all come in the unity of the faith, and of the knowledge of the Son of God, unto a perfect man, unto the measure of the stature of the fulness of Christ:

v.14 That we henceforth be no more children, tossed to and fro, and carried out with every wind of doctrine, by the sleight of men, and cunning craftiness, whereby they lie in wait to deceive;

v.15 But speaking the truth in love, may grow up into him in all things, which is the head, even Christ:

v.16 From whom the whole body fitly joined together and compacted by that which every joint supplieth, according to the effectual working in the measure of every part, maketh increase of the body unto the edifying of itself in love."

1 Having prayed for them 3:14-19, the apostle now beseeches them. The appeal or exhortation comes from one who was a "prisoner of the Lord", lit. "in the Lord" (*en kuriō*). The idea may be "a prisoner for the Lord's sake". Though a prisoner he considers not the enthralment of Nero's chain by reason of his surpassing enthralment with the wonder of the divine call. The parenthetical nature of chapter 3 links "the vocation wherewith ye are called" with chapters 1 and 2. In chapter 1 as the body of Christ the church will yet be seen as "the fulness of Him who filleth all in all" (1:23); and as a building the church will yet be seen as "an holy temple in the Lord" (2:21). To walk worthy of such a vocation (*klēsis*) is ideally beyond the child of God. The exhortation must therefore be to walk in a manner comparable with it: "wherewith ye are (have been) called" at the time of conversion. See Col 1:10, "walk worthy of the Lord" and 1 Thess 2:12, "walk worthy of God". See also Phil 3:14 "high calling" (calling on high); 2 Tim 1:9 "holy calling" and Heb 3:1 "heavenly calling".

2 To walk worthy of their calling demanded two things: (i) solemn attention to their conduct (v.2) and (ii) diligence to give practical expression to the unity of the Spirit (vv.3-6). Both their conduct and giving expression to the unity of the Spirit must be considered against the background of converted Jew and converted Gentile. To walk worthy of their calling was to walk with (*meta*) all lowliness and meekness in relation to self, and with (*meta*) longsuffering, forbearing one another, in relation to others. These graces would require to be very much in evidence where such opposing elements were brought together by the grace of God, and a walk attended by them was a walk worthy of the divine calling. "Lowliness" (*tapeinophrosunē* Acts 20:19; Phil 2:3 in its adjectival form) was used by Christ of Himself in Matt 11:29, and signifies humility of mind, bereft of pride. "Meekness" (*praütēs* 1 Pet 3:15, and again used in adjectival form by Christ of Himself in Matt 11:29) signifies mildness, gentleness, tenderness of spirit. A humble person will always have a tender spirit. "Longsuffering" (*makrothumia*) is patient when evil attacks, while "forbearing one another in love" bears with another's perversity and obstinacy and not in a condescending manner, but with the highest motive "in love".

3   "The unity of the Spirit" must be kept now; "the unity of the faith" (v.13) will be attained ultimately. "One Spirit" (v.4) is rather different from "the unity of the Spirit" (v.3): the former refers to the uniqueness of the Spirit, the latter to a unity the Spirit has made. Similarly the apostle mentions "one faith" (v.5) and "the unity of the faith" (v.13). The unity of the Spirit is one result of the presence in the church of the one Spirit. Remembering the parenthetical nature of chapter 3, the emphasis upon unity (v.3) and oneness (vv.4-6) is seen to be an amplification of the teaching of chapter 2: God's dealings in grace with Jew and Gentile. The prefix "together" (*sun*) was there used with a number of verbs: "quickened together" (v.5), "raised together ... and made to sit together" (v.6), "framed together" (v.21) and "builded together" (v.22). The recurrence of "both" (*amphoteroi*) in vv.14,16,18, and "one" (*heis*) in vv.14,15,16 is important to observe. "The unity of the Spirit" is an extension of this. Here is a unity that has been made and cannot be broken vitally; but where formerly opposing elements are brought together, it can be disturbed in a practical way. The responsibility is "to keep" (*tēreō*, to watch upon, preserve, maintain) and the apostle urges an endeavour to this end - to "endeavour" (*spoudazō*) is to be in earnest about, to strive. For "bond" (*sundesmos*, a bond of union), see also Col 2:19; 3:14. The "peace" mentioned here is again referring to chapter 2 where in vv.14,15,17 it is primarily peace having been made between converted Jew and Gentile.

4   In vv.4-6 there are seven doctrinal unities to be observed in the endeavour to keep the unity of the Spirit. These are related to the three persons in the Godhead: in v.4 the "one Spirit" is connected with one body and one hope and must involve His vital work in the believer; in v.5 "one Lord" in relation to one faith and one baptism widens the circle to a sphere of profession; and in v.6 "one God and Father" embraces all mankind in terms of supremacy and availability. "One body" (v.4) is the unique character of the church and in its oneness there is included converted Jew and Gentile; "one Spirit" in whom both converted Jew and Gentile are incorporated into the one body and whose presence and power is equally necessary and available; and "one hope of your calling" to which both Jew and Gentile were called at their conversion. The Jew had an earthly hope; the Gentile was without hope (2:12); now both have one hope of their calling - not an earthly hope for converted Jew and a heavenly one for converted Gentile, but "*one hope*".

5   There is "one Lord" whom Jew and Gentile must confess, "one faith" the christian faith (Jude 3) to which Jew and Gentile must subscribe, and "one baptism" by which Jew and Gentile confess their allegiance to the Lordship of Christ and subscription to the christian faith.

6   There is "one God and Father of all" in terms of availability whether to Jew or Gentile, not exclusively for the Jew, and also in contrast to the many divinities of the Gentiles (1 Cor 8:5,6), "who is above all", supreme and transcendent over all, "... and through all", in matters of sovereignty, providence and government, "... and in you all", for His vital immanence and relationship is to all believers be they formerly Jew or Gentile.

Having urged the present necessity to keep the unity of the Spirit, the apostle thinks of "the unity of the faith" (v.13) to which all will ultimately attain. This causes him to write assuringly of divine provision in vv.7-11 and divine desire in vv.12-16. In vv.7-11 divine provision, the following three words should be observed: v.7 "every one", *ekastos*, each, v.8 "men" and v.11 "some". In vv.12-16 (divine desire) the following three should also be observed: v.12 "for" (*pros*), v.12 "for" (*eis*) and v.14 "that" (*hina*).

7   "But unto every one" (*hekastos*, each) shows that each receives a "gift (*dōrea*, benefit) of Christ" and with it grace according to the measure of giving to discharge one's responsibility. While each receives a gift, the measure of the giving in terms of allocation rests with the sovereignty of Christ the giver.

8   "Wherefore" shows that in confirmation of v.7 there is a quotation from Ps 68. - "... he saith" (*legei*, it says), the divine voice in the Scriptures. There are three changes in the apostle's rendering of Psalm 68:

(i)   "Thou hast ascended on high" (Ps 68:18) and "when he ascended up on high" (having ascended up on high) (Eph 4:8);
(ii)   "Thou hast received gifts" (Ps 68:18) and "gave gifts" (Eph 4:8); and
(iii)   "for men" (in the man) (Ps 68:18) and "unto men" (Eph 4:8).

"When he ascended up on high" emphasises that His gifts were consequent upon and an evidence of His complete triumph. Ps 68:18 considers what the conqueror himself receives to give to others, or, if it be rendered "thou hast received gifts in the man", what has been received in the exalted man on men's behalf. Although the word "men" in Eph 4:8 is *anthrōpos* (mankind) and not *anēr* (male person), it must not be construed that the gifts of v.8 are given both to men and women. It is simply that these gifts are received in the man for men and not angelic beings. He "led captivity captive" in His triumphal ascension when He led captive those whom He conquered at Calvary (Col 2:15) as He passed through their domain. The gifts He gives are trophies of Calvary's defeat of those forces that would seek to impede the work of God.

9   Though as the ascended and triumphant one He has given gifts, and there is thereby established the heavenly source of gift, ere He could do this, in wondrous grace He descended into the lower parts of the earth. Descending into the lower parts of the earth involved not only His manhood but the depths to which He went. When he ascended (not "was translated") He did not enter where He had not been before, nor any sphere of elevation: He has ascended as a man who has gone into death. While some suggest "... the lower parts of the earth" relates to His incarnation, others refer it to His soul going into hell (hades). If it were His descent to earth, this might well be His incarnation. If the contrast were not with His ascension "far above all heavens" (v.10), then it might be thought to be hades, though the idea of descending might demand explanation. The apostle appears to be thinking of His going into death and the grave (see Ps 139:15; Isa 44:23). Has the apostle a somewhat similar thought in his mind in Rom 10:7 "Who shall descend into the deep? (that is, to bring up Christ again from the dead)". In Rom 10:6-7 there is also the thought of ascending and descending. Is there not also the same sequence of thought in Phil 2:8,9 "obedient unto death, ... wherefore God also hath highly exalted him"? Many authorities omit ... first".

10   The same who descended in grace has ascended in glorious triumph. From the lower parts of the earth He has ascended "... far above all heavens" (all the heavens); far above all that is created and relates to time and space. The end in view is to "fill all things". To fill all things with Himself is the glorious end of His descent and ascension - this could not otherwise have been realised.

11   Until He ultimately fills all things with Himself, He has a present interest; and before He fills all things He will have the church, His body, arrive at "the measure of the stature of the fulness of Christ". With this in view "he gave some, apostles; and some, prophets; and some, evangelists; and some, pastors and teachers". From the giving of Christ to "each" (v.7), we come now to the giving of "some" to be or "some" as apostles, etc: not simply the giving of spiritual powers, but some men as gifts in themselves. While certain are "apt to teach" (1 Tim 3:2), some are "teachers" (Eph 4:11); and while certain might "do the work of an evangelist" (2 Tim 4:5), some are "evangelists" (Eph 4:11). It is necessary to distinguish between having a gift and being a gift. "... some, apostles; and some, prophets": these initiated a new work and laid the foundation (2:20). "Apostles" were invested with authority (1 Cor 5:4; 1 Cor 14:37; 1 Tim 1:20 *et al*); and they were set first in order in the church (1 Cor 12:28). It is important to distinguish between apostles of the Lamb (Rev 21:14; Matt 19:28), apostles of Christ (1 Thess 2:6; Acts 14:14), and apostles of the church (2 Cor 8:23; Phil 2:25). "Prophets" were given revelations (Acts 11:27,28; 13:1; 1 Cor 14:29,30). They were instruments of divine revelation for the church, but did not have the governing power of apostles; they were second in order in the church (1 Cor 12:28). The foundation having been laid (2:20) and revelation now complete (Jude 3), we no longer have apostles and prophets. There remain three gifts, though by reason of the omission of "some" before "teachers" it is thought there might only be two and that the last gift is "pastor-teacher".

"Evangelists (*euangelistēs*) occurs elsewhere only in Acts 21:8; 2 Tim 4:5. This announcer of glad tidings brings the needy soul to the Saviour. To "pastors" (*poimēn*, shepherd), our Lord is the great example (Matt 2:6 JND; 1 Pet 2:25; 5:4; John 10:11; Heb 13:20). The shepherd leads, cares for, separates, feeds. His ministry is towards the heart and conscience, involving warmth and cherishing.

The absence of "some" before "teachers" does not necessarily infer that the same person is both pastor and teacher. This may be true in some instances as, for example, the same person might have been both apostle and prophet, and another evangelist and teacher. The ministries of pastor and teacher are complementary. The teacher imparts the truth of God: in simple and convincing manner lie instructs the saints of God. The prophet gave spontaneous utterance to a revelation; but not the teacher, who by diligent waiting upon God expounds the Scriptures. That the ministries of pastor and teacher are complementary is suggested in 5:29 where the apostle speaks of the Lord (the Christ) nourishing and cherishing the church: nourishing by the teacher and cherishing by the pastor.

12   The apostle now directs the attention to the divine desire or aim in the exercise of the gifts of v.11: "... for (*pros*) the perfecting of the saints, for (*eis*, with a view to) the work of the ministry, for the edifying of the body of Christ", and v.14 "that (*hina*, in order that) we henceforth be no more children". The exercise of the gift is not an end in itself, but is intended to equip the saints to serve each other and to promote the mutual edification of each other so that they be not "tossed to and fro" as children "and carried about with every wind of doctrine".

"Perfecting" (*katartismos*, equipment or adjustment) as a verb occurs in Matt 4:21; Luke 6:40; Gal 6:1; Heb 13:21, and carries the thought of mending a net, of setting a dislocated bone. Gift should not divide the saints, but rather set them individually and subordinately in a right relationship to each other. Gift is "for the work of the ministry" (*eis ergon diakonias*, with a view to the work of service), "for the edifying of the body of Christ", with a view to corporate edification, see v.16. Gifts of v.11 do not monopolise ministry in the church; when they recede, the saints thus helped get busy.

13   "Till we attain unto the unity of the faith, and of the knowledge of the Son of God" RV is the ultimate for the church: "till" assures a permanent provision of gifts until that is attained. "Unity" qualifies both "the faith" and "the Son of God", the latter being explanatory of the former. "The unity of the faith" to which all saints will attain is not faith in the Son of God, nor "one faith" (v.5, uniqueness of the faith); it is rather the faith as a whole, and that will be the knowledge (*epignōsis*, full knowledge) of the Son of God. "Unto a perfect man" suggests the church is considered in its new and heavenly character as "one new man" (2:15) in its ultimate as "a perfect man" ("full-grown man" RV). The full-grown man is now described as "the measure of the stature of the fulness of the Christ" JND. "Stature" (*hēlika*) can refer either to height (Luke 19:3) or age (John 9:21). "Measure" (*metron*) is proper standard. "The Christ" JND is Christ mystically: Christ the head and the church His body viewed as one. "Fulness" (*plērōma*, full development) occurs in 1:10,23; 3:19. The perfect man therefore is the church having reached the proper standard of its adulthood without one member lacking.

14 Gifts have been given for the perfecting of the saints, with a view to stimulating them to engage in mutual help and mutual edification, in order that they be no longer children (infants) "tossed to and fro" (*kludōnizomai*, toss as by waves, agitate) by "every wind of doctrine". Just how serious are the forces arrayed against the saints of God is now stated by the apostle. There was that teaching by men who were versatile in trickery as a man cheating with dice - "sleight" (*kubeia*, from *kubos* a cube, to play at dice); who were artful, thought nothing of knavery and were prepared to do anything - "cunning craftiness" (*panourgia*, see Luke 20:23; 1 Cor 3:19; 2 Cor 12:16); whose teaching was systematised and who therefore handled their error cunningly and with method - "lie in wait" (*pros tēn methodian*, toward methodising: see 6:11 "wiles"); whose aim was delusion, deception "to deceive" (*planē*, schemes of deception: see also 2 Thess 2:11 "delusion").

15 In contrast to the unscrupulous deception of v.14, the apostle urges the need of "holding the truth in love" JND. This would not only act as a preservative from the error, but assist in spiritual growth. "Speaking the truth" is one word (*alētheuō*, to act truly or sincerely). The exhortation is not simply to speak, but instinctively to recognise the truth, to hold it and live it. The speaking must be "in love": truth without love engenders legality, love without truth license. To "grow up into him in all things" implies growing into His mind and in likeness to Him who is the head of the body.

16 Having referred to those five gifts intended to stimulate the saints towards their self-edification in vv.11-12 and to Christ the head in v.15, the apostle now amplifies this teaching with special emphasis upon the body's dependence on Christ and the mutual dependence of each member upon the other. Ideally from Christ the head through the instrumentality of each member the church as the body edifies itself in love. The integration and interdependence of the members is delightfully taught here. All the members of the body are "fitly joined together" (*sunarmologeō*): *sun*, together, (*armos*, a joint), and are moreover "compacted" (*sumbibazō*, united or together) "by that which every joint supplieth" (*dia pasēs haphēs tēs epichorēgias*, through every fastening or ligature of supply). All the members, thus framed together and knit together by ligatures that further the supply of what is necessary according to the appropriate function of each member, affect the increase and self-edifying of the body in love.

2. *Walk not as Other Gentiles*
   4:17-32

v.17 "This I say therefore, and testify in the Lord, that ye henceforth walk not as other Gentiles walk, in the vanity of their mind,

v.18 Having the understanding darkened, being alienated from the life of God through the ignorance that is in them, because of the blindness of their heart:

v.19 Who being past feeling have given themselves over unto lasciviousness, to work all uncleanness with greediness.

v.20 But ye have not so learned Christ;

v.21 If so be that ye have heard him, and have been taught by him, as the truth is in Jesus:

v.22 That ye put off concerning the former conversation the old man, which is corrupt according to the deceitful lusts;

v.23 And be renewed in the spirit of your mind;

v.24 And that ye put on the new man, which after God is created in righteousness and true holiness.

v.25 Wherefore putting away lying, speak every man truth with his neighbour: for we are members one of another.

v.26 Be ye angry, and sin not: let not the sun go down upon your wrath:

v.27 Neither give place to the devil.

v.28 Let him that stole steal no more: but rather let him labour, working with his hands the thing which is good, that he may have to give to him that needeth.

v.29 Let no corrupt communication proceed out of your mouth, but that which is good to the use of edifying, that it may minister grace unto the hearers.

v.30 And grieve not the holy Spirit of God, whereby ye are sealed unto the day of redemption.

v.31 Let all bitterness, and wrath, and anger, and clamour, and evil speaking, be put away from you, with all malice:

v.32 And be ye kind one to another, tenderhearted, forgiving one another, even as God for Christ's sake hath forgiven you."

The fact of their conversion demanded a changed life. They had learned Christ at their conversion, had heard concerning Him and been instructed with regard to Him, and the truth in Him was that they had "put off the old man" (vv.20-22) and had "put on the new man" (v.24). The change of life involved that all kind of falsehood is done with and only truth is spoken (v. 25); only righteous anger now and never nursing one's wrath (v.26); no more stealing but rather giving (v.28); no longer speech that corrupts but only what ministers grace (v.29); and bitterness and wrath now put away and kindness and compassion take their place (vv. 31-32).

17 For "testify" (*marturomai*), see also Acts 20:26 "take to record" AV and Gal 5:3 "testify". These three occasions when the apostle used this verb indicate a solemn enunciation. "In the Lord" gives added weight. Having entered upon the practical section of the epistle, the reference to "Lord" (*kurios*) should now be observed. A change of life on the part of these Gentiles was vital, of the utmost importance. "Henceforth" (*mēketi*, not again) is rendered by the RV as "no longer". "... other Gentiles" - some authorities omit "other". Strictly speaking,

by the grace of God they were no longer Gentiles, although in time past they
were Gentiles in the flesh (2:11). "Vanity of their mind" is not pride but emptiness
of mind. "The creature was made subject to vanity" (Rom 8:20); the apostate
likened to natural brute beasts speaks "great swelling words of vanity" (2 Pet
2:18). The creature has an aimless empty existence and the apostate likened to
wells without water utters empty vain words however high-flown. "Mind" (*nous*)
is the intellectual faculty.

18   "Having the understanding darkened" is translated "being darkened in their
understanding" by the RV. The vanity of the mind (v.17) was the product of the
understanding (*dianoia*, operation of thinking) having been darkened, so that
the light of eternal realities did not penetrate. "Alienated (*apallotrioō*, to be a
stranger to, see 2:12; Col 1:21) from the life of God" does not show that they
once had this life and had become estranged from it; as Gentiles they were born
aliens from the commonwealth of Israel (2:12). And this was similarly true of the
life that God gives: not only in darkness, without light, but in a state of death
toward God, without life. The darkness and death were by reason of "the
ignorance that is in them", and by reason of "the blindness of their heart" (*dia tē
n agnoian*, by reason of the ignorance), (*dia tēn pōrōsin*, by reason of the
blindness). "Ignorance" (*agnoia*, without knowledge) and "blindness" (*pōrōsis*,
hardness without response) show the hardness was of the heart; it was
deep-seated.

19   "Who having cast off all feeling" JND (*apalgeō*, to become insensitive or
callous) is not only the heart hardened toward the voice of God (v. 18), but the
conscience insensible and callous to the wrong of sin (v.19). "Lasciviousness"
(*aselgeia*) is intemperance, licentiousness, wantonness. "To work all uncleanness"
is to make uncleanness (*akatharsia*, impurity) in all its aspects their business,
"... with greediness" (*pleonexia*, inordinate desire for more) insatiable desire for
more uncleanness.

20   "But ye did not so learn Christ" RV for they did not thus learn Christ (the
Christ) when converted. "Ye" is emphatic, as distinct from the Gentiles referred
to in preceding verses. Conversion involves more than claiming Christ as Saviour
and rehearsing facts concerning Him; there is learning Him so as to become His
follower.

21   "If so be" is not of doubt but argument. "Ye have heard him", for to hearken
to Him is to hear about Him. "Him" is emphatic. "Have been taught by him" does
not mean taught by Christ personally but instructed in Him (*en autō*). Having
heard Him they were further instructed in the truth of His person and work. In
"... as the truth is in Jesus", the absence in the original of the definite article
before "truth" and its use before "Jesus" is significant. The truth here is particular

and relates to what is now true for the child of God because Jesus has been here and died and rose again.

22   The apostle now elaborates on the "truth in Jesus" which they had been taught: "(namely) your having put off according to the former conversation the old man" JND, "and (your) having put on the new man" (v.24 JND). By using the infinitive aorist in both verses the apostle is referring to what took place at their conversion. "The old man" (Rom 6:6; Col 3:9) occurs only in Pauline writings. Our "old man" was crucified at Calvary (Rom 6:6); all that we were in our Adam standing had the sentence of crucifixion passed upon it and this was executed at Calvary. Adam and his fallen race are no longer under trial, they have been proved irremediable and were brought to an end under the judgment of God at Calvary. At conversion we put off the "old man"; we broke our link with Adam and put on the "new man", formed a link with Christ. "Concerning the former conversation" (*anastrophē*, mode of life), "which waxeth corrupt after the lusts of deceit" RV, there is therefore no hope associated with the "old man"; its manner of life is such that it goes on increasingly corrupting itself by reason of its being deceived by wrong desires.

23   Read "And being renewed in the spirit of your mind" JND. If the "old man" goes on corrupting itself, the child of God goes on being renewed in the spirit of his mind, becoming a new person in the spirit of his mind in contrast to the vanity of your mind (v.17). The spirit of the mind is in contrast to what might be purely emotional.

24   In "and (your) having put on the new man" JND, again, as in v.22, the apostle employs the aorist infinitive. At conversion a link was formed with Christ, and by reason of the divine work in the soul (2:4-6) all that came to light in the life of Jesus and is communicable characterises the regenerate man, "... which after (*kata*, according to) God", in harmony with His will, "is created in righteousness and holiness of truth" RV. For "holiness" (*hosiotēs*, sacred), see Luke 1:75. Adam, having neither the knowledge of good nor evil, was created in innocence; the new man, created according to God, is characterised by truth - which truth, whether it be in relation to God or man, is regarded not only as right but sacred.

25   "Wherefore" (*dio*, on account of which), on account of the "but" (*de* v. 20) of your conversion as outlined in vv.22-24, here are the practical implications: "lying" (to *pseudos*, falsehood) is put off. Falsehood is not surprisingly mentioned first as belonging to the "old man" since according to vv.14,22 it is characterised by deceit, whereas in v.21 reference is made to "truth in Jesus" and in v.24 the "new man which after God hath been created in righteousness and holiness of truth" RV. Falsehood is not confined to speaking: the first record of trouble in the church was when a man and a woman acted a lie (Acts 5:1-11). Falsehood can be perpetrated too by a silence when something should be said. The emphasis here appears to be on speaking. Everything that savours of deceit, whether it be exaggeration or minimising, is now put off and only truth is spoken to one's neighbour because as members one of another we are vitally linked to each other.

26 Only anger out of devotion and allegiance to God is permitted, and then the temptation to sin must be avoided. The apostle is quoting Ps 4:4 "Stand in awe (tremble), and sin not: commune with your own heart upon your bed, and be still. Selah". This helps us understand that by letting the sun go down upon our wrath our communion is disturbed, and in this we sin; and we give the devil the territory in which he can operate (v.27). For "wrath" (*parorgismos*. provocation), see also 6:4. The child of God must not retire to bed nursing what caused him to be angry.

28 The stealer becomes a giver. Not only must he steal no more, but he must labour (*kopiaō*, to toil to point of weariness) "with his hands". Sanctified hands become engaged in what is good (*agathos*, virtuous) and will instead of stealing rather give to the needy. The child of God does not work merely to have but "to have to give".

29 If in v.28 the work of the hands must be good and be used to help the needy, in v.29 the words of the mouth must be good so as to edify the hearer, not "corrupt communications" (*logos*, word; *sapros*, rotten or putrid as of fruit). Speech therefore that is bad in itself and spreads its badness whether blasphemous, morally injurious or divisive, must never proceed from the mouth of the child of God, "but such as is good for edifying as the need may be" RV. One might never know the deep need in the heart of the hearer and yet one's speech must minister to such need. Instead of the word spoken becoming an instrument to corrupt, it must be an instrument of giving grace.

30 Corrupt speech is one sure way of grieving the Holy Spirit of God who indwells the child of God and by whom he has been sealed. The conjunction "And" forms a connection between v.29 and v.30. One of the personal qualities of the Holy Spirit of God is His sensitivity to opposition. He can be "vexed" (Is 63:10), "blasphemed" (Mark 3:29), "lied unto" (Acts 5:3), "resisted" (Acts 7:51), and here in v.30 He can be "grieved". The full title "the holy Spirit of God" is in sharp contrast to speech that is bad or putrid. "Ye are sealed (see 1:13) unto (or for) the day of redemption": reference is here made to the future redemption of the believer's body (Rom 8:23).

31 The apostle now lists certain evils that the child of God must "put away" (*airō*, to remove or take away) and this is consistent with having put off the "old man" (v.22). The list commences with "all bitterness" and ends with "all malice". These are those inward evils that manifest themselves against others in the variety of ways delineated in the four intervening evils. "All bitterness" (*pikria*) is bitterness of spirit that harbours grudges, seeks revenge, etc.; "all" (*pasa*, in every shape and form) "wrath" (*thumos*, anger) as far as man is concerned, is an attitude of mind, a chronic condition where one is soon angry; "anger" (*orgē*) with man is acute passion in terms of uncontrolled temper. "Be ye angry, and sin not" (v.26) is the exception when the child of God might be angry. Here in v.31 it is anger due to bitterness and refers to a rule of life where the individual is quarrelsome. "Clamour" (*kraugē*) is vociferous assertion of what is right or wrong whether real or imaginary; "... evil speaking" (*blasphēmia*) is injurious language, not necessarily against God but rather slanderous, defamatory, evil speaking against man; all malice" (*kakia*) is bad feeling, malignity.

32   The apostle now lists certain graces to be developed consistent with having "put on the new man" (v.24). "... be" (*ginomai*, to become or come to pass) suggests development; "kind" (*chrēstos*, gentle, gracious, helpful) is used of God in Luke 6:35; Rom 2:4; "tenderhearted" (*eusplanchnos*, compassionate); "forgiving one another" after the divine example, "... even as God also in Christ forgave you" RV. God was the source of forgiveness, Christ the cause and occasion.

3.   *Walk in Love*
   5:1-2

   v.1   "Be ye therefore followers of God, as dear children;
   v.2   And walk in love, as Christ also hath loved us, and hath given himself for us an offering and a sacrifice to God fora sweetsmelling savour."

   The theme of vv.1-14 is love and light: "walk in love" (v.2) and "walk as children of light" (v.8). The example is Christ whose offering and sacrifice to God as a sweet-smelling savour is mentioned in vv.1-2 by way of contrast with those things that characterise the sons of disobedience that bring upon them the wrath of God (vv.3-14). If the child of God follows the example of Christ (vv.1-2), he must not partake with the sons of disobedience in their disobedience (v.7), nor have fellowship with their unfruitful works of darkness (v.11).

1   The appeal to be followers (*mimētēs*, imitator) of God is based on the closing statement of the preceding verse "even as God also in Christ forgave you" (4:32 RV). As children mimic their father so, as "dear (beloved) children", God has to be imitated in the matter of gracious forgiveness (*charizomai* 4:32).

2 "... walk in love" after the example of Christ. God is the source of forgiveness and in this matter is to be imitated by His children (v.1). Christ is the cause of forgiveness and His example in self-sacrificing love has to be followed (v.2). The example of Christ's love is understood in the three words: "himself", "us", "God". "He hath given *himself*" - it was self-sacrificing; He gave Himself "for *us*" - it was in the interest of others; and He gave Himself for us "an offering and a sacrifice to *God*" - it was for the glory of God. The end result was "a sweetsmelling savour". See also Phil 4:18. Thus walking in love the child of God graciously forgives at personal cost in the interest of others and for the glory of God. To forgive is not for personal gain, nor indeed primarily for the good of others, but something that is done for God and the result is pleasurable to Him. "Offering" (*prosphora*) and "sacrifice" (*thusia*) have a specialised significance when mentioned together as here. When, however, they occur separately, there is not the same distinction in their significance: "offering" can be bloodless; "sacrifice" involves the shedding of blood.

4   *Walk as Children of Light*
5:3-14

v.3   "But fornication, and all uncleanness, or covetousness, let it not be once named among you, as becometh saints;

v.4   Neither filthiness, nor foolish talking, nor jesting, which are not convenient: but rather giving of thanks.

v.5   For this ye know, that no whoremonger, nor unclean person, nor covetous man, who is an idolater, hath any inheritance in the kingdom of Christ and of God.

v.6   Let no man deceive you with vain words: for because of these things cometh the wrath of God upon the children of disobedience.

v.7   Be not ye therefore partakers with them.

v.8   For ye were sometimes darkness, but now are ye light in the Lord: walk as children of light:

v.9   (For the fruit of the Spirit is in all goodness and righteousness and truth;)

v.10   Proving what is acceptable unto the Lord.

v.11   And have no fellowship with the unfruitful works of darkness, but rather reprove them.

v.12   For it is a shame even to speak of those things which are done of them in secret.

v.13   But all things that are reproved are made manifest by the light: for whatsoever doth make manifest is light.

v.14   Wherefore he saith, Awake thou that sleepest, and arise from the dead, and Christ shall give thee light."

The appeal in vv.1-2 to walk in love was to "beloved children" (v.1 RV). The appeal to walk as "children of light" (v.8) is on the basis of what becometh saints (*hagios*, holy one) (v.3). There is therefore not only a call to a life of love and forgiveness, but to holiness and abhorrence of sin.

3   Walking as children of light demands much more than not committing the sins here specified. They must not be approved in others, nor spoken about, but reproved. "Named" (*onomazō*) must have a more restricted sense here than "to mention". These sins are mentioned here by the apostle; and in the case of discipline this might also require to be done. When mention is made, this must never be done lightly nor jocularly but tremblingly. As becometh saints these sins must not be mentioned by way of approval or tolerance. Most authorities omit "named" in 1 Cor 5:1. "Fornication" when, as here, it occurs by itself and is not accompanied with "adultery", signifies harlotry in a general sense. In "all uncleanness" (*akatharsia*, impurity 4:19); "all" (*pas*) signifies impurity in every shape or form, be it thought, word or deed. "Covetousness" (*pleonexia*, greediness 4:19, lust of having) is not restricted to lust for money.

4 "Filthiness" (*aischrotēs*, ugliness, obscenity, indecency in act or gesture) is all that is offensive to purity. It occurs only once in NT. "Foolish talking" (*mōrologia* - only once in NT) in the context of indecency might have the suggestion of "indecent talking". See JND footnote. "Jesting" (*eutrapeleia*, buffoonery, ribaldry - once only in NT) is not humour in a general sense, but the ploy of the jester to produce a state of laxity in morals. "Not convenient" (*anēkō*, to pertain to anything, to reach to anything) shows that these evils do not reach to the standard required of saints of God; "... rather giving of thanks" is what befits the saints of God: a mouth opened in thanksgiving to God and not to utter indecencies.

Referring again to the three evils of v.3, the saints are reminded of what they knew (v.5) and are warned about being deceived (v.6). As far as the coming Kingdom of Christ and of God is concerned, they knew that those persons who practise such evils will have no inheritance there (v.5); and as far as the coming wrath of God is concerned, they ought not to be deceived that such evils demand that the perpetrators be the subject of it (v.6).

5 The weight of authority appears to favour JND's rendering: "For this ye are (well) informed of, knowing". "Informed" implies internal conscious knowledge, while "knowing" is what one is acquainted with objectively. The apostle in effect is saying "ye know not only as a fact, but the justice of it". What follows the apostle teaches elsewhere: 1 Cor 6:9-10; Gal 5:19-21. In v.3 the evils are enumerated, in v.5 the persons who practise them and they are spoken of as having no inheritance in the future Kingdom of Christ and of God (Rev 11:15). There is a significant addition in this verse to the evil of covetousness, viz. "who is an idolater". Where there is unbridled lust the true God is excluded as other subjects are enshrined in the heart. It is necessary to understand that the apostle is not thinking in this verse of a child of God falling: he is speaking of character and practice. Nor is the apostle suggesting that those who practise such evils are beyond the reach of God's mercy: 1 Cor 6:9-11 teaches otherwise. This verse relates to those who not only practise these evils, but have made these their choice: who are "the sons of disobedience" (v.6 RV).

6 It is to be deceived to think there can be any escape from coming wrath for those who practise such things and the words of such deception are vain (*kenos*, empty). It might be argued that these evils are a question of heredity, environment, lack of education; that sins of the flesh and of the spirit are to be distinguished. It might be argued that wrath is a figure of speech; that love and wrath are mutually opposed. There is no substance in the argument of such deceivers and their words are vain. Because of these evils the wrath of God cometh or is coming upon the children (*huios*) of disobedience. Since the apostle is thinking of character, the word is "sons", not "children". The wrath of God is not, as with man, an emotional nor arbitrary outburst of passion: it is "on account of these things" (*dia tauta*) the wrath of God is on its way. In 2:2,3 reference has already been made to sons of disobedience and children of wrath.

7 The admonition of this verse is not that they be not partakers with the sons of disobedience in the wrath of God that is coming, but that they be not partakers with them in their disobedience. As far as the "inheritance" in v.5 is concerned, the saints of God have been made meet to be partakers of it (Col 1:12) and have obtained it in Christ (1:11). As far as the wrath of God is concerned (v.6), they are no longer children of wrath (2:3), nor appointed to it (1 Thess 5:9); the blood of Christ is the assurance of this deliverance (Rom 5:9) and His coming the occasion of it (1 Thess 1:10).

8 To reinforce the admonition of v.7 the apostle reminds them of what they were "sometimes" (once, formerly) in their unconverted days. This he has already done in 2:2,3,11,12. Formerly they were darkness itself: not simply in darkness, but morally dark (see 4:18). Now they were "light in the Lord": not "in the light", but light itself in the Lord. The teaching of this verse is quite different from "if we walk in the light" (1 John 1:7). There each child of God is seen to be walking in the light of God as revealed now in His Son; here as children of light the saints walk as those whose souls have been penetrated and gripped by the truth of God.

9 This verse is parenthetical and not only explains what is involved in walking as children of light (v.8) but anticipates the reference in v.11 to "the unfruitful works of darkness". Read "fruit of the light", the weight of authority favours this as does the context. Fruit is produced by walking *as children of light*. Referring to 1 John 1:7 it should be observed that fruit or progress is not associated with walking *in the light*. Fruit usually requires light and walking as those into whose heart the light has shone, fruit is produced "... in all goodness" (*agathōsunē*, virtue, beneficence, Rom 15:14; Gal 5:22; 2 Thess 1:11); "... and righteousness" (*dikaiousunē*, justice, rectitude, Luke 1:75); "... and truth" (*alētheia*, love of truth, veracity, sincerity). "All" indicates the absoluteness of divine requirement. These three qualities are the antithesis of the three evils of v. 3.

10   After the parenthesis of v.9 the apostle resumes the injunction of v.8 to walk as children of light. "Proving" (*dokimazō*) is to try, decide upon after examination, "... acceptable" (*euarestos*) is well-pleasing. Walking as children of light, all matters are put to the test as to whether or not they are well-pleasing to the Lord.

11   If in v.9 reference is to the fruit of the light, the apostle does not now in v.11 by way of contrast refer to the fruit of darkness. He speaks of the "unfruitful works of darkness". Similarly, in Gal 5:19,22 reference is made to "the works of the flesh" and "the fruit of the Spirit". Fruit requires light; works that are unfruitful are produced in darkness. With these works of darkness and shame the children of light must have nothing in common by way of "fellowship" (*sunkoinōneite*). In v.7 the teaching was that the children of light must not be joint-sharers (*summetochoi*) with the perpetrators of evil deeds. "Reprove" (*elenchō*) is to put to shame, expose, prove to be wrong. Not only must there be no fellowship with these works of darkness - they must be exposed. The verses that follow indicate that the exposure is not by condemnator talk but by holy walk.

12   "Done of them in secret" suggests that the darkness of v.11 is not simply that of ignorance, but shame and secrecy. "Shame" (*aischron*) is ugly, offensive to purity and decency and all that is good. Children of light not only have nothing in common with deeds of darkness, they expose them by their holy living and consider it indecent even to speak of them.

13   The RV and some other renderings convey the idea of conversion as a result of exposure by the light. It appears that the apostle is simply explaining what light does in the natural world: it exposes. If this is so, the following rendering is preferable. "But all things having their true character exposed by the light are made manifest: for that which makes everything manifest is light" (JND). This illustration is intended as an encouragement to walk as children of light.

14   There are various suggestions as to the origin of the quotation contained in this verse. Some suggest it is a quotation from a current hymn; while others relate it to the archangel's trump to those who have fallen asleep. There is also the suggestion of an army engaged in hand-to-hand combat and as dusk falls the soldiers lie down exhausted and fall asleep among the dead and dying. When the dawn breaks the trumpet sounds to wake for the sun is risen. It should be observed that "... wherefore he saith" (*dio legei*, it saith) occurs in 4:8 where there is a quotation from Ps 68. It would therefore follow that here also is an OT quotation. There may well be in this one quotation a combination of a number of OT scriptures: Isa 60:1; 51:17; 52:1,2. Isa 60:1 "Arise, be enlightened; for thy light cometh, and the glory of the Lord is risen upon thee" appears to be predominantly in the apostle's mind. There the prophet is speaking of Israel's future awakening to millennial bliss. "Awake" (*egeire*) is to rouse, to stir oneself;

"... arise" (*anistēmi*) to stand up; "... give thee light" (*epiphauō*) to shine upon, to give light to. To those who stir themselves from indifference and lethargy and stand up from among those who are spiritually dead, Christ shines upon them as the sun. Not as a light to expose, but to enlighten, to give warmth and to transform.

5. *Walk Circumspectly*
5:15-21

> v.15 "See then that ye walk circumspectly, not as fools, but as wise,
> v.16 Redeeming the time, because the days are evil.
> v.17 Wherefore be ye not unwise, but understanding what the will of the Lord is.
> v.18 And be not drunk with wine, wherein is excess; but be filled with the Spirit;
> v.19 Speaking to yourselves in psalms and hymns and spiritual songs, singing and making melody in your heart to the Lord;
> v.20 Giving thanks always for all things unto God and the Father in the name of our Lord Jesus Christ;
> v.21 Submitting yourselves one to another in the fear of God."

The appeal to walk circumspectly is based upon what becomes those who are wise (v. 15).

15 It has to be decided if the adverb "circumspectly" (*akribōs*, accurately, exactly) is to be taken in conjunction with the injunction "See then" (*blepete oun*) or, as in the AV, with "... walk". The RV favours the former: "look therefore carefully how ye walk". The difference is between cause and effect and is slight. If *akribōs* is derived as some suggest from going up to the top of a mountain, then the idea of walking with care and diligence is feasible. On the other hand the adverb is, on occasions, associated with searching (Matt 2:8), acquaintance (Luke 1:3), teaching (Acts 18:25), knowing (1 Thess 5:2), etc. The apostle is either saying "look therefore carefully how ye walk, not as unwise" or "look therefore how ye walk carefully, not as unwise". Here is the apostle's fifth and last reference to the believer's walk. Solemn attention must be given to one's walk: the believer must not walk unwisely, "... not as fools" (*asophos*), as if ignorant of spiritual and eternal verities, "... but as wise" (*sophos*), intelligent as to spiritual and eternal verities, and thus must pick his steps and guide his feet.

16 In "redeeming the time", "redeem" (*exagorazō*) is to purchase from, to rescue from loss or misapplication; "... the time" (*kairos*) implies a fitting situation, opportunity, time distinguished by characteristic circumstances. It is not here redeeming time in a general way, but buying up every opportunity as it presents itself, "... because the days are evil" every day is evil and adverse to pleasing God. "The evil day" (6:13) is somewhat different.

17 "Wherefore" indicates a connection with v.16 rather than resuming the thought of v.15. In v.15 the contrast is between "fools" (*asophos*, without wisdom) and "wise" (*sophos*, wise, skilful); in v.17 the contrast is between "... unwise" (*aphrōn*, ignorant, simple, foolish) and "... understanding" (*suniēmi*, to have clear perception). The exhortation is to watchfulness, because the days are evil, so as to perceive what is the will of the Lord - not the will of God (1:1,5,9,11), but rather the will of the Lord related to daily living.

18 Here is one of the many warnings about drinking wine - see also Prov 20:1; 23:30,31; Luke 21:34; Gal 5:21; 1 Tim 3:3. "... be not drunk" (*methuskō*, to grow drunk) signifying the beginning of a state of drunkenness. "Excess" (*asōtia*, riot, Titus 1:6; 1 Pet 4:4) is the negative of the verb "to save" and is the state in which a person ceases to think of saving anything, be it health, character, money. In "... be filled with the Spirit", the absence of the definite article in the original is thought by some to prove that the reference is to the human spirit and that the teaching is to have one's spirit filled with spiritual joy. The definite article however is also omitted in the original in 1:17; 2:22; 3:5; 6:18. In support of the reference being to the human spirit, it is suggested that the comparison of the Holy Spirit with wine would be unthinkable - but see Acts 2:4,13. "Be filled in Spirit" is the present imperative and signifies that here is a general appeal that must remain a continual challenge to every child of God. Acts 2:4; 4:8 are rather different: they were sovereign acts for special occasions. Since "God giveth not the Spirit by measure (John 3:34), there can be no thought of receiving more of the Spirit. The challenge is therefore to deal with those matters that hinder the Spirit of God from being in control. Filled with the Spirit is not an ecstatic experience, as the context here indicates. In a negative way it involves not being unwise (v.17), and not being drunk (v.18); and in a positive way, singing (v.19), giving thanks (v.20), and submitting (v.21).

19 Here is a sharp contrast to v.18 "the song of the drunkard" (Ps 69:12). "Speaking" (*laleō*) is used of the human voice with words; "... to yourselves" (*heautois*) may signify "one to another" (4:32; Matt 16:8); but more often "to yourselves" (Matt 25:9; Luke 21:34; Acts 5:35). Personal and not public worship is the subject. "In psalms" is not necessarily from the OT Psalter but based on an experience with God as those were; "hymns" are directed as praise to God; "spiritual songs" express some spiritual truth. "Making melody" (*psallo*) is to sing accompanied with stringed instruments. "In your heart" (*en tē kardia*, with your heart) is the accompaniment, the stringed instrument; "... to the Lord", Himself the object of the singing and neither self nor men.

20 In v.19 singing is to the Lord; now in v.20 thanksgiving is addressed to Him who is God and Father and in the Name of our Lord Jesus Christ as the basis and cause of approach. Thanksgiving is both perpetual and plenary "at all times for all things" JND. Here is another evidence of being filled with the Spirit.

21 "Submitting yourself one to another". This verse not only affords the final evidence in this section of being filled with the Spirit, but it forms the basis for the teaching of the next section. Since this submission is mutual or reciprocal, there is no thought of superiority nor inferiority. "In the fear of God" (*en phobōchristou*, in the fear of Christ) is the spirit in which submission is shown - not an inward sensation of fear in the sense of terror, but the outward manifestation of respect or reverence of Christ. Here is deference to each other above and beyond natural politeness.

Responsibilities Particular in their Character (5:22-6:9)

The instruction in chapter 5 up to v.21 has been general in its character, addressed to the Ephesians as "dear children" (v.1), "saints" (v.3) and "children of light" (v.8). Now the apostle considers these same people in particular relationships: (i) wives and husbands (vv.22-23), (ii) children and parents (6:1-4) and (iii) servants and masters (6:5-9). Since the teaching stems from submission (v.21), the subject party is introduced first in each section. Submission is therefore considered not as a response to the correct attitude of husband, parents or masters, but rather as a recognition of the mind of God.

1.   Wives and Husbands
   5:22-33

> v.22 "Wives, submit yourselves unto your own husbands, as unto the Lord,
> v.23 For the husband is the head of the wife, even as Christ is the head of the church: and he is the saviour of the body.
> v.24 Therefore as the church is subject unto Christ, so let the wives be to their own husbands in every thing.
> v.25 Husbands, love your wives, even as Christ also loved the church, and gave himself for it;
> v.26 That he might sanctify and cleanse it with the washing of water by the word,
> v.27 That he might present it to himself a glorious church, not having spot, or wrinkle, or any such thing; but that it should be holy and without blemish.
> v.28 So ought men to love their wives as their own bodies. He that loveth his wife loveth himself.
> v.29 For no man ever yet hated his own flesh; but nourisheth and cherisheth it, even as the Lord the church:
> v.30 For we are members of his body, of his flesh, and of his bones.
> v.31 For this cause shall a man leave his father and mother, and shall be joined unto his wife, and they two shall be one flesh.
> v.32 This is a great mystery: but I speak concerning Christ and the church.
> v.33 Nevertheless let every one of you in particular so love his wife even as himself; and the wife see that she reverence her husband."

In the christian home the wife submits to her own husband (v.22), is subject to him in everything (v.24), reverences him (v.33). The husband loves as Christ loved (v.25), loves as his own body (v.28), and loves as himself (v.33).

22   The verb "to submit" (*hupotassō*) of v.21 does not occur in v.22 but must be understood. "Your own husbands" is not in contrast to another, but to emphasise the particular and special and binding relationship of marriage. "As unto the Lord" is somewhat different from "as it is fit in the Lord" (Col 3:18). The submission is of a kind much deeper than what might be the product of human affection or mere etiquette and therefore withstands those tests where submission on a purely human level might collapse. It might be that in terms of character, education, spirituality, the wife surpasses her husband; but when submission is "as unto the Lord" it will be given. There is no thought of unqualified submission; "as unto the Lord" does not mean she submits to her husband as she does to the Lord. There is a safeguard here: her submission must not conflict with supreme loyalty to her Lord.

23   By introducing the analogy of Christ and the church a new dimension is given to christian marriage and an extraordinary reason for the submission of the wife. While "husband" and "wife" might be rendered "man" and "woman", it is evident the marriage relationship is under consideration. The headship of man over the woman (1 Cor 11:3) has a special significance in the marriage bond. Though Sarah called Abraham "lord" (1 Pet 3:6), the husband is never referred to as lord of his wife but head of his wife. Lordship can involve abject subjection; headship is rather affectionate subjection. Christ is not only the head of the church, He is the "saviour of the body". Is the apostle thinking of Christ's saviourhood in redemption to those who are now members of His mystical body, or His being preserver of the natural body since the natural body is a member of Christ (1 Cor 6:15), or is the reference to Christ's present ministry as the preserver of the church, His mystical body? "Saviour" (*sōtēr*) in its range of meaning can signify saviour, deliverer or preserver; (*sōtēria*: health, Acts 27:34; saving, Heb 11:7). Since the apostle goes on to develop Christ's care for the church from the analogy of a man's care for his own body (vv.28,29), it appears he is thinking of Christ as the preserver of His mystical body as in v. 30.

24   "Therefore" (*alla*, but, however, still more). Developing the analogy of v.23, the wife's subjection to her husband is likened to that of the church to Christ. The church is, of course, viewed here according to divine purpose and pattern. "... in every thing" is in every relationship and interest that does not conflict with her supreme loyalty to her Lord.

25   Still comparing the marriage relationship with Christ and the church, the apostle now refers to the duty of the husband to his wife. He loves his wife as Christ also loved the church; if to the same degree is impossible, yet after the same pattern. The love that Christ displayed in the past to acquire His church when He gave Himself for it, He maintains undiminished, sanctifying and cleansing it with a view to presenting it to Himself in the future arrayed in glory. So the husband's first love is to be maintained undiminished. There is here a unique aspect of the sacrifice of Christ: not suffering for sins nor dying for the ungodly, but "giving Himself" a complete sacrifice for He could give no more - and that for the object of His love.

26   Now we have the second expression of Christ's love: what he accomplishes by a spoken word. "The word" (*rhēma*) is that which is spoken, "... the washing of water" (*tō loutrō hudatos*) referring to the new birth (see John 13:10; 15:3). There is no reference here to baptism, nor does the spoken word refer to any preaching or utterance of a formula on such an occasion. The spoken word is Christ's (John 15:3; 5:25,26). "Sanctify and cleanse"; both verbs are in the aorist and cannot therefore relate to a process; they are coincidental with the washing of water by the spoken word. Here then is the present and historical work of Christ in individuals until the church is complete. "Sanctify" (*hagiazō*, to make holy) is to put into a state corresponding to the divine nature. "Cleanse" (*katharizō*, to be free from impure admixture) is to cleanse from natural pollution.

27   Now the third expression of Christ's love, both future and final: it is the glorious result of Christ's love shown at Calvary - He "gave himself for it" (v.25), "that he might present it to himself" (v.27). "Present" (*paristēmi*) is to cause to stand beside or near (2 Cor 4:14; 11:2; Col 1:22,28); glorious" (*endoxos*) honoured, splendid, gorgeous, in unsullied array; without spot" (*spilos*) stain of defilement; "... wrinkle" (*rhutis*) wrinkle, especially in the face through age; "... holy" (*hagios*) sacred, therefore pure and unpolluted. "... without blemish" (*amōmos*) without blame, shame or stain visibly attached (1 Pet 1:19). On the occasion of the marriage of the Lamb (Rev 19:7), Christ shall present the church to Himself in unsullied array, without one spot of defilement or wrinkle of age, sacred, pure, without any stain or blame - a beautiful bride. This the church will be eternally (Rev 21:2). At the marriage supper He will present the church to His invited guests (Rev 19:9). During His millennial reign He will present the church in its glory to the wondering eyes of the nations and kings of the earth (Rev 21:23-26).

28   After this pattern men ought to love their wives: "Ought" (*opheilō*) is to owe a debt, to be obligated. "As their own bodies" is as part of themselves, and therefore with care so as to avoid hurt or harm. Read "their own wives" "their own bodies", "his own wife". "Loveth himself" shows the man does not regard his wife as a possession but as himself.

29   Pursuing the thought of Christ the preserver of the body (v.23), the apostle now refers to a man's "own flesh". A man loves his own body (v.28) and will preserve it from harm: "... no man ever yet hated his own flesh" (v.29) but nourishes it and cherishes it. There is no conflict in teaching between this verse and 1 Cor 9:27, nor indeed in any teaching regarding self-discipline. Notice first of all it is the question of "hating" and this is not necessarily involved in self-discipline nor in asceticism. Secondly, "nourisheth" (*ektrephō*) and "cherisheth" (*thalpō*, to impart warmth) are simply basic to the need of one's flesh involving only food and warmth. Our Lord said "take no (anxious) thought for your life, what ye shall eat, or what ye shall drink; nor yet for your body, what ye shall put on" (Matt 6:25). Nourishing requires eating and drinking; cherishing putting on of garments. To be warmed and filled are things needful to the body (James 2:16). In the marriage bond the husband nourishes his wife by the labour of his hands and cherishes her with the love of his heart. Thus the Lord (Christos, Christ) cares for His church: He nourishes by the teacher and cherishes by the pastor (4:11).

30   Here is the reason for Christ's care for His church referred to in v.29. The church is His body (mystically) and each child of God is a member (*melos*, limb or some part of the body) of that body. There is a vital union between Christ the head of the church and each member since that church is His body. "... of his flesh, and of his bones" most authorities omit.

31   The apostle in this verse quotes almost verbatim Gen 2:24. This he does for a twofold reason: (i) to teach that the pristine beauty of the marriage in Paradise must be maintained - see also Mark 10:2-12; and (ii) to show that there was the secret of Christ and the church in the heart of God when He made the woman and brought her to the man. The pattern for christian marriage is not what obtained during the patriarchal period, nor even the requirements of the Mosaic Law with its adjustments to patriarchal practice; nor is it the Lord's teaching in the "Sermon on the mount"; but it is that teaching that has come from the risen Christ to the church. Here is fully explained why the husband loves his wife as Christ loved the church (v.25); loves as his own body (v.28); and nourishes and cherishes (v.29). In marriage the husband and wife become "one flesh". In Mark 10:7-9 our Lord quotes Gen 2:24 to show to the Pharisees the indissolubility of the marriage bond; and the apostle to give the reason for the husband's unfailing care of his wife. In "... joined" (*proskollaō*, to glue to), the fusion results in the two becoming "one flesh". There is a fusion, a bond unique to marriage, that legitimises and honours what outside of the marriage bond is immoral. It is evident that Gen 2:24 looks down the ages because the first man did not leave a father and mother to be joined to his wife. There is no mention of the woman leaving her father and mother because there is not involved in her leaving her parents what there is in the man leaving his. The woman leaves the place of submission to her parents to assume the place of submission to her husband; whereas the man leaves his place of filial submission to assume the place of headship in relation to his wife (v.23).

32   "This mystery is great" (RV). For an explanation of a mystery see 1:9, and also the introduction to 3:1-12. Two of the NT mysteries are designated "great" (5:32; 1 Tim 3:16). Now we can understand the reason why God deviated in His ways in creation when He made an help meet for the first man. The man was made out of the dust of the ground (Gen 2:7); but the woman was made from bone, from a rib taken from the first man (Gen 2:21-23). What a revelation, that when God made the woman there was a secret in His heart that one day He would have an help meet for His own Son, a bride, a wife that would be His body! "I speak concerning Christ and the church".

33 Returning to the practical implications of the marriage bond, the apostle calls upon the husband to love his wife and the wife to reverence her husband. The fear (*phobeō*) of the wife for her husband must be understood as respect, "not afraid with any amazement" (consternation) (1 Pet 3:6).

2. *Children and Parents*
6:1-4

v.1   "Children, obey your parents in the Lord: for this is right.
v.2   Honour thy father and mother; (which is the first commandment with promise;)
v.3   That it may be well with thee, and thou mayest live long on the earth.
v.4   And, ye fathers, provoke not your children to wrath: but bring them up in the nurture and admonition of the Lord."

Having dealt with husband and wife relationships (5:22-33), the apostle continues his practical teaching in the sphere of the christian home. As would be expected he next refers to children and parents (vv.1-3) and fathers and children (v.4). Then follows in vv.5-9 teaching on servant and master relationship and master and servant relationship. The whole fabric of society is disintegrating because of a turning away from God and His word. The marriage bond is lightly regarded, separation and divorce have been made easy and are alarmingly on the increase; Women's Liberation so-called is eroding all thought of headship and subjection; obedience to and respect for parents have become well-nigh antiquated; and socialistic and communistic ideology is destroying servant-and-master relationships. What a testimony Christians ought to be in such a world both in the home and sphere of employment!

1 That children are addressed directly and their obedience is "in the Lord" means the writer is thinking of christian children. Children are required to obey their parents (v.1) and to honour their father and mother (v.2). "Obey" (*hupakouō*) is to give ear, to render submissive acceptance. In the case of the wife and her husband (5:22) she submits (*hupotassō*, to place under, no doubt as a matter of divine order. Significantly this is the word used of our Lord in Luke 2:51). This obedience is "in the Lord" involving not only the motive, but having confessed Christ as Lord this supreme loyalty becomes a safeguard.

Paul adds "... for this is right" (*dikaion*, just). Where men had only the light of nature and were without the teaching of grace and the fifth commandment, there is condemnation of disobedience to parents (Rom 1:30). The rightness of this obedience is inscribed on the human heart and increases the guilt of disobedience to parents in the last days (2 Tim 3:2). The christian child not only obeys in the Lord but has the Lord's own example to follow (Luke 2:51). In the parallel portion in Col 3:20 the comment is "for this is well pleasing unto the Lord".

2 The quotation extending into v.3 is from Deut 5:16. There is no reference to the Law in the parallel portion in Col 3:20, no doubt because one of the problems at Colosse was the relationship of the believer to the Law of Moses (Col 2:14,16,17,20,21). "Honour" (*timaō*) involves respect and is in advance of "obey" (v.1). In Heb 12:9 where the "fathers of our flesh" are considered the earthly counterpart of "the Father of spirits", we are reminded that we gave them reverence (entrepomai). This respect is toward both father and mother. That the fifth commandment was the first to contain a promise indicates particular divine approval.

3 Here is the promise that attended the keeping of the fifth commandment. There is an obvious omission: "the land which the Lord thy God giveth thee" (Exod 20:12; Deut 5:16). The promise of the land is not given to the Christian, nor the promise of long life. The promise to the Christian is not prolonging of life but quality of life (1 Tim 4:8; 1 Pet 3:10-12). Eph 6:3 is a condensed quotation of the Deuteronomic promise.

4 "Fathers" (*pateres*) may be translated "parents", but this would not be consistent with the context. In v.1 "parents" is the translation of *goneis*, and in v.2 "father and mother" (*patera ... mētera*). It would appear that the apostle is thinking not only of the particular responsibility of the father, but of a peculiar danger: "... provoke not to wrath" (*parorgizō*, to anger, noun in 4:26 "your wrath"). Children obey; fathers exercise necessary self-control so that by not continually looking for faults, nor showing relish and hastiness in correction, nor personal bad example, they do not provoke to anger. A clash of personalities must be avoided; and discipline must be just, never harsh, but exercised in love. To "bring them up" (*ektrephō*) is to nourish, to promote health and strength, to educate (5:29). "Nurture and admonition of the Lord" suggests that the father recognising that his children are given him by the Lord, and himself knowing and experiencing the Lord's dealings, will endeavour to make them strong for the Lord. If the father who knows not the Lord brings up his children to be of note in this world, the christian father's sights are higher, they are heavenly. "Nurture" (*paideia*) is discipline, correction (Heb 12:5,7,8,11): the father who brings up his child for the Lord will not encourage nor sympathise with faults, but will with kindness yet strictness correct. "Admonition" (*nouthesia*) is instruction, warning: as the failures of Israel have been recorded for our admonition (1 Cor 10:11) and the heretic must be admonished twice (Titus 3:10), so fathers cannot omit the warning aspect of instruction (see Deut 6:7,20; 11:18,19; Prov 13:24; 29:15).

3.   *Servants and Masters*
     6:5-9

> v.5   "Servants, be obedient to them that are your masters according to the flesh, with fear and trembling, in singleness of your heart, as unto Christ;
> v.6   Not with eyeservice, as men-pleasers; but as the servants of Christ, doing the will of God from the heart;
> v.7   With good will doing service, as to the Lord, and not to men:
> v.8   Knowing that whatsoever good thing any man doeth, the same shall he receive of the Lord, whether he be bond or free.
> v.9   And, ye masters, do the same things unto them, forbearing threatening: knowing that your Master also is in heaven; neither is there respect of persons with him."

The teaching of these verses would not only ameliorate the then slave-and-absolute- master conditions, it would in time abolish them. Both the christian slave and the christian master had been set free from their spiritual slavery and had now the same Master in heaven. The christian slave served with good will "as to the Lord" (*kurios*); while the christian master recognised he too had responsibilities as a slave to the same Master (*kurios*) in heaven.

5   As "servants" (*douloi*, bondservants) they were considered the absolute property of their masters. Once converted they were not to be concerned about being slaves (1 Cor 7:20-24). By their good fidelity they were to "adorn the doctrine of God our Saviour in all things" (Titus 2:10). "Masters" (*kurioi*, "Lord", vv.1,4,7,10; "masters" v.9) were absolute owners. "According to the flesh" shows the control of the master was only temporal, it did not extend to their spirits. "Fear and trembling" (also 1 Cor 2:3; 2 Cor 7:15; Phil 2:12) was not toward their master according to the flesh but towards Christ; they were to be conscious of weakness, desiring to please Christ and to bring no discredit on His Name. "Singleness" (*haplotēs*) is sincerity, purity or probity of mind. "As unto Christ" was the incentive and object in service, making easier what might otherwise be performed grudgingly.

6   "Eyeservice" (only here and Col 3:22) was only when under inspection. "Men-pleasers" (*anthrōpareskos*) were desirous of pleasing men (Col 3:22): seeking only their master's approval. However "servants of Christ" (*douloi tou christou*, bondslaves of Christ), whether it be apostle (Rom 1:1) or christian slave (Eph 6:6), are bondslaves of Christ; He is their absolute Master and they are bound to serve Him. "Doing the will of God" as it relates to their particular servitude, they serve "... from the heart" (*ek psuchēs*, from soul), not reluctantly nor grudgingly, but with keenness and enthusiasm. With heart (v.5) and soul (v.6) they serve Him.

7   Serving is to be "with good will" (*eunoia*, heartiness, kindliness; 1 Cor 7:3 "benevolence"), and "... not to men": while men benefit from prompt and hearty service, this is because of a higher accountability "as to the Lord". "As unto Christ" (v.5) relates to motive; "as to the Lord" (v.7) relates to accountability.

8   "Knowing" is knowing assuredly. Vv.5-7 is the matter of serving Christ now, to be worthy of being His bondslave; and v.8 is knowing the final assessment will be with the Lord at the Judgment Seat, when whatever good has been done will be appropriately rewarded. This is a general principle whether one is bond or free.

9   Now a brief word for masters (*kurioi*): "do the same things unto them": loyalty must not be one-sided. Slaves have their duties and masters have theirs too. "Forbearing" (*aniēmi*) is to give up, lessen, omit. "Threatening" (*apeilē*) is harshness of language involving no doubt vengeful reprisal. In terms of loyalty, whether it be slave to master or master to slave, there is no difference in responsibility, both have in heaven the same Master with whom there is no respect of persons.

III. Stand against the Foe (6:10-20)

1.   The Whole Armour of God
6:10-20

v.10 "Finally, my brethren, be strong in the Lord, and in the power of his might.
v.11 Put on the whole armour of God, that ye may be able to stand against the wiles of the devil.
v.12 For we wrestle not against flesh and blood, but against principalities, against powers, against the rulers of the darkness of this world, against spiritual wickedness in high places.
v.13 Wherefore take unto you the whole armour of God, that ye may be able to withstand in the evil day, and having done all, to stand.
v.14 Stand therefore, having your loins girt about with truth, and having on the breastplate of righteousness;
v.15 And your feet shod with the preparation of the gospel of peace;
v.16 Above all, taking the shield of faith, wherewith ye shall be able to quench all the fiery darts of the wicked.
v.17 And take the helmet of salvation, and the sword of the Spirit, which is the word of God:
18 Praying always with all prayer and supplication in the Spirit, and watching thereunto with all perseverance and supplication for all saints;
v.19 And for me, that utterance may be given unto me, that I may open my mouth boldly, to make known the mystery of the gospel,
v.20 For which I am an ambassador in bonds: that therein I may speak boldly, as I ought to speak."

Christian experience is one of conflict. The apostle refers to three armours in his writings: for the conflict with the flesh he speaks of "the armour (*hopla*) of light" (Rom 13:12); with the world "the armour (*hopla*) of righteousness" (2 Cor 6:7); and with the Devil "the whole armour (*panoplia*) of God" (Eph 6:13). Here in Eph 6:10-20 the apostle defines the enemy: "the devil" (v.11); "the wicked one" (v.16); "principalities and powers" (v.12); "rulers of the darkness of this world" (v.12); and "spiritual wickedness" (v.12). He also specifies the enemy's province: "high places" (v.12). The method of attack is also referred to: "wiles" (v.11) and "fiery darts" (v.16). The particular time of attack is mentioned: "the evil day" (v.13).

It has to be decided whether the armour as defined is objective in terms of what God has done for us or subjective, what we do for ourselves. Since this armour is complete "the whole armour" (v.11), and is "of God" (v.11), and is an armour to be taken (v.13) or "to have" (v.17 JND), the apostle has in his mind what is objective. Our own armour is not complete, must be defective and is no match for such an enemy. The battle is the Lord's, the foe has been annulled, and it is the matter of faith laying hold of and entering into the good of what God has done for us.

10 "Finally" (*to loipon*, furthermore, for the rest) - not bringing a matter to its conclusion but rather the opening of a new subject (2 Cor 13:11; Phil 3:1; 4:8; 2 Thess 3:1) "... be strong in the Lord". Here is the first requirement: a recognition of the Lordship of Christ. Joshua was deciding the strategy of the attack on Jericho when there stood a man over against him with his sword drawn in his hand and Joshua enquired "Art thou for us, or for our adversaries?". When Joshua was told that here was the captain of the host of the Lord, the arch-strategist in charge of the armies, he fell on his face and said "What saith my lord unto his servant?" (Josh 5:13-15). Thus with the children of God today: there must be submission to the Lordship of Christ and a recognition that He is the arch-strategist and is for us. And what resource is available: "the power of his might"! "Power" (*kratos*) is force superior to all opposition and "might" (*ischus*) inherent vital power! There is with the Lord an inherent ability to employ force greater than anything that might oppose: divine power toward us (1:9), divine power in us (3:16), and divine power for us (6:10).

11 "Put on", use as a garment, "the whole armour" (*panoplia*), the complete suit of armour of God: God's provision is complete both for defence and attack. "Stand" (*histēmi*, stand fast, be firmly placed), for the warfare is mainly defensive hence the emphasis is on standing: standing before the attack (v.11), standing against (*anthistēmi*) during the attack (v.13), and still standing after the attack (v.13). "Wiles" (*methodia*) are schemes of deception: the verb *methodeuō* is to trace, investigate, to handle methodically, to handle cunningly (see 4:14 "to lie in wait"). "The devil" (*diabolos*, slanderer, traitor) strikes with swiftness and from the most unexpected quarters.

12 "... wrestle" (*palē*, the wrestling, swaying backward and forward, the struggle). We wrestle not against "flesh and blood" or better "blood and flesh", for while the agents at times may be human, the real foe is not. "Principalities, against powers", the powers against the child of God are supra-mundane, angelic beings. "Principality" (*archē*) is dignity of position and "power" (*exousia*) is executive authority. There are good principalities and powers (Eph 1:21; 3:10; Col 2:10); and evil (Eph 6:12; Col 2:15). "The world rulers of this darkness" RV (*kosmokratōr*, paramount power in the world, universal lord) are unseen forces of immense power who rule men and keep them in darkness (see Luke 22:53; Col 1:13) and these are arrayed against the children of God. They are the "spiritual hosts of wickedness in the heavenly places" RV - "wickedness" (*ponēria*, malignity, malevolence, delight in evil) is the nature of their work, and "heavenly places" their province. Heavenly places has a very broad significance and is used simply in contrast to earth. There is in it no distinction in the three heavens: hence our blessings are there (1:3); Christ is there (1:20); the saved are there representatively (2:6); principalities and powers are there (3:10); now we learn it is also the province from which the enemy directs his malevolent attack. A host of unseen powerful tactical malevolent spirit-beings is arrayed against the child of God. But God's provision is complete!

13 "Wherefore take up" RV (*analambanō*, to take to one's self, assume) shows the child of God, thankfully, is not left to make his own armour; it is the whole armour of God (see v.11). "... withstand" (*anthistēmi*) is to stand out against. "The evil day" is quite different from "the days are evil" (5:16) where reference is to the whole period since Christ was crucified. A particular evil day is referred to here when the child of God is singled out by the enemy, when everything appears to go wrong and he realises it is not just a coincidence; the pressure is on. The apostle Peter writes to the elect sojourners of the dispersion concerning the fiery trial that had taken place among them (1 Pet 4:12); and our Lord said to the church at Smyrna "ye shall have tribulation ten days" (Rev 2:10). "... and having done all" (*katergazomai*, to effect a result), having taken up the whole armour of God and stood against the wiles of the enemy, remain standing. The battle is not then terminated and there is never a greater need to stand than just then.

14 "Your loins" are the seat of your strength. "... girt" (*perizōnnumi*, to bind roundabout with a girdle) means not to be free from encumbrances only, but prepared for action. "Truth (*alētheia*) is not so much here truth fulness, as truth revealed: the trust of this epistle, "the word of truth" (1:13); and "as the truth is in Jesus" (4:21); gripping and strengthening so as to be able to stand - the truth holding the person rather than the person holding the truth. "The breastplate (*thōrax*) is a covering for the heart and therefore protection for the vitals. "Righteousness", since this is divine provision, is not practical righteousness; the enemy could easily shoot through that. It is the person resting on what they are in Christ. In a yet future day a godly remnant on the earth shall overcome the devil, the accuser of the brethren, by the blood of the Lamb. (Rev 12:10-11). "I hear the accuser roar of ills that I have done. I know them all and thousands more. Jehovah findeth none".

15 "Feet shod with the preparation of the gospel of peace" conveys a twofold thought: having a secure footing in the gospel of peace (2:17) and ready to make it known.

16 "Above all" (*epi pasin*, beside all, added to all, or as an over-all protection), there is "the shield of faith" (*thureos*, large oblong shield), not the small round buckler, but the large oblong, oval, door-like shield of the Romans that covered the whole man. This over-all protection is faith or the faith. Everything about Christianity is an item of faith. Much that is held and cherished may not be fully comprehended, but it is believed. If all that God is and does could be understood and explained, He would cease to be God. "Fiery darts" - the ancient fire-darts that had combustibles ignited on the head of the shaft - are thoughts of disbelief and distrust that can become a fire in the soul. Such thoughts are "quenched" (*sbennumi*, to prevent from spreading, 1 Thess 5:19) by faith. The complete defence to all the fiery darts of unbelief is simply "I believe". "The wicked" (*ponēros*) is the one whose work is malevolent, malignant (v.12).

17 The verb "take" (*dechomai*) can convey the thought of receiving, though not always. Since the other pieces of armour are taken, the change of verb in v.17 suggests the helmet and sword are offered to be received. "The helmet" (*perikephalaia*) is cover for the head. For "of salvation", see 1:13; 2:5,8. The helmet protects the head, the seat of the mind, where a deadly stroke can fall. The believer's mind is under constant attack, doubts about salvation assail, and the only protection is to rest on what one is by grace! "By grace ye are saved" (2:5,8). The believer today does not hope to be saved, it is a fait accompli. When the apostle Paul is thinking of our Lord's coming and the deliverance from coming wrath that will then be brought, he speaks of "an helmet, the hope of salvation" (1 Thess 5:8). "The sword of the Spirit" is the sword of defence given by the Spirit and is "the word of God". "The word" (*rhēma*, utterance or spoken word) is not "the word of God" (*ho logos tou theou*) in a general way, but that word given by the Spirit appropriate to the occasion.

18 "Praying always" (*en panti kairō*, at all seasons) is to be "with all prayer" (in every kind of prayer) "and supplication" (*deēsis*, entreaty). Whereas prayer is of a general nature and is usually for blessing, supplication is particular because of a special need and is to avert evils that are feared. "In the Spirit" is in the power of the indwelling Spirit. "Watching" (*agrupneō*) is to be vigilant (see also Mark 13:33; Luke 21:36). "There unto" (*eis auto touto*, unto this thing) is unto prayer and supplication "with all perseverance" (*proskarterēsis*, persevering constancy), "for all saints" - none is without need.

19 "And for me", Paul adds. Though an apostle he set a value on the prayer of others for him. Committed to the gospel the apostle did not request prayer for his deliverance from prison, but that "utterance may be given". "Utterance" (*logos*) is speech, thing uttered. In Col 4:3 the apostle requests prayer, not only for himself as here, but also that a door of utterance might be opened, suggesting opportunity to speak. In Eph 6:19 it is that the word might be divinely given. "Open my mouth" signifies a public utterance of dignity and gravity. "Boldly" (*en parrhēsia*) is not only fearlessly but with freedom and confidence, also v.20. Since "the mystery of the gospel" is connected with his bond (v.20), the apostle is referring to the gospel of the grace of God going out to both Jew and Gentile and offering blessing to each without distinction (see 3:1-13).

20 Paul is an "ambassador in a chain" (RV footnote). Ambassadors by the law of nations are held inviolable and could not be put in a chain. Bond or chain is singular, suggesting the imprisonment was custodial. "Therein" (*en autō*, in it), in the mystery of the gospel the apostle recognised that he ought to speak boldly. "Ought" (*dei*, right and proper) is not here *opheilō* where a debt is involved.

IV. Conclusion (6:21-24)

1. *Mutual Interests*
   6:21-24

> v.21 "But that ye also may know my affairs, and how I do, Tychicus, a beloved brother and faithful minister in the Lord, shall make known to you all things:
> v.22 Whom I have sent unto you for the same purpose, that ye might know our affairs, and that he might comfort your hearts.
> v.23 Peace be to the brethren, and love with faith, from God the Father and the Lord Jesus Christ.
> v.24 Grace be with all them that love our Lord Jesus Christ in sincerity. Amen."

21 Tychicus was an Asian and was in Paul's company when he went from Corinth into Asia (Acts 20:4). He was frequently sent on missions by the apostle (Titus 3:12; 2 Tim 4:12). Both here and in Col 4:7 he is spoken of as "a beloved brother" dear to the heart of Paul, and "a faithful servant" (*diakonos*), a trusted servant in the Lord. Tychicus had evidently brought to the apostle a report of the saints at Ephesus, and now Tychicus would enable them to know (*oida*, see) the apostle's "affairs" (*ta kat 'eme*, things concerning one possibly in view of allegations made) and "... how I do" (*prassō*, fare). "Make known" (*gnōrizō*) is to declare, reveal. "All things" (*panta*, in all respects) are to be made known.

22 "For the same purpose" (*eis auto touto*) is for this very thing . ..... that ye might know" (*ginōsko*) is to discern, possibly by examination. "Our affairs" (*ta periēmōn*) are the things about or circumstances concerning us. "Comfort" (*parakaleō*, help, encourage) was the reason for Tychicus' commission. How selfless of this ambassador in a chain to desire to encourage others!

23 The benediction with which the apostle concludes the epistle is different in many ways from that in his other epistles and it must be seen as a summing up of the epistle: "Peace to the brethren". As brethren the former enmity between Jew and Gentile had now gone (2:14,15,17) and they had been called upon to give diligence to keep the unity of the Spirit in the bond of peace (4:3). "Love with faith": faith is presupposed and must be accompanied with love to all the saints (1:15); converted Jew and Gentile would bear with one another in love (4:2); and as members of the same body would enjoy self-edification in love (4:16). This love is "from God the Father and the Lord Jesus Christ", conjointly as source and channel and in perfect equality.

24 "Grace" the apostle desired that a sense of divine favour, both in salvation (2:5,8) and service (4:7), should be with "all them that love our Lord Jesus Christ in sincerity" (*aphtharsia*, incorruption). In 1 Cor 16:22 the apostle writes "If any man love not the Lord Jesus Christ, let him be Anathema Maranatha". By way of contrast the apostle here desired this sense of divine favour to be with those who love the Lord Jesus Christ in holiness and purity and constancy, whose love is spiritual and enduring.

PHILIPPIANS
S. Maxwell

PHILIPPIANS
Introduction

1. The History of the City
2. The Locality from which it was Written and Date
3. The Identity of the Author
4. The Assembly to which it was Written
5. The Intimacy and Purpose of its Message
6. Outline
7. Bibliography

1. The History of the City

The city derives its name from Philip of Macedonia. Luke, the historian, describes it thus in Acts 16:12 "which is the chief city of that part of Macedonia, and a colony". The RV reads, "a city of Macedonia, the first of the district, a Roman colony". Amphipolis was in fact the capital, but as W.M. Ramsay comments, "afterwards Philippi quite outstripped its rival; but it was at that time in such a position that Amphipolis was ranked first by general consent. These cases of rivalry between two or even three cities for the dignity of 'first' are familiar to every student of the history of the Creek cities ... the descriptive phrase is like a lightning-flash, revealing in startling clearness the whole situation to those whose eyes are trained to catch the character of Greek city history" (*St. Paul the Traveller and Roman Citizen*, pp.206, 207). Philip took the place from the Thasians about 300 BC. He enlarged the settlement and fortified it to defend his frontiers against the Thasians. At this time a gold-mining industry was developed and gold coins were struck in his name. After the battle of Pydna in 168 BC it was annexed by the Romans; and when Macedonia was divided into four parts for the purpose of administration, Philippi was included in the first of the four districts.

The position of the city dominated the road system of northern Greece, hence it became the centre for the battle of 42 BC in which Antony defeated Brutus and Cassius. After Actium 31 BC Octavian (the future Augustus) constituted the place a Roman colony, housing partisans of Antony whose presence was undesirable in Italy.

It was Octavian who gave the city its notable title *Colonia Julia Augusta Philippensis* which appeared on coins. Of all the privileges which this title conferred the possession of the 'Italic right' was most valuable. It meant that the colonists enjoyed the same rights and privileges as if their land were part of

Italian soil. In the letter to the Philippians two passages, 1:27 and 3:20, speak of citizenship, a term which would have special appeal to the readers. And the virtues listed in 4:8 are those which the Roman mind would appreciate.

There was also a school of medicine in Philippi connected with one of those guilds of physicians scattered throughout the Hellenistic world. It has been suggested for that reason that Luke may have been a Philippian.

2. The Locality from which it was Written and Date

The student of Philippians will have discovered that there is no unity of mind among the scholars as to the location of the writing of the letter. In recent times, two places have been suggested casting some doubt upon the traditional locality, which always has been Rome. Since Paul is a prisoner (1:7-13), it is required that we try to identify the place of imprisonment.

It has been indicated by some that Caesarea was the place of writing. It is contended as evidence that Paul's imprisonment appears to be recent, but this is not apparent from the reading of the letter. The imprisonment at Caesarea in Acts 24-26 rather points out the fact that after Agrippa had listened to Paul's defence he might have been set at liberty had he not appealed to Caesar (Acts 26:32). Festus' ruling had established already that he should go to Rome (Acts 25:12). The tone of the language in Phil 1:20-21 does not suggest the outcome of the imprisonment at Caesarea. The reason suggested for the Caesarea hypothesis is the mention of the praetorium in 1:13. It could be understood in the sense of Acts 23:25 as Herod's palace. However, the mention of "all the rest" (1:13 RV) rather demands the more personal connotation: that of the praetorian guard. Furthermore, the courage of others preaching the gospel (1:14) hardly fits the background of its writing from Caesarea. It has to be said that very few take this suggestion seriously.

The other location of Ephesus has more supporters and would have stronger evidence than Caesarea. The main emphasis for this location is that it allows time for the journeys that are intimated in Philippians. Most NT scholars suggest four journeys. They can be simply set out as follows:

1   The Philippians had received news of Paul;

2   Epaphroditus arrived in Rome with the gift for Paul;

3   He fell ill and the report reaches Philippi (2:26, 4:18);

4   Paul receives word from Philippi of their distress over Epaphroditus.

However, Lightfoot and others give satisfactory evidence that, taking Rome as the place from which the letter was written, sufficient time can be allowed for these journeys. The reference to such Scriptures as Rom 16:3-4 and 1 Cor 15:32

as an Ephesian imprisonment is very weak since the apostle is using figurative language in the context.

It seems best after all that we have noted to the contrary to remain with what is generally held and is more satisfactory to the evidence, that Philippians was written from Rome. The question before us now is, which was the earliest of the letters from this first Roman imprisonment. Lightfoot argues for Philippians. It is best to take the alternative view and see it as the last of the four. The fact that he expects an early verdict (1:12-13, 23-26) does not suggest the early months of his imprisonment. It seems also that considerable preaching had already been done in Rome since Paul's arrival (1:12-18) and the time required for the journeys already referred to satisfies a later dating. It is of interest also to note that Luke and Aristarchus went to Rome with Paul (Acts 27:1-2). They both send greetings to the Colossian church (Col 4:10-14) but neither of them does to the Philippians. This may indicate they were no longer with Paul when he wrote Philippians. Finally, he mentions his bonds in Eph 6:20 and in Col 4:18 in a context that suggests an earlier reference, while Phil 1:13 RV says, "my bonds became manifest in Christ". The language of Phil 1:20-21 indicates that he awaits the verdict and this is more probable at the close of the full two years. Roman authorities were generally in no great hurry to prosecute the case of Paul the Christian, as may be seen from the attitude of Felix (Acts 24:27). We would then suggest the date of writing as approximately AD 63.

3. The Identity of the Author

The writer's claim (1:1) and the historical details, language, style, and tone of the letter all point to Paul as the author. Kennedy, in the *Expositors' Greek Testament* (p. 3407) remarks: ... "perhaps no Pauline epistle bears more conclusively the stamp of authenticity". There is an artlessness, a delicacy of feeling, a frank outpouring of the heart which could not be simulated. A. T. Robertson has this to say, "No one of Paul's epistles stands upon firmer ground than this one". It was the liberal German critic, F. C. Baur, leader of the Tubingen School of Germany who first cast doubts upon the Pauline authorship. The negative views proposed have not been accepted by conservative scholars and, remarkably enough, many of Baur's fellow liberals did not agree with him either.

The unity of the epistle has been questioned by many liberal critics. It is said by them to consist of two letters: the one (1:1-11; 4:21-23) being addressed to the church in general, the other (3:2-4:20) to the more prominent members of it. These critics point out that Paul can hardly have turned abruptly from a grateful and admonitory tone in 1:1-3:1 to a sharp combative one in 3:2. Those who hold this view agree that Paul wrote both letters to the Philippians and that they were later joined together. There is no real difficulty with their problem. If Paul could change from his language in writing 2 Cor 10-13 there is no reason why he should not do so in Philippians when the circumstances demanded it. The language of the letter as we move to the interpretation of it will convince us the more of its author. It came from the pen of Paul, the evangelist, pastor and teacher. These characteristics of this beloved apostle shine out in this delightful letter to his friends at Philippi.

4. The Assembly to which it was Written

Paul's achievements proclaim him as an unexcelled evangelist. His gospel activity is outlined in the Acts (which has been rightly described as the Acts of the Holy Spirit). From his conversion in Acts 9 he was a tireless preacher of the gospel. He left behind him in the strategic centres of Galatia and Asia churches gathered to the name of the Lord Jesus. See Acts 13:1 to 14:28 outlining Paul's first journey with the gospel and Acts 15:36 to 18:22 for his second. A good map of Paul's journeys will be helpful to the student for this interesting study.

It was on Paul's second journey that the positive call to Macedonia was received (16:1-9). The use of the "we" in 16:10 reveals the presence of Luke with the company that sailed for Macedonia and the account of what follows is that of an eye witness. The company crossed the Aegean Sea to Neapolis in Macedonia. The seaport of Philippi lay some ten or twelve miles inland up the Gangites River. Through it passed the trade that flowed from Neapolis along the great Egnatian highway to the west.

The sovereignty of God is noted as the preachers were forbidden to go east but guided to the west. We can hardly contemplate the outcome had the gospel gone eastward. How thankful to God we should be.

There was evidently no synagogue at Philippia but the record tells us that on the sabbath, women gathered by the riverside where prayer was wont to be made (Acts 16:13). It would indicate that few Jews lived in Philippi. The salvation of Lydia from Thyatira, likely a woman of prominence, gave them a foothold for God. The activities of the demon possessed damsel, a clairvoyant no doubt, who had been a source of wealth to her masters, proved the principle is always true that when God is working the devil is never far behind. When Paul expelled the spirit from the damsel, trouble broke out and Paul and Silas found themselves in prison. The account of the praying, the singing, the earthquake and the salvation of the jailor and his household makes stirring reading (Acts 16:23-34). This then was the commencement of the work in Europe and the establishment of the first church in Macedonia. It is to this assembly at Philippi Paul writes to his beloved friends some ten years later.

5. The Intimacy and Purpose of its Message

It is significant that the letter, begotten in the heart of a shepherd separated from saints so precious to him, throbs predominantly with notes of intimacy. He thanks God for the memory of them (1:3); he calls God to witness his deep longing for them (1:8); he makes known to them the results of his present circumstances (1:12); he lets them know how important their prayers for him will be (1:19). Even the choice of remaining in the body in service for God is clearly motivated by the realisation of their need (1:24). And the language of endearment is prominent in the letter (2:12; 4:1). It can be concluded that the Philippian letter is the most intimate of Paul's correspondence to any company of saints.

The purposes of the letter may be gleaned from its chapters, each of which may be seen in a general way to be complete in itself. For the purpose of this commentary, we will view them in that way. The one reason that does seem to have priority is to thank them for their generosity. The reference to the first day (1:5) indicates the spirit of cooperation with the gospel that had manifested itself so quickly in these saints. The circumstances under which he had received their bounty is replete with spiritual lessons. To God, it was sacrificial and fragrant (4:18); to Paul, it was fruit that would abound to their account (4:17); to the saints it was an opportunity to manifest again their love for the servant of God in his work for the Lord (4:10).

The second reason which may be suggested was to encourage them against despondency. The realisation of Paul's imprisonment and the evident fear begotten in their hearts because they were surrounded by enemies (1:28) was sufficient to bring about despondency. However, the apostle assured them of the perdition of their opponents. Also, their circumstances were proof of their salvation, for their call to suffer was also inherent in their believing on the Saviour (1:29; 1 Pet 2:20-21). The great theme of joy and rejoicing prevades the letter (1:4, 25; 2:2, 28; 3:1; 4:1, 4-10) and shows that despondency had no place in the life of the apostle nor in his desire for them.

The third reason was to warn them against disunity. It is evident that Paul was made aware by the visit of Epaphroditus that strife was making insidious inroads among the saints of Philippi. The admonitions of 1:27; 2:1-3 and 2:12-14 confirm this. It was with this in mind that he called on the saints generally "to strive together" (1:27) and then besought two sisters again to be one-minded (4:2). We may conclude from 2:4 that selfishness was the fruit springing from strife and faction (2:3). The great christological section (2:5-11) was the antidote for their difficulty and the emulation of its teaching would be their salvation (2:12).

The fourth and final reason was to strengthen against legality. Paul issues an urgent warning. The repetition of it was not wearisome to the apostle, but for them it was safe (3:3). It was the purpose of the Judaisers to undermine the message of the gospel. They added the rite of circumcision and the keeping of the Law (Acts 15:5) to the sufficiency of the work of Christ. Paul insisted that, if the work of Christ had to be supplemented with legal adjuncts, then in effect it was supplanted. His contemptuous reference to them as the concision (3:2) was in no way to derogate that rite which was a token of a covenant god made with Abraham (Gen 17:11-12), but rather, to establish the fact that the legal and physical rite had been abolished in the cross of Christ and had given way to the spiritual (Col 2:11).

6. Outline

Chapter 1 - Key Thought: The Gospel of Christ

Chapter 2 - Key Thought: The Mind of Christ

II. *The Mind of Christ*   2:1-30

Chapter 3 - Key Thought: The Knowledge of Christ

III. *The Knowledge of Christ*   3:1-27

Chapter 4 - Key Thought: The Power of Christ

IV. The Power of Christ   4:1-23

7. Bibliography

Alford, Henry. *The Greek Testament*. Moody Press.
Alford, Henry. *The New Testament for English Readers*. Moody Press.
Borland, Andrew. *By This Conquer*. John Ritchie Ltd., Kilmarnock.

Eadie, John. *A Commentary on the Greek Text of the Epistle of Paul to the Philippians*. Reprint from 1894 Ed. T&T Clark, Edinburgh by Kloch Publishing Co., Minneapolis, Minn., 1977.

Guthrie, Donald. *New Testament Introduction: The Pauline Epistles*. Chicago Inter-Varsity Press.

Hendrikson, William. *Exposition of Philippians*. Grand Rapids, Baker House, 1962.

Kelly, William. *Philippians and Colossians*. Ralph E. Welch Foundation, 181 Montery Road, Orange, California.

Kennedy, H.A.A. *Epistle to the Philippians*. Expositors' Greek Testament Edited by W. Robertson Nicoll, London, Hodder & Stoughton, 1917.

Kent, Jr. Homer A. *Philippians, the Expositors' Bible Commentary*. General Editor: Frank E. Gaebelein, Grand Rapids, Zondervan.

King, Guy H. *The Joy Way*. Marshall, Morgan & Scott Ltd., London.

Lenski, R.C.H. *The Interpretation of St. Paul's Epistles to the Galatians, to the Ephesians and to the Philippians*. Colombus. Wartburg Press, 1946.

Lightfoot, J.N. *St. Paul's Epistle to the Philippians*. Grand Rapids, Zondervan. Reprint of 1875 Ed.

Moule, H.C.G. *Studies in Philippians*. Grand Rapids. Reprint 1977 of the Cambridge Bible for Schools (1893).

Moule, H. C. G. *Philippian Studies*. Reprint of 1927 Ed. by Christian Literature Crusade, Fort Washington, Pa., 1975.

Ramsay, W.M. *St. Paul the Traveller and the Roman Citizen*. 3rd Ed., London Hodder & Stoughton. 1897 Reprint. Grand Rapids, Baker, 1949.

Robertson, A.T. *Paul's Joy in Christ*. Nashville, Tenn., Broadman Press.

Robertson, A.T. *Word Pictures in the New Testament. Volume 4 Epistles of Paul*. Harper & Brothers, New York and London, 1931.

Vincent, M.R. *Word Studies in the New Testament*. Reprint One Volume. Associated Publishers and Authors, Wilmington, Del., 1972.

Vine, W. E. *The Epistles to the Philippians and Colossians*. Oliphants, London.

Wuest, Kenneth S. *Philippians in the Greek New Testament*. Grand Rapids, Mich., Wm. B. Erdmans.

Text and Exposition

1. The Gospel of Christ (1:1-30)

1. *The Salutation*
1:1-2

> v.1 "Paul and Timotheus, the servants of Jesus Christ, to all the saints in Christ
> Jesus which are at Philippi, with the bishops and deacons:
> v.2 Grace be unto you, and peace, from God our Father, and from the Lord Jesus
> Christ."

The writers of the NT identify themselves at the commencement of their letters instead of at the end as with us. Paul was known as Saul until the commencement of the first missionary journey (Acts 12:9). No doubt the dropping of his Hebrew name Saul from that point may have been in view of his service among the Gentiles. The mention of Timothy's name is formal rather than official. He was well known to the saints at Philippi, having accompanied Paul on the first visit to Philippi (Acts 16:1-3). He had also sent Timothy with Erastus into Macedonia (Acts 19:22). Paul omits mentioning his apostleship, as is also the case in 1 and 2 Thessalonians and Philemon, since this was a letter of affection rather than authority. These saints needed no such reminder of his apostleship.

1   In a letter that emphasises the perfect servant, it is appropriate that Paul and Timothy should be described as bondmen (*douloi*) of Christ Jesus (RV). He writes to Philemon as the prisoner of Christ Jesus. We have Peter, James and Jude also using the word *doulos* to describe themselves. The word *doulos* carries within itself the great truths of redemption, ownership, and devotedness. Paul reminds the Galatians that he bore in his body the *stigmata*, the brand-marks, of the Lord Jesus (Gal 6:17). This is the language of the bondslave. Paul, for the most part, uses the title Christ Jesus since he had met Him as a glorified Man in heaven. The others who had walked with the Saviour on earth spoke of Him as Jesus Christ.

The expression "to all" (*pasin*) here and in vv.4, 7, 8, 25; 2:17,26 as has been intimated by De Wette (quoted by John Eadie), shows the apostle formally embraced them all to indicate his elevation above their parties and conflicts. However, it is best to see it as an expression of the affection he had for them all (v.7). He designates them as "saints in Christ Jesus" literally, "holy ones". Lightfoot notes that even the irregularities and profligacies of the Corinthian church did not prevent Paul's use of the word for his church - "called saints" (1 Cor 1:2). "In Christ Jesus" suggests their position and security; "at Philippi" reminds us of their responsibility and testimony.

"The bishops and deacons" are viewed as forming part of the church. Their separate mention is to indicate their place and service within the company. There are no hierarchical overtones in these two words as accepted in Christendom. They are always used in the plural in the NT. In Christendom we have a bishop over many churches; in the NT we have a number of bishops in one church! It is of interest to note that Alford sees in the words the absence of hierarchical views such as those in the epistles of the apostolic fathers. The word "bishop" (*episkopos*) is translated "overseers" in Acts 20:28; 1 Tim 3:2; Titus 1:7. The overseer and the elder are the same person (Acts 17:28; 1 Pet 5:1-2). Even Lightfoot argues cogently for this in spite of his ecclesiastical background. The word "elder" describes the maturity of the person; the word "overseer" indicates the work. In 1 Pet 2:25 *episkopos* is used of the Lord Jesus to indicate His care over His people. In Acts 14:23; Titus 1:5, we have the appointment of elders by the apostles and their fellowworkers. They are raised up in the midst of the saints by the Holy Spirit (Acts 20:28). The word "deacon" (*diakonos*) is used thirty times in the NT. It is translated "servant" and "minister", simply meaning one who renders service among the saints, whether in secular things or spiritual. The secular side can be seen in Acts 6:20-24; Rom 16:1; 2 Cor 8:4; 9:1. The spiritual work is indicated in Acts 6:4; 2 Cor 5:18; Eph 4:12; 2 Tim 4:5. It must not be thought then that the work of the deacon or servant is only in the secular sphere nor that it is inferior to that of the bishops as in Christendom.

2 Grace is the hallmark of Paul's greeting as he uses it in all of his letters. It is the word charis and is understood to be "free, undeserved favour". We are reminded that it was grace that made us saints in Christ Jesus and now it is grace that sustains, while in 1 Pet 1:13 we are to anticipate grace that is associated with the coming of our Lord Jesus. Peace is the outcome of that grace which reconciled us to God (Eph 2:16-17). The Lord Jesus is our peace (Eph 2:14). The believer should be in the good of both these blessings. In Paul's mind, grace and peace cover the whole of christian experience.

"From God our Father, and from the Lord Jesus Christ" shows Paul had no timidity about associating the Lord Jesus on equal terms with the Father, thus establishing His deity. To Paul the Lord Jesus is the great God and our Saviour Jesus Christ (Titus 2:13). In Rom 9:5 the Lord Jesus is God over all blessed forever (this punctuation we prefer). In the Colossian letter all the fulness of the Godhead dwells in Him bodily (Col 2:9). In this statement we have grace and peace traced to its divine source. He is the God of all grace (1 Pet 5:10) and the God of peace (Phil 4:9). The Lord could say to Paul, "My grace is sufficient for thee" (2 Cor 12:9), and to the disciples He bequeathed His peace (John 14:27). To the saints in Thessalonica Paul could write, "the Lord of peace give you peace" (2 Thess 3:16).

2.   Paul's Pastoral Confidence
   1:3-8

a. His Communication to them (vv.3-5)

> v.3   "I thank my God upon every remembrance of you,
> v.4   Always in every prayer of mine for you all making request with joy,
> v.5   For your fellowship in the gospel from the first day until now;"

3 "I thank my God", John Eadie aptly remarks, is so different from the abrupt "I marvel" of Gal 1:6. In the one there is satisfaction; in the other, surprise and sorrow. The apostle had associated Timothy with him in the salutation, but now uses the first person singular. This indicates the very personal character of the letter. Paul had given testimony to the heathen on the ship to "God, whose I am, and whom I serve" (Acts 27:23). He uses the same expression "my God" in Rom 1:8; 2 Cor 12:21; Phil 4:19. Paul enjoyed an intimacy with God! He was very personal to the apostle. Here as always Paul exhibited a spirit of thankfulness. Some twenty times he uses this word *eucharisteō* throughout his letters. How different from others "because they glorified him not as God, neither were thankful" (Rom 1:21).

For "upon every remembrance of you", the best attested reading is "on my whole remembrance of you", indicating that it is not an isolated or spasmodic remembrance but the complete memory of them. It suggests that he had nothing but happy memories of these saints.

4   J. B. Lightfoot and W. E. Vine with others suggest that v.4 is parenthetic in character. However, in 1 Thess 1:2 Paul moves naturally from his thanksgiving to prayer for them. Here we have the overflowings of a full heart (Henry Alford). There was not only thanksgiving but supplication. The word *deēsis* is used by Paul to describe his intercession for his brethren after the flesh (Rom 10:1), the word being frequently used for intercession. In the *Theological Dictionary of the New Testament* (vol. 2, p.40) Greeven points out that the word in Paul's letters can denote prayer as an expression of piety in general as well as specific petition. This latter sense is still present in the phrase "making petition" (Luke 5:33; 1 Tim 2:1). He embraces them all in his petition.

Request is the same word deesis. The emphasis is now on the way he makes his request; it is with joy. This is the predominant note in the epistle (1:18,25; 2:2,17,18,28,29; 3:1; 4:1,4,10). John Eadie sums up the verse with an interesting note: "The suppliant thanks while he asks, and blesses as he petitions". The apostle might pray for others in his anguish and doubt, but here, as Eadie remarks, no suspicion clouded his soul.

5   The word "fellowship" is *koinōnia*, generally meaning a "partnership", a "having in common". James and John were partners in fishing (Luke 5:10); Titus was a partner with Paul (2 Cor 8:23). Paul used this word for partnership on the part of the churches of Macedonia in the collection for the poor saints in Jerusalem. It is used on two other occasions in the letter (2:1; 3:10). In a material sense it is translated "contribution" (Rom 15:26) and "distribution" (2 Cor 9:13). It may be said that the use of the word "fellowship" in the NT is experimental in character. It pulsates with life and action and is not viewed as positional in its contexts.

The preposition "for" (*epi*) no doubt connects the thankfulness of v.3 and the joy of v.4 and may be translated "over your fellowship unto the gospel". While Paul may have had their contribution in mind, we feel the fellowship here is much wider. H. Alford notes that it does not say "fellowship with me" but rather "among themselves" in the furtherance of the gospel. Their own active participation is in view not only in a contribution to Paul but in the proclamation of the gospel as well.

The first day would revive memories of the gospel reaching Lydia and the jailor. The clause is connected with fellowship and marks the unbroken duration. Remembrance excited his gratitude, but the past merged into the present (j. Eadie). It was not simply a thing of the past but the coming of Epaphroditus to Rome had sustained it until "the now". The article before "now" may be used to give emphasis.

b. His Confidence in them (vv. 6-8)

> v.6   "Being confident of this very thing, that he which hath begun a good work in you will perform it until the day of Jesus Christ;
> v.7   Even as it is meet for me to think this of you all, because I have you in my heart; inasmuch as both in my bonds, and in the defence and confirmation of the gospel, ye all are partakers of my grace.
> v.8   For God is my record, how greatly I long after you all in the bowels of Jesus Christ."

6   The apostle usually places the word "being confident" (*pepoithōs*) at the beginning of the sentence (1:25; 2:24; Philem 21; 2 Cor 2:3) and uses other parts of the verb in a similar way (Gal 5:10; Rom 2:19; 2 Thess 3:4; Heb 13:18). The word is in the perfect tense and consequently reminds us that what he had been assured of in the past was a present reality. This persuasion built on the experience of the past enables Paul to anticipate matter for thankfulness. Paul uses the word "confidence" of the one-mindedness of the Corinthians with him, "that my joy is the joy of you all" (2 Cor 2:3); of the Galatians' recovery (Gal 5:10); of the saints' obedience (2 Thess 3:4); also of his request to Philemon (Philem 21) and the unfeigned faith of Timothy (2 Tim 1:5). It is used in Phil 1:25 in regards to his prospect for future service.

For "he which hath begun a good work in you", the literal reading is "the one having begun in you a good work". The pronoun indicates that it is God who is the divine worker. The good work is primarily the work of regeneration (Titus 3:5) with the resultant evidence being manifested in the lives of these saints in their fellowship in the furtherance of the gospel (v.5) and with the apostle (4:10). The word "work" (*ergon*) is translated "labour" in (1:22) and "work" in (2:22). Its general usage in Paul's writings relates to the works seen in the life as the result of salvation. The two aspects are evident in Eph 2:10; 1 Thess 1:3; 2 Thess 1:11; Titus 2:14.

The word "perform" is "to accomplish" or "perfect". The question is asked by Paul, "Are ye now made perfect in the flesh?" (Gal 3:3). In the Septuagint version of the OT it is used in 1 Sam 3:12 of God "performing" against Eli all the things that he had spoken; in Zech 4:9 of the "finishing" of the house by Zerubbabel. It is no doubt here referring to that final aspect of salvation (Rom 8:23; Phil 3:21; 1 Pet 1:5).

This consummation looks on to the day of Jesus Christ. The present period is called "man's day" (1 Cor 4:3 RV margin and JND). The Lord Jesus will have His day, when He shall be supreme, all being subject to His will. The day is also mentioned in 1:11; 2:16. It is the day of His coming to the air for His own (1 Thess 4:16) and will embrace the Judgment Seat of Christ and the Father's house (1 Cor 3:13-15; 4:5; 2 Cor 5:10; 1 Thess 3:13). It will also involve the marriage of the Lamb (Rev 19:7). It is to that wonderful event Paul draws attention in Eph 5:27. The day of the Lord Jesus (1 Cor 5:5; 2 Cor 1:14) and the day of our Lord Jesus Christ (1 Cor 1:8) refer to the same period. The events that relate to it are heavenly in character, and the Lord Jesus is viewed as the Son of God. It must be distinguished from the day of the Lord (Dan 8:23-25; 2 Thess 2:2 RV). This day relates to earth with its judgment and prior signs and the Lord Jesus is viewed as the Son of man. The synoptic gospels present this view of the Lord Jesus (Matt 24:27; Mark 14:16; Luke 21:27), while John writes his Gospel from the heavenly side (John 11:25-26, 14:2-3). Failure to distinguish these days will lead to much confusion in the understanding of God's purposes for the church, Israel and the nations.

7   The word "meet" (*dikaios*) can be rendered "righteous" or "just". It is the word "just" of 4:8. It is used of God in relation to those that trouble the saints (2 Thess 1:6) and in His attitude to saints who confess their sins (1 John 1:9). To Paul, it was right for him to have such thoughts of these saints. This statement no doubt embraces the thankfulness and joy of v.3 and the confidence of v.6. He embraces them all without distinction and the use of the preposition "on behalf of" (*huper*) indicates this.

WHAT THE BIBLE TEACHES / PHIL 1   183

The marginal reading of the RV and JND indicates "you have me in your heart".
There is little difficulty here for we may be assured it was reciprocal in character.
W.E. Vine thinks the preference should be with the reading of the AV. This would
no doubt be in keeping with the fact that they were his spiritual children. See his
character as a nursing mother and father in 1 Thess 2:7,11.

"Inasmuch as both in my bonds and in the defence and confirmation of
the gospel" is a statement variously interpreted. Perhaps it is better to link
the first words, "inasmuch as", with the expression, "ye all are partakers of
my grace". Most scholars favour this and not the idea, "I have you in my heart
both in my bonds and in the defence and confirmation of the gospel". Paul
was a prisoner when he wrote this letter. Note the references to his bonds
also in Eph 6:20; Col 4:18; Philem 1. The word "defence" (*apologia*) usually
has the thought of an answer made in self- defence (Acts 22:1; 25:16). In this
context is has rather the thought of a personal statement of its message and
Paul had opportunity for this as he tells these saints (1:12). The confirmation
is not prefixed with the definite article and the word is to be considered
linked with the defence of the gospel. The word "confirmation" is used
again only in Heb 6:16. John Eadie points out that the confirmation
resulted from the defence. The confirmation may be seen in Acts 15:32-35;
16:5. W.E. Vine aptly says, "The gospel both overthrows its foes and
strengthens its friends. "

"Partakers" means "partners with" and is the word in v.5 connected with the
preposition *sun*. It is again embracing them all. The grace is not so much the
grace that saves us (Eph 2:5, 8), as the grace that enabled Paul to bear his chain
and to defend and confirm the gospel. The saints at Philippi shared in it (1:29).

8 On a number of occasions, when circumstances demanded it, Paul called
God to record, or witness as the word is (see Rom 1:9; 2 Cor 1:23; 1 Thess
2:5,10). Eadie remarks well, "The apostle wrote only the truth; his words
were the coinage of the heart". The word "how" is a particle which may
indicate the fact of Paul's longing or its intensity. Perhaps the latter is true.
He expresses the same longing in Rom 1:11; 15:23 and regarding Timothy (2
Tim 1:4).

The word "bowels", used always in the plural, is translated very well in 2 Cor
7:15 by the expression "his inward affection" and by "the tender mercy (bowels
of mercy) of our God (Luke 1:78). It is translated "compassion" in 1 John 3:17.
The reading "Jesus Christ" is "Christ Jesus" in most of the translations and reminds
us of a glorified Man in heaven. H.C. G. Moule has an interesting note on this
statement. "The Christian's personality is never lost, but he is so united to his
Lord, one spirit (1 Cor 6:17), that the emotions of the regenerate member are, as
it were, in continuity with those of the ever blessed Head. The ministration of
His life to the member is such that there is more than sympathy in the matter,
there is communication."

3. *Paul's Priestly Concern*
   1:9-11

His Prayer for them

> v.9 "And this I pray, that your love may abound yet more and more in knowledge
> and in all judgment;
> v.10 That ye may approve things that are excellent; that ye may be sincere and
> without offence till the day of Christ;
> v.11 Being filled with the fruits of righteousness, which are by Jesus Christ, unto the
> glory and praise of God."

9   He declared in vv.3,4 that he prayed for them; he now indicates the content of his prayer on their behalf. He uses the word *proseuchomai*, always used in prayer to God, in contrast to *deomai* which is used in requests to men (Acts 8:34; 21:39; Gal 4:12). Lenski points out that *proseuchomai* is the durative present and indicates "I keep praying". The purpose of the prayer is noted by the use of *hina* ("in order that"). "Your love" (*agapē*), which as Lightfoot suggests is not directed to any one individual, is love absolutely, the inward state of the soul. W.E. Vine has a helpful note. "This word is to be distinguished from affection which is more emotional." Its association with knowledge and discernment shows that judgment and not the emotions sways the will. They had already proved in action their love to God (v.5) and to Paul (v.7, 4:10). With tact now, he desires that it may abound yet more and more. Bengel remarks in his quaint way, "The fire in the apostle's mind never says it is sufficient, that past and present attainments are enough". The thought of superabundance suggests far better as in 1:23. It is used of the work of God (1 Cor 15:58); of the liberality of the saints (2 Cor 8:2); of Paul's rejoicing (Phil 1:26); of his circumstances (4:12,18); of love one to another (1 Thess 3:12; 4: 10) and of pleasing God (1 Thess 4:1).

The intensive preposition *epi* before the word knowledge indicates advanced full knowledge. It is the knowledge of the heart instead of the head, as Lenski remarks. It is experimental knowledge in contrast with *gnosis* as W.E. Vine points out. *Gnōsis* can be true or false; *epignōsis* is always true knowledge and that in the spiritual sphere. It is of interest to note that God's knowledge is *gnōsis* (Rom 11:33; Col 13) and not *epignōsis* for, with God, knowledge is absolute and not in degrees. In Paul's prayer for the Ephesians he desired for them a spirit of wisdom and revelation in the full knowledge of Him (Eph 1:17), and for the Colossians the end in view was the full knowledge of His will (Col 1:9). The word "judgment" is "discernment" or "perception". Lightfoot remarks that while knowledge deals with general principles, judgment is concerned with practical applications. This latter word *aisthēsis* does not occur again in the NT. It is not so much intellectual, but moral sensitiveness. The word "all", as Lightfoot points out, answers to the idea of full in the word "knowledge". The two words are linked together in Prov 1:4; 2:1,11; 8:12.

10   This is the end in view for their love, that in full knowledge and in moral discernment they may "approve". This word *dokimazō* is used of discerning the face of the sky (Luke 12:56); of proving the five yoke of oxen (Luke 14:19); of proving the will of God (Rom 12:2); of the trying of every man's work at the Bema (1 Cor 3:13); of examining ourselves in view of the Lord's supper (1 Cor 11:28). It is also used for trying the spirits whether they be of God (1 John 4:1). The wide range of its usage noted indicates "to examine" and then "to choose". Trench says, "to prove a thing whether it be worthy to be received or not". "Things that are excellent" is best understood as "things that differ". The word is *diapherō* meaning "to carry through" (Mark 11:16). Then the thought "to differ" is suggested in Luke 12:24, "are ye better than the fowls", and in 1 Cor 15:41 the stars in their diversity. In Rom 2:18 which literally reads "and approvest the thing excelling", Bengel is to the point when he states, "prove and embrace not merely good in preference to bad, but the best among those that are good, of which none but those of more advanced attainments perceive the excellence". We choose accurately in the case of things eternal, why not among things spiritual? In 1 Thess 5:21, we are exhorted to prove all things; hold fast that which is good. The thought of what is better, value or excellence, is developed in Matt 10:3; Luke 12:7,24.

Again the conjunction *hina* is indicating purpose, "in order that ye may be sincere"; the meaning of the word "sincere" (*eilikrinēs*) is regarded as doubtful. However, Buchsel in the TDNT (vol. 2: p. 397) says it is derived from roots meaning "warmth" or "light of the sun" so that the full sense is "tested by the light of the sun, completely pure, spotless". Arndt and Gingrich in their excellent lexicon render the word "unmixed", the "pure in a moral sense". Moulton and Milligan in the *Vocabulary of the New Testament* indicate "tested in the sunlight". It refers to internal disposition, the absence of impure motives. It describes the purity and sincerity of the heart which is guided by the spiritual tact and discriminative power for which the apostle prays. "Without offence" is one word in the original and is used in Acts 24:16 and in 1 Cor 10:32, where he exhorts the saints to give no occasion of stumbling. A number of writers including Alford, Lightfoot, Eadie and Lenski say the verb is intransitive and thus it is not so much giving offence to others, but is related to the word "sincere": "sincere" is positive and "without offence" negative. It is a question of fitness of the saints in themselves in view of the day of Christ.

The word "till" (*eis*) is "unto", or "with a view to" the day of Christ. For the day of Christ see comments on v. 6.

11   The contrast between vv.10 and 11 should be noted. In v.10 they are to be without alloy and without offence. In v.11 they are to be filled. The word "filled" is in the perfect tense and in the passive voice. Their being without the things indicated in v.10 in view of the day of Christ is because they have been filled and are filled (the force of the perfect). The passive voice suggests also the filling was something not accomplished by themselves but accomplished by another on their behalf. W.E. Vine and H.C.G. Moule suggest it is looking back from the Judgment Seat of Christ, having been filled while they were in the world. We prefer with others, to see that it is a present realisation. The word "fruits" is singular and should be rendered "fruit". It is used in 1:22 and 4:17. The word "righteousness" suggests the character of the fruit. Some refer to this righteousness as justification. However, while that is involved it is better to see it as the moral rectitude of the believer's life being practical rather than positional. It is used in this moral sense in 2 Cor 9:10; 1 Tim 6:11; 2 Tim 2:22; 2 Tim 3:16; James 3:18. The latter reference is really identical to Phil 1:11 (see also 1 Pet 2:24; 1 John 2:29; 3:7,10). In Gal 5:22 we have indicated what the Holy Spirit produces and in Eph 5:9 it is properly the fruit of light in all goodness and righteousness and truth.

It is the preposition *dia*, "through Jesus Christ". In v.1 they are viewed as in Christ Jesus. Here we are to understand that Jesus Christ was in them. This is the reason for the passive, "being filled", the reality of His presence and operation in their lives. He is the righteous in 1 John 2:1 and its is righteousness He produces in the lives of the saints.

The glory of God defines not only the expression of His character but the manifestation of His power. This is the ultimate end of all God's works and, in particular, His work in the believer (Eph 1:6). H.C.G. Moule remarks, "This is the true goal and issue of the whole work of grace. To Him are all things, to whom be glory forever. Amen (Rom 11:36)".

4.   Paul's Prison Comfort
1:12-20

a. His Rejoicing in the Preaching of the Gospel (vv.12-14)

> v.12 "But I would ye should understand, brethren, that the things which happened unto me have fallen out rather unto the furtherance of the gospel;
> v.13 So that my bonds in Christ are manifest in all the palace, and in all other places;
> v.14 And many of the brethren in the Lord, waxing confident by my bonds, are much more bold to speak the word without fear."

12   The phrase, "I would ye should understand" reads literally, "I wish you to know", and does not occur elsewhere in the NT. Because the apostle would not have the saints ignorant of many matters, he uses similar expressions in other passages of the NT. Some of these may be noted: his purpose to visit Rome and how he was hindered (Rom 1:13); the mystery of Israel's blindness (Rom 11:25); the dealings of God with Israel in the wilderness and its lessons (1 Cor 10:1); the matter of headship (1 Cor 11:3); spiritual gifts (1 Cor 12:1); concerning the rapture (1 Thess 4:13). Here he makes them intelligent as to his prison circumstances as he speaks of them as brethren, a term of intimacy and relationship.

"The things pertaining to me as a prisoner" no doubt is the matter for enlightenment. They may have feared that such circumstances would have hindered the gospel. Rather, says Paul, they have advanced it. The word "furtherance" is an interesting word. It is *prokopē* meaning "a striking forward". It is the word used of a pioneer, and it well describes the man in bonds. As to his past, he was such; for the advancement of the Jews religion (Gal 1:14) he had forged ahead. He uses the word in solemn contexts in relation to ungodliness (2 Tim 2:16) and to evil men and seducers (2 Tim 3:13); in a happier context of the saints (Phil 1:25) and of Timothy (1 Tim 4:15).

13 Paul never suggests that he is a prisoner of Rome. He is an ambassador in a chain (Eph 6:19-20) and rejoices in his sufferings for Christ and for the saints (Col 1:24). We are to understand Paul as saying "My bonds became manifest in Christ". M.R. Vincent aptly remarks, "The force of the statement lies in the fact that his imprisonment had become a matter of notoriety for Christ. His confinement as a Christian would stir attention and enquiry. All who came in contact with this prisoner would soon discover that he was in chains, not as a criminal, but as a Christian".

The expression "in the palace" is "in the Praetorium" and refers to the imperial guard. Lightfoot has argued effectively for this and states, "If Paul saw a new face among his guards and asked how he came to be there, the answer would be, 'I have been promoted to the Praetorium'. If he enquired after an old face that he missed, he might be told, 'he has been discharged from the Praetorium' ". See Lightfoot on Philippians (p.102). The expression "in all other places" is best translated "all the rest", and refers to all the inhabitants of Rome, whether civil or military.

14 Paul is speaking of the majority of the brethren and not of all, as no doubt some were not so courageous. Paul writes here of "the brethren in the Lord" but "to the saints and faithful brethren in Christ at Colosse" (Col 1:2). As a general principle, "in Christ" denotes position: "in the Lord" responsibility or practice.

The sphere of their confidence is in the Lord. By Paul's bonds brethren have had their confidence in the Lord strengthened. The grounds of their confidence is "in my bonds". The example of Paul's effective testimony among the guards and all that heard him speak (Acts 28:23-28,30,31) would constrain and incite others who had their liberty to speak the word of God. The "word" (*logos*) in this context is the gospel. To "speak" may indicate personal conversation as well as public preaching.

b. He Reveals Motives in Preaching the Gospel (vv. 15-17)

v.15 "Some indeed preach Christ even of envy and strife; and some also of good will:

> v.16 The one preach Christ of contention, not sincerely, supposing to add affliction
>   to my bonds:
> v.17 But the other of love, knowing that I am set for the defence of the gospel."

15 The "some" who "indeed preach Christ even of envy and strife" are often referred to as Judaizing teachers. However, this can hardly be reconciled with his comments in 3:2 and other references in Gal and 2 Cor. Vincent has this to say, "Nowhere in his epistles does Paul speak of the Judaizers as preaching Christ unless it be another Jesus (2 Cor 11:4)". We may also note Paul's reference to "another" gospel, which is not another, that is, of a different kind from his (Gal 1:6,7). It is best to understand them to be Christians who were personally jealous of Paul, and who sought to undermine his influence. The word "preach" (*kērussō*) means "to preach with authority, as a herald". Philip preached Jesus to the eunuch in Acts 8:35, as Paul did at Thessalonica (Acts 17:3). At Antioch some from Cyprus and Cyrene preached the Lord Jesus (Acts 11:20). This surely emphasises the fact that it is a person we preach: He is the theme of the gospel.

Envy, as W.E. Vine points out, differs from jealousy, in that envy desires to deprive another of what he has whereas jealousy desires as well to have the same or a similar thing for itself. Strife is the expression of enmity, this was directed at Paul personally.

The word "good-will" as related to oneself means "contentment, satisfaction": in relation to others, "benevolence". It is translated "good pleasure" in 2 Thess 1:11. It is used of God's good-will to men (Luke 10:21; Eph 1:5,9; Phil 2:13). Here it is good-will towards Paul and the cause of the gospel.

16 The AV has the reverse order to the majority of the Greek texts. Most read, "these from love knowing that for the defence of the gospel I am set". This order is called a *chiasmus* (the Greeks called it a holding or hanging together, or crosswise as the Latin suggests), a method by which, when two subjects are introduced with more to be said about each, the second of the two receives continued attention before the first. Hence as v.17 in the AV is brought forward first, we have (a) envy and strife (v.15), (b) good-will (v.15), (b) love (v.17), (a) contention (v.16) (see also JND). We will comment on the verses as in the AV to save confusion.

"Contention" is "rivalry" and indicates a solemn matter that we can do a right thing with a wrong motive, as is emphasised in the expression "not sincerely" or "not purely".

The word "supposing" is better rendered "thinking". The word "add" (*egeirō*) is "to awake" or "to raise up affliction to my bonds" and indicates the true motive of contentious preaching. The word "affliction" is used in 4:14 of Paul's need. They thought to distress the apostle in seeking to promote rivalry against him. Lightfoot has a solemn remark, "There was a moral contradiction between the character of their motives and the subject of their preaching".

17   This expression, "the other of love" is linked with the good-will of v.15. Thus we have the outward action of preaching with a true motive. It was out of love. A similar construction is noted in John 18:37, "of" or "out of the truth". See also Gal 3:7, "they which are of faith", or "out of faith".

Note the contrast here, "knowing" in (v.17); "thinking" (v.16). This word *eidotes* is not experimental but intuitive knowledge. It is connected with the unction of the Holy One in 1 John 2:20 and is translated "see in Phil 1:27,30; 2:28; 4:9. The word "set" (*keimai*) is translated "appointed" in 1 Thess 3:3. The word is best understood as "appointed" in the sense "to be discerned" of the Lord Jesus in Luke 2:34. The defence of the gospel has been before us in 1:7 (see comments there).

c. His Reasons for Rejoicing in all the Preaching of Christ (vv. 18-20)

> v.18 "What then? notwithstanding, every way, whether in pretence, or in truth, Christ is preached; and I therein do rejoice, yea, and will rejoice.
> v.19 For I know that this shall turn to my salvation through your prayer, and the supply of the Spirit of Jesus Christ,
> v.20 According to my earnest expectation and my hope, that in nothing I shall be ashamed, but that with all boldness, as always, so now also Christ, shall be magnified in my body, whether it be by life, or by death."

18   "What then?" This question is linked with what immediately precedes. "They think to raise up affliction for me, what does it mean?" asks Paul.

In any event Christ is preached, and Paul means in every way whatever the motive. The word "pretence" (*prophasis*) is used in 1 Thess 2:5 where Paul disclaims any association with such preaching. It indicates using the name of Christ as a mask for personal and selfish ends. We should remember that God is sovereign and can use the word of God for His own purpose, notwithstanding the wrong motive.

Of "I therein do rejoice, yea, and will rejoice", Bengel remarks that the sum of the epistle is, "I rejoice, do ye rejoice?" Joy is the predominant theme (see 1:25). He rejoices presently and anticipates such an attitude in the future.

19   The student of words needs to be cautious in his approach to the word before us. Salvation is a most comprehensive word and is used some forty-five times in the NT. It is always rendered by the word "salvation" with two exceptions. In Acts 7:25, it is translated "deliverance" and, significantly, in Acts 27:34 it is translated "health". We will do well to remember that it is not always the lexical meaning of the word that will determine its significance, but the context. It will give us no difficulty to observe that in v.19 it was not the salvation of his soul, something he had enjoyed for many years. I am not persuaded either from the general context that he had his release from prison in mind: this matter he confidently anticipates (vv.24-26). I would suggest, in view of the use of the word in Acts 27:34, a free translation, "I know (*oida* intuitive knowledge) that this shall turn out to my spiritual well-being and thus I will be lifted beyond the contention of those who are opposed to me". It may be better that it be linked with v.20 "saved from being ashamed".

"Through your prayer, and the supply of the Spirit of Jesus Christ" expresses his personal attitude of rejoicing and the supplication of the saints that he always appreciated (see Rom 15:30,32; 2 Cor 1:11; 1 Thess 5:25; 2 Thess 3:1). He mentions too the bountiful supply which the Holy Spirit affords. For the whole spiritual life of the believer is life through the Spirit who is called in Rom 8:9 the Spirit of God and the Spirit of Christ. Peter uses the latter title in 1 Pet 1:11. The word "supply" (*epichorēgia*) goes back to the Greek chorus, and the custom of appointing a wealthy patron called the *chorēgos* to bear the expense of the entertainment. It is used in Eph 4:16 of that which every joint supplieth and in Col 2:19 of having nourishment ministered.

20   The word "earnest expectation" is found in Rom 8:19 of the anxious watching of the creation. It is the watching with outstretched head and has the thought of eager longing. Hope stands related to the future (Rom 8:24). It is always linked with confidence and not uncertainty for hope maketh not ashamed (Rom 5:5).

"I shall be ashamed" is here in the passive voice. "Put to shame" (*aischunomai*) is used relative to suffering in 1 Pet 4:16, and in view of the Lord's coming (1 John 2:28). It is here connected with the circumstances related in vv. 15,16,17 and because of them, with being prevented from magnifying Christ.

The word "boldness" has the thought of freedom of speech. It is the contrast to being ashamed. It is used with access in Eph 3:12 and is translated "confidence" in Heb 3:6. The privilege to enter into the holiest in Heb 10:19 is something they were not to cast away in Heb 10:35. Confidence before Him at His coming (1 John 2:28) is boldness in the day of judgment (1 John 4:17). The prospect of being called before Caesar is in view with the words "as always, so now". Through the instrumentality of his body, the vehicle of expression and action, Christ shall be magnified.

"Whether it be by life, or by death" shows the issue of his trial is unknown, but for Paul, one way or the other, the glory of the Lord was his ardent ambition.

5.   *Paul's Personal Contemplation*
   1:21-26

His Contemplation of Life or Death

> v.21 "For to me to live is Christ, and to die is gain.
> v.22 But if I live in the flesh, this is the fruit of my labour: yet what I shall choose I wot not.
> v.23 For I am in a strait betwixt two, having a desire to depart, and to be with Christ; which is far better:

> v.24 Nevertheless to abide in the flesh is more needful for you.
> v.25 And having this confidence, I know that I shall abide and continue with you all for your furtherance and joy of faith;
> v.26 That your rejoicing may be more abundant in Jesus Christ for me by my coming to you again."

21   "For me to live is Christ" is connected with the previous verse. With holy "indifference" he was able to meet life. As H.C.G. Moule remarks Paul in this verse is saying, "Whatever may be the life I live, its principle and end is Christ"; literally it reads, "For to me to live Christ". He is not so much speaking of the source of his life; he is rather emphasising the secret of his whole living, Christ. "To live" is in the present tense and indicates that this is characteristic of Paul's living.

The verb "to die" is the translation of *apothanein*. Being the aorist tense, it may indicate not only the act of dying by execution which at this stage was not far from the apostle's mind, but must go beyond this and entail the state after death that he describes as "gain" inasmuch as he would be with Christ. The word "gain" is found again in 3:7.

22   In this statement the article is not used and reads, "if I live in flesh". The word *sarx* is used some 151 times in the NT. In Rom 1:3 and 9:5 it is used regarding the lineage of our Lord Jesus Christ. It is also related to kindred in Rom 4:1; 9:3; 11:14, and is used in describing the material of which the human body is composed (Rom 2:28; 8:3). It is used of men in general (Rom 3:20) that "no flesh" be justified in His sight. It refers to man's natural state (Rom 7:5,25; 8:6), to the nature which is morally evil and cannot be improved (7:18,25) and is used of human frailty (Rom 6:19; 8:37). These references will impress us with the variety of ways in which the word is used. In Phil 1:22 it should be clear that to live in flesh is a physical connotation and not a moral one. It is in keeping with the similar expression in Gal 2:20 and Phil 1:24.

This tireless worker recognised that to live would give opportunity for further fruitful service for the Lord. Here "fruit" is defined as that which is the result of labour. He refers to fruit again in 4:17, but there the meaning is different; it is the reward of love expressed in giving sacrificially. He desired fruit also among the Gentiles at Rome, and for that reason longed for a visit (Rom 1:13). The expression in v. 22 is literally "fruit of work". The fruit is what God grants in the preaching of the gospel, whereas the fruit of the Spirit (Gal 5:22-23) is the moral features of Christ produced by the Spirit in the life of the believer and is indeed conformity to Christ.

For "yet what shall I choose", we should read "and what I shall choose?" The choice is between departing to be with Christ or remaining here and having more fruit to his credit. The Greek word for "wot" (*gnōrizō*) is used 24 times in the NT. In all the occurrences it means "to make known" as in Paul's writings. In view of this Paul is not saying in the passage, "As to choice I don't know", but rather, as in the RV margin, "I do not make it known.

23   The word strait (*sunechō*) is used 12 times in the NT, The Lord used it in Luke 12:50, "How am I straitened until it be accomplished", in relation to His baptism of suffering at Calvary. It is used in relation to Jerusalem's coming judgment, no doubt under Titus in AD 70 (Luke 19:43); of Paul in Acts 18:5 as he was pressed in spirit. It is used of the love of Christ constraining in 2 Cor 5:14. Paul was pressed from both sides: there was the pull of the gain of being with Christ and fruit of further labour in living. The word "betwixt" is simply "between the two".

Generally speaking the word "desire" (*epithumia*) is of evil connotation. It is used 38 times in the NT. However it is used in Luke 22:15 of the Lord's desire to keep the Passover, and here it is used also in a good sense of strong desire for that which is essentially and inherently good. The word "depart" (*analuō*) is used twice in the NT. In Luke 12:36 its meaning is "to return". In the context of v.23 it has rather the thought of loosing the moorings of a ship or the breaking up of a camp. In the *Vocabulary of the Greek New Testament* by Moulton and Milligan (p.36) they cite the word as used in a memorial inscription of a person dying. There is no doubt that Paul uses *analusis* in this sense in 2 Tim 4:6. Paul was accustomed to what was involved in sailing and soldiering.

"To be with Christ" surely indicates that death introduces the saint immediately into the presence of the Lord Jesus. It is a grave error to teach that saints sleep as to their souls and have no consciousness of anything until the Lord comes. It is only the body of the saint that is viewed as sleeping, never the soul. The souls under the altar in Rev 6:9,10 are certainly not sleeping. The language of Paul is a denial of such error. In the statement "which is far better" we have three superlatives used to try and get beyond the failure of language to express what it means to be with Christ, for Paul says to be absent from the body is to be at home with the Lord (2 Cor 5:8).

24   J.B. Lightfoot translates this, "To abide by the flesh, that is, to cling to this life in the body" with the present circumstances that he was enduring for Christ.

H.C.C. Moule has a fine comment on "is more needful". "Desire and the sense of bitterness lie on the side of death; obligation in view of the claims of others lies on the side of life". Bengel puts it succinctly, "It is more important for me to be serviceable to you, than a little sooner to enjoy heaven. Heaven will not fail to be mine at last, notwithstanding the delay" (vol.4, p.127). Paul was the true bondslave of Christ Jesus (1:1) and so to secure the interests of his risen Lord was the consuming passion of his life.

25   "And having this confidence" is capable of being linked with the previous verse "to abide in the flesh", or with what follows "that I shall abide". Either way makes little difference to the sense.

Here the apostle uses the word *oida* for knowledge that is not experimental but intuitive. Paul had no doubt as to the mind of God, and that he had the privilege of returning to Philippi is indicated in 1 Tim 1:3. The first word "abide" (*menō*) has in view his remaining in the flesh. In the word "continue" (*sumparamenō*) the preposition *sum* indicates "together" and *para* "alongside of". With *menō* the word is now pointing to his close association with these saints upon his release from imprisonment.

We have had the word "furtherance" (*prokopē*) before in v.12. The emphasis there was upon the advancement of the gospel; here it is advancement and joy in the faith. The one is related to sinners: the furtherance and joy of the faith is regarding ministry to the saints. The one is linked with the evangelist; the other with the teacher, Paul being gifted in both these spheres. We have joy linked with initial faith in Christ in Rom 15:13 and also in 2 Pet 1:5-7 where we have faith developed. It may be, as W.E. Vine points out, that even with the presence of the article before "faith" the strengthening of their faith is the thought here.

26 "That" (*hina*) means "in order that". The word "rejoicing" (*kauchēma*) is translated "rejoicing" four times; "glorying" twice; and "boasting" six times. The RV translates, "that your glorying may be more abundant". The word indicates the ground or matter of glorying (W.E. Vine). For the words "more abundant" we should read "may abound". It is the word *perisseuō* and has been before us in 1:9 regarding their love; it is also in 4:12,18. Here it is in regards to their boasting. We should read, "in Christ Jesus, in me". He was not so much boasting or glorying in them, but it is a reference to their boasting in Christ Jesus, because of him. He had brought the gospel to them.

In "by my coming to you again", the word "by" is the preposition "through" (*dia*). The word "coming" (*parousia*) is used of the coming of Stephanus (1 Cor 16:7) and of Titus (2 Cor 7:6) and of Paul's presence with the Philippians (2:12). In the majority of its references it points to the coming of the Lord. W.E. Vine points out that *parousia* always refers to a period of time and must be so understood when used prophetically of the period beginning with the descent of Christ to the air to receive his saints (1 Thess 4:16,17) and ending with His revelation to the world (2 Thess 1:7). The words "to you" should be understood as "with you".

6. *Paul's Practical Communication*
   1:27-30

His Desire for their Steadfastness

> v.27 "Only let your conversation be as it becometh the gospel of Christ: that whether I come and see you, or else be absent, I may hear of your affairs, that ye stand fast in one spirit, with one mind striving together for the faith of the gospel;
> v.28 And in nothing terrified by your adversaries: which is to them an evident token of perdition, but to you of salvation, and that of God.

v.29 For unto you it is given in the behalf of Christ, not only to believe on him, but
also to suffer for his sake;
v.30 Having the same conflict which ye saw in me, and now hear to be in me."

27   The word "only" is indicating Paul's desire for them in prospect of his release and return. The word "conversation" (*politeuō*) is here used in the middle voice and is an imperative. It is then a command that we are to carry out for ourselves. It is associated with the words "city" (*polis*) and "citizen" (*politēs*). It is used metaphorically of our manner of life becoming our heavenly citizenship referred to in 3:20.

The word "becometh" is used in relation to the reception of Phebe as becometh saints (Rom 16:2) and is translated "worthy" in Eph 4:1; Col 1:10; 1 Thess 2:12. It can be summarised this way: our walk is to be consistent with what we announce (Phil 1:27); with what we are associated (Eph 4:1); with what we acknowledge (Col 1:10); and with what we anticipate (1 Thess 2:12).

His presence or otherwise was not to be the motivating power in their behaviour, but rather, Christ Himself, who was the theme of the message they heard and now proclaimed.

"Affairs" refers to the things concerning you as in 2:20. With "that ye stand fast in one spirit, with one mind", Paul encourages the saints. At Corinth they are to stand fast in the faith (1 Cor 16:3); the Galatians are to stand fast in liberty (Gal 5:1) and the Thessalonians to stand fast in the Lord (1 Thess 3:8). In 4:1 also the word "stand fast" means "to hold your ground". The expression "in one spirit" is in relation to the purpose and aim, with one mind and with one soul. It is the translation of *psuchē* the seat of the will as seen in Eph 6:6 doing the will of God from "the heart". It is translated "life" in 2:20 and "mind" in Heb 12:3. The spirit (*pneuma*) differs from the soul (*psuchē*). The spirit, the principle of the higher life, is distinguished from the soul, the seat of the affections, passions (J.B. Lightfoot). This distinction can be noted in 1 Thess 5:23.

"Striving together" is one word *sunathleō*. It is the word associated with the athletic games with which Paul was so familiar. It is used in 4:3 of those women that "laboured with" Paul in the gospel. It has generally the idea of combined and earnest effort (W.E. Vine). "The faith of the gospel" is the content of the gospel or teaching. The phrase is objective in character. The summing up of v.27 indicates the apostle's concern about disunity, and his encouragement to stand their ground against opposition.

28   These saints were well acquainted with the opposition and persecution that attended the preaching of the gospel in their midst (Acts 16). The word "terrified" (*pturō*), found only once in the NT, is used in classical Greek of the starting or shying of a frightened horse and thus of alarm in general. Adversaries, those that oppose, the Lord Jesus had in His lifetime (Luke 13:17). Paul speaks of them also at Corinth (1 Cor 16:9). The flesh is an adversary to the Holy Spirit (Gal 5:17). The man of sin is an adversary of God (2 Thess 2:4).

Their attitude of courage in the face of opposition is to the adversaries an evident token of perdition. The words "evident token" translate *endeixis*, the word "proof" in 2 Cor 8:24, and "to declare" in Rom 3:25, 26. So it is a declaration and a proof to their enemies. The word "perdition" is also translated "destruction" in 3:19; 2 Pet 2:1 and "damnation" in 2 Pet 2:3. W.E. Vine has this to say about the word, "It never implies loss of being, but loss of well-being; not extinction, but ruin". It indicates their spiritual and eternal loss and ruin.

In v.27 Paul has described what is outward in character, a manner of life becoming the gospel, in other words, consistency. Then he turns to what is inward, a oneness of spirit bespeaking harmony. In v.28 he is pleading for serenity in the face of opposition. He now speaks of certainty in relation to perdition and their own salvation. The content of their suffering in v.29 is linked with their believing and is inseparable from it. From these observations we conclude that primarily it is the salvation of their souls that is in view and the present assurance of it flowing from their suffering. Then we may note, without straining the context, that seeing the perdition of these men lies in the future, so also does the salvation of the saints (Rom 13:11; 1 Thess 5:9). The words "and that of God" indicate not only the source of their salvation but the power to stand against the enemy.

29   With "unto you it is given in the behalf of Christ", Paul is anticipating the next statement in the verse. To these saints was granted the privilege to suffer for Christ. The word "given" (*charizomai*) is translated "freely given" (Rom 8:32; 1 Cor 2:12). It is used of the name that God has given Christ (2:9).

"To believe in him" is in the present tense pointing to the continuousness of the action of faith. Faith in Christ is here incidentally spoken of as a grant of divine grace (H.C.G. Moule). Another writer Puts it this way, "God has given you the high privilege of suffering for Christ; this is the surest sign that He looks upon you with favour" (J.B. Lightfoot). "Suffering is a means of achieving His gracious purposes both in His own Son (Heb 5:8,9) and in all believers (James 1:3,4; 1 Pet 1:6,7)" (H.A. Kent Jr.).

30   The word "conflict" (*agōn*) which means a contest, is translated "contention" in 1 Thess 2:2, the "fight" of faith in 1 Tim 6:12; 2 Tim 4:1 and the "race" that is set before us in Heb 12:1. In Col 2:1 it is used of a "conflict" that was inward and had to do with his prayer life for the Colossian and Laodicean saints. He reminds the Thessalonian saints of the suffering at Philippi and the contention at Thessalonica (1 Thess 2:2); this was outward in character. In the prayer life of the apostle, spiritual foes brought about the conflict, as is also indicated in Eph 6:12. At Philippi and in other places it was the opposition of men, yet stirred up by the devil. So it is difficult to isolate the two aspects of the conflict. Since they had witnessed the conflict at Philippi he says, "Ye saw in me".

"And now hear to be in me" shows his confinement in Rome was news that they already had. He sets himself as an example and encourages them in the fact that it is the same kind of conflict in which they were engaged.

CHAPTER 2 - KEY THOUGHT
THE MIND OF CHRIST

II. The Mind of Christ (2:1-30)

1. *The Exhortation to Unity*
2:1-4

The Ordering of Humility

v.1   "if there be therefore any consolation in Christ, if any comfort of love, if any fellowship of the Spirit, if any bowels and mercies,
v.2   Fulfil ye my joy, that ye be likeminded, having the same love, being of one accord, of one mind.
v.3   Let nothing be done through strife or vainglory; but in lowliness of mind let each esteem other better than themselves.
v.4   Look not every man on his own things, but every man also on the things of others."

1   The apostle's mind had been occupied with the hostility against the Philippian church in the closing section of ch.1. He now reverts back to the admonition in v. 27. The use of "if" (*ei*) does not suggest the uncertainty of these graces among the Philippians, but can be better understood by reading "since". The formula (*ei tis*) precedes the four clauses, and, as J. Eadie suggests, marks the intensity of the apostle's desire. The word "consolation" (*paraklēsis*) is translated "consolation" in Luke 2:25; 6:24; Acts 15:31. It is used for "exhortation" in 1 Cor 14:3; 1 Thess 2:3; 1 Tim 4:13; Heb 12:5; 13:22. It is also translated "comfort" in Acts 9:31; Rom 15:4; 2 Cor 1:3, 4; 7:4,13. Its meaning (to call to one's side) emphasises here comfort, and thus encouragement. The sphere of this grace is "in Christ" and because of our union with Him, we have it vouchsafed to us. The word "comfort", imparted as the effect of love is *paramuthion*. Its cognate *paramuthia* in 1 Cor 14:3 has the same meaning, that of consolation. The latter stresses the process, the former the act or instrument adopted (W.E. Vine). Vine also states that it means "a speaking-closely and indicates a greater degree of tenderness than *paraklēsis*.

We have discussed the word "fellowship" (*koinonia*) in 1:5. This is a fellowship that is imparted by the Holy Spirit, and His ministry is always indicative of unity; it is so used in 2 Cor 13:14; Eph 4:3 (see note).

The word "bowels" (*splanchna*) has been noted before in 1:8. The word "mercies" is a translation of *oiktirmos* from a root (*oiktos*) meaning "pity" and can be understood as "pities" here. The two words, "bowels and mercies", are found together in Col 3:12 and translated in the RV "a heart of compassion". We may have suggested what is first of all inward, bowels, then what is outward, mercies. In the expression "any consolation in Christ" we have root: the fruit is the "comfort of love". In the "fellowship of the Spirit" we have the root, and the fruit is suggested in "tender mercies and compassions" (RV).

2   "Fulfil ye my joy" reminds us that he had joy in them (1:4,9). The word "fulfil" (*plēroō*) is used here in the aorist tense suggesting that the action of their fulfilment was to be immediate and decisive. Since this point tense never suggests a process, it is the completion of his joy that is in his mind in the phrase "that ye be likeminded". The *hina* clause is rendered "in order that ye think the same thing-, as the word "likeminded" (*phroneō*) is from "to think". It is used in Rom 12:3; 1 Cor 4:6.

In 1:9, he desired their love to abound; here it is the mutual character of it that is indicated.

"Being of one accord" is a translation of one word (*sumpsuchos*) in the original. It is used only once in the NT and literally means "being one in soul".

"Of one mind" or "minding the one thing" is used above in this verse. H.C.G. Moule suggests the word *phroneō* represented by "mind" in these clauses denotes not so much intellectual as moral action and attitude.

3   In saying "Let nothing be done through strife or vainglory" it is noticeable in the original that no verb appears, reading very forcibly "nothing through strife or vainglory". The exhortations of the previous verse would highlight the word "nothing" in our verse. The word "through" (*kata*) literally means "according to" and suggests that the standard of conduct or motive is not strife. The word *eritheia* has been before us in 1:6 and denotes rivalry and faction, the fruit of jealousy. The word "vainglory" (*kenodoxia*) is used only here in the NT and means "vanity and conceit". It is made up of *kenos* (empty) and *doxa* (glory).

In Col 2:18,23 this word *tapeinophrosunē* ("lowliness of mind") is used of a false humility as the context will indicate, but in all other references it is used in a good sense. In Acts 20:19 it is translated "humility of mind", in Col 3:12 "humbleness of mind", and 1 Pet 5:5 "be clothed with humility". This last reference may well give us the vivid picture, which was likely on Peter's mind, that of the Lord girding Himself with the towel to wash the disciples' feet (John 13:4). What an example for us!

The word *hēgeomai* of "let each esteem other better than themselves is translated in 2:6 "thought", RV "counted", also in 3:7,8 "counted". It is the word "judged" in Heb 11:11, and "chief in Acts 15:22. These words will supply the meaning, "to esteem", "to count" and "to judge" others to be "chief". This is something the flesh is not prone to do.

4   In "Look not every man on his own things", the word "look" is *skopeō*, translated "take heed" in Luke 11:35. In Rom 16:17 and in Phil 3:17 it is translated "mark". Arndt and Gingrich in their lexicon of the NT give as the meaning of this word in its six occurrences in the NT "to look out for", "notice", keep one's eyes on", so in our passage, "to look out for one's own interests". The RV reading of the plural is to be preferred here, not looking "each of you" to his own things. See note on this preference.

Notes

1 The absence of the article before "spirit" has led expositors to interpret the statement as a "community of feeling" among themselves. However, the context would rather indicate that it is the Holy Spirit that is in view. This is also indicated in 3:3, and should also be interpreted so in Eph 1:17. In these instances it is impossible to divorce the Holy Spirit from a man's own spirit.

4 The AV uses the singular *hekastos* translated "each one". However, it is best to retain the plural (*hekastoi*) as in the Nestle text and in the RV in view of the emphasis of plurality in the epistle.

2. *The Example of Humility*
2:5-8

The Outshining of Humility

> v.5 "Let this mind be in you, which was also in Christ Jesus:
> v.6 Who, being in the form of God, thought it not robbery to be equal with God:
> v.7 But made himself of no reputation, and took upon him the form of a servant, and was made in the likeness of men:
> v.8 And being found in fashion as a man, he humbled himself, and became obedient unto death, even the death of the cross."

5 The word "mind" (*phroneō*) has been considered in 1:7; 2:2,3. It is here a present imperative and is plural and can be rendered "minding", seeing it is an attitude he desires them to have. It may be read "think this yourselves".

Christ Jesus, the title used of our Lord Jesus, is in keeping with 1:1 and again reminds us that the apostle first met Him as a glorified Man in heaven. The exhortation in this verse is based upon v.4, having regard to the needs of others, and the Lord Jesus being the unique example of this virtue.

6 In "Who, being in the form of God ...", "Who" is the pronoun in reference to Christ Jesus: He is now contemplated in this wonderful unfolding of christology. We should bear in mind it was not drawn forth from any error relative to His person doctrinally, but rather, to set forth morally the lesson of humility. This is in contrast to Paul's unfolding of His person in Col 1:15-19. The word "being" is a translation of *huparchō*; it is a present participle and indicates prior existence in relation to our Lord. It is translated by JND as "subsisting", and consequently denotes what remained true of the person after He came into manhood, that is, the form of God. J.A. Bengel has this to say regarding "being", "The Son of God subsisted in that form of God from eternity, and when He came in the flesh He did not cease to be in that form, but rather, so far as the human nature is concerned, He began to subsist in it" (vol. 4, p.131). "Form" is the word *morphē*. There are some commentators who teach that the "form of God" means "the divine appearance" of which Christ by His incarnation divested Himself. Alford says: "He emptied Himself of the form of God (not His essential glory, but its manifested possession)" (vol. 3, p.168 Greek text). To this we cannot subscribe. "Form", says Lightfoot, "means not external accidents but the essential attributes" (*Epistle to the Philippians*, p.110). W.E. Vine quoting Gifford on the "Incarnation" says "*Morphē* is properly the nature or essence, not in the abstract, but as actually subsisting in the individual, and retained as long as the individual itself exists". The expression, therefore, insists on the pre-existent and unoriginated deity of Christ previous to His birth and its continuance. This surely is the meaning of "the form of God".

In "thought it not robbery", the word "thought" (*hēgeomai*) has been considered in v.3. The word "robbery" is a translation of *hapagmos*. It is used only once in the NT. It has two meanings (as to the first meaning see notes). We believe the second meaning, suggested by Gifford, Vine and others, to be in keeping with the context, "who, though He was subsisting in the form of God did not count it as a prize to be held fast" (see RV).

The prize was "to be equal with God". It is of interest that in John 5:18, they charged Him with being equal with God because, as the RV reads, "He called God His own Father". It is strange that these his enemies had no difficulty with His being equal with God, yet many theologians have! The word "equal" here is isa, the neuter plural of *isos* (J. Stegenga, *Greek English Concordance* p.367). The RV therefore translates properly "equality with God". W.E. Vine states it signifies the various ways or conditions in which He who was possessed of the nature and attributes of deity could and did exist and manifest Himself as such.

7   The word "but" (*alla*) in "But made himself of no reputation" is a word of contrast. It is indeed the contrast to what Christ would have done had He regarded His equality with God a prize to be held on to, or as Williams translates it, "He did not think His being on an equality with God a thing to be selfishly grasped". The emphasis is on the word "himself", indicating to us the voluntary act of His *kenoō*, which means "to empty". This self-emptying must be understood by the context. The expression "made himself of no reputation" is *ekenōsen* which, being the aorist active of *kenoō*, points to the action in the past, and, being active emphasises its voluntary nature as carried out by Himself. This word has entered into theological language as the Kenosis Theory. We do not enter into it here (see notes). We are assured that He could not empty Himself of His deity, for then he would have ceased to be God. We may ask of what did He empty Himself? It was those equalities of majesty and glory, not the essential attributes

of deity. We must see the distinction between "the form of God" and being on "equality with God". It will help us if we remember in John 17:5, his prayer was that the Father would glorify Him with the glory that he had with the Father before the world was. Surely this indicates His self-emptying.

He "took upon him the form of a servant". In this statement we have the explanation of the outcome of his emptying himself. He laid aside his glory in taking upon him the form (*morphē*) of a servant. The word *morphē* indicates all that is essentially the character and nature of a servant (see notes regarding this word). The word "servant" (*doulos*) is usually translated "a bond-servant". We must insist that this was not in relation to men, but to His entire submission to the will of God. He never was the bondslave of men. He was indeed God's perfect servant (Isa 42:1), and perfectly portrayed as such through the chapters of Mark's Gospel, which is indeed the Gospel of the Servant.

The AV reads "was made in the likeness of men", but "was made" is wrong! It is the word *genomenos* which grammatically is the aorist middle participle of *ginomai*. It indicates an action complete in itself and carried out by Himself. Thus it is not "made", it is "becoming" what He was not before (JND). Of the word "likeness" (*homoiōma*) W.E. Vine states, "it does not indicate any diminution of the reality of the human nature He assumed". He was a perfect man (Rom 5:15; 1 Tim 2:5). He was a real man, but not a mere man. He was the Son of God and possessed at all times all the full attributes of deity. He could say "before Abraham was, I am" (John 8:58). The statement "the likeness of men", while indicating His perfect humanity, guards against any thought that He was not God. H.C.G. Moule remarks, "of men, not of man", as if to make the statement as concrete as possible. He appeared not in the likeness of some transcendent and glorified manhood, but like men as they are. However, we must add that He was without sin, and in this He was unlike men.

8 In the phrase, "and being found in fashion as a man", the conjunction "and" gives the continuity in the down-stooping of the Saviour. The word "found" (*heuriskō*) is consistently translated "found" or "find" in the NT. It is used of Paul in 3:9 of our epistle. It carries the thought of a search in 2 Tim 1:17, but has no such connotation in this verse. The thought here is that he was seen by presenting Himself in the character described.

The word "fashion" (*schēma*) denotes the reality of what was discerned by men. W.E. Vine points out that the preceding words *morphē* and *homoiōma* describe what He was in Himself as man. J.B. Lightfoot remarks that v.7 dwells on the contrast between what He was *from the beginning* and what He became *afterwards*. In the present verse, it is between what He is in Himself and what He appeared to be in the eyes of men. The statement in this verse counteracts the theory which considers Him to have been a mere appearance.

In "he humbled himself", the word "humbled" is the translation of *tapeinoō*. The verb is in the aorist tense and the active voice, reminding us that it sums up the whole action and character of His life, which for a season He assumed of His own volition.

In "became obedient unto death", the word "became" *genomenos* has been before us in v.7, and should read here "becoming obedient unto death", the middle voice of the verb indicating an action He understood for Himself. In this particular voice, the stress is laid upon the subject producing the action. We must not construe His obedience as if He became subservient to death as a master, but rather, His obedience is stressed as unto death. The preposition being used is *mechri* (Nestle Greek Text) and so the RV reading "even to death". H.C.G. Moule well remarks, "He did not obey death: He abolished it" (2 Tim 1:10). In Heb 5:8 He learned obedience in the experience of His manhood, but never at any time had He to learn to obey. His perfect obedience to the Father is expressed in John 6:38; 8:29; 15:10. The will of His Father was His constant delight (Ps 40:8) and in this perfect submission the Father found infinite delight (Matt 3:17).

This form of death, the death of the cross, was the climax of His humiliation. It was reserved by the Romans for criminals and slaves, and never for their citizens. It was the stumbling block to the Jews and foolishness to the Greeks (1 Cor 1:23). To the Jews, it was a reminder that such an one was under the curse of God (Gal 3:13; Deut 21:23). The Greeks associated all forms of grace and beauty with their deities, even though all forms of debauchery were linked with their worship. The Christian's attitude to the cross is much different (Gal 6:14).

Notes

6 The words *morphē* and *schēma* (v.8) are most important to a proper understanding of the interpretation of Phil 2:6-8. The contrast in these two words should be considered fully in Synonyms of the New Testament by R.C. Trench, pp.261-267. He emphasises that *morphē* is the "essence" of a thing. The word *schēma* or "fashion" is the outward expression of a thing, such as the whole outward array and adornment of a monarch. J.B. Lightfoot is voluminous in his treatment of the words (no doubt aware of their importance) in his excellent commentary on the epistle, pp. 127-133. The reading of this is useful and in its summing up indicates that *morphē* never changes, being inherent quality, while *schēma* may change seeing it is linked with outward appearance (see 1 Cor 7:31).

The first meaning of the word *harpagmos* is to be rejected for this particular reason. It surely could not be an act of robbery (AV) to be on equality with God. In His pre-existent state He had this. In view of this, the second meaning is retained and preferable seeing that what He already possessed He did not selfishly hold on to.

7 The Kenosis Theory is the outcome of the expression "He emptied himself", a translation of the word *ekenōsen*. We may say the AV reading "he made himself of no reputation" is more of a commentary on this than a translation. Liberal theologians have taught that He emptied Himself of His deity in becoming man. This is surely repugnant to the Spirit-instructed believer, and is to be totally rejected. We may quote J.B. Lightfoot in his excellent statement, "He stripped Himself of the insignia of His majesty" (p.112). We may conclude by stating the outward manifestation of deity - *yes*: the essential character of deity - *no*! In His manhood the miracles He performed were evidences of His deity, and yet He never exercised such power for His own advantage (Matt 4:3,4), but always for the blessing of others (John 6:10-14).

3. *The Extent of His Glory*
   ## 2:9-11

The Outcome of His Humility

> v.9 "Wherefore God also hath highly exalted him, and given him a name which is above every name:
> v.10 That at the name of Jesus every knee should bow, of things in heaven, and things in earth, and things under the earth;
> v.11 And that every tongue should confess that Jesus Christ is Lord, to the glory of God the Father."

9 The "wherefore" is resultant upon the facts that our Lord had the mind to look upon the things of others (vv.4,5); that His was a downstooping rather than a holding on to equality with God (v.6); that He became a servant and stooped to the death of the cross (vv.7,8). The word "also" in the sentence is important. The previous verses sum up what Christ has done. The "also" is to point out what God has done by way of reciprocation.

The word "highly exalted" (*huperupsoō*) occurs only here in the NT. It is one of Paul's superlative words. It is prefixed by the preposition *huper* which has the meaning "over and above" (Arndt and Gingrich Lexicon of NT). *Hupsoō* ("lift up") is the word used of the Lord's lifting up on the cross (John 3:14; 8:28; 12:32,34). The aorist tense indicates an act in the past, so it is in resurrection and ascension that He has been highly exalted (see Acts 2:23; 5:31) "and given ... a name which is above every name". We should read literally, "and gave Him the name"; the definite article is used also in the RV. The expression "gave" is an aorist and used in the middle voice, a translation of the word *charizomai*. It is used in the epistle in 1:29. Arndt and Gingrich give as its meaning "to give freely or graciously as a favour". This usage will be discerned especially in Rom 3:32; 1 Cor 2:12.

"The name which is above every name" has produced many suggestions. Is it the personal name Jesus? It is claimed by many that it is. Some are sure it is the name "Lord", but is not that a title? "God hath made that same Jesus whom ye have crucified, both Lord and Christ" (Acts 2:36). I am more inclined to believe that it is the name Jehovah, and if the name Lord is used in that sense, then I can appreciate that. The unique thing about the phrase is that He takes that wonderful name in glorified manhood. (See note on this name.) The apostle again uses the preposition *huper* in denoting its exaltation above all other names.

10   We should read here, "that *in* the name of Jesus". It indicates authority as will be seen from John 5:43; 1 Cor 5:4, the preposition *en* often being used in this way. The name also suggests character, that is, all that He is in Himself. The next statement, "every knee should bow", is no doubt an echo of Isa 45:23 as most marginal references will show and also stands related to Rom 14:11. W.E. Vine says that the word "bow" (*kamptō*) is used especially of religious veneration here, in Rom 11:4 and Eph 1:20-22 and is a recognition of the deity of Christ.

   H.C.G. Moule says "of things in heaven, and things in earth, and things under the earth" that created existence in its height and depths is in view. The language of Eph 1:20-22 is expressive of this, as also Rev 5:13. It may be appropriate to note here that, when it is a matter of acknowledgment, "under the earth- is included. However in the passage in Col 1:20, it is the great truth of reconciliation that is being treated, and "under the earth" is not involved. This surely guards against any idea of universalism in salvation. It is of interest to note that inanimate creation is viewed as giving praise in Ps 148:3-10, no doubt a millennial psalm.

11   The word "confess" (*exomologeō*) is of interest in light of its occurrences; it has the thought of confessing or admitting sin. In two references in connection with the Lord Jesus who had *no* sins to confess, it is translated "thank" in Matt 11:25; Luke 10:21. W.E. Vine says the word means "to speak the same thing" and has to do with confession openly and publicly. In the *Vocabulary of the New Testament* by Moulton and Milligan, see p.224 for some interesting sidelights on this word.

   The emphasis in the phrase "that Jesus Christ is Lord" is upon the word "Lord" (*kurios*). It will be seen from a concordance of the Septuagint (Samuel Bagster) that *kurios* is used as the equivalent of Jehovah in the Hebrew. Also, the Lord's use of it to Satan in the Temptation is indicative of the same connotation (Matt 4:7,10). Also in relation to Job and his experience (see James 5:11); see also the title of our Lord Jesus in Rev 19:16, "King of kings, and Lord of lords". A final reference will suffice: John had no difficulty by the divine Spirit identifying the enthroned Lord of Isa 6:5 with the Lord Himself (John 12:38-41), an eloquent claim to His Lordship indeed.

   The Saviour's words come to mind in this final statement, "to the glory of God the Father"; He could say "I have glorified thee on the earth" (John 17:4). In all the work of the Son and in His exaltation and praise, the ultimate result is the glory of God the Father. As we conclude this section, we have cause to worship. We have followed our glorious Lord from the pre-existent glory to the depths of suffering and back to the heights of universal acclaim in exalted manhood. We marvel that such unfolding should be brought in incidentally to enforce the practical exhortation to unselfish living among saints.

Notes

9 "The name" given to the Lord Jesus is indicated by W.E. Vine to be the name Jesus. He also says that the historical fact, stated in the aorist tense of "gave", coming after the statement of His exaltation, does not rule this out. Moreover, that name contains in itself the very title Jehovah. This is confirmed by the Lord's statement in John 17:11,12 (*Epistle to Philippians*, pp.61-62). J.B. Lightfoot in his commentary (p.113) says we should probably look to a very common Hebrew sense of "name" not meaning a definite appellation, but denoting office, rank, dignity. However, we feel that what is demanded in v.10 in the name of Jesus, rules out such a suggestion and demands a proper name, as we have suggested in the commentary.

4. *The Exercise of the Assembly*
   2:12-18

a. The Object of Humility (vv.12-15)

> v.12 "Wherefore, my beloved, as ye have always obeyed, not as in my presence only, but now much more in my absence, work out your own salvation with fear and trembling.
> v.13 For it is God which worketh in you both to will and to do his good pleasure.
> v.14 Do all things without murmurings and disputings:
> v.15 That ye maybe blameless and harmless, the sons of God, without rebuke, in the midst of a crooked and perverse nation, among whom ye shine as lights in the world;"

12   The "wherefore" carries us back to the exhortations of 1:27-2:4 and to the example of our Lord Jesus Christ. The language of this verse includes both the passages cited. The term of endearment "my beloved" is used also in 4:1; indicates the affection the apostle had for these saints (see 1:8). Then obedience is no doubt linked to the teaching he had given them after their salvation. This may be illustrated in the experience of the saints at Rome. Paul says "ye obeyed from the heart" (Rom 6:17) or "ye became obedient" (RV). The apostle had happy memories of his presence with them, short though it was, and it is to this he is referring.

They had been obedient, but now he adds, "but now much more in my absence". He had longed for his presence with them (1:25); now he desires that in his absence there would be a stronger reason for their obedience, suggested by the phrase "much more". This obedience would be in regard to the exhortations he had given and will yet give in the epistle.

They are to "work out" their own salvation with fear and trembling. The words "work out" (*katergazomai*) in the context is used in the middle voice, and is imperative, thus indicating that they are to do this for themselves and to do it immediately. JND translates in his marginal notes "to work out unto result". This is the final reference to salvation in the epistle. The meaning of the word here is to be found in the general context. In 2:5-11 we have had an unfolding of the stoop (vv.6-7), suffering (v.8) and the consequent supremacy of our Lord Jesus Christ (vv.9-11). Now the apostle applies the practical outcome of such grace in the verse before us. Most commentators suggest that the Philippians are to work out that which is within, their salvation. This I would suggest is the theme of 1:6. The apostle is rather saying here, I am aware of your internal problems and I have given you an example to follow (2:5-7); now work out your own salvation as an assembly. The word clearly indicates that they needed to be saved from that which would finally be destructive to the testimony, if they did not move to end their strife (2:3,14). Fear and trembling is the attitude in which it must be worked out and would be in contrast to the spirit of strife and vainglory (v.12).

13   In the phrase "For it is God which worketh in you", the emphasis is upon "God", reminding us that every work of grace, whether individual or collective in the saints, must be attributed to His divine power, operating by His Holy Spirit (2:1). The word "worketh" (*energeō*) is used of God's working (1 Cor 12:6) and of the Spirit's (1 Cor 12:11) in the matter of gifts, and also of God working in Peter and Paul in the preaching of the gospel (Gal 2:8).

In "both to will and to do of his good pleasure", the word "will" (*thelō*) is translated "for it is God who works in you both the willing and the working" (JND). Of the word "do" (*energeō*) JND says in his marginal notes, "It is internal operation of power though seen in results". It is to be distinguished from the words "work out" in v.12, which have the thought of achieving something. There is a striking contrast in Eph 2:2: the devil is working in the children of disobedience, plotting their course. How different the result of God's working in the saints! "Good pleasure" (*eudokia*) is used in Eph 1:5 of God's good pleasure in our position; in Eph 1:9, in his purpose, and in our verse, it has to do with our practice.

14   In the phrase, "Do all things without murmurings and disputings", "all things" stands first in the sentence of the Greek text and emphasises the all-inclusive nature of the command. The word "do" (*poieō*) is translated "making" (1:4) with regard to their requests and in 4:14 in the matter of their fellowship with the apostle. In this verse it has to do with every practical outworking of assembly life. "Without murmurings" is translated "without grudging" in the matter of hospitality in 1 Pet 4:9. H.C.G. Moule notes that in the use of the two words "murmurings and disputings", it is not so much against God but amongst and against one another. The latter word "disputings" (*dialogismos*) is generally translated "thoughts", whether evil (Matt 15:19) or doubtful, as in the case of the disciples (Luke 24:38).

15   Paul's desire is "that ye may be blameless and harmless". The word "that" (*hina*) is translated "in order that". The word "may be" (*ginomai*) is an aorist in the middle voice, so we may read literally "that ye may become blameless", which is an outward condition, no charge rightfully laid against them. Harmless, which is inward, is the word *akeraios* used in Matt 10:16, "harmless as doves"; it is translated in Rom 16:19 "simple" concerning evil. It is better to translate it "pure and innocent" (*Greek English Lexicon*, Arndt and Gingrich).

"The sons (*tekna*) of God" should read "children". It is without the article indicating not so much a title, but emphasising character. The RV translates "without rebuke" as "without blemish"; JND "irreproachable". In other words, they are to be above reproach. Paul has indicated the character; now he points out conditions in which they find themselves. They live among people who are crooked and perverse. The word "crooked" (*skolios*) is translated "untoward" in Acts 2:40 and "forward" in 1 Pet 2:18. Arndt and Gingrich give the meaning as "unscrupulous, dishonest". The word "Perverse" (*diastrephō*) is translated "to turn away" in Acts 13:8, and "to pervert" in Acts 13:10. It has the thought of being depraved. The same words are used of Israel in Deut 32:5.

For "among whom ye shine as lights in the world" the reading of the RV is "among whom ye are seen"; JND translates "among whom ye appear". W.E. Vine points out that this is not a command "not shine ye", but a statement of fact. The difference is always marked between the child of God and the unregenerate. The word "lights" is translated "luminaries"; it is *phōstēr*, the word used for the light of the city (Rev 21:11).

We should remember the world is a dark place. We have been delivered from the power of darkness (Col 1:13). We walk in the light of the divine presence (1 John 1:7). We should reflect the character of the One who declared, "I am the light of the world" (John 9:5). He has gone back to the glory, so that the only light the world has is the people of God.

b. The Explanation of the Apostle (vv. 16-18)

> v.16 "Holding forth the word of life; that I may rejoice in the day of Christ, that I have not run in vain, neither laboured in vain.
> v.17 Yea, and if I be offered upon the sacrifice and service of your faith, I joy, and rejoice with you all.
> v.18 For the same cause also do ye joy, and rejoice with me."

16 Lightfoot and others suggest that this expression "Holding forth the word of life" should be linked with v.15 "that ye may be blameless and harmless" thus making "children of God as lights in the world" a parenthetical statement. This no doubt is to divorce the thought of "shining as lights" from the first statement of v.16. The word "holding forth" (*epechō*) is translated "gave heed" in Acts 3:5, and to "take heed" in 1 Tim 4:16, notwithstanding the fact that Lightfoot finds an incongruity in the images of the light and holding forth the word of life. We may find a relationship in the shining and holding forth the word of life. The one has to do with what we are; the other with what we do. It is the word which has life in itself and in its message which is the gospel.

For "that I may rejoice in the day of Christ", the RV reads, "that I may have whereof to glory". Paul speaks of the Corinthian saints as glorying in those who brought them the gospel and also of the messengers glorying in the converts (2 Cor 1:14). This theme is also indicated in 1 Thess 2:19. W.E. Vine says "what a man glories in is an index to his character", and quotes Prov 27:21, "a man is tried by his praise". Thus it will be at the Judgment Seat of Christ, in the day of Christ. For this expression see 1:6.

In the phrase, "that I have not run in vain, neither laboured in vain", the apostle has in mind the Grecian games and views himself as a runner. The following scriptures note the same theme and aspirations of the apostle: Phil 3:14; 1 Cor 9:26; Gal 2:2; 2 Tim 4:7. The word "laboured" (*kopiaō*) is "to toil". It is the word used of the fishermen in Luke 5:5, "we have toiled all night"; of the weary Saviour in John 4:6; of the elders labouring among the saints in 1 Thess 5:12; and of the husbandman in 2 Tim 2:6. The word "vain" (*kenos*) is often translated "empty".

17   "Yea, and if I be offered upon the sacrifice and service of your faith": the apostle now uses language associated with the Levitical system in the OT. He views himself as the libation or the drink offering as in Exod 29:40; Lev 23:13. The word "offered" (*spendō*) means "to pour out", and is used again only in 2 Tim 4:6. In v.17, it is used in the passive voice in the contemplation of martyrdom. A. Borland writes succinctly, "So greatly had he imbibed the spirit of his Lord that, in consideration for the saints whose faith he wished to further, he was willing to count his death a joyful libation poured out on the sacrifice and service of their faith" (*By this Conquer*, p.97). The word "sacrifice" is *thusia*, the thing sacrificed (Rom 12:1) and not the act of sacrificing. Of the word for service (*leitourgia*), W.E. Vine says it is always used for priestly and sacred ministration. It is used in 2:30, of Zechariah in Luke 1:23,30, and of the Lord in Heb 8:6. Paul envisages the Philippian saints as the burnt offering; he is willing to be poured out as the libation, to give his life, if need be, for their spiritual well-being. Such progress to Paul was a source of mutual joy and in keeping with the character of the drink offering So he speaks of rejoicing with them all.

18   He adds, "For the same cause also do ye joy, and rejoice with me". The RV has "and in the same manner", which is preferable. The same manner or reason is no doubt the advancement of their faith. The expression "rejoice with me" is an imperative and has the force of an exhortation, "do ye rejoice with me".

5.   *The Exhibition of Conformity*
   2:19-30

a. The Outreaches of Humility (vv.19-24)

> v.19 "But I trust in the Lord Jesus to send Timotheus shortly unto you, that I also may
> be of good comfort, when I know your state.

> v.20 For I have no man likeminded, who will naturally care for your state.
> v.21 For all seek their own, not the things which are Jesus Christ's.
> v.22 But ye know the proof of him, that, as a son with the father, he hath served with me in the gospel.
> v.23 Him therefore I hope to send presently, so soon as I shall see how it will go with me.
> v.24 But I trust in the Lord that I also myself shall come shortly."

19   The phrase "in the Lord" or "in the Lord Jesus" suggests in the NT the sphere of responsibility, in contrast to "in Christ", which denotes position. The expression "I trust" (in the RV reading "I hope") breathes out Paul's confidence for the future, all in keeping with the mind of the Lord for him. His dearly beloved Timothy had been with him at the beginning of his labours in Philippi (Acts 16:1-5) and no doubt would be warmly welcomed among the saints at Philippi. The word "shortly" (*tacheōs*) is translated "quickly" in relation to the servant in Luke 14:21, and in the language of the steward in Luke 16:6. Paul desires Timothy to come to him shortly in 2 Tim 4:9. It has the thought of urgency, that is, without delay.

Paul continues, "That I also may be of good comfort, when I know your state". The "also" indicates the good comfort or cheer that the saints at Philippi would have at Timothy's arrival. Paul also would share in it, as his fellow-worker would bring him news of them concerning their spiritual state. This surely reveals the heart-yearning of a great shepherd.

20   The word "likeminded" (*isopsuchos*) means "of equal soul" or "of like soul". He was of one mind with Paul, in genuine sympathy with the saints to whom the apostle was writing. A similar expression is used in Deut 13:6, "which is as thine own soul". The Septuagint version of Ps 55:13 reads "But thou, O man likeminded." In "will naturally care for your state..." the words "will" and "care" are the translation of the one word *merimnaō*. It is used concerning Martha in Luke 10:41, "thou art careful and troubled"; of the married person's care for his partner (1 Cor 7:33). These and its use in 4:6, "be careful for nothing", suggest an anxious care. Timothy would not be distracted from his task. The word "naturally" of the AV is *gnēsiōs*, literally meaning "sincerely or truly".

21   The word "all" with the article suggests one and all, without exception. This surely is going back to the exhortation of 2:4. Bengel suggests a link with the song of Deborah in Jud 5:17,23. Indeed a reading of the section will surely indicate a similarity. He remarks when some sacrifice must be made, the man does not fight, but flees, and excuses himself with the hope of fighting at another time. Those others, in whom Paul may have had confidence, may have been absent at the time of writing. The point in the passage is, however, that Timothy stands in contrast to them all. The word "seek" (*zēteō*) suggests an earnest and determined seeking as may be seen in 1 Pet 5:8, where it is used of the devil as a roaring lion seeking whom he may devour.

22   "But", says Paul, "ye know the proof of him". The word "know" (*ginōskō*) is an experimental knowledge, something that had been gathered from observing Timothy in the past. The word "proof" (*dokimē*) has the meaning here of the result of proving. It is translated "experience" in Rom 5:4, and Paul uses it of himself in 2 Cor 13:3, "since ye seek a proof of Christ speaking in me". Hence it has the thought of approval and character.

Timothy was "a son with the father". The son here is rather a child (*teknon*), and, while he was Paul's fellow-worker, yet there was that filial regard for Paul by this younger man. It may be we have a parallel in 2 Kings 2:12, "My father! my father!", language used by Elisha concerning Elijah. What harmonious working in such a happy relationship! The due regard for the older by the younger.

Timothy "hath served with me in the gospel". The word "served" (*douleuō*) is the service of the bondslave. It is used here in the aorist tense suggesting the whole of his service while at Philippi. The RV reads "in the furtherance of the gospel". This message was dear to the hearts of these two men.

23   "Him therefore I hope to send presently" reads literally "this one" emphasising the suitability of Timothy for the task. The word "presently" (*exautēs*) is translated "immediately" in Acts 10:33; 11:11; 21:30, and "straightway" in Acts 23:30. This seems to suggest perhaps a note of urgency in Timothy's mission on Paul's behalf.

"So soon as I shall see how it will go with me" indicates that the immediate sending of his fellow-worker was dependent on the matters concerning Paul, that is, on the outcome of his present imprisonment. The word "see" (*aphoraō*) in the received text is translated "looking" in Heb 12:2. A number of texts have the word *aphidō*. The thought is that he is looking beyond his present circumstances to what is going to happen and to what he confidently anticipated (see 1:25). It is the time factor he has in mind.

24   In "But I trust in the Lord that I also myself shall come shortly", the word "trust" is *pepoitha*, translated "persuaded" in Luke 20:6, and "confidence" in Phil 1:6,14,25. This confidence of Paul is of course subject to the authority of the Lord and to His will, thus the expression "in the Lord". It would be a cheer to the saints at Philippi to contemplate the prospect of a visit from Paul, as well as of Timothy.

b. The Outgoing of His Sympathy (vv.25-30)

    v.25 "Yet I supposed it necessary to send to you Epaphroditus, my brother, and companion in labour, and fellowsoldier, but your messenger, and he that ministered to my wants.

    v.26 For he longed after you all, and was full of heaviness, because that ye had heard that he had been sick.

    v.27 For indeed he was sick nigh unto death: but God had mercy on him; and not on him only, but on me also, lest I should have sorrow upon sorrow.

v.28 I sent him therefore the more carefully, that, when ye see him again, ye may rejoice, and that I may be the less sorrowful.
v.29 Receive him therefore in the Lord with all gladness; and hold such in reputation:
v.30 Because for the work of Christ he was nigh unto death, not regarding his life, to supply your lack of service toward me."

25 The contrast can be seen between the possible visits of Timothy and himself and that of Epaphroditus. The word "necessary" (*anankaios*) of v.25 stands in the emphatic place in the sentence, i.e., "necessary I supposed it". It is the word "more needful" of 1:24. The word translated "supposed", *hēgeomai*, is rendered "that is chief" in Luke 22:26; in Acts 14:12 the "chief speaker" and in Acts 15:22 "chief men among the brethren". It is the word "counted" in 3:7. Paul counted this sending of Epaphroditus to be the chief matter before him.

We know nothing of Epaphroditus apart from the record of the Philippian letter, and yet it is sufficient to conjure up in our mind's eye the portrait of a faithful man. His name means "lovely", "fascinating" (*Dictionary of Proper Names*, J.B. Jackson). John Ritchie in his book of proper names is in agreement. The record indicates the name suited him well, as we shall see further.

Paul says "my brother, and companion in labour, and fellowsoldier, but your messenger". In the *family* of God, we think of him as a brother: in the *field* of service, he is a companion in labour. The word is *sunergos*; it is made up of *sun* ("together") and *ergon* ("labour"), used in 1:22. Priscilla and Aquila stood in the same relationship (Rom 16:3). In the *"fight"* we think of this man as a fellowsoldier, (we find Archippus mentioned in the same category in Philem 2), and in the *fellowship* (this is his assembly relationship) he is their messenger. This word "messenger" is the translation of *apostolos*. Its interpretation is found in its translation in John 13:16 "he that is sent". It is rendered "messenger" only one other time, in 2 Cor 8:23, and then in the plural. It is rendered "apostle" seventy-eight times in the NT.

To Paul Epaphroditus was "he that ministered to my wants". The word "ministered" (*leitourgos*), among the Greeks denoted one who discharged a public duty at his own expense, then in general, a public servant, minister (W.E. Vine, *Expository Dictionary*). It is used of Paul in Rom 15:16 as a serving priest in respect of his gospel preaching, and now Epaphroditus is seen as a representative of the church at Philippi ministering to Paul's needs on their behalf.

This man is not to be confused with the Epaphras of the Colossian letter, even though Epaphras was a common contracted form of Epaphroditus. In his *Personalities around Paul*, Hiebert suggests that it may well be that his parents were devotees of the cult of Aphrodite, the goddess of love and beauty. If this be so, we have another instance of a Christian being known by his pagan name. However, what a transformation God's salvation effects.

26 He who "longed after you all, and was full of heaviness" was a man who indeed was homesick (the expression "longed after" comes from a root *potheō*, "to yearn"). "Full" of heaviness comes from another root *adeō*, "to be sated". It is used of the Lord in the garden (Matt 26:37; Mark 14:33), the only other two occasions it is used in the NT.

"Because that ye had heard that he had been sick": it was of deep concern to this worthy servant that news had reached Philippi of his sickness. It is indicated that he did not wish to give the saints any undue concern for him.

27 The extent of the sickness of this faithful man is indicated in the statement "nigh unto death": we would say that he was at "death's door". It is of interest to note that in 2 Tim 4:20, Trophimus was left at Miletum sick. In an earlier day (Acts 19:11) God wrought special miracles by the hands of Paul. It is evident that in the case of Epaphroditus, Trophimus and even Timothy, (see 1 Tim 5:23), sign-gifts had ceased. In the Acts 9:40,41; 20:9,10, these sign-gifts included the resurrection of the dead. Here we have a case of divine healing, God was gracious and had mercy upon this man, raising him up.

"And not on him only, but on me also, lest I should have sorrow upon sorrow", says Paul. The apostle had sorrows enough of his own associated with his prison circumstances, but the added sorrow attendant upon the death of his companion in labour is what he has in mind, "sorrow upon sorrow". He gratefully acknowledges the good mercy of God.

28 In the phrase, "I sent him therefore the more carefully", the expression "more carefully" is the translation of the word *spoudaioterōs*. It is rendered "instantly" in Luke 7:4 and "diligently" in Titus 3:13. We have a similar word in 2 Tim 1:7 regarding Onesiphorus: he sought Paul out ,'very diligently". The fact of his recovery would make Paul eager to send him back home with greater dispatch.

For "that, when ye see him again, ye may rejoice", we may read "in order that, seeing him again, ye may rejoice". His arrival home to Philippi as one really alive from the dead (as we speak metaphorically) would cause great rejoicing.

Paul then would be the less sorrowful. The sorrow of captivity would still remain but would be alleviated by the thought of their joy at the return of Epaphroditus.

29 The word "receive" (*prosdechomai*) is used of the Lord receiving sinners, and this context would surely give the meaning of the word. He received sinners eagerly and lovingly to Himself. It is used regarding the reception of Phebe (Rom 16:2). We have again the sphere of responsibility indicated, "in the Lord". The word "gladness" (*chara*) is translated "joy" in 1:4,25; 2:2; 4:1.

For "and hold such in reputation", the RV margin has "honour such". The word "reputation" is a translation of *entimos* translated "dear" in Luke 7:2; "more honourable" in Luke 4:18 and when used of the Lord Jesus "precious" (1 Pet 2:4,6).

30 Paul emphasises that "for the work of Christ he was nigh unto death". It is interesting to note that the bounty Epaphroditus carried from the saints at Philippi to Paul is designated by this dignified title "the work of Christ". Here it was not so much public preaching, but a very practical and appreciated task. For the expression "nigh unto death" see v.27.

The word "not regarding his life" (*parabouleuomai*) is used only once in the NT. It means to expose to danger, to risk (Arndt and Gingrich Lexicon). In the *Vocabulary of the New Testament* (Moulton and Milligan) it is stated that the word is from *parabolos*, "venturesome". They quote an example of a man to whom "to the ends of the world it was witnessed of him that in the interests of friendship he had exposed himself to dangers as an advocate in legal strife (by taking his client's causes even up to emperors)". We find also that it is a gambler's word: he gambled with his life; he hazarded his life. To this man in our passage the work of Christ was more dear than life itself.

"To supply" is from the word *anaplēroō*, "to fill up" (see 1 Thess 2:16; also 1 Cor 16:17 "they have supplied"). The thought of lack is not to be construed as a lack of exercise, rather it was a lack of opportunity. The word "service" (*leitourgeia*) is noted in 2:17; representative service is in view.

In concluding this chapter, these three men, Paul, Timothy and Epaphroditus exemplify the spirit of the Lord Jesus in sacrifice, shepherding and suffering. They had imbibed something of the mind of Christ (2:5).

CHAPTER 3 - KEY THOUGHT
THE KNOWLEDGE OF CHRIST

III. The Knowledge of Christ (3:1-21)

1. The Peril of which he Warns
3:1-3

The Message for their Safety

v.1 "Finally, my brethren, rejoice in the Lord. To write the same things to you, to me indeed is not grievous, but for you it is safe.
v.2 Beware of dogs, beware of evil workers, beware of the concision.
v.3 For we are the circumcision, which worship God in the spirit, and rejoice in Christ Jesus, and have no confidence in the flesh."

1 The word "finally" is not to infer that the epistle is drawing to a close, but simply means "for the rest". This can be seen in 1 Cor 7:29 "it remaineth", literally, "for the rest". It is also used in 4:8. In v.1, it is a change of subject matter. The phrase "my brethren" is a term of family relationship and thus, endearment, particularly in view of the warning to follow.

For "rejoice in the Lord" the RV margin reads "farewell". However, we prefer the AV here. It is the word *chairō* and its usage in the NT is "to rejoice, to be glad"; this will be noted in 1:18; 2:17,18,28; 4:4. The term "in the Lord" has been noted in 1:14; 2:19,24,29.

"To write the same things to you" need not suggest the idea that he had written something in a letter now lost. It is likely he is referring to earlier matters in the epistle regarding those who were opposed to him (1:15); the matter of dissension and the great remedy to be occupied with Christ (2:5-11). We cannot but think that it is the matter of not seeking one's own things he has still in mind.

The word "grievous" in "to me indeed is not grievous" is a rendering of the word *oknēros*, translated "slothful" in Matt 25:26 and in Rom 12:11. The RV reading is "irksome". Arndt and Gingrich translate "it is not troublesome to me". The word "safe" (*asphalēs*) is rendered "certainty" in Acts 21:34; 22:30; 25:26. In Heb 6:19 it is the word "sure" We can conclude then that what he was to say would give them certainty and consequently was safe and trustworthy. There follows now an example of men who minded their own things.

2 The word "beware" (*blepō*) used three times is often translated "take heed" and "to see". He refers contemptuously to these men as dogs, for to Paul this was indeed their character. The dog was an unclean animal according to the Levitical law. In Deut 23:18 the price of a whore and the price of a dog were not allowed to be brought into the house of the Lord, for both were an abomination unto the Lord. The Gentiles were termed dogs by the Jews (Matt 15:27). The emphasis here is upon the impurity of the false teachers, the Judaistic opponents of Paul in contrast to the true believer. As to their course of action, they were evil workers. They were opposed to the preaching of justification by faith. They were the ones who hucksterised the word of God (2 Cor 2:17). He calls them the concision, the mutilators, in contrast to the true circumcision; the word here is *katatomē*, "a cutting off". Paul likens these men to the idolatrous priests who mutilated their bodies (see 1 Kings 18:28). We are taught by Paul's intelligent zeal not to have anything to do with cults that destroy the true element of the gospel. These men are to be distinguished from those who preached Christ from ulterior motive in 1:15-17.

3 The circumcision referred to here is not ceremonial but spiritual (see Col 2:11). This took place in association with the death of Christ. It was to those already circumcised ceremonially the exhortation was given, to see to it that it was effected spiritually and practically in holy living (Deut 10: 16; Jer 4:4).

We "worship God in the spirit, and rejoice in Christ Jesus", for the Lord Jesus declared in John 4:23,24 that worship must be in spirit. The RV reading is to be adopted here, "who worship by the Spirit of God". It denotes here that all worship to the Father must be through the instrumentality of the Spirit of God. The word for "worship" (*latreuō*) is used in Luke 2:37, "but served God with fastings". Paul uses it in Rom 1:9, "whom I serve with my spirit". It is also rendered in 12:28 "we may serve God acceptably". Thus we can see that the word defines any service that brings glory to God. To define "worship" is difficult, but it is surely to be occupied with the greatness and glory of God and of His Son. In other words, the "worthship of divine persons". The "rejoicing in Christ Jesus" is rather boasting. It is the translation of the word *kauchaomai*, from the root *aucheō*, "to boast". This is in contrast to those he has been speaking of in v.2. Their boasting was in outward ritual: Paul's was in inward relationship with Christ.

In the phrase "have no confidence in the flesh", the word "confidence" is *peithō*, "trusting" and it is interesting to note that it is in the perfect tense, intimating something he learned in the past, and was presently in the good of. The word "flesh" (*sarx*) is man in his unregenerate state. For it usage in the NT, see 1:24.

2. *The Past of which he Writes*
   3:4-6

The Confidence of which he could Boast

> v.4 "Though I might also have confidence in the flesh. If any other man thinketh that he hath whereof he might trust in the flesh, I more:
> v.5 Circumcised the eighth day, of the stock of Israel, of the tribe of Benjamin, an Hebrew of the Hebrews; as touching the law, a Pharisee;
> v.6 Concerning zeal, persecuting the church; touching the righteousness which is in the law, blameless."

4   In vv.4-5 we have the matters of which he could boast, "though I might also have confidence in the flesh". In seeking further to expose the character of the Judaizers and their teaching, Paul indicates that on the basis of their trust in the flesh he had more to trust in than they had. The expression "in the flesh" is noted in v.3.

"If any other man thinketh that he hath whereof he might trust in the flesh, I more" says Paul. Here, as it were, the apostle throws out a challenge to any man that "thinketh" thus. This word "thinketh" (*dokeo*) is translated "seemeth" in the RV margin. It is used in Gal 2:2 of them "which were of reputation", also in Gal 2:6 "who seemed (to be somewhat)" and in v.9 "who seemed to be pillars". Its use in Matt 3:9 helps us, "think not" to say within yourselves. Paul then is addressing those who seemed to have something to boast about in the flesh. The apostle concludes "I more". He uses this word *mallon* in our epistle in 1:9 in relation to their love abounding "more and more", also in 2:12 "much more in my absence". These occurrences in this letter interpret the meaning of the expression "I more".

5   "Circumcised the eighth day" is the first credit Paul marks up for himself relative to the past; it was "covenantal". Circumcision was instituted after the covenant with Abraham (Gen 17:11,12; 23:27) as Paul makes clear in Rom 4:9-11.

It is also he that repudiates that it has anything to do with a standing in Christ (Gal 5:6). Finally, he intimates the motive of those who would force circumcision upon the Gentiles (Gal 6:13). The eighth day was that appointed by God in Gen 17:12 before the Law was instituted and in Lev 12:3 after the Law was given.

"Of the stock of Israel" has to do with Paul's national relationship. The word "stock" (*genos*) is used by the apostle in his preaching in Acts 13:26. He addresses his hearers as the "stock" of Abraham. It is also used of the Lord Jesus as the "offspring" of David (Rev 22:16). It can be seen to be national in its connotation in Gal 1:14 where the word is translated "nation" The contrast is to be noted in Rom 11:17 where it is emphasised that the Gentiles have been grafted into the olive tree, symbolic of Israel as a nation.

"Of the tribe of Benjamin" is now his boast in what we may speak of as "tribal". He might well glory in this relationship. The prowess of this tribe can be seen from the character indicated of them by Jacob in Gen 49:27. It was Ehud, the Benjamite, a left-handed man who delivered the children of Israel from the power of Moab (Jud 3:15-30). It was from this tribe that Israel received their first king (1 Sam 9:1-2). It is a profitable study to contrast Saul the son of Kish with Saul of Tarsus. Saul of Tarsus surely ravined as a wolf in Acts 9, breathing out slaughter against the disciples of the Lord. The comparison ends there. Saul the son of Kish near the close of his chequered career said "I have played the fool and have erred exceedingly" (1 Sam 27:21). The writer of our epistle could say at his close "I have kept the faith" (2 Tim 4:7). The man Mordecai who had so much influence upon Esther was of the tribe of Benjamin. He was great among the Jews seeking the wealth or good of his people and speaking peace to all his seed (Esther 10:3).

"A Hebrew of the Hebrews" is Paul's filial or family relationship. The purity of his parentage is before his mind. This is the language of superiority. He was a Hebrew of Hebrew parents, unlike Timothy, whose mother was a Jewess and his father a Greek (Acts 16:1).

"As touching the law a Pharisee" is a reference to the ceremonial character of his life prior to salvation. There is no article before law, but there is no doubt that it is to the Mosaic law he is referring. It is of his zeal for the law that he makes mention. It was that which motivated his whole thinking (see Gal 1:13,14). The Pharisees in Paul's own words tell out plainly their character. He said to Agrippa "that after the most straitest sect of our religion I lived a Pharisee" (Acts 26:5). They were the most vehement enemies of the Lord Jesus and against them He pronounced His woes in Matt 23.

6 "Concerning zeal, persecuting the church" is a statement of the consuming passion of a blinded Pharisee. His own language is descriptive, "and being exceedingly made against them, I persecuted them even unto strange cities" (Acts 26:11). The church referred to was the church at Jerusalem, described as the church of God in Gal 1:13.

"Touching the righteousness which is in the law, blameless" touches upon the "moral" character of Paul's life. This righteousness stood related to obedience to what the Law demanded. The fact that he uses the word "blameless" indicates to us that this obedience was outward. He was in this respect so like the rich young ruler who could say to the Saviour "all these have I observed from my youth- (Mark 10:20). It was in the matter of what was inward he failed, in the principle of covetousness (Mark 10:21-22). It is to this Paul refers in Rom 7:7-9, regarding his own experience. Hence, in vv.4-5 we have the matters that were credits, and in v.6 the morality that he claimed.

3.   The Purpose for which Judaism was Worthless
    3:7-12

a. The Change of his Pursuit (vv.7-9)

> v.7   "But what things were gain to me, those I counted loss for Christ,
> v.8   Yea doubtless, and I count all things but loss for the excellency of the knowledge of Christ Jesus my Lord: for whom I have suffered the loss of all things, and do count them but dung, that I may win Christ,
> v.9   And be found in him, not having mine own righteousness, which is of the law, but that which is through the faith of Christ, the righteousness which is of God by faith:"

7   The word "gain" (*kerdos*) has been before us in 1:21. Here, however, it is plural and reads literally, "but what things were to me gains". The things he has already referred to in vv.5-6 are his gains.

Those Paul had "counted loss for Christ". The word "counted" (*hēgeomai*) is used here in the perfect tense, which is an action in the past with present results. It has been considered in 2:3; 2:6; 2:25. In this context, it is the spiritual accountant working on his ledger. He is surveying the profit and loss columns. In this section, we have the crisis of his conversion before us, and for Paul, this was the death of Judaism in his experience. The word "loss" (*zēmia*) is translated "damage" in Acts 27:10, and "loss" in Acts 27:21. It is a singular word and indicates that all the gains linked with his pre-conversion day are now transferred to the loss side of the ledger of his life. "For Christ" (*dia*) should be read "on account of Christ". On the Damascus road he learned that Jesus the Nazarene was the true Messiah. He was the fulfilment of the order that had become obsolete. In his ignorance, he had sought to destroy what was of God.

8   The phrase "yea doubtless" is a translation of *menounge*, rendered "yea rather" in Luke 11:28; "yea verily" in Rom 10:18. He has changed the tense of the word "count" from the perfect in v.7 to the present tense here. We should remember that he is writing now after thirty years of christian experience. In the use of the present tense, he has no need to alter the ledger as it were, but adds all things, in contrast to "what things" (v.7).

In the phrase "the excellency of the knowledge of Christ Jesus my Lord" the word "excellency" (*huperechō*) is rendered "higher powers" in Rom 13:1 and in 1 Pet 2:13. However, its use in Phil 4:7 is helpful to its interpretation here. It is the knowledge "which passeth all understanding". It is for Paul the realisation of the Lordship of Christ. He had seen His glory in his soul, "the light above the brightness of the sun". The utter devotion of his soul is expressed in the term "Christ Jesus my Lord". How emphatic this is! David used it in Ps 110:1; Elizabeth, the mother of John, used it in Luke 1:43; Thomas used it in John 20:28.

In "for whom I have suffered the loss of all things", "for" (*dia*) can again be rendered "on account of". The word "suffered" is used in the aorist tense, of something that took place in the past. Also it is in the passive voice, indicating to us that Paul was not the doer of the action; it was something that happened as the result of trusting Christ.

For Paul it was to "count them but dung, that I may win Christ". The word "count" has been before us in this verse. It is used in the present tense and in the middle voice. It is something he does for himself now. The word "dung" (*skubalon*) is used only here in the NT and is translated "refuse" in the margin of the RV. Here was the estimate of the "all things- that would have given him prominence as a man in the flesh.

In "that I may win Christ" the word "win" (*kerdainō*), a verb in the aorist tense, corresponds to the noun *kerdos* in v.7. It is to gain Christ, not the mere experimental knowledge of Christ, but to receive Him as Saviour and Lord. This is indicated in the next verse.

9   To "be found in him, not having mine own righteousness" was for Paul the end of all self-effort and human attainment. This verse is indeed a summary of the doctrinal section of the epistle to the Romans. It has been well said that Paul left the Pharisee position for that of the publican (Luke 18:9-14). The expression "be found in him" is the position of every child of God. We do not consider, as W.E. Vine does, that this has any reference to the Judgment Seat of Christ.

"Not having mine own righteousness" bears out the fact that Paul is looking to his position before the throne of God, where all man's righteousness avails nothing to give a standing before a holy God.

This righteousness is "of the law", The preposition "of" (*ek*) is "out of the law", as a source. It is quite clear that Paul, who wrote the epistle to the Romans, indicates the futility of any acceptance in law-keeping (see Rom 3:20).

He seeks "that which is through the faith of Christ". The preposition in the former clause *ek*, "out of", is now changed to *dia*, "through" faith in Christ, and this is the only basis of salvation (Rom 3:21-22). The apostle is not speaking derogatorily of the Law. He has already indicated that it is holy and the commandment holy and just and good (Rom 7:12). It is rather a complete repudiation of his own self -righteousness as merit before God.

In "the righteousness which is of God by faith" the emphasis is on the source of this righteousness; it is "out of" (*ek*) God. It is a divine imputation of a right standing before God (Rom 4:24). It is upon (*epi*) the ground of faith and not on any other merit (Rom 3:22,27; 5:1). Thus in this section we have noted the apprehension of his credits (v.7); the abandonment of all for Christ (v.8); and the acknowledgement of his confidence.

b. The Challenge of his Passion (vv.10-12)

> v.10 "That I may know him, and the power of his resurrection, and the fellowship of his sufferings, being made conformable unto his death;
> v.11 If by any means I might attain unto the resurrection of the dead.
> v.12 Not as though I had already attained, either were already perfect: but I follow after, if that I may apprehend that for which also I am apprehended of Christ Jesus."

10 In the phrase "that I may know him" the verb "know" (*ginōskō*) is in the aorist tense denoting a definite experience. W.E. Vine says the word indicates not mere knowledge, but recognition involving appropriation. This is something beyond the fact of being found in Him. It rather stresses the thought of experimental acquaintance. Paul yearns to know deeper communion with Christ and for a greater insight of His person .

As Paul continues, it is interesting to note the reference to resurrection first. This is not strange; this is what brought about Paul's conversion on the Damascus road; the sight of a risen Saviour. From the moment Paul heard the voice from heaven declare "I am Jesus whom thou persecutest", there came with it the desire to know the quickening power of resurrection in his moral and spiritual being. Is it not this same power that is the basis of Paul's prayer in Eph 1:19-20? Surely it is, and Col 1:11 is no different.

Paul desires to know "the fellowship of his sufferings". The word "fellowship" is the translation of the word *koinōnia*. We have noted it in 1:5 related to their partnership in service. It is used in 2:1 regarding the Holy Spirit. The present context indicates the matter of suffering. The emphasis on suffering takes us back to Calvary. It should be understood that the apostle has in mind exemplary and not propitiatory sufferings in which none can share. We may see this distinction in 1 Pet 2:21 and 2:24. A further clarification of this is seen in Col 1:24. Paul's suffering on behalf of Christ is a filling up on his part of that which is lacking (or properly, comes after) of the afflictions of Christ for His Body's sake, the church. In this way, we are partakers of Christ's suffering according to 1 Pet 4:12,13, where the word "partakers" (*koinōneō*) is akin to the word "fellowship" in our verse, each being a derivative of *koinōnos*. This fellowship then is experienced in the life of the child of God in the measure that he is in the good of being crucified with Christ (Gal 2:20).

For "being made conformable unto his death" the RV reads "becoming conformed unto his death". The expression "being made conformable unto" is one word in the Greek NT. It is the present participle of the verb *summorphizō* and is used in the passive voice (see *A Parsing Guide to the Greek NT* by Han). This is Paul's desire, to be in spiritual harmony with the Lord's death. The language of Ruth may be appropriate here, "where thou diest, I will die" (Ruth 1:17). We can gather from the exposition of this epistle thus far that Paul was prepared to die as a martyr. However, it is moral conformity in this verse, a reckoning to have died unto sin (see Rom 6:11-12). In this intimate association with the cross, the believer is never viewed as dying with Christ in the NT, but rather as "having died". It is always a past reckoning (Rom 6:11) with a present result in the life (Rom 6:12).

11 In the clause "if by any means I might attain unto the resurrection of the dead", the phrase "if by any means" is the translation of the word *eipōs* and literally reads in the Greek NT "if somehow". The words "might attain" are a translation of the verb *katantaō* used in the aorist tense here in the subjunctive mood, which is the mood of probability and potentiality. We need to stress that Paul is not doubting that he would have part in the resurrection of the dead. The word used here regarding this event is *exanastasis*, an out-resurrection. He has assured this experience to all believers in the day of the Lord's coming to claim his own (1 Cor 15:52,53; 1 Thess 4:16). This passage has been the basis for what has been termed a "partial rapture". Such is foreign to the teaching of the NT, and must be rejected. It is rather the continuation of Paul's moral teaching in this section. Here we have the earnest desire of a saint to live presently in the good of the fact that he has been raised with Christ (Rom 6:4; Col 3:1). He desires that his life will manifest the power of the resurrected Christ. Thus we see in this section the deep radical moral change in a man when he ceases to be the centre of his moral existence. The grace of God inspires moral conformity to Christ. It permeates the life with His fragrance and promotes assembly unity (2:13).

12 The RV reads "obtained" for the AVs "attained". This change indicates to us that such spiritual attainment outlined in these verses is realised not by fleshly effort, but by the power of God in the life.

The word "perfect" is the translation of *teleioō*, to bring to completion". It is rendered "fulfilled" in Luke 2:43, and "fulfilled" regarding the Scripture in Acts 19:28. It is the word of Paul to "finish" his course in Acts 20:24. He is not referring to the resurrection state that will result in a changed body in that day, but the power of Christ continually living in him.

The word "follow after" (*diōkō*) has been translated "persecuting" in 3:6. How different the tone of this passage. While the man has been changed by the grace of God and his pursuit is different, yet intact in this expression is all the zeal and drive of his former days. That energy, boundless in his past, is now channelled into the obsession of living for Christ.

"If that I may apprehend that for which also I am apprehended of Christ Jesus" allows us to say that in his past it was laying hold of persons (Acts 9): now it is a purpose. If only we, too, could channel the zeal of unsaved days, with which we pursued everything that was contrary to God, into our christian living. What progress there would be in spiritual things. This beloved saint recognised he was not yet perfected. Yet the bent of his life was to grasp the purpose for which he had been saved by the grace of God. The tragedy of our times is the measure in which we take our salvation for granted.

The word "apprehend" (*katalambanō*) is used of Paul in relation to a prize and translated "obtain" in 1 Cor 9:24; in regard to a purpose in Eph 3:18 and translated "comprehend"; and to a prospect in 1 Thess 5:4, and translated "overtake". In our verse it is the pursuit of true christian experience, the realisation of his arrest on the Damascus road.

4. The Progress to which he Witnessed
3:13-16

The Prize and its Character

>v.13 "Brethren, I count not myself to have apprehended: but this one thing I do, forgetting those things which are behind, and reaching forth unto those things which are before.
>v.14 I press toward the mark for the prize of the high calling of God in Christ Jesus.
>v.15 Let us therefore, as many as be perfect, be thus minded: and if in any thing ye be otherwise minded, God shall reveal even this unto you.
>v.16 Nevertheless, whereto we have already attained, let us walk by the same rule, let us mind the same thing."

13 "Brethren, I count not myself to have apprehended" shows that the apostle looks backward and indicates that as far as he himself is concerned he has not yet apprehended (RV). Others professed to have reached the ultimate albeit in Judaism, to whom he referred in 3:2-4. The word "count" (*logizomai*) is rendered "reckoned" in Luke 22:37; "think" in 2 Cor 10:3; "suppose" in 2 Cor 11:5. These three renderings give the meaning of the word "count". The word "apprehended" is the word used twice in 3:12 (*katalambanō*).

"But this one thing I do" is really the exclamation of a priority in his life. "Forgetting those things which are behind, and reaching forth unto those things which are before" shows a forward look characterised by two decisions. Firstly he is to "forget" those things which are behind. These no doubt are the matters considered in 3:5-7. Then like the runner in the games with his eye fixed on the finishing line, he is to forge ahead for the prize. The "things which are before" relate to the aspirations of his heart in vv.10-11. The word "reaching forth unto" is the translation of one word (*epekteinō*) in the Greek NT, and used only once; it is in the middle voice stressing Paul's desire to do this for himself. Arndt and

Gingrich in their lexicon give the meaning "to stretch out" and to "strain towards something". It is surely the word of the runner.

14   The words "I press" are the translation of the word *diōkō*, noted already in 3:6; 3:12. "The mark" is rendered "the goal" in the RV. It is the word *skopos* and comes from the root *skeptomai*, "to peer about" and so "to fix the eye on a mark". The writer to the Hebrews puts it well in 12:1-2 "looking off unto Jesus".

I shall never forget seeing a prize-winning picture of two great runners, the one pictured giving a glance backward to see his rival, the other runner, breasting the tape on the other side. The photographer captured in that tense moment a race lost by a backward glance.

The prize, I would suggest, is not the high calling of God, but rather, that which is associated with the high calling. The preposition eis should be translated "unto" and not "for" as in the AV. The prize looks on to reward at the Judgment Seat of Christ (see 2 Tim 4:8). The high calling is indeed the heavenly calling (Heb 3:1) and all saints share in it. It is spoken of as a holy calling (2 Tim 1:9). It has very practical implications in the present (2 Pet 1:10; Eph 4:1), so we may suggest it looks back to conversion, demands consecration, and it will be consummated at the Bema.

15   "Let us therefore, as many as be perfect, be thus minded" is the call to the perfect; it demands some elucidation. The apostle has made the statement in v.12 that he was not yet perfect. The word in v.12 is the verb *teleioō*, here it is the adjective *teleios*. The word in v.12 we have noted means "to bring to completion, or to an end". It is the word that is used of the Lord in Heb 5:9. With what care we should interpret it in that context! In the person of Christ it can have no relationship to spiritual growth or maturity; it is rather that official completeness resulting from the circumstances through which He passed. The word before us in v.15 is used in the sense of full growth or maturity in the things of God. It was Paul's desire to present men complete or mature in Christ Jesus (Col 1:28). The writer to the Hebrews indicates that the strong meat belongs to them that are of full (mature) age (Heb 5:14).

The word "minded" (*phroneō*) we have considered in 1:7; 2:2,5. Paul adds "if in any thing ye be otherwise minded". This is not to think differently, which at times may be quite correct. The apostle is stressing the fact that they may be thinking wrongly, and surely this is indicated by the exhortation in 2:2 "to be likeminded", "minding the one thing"; also his strong emphasis on the mind of Christ strengthens the idea.

In the matter of brotherly love, the apostle reminded the saints at Thessalonica (1 Thess 4:10) that this grace was the result of being taught of God (see also 1 John 2:27). The work of the divine Spirit is to bring believers to oneness of mind in the things of God (see 1 Cor 2:10-12). It is a divine principle that further light will be given only to those who are prepared to walk in light already revealed.

16   The apostle includes himself in the exhortation, "Nevertheless, whereto we have already attained". H.C.G. Moule suggests that the race may still be in the mind of the apostle. He is surveying the course with its difficulties and suggests a translation, "whereunto we have succeeded in arriving". W.E. Vine indicates also that the race ma be in the mind of Paul.

In "let us walk by the same rule", the word "walk" (*stoicheō*) comes from the root *steichō*, "to line up". Here the thought is of walking in line with others. This can be seen in Acts 21:24 where the word is translated "walkest orderly". The word "rule" is *kanōn* from the root *kanē*, a "reed". The thought is of a measuring rod. Paul speaks of a man's "line" of things in 2 Cor 10:15. In Gal 6:16 Paul uses it in relation to the Galatians where the rule, no doubt is, "for, in Christ Jesus neither circumcision availeth any thing, nor uncircumcision, but a new creature (Gal 6:15). It is most likely that Paul's rule is indicated in vv.13-14, and he encourages them to walk with him according to this principle.

The word "mind" in "let us mind the same thing" is familiar to us now in this epistle. It is *phroneō* (see 1:7; 2:2,5; 3:15). One translation sums up the word used in Matt 16:23 "savourest". Paul says then, let us appreciate the same thing.

5.   *The People over whom he Weeps*
3:17-19

The Warning regarding False Brethren

> v.17 "Brethren, be followers together of me, and mark them which walk so as ye have us for an ensample.
> v.18 (For many walk, of whom I have told you often, and now tell you even weeping, that they are the enemies of the cross of Christ:
> v.19 Whose end is destruction, whose God is their belly, and whose glory is in their shame, who mind earthly things.)"

17   He uses "Brethren", a term of relationship and endearment in v.13. The words "followers together" are the translation of one word in the original (*summimētai*), rendered correctly in the RV "be ye imitators together of me". The word "be" (*ginomai*), a verb in the middle voice, should be read "become" imitators. The word imitator is used in a good sense in the NT. It is the word *mimētēs*, used in 1 Cor 4:16; 11:1. Paul here is the example. In Eph 5:1, we are to be imitators of God, in 1 Pet 3:13, imitators of that which is good. It is used seven times in all in the NT. Here Paul can confidently set himself as an example for them to follow. His life was truly christian, so were his desires. He was a pattern in salvation (1 Tim 1:16) and also in behaviour and sanctity.

In the clause "mark them which walk so as ye have us for an ensample", the word "mark" is a rendering of *skopeō*. It is translated "take heed" in Luke 11:35; "considering" in Gal 6:1 and "look" in Phil 2:4. The word "walk" (*peripateō*) has to do with the individual. It is a word here that denotes what is characteristic of the walk. The use of the plural "us" would include Timothy, Silas, Epaphroditus and others known to the saints in Philippi. The word "ensample" is a rendering of *tupos*. It is rendered "print" in John 20:25. In Rom 5:14, it is the word "figure". In the pastoral letters, it is translated "pattern" (1 Tim 4:12; Titus 2:7) as also in Heb 8:5. The word used here of the moral life indicates a pattern to follow. In this verse we have true imitation in conduct.

18   The word "walk" is the same as that in v.17 and suggests what is habitual, whether right or wrong. In contrast to v.17 it is now a wrong walk of which he speaks. The words "have told", the translation of *lego*, are in the imperfect tense, suggesting that he kept on telling them. The word "often" (*pollakis*) is translated "oftentimes" in Rom 1:13 regarding Paul's purposed visit to Rome and in Heb 10:11 relative to the continuity of the sacrifices. The weeping is viewed in the present tense. The parchment of Paul's correspondence may have been stained by the tears of this tender man.

"The enemies of the cross of Christ" here are in opposition to the cross. Those of whom he now speaks are not the ones in 1:15 nor the Judaistic teachers of 3:1-2. They are the antinomian traitors. The class of people in view profess to be followers of Christ, but use it simply as a cloak for their own impurity. Although they spoke of the cross, they were bereft of its power in their lives. They turned the grace of God into lasciviousness and are well described in Jude 4.

19   The end here indicates the issue and destiny of these ungodly men. The word "destruction" (*apōleia*) is used in 1:28 but translated "perdition". It is also translated "damnation" in 2 Pet 2:3. "Whose God is their belly, and whose glory is in their shame" shows that the only God they worshipped was their sensual appetites. The RV reads "whose God is the belly". The antinomian boasted of an exalted spiritual liberty and special intimacy with God. It was no doubt that such persons were in Paul's mind in Rom 6:1, "Shall we continue in sin, that grace may abound?" He speaks now of their glory, but it is in their shame. They likely gloried in their professed liberty which might be better described as unbridled license.

In the AV it will be noted that vv.18-19 are a parenthesis ending with the statement of the goal. The words "who mind" (*phroneō*) stand in stark contrast to the word we have noted in other contexts. The things they are occupied with are described as earthly. It is the word *epigeios* and again is in contrast to what follows to close this chapter. Paul has given us then a full and graphic description of their character.

6. *The Prospect for which he Waits*
3:20-21

The Change at His Coming

v.20 "For our conversation is in heaven; from whence also we look for the Saviour, the Lord Jesus Christ:
v.21 Who shall change our vile body, that it may be fashioned like unto his glorious body, according to the working whereby he is able even to subdue all things unto himself."

20 This verse is connected with v.17; as we have noted vv.18-19 are an aside. Here then is a marked contrast from those antinomian libertines. The word "conversation" is *politeuma*. The apostle uses the synonym *politeia* in Acts 22:28 rendered "freedom" or literally "citizenship". Arndt and Gingrich in their lexicon quote M. Dibelius, "Our home is in heaven, and here on earth we are a colony of heavenly citizens". The politics of earth mean nothing to those whose lives are governed by the edict of a heavenly city (Heb 11:16). Abraham maintained a pilgrim character because he looked for this heavenly city (Heb 11:10) and so should we, seeing we already belong to it.

Paul adds, "from whence also we look for the Saviour, the Lord Jesus Christ". The eyes of the child of God are ever turned heavenward. Paul reminds us that we wait for His Son from heaven (1 Thess 1:10). The saint is not looking around for signs, he is rather looking up for the Saviour. The term "Saviour" reminds us that an aspect of salvation still awaits us.

The word "look" (*apekdechomai*) is in the middle voice and indicates that we participate in this action for ourselves. It is translated "waiteth" in Rom 8:19; "waiting" for the adoption in Rom 8:23; and to "wait" in Rom 8:25. Its lexical meaning is to "await eagerly".

He is our Lord Jesus Christ. Here is the full title as indicated in the apostolic preaching in Acts 2:36.

21 The RV reading is to be preferred, "who shall fashion anew the body of our humiliation". The word "change" of the AV is *metaschēmatizō*. It is used of the false apostles and deceitful workers "transforming themselves" into the apostles of Christ (2 Cor 11:13). In the same context, Satan is "transformed" into an angel of light and his ministers "transformed" as the ministers of righteousness (2 Cor 11:14-15). It should be emphasised from such contexts that the change indicated by this word is outward. The word is made up of *meta* and *schēma*. The latter word is used in 2:8 where we have noted it in that context.

For "that it may be fashioned like unto his glorious body", the RV reads "that it may be conformed to the body of his glory". The word "fashioned" is much different from the word "change" we have considered. It is the rendering of the adjective *summorphos*. It is made up of *sun* and *morphē*. The word *morphē* has been fully considered in 2:6,7. This word indicates the reality of an inward change in contrast to schema. It is used in Rom 8:29 "to be conformed to the image of his Son".

"The body of his glory" is referring to the body of our Lord Jesus in exaltation. His glory is the manifestation of all that He is beyond the cross (see 2:11). It is to this glory that Paul refers in Col 2:9. Peter remarks that God raised Him from the dead and gave Him glory (1 Pet 1:21). The writer to the Hebrews reminds us that He is crowned with glory and honour (Heb 2:9).

Paul notes "the working whereby he is able even to subdue all things unto himself". The word "working" is the translation of *energia*, from which we get our word energy. The phrase "is able" (*dunamai*) suggests to us His divine ability. It is used in Eph 3:20. The word is akin to *dunamis*, used in Phil 3:10, the "power" of his resurrection.

"To subdue" (*hupotassō*) is rendered "subject" and "subjection" in most cases in the NT, The Nestle Greek Text reads "to subject to him all things", that is the Lord Jesus has subjected all things to the Father. This would be in keeping with the context of 1 Cor 15:24-28.

We conclude this great chapter and this section with this summary: - He has spoken of the Citizenship of the Saints (v.20a); the Coming of the Saviour (v.20b); the Change to His Similitude (v.21), which is the redemption of our bodies (Rom 8:23).

CHAPTER 4 - KEY THOUGHT
THE POWER OF CHRIST

IV. The Power of Christ (4:1-23)

1. *The Appeal and its Purpose*
4:1-3

The Call to Stability and Unity

> v.1   "Therefore, my brethren dearly beloved and longed for, my joy and crown, so stand fast in the Lord, my dearly beloved.
> v.2   I beseech Euodias, and beseech Syntyche, that they be of the same mind in the Lord.
> v.3   And I intreat thee also, true yokefellow, help those women which laboured with me in the gospel, with Clement also, and with other my fellowlabourers, whose names are in the book of life."

1   The "therefore", or as the RV reads "wherefore", links this practical section with the end of the previous chapter, and the coming of the Lord with its effects upon our bodies is a basis for appeal to these saints. He uses the term of relationship in the family of God in 1:12; 3:1,13, 17; 4:8. The expression "dearly beloved" is an adjunct to the other passages noted and is the rendering of *agapētos*. The phrase "longed for" (*epipothētos*) is from the root *potheō* meaning "to yearn". It is the language of deep heart longing for these saints.

"My joy and crown" fit together. The joy is the emotion expressed by the evangelist who has children in the faith, and the crown (*stephanos*) is the reward for the fruit of such labour. As Paul's crown, this would be the evidence that he had not run in vain (2:16). 1 Thess 2:19 is to be taken in the same context, "or joy, or crown of rejoicing".

"So stand fast in the Lord, my dearly beloved" shows that the apostle desires their stability. It is the word *stēkō* and has been noted in 1:27. "In the Lord" is the sphere of responsibility (see 1:14; 2:29; 3:1). It is in the imperative mood which is akin to a direct command. To be done without delay, the command is softened by the loving appeal. He uses the expression "my dearly beloved" for the second time in the one verse.

2   We cannot identify these two women, Euodias and Syntyche. However, their names are significant. The dictionaries give for the first "fragrant and prosperous journey" and for the second "fortunate". The word "beseech" is *parakaleō*, generally used for exhortation.

For "that they be of the same mind in the Lord", Nestle's text reads "the same thing to think". The word "mind" is familiar to us now in the letter; it is the word *phroneō* (see its use in 1:7; 2:2,5; 3:15,16,19). "In the Lord" is the repetition of verse one.

3   In v.1, it is a call to steadfastness, and in v.2, a concern for oneness. Now, he refers to a co-worker for helpfulness.

In "I intreat thee also, true yokefellow", the word for "intreat" is *erōtaō*. It is used of Joseph in his approach to Pilate for the body of the Lord Jesus, translated "besought". Paul uses it in 2 Thess 2:1 in view of the coming of the Lord, where it is rendered "beseech". The RV uses the word "beseech". The word "true", the rendering of *gnēsios*, is used of the love of the Corinthians, and translated "sincerity" (2 Cor 8:8).

In the pastoral epistles, Paul calls Timothy my own "genuine" son in the faith (1 Tim 1:2) and similarly Titus (Titus 1:4). The word "yokefellow" (*suzugos*) is used only once in the NT. It has been suggested that this is a proper name and its meaning given. However, we are not impressed with this suggestion. We are much happier with the suggestion of J.B. Lightfoot that in all probability it was Epaphroditus for whom he had so much esteem, called by Paul "my companion in labour and fellowsoldier" (2:25). Paul and this dear man had pulled well together in the yoke of service.

"Those women which laboured with me in the gospel" are not different women, but the two already referred to; the RV reads "these women". They are noted as labourers in the gospel. The word rendered "laboured" (*sunathleō*) is used by

Paul in his injunction in 1:27, "striving together for the faith of the gospel"; see the use of the word in that context.

The man Clement is unknown to us, but evidently well-known to the apostle. He associated all those who had worked with him as fellowworkers. This word fellowlabourers (*sunergos*) is used in 2:25, where its meaning is discussed.

Their "names are in the book of life". The OT makes reference to a book of those who had spiritual life (Exod 32:32; Isa 4:3; Dan 12:1). As H.G. Moule remarks, "the book of life indicates God's perfect knowledge of those that are His" (2 Tim 2:19). We should note also the assurance of John 10:27,28, "they shall never perish", hence the impossibility of being blotted out of the book. The strong negative used in Rev 3:5, rather than indicating the possibility of a name being blotted out, assures of the permanence of the inscription. The Lord bade the disciples to "rejoice, because your names are written in heaven" (Luke 10:20). The writer to the Hebrews, speaks of the "church of the firstborn, which are written in heaven" (Heb 12:23). The right of entrance into the city is to be enrolled in the Lamb's book of life (Rev 21:27). The awful prospect of the lake of fire awaits those whose names are missing in that solemn search (Rev 20:15). With the unnamed in our verse, we too may rejoice that our names are written in heaven's register of life.

2. *The Assurance of Peace*
   4:4-7

The Call to Rejoicing

> v.4 "Rejoice in the Lord alway: and again I say, Rejoice.
> v.5 Let your moderation be known unto all men. The Lord is at hand.
> v.6 Be careful for nothing; but in every thing by prayer and supplication with thanksgiving let your requests be made known unto God.
> v.7 And the peace of God, which passeth all understanding, shall keep your hearts and minds through Christ Jesus."

4 "Rejoice in the Lord alway: and again I say, Rejoice" is Paul's reminder to joyfulness. The word "rejoice" (*chairō*) is the dominant note in this letter (1:18; 2:17,18,28; 3:1). The RV margin has "farewell"; however, we prefer the word "rejoice", and especially when he uses it for the second time, as if to give emphasis and impress them with the need for its continuance.

5 The word "moderation" (*epieikēs*) is rendered "patient", a requirement for the overseer (1 Tim 3:3). In the context of behaviour, it is rendered "gentle" (Titus 3:2), and with respect to the wisdom that is from above, it is rendered "gentle" (James 3:17). We should understand that in the matters where the word of God is involved, we must not compromise (see Gal 2:5). It is clear from the general theme of the epistle, that it is the question of attitudes among the saints that leads to disunity and strife (see 2:3). It is the opposite of self-seeking and contention, and the word indicates a behaviour that can be seen.

The phrase, "the Lord is at hand" may be taken to indicate the nearness of the Lord's presence at all times (Ps 119:151). However, in view of the fact that in 3:20 the Lord's coming has been in Paul's mind, we may perhaps put the emphasis on the nearness of His coming (Rom 13:11; Heb 10:37; James 5:8).

6 In the previous verse, he has made a request for yieldingness; now he notes the requirement of prayerfulness. The word "careful", the translation of *merimnaō*, has been used of the care of Timothy for the Philippian saints (2:20). In Matt 6:25, the Lord instructed them in His sermon, take "no thought" for your life. The RV reads, "in nothing be anxious", and this suggests the matter of over-anxiety in daily living. The antidote for such a malady is prescribed by Peter, "casting all your care upon him for he careth for you" (1 Pet 5:7). The word used by Peter is *merimnaō*.

In the clause "but in every thing by prayer and supplication with thanksgiving", the emphasis in the last phrase has been upon "nothing". The word that is prominent here is "everything". It is indeed a marked contrast. The word for "prayer" (*proseuchē*) is used for prayer in general; it is the word in 1 Tim 2:1, where assembly prayer is in view. The word "supplication" is the rendering of *deēsis*, also used in 1 Tim 2:1. The use of this word in the NT indicates petition in view of special need. This can be noted regarding Zacharias (Luke 1:13), and Paul's desire for Israel (Rom 10:1). It is used regarding the Lord Jesus in Heb 5:7, and it can be noted in our epistle in 1:4,19. The added ingredient in the passage is "thanksgiving". We may be sure that it looks back to what has already been received and the confidence that there will be further answers to prayer.

"Let your requests be made known unto God" is Paul's conclusion. The word "requests" is the rendering of *aitēma*, translated "required" in Luke 23:24, and reads literally, "the requests" in 1 John 5:15, "we have the petitions that we ask for". The word gathers up the first two that we have considered and is the substance of what we require or request from our Father.

7 Here we have the realisation of peacefulness. This is the result of taking everything to God in prayer. "We have peace with God" (Rom 5:1): this is positional, and is based upon our justification. The peace of God is here experimental, something we may or may not enjoy. It is the word of Paul's salutation in 1:2.

This peace "passeth all understanding". The word "passeth" (*huperechō*), Paul uses in Rom 13:1 regarding our subjection to the "higher" powers. It has been observed in our epistle already, where it is translated "better" in 2:3 and "excellency- in 3:8. The word "understanding" (*nous*) is translated "mind" in Rom 1:28; 7:23, 25; 1 Cor 1:10; Eph 4:17, 23. It is the faculty of thinking and of judging. Arndt and Gingrich translate the phrase, "which surpasses all power of thought". It reminds us that it is like the love of Christ which passeth knowledge (Eph 3:19). The word passeth" in that verse, however, is *huperballō*.

The peace "shall keep your hearts and minds through Christ Jesus". The word "keep", the translation of (*phroureō*), is a military word as can be seen from 2 Cor 11:32, where the context speaks of a garrison being kept. In Gal 3:23, we were kept under law. In 1 Pet 1:5, we are kept by the power of God. The RV margin properly translates it "guard".

The heart and the mind are linked together, and stand related to each other in Prov 23:7. The heart (*kardia*) is the secret spring of all activity, as can be seen from its many references in Old and New Testaments. Peter speaks of the hidden man of the heart (1 Pet 3:4). "The mind" (*noema*) is translated "device" in 2 Cor 2:11 relative to Satan. It is also the word "thought" in 2 Cor 10:5. The RV reads properly, "in Christ Jesus" and suggests the sphere of our preservation. The order of the titles is important; it is the Lord Jesus as risen and ascended to glory.

3. *The Accounting and God's Presence* 4:8-9

The Call to Meditation

> v.8 "Finally, brethren, whatsoever things are true, whatsoever things are honest, whatsoever things are just, whatsoever things are pure, whatsoever things are lovely, whatsoever things are of good report; if there be any virtue, and if there be any praise, think on these things.
> v.9 Those things, which ye have both learned, and received, and heard, and seen in me, do: and the God of peace shall be with you."

8 In this verse, we have set forth in these principles the preservation of their thinking.

"Finally, brethren, whatsoever things are true", says the apostle, now drawing to a conclusion the salutary matters of the epistle before he speaks of things that are of a personal nature, yet involving them.

In "the things that are true," this word "true" (*alēthēs*) is used in contrast to what is error, as in John's testimony to the Lord Jesus (John 5:32; 10:41), the Lord's own record of Himself (John 8:14) and of His judgment (John 8:16). It is used of the anointing the child of God has received, which is true and no lie (1 John 2:8).

In "whatsoever things are honest", the word "honest" is *semnos*. It is translated "grave" in regard to the deacon in 1 Tim 3:8, and of the aged men in Titus 2:2. Its meaning is "worthy, noble and venerable". The RV margin is nearer to its meaning with "honourable or revered".

Paul draws attention to "whatsoever things are just". The word "just" (*dikaios*) is translated "righteous" forty-one times in the NT, "just" thirty-three times, "right" five times and "meet" twice. Paul uses the word in 1:7 (see this context). It is things that are right or just.

And there are things that are "pure". Here we have the word *hagnos*, rendered "chaste" in Titus 2:5 and in 1 Pet 3:2. This word is akin to *hagios*, which means "hallowed or consecrated", therefore, "most holy". It would be in keeping with the apostle's exhortation that the things in Eph 5:3-4 are to have no place in the conversation, far less in the thinking of the child of God.

In "whatsoever things are lovely", the word "lovely" is the translation of *prosphilēs*. Arndt and Gingrich render the word "agreeable, amiable" and thus "acceptable".

They were also to think on "whatsoever things are of good report". The word *euphēmos* here means "something well spoken of", i.e. "reputable" (James Strong). The RV margin reads "gracious" and this would gather up Strong's lexical meaning. Arndt and Gingrich render it "auspicious, well-sounding and praiseworthy", "attractive and appealing". In a word akin to it, *euphēmia*, Moulton and Milligan quote an example on p.267 of their *Vocabulary of the Greek New Testament*: "The well born and nicely nurtured must carefully abstain from evil speech even in misfortune"; also, "Let the shrine be held in good repute" along the Leucadian shore. This indicates the use of the word in the literature of the Greeks.

"If there be any virtue, and if there be any praise, think on these things", says Paul. The word "virtue" (*aretē*) is translated "praise" in 1 Pet 2:9, and rendered "virtue" in 2 Pet 1:3,5. It is to be added to our faith in Peter's context. It has the thought of excellence. H.C.G. Moule in his commentary remarks that in Greek ethics it was connected with manliness, courage and self-reliance. The expression "if there be any" would suggest that nothing was to be left out that was basically virtuous.

The word "praise" (*epainos*) has the thought of what is praiseworthy. It is used in 1:11. It is used of one whose praise is in the gospel (2 Cor 8:18). It is used also in 1 Pet 2:14 of the praise of them that do well. It is used as relating to the Judgment Seat of Christ (1 Cor 4:5).

The expression "think on" is one word in the original; it is the translation of *logizomai* and has been noted in 3:13.

9 The word "learned" is the word of the disciple, *manthanō*. The Lord uses it in Matt 11:29, "learn of me". Paul uses it in Eph 4:20, "ye have not so learned Christ". It is used of the Lord Jesus Himself (Heb 5:8), "he learned obedience" we should add experimentally. This was the impartation of teaching. The word "received" (*paralambanō*) is made up of *para* ("alongside of") and *lambanō* ("to receive"), thus to receive from a person. It is used by the apostle regarding what he had received of the Lord: the revelation of the supper (1 Cor 11:23) and of the gospel which they had received from Paul (1 Cor 15:1).

The word translated "heard" is *akovō*. Paul has used it in 1:27 as to their affairs; in 1:30 as to what they had seen in him while among them; now of what they heard. They had heard regarding Epaphroditus (2:26). The word "seen" (*oida*) means to "be aware of", to "consider and understand". It is used in 1:27 of Paul's visit to them; in 1:30 of the conflict they saw in him, and also in 2:28 of their seeing Epaphroditus again. The emphatic word "do" (*prassō*), is an imperative. The balance of teaching and practice is to be noted in this verse. The order also is most important. There must be instruction in the doctrine, then the working it out in the life, and Paul had no hesitation, setting himself forth as a pattern for them.

Paul now speaks of "the God of peace". He has already spoken of the peace of God in v.7. The thought in that passage was "supply". Here it is different; it is rather the "source of supply", the God of peace. It is used in 1 Thess 5:23, "the very God of peace sanctify you wholly". He is the God of peace because He has made peace (Col 1:20). He ministers it to the sinner trusting His Son (Rom 5:1), and to the child of God it can be multiplied (1 Pet 1:2). It is used also in Heb 13:20 as the title of the One who brought Christ from the dead.

It is one thing to have the provision of our God, but how much more blessed to know His continual presence. In concluding this section, we have intimated the presence of God and their task.

4. *The Assessment of His Position*
   4:10-13

The Contentment of the Servant

> v.10 "But I rejoiced in the Lord greatly, that now at the last your care of me hath flourished again; wherein ye were also careful, but ye lacked opportunity.
> v.11 Not that I speak in respect of want: for I have learned, in whatsoever state I am, therewith to be content.
> v.12 I know both how to be abased, and I know how to abound: every where and in all things I am instructed both to be full and to be hungry, both to abound and to suffer need.
> v.13 I can do all things through Christ which strengtheneth me."

10   "But I rejoiced in the Lord greatly-, says Paul. The word "rejoiced" (*chairō*) has been noted thus far in the epistle (see 1:18, 2:17,18,28; 3:1; 4:4). Here it is in the passive voice, aorist tense, and tells us that he "was made to rejoice".

"In the Lord" denotes the sphere of responsibility and service in 1:14; 2:19,24,29; 3:1; 4:1,2,4.

The word "greatly" is the translation of *megalōs* and is used only here. It is akin to *megas* translated "great" throughout the NT. The abundance of his rejoicing must be made known to them, and the use of the word "but" indicates that he did not desire to omit matters he is about to speak of.

Now at the last their care of him had flourished again. The word "at last" (*pote*) is translated "in time past" in Eph 2:2; Heb 1:5,13; in 2:1 as "any time". The word "care" (*phroneō*) is also used in 1:7; 2:2,5; 3:15,16,19; 4:2. The meaning of it in this context is to "take thought or to be "mindful of" him. The statement in this verse recalls a grateful remembrance of their past communications.

The phrase "hath flourished again" is the translation of one word, *anthallō* from *thallō* ("to flourish"). Arndt and Gingrich indicate its meaning as "to cause to grow, or bloom again like a plant". It is used in the LXX version of the OT in Ps 27:7; Ezek 17:24; Hos 8:9.

Paul adds "ye were also careful, but ye lacked opportunity". The word "careful" is again *phroneō*, already rendered "care" in this verse. The phrase "lacked opportunity" is one word in the original (*akaireomai*), used only here in the NT. The word *akairōs* is akin to it and is translated "out of season" in 2 Tim 4:2. It is evident that Paul is indicating they had no means of communicating with him, so in this verse, we have the intimation regarding their care.

11   Paul did not "speak in respect of want". The word "speak" (*legō*) is used in 3:18. The word "want" (*husterēsis*) is used regarding the widow in Mark 12:44; it has to do with the thought of need.

"For I have learned, in whatsoever state I am"; here is a man who has been in God's school, as the word "learned" indicates. It is the word *manthanō* used in 4:9. "In whatsoever state" simply means the circumstances of life that a person may be found in.

He had learned therewith to be content. Of the word "content" (*autarkēs*), Arndt and Gingrich tell us it means "self-sufficient, independent of circumstances".

12   Paul tells them, "I know both how to be abased, and I know how to abound". The word "know" in both cases is *oida* and is in the perfect tense. It is used in 1:17,19,25. It is not so much experimental knowledge, but the word indicates what is intuitive. It is to be distinguished from *ginōskō*. Paul is indicating what he perceived. The word "abased" (*tapeinoō*) has been noted in the self-abnegation of our Lord Jesus in 2:8. It is the word James uses in his exhortation, "humble yourselves" (James 4:10) and Peter in 1 Pet 5:6. The word "abound" is the word *perisseuō* (see its use in 1:9,26).

"Everywhere and in all things I am instructed both to be full and to be hungry", he adds. The apostle is again speaking of every circumstance of life. The secret of this contentment in vv.11-12 is the fact of his initiation which the word "instructed" means. It is *mueō* and means to "initiate into the mysteries". The RV margin gives "I have learned the secret": Nestle's text reads "I have been initiated".

"To be full" (*chortazomai*) was primarily used of animals being gorged (Arndt and Gingrich). Here it means to be "well-fed". Its use in this way can be seen in Rev 19:21 where the fowls were filled with flesh. "To be hungry" was something that Paul knew all about. He refers to it in 1 Cor 4:11. The Lord Himself understood it properly (Matt 4:2). He knew how "both to abound and to suffer need". The word "abound" has been noted in this verse; he uses it now for the second time. "To suffer need" is the translation of one word, *hustereō*. It is rendered "to come short" in Rom 3:23. Paul uses it in writing to the Corinthians, "I was present with you and wanted" (2 Cor 11:9). It is used in Heb 11:37 of those who were destitute.

13 In this verse the apostle gives indication of his confidence, "I can do all things through Christ which strengtheneth me". The phrase "can do" is the rendering of *ischuō*, translated "prevailed" in Acts 19:16; also translated "availeth" in "the prayer of a righteous man availeth much". It is spiritual strength that Paul is indicating here. It has a wider connotation than the immediate context of abounding and being in need; it refers to every circumstance of his suffering and service for God. The proposition is "in" rather than "through". It is "in Him" that the apostle finds prevailing strength. The word "strengthen" is *endunamoō*. He gives testimony to it in 2 Tim 4:17. It is used of Abraham, "he was strong in faith" (Rom 4:20). It is akin to *dunamis*, used of the *"power"* of his resurrection in 3:10. It surely has been made good to Paul in the context of 2 Cor 12:9, "My strength is made perfect in weakness".

5. The Appreciation of their Provision
4:14-20

a. The Commendation of their Stewardship (vv.14-16)

> v.14 "Notwithstanding ye have done well, that ye did communicate with my affliction.
> v.15 Now ye Philippians know also, that in the beginning of the gospel, when I departed from Macedonia, no church communicated with me as concerning giving and receiving, but ye only.
> v.16 For even in Thessalonica ye sent once and again unto my necessity."

14 "Notwithstanding ye have well done", says Paul. The word "notwithstanding" (plen) has been noted in the epistle in 1:18; 3:16. The apostle would not give the impression that their gracious ministry was not fully appreciated, so here he returns to it again and acknowledges that they did well.

The phrase "did communicate with" is the rendering of the word *sunkoinōneō*. It is made up of the preposition *sun* ("with") and *koinōneō* (rendered "distributing" in Rom 12:13, and "communicate" in Gal 6:6). The noun *koinōnia* has been noted in our epistle as "fellowship" (1:5; 2:1; 3:10), It was not so much that they shared together in sending the gift, but they had reckoned his affliction to be their own. The word "affliction" (*thlipsis*) Paul has used in 1:16.

15 The RV reads "and ye yourselves also know ye Philippians". The word "know" is *oida* (see its use in 1:17,19,25; 4:12). The use of the expression "ye Philippians" denotes here his great love for them as indicated in 4:1, "longed for". In other words, we see his deep appreciation for them in contrast to 2 Cor 6:11 and Gal 3:1, i.e. to the Corinthians for their narrowness and to the Galatians for their foolishness. We may say then of the Philippians, it is devotedness.

"The beginning of the gospel" would no doubt go back to when the gospel reached them. The stirring account of it may be read in Acts 16.

"When I departed from Macedonia" was some ten years before and the historical record of the period is given in Acts 17 and 18.

Paul recalls that "no church communicated with me as concerning giving and receiving, but ye only". The word "church" is *ekklēsia*, made up of *ek* ("out of") and *klēsis* ("a calling"). A New Testament church then is made up of saints called out of the world, baptised and gathered to the name of the Lord Jesus. The gatherings of such companies are indicated in the Acts. These churches are to be distinguished from the church which is His Body (Eph 1:23) which embraces every believer. It is well for us to mark the distinction in view of the confusion that exists in christendom.

The word "communicated" is *koinōneō*; see its use in v.14. The giving and receiving indicates the matter of giving the gifts, and Paul being in receipt of them. The emphasis upon "ye only" again points out his appreciation of these saints that supported him in the work of God.

It should be pointed out that this section indicates to us how the work of God was carried on and maintained. It is a far cry from what we see in the religious world, which things must be obnoxious to God. This is the principle to which John refers, "because that for his name's sake they went forth, taking nothing of the Gentiles", i.e. of the unregenerate (3 John 7).

16   Even in Thessalonica they had sent once and again to Paul's necessity. The history of these early pioneering days is thrilling reading indeed. It can be gleaned from 1 Thess 2:9 and 2 Thess 3:8 that Paul took nothing from the Thessalonians, but wrought with his hands at tent-making. In view of this, the gifts of his beloved Philippians would be much appreciated. The word "again" (*dis*) is rendered "twice" in relation to the cock crowing (Mark 14:30, 72); as to the Pharisee fasting "twice" (Luke 18:12); and to the apostates "twice" dead (Jude 12). The word "necessity" (*chreia*) is translated "need" relative to the Lord (Mark 2:25); in the epistle in 2:25 it is translated "wants".

b. The Character of their Supply

> v.17   "Not because I desire a gift: but I desire fruit that may abound to your account.
> v.18   But I have all, and abound: I am full, having received of Epaphroditus the things which were sent from you, an odour of a sweet smell, a sacrifice acceptable, wellpleasing to God.
> v.19   But my God shall supply all your need according to his riches in glory by Christ Jesus.
> v.20   Now unto God and our Father be glory for ever and ever. Amen."

17   In this verse, we have Paul's desire regarding their account. The lack of covetousness is marked in the heart of this great servant, and no doubt, much of this is in his mind in 2 Cor 4:2. The word "desire" is *epizēteō* and perhaps as W.E. Vine suggests, Paul did not desire a repetition of their giving. The word "gift" (*doma*) has the article before it and indicates the gift which they had sent him.

The word "fruit" (*karpos*) is used in 1:11,22. It has to do with the recompense they will receive from the Lord Jesus in that coming day. The word "abound" (*pleonazō*) is translated "abundant" in 2 Cor 4:15, and "to increase" in 1 Thess 3:12. The word "account" is a rendering of *logos*, "settlement" (Arndt and Gingrich). It is a financial word used of debit and credit. Here it was to their credit to give to the Lord's servant.

18 "But I have all, and abound", says Paul. The word "to have" (*apechō*) is used by the Lord in Matt 6:2, "they have their reward", that is, they have in full here and now, and they will receive nothing more. It is again a financial expression. Paul seems to say "you have paid me in full". The word "abound" is used twice in v.12.

The word "full" (*plēroō*) we have noted in 1:11; 2:2. It is here used in the perfect tense and the passive voice; by their exercise and devotion he had been filled.

Paul had "received of Epaphroditus the things which were sent". Here the preposition "of" (*para*) is translated "from" in the RV. He now speaks of the faithful messenger and their bountiful mercies. The character of this man Epaphroditus may be noted in 2:25-30.

Their gift was "an odour of a sweet smell, a sacrifice acceptable, wellpleasing to God". The word "odour" (*osmē*) is used of Mary's box of ointment (John 12:3). This was surely God's estimation of the Lord's sacrifice at Calvary, as the whole burnt-offering (Lev 1; Eph 5:2), and now of the gift of the saints. The "sweet smell" (*euōdia*) is rendered a "sweet savour" in Eph 5:2.

The word "sacrifice" (*thusia*) is used in Rom 12:1 of the believer's body. It was noted in our epistle already (2:17) and is used of the spiritual sacrifices offered up in 1 Pet 2:5. It is a remarkable thing that the Spirit of God places the gifts of His people, given in this sacrificial way, as going up to God in the same way as the sacrifice of the Lord Jesus. The word "acceptable" (*dektos*) is used of the acceptable year of the Lord (Luke 4:19), and of a time accepted (2 Cor 6:2). The word "wellpleasing" is the rendering of (*euarestos*) used of the sacrifice in Rom 12:1; of the saint at the Judgment Seat of Christ (2 Cor 5:9); of the conduct of the believer (Eph 5:10) and of God's working in us to produce what is wellpleasing to God (Heb 13:21). Here then, it has the thought of what is well-pleasing to God.

19 "But my God shall supply all your need" is Paul's declaration and assurance. Paul can speak out of experience, for the God who met his need through them, in turn will meet their need. As we come close to the end of this epistle, we can trace the God of the epistle.

Have we not here suggested Jehovah-Jireh, which means the Lord will provide (Gen 22:14) - Divine Provision? In 1:28 we have an indication of Jehovah-Nissi, the Lord our Banner (Exod 17:15) - Divine Protection. In 2:27 - we are reminded of Jehovah-Ropheca, the Lord that healeth thee (Exod 15:26) - Divine Pity. In 3:9 we have Jehovah-Tsidkenu, the Lord our Righteousness (Jer 23:6) - Divine Position. In 4:5 we may see Jehovah-Shammah, the Lord is there (Ezek 48:35) - Divine Presence. Finally, in 4:9 we have Jehovah-Shalom, the Lord is Peace (Judg 6:24) - Divine Peace.

God's supply is "according to His riches in glory by Christ Jesus". The word "riches" (*ploutos*) is used in Eph 1:17 where it is describing grace. In 1:18 it describes the glory of His inheritance in the saints; in 2:7 the exceeding riches of His grace; the unsearchable riches of Christ (3:8), and finally in 3:16, the riches of His glory. These riches in the context of our passage are in glory, in the heavenly sphere. H. C. G. Moule remarks "His resources, consisting in, and so lodged in His own glory of divine power and love". The word "glory" is *doxa* (see the comments in 1:11; 2:11; 3:19,21). The Lord Jesus is the divine reservoir of divine glory. All the fulness of the Godhead dwells in Him (Col 1:19; 2:9).

20   Here in the verse that closes this section, we have the doxology with its Amen. "Now unto God and our Father be glory for ever and ever. Amen." The RV reads, "unto our God and Father", as does JND. The apostle joins the saints with him in this wonderful family relationship. In the first statement we have an association. Then Paul breaks forth in an ascription of praise. The article is used with glory; it is "the glory". This is a recognition of His nature, attributes and activities. "Forever and ever" simply means "increasing", and it will be the activity of saints throughout eternity to give our God the glory. In the context of our verse it is used as in Gal 1:5. In Eph 3:21 it is in the sphere of the church that glory is ascribed.

The expression "Amen" in this context means, according to Arndt and Gingrich, "so let is be". It is translated a number of times "verily, verily". In Rev 3:14, it is a divine title of the Lord Jesus. It is given as trustworthy and faithful, when referring to divine persons. This can be seen in Deut 7:9 and Isa 49:7, where the Hebrew word is *aman*. The RV margin of Isa 65:16 reads, "the God of Amen".

6.   The Appendage and its Praise
4:21-23

The Conclusion of the Letter

v.21 "Salute every saint in Christ Jesus. The brethren which are with me greet you.
v.22 All the saints salute you, chiefly they that are of Caesar's household.
v.23 The grace of our Lord Jesus Christ be with you all. Amen."

21   "Salute every saint in Christ Jesus", says Paul. The word "salute" (*aspazomai*) is translated "greet" in 1 Thess 5:26 and again in 2 Tim 4:21. Peter uses "greet" in 1 Pet 5:14, although in 5:13 it is rendered "salute". It is only once translated "embrace", namely in Heb 11:13, where it is speaking of the promises. It has come to mean today "to greet". The greeting is all-embracing; it is meant to enclose all who are in Christ Jesus.

Intriguingly Paul speaks of "the brethren which are with me". We cannot say who they are but evidently they are Christians who were with him at the time of writing.

22   "All the saints salute you, chiefly they that are of Caesar's household" is a greeting from all the Christians in Rome. He especially mentions some whom the gospel in its power had reached. Perhaps some were the slaves and freed men attached to the palace (Lightfoot). The writer mentioned has an interesting additional note on pp.171-178 of his valuable commentary. He notes that it is a term including vast numbers of persons, not only in Rome, but in the provinces. However, most likely it is those with whom he was particularly acquainted during his imprisonment mentioned in the epistle (1:13).

23   "The grace of our Lord Jesus Christ be with you all. Amen". The RV reads, "with your spirit". This is seen as well in Gal 6:18; 2 Tim 4:22. It is really used for the person; after all, a man takes character from his spirit. We speak of the "spirit of the man".

It is interesting that in Paul's letters **grace** forms part of the greetings as he opens his correspondence; now it comes at the close. The Lord Jesus Christ is His full title (note it in 3:21). The difference is interesting. Here He is linked with grace: in 3:21 He is linked with glory. The first time He came to earth, He brought us grace, and maintains us in that grace; when He returns, what glory will be ours (3:21)! The word "Amen" has been considered. How good to conclude such a letter with "so be it"!

We conclude the exposition of this epistle, so rich in christology, and rightly described as the Epistle of Christian Experience. In the man who wrote it we see in 1:20,21 the Purpose of an Ambitious Life; in 2:5 the Pattern of an Attentive Life; in 3:10 the Prize of an Abandoned Life; in 4:13 the Power of an Assessed Life. In these themes, we have the Exercise, Example, Expression and Experience of Paul's life. They define for us the hallmarks of true christian experience.

COLOSSIANS
T. Bentley

COLOSSIANS

Introduction

1. The City
2. The Colossians
3. The Church at Colossae
4. The Communication from Paul
5. Outline
6. Its Plan
7. Bibliography

1. The City

A hundred miles or so to the east of Ephesus lay three cities, famous in the Roman province of Asia for their dyed wools. Of these cities Laodicea, Hierapolis and Colossae, the third lay some ten to twelve miles farther inland from the other two. Laodicea, wealthy and magnificent, was the oldest and least faithful of the Seven Churches of the Revelation. Hierapolis, in addition to the dyed-wool industry, was renowned for its medicinal springs that attracted many visitors to its baths. It advanced in importance as Colossae declined. Colosse (AV), Colossae (RV) or Colassae, was in Paul's day a decaying city. Ancient records once described it as "a populous city, prosperous and great", but by the time Paul wrote to the church there, it was no more than a country town. Nevertheless, its position made it influential. It stood on the great highway between Ephesus and the Euphrates; it was, therefore, a place where new ideas and new thoughts were always likely to flourish. It was the least of the cities which were honoured with letters from Paul. Lees speaks of it appropriately as "an outstation". Not many generations after Paul's time Colossae disappeared altogether from the pages of history. This was not completely strange since earthquakes were frequent, the entire area being volcanic. It is not mentioned in the NT outside the epistle itself, to which it owes its glory now, for the letter has given the place addressed undying fame.

2. The Colossians

Colossians in NT times comprised three ethnic groups: (1) the indigenous Phrygians, (2) the Greek traders who found a ready livelihood because Of the rich trade on the great highway, and (3) the Jews, of which there was a considerable colony. It is of interest to remember that Antiochus the Great had transplanted a sizeable number of Jews from the east into Phrygia, which Paul might have had in mind when he spoke of God as translating the believer "into the kingdom of the Son of His love" (1:13 RV). There were Phrygians present at Jerusalem on the day of Pentecost (Acts 2:10). They were, of course, Jews or Jewish proselytes.

3. The Church at Colossae

It is impossible to furnish a firm date for the introduction of Christianity to Colossae and its neighbouring cities. There is, however, the possibility that amongst those "of Phrygia" who listened to the apostles on the day of Pentecost, were some from the Lycus valley. If such were the case, the gospel would have been brought into Colossae from the earliest days of the church. Internal evidence precludes any idea that Paul had himself visited Colossae (2:1). Paul had twice been through Phrygia, and yet there is no evidence that he actually came to Colossae. On his first journey through Phrygia he went from Lystra to Mysia and if he had turned aside to Colossae, it is highly improbable that Luke would not have mentioned such a fact. The second of Paul's journeys through Phrygia consisted of calling upon the churches already founded (Acts 18:23).

The assembly at Colossae appeared to have been founded as a result of the evangelistic labours of Epaphras, who himself was a Colossian (4:12). Epaphras stood in intimate relation to the assembly. He had shown Paul their love (1:8), he was a faithful minister of Christ on their behalf (1:7), and it was from this distinguished servant of God that the Colossians had learned the gospel in its original simplicity.

The relevant facts concerning the church at Colossae, which may be gathered from the NT, may be tabulated as follows: -

(a) Earliest contact with the gospel was possibly on the day of Pentecost (Acts 2:10).

(b) The assembly was founded through the preaching and teaching of Epaphras (1:7).

(c) Paul did not visit the church before his first imprisonment (2:1).

(d) Paul probably visited Colossae in the period between the two imprisonments (Philem 22).

(e) The assembly was composed of the highest as well as the lowest class - masters and slaves (3:22; 4:1) - Philemon, Apphia, Archippus, Epaphras, and eventually Onesimus. These known by name were included in the company.

(f) It had spiritual vitality (1:4) and stability (2 :5,6) and yet it was the subject of heartfelt prayer both on the part of the apostle (1:3,9; 2:1) and of Epaphras (4:12-13).

(g) It was assailed by a vicious heresy that threatened its very life (2:4).

(h) The assembly received the letter from Paul and preserved it, likely obeying its commands and heeding its precepts.

4. The Communication from Paul

I Its Penman

While there are some who will challenge the claim to Pauline authorship, there is, by and large, a greater percentage of Biblical scholars who agree that Colossians is, as it is declared to be (1:1; 4:18), from the hand of Paul. There is sufficient evidence from within the epistle to establish beyond any reasonable doubt that we are considering one of Paul's epistles. Early christian writers support the reception of the epistle as the genuine work of Paul. One of the earliest direct allusions to the epistle is found in Justin Martyn. Direct quotations are found in Irenaeus and Tertullian, both of whom cite passages from every chapter. The external evidence is strong, thus confirming the unwavering witness from the first, to the genuineness of the epistle.

Critics who voice objection to the Pauline authorship base it on the vocabulary and especially on the number of the hapaxlegomena. A.T. Robertson says, "This objection overlooks the fact that style is purely a function of subject. Vocabulary varies largely with the theme discussed" (*Paul and the Intellectuals*, p.15). It is true that words such as "believe", "justification", and "righteousness" do not appear in Colossians, but then "righteousness", for example, does not appear in 1 Thessalonians either. That "cross" is absent from Romans and "law" is not found in 2 Corinthians does not impugn the genuineness of Pauline authorship of the epistles. The apostle uses language adequate to the occasion, so the absence of terms which are found in Paul's other epistles, is because he is dealing with circumstances that are unique in Colossae.

Above all, it is not Paul who decides to write upon receiving the report from Epaphras. Far beyond his own exercise, and yet not contrary to it, is the operation of the Holy Spirit of God. It is He who takes up the human Penman and uses him to express divine thoughts in words which the Holy Spirit speaketh. The epistle is the work of the Spirit of God in divine inspiration, and being so, it is "profitable for doctrine, for reproof, for correction, for instruction in righteousness" (2 Tim 3:16).

II Its Period

There are four Prison Epistles, so-called because they come from the apostle during the time of his imprisonment in Rome, namely Colossians, Philemon, Ephesians and Philippians, and probably written in that order. That these are written *late* in the first imprisonment appears from the fact that in both Philemon (v.22) and Philippians (1:25) the apostle seems to be expecting an early release. An appropriate date for the writing of the epistle is AD 62 or 63. A general arrangement of Paul's epistles according to chronological order provides three groups:

FUNDAMENTAL:	1 and 2 Thessalonians	Instruction for young converts
(The firm base of the gospel)	1 and 2 Corinthians	Correction for the local assembly
	Romans	Doctrine of the gospel
MYSTICAL:	Colossians	The glories of the Head
(The Superstructure of union with Christ in mystical oneness)	Philemon (Personal)	
	Ephesians	The privileges of the Body
	Philippians	The corresponding practical walk
PASTORAL:	1 Timothy	The house of God
(The topmost stone of godliness and good works)	Titus	The house of God
		The man of God
	2 Timothy	

Galatians and Hebrews are undated, but closely linked in teaching. Saints are introducing legalistic practices into the assembly, causing bondage and bitterness in Galatians, while Hebrews reveals that saints are forsaking the assembly and are going back to the ceremony and ritual of a system which has been set aside in the Person and work of Christ.

III Its Purpose

There is heresy at Colossae, threatening the spiritual vitality of the church. The identifying of the heresy that assailed the testimony has given rise to an endless amount of discussion. Lightfoot's survey and suggestions are in his volume on this epistle in which the reader, in his own time, can read more fully the various and varying pronouncements on this subject.

It would appear from the epistle that Paul is dealing with a certain class of false teachers, more properly - *one class only*. The errors may vary but one set of teachers is responsible for all. These errors seem to divide themselves into three divisions, namely:

1 Those of Jewish origin:

   i. The Jewish observances with regard to food.
      2:16 "Let no man judge you in meat or in drink".

   ii. The Jewish celebration of feasts.
      2:16 "... or in respect of an holy day, or of the new moon, or of the sabbath days".

   iii. The Jewish ordinance of circumcision.
      2:11 "Ye are circumcised with the circumcision made without hands".

   iv. The Jewish adherence to Law.
      2:14 "Having blotted out the bond written in ordinances that was against us" (RV).

2 Those evidently of oriental mysticism and Greek philosophy:

   i Speculative philosophy derived from human reasoning.
      2:8 "Take heed lest there shall be any that maketh spoil of you through his philosophy and vain deceit, after the tradition of men ... and not after Christ" (RV).

   ii. Selective patrons, a coterie for whom this "wisdom" was reserved.
      1:28 "Whom we preach, warning every man, and teaching every man in all wisdom; that we may present every man perfect in Christ Jesus". Note the emphatic occurrence of the term "every man".

   iii. Seductive interpolation of intermediaries between God and men, and the consequent relegation of Christ, who is to have pre-eminence.
      2:9 "In him dwelleth all the fulness of the Godhead bodily".
      1:19 "For it pleaseth the Father that in him should all fulness dwell".

   iv. Sensitive observance of a rigid asceticism.
      2.20 "why... are ye subject to ordinances, (Touch not; taste not; handle not...) after the commandments of men".

3 Those a combination of (i) and (ii) with present Christianity:

i. That salvation came not by faith but by knowledge (*gnōsis*).
    1:4 "Since we heard of your faith in Christ Jesus".
    2:12 "...risen with Him through faith in the working of God" (RV).
ii. That matter was sinful such as the human body.
    1:21,22 "... yet now hath he reconciled (you) in the body of his flesh through death".
    2:9 "In whom dwelleth all the fulness of the Godhead bodily".
iii. That Christ did not occupy the one essential position as the only Saviour.
    1.19 "For it pleased the Father that in him should all fulness dwell".
    2:6 "As ye therefore received Christ Jesus the Lord so walk in Him" (RV).
iv. That perfection is obtainable by means known only to the initiated, and not by Christ alone.
    1:28 "... present every man perfect in Christ Jesus".
    3:4 "When Christ who is our life shall be manifested then shall ye also with Him be manifested in glory" (RV).

With such a background it is not surprising that the epistle is priceless in its description of the Person and work of Christ. Nowhere else does Paul touch such heights on this theme and it is impossible to read it without realising that Christ possesses a glory and station which can only move the soul to worship when the tremendous impact of the epistle reaches the mind. The theme of the epistle then is the pre-eminence of Christ.

The Person of Christ
In relation to God - His image: fully God, perfect Son seated at His right hand (1:13,15; 2:9; 3:1).
In relation to Creation - Its Designer, its Creator, its Sustainer (1:15,16,17; 2: 10b).
In relation to the Church - The First of firstborn sons: the prototype spiritual man, the expression of obedient Sonship; Its Head: its fulness, its storehouse of wisdom and knowledge (1:13,18; 2:3,10).

The Work of Christ
In relation to heaven and earth - Perfect reconciliation (not inclusive of the unrepentant) through His blood (1:20) of all things out of harmony with His will.
In relation to the Church - Redemption; forgiveness; life; glorification (1:14; 3:14).
In relation to the Law - Its power and penalty cancelled: its ordinances no longer obligatory (2:14,20-23).
In relation to Satan and his hosts - Overwhelming and final victory (2:15).
Paul's purpose in the writing of this epistle is, above all, so to expound the doctrine of Christ as to refute the false teaching that is threatening the Colossian church. This over-riding interest enables him to express his personal prayerful interest in the saints whom, having not seen, he loved.

(d) Its Personalities

Biographical Notes

Paul

Notices in the epistle concern mainly (1) his apostolic call, (2) his situation at the time of writing, (3) his connection with his readers and (4) the circumstances under which the epistle was to be carried to Colossae.

1. *His Apostolic call*
It was:
  i. through the will of God (1:1).
  ii. to proclaim the gospel (1:23).
  iii. more particularly to minister the long hidden mystery (1:25-28). This he proclaimed with earnestness of spirit (1:28,29), in order to present every man perfect in Christ (1:28).

2. *His present condition*
He is:
  i. in bonds, on behalf of the mystery (4:3,18).
  ii. (after Tychicus and Onesimus depart) with
       a) "of the circumcision", Aristarchus, Mark and Jesus (called Justus),
       b) of Gentile converts, Epaphras, Luke, Demas.

3. *His connection with the saints at Colossae*
  i. He had never seen them in the flesh (2:1). Epaphras laboured in Colossae with abounding fruit in the gospel (1:7).
  ii. He was constantly suffering for them as for Gentiles generally (1:24).
  iii. He beheld their order with joy (2:5).
  iv. Having heard from Epaphras of their faith and love (1:4,8), they are the subject of his constant thanksgiving and prayer (1:3,9). His continual anxiety is for them and the saints of Laodicea.
  v. He pleads for their prayers on his behalf that God will "open a door" (4:3).

4. *His directions regarding the sending of the letter*
  i. Tychicus sent to relate Paul's circumstances, and to comfort them (4:7,8).
  ii. Onesimus sent to accompany Tychicus (4:9).
  iii. The letter bears Paul's signature (4:18).
  iv. It is to be sent to Laodicea, and "the letter from Laodicea" is to be read in Colossae (4:16).

Archippus

Just as the epistle closes Paul refers to Archippus (4:17), whereas at the opening of the letter to Philemon he finds early mention (Philem 2). There Paul acknowledges him as "our fellowsoldier" and connects him with Philemon and his wife Apphia, suggesting to most readers that he is their son. The passage in 4:17 does not make clear whether he is in Colossae or Laodicea but it does reveal that he has a responsible ministry to perform and in this Paul advises him to be watchful and thorough. His association with Philemon and Apphia seems to suggest that he is in Colossae and with them is being asked to receive the escaped and now converted slave, Onesimus.

Aristarchus

He joins with the apostle in saluting the saints at Colossae (4:10). It is the first indication that he is a Jew, assuming that the term "of the circumcision" is inclusive of him, with mark and Jesus (called Justus). He was a Macedonian from Thessalonica (Acts 27:2) and went with Paul on his third missionary journey. In Ephesus he was arrested with Paul during the riot of Demetrius (Acts 19:29). He journeyed again with Paul in "Asia" (Acts 20:4), and waited for him at Troas (v.5). It is likely that he accompanied the apostle on his voyage to Rome (Acts 27:2), where according to the allusion in Colossians and Philemon, he remained with Paul during the first imprisonment. Tradition observes that he dies a martyr's death under Nero's persecution.

Barnabas

The reference to him is brief (4:10) and yet blessed. Paul honours him with his mention so as to give endorsement to Mark, the "cousin" of Barnabas (RV). He was highly esteemed by the apostle who surnamed him Barnabas, that is "the son of consolation". Joseph, as he was known, was a Levite of Cyprus, a wealthy convert who in the early days of the testimony gave over his wealth (Acts 4:36,37). It was he who introduced the newly-converted Saul of Tarsus to the apostles. Later the two were sent forth by the church at Antioch to engage in the work to which they had been called. The two men disagreed eventually over the defection of Mark. He appears to have had much influence upon Mark which Paul tacitly admitted in the final mention of his former colleague (4:10).

Demas

He is mentioned by name only as sending greetings to the Colossian saints (4:14). It appears from v.11 that he was a Gentile. He is given a further mention in Philem 24. At a later period, during Paul's second imprisonment, he is noted as having left the side of the apostle and having gone to Thessalonica, "having loved this present world" (2 Tim 4:10).

Epaphras

The only notes of Epaphras occur in Colossians and Philemon. Paul seems to infer that this faithful servant of Christ was a Colossian (4:12), and it is to him that the evangelisation of Colossae and the neighbouring cities of Laodicea and Hierapolis is accredited. He continued in such pastoral care for the saints that when serious heresy threatened, he went to Rome and made the situation known to the apostle. While with the apostle, his earnest and affectionate intercession in prayer so impressed the heart of Paul that he gives the Colossians deep insight to his solicitation on their behalf. He joins in the concluding greetings where Paul gives him high honour in the title "servant of Christ". The name Epaphras is a shortened version of Epaphroditus, but Epaphras is not the Epaphroditus of Phil 2:25.

Jesus Justus

A convert from the circumcision who sends greetings by Paul to Colossae. Nothing is known of him beyond the mention in Col 4:11. He is not among those who send greetings in the letter to Philemon. He is, however, a comfort to the apostle when the vast majority "of the circumcision has left the apostle's side.

Luke

Luke, "the beloved physician" (4:14), the writer of the Gospel which bears his name and of the book of the Acts of the Apostles, is a loyal companion of Paul for the most part of his christian life. His first appearance with the apostle is at Troas (Acts 16:10). We may learn more of him from the Acts, in which he intimates his presence with Paul during certain sections of the latter's missionary journeys by the use of "we" or "us" in the narrative (Acts 16:10-17; 20:5-21:18; 27:1-28:16). He seems to have been personally active in the preaching of the gospel, "the brother, whose praise is in the gospel throughout all the churches" (2 Cor 8:18). Luke is with Paul while this epistle and that to Philemon are being written, and it is affecting later to read the words of the faithful servant of Christ shortly before he is martyred: "Only Luke is with me" (2 Tim 4:11). As Luke is not linked with those of circumcision (Col 4:11) it implies that he is a Gentile; and so he is the only Gentile writer of the NT. His two great contributions, under God, are of inestimable value to the people of God.

Marcus

Mark, the friend of two apostles, Peter and Paul, is the writer of the second Gospel. Mark is his surname (Marcus in AV, Col 4:10; Philem 24; 1 Pet 5:13), his first name John, by which alone he is designated in Acts 13:5,13. His mother Mary was evidently in comfortable circumstances and her house was a meeting place of the Christians (Acts 12:12-17). Mark was also the cousin of Barnabas

(4:10 RV). He accompanied Barnabas and Paul on the first missionary journey as far as Perga and returned to Jerusalem (Acts 13:13). Later when Barnabas proposed that Mark should join them in another journey, Paul disapproved. This led to the separation of Paul and Barnabas, the latter taking Mark to Cyprus (Acts 15:39). Mark does not appear again till he is mentioned as sending greetings to the church at Colossae, which indicates that he is again with Paul as a cordial and comforting companion in the apostle's imprisonment. Before Paul lays down the pen forever, he writes of Mark in highly commendatory terms reflecting the value he attached to this able servant of God (2 Tim 4:11).

Nymphas

Some take the name to be feminine - Nympha (4:15RV marg.). Nymphas was an influential Christian residing either in Hierapolis or Laodicea, in whose house the church met. It appears that he was known to the apostle; possibly they met when Paul laboured in Ephesus for three years.

Onesimus

The reference in 4:9 suggests that Onesimus was a Colossian. From the epistle to Philemon, we gather that he was Philemon's slave. He escaped from his master and reached Rome as a fugitive. There he came into contact with Paul, hence with the gospel and was gloriously saved. It appears that he became an intimate associate of the apostle and his companions, but Paul took the opportunity of sending him back to Philemon that things needing to be righted between him and the master might be so adjusted as to provide the maturing Onesimus with an unrestricted path in service for his Lord. The warm recommendation of Onesimus to the Colossian church indicates the value and potential Paul saw in the one he begat in his bonds.

Timotheus

Timothy, in the AV usually Timotheus, is linked by Paul with himself in the opening of the epistle (1:1). He is thus mentioned in all the epistles of the first imprisonment except the letter to Ephesus. He was the close companion of Paul, possibly one of the most trusted of all those associated in labour with the apostle. Timid and sickly, yet he travelled far and wide in pursuit of the gospel and its truth. Once he was imprisoned; when we do not know, but the mention of it also tells of his release (Heb 13:23). The convert from Lystra joined Paul in his second missionary journey and probably accompanied him throughout the first. He was with him during the first imprisonment at Rome, was advised by Paul to "abide still at Ephesus", where he still was when the imprisoned apostle earnestly solicited his presence to Rome. It is probable that Timothy reached Paul before the latter's death, but we cannot ascertain this definitely.

Tychicus

Tychicus is identified as the bearer of two letters: Colossians and Ephesians. He was a companion of Paul during one stage of the third missionary journey (Acts 20:4). He did not proceed with the apostolic band to Jerusalem, but was left behind in Asia. He endeared himself to the apostle, being faithful in his ministry and fervent in his labours. On his arrival at Colossae he would relate the circumstances of Paul's imprisonment as well as deliver the letter he carried for the church there. Beyond the reference in this epistle, there are two more; one suggesting that he might have been sent to Crete (Titus 3:12), the other stating that he was sent to Ephesus (2 Tim 4:12). Paul could scarcely spare him from his side in those days of his final imprisonment, yet the claim of the testimony must be met even though Paul suffered through the absence of his trusted companion and "fellowservant in the Lord".

Summary

1. Christians at Rome

    i. Paul and Timothy
    ii. Associates from "the circumcision"
        Aristarchus
        Marcus
        Jesus Justus
    iii. Associates of Gentile origin
        Epaphras
        Luke
        Demas

2. At Laodicea or Hierapolis
        Nymphas

3. Either at Colossae or Laodicea
        Archippus

4. The bearers of the letter
        Tychicus (bearer also of Ephesians).
        Onesimus (bearer also of Philemon).

V Its Parallels

In the epistle of Paul to the Colossians we have a statement of doctrine concerning the deity of Christ. This statement is such that Paul gives us the whole content of the Logos doctrine, as we find it in the Gospel of John, without actually using the term "Logos". Read, for example, ch. 1:15-18 and then compare John 1:1-3,14. Other parallels exist between the Gospel and this epistle:

Col 1:17 "And he is before all things".	John 1:1-2 "In the beginning was the Word. ... The same was in the beginning with God".
Col 1:16 "In him were all things created ... all things were created by him and unto him".	John 1:3 "All things were made by him and without him was not anything made that was made."
	John 1:10 "the world was made by him".
Col 1: 15 "Who is the image of the invisible God".	John 1:18 "No man hath seen God at anytime; the only begotten Son, who is in the bosom of the Father, he hath declared him".

What is attributed to Christ in the epistle and in the Gospel alike is:

(1) Eternal pre-existence; He did not begin to be, but ever was;
(2) He is Creator of all things; therefore He is not a creature;
(3) He is the One who has revealed God perfectly and fully.

The subject could be further investigated, for example:

Col 2:12 "Through the faith of the operation of God, who hath raised him from the dead".	John 11:40 "If thou wouldest believe believe, thou shouldest see the glory of God".
Col 2:13 "And you, being dead in your sins ... hath he quickened".	John 11:44 "And he that was dead came forth".
Col 3:1-4 "If ye then be risen with Christ... then shall ye also appear with him in glory".	John 11:23,25 "Thy brother shall rise rise again... I am the resurrection and the life".

There are also evident parallels between this epistle and the Apocalypse, where coincidences of thought and even of expression occur.
Some of these are:

| Col 1:18 "who is the beginning". | Rev 3:14 "the beginning of the creation of God". |

Col 1:18 "the firstborn from among the dead"	Rev 1:5 "The firstborn of the dead".
Col 3:1 "... seated at the right hand of God".	Rev 3:21 "... as I also overcame and sat down with my Father in his throne".

The closest parallel of all, however, exists between the epistle to the Ephesians and this epistle. The two epistles throw considerable light each upon the other. A comparative reading of this epistle with that of the Ephesians is strongly recommended. While the distinct purpose of each is always present and dictates the particular phrasing of the passage, the parallel reading is always helpful. It will be seen that sometimes Colossians *supplements*, sometimes it is *supplemented by* Ephesians; sometimes a difficult and obscure passage in the one is made the clearer by the context of a similar passage in the other.

There follows three main points of resemblance

1. Similarity of time and occasion of writing.

(i) Paul is in bonds.

Eph 6:20 "For which I am an ambassador in bonds".	Col 4:18 "Remember my bonds".

(ii) Tychicus is his messenger.

Eph 6:21-22 "But that ye also".	Col 4:7-8 "All my state".

2. Similarity of plan in the Epistle.

Ephesians	**Colossians**
(i) Introduction	(i) Introduction
Salutation	Salutation
Thanksgiving	Thanksgiving
Prayer	Prayer
(ii) Doctrinal Section	(ii) Doctrinal Section
The Gospel for the Gentiles	The Gospel for the Gentiles
The Unity of the Body which has Christ for its Head. its Head.	The Greatness of Christ the Head of the Body.

(iii) Practical Section

Responsibility arising from
the Unity of the Church.
Exhortation to:
  Husband and wife
  Child and parent
  Master and slave
Concluding appeal for
watchfulness and prayer.

(iv) Conclusion

Mission of Tychicus

Benediction

(iii) Practical Section

Responsibility arising from
vital Union with the Head.
Exhortation to:
  Husband and wife
  Child and parent
  Master and slave
Concluding appeal for
watchfulness and prayer.

(iv) Conclusion

Mission of Tychicus
Salutations
Benedictions

3. Similarity of detail in both language and theme.

Ephesians 1:7	Colossians 1:14
1:17,18	1:9
2:1	2:13
2:11	2:11,13
3:6-9	1:25,27
4:15,16	2:19
4:22-24	3:9,10
5:15,16	4:5
5:19,20	3:16,17
5:22-6:9	3:18-4:1
6:18-20	4:2-4
6:21,22	4:7-8

5. Outline

I. *Personal*	1:1-8
1. The Salutation	1:1-2
2. The Fruits of the Gospel at Colossae. The Messenger Confirmed	1:3-8
II. *Expositional*	1:9-23
1. Prayer for the Saints	1:9-14
2. Pre-eminence of the Saviour	1:15-23
III. *Ministerial*	1:24-2:7
1. Paul's Ministry and the Mystery	1:24-29

6. Its Plan

1. Chapter 1:1-1:8	The Service of Christ Endorsed
2. Chapter 1:9-1:23	The Supremacy of Christ Expounded
3. Chapter 1:24-2:7	The Secret of Christ Expressed
4. Chapter 2:8-2:19	The Sufficiency of Christ Experienced
5. Chapter 2:20-3:4	The Results of Identification with Christ
6. Chapter 3:5-4:6	The Responsibilities of the interpretation of Christ
7. Chapter 4:7-4:18	The Records of Involvement for Christ

7. Bibliography

Bible Texts and Versions Cited

Text

The Greek New Testament. 1st edition 1966; 3rd edition 1975. K. Aland, M. Black, C.M. Martini, B.M. Metzger and A. Wikgren, eds. Stuttgart: United Bible Societies.

Versions

King James Version. 1611. Cited as AV.
Revised Version. 1881. Cited as RV.
New American Standard Bible. 1960. Cited as NASB.
The New English Bible. 1st edition of New Testament 1961; 2nd edition 1970. London: Oxford University Press, and Cambridge University Press. Cited as NEB.
The New Testament: a new translation by James Moffat. 1922. London: Hodder & Stoughton. New edition, revised: 1934. New York: Harper and Row. Cited as Mft.
New Testament in Modern English. 1962. J.B. Phillips. New York: The Macmillan Co. Cited as Phps.
New Testament in Modern Speech. R.F. Weymouth. 1929. Newly revised by J.A. Robertson, 5th edition. London. Cited as Wey.
New International Version. 1973. Grand Rapids, Michigan: Zondervan Bible Publishers. Cited as NIV.
Revised Standard Version. 1952. New York: Nelson & Sons. Cited as RSV.
The Holy Scriptures, A New Translation from the original languages. J.N. Darby. 1939. Stow Hill Bible & Tract Depot. Cited as JND.

General Bibliography

Alford, H. *The Greek Testament.* Vol. III. Galatians-Philemon with revision by Harrison, E.F. Chicago: Moody Press, 1968 edition.
Arndt, W.F. and Gingrich, F.W. *A Greek-English Lexicon.* University of Chicago Press, 1957.
Boyd, J. "Epistle to the Colossians" from *Assembly Testimony.* Nos. 147-162, Jan. 1977 to Aug. 1979.
Bratcher and Nida. *A Translator's Handbook on Paul's letters to the Colossians and to Philemon.* Vol.XX. Stuttgart: United Bible Societies, 1977.
Bruce, F.F. *An Expanded Paraphrase of the Epistles of Paul.* Exeter: The Paternoster Press, 1965.
Bullinger, E.W. *Figures of Speech.* London: Messrs Eyre & Spottiswoode, 1898.
Carson, H.M. (1960) "The Epistles of Paul to the Colossians and Philemon" from *The Tyndale New Testament Commentaries.* General Editor: Tasker, R.V.G. Grand Rapids, Michigan: Eerdmans Publishing Co. 7th edition, 1977.
Davies, J.M. "The Epistles to the Colossians and to Philemon" from *Precious Seed.* Bath: Somer Press, 1972.

Eadie, J. (1856) *Commentary on the Epistle of Paul to the Colossians*. Reprint. Minneapolis: James and Klock Christian Publishing Co., 1977.

Ellicott, C.J. *St. Paul's Epistles to the Philippians, the Colossians and Philemon*. London: Longmans, Green & Co., 1875.

Gaebelein, F.E. (ed.) *Expositor's Bible Commentary*. Vol. eleven. London: Pickering & Inglis, 1978.

Garrod, G.W. *The Epistle to the Colossians*. London: Macmillan & Co. Ltd., 1898.

Han, N.E. *A Parsing Guide to the Greek New Testament*. Scottdale: Herald Press, 1971.

Harrison, E.F. *Colossians, Christ All-Sufficient*. Chicago: Moody Press, 1971.

Hendriksen, W. *Colossians*. The Banner of Truth Trust. First British edition 1971.

Johnson, S.L. "The Epistle to the Colossians" from *Bibliotheca Sacra* Vol. 118, No. 471 to Vol. 119, No. 476. 1961-62.

Kelly, W. (1869) *Lectures Introductory to the Epistles of Paul the Apostle*. Bible Truth Publisher. Reprint 1970.

Kelly, W. *Lectures on Colossians with New Translation*. London. Paternoster Square.

Kent, H.A. (Jr.) *Treasures of Wisdom, Studies in Colossians and Philemon*. Grand Rapids, Michigan: Baker Book House, 1978.

Kubo, S. *A Reader's Greek-English Lexicon of the New Testament*. Grand Rapids, Michigan: Zondervan Publishing House, 1978.

Lenski, R.C.H. *The Interpretation of St. Paul's Epistle to the Colossians, to the Thessalonians, to Timothy, to Titus and to Philemon*. Minneapolis: Augsburg Publishing House, 1964.

Lightfoot, J.B. *St. Paul's Epistle to the Colossians and to Philemon*. London: Macmillan & Co., 1892.

Lightfoot, J.B. *Notes on the Epistles of Paul*. Michigan: Zondervan Publishing House, 1957 (Classic Commentary Library).

Lincoln, W. *Lectures on the Epistle to the Colossians*. Kilmarnock: John Ritchie.

Martin, R.P. *Colossians: The Church's Lord and the Christian's Liberty*. Exeter: The Paternoster Press, 1972.

Metzger, B.M. *Textual Commentary on the Greek New Testament*. London-New York: United Bible Societies, 3rd edition 1971.

Moule, C.F.D. *The Epistles to the Colossians and to Philemon*. The Cambridge Greek Testament Commentary. Gen. Editor, 1962.

Nicholson, W.R. (1903) *Colossians: Oneness with Christ*. Grand Rapids, Michigan: Kregel. Reprint. 1973.

Robertson, A.T. *Paul and the Intellectuals (The Epistle to the Colossians)*. Revised and edited by W.C. Strickland. Nashville, Tennessee: Broadman Press.

Robertson, A.T. *Word Pictures in the New Testament Vol. IV. The Epistles of Paul*. Nashville, Tennessee: Broadman Press, 1931.

Robertson, N.W. (ed.) *Expositor's Greek Testament Vol. III*. Grand Rapids: Eerdmans Publishing Company. Reprint. 1974.

Rutherfurd, J. *St. Paul's Epistles to Colossae and Laodicea*. Edinburgh: T & T Clark, 1908.

Simpson, E.K. *Words worth Weighing in the Greek New Testament*. London: Tyndale Press, 1946.

Simpson, E.K. and Bruce, F.F. *Commentary on the Epistles to the Ephesians and Colossians*. (The New International Commentary on the New Testament). Eerdmans Publishing. Grand Rapids. Michigan. 1957.

Stott, J.R.W. *God's New Society. The Message of Ephesians*. Inter-Varsity Press. 1979.

Thomas, G.W.H. *Studies in Colossians and Philemon*. Baker Book House. Grand Rapids. Michigan. 1973.

Vaughan, C. *A Study Guide: Colossians*. Zondervan Publishing House. Grand Rapids. Michigan. 1973.

Vaughan, C. "Colossians" from *Expositor's Bible Commentary*. Vol. eleven. Gaebelein, F.E. (ed). Pickering & Inglis. London. 1978.

Vine, W.E. *Expository Dictionary of New Testament Words*. Oliphants Ltd., Edinburgh. London. 1940.

Westcott, B.F. *A Letter to Asia*. Macmillan & Co. Ltd. London. 1914.

Winter, R.D. and Winter, R.H. (eds). *Word Study, New Testament and Concordance*. Tyndale House Publishers. Wheaton. 1978.

Text and Exposition

1. Personal (1:1-8)

1. *Salutation*
1:1-2

> v.1   "Paul, an apostle of Jesus Christ by the will of God, and Timotheus our brother,
> v.2   To the saints and faithful brethren in Christ which are at Colosse: Grace be unto you, and peace, from God our Father and the Lord Jesus Christ."

1 Paul is following contemporary conventions as he opens with this salutation. The writer is identified; the recipients are introduced and the greeting imparted. The form is standard but the content is spiritual. The apostle transforms the customary formula by presenting himself in relation to Christ ("apostle of Jesus Christ"); his readers in respect of their position in Christ ("brethren in Christ") and the greeting as the rich provision from Christ ("grace be unto you, and peace, from God our Father and the Lord Jesus Christ").

Practically in all his epistles Paul asserts his divinely-given commission as an apostle, literally "a sent one", the exceptions being the epistles to the Thessalonians, the Philippians, Philemon and the Hebrews (accepting that Paul is the human penman). The absence of the title of authority in Thessalonians and Philemon is due to the specially-affectionate relationship between the writer and his readers, while in Philippians "...made Himself ..." (2:7) and Hebrews "... *the* Apostle" (3:1) it is the relationship of the writer and his Lord.

The substitution of "Christ Jesus" (RV) for "Jesus Christ" is one of many approved variant readings. (*Word Study Concordance* by G.V. Wigram and R.D. Winter, p.1094). It was on resurrection ground that Paul received his commission as an apostle. In 1 Cor 15:8 the term "last of all", if taken as it stands, precludes apostolic succession. The term "Christ Jesus" is exclusively a Pauline one. Its significance is best sought within the context of the apostle's spiritual history. With the genitival use of possession it denotes the relation between Paul and Christ. He belongs to Christ as His representative, commissioned to speak on His behalf and to act for His honour. Paul was not of the Twelve, nor was it ever God's intention that he should have been so. The apostle to the Gentiles has a ministry distinct from and yet complementary to those who were appointed by the Lord to be with Him (Mark 3:14). Notice that Peter justifiably terms himself "an apostle of Jesus Christ" (1 Pet 1:1; 2 Pet 1:1). Both in grammatical usage and in doctrinal significance, the name *Christ Jesus* stands in marked contrast to that of *Jesus Christ*. Paul carefully distinguishes between the two, while at times he uses both forms in a single passage with evident discriminative meaning (Gal 2:16 RV; Eph 1:5). Rom 5 and 6 (RV) provide an interesting contrast in this connection.

We meet this expression "by the will of God" relative to Paul's appointment to his apostleship in four epistles, namely 2 Corinthians, Ephesians, Colossians and 2 Timothy. It was through the will of God that his vocation came, not by personal assumption nor from outward persuasion but by divine intention. We should always be conscious of the directive of God's will in our service. It is a sense of certainty that begets a spirit of constancy. The operative power of the will of God is conveyed by the preposition *dia* ("right through"). It is not something that begins and stops half way due to circumstances, but a power that enables the believer to remain unswayed by even the most discouraging conditions. This is seen in Paul. In 2 Corinthians he is reviewing an experience in which he even faced death (1:8). The two letters, Ephesians and Colossians, came from prison in Rome and his final captivity before eternal release gave birth to 2 Timothy (1:1), where again, he is fully satisfied that his stewardship continued unaltered.

Paul kindly involves his faithful associate, Timothy. Nevertheless the inclusion is stated in terms that are meaningful. He does not extend to Timothy the status of an apostle or the sense of apostleship although it is true that in 1 Thess 2:6 the term "apostles of Christ" appears to include Silvanus and Timothy. If it does, it is only in what may be termed a "weakened" sense and not in the way that Paul understands of himself. The same can be said of Barnabas (Acts 14:14); of Andronicus and Junias (Rom 16:7). The description that Paul gives of Timothy is one of honour and commendation. The RV renders "the brother" which suggests Timothy's unfailing fidelity in every conceivable circumstance. Following the AV the term "our brother" would link him with the Colossians in an undying fellowship. There are those who suggest that Timothy was the founder of the church at Colossae. Later exposition in this volume will indicate that the present writer favours Epaphras as the one who laid the foundation to the commencement of the church at Colossae.

2   In Paul's earlier epistles (1,2 Thessalonians; 1,2 Corinthians; Galatians) his mode of address differs considerably from what appears in every church epistle from Romans onwards. The churches are addressed as such. It is obviously the mind of the Spirit, that believers may be made conscious of their corporate testimony. The term "the saints", which with varying associations begins Romans, Ephesians, Philippians, and Colossians, serves to establish what churches are actually composed of: those who are saints by calling and are constituted "holy ones". Darby, for example, takes the term as a description of "brethren", namely, "to the holy and faithful brethren in Christ" (JND). Others treat *hagiois* as a noun, which it is in most passages. This requires that *pistois* also be taken as a noun. Then the translation would run: "to the saints and believers in Colossae as brethren in Christ". The whole expression is objective. Observe that four important relationships of the believers obtain. (1) Their relationship to God as "saints". No order or ordination of men confers sainthood. It is a work of God. It is not because of any perfection in the believer but due to the work of a perfect Saviour. The sinner who believes in Christ is set apart by God, for God and unto God. This is NT sainthood. (2) Their relationship to one another as "brethren". Saints who are essentially believers are here denominated "brethren". How vital it is to regard this act of the Spirit of God! All denominational titles that add to this are clearly not the mind or the work of the Holy Spirit. (3) "In Christ", their relationship to Christ. It is to the mystical union in the one body that this epistle and its companion epistle (Ephesians) refer. This term we must accept as embracive of every believer in Christ that forms part of and is a member of the Body of Christ. Strictly speaking, the formula "in Christ" cannot apply to any but those who are members of the Church which is His body. (4) "At Colossae", their relation to the world. This was the sphere of their testimony providing ample opportunity for the display of not only a life of holiness consistent with their divine calling, but also of harmony in keeping with their fellowship and of honour in view of their spiritual union with Christ.

There are those who see two distinct classifications in this expression, those who are "saints" and those who are "faithful brethren". First of all, the definite article indicates that only one group is in view. In the light of 2:5 it cannot be conceived that "unfaithful brethren" existed in the assembly at Colossae. Therefore, in spite of threatening error the door has not yet been opened for its entrance. If the normal greetings of the day were withheld from the saints at Colossae because of their faith in Christ, they would be assured that God their Father had not turned His back upon them. It is assumed that in the assembly the two ethnic groups, Jew and Gentile, were side by side, now one in Christ. So if the "Gentile" brother felt deprived of the customary greeting from his friends, Paul brings "grace" from God; likewise the Jewish brother was saluted with "peace", and both grace and peace were mutually shared. Darby has "and the Lord Jesus Christ" in brackets by which he indicates the words are not in the majority of manuscripts. The AV, copying from the other manuscripts, carries the expression and follows the opinion of those who impose the addition that it is in harmony with all of Paul's other salutations. If the expression is not in the original manuscript it is the only time Paul brings the greeting from the Father alone. This in no way undermines the glory of the Lord Jesus. Nowhere else does Paul say more regarding that blessed One than in this epistle.

2. The fruits of the Gospel at Colossae. The Messenger Confirmed 1:3-8

v.3   "We give thanks to God and the Father of our Lord Jesus Christ, praying always for you, v.4   Since we heard of your faith in Christ Jesus, and of the love which ye have to all the saints,

v.5   For the hope which is laid up for you in heaven, whereof ye heard before in the word of the truth of the gospel;

v.6   Which is come unto you, as it is in all the world; and bringeth forth fruit, as it doth also in you, since the day ye heard of it, and knew the grace of God in truth:

v.7   As ye also learned of Epaphras our dear fellow servant, who is for you a faithful minister of Christ;

v.8   Who also declared unto us your love in the Spirit."

3   Thanksgiving is one of the leading features of this epistle 1:3,12; 2:7; 3:15,17; 4:2. Prayer appears in 1:3,9; 2:1; 4:2,3,12. Prayer makes request: thanksgiving returns praise for the request realised. These are essential exercises in the Christian's communion with God. The epistle shows how the Spirit weaves them inextricably in perfect blending, thus recommending a similar practice on the part of the Colossians themselves, and us too. Paul's gratitude for the transforming work of grace in the lives of the Colossians is expressed in thanksgiving to God as the source of their blessing.

Many retain the plural "We give thanks", thus embracing Timothy and others in the giving of thanks. Yet it can be safely taken as the epistolary plural. Often and whenever he chooses Paul speaks of himself in the plural. The example which Paul sets in his giving of thanks shows that he is practising what he exhorts the Colossians to do (see 4:2).

"The God and the Father of our Lord Jesus Christ" is an appropriate title for the One who is responsible for all that has occurred as a result of believing the message concerning His Son. Six times in the NT the expression is used.

1. Rom 15:6: "The God and Father of our Lord Jesus Christ" is the Subject of our glory and praise.

2. 2 Cor 11:31: He is the Searcher of our hearts, the silent Observer of every motive.

3. Col 1:3: He is the Source of all blessing to whom thanksgiving is ascribed.

4. Eph 1:3: From the countless ages of eternity He has chosen us in Christ.

5. 2 Cor 1:3: In all our circumstances bounded by time He ministers His consolation and comfort.

6. 1 Pet 1:3: The future is secure in His abundant mercy, who has begotten us unto a living hope.

As the God of Abraham, Isaac and Jacob He manifests His grace in linking Himself with the patriarchs. He will fulfil all that He has promised to them, not because of what they are, but because of all that He is. As the God and Father of our Lord Jesus Christ, He manifests His pleasure in owning Christ as the perfect Man and the obedient Son, in whom all His purpose and grace will be consummated in perfection.

"Praying always for you" would seem to mean "on every occasion when I am praying for you", that is "whenever my prayers include you". Some will link the

word "always" with the phrase "we give thanks" rather than with the word
"praying". It would imply that when Paul prayed for the Colossians he always
gave thanks to God for them. It is wholesome to be always able to discover fresh
causes for the thanksgiving in the saints. Largeness of heart will never allow failure
to dim the eye to the work of grace in others. The form of the word conveys the
personal joy and benefit Paul derived from his exercise in prayer in respect of
the Colossian believers.

4   The participle *akousantes* ("having heard") gives the reason for this constant
thankfulness on the part of the apostle. It is needless to question the source of
Paul's information. It came through Epaphras. Paul had no direct contact with
the saints at Colossae. However, the present writer wonders how it was that Paul
had spent three years in Asia and that he never went into the city, an outstation
in the Lycus valley only one hundred miles from Ephesus.

The three cardinal graces of Christianity, as Darby calls them, are specified
here in association with each other (see 1 Cor 13:13; 1 Thess 1:3; 5:8 and compare
1 Pet 1: 21-22; Heb 10: 22-24). It is hope that is emphasised in the Thessalonian
writing where Paul teaches the truth of the coming. Love is clearly the point of
emphasis in 1 Corinthians for it was visibly absent though gift figured prominently.
Faith has the prime place of the familiar triad in Colossians as there was evil
teaching assailing the testimony and the belief in Christ as the all-sufficient One.
The term "faith in Christ Jesus" conveys, as in most translations, that Christ Jesus
is the object of faith. In this verse their faith is sure, whereas in 2:5 it is steadfast.
It is always a matter for sincere thanksgiving to hear of a person or persons
placing their trust firmly in Christ.

"And of the love which ye have to all saints" shows that the One who has
brought them to Himself in living faith will bring them into filial love one for
another and for all who own His Name, wherever or whoever they may be (1
John 5:1). Their love was of a far-reaching kind. It extended to all saints - the
proper relationship that should exist between all believers in Christ Jesus. Four
times Paul refers to love in the epistle (1:4,8; 2:3,14). It is a love which finds its
origin in the Spirit (1:8) and it surpasses all barriers in embracing all saints (1:4).
It creates a holy oneness, a togetherness of saints (2:2) and it completes the
dress of the new creature in Christ (3:14).

5   The RV renders "because of the hope" which suggests that the Colossians
loved all saints because they shared a common hope: being together in glory
forever. By making the hope objective it is to be understood that it denotes the
thing hoped for (cf. Gal 5:5; 1 Pet 1:3). "Hope" (*elpis*) in the NT alternates between
the subjective sense and the objective realisation, Rom 8:24 being a clear example
of its imperceptible movement from one to the other.

The verb translated "laid up" (*apokeimenēn*) occurs in only three other
passages in the NT (Luke 19:20; 2 Tim 4:8; Heb 9:27). It conveys the idea of

reservation and security. The hope is certain. Its ultimate realisation is beyond doubt as it is wrapped up in the napkin of divine promise. It is kept safely and will certainly be possessed. Paul assures that when Christ shall appear they will appear with Him in glory (3:4). Before this appearing with Him can take place, the dead in Christ must be raised, the living transformed and together be caught up to meet the Lord in the air (1 Thess 4:13-19). This great event will bring us into the eternal enjoyment of the reserved hope, our inheritance in light (1:12), that which, according to Peter, is imperishable, undefiled, unfading, reserved in heaven (1 Pet 1:4).

With "for you", the Colossians were assured that their future was secure in Christ. Nothing could hinder their attainment; their realisation of future good and eternal bliss was sure.

"Heaven" (*ouranos*) is an all-embracive word, including the ethereal heavens right up to the abode of God (Matt 5:16). The corresponding word in the Ephesian epistle is *epouranios*, an objective, used of the sphere to which the Lord Jesus has ascended (Eph 1:19-23). The latter, being more restricted, is contained in the former, so no problem exists. High in that region of effulgent delight is our hope, safely guarded at God's right hand. Contemplation on this hope will provide a reflex action. Heavenly mindedness will result. Then love to the saints will be enkindled, regarding each other with an ever-deepening family affection.

"Whereof ye heard" is the second remark Paul makes regarding the hope. "Whereof" refers, of course, to the hope. *Proēkousate* speaks of the conversion of the Colossians. Upon believing the word of the gospel they possessed the promise associated with the hope. Paul is stating the genuineness of the gospel, that revelation of God's salvation, truth in its essence, and he is also confirming the veracity of the witness borne by Epaphras. However, what is uppermost in Paul's mind is to be seen in his use of the preposition "before". He is referring to the period prior to the coming of the errorists and their heretical teaching. Ultimate faith is found alone in a Person. This is why in the next expression Paul gives an almost *personal* touch to the gospel.

6   "Which is come unto you" (*pareimi*) is usually the word reserved for the coming of a person. Is this not, however, what happens when the gospel arrives? A Person is present; a Person is presented; otherwise it is not the gospel of the glory of Christ. The word continues to refer to the abiding presence of the gospel. Its glorious effects remain, not in a passive presence but in a productive power bringing forth evidences of life. This addition is to confirm the greatness of the gospel. The Colossians are here reminded that the gospel is world-wide. What they experienced in Colossae is happening in "all the world".

Is Paul saying that all the world has heard the gospel? This would not be true, even though he must be thinking of the vast expanse of the message. Paul indicates here that the gospel establishes its truth by its suitability to all men everywhere. It is the only means by which ruined men, wherever found, can know forgiveness of sins and peace with God. The rapid progress of the gospel in those early days could also be in the apostle's mind, for as Lightfoot says in his *Epistle to the Colossians* p.132, "More lurks under those words than appears on the surface". The gradual build-up toward confirmation of Epaphras' ministry must be noted. What the Colossians heard is the same gospel as is proclaimed worldwide. They were in no inferior lot simply because it was not an apostle who evangelised them. Anything less than the apostolic gospel is false, even today. Changes have certainly introduced circumstances which are vastly different from the apostle's day, but they have never caused so much as the slightest need for any alteration in the message. Man is still a depraved creature needing God's salvation which only the gospel of the grace of God brings.

In the previous expression, the suitability of the gospel is established. Now in these words "bringeth forth fruit" it is the superiority of the gospel over all ethnic religions that is advanced. The fruitfulness of the gospel, wherever it goes, demonstrates its veracity. It is the credential which answers the spurious claims of the enemy and his counterfeit product. The form of *karpophoreō* in the middle voice stands out more significantly in contrast to the active form of the same verb in v.10. The gospel contains in itself that power to germinate and to produce fruit of itself (Gen 1:11) and after its own kind (Gal 5:22). The inward energy of the gospel, its outward expression of spiritual fruitage and its onward expansion in external growth, is what Paul avers. The RV, to give this threefold verification, reads: "bearing fruit and increasing", thereby the continuity of the gospel and its power is the more forcefully declared. This attestation to the fructifying power of the gospel cripples the theorists' claim that much more than faith in Christ is needed. But Paul strikes the triumphant note of thanksgiving and thanks God for their "faith in Christ Jesus".

"As it doth also in you" shows the local evidence of that productive gospel is noted. Away in the Lycus valley, Paul sees a fertile work of the Spirit, a company formed by the work of God who ever gives the increase (1 Cor 3:6). The "in you" being corporate, makes the assembly at Colossae what the assembly at Corinth is, "God's husbandry". Amid all the barrenness and outcrop of tares, there is in Colossae "a garden enclosed". They too knew the gospel's compelling influence. Paul's deepest concern is that the fruit, begotten by the energy of the gospel, in the power of the Spirit, will be kept entirely for the pleasure of the Lord.

In the Pauline epistles the mention of fruit incites consideration (Rom 6:22; 1 Cor 3:6; Gal 5:22; Eph 5:9; Phil 1: 9; Col 1:10).

1. Rom 6:22: The fruit of yielded members.

2. 1 Cor 3:6: The fruit of a co-ordinated ministry which God favours with increase.

3. Gal 5:22: The fruit of the Spirit in evidence in those who are energised by Him.

4. Eph 5:9: The fruit of the light (RV) displayed in a consistent walk of goodness (manward), righteousness (self-ward) and truth (Godward).

5. Phil 1:9: The fruit of righteous conduct.

6. Col 1: 10: The fruit of infinite variety.

The inevitable results of the gospel are "beautiful lives" (*karpophoroume non*) and "expanding influence" (*auxanomenon*, RV "increasing"). Every servant knows this, as did Epaphras.

Their spiritual growth has been independent of later human additions. The word "since" denotes the total sufficiency of what they had heard when the gospel reached them. No subsequent teaching of either Gnostic or Judaistic origin has contributed to their state either in the sight of God or man. Paul is consolidating the saints against every inroad of evil. It is always of serious consequences to insinuate that initial faith in Christ is insufficient for mature growth. Modern tactics have not altered. Younger believers are often upset by the approach of those who question whether what happened at conversion is potentially adequate to acquire full growth. Paul, for the second time, stresses their original acceptance of the message, "ye heard" (v.4) and again in this expression before us.

The RV places the words in this order "since the day ye heard and knew the grace of God in truth". There are those like Eadie (p.15), who give the word "knew" (*epiginōskein*) the same sense as "full knowledge". Lightfoot explains it as: "advanced knowledge, thorough appreciation'; in p.134. Others suggest it carries the idea of "acknowledge". W. Hendriksen translates: "and to come to acknowledge the grace of God" (p.52). Alford, with Lightfoot, subscribes to the intensive form of the word and adds: "but too delicately so to be expressed by a stronger word in our language" (p.198). Lenski blends the expression by reading it as follows: "they got to hear effectively, that is, got to realise" (p.28).

In this second occurrence of "grace" (*charis*) we again meet Paul's signature word. The term "grace of God", occurring some twenty-five times in the NT, is variously used. Each context will determine the sense in which the Spirit of God will have us to understand it. Hence in Titus 2:11 it is the unmerited favour of God in Christ in its sovereign, saving display of love which saves those who believe, undeserving though they be. The grace of God takes no account of "works", that is works that man may perform to merit divine favour. The only work it honours is the work of Christ on the cross. On this ground alone can God "justify the ungodly" (Rom 4:5).

"Thus", says Dr. J. Boyd, "the grace of God (v.6) is truly known by the believer". Paul is speaking of the unadulterated message proclaimed by the faithful Epaphras and tacitly infers that the "gospel" but lately introduced by the errorists is a travesty. For it is not "grace" but ordinances (2:14), neither is it of God but of the world and of men (2:8,20,22).

The present day interpreter of the "grace of God" would require to possess a correct grasp of the scheme of grace, a true knowledge of the plan of mercy if he is to gain the well-deserved compliment earned by Epaphras. The paragraph ends on this note.

7 The sense of "as ye also learned" is: "even as ye were instructed in it". Paul leaves no room for additions. The hearing, the knowing, the learning belong to the period of the gospel's presentation among them by Epaphras. These are to be understood not as stages in the christian life but as describing the experience of conversion, the historical point in one's experience when the gift of God in Christ Jesus is received. The herald of the gospel should be articulate so that men may "hear" without beclouding the gospel's glory to darken the bright horizon of its hope, nor curtailing its doctrines to impair its veracity nor mutilating its facts to distort its historical credibility.

Now the servant is named - Epaphras, the one through whom the Colossians "heard" and "learned" the truth of the gospel. The relationship of Epaphras as preacher and teacher to the Colossians is the first of three which Paul sketches in favour of Epaphras. It is by the labour of such men that a testimony to the grace of God is established in any locality. Guidelines for service are to be observed. Was this honoured servant to be content with merely preaching the gospel, seeing men and women saved and then to leave them without further instruction in the things of God? The fact that a church exists in Colossae reveals the faithfulness of Epaphras in declaring the "whole counsel of God". All gospel outreach should have as its goal the formation of a NT assembly or the establishing of an already-existing one. If, with the mention of Laodicea and Hieropolis (4:13), we are to understand that these assemblies were the fruit of Epaphras' toil, then great commendation becomes this devoted servant of Christ.

The relationship of Epaphras to Paul and Timothy is that of a "beloved fellowservant" (RV). Four people in the letter, inclusive of Epaphras, are described as "beloved": the Courier entrusted with the mail, Tychicus (4:7), the Convert not yet entrusted with the ministry, not until at least he has righted things with Philemon (4:9), Luke the Comforter (4:14).

The term "fellowservant" occurs once again in the NT (4:7). Tychicus is the one thus described. Paul kindly confirms the fidelity of Epaphras by the usage of this term and places his stamp of approval upon all that he taught. If the Colossians were disposed to adhere to specious teaching from sources the apostle could not commend, then it would mean that they were setting aside not only the credibility of Epaphras but also that of Paul and Timothy. Both Paul and Timothy found a common bond with Epaphras, for he, along with them, served the same Lord. To reject one was to reject the others and ultimately the Lord whose servants they were. Cordial relationships among fellowlabourers exist in so far as they serve the Master and Lord in accordance with His Word. Paul testifies to this as being so in Epaphras' case.

In the following clause Paul deals with the relationship of Epaphras to Christ, "who is for you a faithful minister of Christ": Epaphras is one to be trusted. If error existed in Colossae it would not have been introduced by him. He ever taught the truth and now his commendation, brief but noble, is written eternally.

It could be that there were some misgivings that the one who founded the assembly at Colossae was not an apostle. Nevertheless, Paul has clearly endorsed the service of his fellowservant and consummates it in the term "minister of Christ" (*diakonos tou christou*), which denotes the servant in relation to his Lord.

There is great uncertainty as to the reading "for you". The RV, ASV, Wey, RSV and NIV favour "on our behalf" for which manuscript evidence is preponderant. Alford, Lightfoot, Peake and Moule offer a strong case for its adoption. On the other side, J.N. Darby, Moffat, Panin, Ellicot, Eadie comply with the AV and retain the form "for you", while F.F. Bruce in his Expanded Paraphrase of the Epistles of Paul p.247 reads: "on your behalf". The U.B.S. Textual Commentary on the Greek New Testament has an explanatory note as to why a majority of the Committee prefers "for you" (*huper humōn*). "On your behalf" suggests the devotion Epaphras displayed in his service for the Colossians. He preached a pure gospel, taught right principles, endorsed it with exemplary living and agonised in prayer with and for them. Now he carries an unbiased report to the apostle of their love, as is seen in the next verse.

8   The faithfulness which Epaphras exhibited before the Colossians in his service among them marked him when he was absent from them. Paul is thoughtfully sustaining Colossian confidence in their own leader by highly esteeming the report of their love. The love of the Colossians had evidential support. Rotherham captures the meaning of "declared" (*dēlōsas*) in his translation "who also hath made evident unto us your love ..." (ENT 4th edition 1903). That there is tangible evidence of an indwelling love to enable Epaphras to declare it reminds us that love can only be known by the actions it prompts (John 3:16). The absence of the article need not present a problem. Literally it reads: "in Spirit" (*en pneumati*). The love of which Epaphras has abundant proof and now reports to Paul, has its source in (the) Spirit. Ephesians differs from Colossians in this: the former contains many references to the Spirit, whereas in the latter this is the only mention of the Spirit. Probably the errors that assailed the church restrained Paul from bringing in the Spirit more often. From the divine side, however, this is one epistle where the Spirit takes of the things of Christ and reveals them to us. Nevertheless, the reference here indicates that Paul is taking account of conditions which are of God amongst them, and certainly wrought by the Spirit of God. The more this love is seen in its vivid manifestation, the more its impulses are felt - the evidence that the Spirit of God has been in demonstrative and characteristic display (Rom 15:30; Gal 5:22; Eph 3:16-17).

The trend of thought from v.3 is easily marked by the thoughtful reader. Christian life, both personal and corporate in Colossae, finds its source in the gospel. A gospel that is of God, when believed, brings us into a right and eternal relationship with Him. The issues that stream forth prove its total reliability. The object it presents for faith is a risen and glorified Saviour. The outcome it promotes in love reaches out to all saints and the outlook it preserves in hope will neither rust nor tarnish nor thief take away.

This gospel is not to be compared with religion, past or subsequent. The stamp of divinity is upon it - "the truth of the gospel". The gospel is not confined to the narrow limits of class, creed or condition among man. It is gloriously universal. Paul said in another epistle, "it is unto all" (Rom 1:16) without exception and distinction. The inherent power of the gospel produces lasting fruit and never is drained of its life energy - it ever increases. The transforming power of the gospel is universally acknowledged in history and experience. If it were of works then grace is no more grace. The gospel is distinctly the message which tells of grace. The fact that the treasure has been put into the earthen vessel demands a human channel. Human lips, anointed by the Spirit, declare the gospel that man may hear, know and learn. Angels would fain proclaim it. The possession of the gospel involves the responsibility to propagate it far and wide. On the human side, there is a trinity of co-operation and unselfish concern for the testimony in Colossae - Paul, apostle of Christ Jesus by God's will, Timothy the brother whose genuineness is unquestioned and Epaphras, servant beloved and faithful minister. On the divine side the holy Trinity, eternal and gracious, co-exists in mediatorial grace - God the Father with resources of grace, Christ Jesus our Lord, the sole object of trust and devotion, and the Holy Spirit producing in liberal effusion His love in the recipients of the grace of God. With such a testimony of these spiritual dimensions abounding, it bowed the heart of the apostle in a twofold exercise in the sanctuary: one, in thanksgiving for its existence (v.3) and two, in prayer (v.9) that it might thrive and develop.

II. Expositional (1:9-23)

1. *Prayer for the Saints*
1:9-14

> v.9 "For this cause we also, since the day we heard it, do not cease to pray for you, and to desire that ye might be filled with the knowledge of his will in all wisdom and spiritual understanding.
> v.10 That ye might walk worthy of the Lord unto all pleasing, being fruitful in every good work, and increasing in the knowledge of God;
> v.11 Strengthened with all might, according to his glorious power, unto all patience and longsuffering with joyfulness;
> v.12 Giving thanks unto the Father, which hath made us meet to be partakers of the inheritance of the saints in light:
> v.13 Who hath delivered us from the power of darkness, and hath translated us into the kingdom of his dear Son:
> v.14 In whom we have redemption through his blood, even the forgiveness of sins:"

Not one of the writers of the Holy Scriptures has given so much of his personal devotions in prayer as the apostle, David apart. Others have prayers recorded, of these Solomon, Daniel and Nehemiah deserve special mention. One can scarcely conceive the untold blessedness derived from those seven times in the life of the Lord Jesus when the actual words He used in prayer are sublimely recorded.

Besides our blessed Lord, we do well to emulate the spirit of Paul in prayer. It is the first notification we have from the Lord regarding him: "Behold, he prayeth" (Acts 9:11). Saul, at the time of prayer, would have been found in the temple, in the synagogue or on the house-top engaged in prayer; accepting as we do his words in 1 Tim 2:2. It can be safely assumed that when he prayed in Acts 9:11 it was the first time, in the language of the well-known hymn, he breathed "that holy Name in prayer" - Lord Jesus Christ!

Nothing proved a more influencing force in his experience than the praying Stephen. Others were moved by Stephen's preaching, but the Saul of Acts 7-9 was touched by his praying. Note the elements that continued to give this future apostle a veritable baptism in prayer. The final moments of Stephen's life on earth caused the young man Saul to perceive (1) a Holy Spirit fulness, (2) an opened heaven, (3) a glorified Lord and (4) a kneeling, praying, pleading servant in touch with heaven. How Christ-like! Bring into line that praying One at the baptismal scene on Jordan's banks. Observe the opened heaven and the descending Spirit. Moreover, on the Holy Mount behold the transforming power of prayer in radiant glory. Then, with unshod feet, penetrate the shade of the Olive Garden and behold Him prostrate. It was never Paul's experience to follow Christ as one of His favoured few from His selected band, but God did not deny His servant-to-be the experience, even though it was seen in one who was as human as he.

Paul, never allowing that hallowed insight to fail in its intent, learned from Stephen on his knees far more than he ever learned at the feet of Gamaliel. He observed in Stephen a man with the ability to possess himself amid suffering, with the capacity to perceive the ministry of a glorified Man in heaven and with the Christ-like sympathy to plead on behalf of others. This the apostle himself reveals in his own prayer exercise.

Prayer is prominent in this epistle as it is in the most of Paul's writings. The constituent elements of prayer are readily recognised in the letter.

1. *Salutation* (1:2). Grace and peace. In the one, all that the goodness of God can bestow and in the other, all that the weakness of man requires.
2. *Benediction* (4:18). In Paul's case, his seal of genuineness, the hallmark of his authority is grace, grace to begin with and grace to end with. It can be observed that nothing should begin without prayer drawing upon grace (1:2) and nothing should end without prayer deserving grace.
3. *Thanksgiving* (1:3,12; 2:7; 3:15,17; 4:2). The six occasions relate in one way or another to the hope.
4. *Supplication* (1:9-14). A prayer for the knowledge of His will.
   (2:1-3). A prayer for the knowledge of His mystery.

Prayer in this epistle is expected and expressed as being characterised by steadfast continuance. What the apostle desires (4:2) he displays (1:3). It is a blessed mutuality in prayer. The two prayers of Paul (1:9-14; 2:1-3) and that of Epaphras (4:12) cause us to discern that prayer should be marked by special concern. Vagueness and wordiness in prayer are to be avoided. Detailed desire and direct demand become the character of prayer. There is a word used in this epistle which contributes to a proper concept of prayer. It is the word "striving" (*agōn*, 1:29; 2:1 and 4:12).

The prayer has three instructive features which come as a structure for consideration, that is an occasion, an objective and an order. The opening words of v.9 provide the *occasion*.

9 Paul speaks of "the day we heard of it". Heard what? The news of the gospel's fruit among them and their progressive faith and love bestir the apostle's urgency in prayer. Such seals of genuineness are always a cause for thanksgiving, but they should also generate an immediate and constant prayer exercise that they may not be broken by evil of life or lip.

The phrase "for this cause" has a particularly close parallel in Eph 1:15. It is also well illustrated by 1 Thess 2:13. The report of the spiritual progress of others should stimulate our intercessory prayers on their behalf.

"Do not cease" (*pauometha*) is the middle form of the verb *pauō*, "to cause to pause or cease". If the spiritual interests of Paul in the Colossians were to be maintained then it became imperative that he never gave up praying for them. It is this spirit of steadfast continuance that became his word of exhortation in 4:2. The apostle was a living example of his exhortative ministry. The expression conveys constancy in prayer when expounded as: "from the day we heard it" down to the period of his writing this letter, "we cease not" (Eadie).

For a similar combination to "pray for you, and to desire", see Mark 11:24. The word rendered "to pray" (*proseuchomai*) is the general word used in the NT for prayer. Prayer always serves our interests. This point is endorsed by the middle form of this word in its occurrences throughout the NT. If the general idea is to be read into the word "praying", for it is a participle, then in "desiring" or "asking" (*aitoumeoi*) there is contained something special and specific. The prefix of this compound word "to pray" (*proseuchomai*) shows that the supplicator is before the person of whom he makes request. Being face to face with God in prayer demands holiness. We are in the presence of a holy God. Then the word "desire" that Paul chooses here is the word used of an inferior making request for something to his superior. (Observe JND's note on John 14:16 in his New Translation.) This involves us in humility and godly reference when praying. The "we" (*hēmeis*) implicated not only Paul and Timothy but Epaphras also. Focus in prayer generates power. Oneness of mind and heart is often missing, hence ineffectual prayer (Matt 18:19). The fact that Paul can quote from the prayer of

Epaphras gives ample evidence to indicate that they often bowed the knee together in Rome.

"That ye might be filled with the knowledge of his will" is Paul's desire. As expressed in these words, it shows how accountable we are to the Lord to know His will. The Colossians had knowledge of the grace of God (v.6) but this is to be followed by the knowledge of the will of God (v.9) and such experiential knowledge will lead to a knowledge of God in intimacy and communion. Paul longs for development. All the epistles of the collection known as the Prison Epistles contain a similar petition (Eph 1:17; Phil 1:9; Philem 6). In the present epistle, however, it is repeated again. Compare

2:2 (RV) "that they may know the mystery of God", and

3:10 (RV) "the new man which is being renewed unto knowledge".

It is to be readily discerned that in Paul's reference to knowledge, he raised an early protest against the spurious claim to knowledge of the heretical teachers in Colossae. Thus he implies that the greatest safeguard against error is the knowledge of God's will as revealed in the word of truth.

The measure of this spiritual knowledge is to be thoughtfully considered - "*filled* with the knowledge of his will". "Ye might be filled" is the subjunctive form of the verb *plēroō* suggesting that the filling is experimental. Believers can be possessors of the saving grace of God and fail to make progress by not apprehending the mind and will of God. The verb, being in the passive voice, shows that the filling is the work of a power outside the believer. It is God who fills the submissive and obedient saint with this spiritual knowledge. The Lord Jesus taught this in His ministry (John 7:17). Notice that the plural form of the word stresses the corporate nature of the experience. Paul is addressing the assembly, so corporate experience is in view. Not only some individuals of the company in Colossae, but the whole company as a whole is to know the work of God in them. Paul is requesting that the saints may have a conscious infilling of the knowledge of God's will, and that it will be constant, an ever-continuing process.

Paul, by the Spirit, uses a stronger word *epignōsis*. This is in contrast to the simpler word found in the language of the Gnostics. It would seem to mean that it is not only "recognition" but "further additional knowledge". This richer knowledge is thorough and deep: a comprehensive acquaintance with God's revelation of Himself in His Word. Here is the marvellous privilege of all believers, not as the Gnostics infer that the opportunity is open only to the initiated ones.

The subject is God's will. The will of God is the expression of the character of God, that is, the divine will partakes of the same infinite perfection as is inherent in the Godhead. It is possessed of the full perfection and authority of God. Any claim to a possession of the will of God which does not conform to its full intrinsic moral and spiritual values is certainly not the will as revealed to us in the Holy Scriptures. It can only be judged as spurious. The Spirit of God never leads contrary to the revealed mind of God.

The term "his will" occurs in the companion epistle, Ephesians (note 1:5; 1:9 and 1:11,12). Such passages reveal the will of God in active exercise as the expression of His divine sovereignty. This may be defined (as far as definition is possible) as God's holy limitless and purposeful activity at work for the eternal blessing of all who willingly respond in obedience to His Word.

The will of God is also expressive of His divine holiness. To flout His commands and appeals is to deny His holiness and the challenge it makes in our own lives (1 Thess 4:3; 1 Pet 1: 15-16).

Furthermore, the will of God is expressive of divine wisdom. "His will is best" sounds like an over-simplification; yet it is verily true. The path marked out for the people of God in His Word is that which best serves divine pleasure, for He knows. None can improve upon the divine pattern. Its design displays His wisdom and governs our approach in worship, service and testimony. This is the purport of Paul's petition "that ye might be filled with the knowledge of his will". The infinite sufficiency of divine grace will strengthen us on the one hand to meet the requirements of the sovereign Lord, and on the other hand to conform to the claims of a holy God, so that we shall be able to enjoy such mutual fellowship with Him as no heart can conceive and no tongue express.

The phrase "in all wisdom and spiritual understanding" conveys (i) the perception of the will of God and (ii) the application of the will of God. The former supplies the means whereas the latter suggests the manifestation of the will of God. No doubt the RV rendering offers this concept more clearly by "in all spiritual wisdom and understanding". Paul avers, perhaps in a veiled way, that the wisdom of which he speaks is not the wisdom of this world, but of the Spirit. The wisdom of which James writes as being "from above" (3:17) possesses other delightful and divine characteristics. Joseph perceived the mind of God for his life and the moment came when he displayed practical understanding of that will and fled from evil. Sadly, David likewise had a clear perception of that will but when tempted he did not apply what he knew and hence fell while Joseph fled.

The Colossians will do well to acquire a divine infilling of the knowledge of His will by means of the Spirit imparting a clear perception of that will, so that when evil in any form approaches and appeals, they will know, as a result of experience, how to deal with the situation. It must appear evident that Paul never prays for knowledge as an end in itself. The Spirit would enable the saint to use the knowledge aright in applying it to his daily life in every circumstance.

10 "That ye might walk worthy of the Lord" is taken by some to be the second petition of the prayer. Is it not more correctly the objective of the prayer? It leads on from the application of spiritual wisdom into a walk that is well pleasing unto the Lord. How different from the bombastic claims of the Gnostics with their emanations, demigods and esoteric knowledge. Paul, in a down-to-earth way, presents a truly humbling objective - "that ye might *walk*". It is the norm of

Christianity for our conduct to correspond to our calling. The aorist tense presumably regards the "walk" as whole and one. In *A Letter to Asia* (1914) p.39, observe how B. F. Westcott paraphrases the text: "that your walk may be worthy". This is good, for it is not merely part of the walk that is in view, but the conduct and course of life in its entirety.

Paul in his earliest epistle gives nearly the same phrasing as here - we have "to walk and to please God" (1 Thess 4:1). In this verse it is "worthily of the Lord" (RV), undoubtedly meaning Christ. In other passages Paul uses similar language (1 Thess 2:12; Phil 1:27; Eph 4:1). Dr. G.W Thomas calls these lovely exhortations "some of the possibilities of grace". A walk worthy of the Lord would be worthy of His Person and work. This brings us yet again to the basic requirement for the believer's life - the knowledge of Himself as revealed in the word of God.

Areskeian ("pleasing") is giving *complete satisfaction*. The exhortation, we have seen, is "to walk and please God". The example reminds us of its possibility, Enoch "walked" and "pleased" God (Heb 11:5). The word in early times had a bad sense. Lightfoot offers usages, explaining it as descriptive of "ingratiating oneself with a sovereign or potentate and beautifully adds, "towards men this complaisance is always dangerous, and most commonly vicious... but towards the King of kings no obsequiousness can be excessive" p.137. The aim in the believer's life is to be constantly anticipating *His* will so that in everything he may be well pleasing unto the Lord (2 Cor 5:9).

The source of this river of spiritual life is in the "*thorough* knowledge of his will". Its main stream flows steadily in the course of a life "well-pleasing" unto the Lord. Like the Edenic river it opens out into four. If we compare the figure of the blessed man of Psalm 1, the root of this spiritual tree is "the knowledge of his will"; its strong trunk "the walk worthy of the Lord". The four present participles that follow form the branches. The figure of the tree is suggested by the reference above in 1:6.

Four aspects of the believer's life and conduct are presented in these four participial phrases, namely:

    v.10 *karpophorountes* - being fruitful or yielding

    v.10 *auxanomenoi* - increasing or growing

    v.11 *dunamoumenoi* - being strengthened or empowered

    v.12 *eucharistountes* - giving thanks or offering thanks

"Being fruitful in every good work" shows that variety marks the fruitful life of the Christian. Every deed of righteousness would be in view. Usually a tree produces one kind of fruit, but this tree of spiritual life is omnifarious - all kinds of fruit abound. Fruitfulness in *every* good work of every kind is the holy effect of union with Christ (John 15). There is no excuse for an inactive Christian. He is called to serve in a God-given capacity under the direction of the Holy Spirit (1 Cor 12) and in the anticipation of the soon-coming Lord (Mark 13).

"And increasing in the knowledge of God" suggests an experience of spiritual growth and enlargement. The reading is not clear. It is variously rendered:

"increasing *by* (as a result of) the knowledge of God" (RV margin). As dew or rain nurture, so the life of the believer matures as a result of personal communion with God. True development results from a knowledge of His grace (v.6), then a knowledge of His will (v.9) and also from a knowledge of Himself.

11 "Strengthened with all might" implies the continual impartation of divine strength which comes by the power of the Spirit (Eph 3:16). If this spiritual outgrowth of divine life is to withstand opposing elements, it will require stamina. Paul draws deeply on power in his prayers, and as here, he is assured God will habitually supply the needed strength to stand and withstand. The expression concentrates upon the root idea of power, "empowered with all power". There is no limit to "all" power. The "all's" in the prayer are embracive: all wisdom, all pleasing, all might and all patience.

The power is not proportional simply to the recipient's need, but to the divine supply, as the next expression suggests - "according to his glorious power". The full outshining of God's moral excellence toward man is displayed in the gospel. He has an undiminished supply of power for the recurring needs of His people. This He liberally dispenses in a manner consistent with His glory. But to what purpose? Here it is not the achievement of heroic acts, but the passive evidence of spiritual qualities.

"Unto all patience and longsuffering with joyfulness" is certainly a tremendous aim if not indeed somewhat surprising. Trench, with typical skill, distinguishes thus:

Patience is bearing the *ill-will* of persons.
Longsuffering is bearing *evil things*, such as pain, or distress, which God may send.

Lightfoot explains:

Patience or endurance is the temper which does not easily succumb under suffering: its opposite is "cowardice" or "despondency".
Longsuffering is the self-restraint which does not hastily retaliate a wrong: its opposite is "wrath" or "revenge".

Those worthy definitions lead to this conclusion: (1) Patience means "no giving-up", (2) longsuffering infers "no giving-back", while (3) "with joyfulness" suggests "no giving-in". The first illustration is that of Job on the ash-pit, bereaved, boil-stricken, beset, yet God blesses. The second is Stephen, battered, yet bending to pray for his assailants. The third is Paul and Silas, bound and bleeding, yet bending in praise to God.

Paul is on target as he prays, for he knows nothing puts more strain on the Christian's strength than the passive virtues he himself knows "as sorrowful, yet always rejoicing" (2 Cor 6:10, RV).

12 "Giving thanks unto the Father" is the fourth of these continuous features of spiritual life and vitality. Trench (p.191) states it is "one manner of prayer...

which ought never to be absent from any of our devotions (Phil 4:6; Eph 5:20; 1 Thess 3:18; 1 Tim 2:1), namely, the grateful acknowledgement of past mercies as distinguished from the earnest seeking of future". He goes on to note: "it will subsist in heaven (Rev 4:9, 7:12)".

This is the only aspect of prayer that will continue when the journey on earth is over. Prayer is the crowning point of christian effort. Our relationship with God as Father must never be denied nor dismissed from the mind of the believer. Modern claimants in the name of feminine equality clamour for the removal of every vestige of the Fatherhood of God from christian prayer, praise and preaching. Colossians is still timely: "Continually giving thanks unto the *Father*", no matter who or what opposes.

"Which hath made us meet to be partakers of the inheritance of the saints in light" is the first of four causes of gratitude to the Father. The word Paul uses does not suggest any thought of merit on the part of the believer. *Hikanōsanti* ("made meet") used only here and in 2 Cor 3:6 means "to make fit, or competent". A.T. Robertson renders the expression as "to the Father who qualified you". The aorist indicates when this began. It points to the time when the Colossians were converted to God. Then they were given the new nature, they were born of God; not only providing them with a title to the inheritance - the authority to possess it but also the capacity to enjoy that to which they have been introduced.

The only places in the NT where *meris* ("partakers") is found are worth noting, namely, Luke 10:42; Acts 8:21; 16:12; 2 Cor 6:15. Those places where *klēros* ("inheritance") is found are: Matt 27:35; Mark 15:24; Luke 23:34; John 19:24; Acts 1:17,25,26; 8:21; 26:18; 1 Pet 5:3 and, as with *meris*, in Col 1:12. Of these occurrences there is only one other passage, which along with our verse here, contains the two words now translated as "share" and "lot", that is, Acts 8:21. Is Simon to be viewed in eternal contrast with the Colossians who had something he had not? I judge so. How eternally grateful we will be to the work of God in making us competent to share the sainted heritage in light.

En tō photi may represent "that is in light" or "that are in light". "The portion of the saints", writes Lightfoot, "is situated in the kingdom of light".

13   If in the previous verse we were taken in mind to the Passover of Josh 5, then in this one we are carried further back in thought to that of Exod 12. Thanksgiving abounded on both of these occasions. As a mighty victor would rescue captives from the tyrannical power of a vanquished foe, so God has rescued us out of the kingdom of darkness.

The aorist form of the verb *rhuomai* (RV "delivered") also directs to the moment of conversion when as sinners we trusted Christ for salvation. It was then that the deliverance was effected absolutely and completely. However, it also summarises the means by which the rescue was affected for the word used by the Spirit of God cogently portrays the inceptive and vigorous activity of God which operated towards us in spite of our total inability to release ourselves from the clutches of darkness. There is also an emphasis on the difference between the two modes of existence - where we once were *under* "the power of darkness", and where we are now *in* "the kingdom of his dear Son".

"The power of darkness" means the domination which darkens exercises in the unregenerate. "Darkness" (*skotos, skotia*) is absence of light. It can be viewed in different aspects.

1. Literal - John 6:17; 20: 1.
2. Symbolical of what is either spoken or done in secret - Matt 10:27; Luke 12:3; 1 Cor 4:5.
3. Moral and spiritual - Matt 6:23; John 3:19; Acts 26:18; 2 Cor 6:4; 1 Pet 2:9; 1 John 1:6.
4. Mental or intellectual - Rom 2:19 (note the passive form of the verb in Rom 1:21 and Eph 4:18).

It is used descriptively of:

5. The world in its present state before God - John 1:5; 12:35; Eph 6:12 which is symptomatic of the powers that exercise their authority over it, Luke 22:53; Col 1: 13.
6. The place of punishment - Matt 22:13; 2 Pet 2:17.
7. The unenlightened state of those who know neither God nor His prophetic counsels *in futuro* - 1 Thess 5:4,5.

Paul would have the Colossians know that the completeness of their deliverance prohibits any predisposition to seek either the aid or advice of those agencies the power of darkness utilises. Many today, not in the good of this truth, find themselves bitterly oppressed, having a predilection for these spiritual forces of wickedness to which they were once in bondage.

Metestēsen ("translated" RV) is "an old word", says A.T. Robertson in *Word Studies* p.477, Vol.1, "used to signify the deportation of whole peoples to distant lands by arbitrary conquerors (compare 2 Kings 17:6). The expressive term declares the action of God's saving power, which does not stop with deliverance from the power of darkness but continues in our transference into the kingdom of His dear Son. Once again the tense points to the moment of conversion when upon believing we were lifted out of our original state and dwelling - darkness - and were carried (brought NIV) into the glorious reality of Christ's moral sway in our hearts by grace. The Pauline use of *basileia* (AV "kingdom") is usually futurist, referring primarily to the visible manifestation of the kingdom when Christ comes to reign. Seven times in the epistles the kingdom is assigned to the Lord Jesus; of these, only two would appear to have application to the present phase of the kingdom, which are: (1) Eph 5:5 designating those who do not constitute His kingdom and (2) here in the present verse indicating those who do.

"The Son of His love" (JND) can be understood in two ways:

1. The Son who *reveals* the Father's love (Lightfoot), or
2. The Son who *is the object* of the Father's love (Ellicott).

The expression is comparable to that of Matt 3:17 and 17:5 where divine, unoriginated and uninterrupted affections are expressed by the Father for the Son.

14 Three issues emerge from a consideration of this delightfully assuring statement, "in whom we have redemption":

1. that redemption is a deliverance as a result of a ransom paid;
2. that there are those who are in present permanent possession of this redemption;
3. that union with Christ is the only means by which redemption is possessed.

The first observation (as above) is derived from the meaning of the word *apolutrōsis* (redemption), used ten times in the NT. Its meaning declares not only a deliverance *per se*, but also a deliverance brought about by the payment of a ransom price. In nine of the occasions where this word occurs, it is the costliest of "king's ransoms", to quote E.K. Simpson (see below), the infinitely precious blood of the Lamb, the flawless counter-ransom.

The words for redemption and its associated themes, employed by the Holy Spirit in the NT, can be collected under two groups:

1. Those which present the idea of purchase at a price;
2. Those which stress the thought of release by a ransom.

The first group is composed of three great words which deserve greater development than is possible here.

i) *Agorazō* translated "bought" in 1 Cor 6:20; 7:23; 2 Pet 2:1; Rev 5:9 (JND note); 14:3,4 (JND). This verb is derived from a word which means "a forum or a market-place" and therefore conveys the action "to buy or purchase". Each of the passages noted will clearly infer, if not directly state, the immensity of that price - the blood of Christ.

ii) *Exagorazō* ("redeem") occurs four times in the NT and means "to buy back". See Gal 3:13; 4:5 where the price is again the precious blood of Christ.

iii) *Peripoieō* ("purchase") has an explanatory occurrence in Acts 20:28 showing that the object acquired has not only an irreducible price, but that it is also obtained in the interest and for the pleasure of the purchaser.

   The second group includes:

i) *Lutroō* ("redeem") finds three occurrences in the NT (Luke 24:21; Titus 2:14; 1 Pet 1:18). In the last two references the death of Christ is stated as the means of redemption.

ii) *Lutron* ("ransom") is found in Matt 20:28; Mark 10:45 again, where both usages constitute the death of Christ as the ransom by which the sinner is freed.

iii) *Antilutron* ("ransom") has a singular usage in 1 Tim 2:6. The emphasis is on the substitutionary character of the ransom.

iv) *Lutrōsis* ("redemption") is used of the redemptive work of Christ providing deliverance through His death, from the guilt and consequences of sin (Heb 9:12).

v) *Apolutrōsis* ("redemption") is used in Rom 3:24, where justification is made possible by the ransom having been paid. Likewise, deliverance in Eph 1:7 and Col 1:14, is accomplished on the basis of a ransom paid. See Luke 21:28; Rom 8:23; 1 Cor 1:30; Eph 1:14; 4:30; Heb 9:15. Even in Heb 11:35, where the word appears to be loosely employed, the deliverance not accepted resolves itself into a ransom refused, observed E.K. Simpson (*Words Worth Weighing*, Tyndale Press 1946).

The expression "we have" affords little comfort to the errorists assailing the Colossian saints. Here was something the Colossians had already and nothing could terminate their possession. It was permanently theirs as it is indeed the possession of all who, by faith, have been brought into living union with Christ, the Son of the Father's love. Diffidence has no portion here. The Christian can rest with undisturbed repose upon the faithful testimony of God's word. What the Colossians had was not a mere initiation "but a glorious redemption because of the accomplishment of Christ upon the cross when He gave Himself".

It must now be noted that the sentence begins with a pronoun "in whom". By the use of this relative pronoun *hoi*, which has its antecedent in "the Son of his love", a stupendous sentence about Christ has commenced. Before considering how this Christological sentence continues, notice that the expression "in whom" means "in union with Christ". This living union with the risen Christ is brought into operation the moment the soul trusts the Saviour. It is then that the deliverance is effected, not to be followed by a later bondage. The price will never have to be paid again nor will the procured release ever relapse. How gladly we sing:

> "Payment God will not twice demand,
> First at my bleeding Surety's hand
> And then again at mine."

Let not the omission of "through his blood" in JND, RV or NIV offend. Textual authorities are for the most part agreed. The interpolation in certain manuscripts is simply a copy of Eph 1:7. The word "redemption" as we have seen, infers that the price has been paid and if, as we believe, Paul did not include it here, it was not because he questioned the means of redemption nor had he any compunction about mentioning the blood in his Colossian letter, for v.20 has it with eternal imprint. The Christological passage which follows lays stress on the glories of the Redeemer, so the words "in whom we have redemption" conform to the

Holy Spirit's pattern and purpose to focus attention upon the personal glory of our Lord Jesus Christ.

Aphesis means "forgiveness or dismission", that is, our sins can never be recalled against us, who in union with Christ through faith possess this redemption. Eadie (1856) puts it well when he says, "but forgiveness passes through no intervention - it comes at once from the cross to the believing soul". The phrase we are now considering is spoken of as being in apposition with redemption (*apolutrōsis*). The significance of this concept lies in the fact that "forgiveness of sins" is the central feature of redemption. If this main theme of the gospel is absent from our preaching, then it is a powerless message verging on the philosophy which Paul denounces later. Man needs release through a ransom paid. This provides the removal of all the consequences of his sins on a basis that establishes the righteous character of God. This the cross provides. This we must preach. A comparative reading with Eph 1:7 will disclose that the word used for sins in that verse is not the same as the one used here in Colossians. There is, however, no real difference in the import of the two words, the difference lies in the figure of speech used.

Before studying the passage ahead, take account of the close parallel between vv.12-14 and Acts 26:18. Common to both passages are four words: *exousia* (power), *klēros* (inheritance), *aphesis* (forgiveness) and *hagioi* (saints). Does it not reveal the unchanging nature of the message? Is any alteration required that a challenging situation must be met by a new set of ideas? The language of Paul's testimony in Acts 26 is that of the commission he received from the glorified Christ at God's right hand. It is gloriously comforting that Paul does not need to derive his terminology from that of his opponents. The stream of divine truth still provides resources, unformed by human touch, that are sufficient, in the power of the Spirit, to bring down those who oppose. Neither will Saul's armour suffice even though it gleamed like Goliath's.

2. *Pre-eminence of the Saviour*
1:15-23

v.15 "Who is the image of the invisible God, the firstborn of every creature:

v.16 For by him were all things created, that are in heaven, and that are in earth, visible and invisible, whether they be thrones, or dominions, or principalities, or powers: all things were created by him, and for him:

v.17 And he is before all things, and by him all things consist.

v.18 And he is the head of the body, the church: who is the beginning, the firstborn from the dead; that in all things he might have the preeminence.

v.19 For it pleased the Father that in him should all fulness dwell;

v.20 And, having made peace through the blood of his cross, by him to reconcile all things unto himself; by him, I say, whether they be things in earth, or things in heaven.

v.21 And you, that were sometimes alienated and enemies in your mind by wicked works, yet now hath he reconciled

v.22 In the body of his flesh through death, to present you holy and unblameable
and unreproveable in his sight:
v.23 If ye continue in the faith grounded and settled, and be not moved away from
the hope of the gospel, which ye have heard, and which was preached to every
creature which is under heaven; whereof I Paul am made a minister."

We have already noted how this great sentence about Christ is begun with the
relative, *hoi* (whom), referring to the Son of His love. The sentence is carried on
by two more relatives *hos* v.15; *hos* v. 18 and the recurring personal pronouns
autos as follows:

Whom:	"in whom" v.14	- The Saviour of redemption;
Who:	"Who is" v.15	- The Image of the Invisible God;
Him:	"for in him" v.16	- The Originator of Creation;
Him:	"through him" v.16	- The Instrument by which Creation came into existence;
Him:	"unto him" v.16	- The Goal of Creation;
He:	"and he" v.17	- The Pre-existent One;
Him:	"and in him" v.17	- The Sustainer of all things;
He:	"and he" v.18	- The Head of the body;
Who:	"who is" v.18	- The Beginning of the new creation;
He:	"that he" v.18	- The Pre-eminent One;
Him:	"for in him" v.19	- The All-sufficient Saviour;
Him:	"and by him" v.20	- The Means of reconciliation;
His:	"... his cross" v.20	- The Suffering One, whose death makes peace.

It is clear from the foregoing that Paul has reached the heart of the epistle.
We now approach a passage, which for depth of thought and sublimity of
doctrine, stands unsurpassed in all the wonderful pronouncements of divine
revelation. It is our privilege to gaze upon the Person of the Lord Jesus Christ
whose glory pervades the whole passage. The comparison can be made with
the Tabernacle of which the ark is the centre of attraction. We have known
emancipation from Egyptian thraldom and the promise of an inheritance into
which we have fitness to enter. We have been to the altar where the ransom
price has been paid and forgiveness received. Now the light of God shines
upon the anti-type of the ark which stands in that earthly sanctuary, and we
behold His glory! The passage, unique in itself, blends in perfect harmony
with other references and supplies its complementary portion and
supplementary detail to the Christological teaching of the NT. Evident parallels
appear if a comparative reading of this passage is made with John 1:1-18; Phil
2:6-9 and Heb 1:1-3. The Spirit of God is pleased to give each of these passages
a uniqueness readily observed in the key word used with reference to the
Person of Christ. *Logos* (Word) is John's significant and singular term. *Eikōn*

(image) is, as we shall see, the word of consequence in the Colossian passage. *Morphē* (form) provides Paul with the decisive term that infers the deity of Christ in the Philippian letter. *Charaktēr* (express image) suits the purpose of the Hebrew letter, for no one, either angel or man, can be the express image of God's substance but the Son.

In the verses before us, the Person of Christ Jesus our Lord is presented in a threefold relationship, namely:

1. v. 15a In relationship to God - "image (*eikōn*) of the invisible God
2. vv.15b-17 In relation to Creation - "firstborn (*prōtotokos*) of all creation";
3. v.18 In relationship to the Church - "head (*kephalē*) of the body".

The related aspects of His Person and work are continued through vv.19-22, namely,

v.19 God's pleasure is that all saving fulness is to dwell (infinitive) in Him;

v.20 God, by Him, is to reconcile (infinitive) all things unto Himself;

vv.21-22 All those reconciled (in the church) He is to present (an infinitive) blameless.

15   Paul's statement, "Who is the image of the invisible God" is confirmed in 2 Cor 4:4 which is another evidence that Paul is not merely adopting the language of his opponents, as is postulated by so many late and modern exegetes. The repeated inference that Paul is borrowing from contemporary language to defeat the errorists deprives the Spirit of God of His sovereign originality of thought and word, and ignores the plain statement of 1 Cor 2:13 which JND renders succinctly: "which also we speak, not in words taught by human wisdom, but in those taught by the Spirit, communicating spiritual (things) by spiritual (means)".

The text begins with the relative "Who", which refers to Christ as the Son of His love (v.13 RV). The term "Who is" confirms the ever-existing nature of the truth stated. Questions are raised as to whether the apostle is referring to Christ in His pre-existent state, incarnate, or glorified state. Does not the term imply all three? Primarily, in deference to the contextual development of the Son's glories, His pre-existence is in view. If that is established, then in Incarnation what He ever was He continues to be, and so too in the present as a glorified Man at God's right hand. Here is something that is inherent in Himself, not the result of creative intent, as in the case of man (Gen 1:26-27). Language fails us, as always, when the essential glory of Christ is being expressed, but it would be understandable to say that there was never a point in time or eternity when Christ as Son was not what He is "(the) image of the invisible God". Paul's is beginning antecedent to time. Let us understand it in this light, then we shall see clearly Paul's use of the word "image" in this its august application. See Trench pp.49-53 (1953).

In the word "image" we have not merely the idea of

(a) representation, that is, the divine "copy" or "likeness" and
(b) manifestation, that is, the visible representation, but also
(c) real, essential embodiment.

While "likeness" is implied in the word "image", "image" is not involved in the word "likeness". This explains why Paul never speaks of Christ as "the likeness of God". Due to Arian error the early church exponents of truth became rightly aware of the inherent weakness of "similar" as compared with the unquestionable force of "same", though their form has only a diphthong to distinguish them. Perfect resemblance pertains but much more. Ellicott, in this instance snubbed by A.T. Robertson (strangely enough), puts it well when he observes: "that christian antiquity has ever regarded the expression 'image of God' as denoting the eternal Son's perfect equality with the Father in respect of His substance, nature and eternity" (p.125, 1875).

Paul has therefore established irrevocably the exactness of the Son's likeness to the Father, nevertheless, it is not so much the exactness that is emphasised here but its visibleness. *The Incarnation did not create visibleness: it only displayed it.* This is the whole import of "image" in this context. It is the Son's uncreated, inherent, self-subsisting nature to be what He is - the visible representation of God. This He unfolds in the reply to an enquiring Philip, "He that hath seen me, hath seen the Father also" (John 14:9). Oriental religions, like their predecessors, challenge this truth. What is needed today is a clear presentation of the unquestionable supremacy of Christ based on a sound spiritual exposition of these statements of divine truth. It is true that Paul was dealing with Gnosticism and Judaism, but their offsprings abound today. They are all too eager to cast a shadow upon the glories of our Lord Jesus Christ as the all-sufficient One. Apostate Christendom houses those who impugn this doctrine. Presentation of the truth of Christ is best accomplished by sound propagation of the truth concerning Him.

The Christian's Christ is One to whom is attributable all that is conceivable of God according to divine revelation. This is the import of the expression "image of God" in this context. John Heading has a useful paragraph on other uses of the word "image" as well as its comparative reading in 2 Cor 4:4 (see Second Corinthians, J. Heading, 1966).

For "the firstborn of every creature" the RV reads "the firstborn of all creation". The first part of v.15 tells us what Christ is in Himself in relation to God - "the image of the invisible God". Paul now unfolds in the second part of the verse what Christ is in Himself in relation to creation. He is "the firstborn of all creation". Great caution is required as we approach this phrase, for both ancient and modern Arians contend that Christ is here called a "creature", albeit the chief one created by God.

Paul's language in this and the verses following nullifies such a notion. He uses *prōtotokos* ("firstborn"), not *prōtoktistos* ("first created"). In the context, "first" has nothing to do with time or a date. The appearance of the Son (as we sing, "late in time behold Him come") does not alter the divinely-stated fact that He is "the firstborn of all creation". "Firstborn" denotes rank. The title indicates Christ's pre-eminence over all creation, while it does not imply a commencement of His Being for He is not only the pre-existent One, but also eternally pre-existent as the passage so clearly affirms. The objective construction of the text prevents His being regarded as belonging to the class of created beings. All creation having been produced by His creative power marks Him out as distinct from it in firstborn dignity. Since Christ occupies His place relatively as "firstborn of all creation-, He exercises the right of primogeniture as the Lord of all creation, confirming the words of Heb 1:2 "heir of all things".

The title "firstborn" is used of Christ here and in v.18. It is also applied to Him in Rom 8:29; Heb 1:6 and Rev 1:5. There is a clear Messianic reference in Ps 89: 26-27 which heralds Christ's millennial rule. Each of these occurrences confirms the meaning of "firstborn" as being one of honour, rank and dignity. The time factor does not appear in these usages. Ephraim, for instance, is spoken of by Jehovah as "my firstborn" (Jer 31:9), and earlier in Exod 4:22, Israel as a nation is similarly described. God speaks of His earthly people in this way because of their covenant relationship with Himself, their special rights and privileges, their rank and their destiny. Job speaks of "the firstborn of death- to denote the one who has pre-eminent power over death (Job 18:13). Compare Col 1:18. Isaiah, enlarging upon the period of millennial peace, writes, "the firstborn of the poor", that is, the One who is pre-eminently poor (compare 2 Cor 8:9) "shall feed, and the needy shall lie down in plenty" (Isa 14:30). So they are not strange terms that Paul is using. His readers will at once acknowledge their exactness in stating what the Son of God is.

16   In the phrase "for by him were all things created", *hoti* ("for" or "because") is used to give the reason and explanation of the title given to Christ, firstborn of all creation. He is not only superior to every creature, but He is also Himself the agent in the work of creation. Six times Paul uses the phrase "all things" (vv.16-20), which in his day was taken to denote the universe. This doubtless is the meaning of the expression though the word "universe" itself is not a NT word.

Ektisthē ("were created") is the aorist indicative of the verb *ktizō*, "to create". In Christ *creation took place* as a definite historic act. This truth conforms to what we have in John 1:3 concerning the Word. "All things were made by him; and without him was not anything made that was made" (compare 1 Cor 8:6 RV). The phrase "by him" or as in RV "in Him" has two prepositional counterparts in the verse. They are meaningful expressions revealing Christ's creative power and supremacy.

1. *In Him*: Christ is acknowledged as the conditioning cause of creation. His intrinsic power gives character, meaning and unity to "the" all things that are created. So creation exists because of His inherent power.
2. *Through Him*: Not as a mere passive instrument, but as the Divine cooperating Agent, He is the conserving cause of creation. Its continuance depends upon His mediating power.
3. *Unto Him*: Creation's goal is Christ. He is the intent of creation. As He is its beginning, so He must be its end (Rev 22:13).

In the words, "that are in heaven, and that are in earth, visible and invisible", we observe the chiastic structure, for the "visible" relates to what is on earth, and "invisible" to what is in heaven. Regard all things from any point of view you desire, and the glorious fact remains: the existence of everything depends upon the Son.

"Whether they be thrones, or dominions, or principalities, or powers" are the descriptive terms by which Paul expounds what he observes to be invisible in heavenly regions. In the corresponding passage of the Ephesian epistle (Eph 1:21), the word "thrones" is omitted. There Paul asserts of the Son that God has exalted Him. Here in our verse the word "authorities" (cf. Eph 1:21) is not included. It is the characteristic feature of this epistle that all authority, earthly and otherwise, is wholly subordinate to the authority of the Son. A descending order of dignity may be only accidental but nonetheless discernible in Paul's order. While in the Ephesian passage an ascending order appears it is to be observed that He, Christ, has ascended far above all. If any would be so foolish as to select the highest of these creatures or whatever to interpose between God and man, it would be considered by Paul as a gross interference with the prerogative of the Son. So far as they have being, they owe everything to Him; hence these are subordinate to His authority. The theme of the epistle and also the fact that these words are used after *aorata* ("invisible") emphasise that the celestial beings are discussed and not the terrestrial dignities.

In "all things were created by him, and for him", a notable change in tense has occurred in that the perfect passive indicative of *ktizō* is used now, whereas it is the aorist in the beginning of the verse. What is the significance of this change? Paul is establishing in the earlier part of this verse that the very existence of the creation is due to the creative activity of Christ. Now he employs the perfect tense to convey the transcending fact that the permanence, progress and purpose of creation rest on Christ. The creation exists because of Him, but it likewise subsists through Him. This thought is beautifully expressed in those words: "upholding all things by the word of his power" (Heb 1:2).

17 Of "and he is before all things, and by him all things consist", it has been remarked by scholars that this whole verse is emphatic. "And he is" sets forth the eternity of being possessed inherently by the Son. "Prior to His creative work", says Eadie, "He had filled the unmeasured periods of an unbeginning eternity". This is the Immutable. No measure of His existence is possible. At every point of His existence it can be said of Him, He is. Compare this with the "I am" of Exod 3:14 and the "I am" of John's Gospel. The RV translates the next part of the verse as: "and in Him all things consist" ("hold together", RV margin). Another translation has: "and in union with Him all things have their proper place". The verb *sunistēmi* ("consist", RV) carries the idea of congruence, harmony, correspondence; it represents the unifying power, the integrating principle. Christ is the unifying power or else the cosmos would be chaos.

Vv. 15-17 have set forth with appealing clarity the glory of the Son in regards to deity and in relation to all creation. These glories are entirely unique, and contribute to the epistle's theme that "Christ is all". Now we must contemplate His relation to the church. As with the creation, so it is with the church. Here again, there is one great term to describe His supreme position, as the opening words of the next verse reveal.

18 *Kephalē* ("head", also in 2:10 and 2:19) implies in this verse that Christ's Headship is assumed in resurrection. In 2:10 His Headship is asserted in His government of "all principality and authority". The reference in 2:19 shows that the Headship of Christ must be acknowledged. Headship involves Christ being the One to whom the body owes its life and from whom it derives its sustenance. The figure also includes the idea that Christ alone directs and controls the body. He has never appointed another to perform this organic function. In the epistle to the Ephesians the same relation of Head to the body is set forth; but while here the attention is mainly directed to the Head, in Ephesians the attention is rather centred on the body. In keeping with the theme of Colossians, the glories of the Head are emphasised, whereas in Ephesians the privileges and the blessings of the body are stressed.

The truth of Christ's Headship appears in other passages.

1. He is "the head of every man" (1 Cor 11:3). This statement occurs in connection with the deportment of the sexes in the local assembly. The man with the uncovered head displays the headship of Christ. The covered (veiled) woman conceals the headship of the man. It is not optional nor is it even a cultural preference. It is clearly a question of headship.

2. He is "the head over all things to the church" (Eph 1:22-23). Reference here is to that momentous day of glory when all that Christ is in manifested glory will be shared by His Body in nuptial oneness. Her role as the "fulness of Christ" will then be revealed and displayed.

3. He is "the head of all principality and power" (Col 2:10). They yield to Him in subjection. Owning His authority they serve His pleasure. Peter stated this

fact (1 Pet 3:22). This has a very practical bearing on ancient and modern claims to having received communications from angels. Given that such a communication was possible, it would be surprising if it challenged the authority of Christ, cast reflections upon His deity, Sonship and glory as a divine Person or questioned the efficacy of His sacrificial work on Calvary. It would be right to assume from this verse that the angel is not one of those who is subject to Christ. The communication would therefore be invalidated.

4. He has a headship which will be seen in millennial glory. David blessing Jehovah in the sight of all the congregation says, "Thine, Jehovah, is the greatness, and the power, and the glory, and the splendour, and the majesty; for all that is in the heavens and on the earth is thine: thine, Jehovah, is the kingdom, and thou art exalted as Head above all; and riches and glory are of thee, and thou rulest over everything; and in thy hand is power and might; and in thy hand it is to make all great and strong" (1 Chron 29:11-12). Here is language which delineates not only David's Lord because He is God; but David's Son because He is God Incarnate.

Paul frequently uses the figure of the body for believers as united to their risen Head. The earlier occasions of its mention show the relation of the members to the body, illustratively (1 Cor 12:12), descriptively (1 Cor 12:13), characteristically (1 Cor 12:27). The central reference of the three here mentioned is the doctrinal explanation of what happened on the day of Pentecost when such a union was brought about by the baptism in the Holy Spirit. Is not this the reason why in 1 Cor 10:16 the bread is spoken of as the "communion of the body of Christ"? Paul's later references largely expand upon the relationship of the Head to the Body, one of the great passages being Eph 4:15-16. The order here is reversed in the Ephesian letter, which reads, "The church which is his body". As there, so here, the church (*ekklēsia*) is viewed not as a local company of believers gathered to the Name of the Lord Jesus, but is embracive of all believers from Pentecost till the rapture. The fact that many differences exist between these two concepts can be gathered from relevant Scriptures.

In the phrase "who is the beginning" (*hē archē*) A.T. Robertson affirms that the article *hē* is uncertain, but adds, "It (beginning) is absolute without it". Lightfoot labours to establish the reason of its absence, whereas it is rather its presence which would have called for apology. This title has reference to the new creation. He is its origin. Headship takes care of authority and safeguards the thought of rule and control, while the Beginning puts before us the idea of what might be called creative initiative. Headship clearly establishes what is organic. Beginning reveals what is originative. An occurrence which illustrates this use of *archē* can be found in Revelation. There, not only have we the statement (in chs. 21 and 22) that He is the Alpha and the Omega, the Beginning and the End, but it is also said of Him that He is "the beginning of the creation of

God" (Rev 3:14). The church in Laodicea had this epistle many years before the Johannine letters, so they would understand the significance of Christ's address to them as "the beginning of the creation of God". As in this epistle, the new creation is in focus. The order of the three titles demands this consideration. "The Amen" refers to His essential deity. His perfect manhood is revealed in "the faithful and true witness" as the vehicle of divine revelation. As "the beginning of the creation of God" all that He is in resurrection fulness, the source of the new creation is His. He is the Originator of it and it owes not only its existence to Him, but also its position under His Headship. He is the Head of the new creation. This is a truly comforting thought. It means that there will never be another Fall. Everything is secure in Him who is the Beginning, the Head of the body, the Church.

"The firstborn from the dead" is literally, "out from among the dead ones". To Him, as the Son of God, resurrection was not only foreordained, but it was also His presumptive right. His inherent sinlessness demanded it. For all others, resurrection was a matter of divine mercy: for Christ it was His due. It is therefore, in resurrection that he becomes Head of a new race (compare 1 Cor 15:20). In Rev 1:5 the Saviour is called *the first begotten of the dead*. That phrase, as here, not only marks the reality of His death but it also establishes the fact of His resurrection. All honour of rank and dignity are His as the mighty Conqueror, who triumphed over the forces which held men captive (Heb 2:14; 1 John 3:8). He has risen to die no more, and He is the first to rise to die no more. He is called the firstborn from among the dead for more than this. In resurrection He is the Head of a new order; a note of generation is struck in that the church is an entity instinct with spiritual life in Him, its risen Head. His resurrection is the pledge that the redeemed shall also be raised (Rom 8:11; 1 Cor 15:20; 1 Thess 4:14 RV margin).

In "that in all things he might have the preeminence", *hina* (that) introduces a purpose clause. It indicates the objective of all Paul has said from v.15. It is ordained of God that Christ should have first place in all things. The expression, however, has a close relation with what has immediately preceded. It is true He has full right to pre-eminence as the Son, the Image and the Firstborn, but in resurrection He enters into an even wider and more momentous supremacy. Some have taken the "all things" as masculine, meaning "all persons". The context endorses the neuter expression, putting emphasis upon the totality of His preeminence. This then is the goal of God's economy, that He might become in all things what He is in Himself, pre-eminent. There is no sphere where He is not supreme, not the least in the thoughts and affections of believers. It affects corporate life as well. Assembly testimony will be the richer when His pre-eminence is manifestly unchallenged and unquestioned. No one, however important he considers himself to be, can aspire to such a place without receiving divine censure (3 John 9). John saw Him "in the midst of the throne ... and in the midst of the elders" (Rev 5:6). Today, He takes that place amongst His own who are gathered unto His Name alone (Matt 18:20).

The apostle has concluded his exaltation of the person of Christ. The transcendent glory of the Son has been Paul's theme. We can hear him, as it were, borrow the words from the Psalmist: "He is thy Lord, worship thou him". From this superlative exposition of the person of Christ Paul turns to a treatment of the work of Christ. The pattern Paul follows in his treatment of the person of Christ is the same as he now treats of His work, because His work, as His person, is related in the same order to God (1:19), the creation (1:20) and the new creation (1:21-23).

19   The statement "for it pleased the Father that in him should all fulness dwell" assigns another reason for the pre-eminence of Christ. The use of the conjunction "for" provides a close connection in thought with what precedes. The verb *eudokeō* is repeatedly used for God's will and pleasure (see Matt 3:17; Luke 12:32; 1 Cor 1:21; 10:5; Gal 1:15; Heb 10:6,8,38; 2 Pet 1:17). Naturally a nominative is required, but this is not found in the Greek text even though varying subjects appear in English translations. JND supplies, "all the fulness" and Ellicott, after elucidating three alternatives chooses the same phrase as Darby. Conybeare makes the nominative Christ. This would offer a rendering, "... because He (the Son) was pleased that in Him should have its dwelling the totality of deity". This would imply that Christ is not only the means, but also the end of reconciliation, giving a reading of the next verse a form of speech out of keeping with the tenor of Scripture. It is preferred that "God" is the subject of the sentence, or as the AV and the RV "the Father" is the subject. Then "all the fulness" will become the object of the verb, as Lightfoot and such translations as NEB, NIV, TNT propound. The Gnostics have the fulness of the divine nature interspersed among various aeons. Paul counters such a notion in this glorious affirmation that "all the fulness" dwells permanently in Christ. One of the key words of this epistle is *plērōma* ("fulness"). It means "filled full". There are various uses throughout the NT (eg. Mark 8:20; Rom 11:12,25; 13:10; 15:29; Gal 4:4; Eph 1:10). It is to be observed that all that is essential to the Son as a divine Person is not His by the Father's counsel or consent but His essential Godhead fulness is independent of the Father's pleasure, though not contrary to it. "Whatever dwells in Christ by the Father's pleasure", says Eadie (1856) "is official, and not essential; relational, and not absolute in its nature". All the fulness of deity is His as the Image (v.15), the fulness of power in creation (v.16), the fulness of power in the new creation (v.18) and the fulness of reconciliation (v.20). This is the gospel that wrought such fruit for God in Colossae. This is the message which proclaims Christ as the all-sufficient Saviour, and gives expression to the infinite power of His mediatorship between God and man. The infinitive "to dwell" must be noted as it is one of three in these verses. It means "to abide" or "to be at home". All the attributes of deity, all the fulness of grace, all the saving fulness are at home in

Christ. The indwelling, or even more literally, the down-dwelling of this fulness in Christ is God's pleasure, thus excluding any prevailing idea of rivalry in the Godhead. Jehovah will proclaim in the OT, "Look unto me, and be ye saved, ... for I am God, and there is none else" (Isa 45:22). Peter will unashamedly announce to the multitude in Jerusalem when speaking of Christ, "Neither is there salvation in any other, for there is none other name under heaven given among men, whereby we must be saved" (Acts 4:12). There is no incongruity for it is God's pleasure that in Christ should all saving fulness be made to dwell.

20   The supplied nominative "God" to "was pleased" agrees with the verb *eirē-nopoiēsas* ("having made peace"). God, having made peace through the blood of His cross (Christ's), was pleased to reconcile by Him (Christ) all things unto Himself. The procurement of peace is through the shed blood of Christ on the cross. Reconciliation cannot be secured by any other means. Peace is not that which man makes with God. It is something which God has already made for man. The responsibility rests upon every guilty sinner to accept it by faith. This is the gospel Paul expounds in other places: in Rom 5:1 he speaks of "peace with God", the portion of those justified by faith. This is one of five mentions Paul makes of the cross in this group of epistles commonly known as the Prison Epistles. There would be purpose in listing those references if only to refresh our souls in the consideration of them.

1. Eph 2:16: "the cross". Its distinctiveness is apparent by the use of the article "the". It is wholly distinct from all others because of its singular achievements.
2. Phil 2:8: "the death of the cross". Its depth is here emphasised. The step that consummates His unfathomable humiliation is cross death.
3. Phil 3:18: "the cross of Christ". Its dignity, suggesting the glory He gave it as being the scene of His glorious triumph and apparent reproach and shame.
4. Col 1:20: "the blood of his cross". Its demand is essentially involved in this phrase. No question here of Him being taken down from the cross before He died and another replacing Him. Nothing but the life blood of the Saviour poured out at Calvary could procure peace.
5. Col 2:14: "his cross". Its devotion is evident, for it was the one that He accepted voluntarily and made it *His*.

"By him to reconcile all things unto himself" continues the thought of the Father's pleasure. He was pleased that all fulness should dwell in Christ. It follows that the Father was pleased to reconcile all things to Himself through Christ's peacemaking work on the cross. Paul stresses that God works in His reconciling grace through (RV) Christ alone. No other agent is required or even considered. Here the Person includes His work: they can never be separated. The word "reconcile" opens up to the reader a very important doctrine in the NT. There are three words which have an essential bearing on the teaching of reconciliation.

They are:

1. *Katallassō* properly denoting "to change", "to exchange" (especially of money), hence of persons, "to change from enmity to friendship", "to reconcile" (see Vine's *Expository Dictionary*). This is Paul's great word. It occurs in Rom 5:10; 2 Cor 5:18,19,20 in connection with the reconciliation of man to God. Its noun form *katallagē* ("reconciliation") has four occurrences: Rom 5:11 (RV); 11:15; 2 Cor 5:18,19.

2. *Apokatallassō*, an intensive word meaning "to reconcile completely". Vine adds, "to change from one condition to another so as to remove all enmity and have no impediment to unity and peace". It is used three times, twice in Col 1:20,21 and elsewhere in Eph 2:16.

Neither (1) nor (2) denotes mutual reconciliation after mutual hostility. Lightfoot, quoted by Vine and others, has an excellent paragraph on this in his *Notes on the Epistles of Paul*, Zondervan 1957, p.288.

3. *Diallassō* meaning "to effect an alteration", "to exchange", hence "to reconcile" in cases of mutual hostility yielding to mutual concession (Vine). Matt 5:24, the only occurrence, is the illustrative use of the word. It is never used by the apostles in connection with reconciliation.

The passages which are related to our subject make evident that:

(a) Man's sin resulting in alienation from and enmity to God necessitates reconciliation.

(b) God is the Reconciler, not the One reconciled (for further discussion on this point which is not possible here, see Alford, *Greek New Testament* Vol. 2 p.665; H.P. Liddon, *Explanatory Analysis of Romans* pp.101,102; Lightfoot, *Notes on the Epistles of Paul* p.288).

(c) Christ is the One who effects the reconciliation by His death (Rom 5:10), by his blood (Col 1:20) and by His cross (Eph 2:16).

(d) The nature of reconciliation is to change from enmity to amity.
   i. The bringing of man back to God in amity (Rom 5:10).
   ii. The cleansing of things in the heavens (Col 1:20).
   iii. The removal of the curse from the earth (Rom 8:20).

(e) The scope of reconciliation is universal, ethnical, cosmical and personal.
   i. As to the world, there is a forensic provision for the entire world (2 Cor 5:19).
   ii. As to the Jew and Gentile, enmity has been removed by the cross (Eph 2:16).
   iii. As to the universe, "all things" are to be reconciled with an unlimited application to heaven and earth (Col 1:21; Rom 8:18-23). Special attention must however, be given to the accuracy of divine language when the scope of divine restoration is being affected. Both Eph 1:10 and Col 1:20 specify, howbeit inversely, "heaven and earth", never "under the earth" as in Phil 2:10.

iv. As to the individual, its application is specifically to all those who, in responding to the call of the gospel, believe (2 Cor 5:18-19).

(f) The gospel is the proclamation and appeal of this reconciliation (2 Cor 5:18-19). Chrysostom is recorded as saying, "It is great 'to reconcile'; greater 'through Himself', greater again 'through His blood'; greatest of all 'through His cross' ".

21 "And you, that were sometimes alienated and enemies in your mind by wicked works" is Paul saying, "You Colossians shared in the blessings of reconciliation when you received Christ". Paul is now showing the application of reconciliation in relation to the new creation. The participle "estranged" (*apēllotriōmenous*) bears witness to the Fall. By man's sin he removed himself from God and so his posterity (compare Eph 2:12 RV "separate from Christ"; Eph 2:13 RV "Ye that once were far off are made nigh"). Hostility in a most active sense comes out in the word "enemies" as in Matt 13:28; Rom 8:7. The mind (*dianoia*) is the source, the works (*ergois*) the sphere, and evil (*ponērois*) the strength. In spite of this God acts in reconciliation revealing his infinite grace and love towards those who displayed such rebellion and were at such a distance from Him. All that has hindered fellowship between God and us He has removed now in this work of grace.

Both the text and punctuation are difficult here. There seems to be considerable textual authority to begin v.22 after "works" as do JND, RSV, NIV, NASB, Robertson, Bruce.

In "yet now hath he reconciled" God is the Reconciler. The present period of grace is in view in the word "now". Not so much, at the present moment, but in the economy of God's saving grace which characterises this era, and is presented in the gospel.

22 "In the body of his flesh through death" is another reference to the death of the Lord Jesus Christ (see v.20 above). There Paul is stressing the efficacy of His blood, securing peace and providing reconciliation. This reference with its special notice of "body" and "flesh" seems to accomplish a double purpose:

1. It distinguishes the physical body of Christ (as Rom 7:4) from the mystical body of Col 1:18.
2. It combats error:
   (a) The Gnostics viewed all matter as evil.
   (b) The Docetic error postulated that the Lord existed on earth only as a phantom.

The verity of the incarnation is established beyond doubt, not without intention as the Spirit foresaw the errors that would abound then and now. The close relationship between the incarnation of Christ and His sacrificial death is also declared in this incomparable passage. It tells us:

1. Christ's body was real - not a phantom.
2. That Christ's body was subject to death, bearing in mind Phil 2:6-9.
3. That this death reconciled man to God.

With "to present you holy and unblamable and unreproveable in his sight", compare Rom 12:1 for the word "present". The infinitive *parastēsai* ("to present") reveals the ultimate purpose of God in His work of reconciliation. He will place us before Him free from every trace and taint of sin. That we are already in God's accomplished purpose bears out the Ephesian aspect of the ministry. Paul sees it as existing now in the heavenlies in Christ (Eph 1:4). Here in Colossians he is looking on to the moment when it will be fully realised. Then we shall be holy, free from all inward impurities and defilement. In that day of presentation our state and standing will harmonise in manifest perfection. The three adjectives are used for effect to denote complete and total purity, the result of Christ's redemptive work on the cross in purifying each member of the body from all sin, blemish and fault. Perhaps no precise meaning is to be attached to each separate adjective, but it does not hinder William Lincoln from distinguishing them as: holy before God, blameless before others and unreproveable by Satan. No angelic mediator or any number of them could accomplish this. There was falsity and heresy assailing the testimony and undermining the faith of believers in Colossae, but Paul has effectively withstood the onslaught of the enemy by a full-orbed ministry of Christ. He has exalted the Person of Christ and carefully expounded His personal, essential and eternal glories. Neither has he overlooked His moral, official and acquired glories. They are all in these amazing verses. The length of these verses is beyond measure. Paul starts in eternity, he comes through the corridors of time and describes a day of glory the fulness of which eternity will never exhaust. When will it ever be otherwise, that we shall be before Him holy, without blemish and unreproveable? Look at the depth Paul has struck within the compass of these verses - an unfathomable depth, twice mentioned: "the blood of the cross", "through death". Neither can the height be scaled, that pinnacle of glory on which He alone sits as Firstborn from among the dead, as Head. When it comes to breadth no other passage is so embracive, "all things" in heaven and in earth. If there remains a doubt in any Colossian Christian after this matchless unfolding of Christ and His glory, then what follows in the next verse will appear necessary. But we think that as the epistle was read in the assembly at Colossae, by this stage there would echo in every exercised heart: "My Lord and my God".

23   In "if ye continue in the faith", the *ei* (if), introduces a conditional clause, which in itself expresses a hypothesis. But because the indicative mood follows, the hypothesis is converted into a hope. The expression can then be read, "If, as the case is, ye continue in the faith" (Eadie). Note that the clause depends on the infinitive "to present" of the previous verse, not on "reconciled". This future blessedness is the portion of all them that believe. But believe they must. Their continuance is the proof of their faith. Thus Paul assumes the Colossians will abide in the faith. The words do not in any way contradict the truth of the eternal security of the believer. They are tests for the unreal. If there was a danger, it was love on Paul's part to administer a word of caution in the confidence that they would continue faithful. Once again the translations differ as to what the word "faith" here denotes. Often it stands for the body of revealed truth as, for example, in Jude. Most commentators read the expression as referring to personal faith, so it would then read: "If ye continue in your faith". Matters concerning the faith predominate in the epistle writer's mind, as directed by the Spirit, so it would be in line with the character of the epistle to retain the thought that it is *the faith* that Paul has in mind. Contending *for* the faith and continuing *in* the faith are wholesome features in any that name the Name of Christ. *Epimenō* is used three times in Romans (6:1; 11:22,23), each time, as here, with the dative. As "sin" and "unbelief" have the definite article there, so "faith" has it here.

"Grounded and settled, and be not moved away from the hope of the gospel which ye heard" gives three modifiers agreeing with the idea conveyed in the word "continue". "Grounded" is a perfect passive particle which expressed literally reads "having been placed and remaining on a foundation". The sense in which the Lord uses it illustrates the fixity of the building irrespective of what pressures come upon it (Matt 7:55). This reference is a tacit endorsement of Epaphras' ministry at the time when the Colossians were placed upon the sure foundation of the faith. It enhances the work of teaching for when truth is taught it places saints upon a foundation tried and sure. The adjective which follows describes the effect of being founded as "firm, steadfast" (1 Cor 7:35; 15:58). The next statement expresses the result of the foregoing "steadfastness". We meet with it only here, so it is unique to Colossians. We judge the sense is "not inclined to move". How beautifully do these two participles blend. "Grounded" we have seen is a perfect passive participle to express a condition that began in the past and now continues. This latter is a present passive participle to express a condition that continues from now on. The present writer submits that this reflects Paul's confidence in his own ministry. This epistle will have the desired effect that the Colossians will not have the slightest inclination to be moved away from the hope of the gospel. As for "the hope" it is simply the hope that belongs to "the gospel" or is presented in the gospel. Once again Paul is confirming the witness of Epaphras. The spurious teachers in Colossae have neither gospel nor hope. Paul is confident the saints will remain unshaken and rejoice in hope.

"And which was preached to every creature which is under heaven is added to show simply the gospel has been preached to everybody in the world. Paul is showing in the same pointed way as in v.6 the world-wide reach and range of the gospel in its universality. The gospel is the one constant unchanging message for all men everywhere. The term "to every creature" follows the language of the Lord Jesus Christ when he commissioned the apostles. Compare "all nations" (Matt 28:19), "all the world, to every creature" (Mark 16:15) and "unto the uttermost part of the earth" (Acts 1:8). Paul also makes appeal in these words to the gospel's publicity as opposed to the secret mysteries of the errorists.

"Whereof I Paul am made a minister" (RV "was made") refers to his conversion when he was commissioned to preach the gospel to the Gentiles (Acts 26:17). This is the only occasion in the epistle where Paul employs the emphatic "I, myself" (*egō*). Noticeably, he uses it in relation to his being a servant, a deference that becomes the revelation of this epistle concerning the glories of Christ. The emphasis is not to magnify himself, but to imply his faithfulness to the authority under which he had acted in his past course of service. He was loyal to the One who had sent him forth on such an honoured mission. It was also calculated to impress on the Colossians that the gospel, which Epaphras preached and was bearing fruit in them as it is in all the world, was also the same gospel to which he was attached in ardent labours and in abounding loyalty to Him whose servant he was.

III. Ministerial (1:24-2:7)

1. *Paul's Ministry and the Mystery* 1:24-29

v.24 "Who now rejoice in my sufferings for you, and fill up that which is behind of the afflictions of Christ in my flesh for his body's sake, which is the church:
v.25 Whereof I am made a minister, according to the dispensation of God which is given to me for you, to fulfil the word of God:
v.26 Even the mystery which hath been hid from ages and from generations, but now is made manifest to his saints:
v.27 To whom God would make known what is the riches of the glory of this mystery among the Gentiles; which is Christ in you, the hope of glory:
v.28 Whom we preach, warning every man, and teaching every man in all wisdom: that we may present every man perfect in Christ Jesus:
v.29 Whereunto I also labour, striving according to his working, which worketh in me mightily."

The apostle has just concluded his excellent exposition of the Person of Christ (1:15-18) and proceeds with a crucial treatment of His work, centring his discussion upon the term reconciliation (1:19-20). He then outlines the application of it to the Colossians (1:21-23). The section ends with a brief and distinct reference to himself in the words "whereof I Paul am made a minister". These words form a smooth transition into the present paragraph (1:24-29) in which he sets forth what is implied and involved by his being made a minister. This is the first time in the epistle that Paul speaks of himself directly. While the paragraph is clearly autobiographical, it is not intended to draw attention to the man as such, but to his service and its objectives. As the paragraph develops, Paul mentions his sufferings in which he is rejoicing (1:24), his stewardship in which he is responsible (1:25-27) and his service in which he is resolute (1:28-29).

24   Paul views himself as one "who now rejoice in my sufferings for you" (see 2 Cor 1:6; Rom 8:18; 2 Tim 3:11). As Paul thinks of his own high privilege and of the great hope that has become the portion of those whom he is addressing, he breaks out into jubilant thanksgiving. The hardships which he experiences weigh lightly upon his spirit, for in them he can rejoice. In other portions he gives reasons why he can rejoice in such trying circumstances (Rom 5:3; 2 Cor 12: 10). Sometimes he refers to the good results of his sufferings as in Phil 1:12, or alludes to the cause of them, as here and in Eph 3:1,13. The word "now" means "at the present time" which serves to remind us of his bonds which compel Eadie feelingly to remark, "with the chain upon my wrist, I rejoice". These sufferings are said to be "for you". The preposition *huper* ("for") has here the sense of "on account of". This use will bring out the cause of the sufferings which is the point of the passage. Good effect has certainly abounded from Paul's sufferings, an issue which he details for the benefit of the Corinthian saints (2 Cor 1:5-8). Paul was ever conscious of his distinctive calling and responsibility. When the Lord Jesus spoke of him to Ananias, He said, "... he is a chosen vessel unto me, to bear my name before the Gentiles, and kings, and the children of Israel" (Acts 9:15). Because Paul was faithful in his ministry suffering ensued. When the servant of God is aware of divine calling which places him in unreserved devotion to His will, no amount of suffering, however intense, will cause him to relinquish his holy charge. Paul has become the recipient of divine communications as he tells us in this epistle. That revealed truth, the Mystery, brought great responsibility upon him, especially in relation to the Gentiles. Had he chosen an easier path, sufferings might well have been averted. But what then of the ministry and those for whom it was divinely intended in the economy of God? If saints are to enjoy the fulness and fruit of divine revelation, it is incumbent upon all servants of God that they declare the whole counsel of God. Thus Paul, as the instrument that the Lord employed to make known the character of the church, its calling and constitution, suffers, yet rejoices, knowing that he has been faithful in his stewardship.

His stewardship involves the responsibility to "fill up that which is behind of the afflictions of Christ in my flesh for his body's sake, which is the church". "Fill up" translates the double compound verb *antanapléroó* found only here in the NT. The verb *pléroó* means "fill, fulfil" and the single compound *anapléroó* is an emphatic form "fill completely". The prefix *anti* ("in the place of" or "on behalf of") means that this is done in the place of or on behalf of someone else. Therefore it means "complete on Christ's behalf" or "in the place of Christ". Next in this difficult verse in the plural noun *husterémata* which the RV translates, "that which is lacking". This appears to be the sense of its usage in this context. The word rendered "afflictions", occurring forty-five times in the NT, is used only here of Christ, and never of His vicarious sufferings. One thing must be made clear. The apostle is not speaking of the sufferings and death of the Lord Jesus. Every passage in the NT which refers to His sacrifice for sin speaks of its finality and completion. There is no element lacking in the work which Christ accomplished to the entire and eternal satisfaction of God. Paul views his sufferings as the sufferings of Christ because He suffered in and with him. The Lord Jesus says, "In the world ye shall have tribulation" (John 16:33), so His own sufferings whilst here on earth did not cause suffering to cease. It is an integral part of the ministry of Christ's servants, as it was of Christ Himself. The words of the risen Lord gave Paul the sense he here expresses, when on the Damascus road he heard Him say, "Saul, Saul why persecutest though *me*" (Acts 9:4). In the same chapter and v.16, the words spoken of him would augment what he already heard, "For I will show him how great things he must suffer for my name's sake". It appears there is a quota of suffering still remaining which Paul is filling up gladly for it brings not only joy to him but also benefit to the body of Christ, the church. They are sufferings which Christ experiences because of our union with Him. He suffers in us. It was this that transformed the sufferings which Paul experienced when he viewed them in the light of his union with Christ. Believers are exhorted "to go forth unto him without the camp, bearing his reproach", not so much reproach on His account, but the reproach which is His, and which He still bears in us.

25 "Whereof I am made a minister, according to the dispensation of God which is given to me for you, to fulfil the word of God" shows that not only does Paul suffer, he also serves and that with a realised sense of his special calling and its significance. Paul has a service in the gospel to which he refers in v.23. He uses the same term here to denote the responsibility he bears to the truth God has chosen him to declare. That must be the sense here. Paul is a minister of the church in the sense that he proclaims the truth concerning its distinctive character, constitution and consummation and is intimately concerned about its confirmation in present truth. This dual sense of divine commission Paul speaks about is also to be found in Rom 16:25-26; 1 Cor 2:1-10 and Eph 3:2-10. The conception of stewardship, often used by Paul (cf 1 Cor 4:1; 9:17; Eph 3:2) comes directly from the Lord's ministry. It is He who describes His servants by the figure of stewardship, a steward being one who is responsible for the economy or administration of the household (Luke 12:42). This "dispensation" (stewardship, RV margin) of which Paul speaks is "of God" which means it is of God's arranging. It is God who has so ordered His household affairs to give Paul this distinctive responsibility. It was unique to Paul, for he always said that it was "given" to him. God appointed the apostle to this position of trust for the benefit of the Colossians, "for you" or "with a view to your good", meaning, of course, for their spiritual well-being, their spiritual perfection (v.28). The infinitive clause "to fulfil the word of God" tells what Paul is to discharge by this "stewardship". A parallel passage Rom 15:19 has led some to suggest that the preaching of the word of God in the widest scope possible is here viewed, hence the full proclamation of the Mystery. Doubtless that is the sense conveyed about the gospel as Paul gives geographical boundaries that reveal his extensive engagements in the gospel. What is entrusted to Paul is the responsibility of filling up, or bringing to completion the word of God with respect to the Mystery. This he has done by the very existence of what we possess in the epistles of Ephesians and Colossians. "He was not the last to add to the edifice of Scripture; he did not complete the canon of Scripture, but any later writings only confirmed or expounded what had already been taught. They do not contain anything like the 'mysteries' referred to in Paul's letters. Doctrinally, it may be said that he completed the canon" (J.M. Davies p.35).

26   In "even the mystery which hath been hid from ages and from generations, but now is made manifest to his saints", *mustērion* (mystery) is the word translated in the LXX as "a secret" nine times in Daniel (Dan 2:18ff; 4:9). Twenty-seven times the word "mystery" occurs in the NT - three times in the Gospels (Matt 13:11; Mark 4:11; Luke 8:10) and four times in Revelation (1:20; 10:7; 17:5,7). In Ephesians it is used six times, hence more often than in any other book of the NT (1:9; 3:3,4,9: 5:32; 6:19). Here in Colossians the word occurs four times (1:26,27; 2:2; 4:3). A mystery in NT usage is not something mysterious, but rather a divine secret concealed but known to man only by divine revelation. The classical meaning attached to the word was, namely, something that was revealed only to a few specially initiated, which was the current term employed by those whose teaching assailed the Colossian saints. It must be understood that the word "mystery" here is in apposition to the words "the work of God" in v.25, which confirms that Paul's fulfilling the word of God was his completing that word by the communication of what was given him by divine revelation. "Ages" and "generations" are terms describing successive periods in the history of mankind. Several "generations" go to make up one "age". When it is said here that the revelation of the mystery has been hidden away "from ages and generations", it means that it has been hidden away from men during countless years. It is "hidden away" no more. It has been revealed "to his saints". The full splendour of this glorious purpose of God has now been made fully known. We ought to be thankful that such a radiant revelation of divine purpose has become ours in this administration of God's economy through Paul's ministry.

27   The three verses may be summarised:
   v.25 The Instrument by which the Mystery is declared.
   v.26 The Announcement by which the Mystery is disclosed.
   v.27 The Portrayal by which the Mystery is defined.

The "riches of the glory" is a regular Pauline expression. He is specially drawn to "riches" as a figurative term. He has already spoken of the Mystery; now he adds thereto and one can read of "the glory of this mystery". But even that does not fully expand the wealth of his subject, so he writes: "the riches of the glory of this mystery". The mystery so defined in Eph 3 shows that the Gentiles are "fellow heirs", "fellow members of the body" and "fellow partakers of the promise in

Christ Jesus". The complementary passage which is here before us represents the mystery as being "Christ in you", by which is revealed the nature of the blessing and privilege. The term is expanded to read: "the glory of this mystery". The mystery displays all the excellence of God's purpose which is always realised by the perfect operation in harmonious blending of His attributes. In granting this undiscovered and undiscoverable blessing to the Gentiles not one particle of divine glory is forfeited. Like all His works, the mystery declares the glory of God. The full expression reads, "the riches of the glory of this mystery". The word is "wealth" and it disclosed the liberality of God in bringing this His purpose into living reality. It demonstrates the wealth of His grace, the wealth of His wisdom, the wealth of His glory. The verse concludes by indicating that the indwelling of the Christ is the pledge of future and eternal glory (cf 3:4). Such was the mystery, so rich with glory that God desired to make it known. The strength of the word *ēthelēsen* (AV "would", RV "was pleased") appears to be, "desired with intent" or "resolved" or "willed" and thus declares God's purpose in this unfolding of the mystery as well as the pleasure God knew in thus instructing His people as to their privilege and blessing.

28   Christ "whom we preach, warning every man, and teaching every man in all wisdom" and Christ alone is the subject of apostolic preaching. So it was with Paul as this epistle affirms. Paul was fully resolved in his service. He was resolute in the subject of his preaching. His theme is Christ, not merely His doctrine, but Himself. He is the centre and circumference of our message. To the lost and perishing we announce His saving power and grace and see men brought to repentance and faith, and to those who believe in the teaching we impart for their spiritual growth and well being. The preaching involves two elements, one which looks at the negative side "warning" and the other which points to the positive side "teaching". There is no need to go beyond the scope of this epistle to see these elements clearly displayed in Paul's approach in the ministry. From 2:4 to 3:4 Paul is admonishing relative to practice and teaching, while from 3:5 to 4:18 he is teaching in respect of doctrine. Herein lies the secret for faithful service, a pattern for every servant of God to follow. The preaching of Paul was in the character of an evangelist, with ardour and authority. His warning was in the concern of a pastor, with compassion and consideration. His teaching was in the clarity of a teacher, with precision and power. Paul never narrows his ministry to the few. The threefold occurrence of the words "every man" shows Paul's undying interest in every man, irrespective of his character, creed or class. There is likely a hint at the exclusiveness of certain teachers who confine their interests to an intellectual few. The next expression "in all wisdom" has been taken to convey the method or manner in which the ministry has been carried out. It certainly would be expected that all activity for God and His glory would be discharged in such a way as to display divine wisdom. The sublime message of the gospel never requires the embellishment of man's worldly wisdom to give it effect or attractiveness. Paul has none of this and it must be judged that his approach here is not merely prescriptive but also directive. What shall we say of the mystery of which Paul is the instrument for its proclamation? Here again there is no innovation needed. Christ is the theme. Surely He is sufficient! Others, however, discern that Paul is referring to the content of the preaching when he says "in all wisdom", referring largely to the scope of the material presented. Some of those who preach can be severely selective having a studied preference for certain areas or aspects of divine truth. Thus the "all" here gives the unrestricted range of knowing that the whole counsel of God must be declared.

Paul is resolute in the sublimity of his purpose. He has a goal. His activity for God is not aimless. It is "to present every man perfect in Christ" (RV). At the end of the previous section mention is made of a presentation (v.22). Arising out of that is the presentation which closes this present section. In the one the believer is assured that he is accepted and will stand before God, holy, unblameable and unreproveable. The question may well be asked; how can Paul speak of "presenting" the same believers "perfect" through the preaching, admonishing and teaching? Paul has no thought of adding to the work of Christ as though it were insufficient. His aim is to have every man, reached by divine grace, so instructed as to his position in Christ that he will walk in the power of living union with Christ. He wishes to see saints mature and realise the purpose for which they have been saved. No parents will be content with their child merely possessing life and not having a commensurate growth into youth and adulthood. So with Paul, it is a task demanding so much that were it not for divine enablement, the achievement would be impossible, for there are many adversaries. Life attracts enemies. Legality had crushed out every feature of Christ in the Galatians causing Paul to say, "My little children, of whom I travail in birth again, until Christ be formed in you" (Gal 5:19). Carnality dwarfed and divided the Corinthian believers to whom Paul wrote, "... my beloved children, for though ye should have ten thousand tutors in Christ yet have ye not many fathers: for in Christ Jesus I begat you through the gospel" (1 Cor 4:14b-15). As a mother he travailed, as a father he begat.

29   "Whereunto I also labour, striving according to his working, which worketh in me" says Paul, resolute because of the source of his power. God empowered him mightily. The strenuous nature of the service of God for Paul is disclosed in the word "labour" which means toil to the point of weariness. Physical exertion is included with all that that demanded upon a frame beset with sustained restrictions (2 Cor 12). The word which follows is *agōnizomenos* (striving), and it stems from the word Luke uses of the Lord Jesus in His agony in Gethsemane (Luke 22:44). Spiritual toil appears to be what the apostle is speaking of: the many wrestlings in prayer, the intense struggle to achieve the goal. He ends by tracing his support to the working of the very energy of God in him, and that mightily. God energised Paul's exercises in prayer by His dynamic power. The accomplishments in service by Paul were due to the One who strengthened him. It is the lack of this power that has resulted in recourse to human resources to prosper a work which can only be accomplished in the strength God supplies.

WORDS PECULIAR TO COLOSSIANS 1 ARE:

Antanaplēroō	: fill up completely	1:24
Areskeia	: desire to please	1:10
Eirēnopoieō	: make peace	1:20
Metakineō	: not move away	1:23
Horatos	: visible	1:16
Proakouō	: hear before	1:5
Prōteuō	: be first, pre-eminent	1:18

WORDS COMMON TO COLOSSIANS AND EPHESIANS, IN COLOSSIANS 1 ARE:

Apallotrioō	: alienate, estrange	1:21; Eph 2:12; 4:18
Apokatallassō	: reconcile	1:20,21; Eph 2:16

2. Paul's Conflict and the Colossians 2:1-5

v.1   "For I would that ye knew what great conflict I have for you, and for them at Laodicea, and for as many as have not seen my face in the flesh;

v.2   That their hearts might be comforted, being knit together in love, and unto all riches of the full assurance of understanding, to the acknowledgement of the mystery of God, and of the Father, and of Christ;

v.3   In whom are hid all the treasures of wisdom and knowledge.

v.4   And this I say, lest any man should beguile you with enticing words.

v.5   For though I be absent in the flesh, yet am I with you in the spirit, joying and beholding your order, and the stedfastness of your faith in Christ."

1   Verses 28 and 29 of the previous chapter describe the general character of Paul's labours, what he and his fellow-workers do for "every man". Paul toils, "striving" (*agōnizomenos*) with the energy God gives him in his service. The "for" of v.1 connects with the foregoing verses to describe the nature and the object of the struggle.

The opening formula "I would that ye know" presents us with the less common positive variation of the more usual negative "I would not have you ignorant". Paul unveils something of his prayer life so that the saints of the Lycus valley may be encouraged to know that he has a personal and unremitting concern for them. There is a welcome openness in Paul's approach which can be suitably emulated. How encouraging it can be to hear some say, "I would have you know I pray for you every day".

"What great conflict I have for you" is literally "how great a contest I am having". *Agōn* carries the metaphor of *agōnizomenos* of 1:29, and specifies the struggle experienced for his readers in their prevailing situation. The struggle is one of prayer, an inward anxiety that finds relief only at the throne of grace. Earnestness marks his prayer-exercise for these saints. The word "great" (*hēlikos*) occurs only here and in James 3:5.

The conflict is "for them at Laodicea, and for as many as have not seen my face in the flesh". The "for" in both cases is inserted by the translators: there is only one preposition which makes one group of those for whom Paul "strives" and not two or more groups: "for you", the Colossians, "those of Laodicea" and "as many as have not seen my face in the flesh" (JND). No doubt Hierapolis was among the "many". This bespeaks Paul's unselfishness in prayer. The real spring of prayer arises out of a deep consideration of others. The honoured prisoner could justifiably be fully occupied about his own circumstances, deprivation and restriction. Rather he is wrestling in prayer for the spiritual preservation of those unseen, yet not unknown. For Paul to pray so earnestly for those whom he had never met is great tenderness. There is much to be learned from this verse which gives such an insight to Paul's prayer exercise.

2 The literal heart viewed as a bodily organ is the seat of strength and of physical life (Ps 38:10; Isa 1:5). Hence the word is used metaphorically as the spring of man's personal, spiritual and intellectual life, the inner nature of man. The heart is the seat of:

1. emotions:	of joy (Deut 28:47; John 16:22), of pain (Jer 4:19), of tranquility (Prov 14:30), of grief (John 14:1; Rom 9:2; 2 Cor 2:4), of affections (Luke 24:32; Acts 21:13);
2. understanding:	of knowledge (1 Kings 3:12; Matt 5:9), of perception (John 12:40; Eph 4:18), of thoughts (Matt 9:4; Heb 4:12), of rational powers (Mark 2:6; Luke 24:38), of imagination (Luke 1:51);
3. will:	of intentions (1 Kings 8:17; Rom 6:17; Heb 4:12), of decisions (Exod 36:2), of purpose (Acts 11:23; 2 Cor 9:7);
4. trust:	of faith (Mark 11:23; Rom 10:10; Heb 3:12), of obedience (Rom 6:17; 2 Thess 3:5), of conscience (Acts 2:37; 1 John 3:20).

Paul is deeply concerned about the state of those believers' faith in Christ, their confidence in His work as being, like Himself, totally sufficient to maintain them in the closest of relationships with God. He is likewise in conflict that their obedience to his letter will be manifest in a total rejection of all the spurious teachings the errorists have spread among the saints.

"Might be comforted" translates the word *paraklēthōsin* which signifies such ideas as comfort (1 Thess 3:7), exhortation (1 Thess 4:1; 2 Thess 3:12) and encouragement, the most appropriate of the three to this context. What they needed in such an opposing situation was confirmation that what they believed was in very essence the truth and the revelation of God in His Son, in whom all treasures of wisdom and knowledge permanently reside. This would make them courageous in the conflict with error, and would preserve them from yielding one iota of the faith. The Holy Spirit is termed the Comforter (John 14:26). His work today, through the Holy Scriptures, brings confirmation and encouragement to all believing souls. This divine ministry can be augmented by the ministry of those who partake of Paul's "conflict", and seek only the spiritual and moral preservation of the testimony.

"Being knit together in love" (*sumbibasthentes*) is equivalent to a new clause "and that they (as opposed to their 'hearts') be knit together in love". Sometimes the word means "instruct" (1 Cor 2:16), sometimes "conclude", "infer" (literally, Putting two and two together) as in Acts 16:10. The required meaning here, v.19 and the parallel in Ephesians is that of "compacting" or "building up". This is because of the corporate result the apostle has in view. It is the collective oneness of the assembly about which Paul is deeply concerned. Love is the bond of that unity. Love to the Person of Christ in all His worth and work, love to one another as being united to Him by one common faith, is the causal force of Paul's intensity in prayer. This love is born out of a conviction that He, the Lord Jesus, is worthy of that love because of all that He is, which has been so thoughtfully discoursed by Paul in this letter, and because of all He has become that He might accomplish complete reconciliation. A proper insight into all that He is to God and to His own, produces conviction in knowing that the truth we know is the truth. The love here is therefore not a sentimental one, but it is a love that is intelligent, and that becomes the sphere in which the compactness is realised.

In the phrase "and unto all riches of the full assurance of understanding", the noun *plērophoria* is full of certainty and assurance. It occurs four times in the NT:

1. 1 Thess 1:5 describes the conscious certainty that fills the heart of the apostle and his fellow-workers, knowing that, as they preach the gospel in Thessalonica, the sovereign purpose of God is being realised in the salvation of those who believe.

2. Heb 6:11 desires that the saints be fully aware of the absorbing power of the hope that the promises of God will be brought to full fruition and entire fulfilment.

3. Heb 10:22 speaks of the faith that makes one conscious of divine acceptance in the presence of God and excludes all fear of the judgment of God.

4. Col 2:2 shows the "liberty of the mind consequent upon an understanding in Christ" (Vine). It is the complete understanding that what has been comprehended is indeed the truth.

The compactness in love corporately will lead purposefully to this conviction. This is the sense of *eis* ("with a view to"); the object and purpose of being "compacted together in love" is that all the saints will be fully assured that what they believe is worthy of their faith as it is the truth. When this certainty is lost and strange impressions chase away convictions once held, dubiety becomes fructifying soil for the growth of error. The fear that such may be the case in the Colossian assembly causes Paul the intense anxiety these verses unveil.

"To the acknowledgement of the mystery of God and of the Father, and of Christ" can be taken as virtually synonymous with the foregoing expression; the second defining more clearly the language of the first. JND rightly gives the sense when he renders *epignōsis* as "full knowledge" (so Newberry). Any thought of a limited knowledge in divine things is foreign to the Spirit of God, especially when revelation is complete and completed (1:25). The thought of the mystery is taken from vv.26,27 of the former chapter. Paul is stressing in this expression not so much the recognition of the mystery, but its comprehension. And at this point there are variants. Readings based on various manuscripts differ, as do the consequent interpretations. The RV accepts the simplest reading, "the mystery of God, even Christ", which meets the general requirements of the context. It follows that Christ is "the mystery of God", no longer hidden, but manifested (1:26) and meant for us to know to the fulness of our capacity (A.T. Robertson). The Pauline position is clear - "Christ first, Christ last, Christ all the way".

In this prayer of Paul's we discern the great features which mark a faithful company of God's people. (1) It should be a confirmed company - a concentration of courageous hearts. He has prayed for divine enablement that will strengthen the saints to meet every challenging situation with confidence and with courage. (2) It should be a compacted company, "knit together in love" - love to Christ and love to one another. (3) It should be a convicted company, filled with a wealth of certainty which an understanding of the truth brings. (4) It should be a consummated company - fully absorbed with Christ and none else.

3 "In whom" indicates that it is Christ in whom all the treasures of wisdom and knowledge are hidden. The alternative reading translates the relative in the neuter "in which" (so Eadie, Alford, JND, Kelly), referring it to the word "mystery" (v.2). Ellicott considers this as "unusually perplexed". The apostle is not speaking of the mystery, he is here contributing further to the sufficiency of Christ in His essential and eternal fulness. In Him and in Him alone are all these treasures to be found. He is the storehouse of divine wealth; the embodiment of God's wisdom. Paul stresses that *all* these treasures are in Christ. He needs no supplement. No one can add anything to Christ. All that a man requires to be brought into an eternal relationship with God is to be found in Christ and in His work. This is why it is vitally important that man should have a clear understanding relative to the Person of Christ. In Christ there comes the full and final revelation of God, and nothing more is needed; Christ is all. The "wisdom" and "knowledge" presumably are divine and not just in general. "Knowledge" denotes the apprehension of truth as needed in Christ. "Wisdom" is the enlightenment which springs from accepting the revelation of God in Christ. The words *sophia* and *gnōsis* may not require to be carefully distinguished at all. Paul may simply be describing the one thing from different standpoints and in effect be saying, "Call it what you will! Call it *sophia* (wisdom) if you are an adherent of Jewish ideas, or *gnōsis* (knowledge) if you are influenced by Grecian thought; *all* of it - all 'knowledge' that is really worth having - is centred alone in Christ". The position of *apokruphoi* (RV "in whom are all the treasures of wisdom and knowledge hidden") places undoubted emphasis on it. The treasures are "hidden away" in Christ, but are there for our repeated discovery. They are "laid up" in Christ and are available to every believer in the Lord Jesus Christ. He opens up His treasures to us and presents us with wealth inestimable. We then, from our treasures, which are really His wealth acquired, present to Him our gifts which conform to His Person and glory. The OT opens with God giving gold to men; the NT begins with men giving gold to the One who is God incarnate. It is through the acquiring of all that Christ is that we can the more fully worship and adore Him. The wise men possessed the gold before they could present it. These treasures are in Christ but we must make them ours by growing daily in our understanding of Christ.

4 "And this I say" is a formula which generally refers forward (see 1 Cor 1:12; Gal 3:17; Eph 4:17; 1 Thess 4:15). It normally stands for "this is my meaning", introducing an explanation. Here the clause has a reference to the preceding statements of vv.1-3. Paul has mentioned his anxiety and the prayer which that creates in him. Then in the clause immediately preceding he lays great claim for Christ, that the Colossians may not be deluged by specious arguments of those who claim inner wisdom and knowledge.

He fears "lest any man should beguile you with enticing words". *Paralogizomai* ("beguile") is used elsewhere only in James 1:22, and means "to delude, mislead, lead astray, to deceive by false reasoning". Saul used the word when he reviled Michal his daughter for enabling David to escape, saying, "Why hast thou *deceived* me so, and sent away mine enemy, that he is escaped?" (1 Sam 19:17 LXX; cf. Gen 29:25; Josh 9:22). The middle voice of the verb suggests the selfish interests of the deceitful teachers. Their subtle language masks their selfish intent. Neither the glory of Christ nor the good of His people forms their objective. Evil teaching is not so easily discerned when it is presented with "enticing words". Many

Absaloms can persuade by appearances and sympathetic advances which win the hearts of the unwary. When a believer allows himself to be deceived about truth concerning Christ and His glory, the results can be tragic. It is this which gives rise to Paul's anxiety on behalf of the Colossians. Yet he is also conscious of the preservative power of the truth which dispels false teaching and delivers the saints from deceitful workers. The language of Paul puts into bold relief the true manner and matter of the suspects. In the word *pithanologia* ("enticing words") which occurs only here, *pithanos* suggests credibility and *logia* long-windedness. It has the sense of specious, plausible reasoning. It is probable that Paul has in mind his words of 1 Cor 2:4, where the antonym *apodeixis*, "demonstration" or "proof" occurs. The warning which Paul gives should be heeded today for the peril of the persuasive preachers continues to plague believers. If it were a sword that the devil's emissary wields it would be readily discerned, but today it is a Bible, usually a translation that serves his teaching, backed by the attractive brochure and sales talk that wins the unsuspecting and convinces the unwary. Saints are exposed to the employment of every psychological weapon in the armoury of Satan as he seeks to undermine their faith. The need is for leaders who possess a pastoral care for the flock to exercise vigilance and so minister the truth of God as to thwart the intentions of the Evil One. Believers themselves must be fully aware of the danger and so apprehend the teaching of God's word as to withstand the prevailing attack the enemy mounts upon the testimony.

5 Two factors which gripped Paul very strongly were: (1) the presence of deceitful teachers assailing the testimony at Colossae, and (2) his absence, his inability to be present among them to take a more personal part in refuting the teaching threatening the stability of the saints. The ways of God with His servants are often past finding out. Paul knew how much his presence would have meant to the saints at Thessalonica, yet he was hindered in coming among them. His movements were under the control of One who knows the end from the beginning, so his very absence won for them and us this epistle of such spiritual wealth. The Lord knows how to put even the most needful of His servants out of circulation that He may display His resources and make them available to the saints. Would we have had the letters to the seven churches of Asia if John had been at liberty? Would we have possessed the universally-acclaimed Pilgrim's Progress if the Bedford preacher had been given unrestricted movement in his service?

Compare "yet am I with you in spirit" with 1 Cor 5:3,4. Paul had continual concern and prayer for the Colossian saints which gave him a sense of awareness and belonging. The term "in spirit" doubtless speaks of Paul's own spirit, not of the Holy Spirit. This is evident from its antithesis "the flesh" which refers to Paul's physical presence. The epistle when read in their hearing would substantiate the truth of his personal interest in them. Many believers affirm that they are with you in spirit, and that may indeed be true, but it is more assuring when such a pledge is supported by some practical token of their professed interest. The practical demonstration of Paul's concern for the Colossians and evidence of his oneness with them in their stand against evil teaching are seen by (1) his prayerful remembrance of them and his intercession for them, (2) the epistle which he wrote and (3) the sending of Tychicus, the beloved brother and faithful minister who would encourage their hearts. These came as a practical endorsement of his language in this verse.

Paul's encouragement lay in "joying and beholding your order, and the stedfastness of your faith in Christ". If there had been any defection from the ranks of the faithful in Colossae, it was slight for there did not appear to have been any sizeable breach made in the lines. Often in Paul's writings military terms appear: the armoury of Eph 6, the garrison of Phil 4 are some of the figures he employs in conveying his message. It gladdens the heart of the apostle to know that he is helping a company that is standing firm in the face of such an onslaught. What causes him to rejoice? It is the sight of an assembly of saints ordered in rank (*taxis*) and solid in strength (*stereōma*). *Taxis* (AV "order") and *stereōma* (AV "stedfastness") are military terms, the former occurs in nine other passages in the NT whereas the latter is used only here. The boards of the Tabernacle were each supplied with gold rings which gave them a means by which they yielded to the bars of gold. These kept the boards in line thus forming an orderly sanctuary. Collective order amongst God's people is not realised by legal rules and regulations. To each believer there is a given capacity to respond to that which will maintain divine order in God's assembly. Paul sees the Colossians in this light and observes their order with joy. Their faith reposed in Christ. If this is the state of the Colossians why then is Paul so anxious? The answer lies in the presence of the persistent foe. Paul is looking ahead. They are standing firm, but he wishes that they will stand even more firmly as the insurgence of the adversary increases. It is better to fortify in advance than to salvage the remains.

3. The Reception of Christ and its Results
   2:6-7

v.6 "As ye have therefore received Christ Jesus the Lord, so walk ye in him:
v.7 Rooted and built up in him, and stablished in the faith, as ye have been taught, abounding therein with thanksgiving."

The RV wisely forms these two verses into a paragraph which provides a fitting conclusion to the section (begun at 1:29) on Paul's ministry. In this short paragraph Paul reminds the Colossians of their initial experience in which they have accepted Christ as their Saviour and lord. He also urges them to progress in the life of faith.

6 I "as ye have therefore received" *paralambanō* ("received") signified "to take to oneself", usually with respect to personal objects e.g., "his own *received* him not" (John 1:11). It is used emphatically to denote the appropriation of teaching or instruction through transmission (1 Cor 11:23; 15:1,3; Gal 1:9,12; Phil 4:9; 1 Thess 2:6; 4:1; 2 Thess 3:6). The apostle once again confirms the preaching of Epaphras (1:7). What they have heard from him is that which has brought them to a saving faith in Christ, and it requires no supplement. It is the gospel, substantiated by sound doctrinal facts about the Christ which has been instrumental in bringing them to faith in Christ. The fact that Christ has been received is what is uppermost in Paul's mind. Not now the messenger, however faithful, nor the manner of reception, no matter how vital, but the Person received, is the point of Paul's reminder. Paul is not speaking of the Colossians having received the doctrine about Christ, as some aver, it is Christ Himself that they have received - the sum and substance of the evangel of God.

This extended form, "Christ Jesus the Lord" appears nowhere else in Paul, but Eph 3:11 has a slight variation. These have the article before Christ, and read literally:

"the Christ, Jesus the Lord" (Col 2:6)
"the Christ, Jesus our Lord" (Eph 3:11)

It would be appropriate to list other grammatical constructions of the Name combined in various forms with *Kurios* ("Lord").

1. CHRIST JESUS OUR LORD

Rom 6:23	"... is eternal life in Christ Jesus our Lord" (RV).
Rom 8:39	"the love of God in Christ Jesus our Lord".
1 Cor 15:31	"... which I have in Christ Jesus our Lord".
1 Tim 1:2	"peace from God and Christ Jesus our Lord" (RV).
1 Tim 1:12	"And I thank Christ Jesus our Lord".

2. CHRIST JESUS MY LORD

Phil 3:8	"the knowledge of Christ Jesus my Lord".

3. CHRIST JESUS (AS) LORD

2 Cor 4:5	"not ourselves, but Christ Jesus as Lord" (RV).

With these forms of dignity and honour, compare Paul's use of the title "our Lord Jesus Christ".

The construction with the article which appears in the verse before us is found in various passages:

Acts 3:20	"the Christ who hath been appointed for you, *even* Jesus" (RV).
Acts 5:24	"they ceased not to preach Jesus (as) the Christ".
Gal 5:24	"they that are of (the) Christ, Jesus".
Eph 3:1	"the prisoner of (the) Christ, Jesus".

"The Christ" signifies the Messianic office with all its rich meanings. It is an appellative rather than a proper name. (See an excellent note on this subject by JND on 2 Cor 1:5.) In the four passages quoted above the title stands by itself as a distinct term and *not* in immediate connection with "Jesus" as part of a compound title.

Here in 2:6 we can take the article as resuming the mention of Christ in v.5 which strengthens the construction, for "the Christ" then refers to Him as "that" Christ whom they have received. The principal term is "the Christ" and the words "Jesus the Lord" define who the Christ is: He is Jesus, the Lord. Paul establishes the true humanity of the Saviour which accords with Paul's own experience (Acts 9:5). The glorified Christ who has appeared to him is none other than that same Jesus who has been crucified, but who is alive forevermore, and of whom he, Paul, is found the persecutor. The identification is carried further: He is the Lord. The article before "Lord" emphasises the absolute nature of His Lordship. It is not only that Christ is Lord, but that He is *the Lord*. The title implies His essential deity. This is the very aim of the epistle, to set forth the unique dignity of His Person in contradistinction to principalities and powers. So Paul speaks of Him as *the* Lord while in the Ephesian letter, which treats of His gracious relations to His people he speaks of Him as *our* Lord.

"So walk ye in him" can be taken as an imperative. *Peripateite* ("walk") is the first such form in the epistle. The durative tense stresses the permanent character of this walk in Christ: "go on walking in Him". He is not only the object of faith, but He is also the sphere in which the believer must live out his life to the glory of God. The conduct of life must be consistent with the profession of Christ. The once-for-all reception of Christ at conversion is to be balanced by the continuing to walk in the Lord. Truth never creates an imbalance. If the Christian keeps walking in Christ he will be fortified against the destructive teachings of error. This walking in Him affects not only the individual life and course of the believer, but also his collective testimony. To be walking in union with Christ as Lord would mean to be gathered alone in His Name, not gathered in His Name associated with other names. This is not envisaged in the NT. Most believers will never reject the functions and claims of the Lord as Christ. They know He is God's Anointed and will be fully manifested as such. Nor will they depreciate His work as Saviour, knowing all their sins are forgiven and the fulness of resurrection life is theirs in Him. But when it comes to walking in Him as the Lord reasonings arise, arguments abound and the course taken is often one with which the Name of the Lord cannot possibly be associated even though all too often it is. Among many other things, the believer walking in Him as the Lord, will be found in association with a company of likeminded saints, separated from every sectarian and denominational system, and gathered in the Name of the Lord Jesus Christ alone. This and very much more is involved in fulfilling the imperative exhortation which Paul gives in this amazingly-concise expression, "walk ye in Him".

7 "Rooted" is literally "having been rooted" as the verb denotes a past act, with continuing effect, or with a prevailing result. The reference is to the conversion of the Colossians when they first exercised faith in Christ. God rooted them in Christ, as a plant is firmly rooted in soil. It is from Him sustenance is derived that gives the believer tree-like stability to withstand the contrary winds which blow from every quarter. The imagery Paul employs stresses the impossibility of eradication. No force can uproot the believer who is firm-rooted in Christ. There is abiding fixity in Him. What God does He does once and for all. But Paul desires that collectively as an assembly of God's people they may consciously know the abiding effect of the Father's planting. There will also be the production of fruit, which organic union with Christ promotes (John 15). The emphasis in the passage before us is abiding fixity. By this figurative word Paul reveals the true nature of their walk. It is a walk circumscribed by all that they are in Christ and not in anything outside of Him, however plausible it may appear.

"And built up in him", literally, "being built upon" (cf 1 Cor 3:10,12,14; Eph 2:20; Jude 20), presents the figure of a building. Both figures have basically the same issue: growth is the expectation of christian living. The present tense of the verb suggests the attitude of the believer toward Christ which enables him to be constantly and consistently growing, as a building rises progressively toward its completion. God cannot promote the spiritual process by which His people progress if the heart and mind are turned away from Christ. Occupation with Christ and with Christ alone is God's means of developing the life He has imparted to those who believe. A daily dependence upon what He teaches us in His word will preserve us from a change of attitude toward Him, while at the same time it will prosper our spiritual use in what He expects from us. Laodicea was favoured to have those words read to them. Did they heed the injunction? Why then in the last view given of them is their attitude to Christ changed? He is outside. They are poor, blind and naked and are not aware of their spiritual penury (Rev 3). It would appear from this record that it is tragically possible for an assembly to be large numerically, rich materially but stunted in growth spiritually.

They are to be "stablished in the faith". *Bebaioumenoi* ("established") conveys the idea of being confirmed or assured (Rom 15:8; 1 Cor 1:6,8; Heb 2:3). The question arises: is the faith spoken of here the believer's faith or the body of truth? Either makes good sense, though if the preposition is taken as instrumental we adopt the idea that they are "established by means of the faith" which frees them from the doubts the errorists would seek to create by false teaching. There are those who feel that it is "their" faith which calls for greater vigour and render the expression as "established in faith".

"As ye have been taught" alludes to 2:6 and 1:7, and is a reiteration of the statement as to the absolute reliability of what they are taught at first, in all likelihood by Epaphras. The word "taught" seems to confirm the view that "the faith" as the content of the things believed is what the apostle has in mind in the previous expression, which the NEB significantly translates "be consolidated in the faith you were taught". Paul sees the Christ-centred message which was first presented to them as sufficient, therefore he need not go back over the ground as though they lacked anything. His purpose is rather to exhort and build up and strengthen the saints in Christ.

There would be thanksgiving for the truth brought to them, the message of an all-sufficient Christ, the sum total of divine fulness and revelation. There would be thanksgiving for the fact that the truth was presented to them, and that their hearts were opened to receive Him who is the Truth. There would be thanksgiving because all that they needed for spiritual stability and growth was in Christ, their Saviour and Lord. This overflow of gratitude to God would be a preservative from the temptation to doubt the faith once and for all delivered to the saints. As we move through the epistle we shall find a constant insistence upon the holy obligation of thanksgiving. It sounds almost like a refrain, a sweet cadence through the exhortation (1:12; 2:7; 3:15, 17; 4:2).

The summary of vv.6,7 in sermonic dress is:

1. The Confirmation of initial Experience of Christ.
2. The Consolidation of vital Establishment in Christ.
3. The Composition of spiritual Expression to Christ.

IV. Polemical (2:8-19)

1. *The Falsity of the Teaching, the Sufficiency of the Person of Christ 2:8-15*

> v.8 "Beware lest any man spoil you through philosophy and vain deceit, after the tradition of men, after the rudiments of the world, and not after Christ.
> v.9 For in him dwelleth all the fulness of the Godhead bodily.
> v.10 And ye are complete in him, which is the head of all principality and power:
> v.11 In whom also ye are circumcised with the circumcision made without hands, in putting off the body of the sins of the flesh by the circumcision of Christ:
> v.12 Buried with him in baptism, wherein also ye are risen with him through the faith of the operation of God, who hath raised him from the dead.
> v.13 And you, being dead in your sins and the uncircumcision of your flesh, hath he quickened together with him, having forgiven you all trespasses;
> v.14 Blotting out the handwriting of ordinances that was against us, which was contrary to us, and took it out of the way, nailing it to his cross;
> v.15 And having spoiled principalities and powers, he made a shew of them openly, triumphing over them in it."

The long sentence beginning at v.8 and ending at v.9 is one of the most complex in the epistle. The relation between the various expressions is not always clear and there is difficulty in establishing the subject of the verb. While authoritative counsel and warning are the prevailing notes throughout the section, with these there are interspersed solemn words of caution, affirmatory statements concerning the sufficiency of Christ and His work. The section may be divided into four main parts:

1. The warning against being seduced by pretentious philosophy (v.8).
2. The reasons why the teaching is false (vv.9-12):
   (a) who Christ is (v.9),
   (b) what saints are through union with Him (vv.10-12)
     i. Their position in Him (v.10).
     ii. Their circumcision through Him (v.11).
     iii. Their identification with Him in baptism (v.12).
3. The state before and after conversion (vv.13-14):
   (a) Dead in sins (spiritually) and uncircumcised (judicially) v.13a.
   (b) Quickened together with Him, and forgiven.
4. The victorious accomplishment of the cross (v.15).

8 "Beware", "take heed" (RV) as Mark 13:5,9,23,33 or simply "see" (JND) is more literally "see to it" (RSV); also in Eph 5:15; Heb 12:25. Paul is alerting his readers to an existing danger which he considers is real and not hypothetical. Lightfoot speaks of the imminence of the peril. The pastoral heart of Paul is again revealed as he exposes the imposter and warns the flock of the wolf in sheep's clothing. No true shepherd can remain indifferent when the marauder stalks the flock and endangers the security of that which is dependent upon his care.

"Lest any man spoil you" uses a construction which is unique to the NT. Alford suggests that the expression points at some known person, while Lightfoot explains that the construction is frequently used by Paul when speaking of opponents he knows well enough but does not care to name; he cites Gal 1:7 as an example. The RV translation, "take heed lest there shall be anyone", suggests the proximity of the deceiver. The next point of importance in this warning is the intent of the false teacher or teachers. Vivid yet vicious imagery is contained in this essentially invidious word *sulagōgon* ("spoil"). Only used here, it recurred later in classical Creek literature having the sense of "kidnap" according to authorities. That is what it means here. Paul is not warning the readers about simply being robbed of their precious possessions as "despoil" would suggest , but of the fact that *they themselves* could be carried off as booty. Confirmation of this view can be gathered from the emphatic "you" in the text. The sinister activities of these misleading teachers would be to enlist the believers under their banner that they might claim their allegiance.

"Through philosophy and vain deceit" is the means which the adversaries employ to enslave their unwary victims. The speculations of the false teachers at Colossae are specifically deplored by the apostle as can be seen in the expression which literally reads: "his philosophy", as the article before *philosophias* can be taken as a personal pronoun. It was clear that what was being taught by these men in Colossae was not in harmony with divine revelation. It offered no help but was only a deception. Christ was dethroned, displaced and denied; therefore there was no hope offered in their specious arguments and theories. The highest attainments of human intellect are valueless compared with the "wisdom of God". Paul writing to the Corinthians says, "the world through its wisdom knew not God". The world has its wisdom, its philosophies; yet they are totally powerless and inadequate in bringing a soul into eternal relationship to God. In these there is no solid ground for faith (1 Cor 2:5). Mark carefully Paul's language for he never links the word "philosophy" with Christ or with christian doctrine. The hallmark of the christian faith is revelation; hence it is never viewed in Scripture as a philosophy. Liddon rightly observes, "The teacher occupies the third place after the apostles and prophets in 1 Cor 12:28, the fifth in Eph 4:11. Had the church been only a school of philosophy, he must have always been first" (*Explanatory Analysis of Romans*, 1961, p.236). The next part of the expression raises the question: Has Paul two items in mind when he speaks of "philosophy and vain deceit"? If the construction offers the answer then it will be observed that "philosophy" and "deceit" are governed by the one preposition "through". There is no article with "vain deceit". It is assumed that Paul denominates the philosophy as vain deceit. No doubt, the false teachers at Colossae employed some imposing appellations to describe their *medley* of angelology, asceticism and whatever, but Paul's description reveals it for what it is - vain delusion.

"After the tradition of men, after the rudiments of the world" give two prepositional phrases which further describe the "philosophy" as regards its origin and its subject matter. "Tradition" (*paradosis*) means that which is handed on, and is used in the NT of the teachings of the Jewish rabbis (Matt 15:2; Gal 1:14) whose interpretations were transmitted orally from one generation to another, and were committed to writing only at a much later period (Vine). Sometimes it is used of christian doctrine given by the apostles (1 Cor 11:2; 2 Thess 2:15; 3:6). Paul uses it here to show the origin of the philosophy advanced in Colossae: it was man-made, it had no supernatural source, whereas the ministry by which Paul would strengthen the Colossians was the direct result of divine revelation. Nothing less will satisfy the spiritually-rooted believer; nothing more is required. The phrase which follows has received a wide range of interpretations as commentators conceive Paul's meaning in this passage. The noun *stoicheia* is never used in the NT of:

1. the elements of matter (2 Pet 3:10,12);
2. the elementary principles of religion (Gal 4:3,9; Col 2:8,20);
3. the basic elements of instruction in the word of God (Heb 5:12).

Here in v.8, v.20 and also in Gal 4:3,9, the word "rudiments" has the qualifier *of the world* which does not occur in either Heb 5:12 or 2 Pet 3:10,12. The term "of the world" indicates the physical not the spiritual, so it marks the nature of these rudiments. The Galatian passage gives the expression a definite meaning. There Paul wrote about Jewish ritual and worship connected with the Mosaic law. In Gal 4:9, 10 he terms them "weak and worthless elemental things" (NASB), as he chides the Galatians who were reverting to the observation of days, and months, and seasons, and years, and such practices as the Judaizers sought to impose. This return to legal ordinances would crush out every feature of Christ and of the new creation. In Colossae, the false teachers were of the same ilk; they advanced religious practices, particularly ceremonial observances which were purely physical, legal and material, hence devoid of power and efficiency in accomplishing anything spiritual. As in Galatia, such teaching could only bring enslavement and bondage.

It will be noted that the majority of modern commentators and translations favour a different interpretation. The word "rudiments" is taken to mean spiritual powers, "elemental beings" such as supernatural agencies, angels or demons which are believed to preside over the elements of nature, the stars and the planets. Such translations as Mft, RSV, NEB, are inclined towards the "elemental forces" idea. A.S. Peake arrives at the same conclusion after what is generally a helpful discussion in the ECNT, pp.522-523. F.F. Bruce in his *Expanded Paraphrase of the Epistles of Paul* has "elemental powers" in Gal 4:3,9 and Col 2:8, while in v.20, he renders it "elemental spirits". Moule presents a useful treatment of the problem in clear terms (C.F.D. Moule, *Epistles of Paul to the Colossians and to Philemon*, 1962, pp.91-92). Lightfoot, Ellicott, Eadie, Lenski, Hendriksen, Kent, Harrison are among those who interpret the passage with reference to rudimentary teachings, either Jewish or of pagan origin, or a commixture of both.

In "and not after Christ", a strong negative is set against the two positive phrases Paul has set forth to identify the spurious teaching circulating in Colossae. Christ is neither its source nor its subject. Thus Paul condemns the philosophy which threatens the testimony in Colossae on many grounds:

1. It is *vain deceit*   -   Its result is delusion; the truth of the gospel delivers.
2. It is *traditional*   -   Its reliability is questionable, hence unsatisfactory.
3. It is *of men*   -   Its reasoning is human; the gospel is of God.
4. It is *elementary*   -   Its range is infantile; maturity is the Christian's aim.
5. It is *of the world*   -   Its resource is material; the blessings in Christ are spiritual.
6. It is *not after Christ*   -   Its relevance (to man's need) is non-existent; Christ is all.

9 "For in him" or "because in him" introduces additional cause for the implied exclusion of all other teaching which is not after Christ. The contrast between the philosophy and the Son is made the more significant by the emphatic position of the phrase *en autō* ("in him"). Paul directs his readers away from the pretentious philosophy of man to the peerless Person of Christ; away from the traditions of men to Him who is the Truth, and away from the mere rudiments of the world to the One in whom all fulness permanently dwells. Philosophy is an idol of man, a blind substitute for the knowledge of God. It is false and ruinous, whether it leaves Him out or brings Him in. Tradition invariably puts man as far off from God as it can, and calls this religion. The ultimate end of both is that God is set aside. Therein lies its condemnation. So with the mention of Christ Paul launches into a lengthy presentation of the Person and work of Christ (vv.9-15) which resembles 1:15-22.

"Dwelleth" (*katoikei*, 1:19) stresses a permanent dwelling, not something transitory. The tense of the verb points to the present abiding dwelling of the fulness of the Godhead in the glorified Son of God at God's right hand, while the compound form signifies the permanent indwelling of the fulness in Him.

Theotēs ("Godhead") is a word quite different in meaning from *theiotēs* ("divinity", Rom 1:20), because the latter describes the quality of God whereas the former looks at the essence of God. There dwells in Christ not certain aspects of God but the totality of God's attributes, powers and glories. This is conveyed in the term "all the fulness" by which Paul asserts there can be no sharing of His divine power and majesty with other beings, such as angels or the like. Every word in this verse is pregnant with meaning, making it one of the outstanding verses affirming the deity of Christ. This fulness of the Godhead dwells in Christ, in bodily fashion, in His bodily manifestation, that is when He became incarnate - both when on earth and now in heaven, in His present glorified body. This is the sense of the adverb *sōmatikōs* ("bodily"). This verse at once asserts Christ's essential Godhead and His perfect manhood as:

In Him	- No contemporary in angels or men,
dwelleth	- No change, it permanently resides,
all	- No computation, not given by measure,
the fulness of	
the Godhead	- No comparison, the unique Son of God,
bodily	- No corruption, in perfect manhood enthroned.

10   For "and ye are complete in him", the RV has "and in Him ye are made full". "Made full" translates the perfect passive participle of the verb *plēroō*, which is the cognate of the noun *plērōma* ("fulness") in v.9. The subject matter of v.9 is the fulness of the Son, while here it is the fulness of the sons, a cycle often seen in Paul's writings. Compare Gal 4:4 where Paul begins with the singularity of the Son and in v.5 ends with the plurality of the sons. The abiding permanency of all God has made us in connection with His Son is very strongly connoted in the periphrastic perfect: "you have been made full, are so now, and continue so". This is not achieved by any self-effort, for the passive denotes God has made us full in union with His Son. The believer needs no supplement. He requires no help from any subordinate whether he is high or low, angelic or demonic, for Christ is all.

In the phrase "which is head of all principality and power", the reference is to celestial dignities, and to such as are unfallen. Paul has shown in 1:16 that all such beings have been created by God. However high and holy they may be, they are inferior, subordinate as His creatures. Nevertheless they are high, but Christ is higher still. He has first place. He is their head; they owe their allegiance to Him. He is their sovereign Lord; they form a portion of His spiritual dominions. The time will come when they will publicly bow in worship to Him at God's command (Heb 1:6) even as now in His presence they veil their faces (Isa 6:2). The imagery expresses not only the sovereignty of Christ, but also His power to energise and direct these angelic hosts. How then can anyone assign to such provinces of operation which belong to the Son of God? Yet is this not the folly which Paul tacitly evinces, prevailing in Colossae? No believer need adopt even the highest created intelligence as a mediator. He has Christ whose power avails, whose grace abounds, whose love abides and whose blood atones! And yet Roman Catholic teachers still advance the mediation of saints between God and man. Mary is acclaimed as a necessary supplicant, and added indulgences such as Paul denounces in this chapter are accorded a value which can only devalue the Person and work of Christ.

11   The formula "in whom" has its usual significance - union with Christ. Let us not, however, miss the grandeur of this theme which is the very heart of Paul's message, due to its reiteration and peculiar frequency in the epistle. The incorporation of the believer in Christ fully appreciated will impart a much needed vitality and freshness in heart and mind. The theme is introduced by the apostle in 1:4. Our conversion is in view. The moment genuine faith is exercised all the accomplishments of the Person and work of Christ are made good to us by the divine activity of uniting us to Him in an eternal and indissoluble union. In 1:14 it is our clearance that is mentioned. By union with Christ we possess the fulness of redemption which among other things includes the complete forgiveness of our sins. It is through association with Christ that we have a clear sky between God and our souls. V.6 of this chapter introduces us to the first imperative. We have a capacity to respond to divine desires. Here our course as the sphere of spiritual progress is presented as "walk *in him*". The constant rise toward spiritual maturity continues the theme in v.7, where the figure of a building in course of construction endorses the truth that only in association with Christ can real and consolidated maturity be realised. Our completeness has been before us in v.10 and now in this verse, our circumcision opens up further results of our union with Him.

Perietmēthēte ("were circumcised" RV) being an aorist points to conversion when spiritually it took place. It is in union with Christ that true circumcision occurs, a circumcision of an infinitely higher form than is possible under the

Abrahamic covenant or the Mosaic law. The rite in the OT stands in clear contrast to the Christian's circumcision. Several facts concerning the rite will help to bring out the differences. (1) The fact that it is performed by human hands makes it *manual*. (2) That this rite is performed on the body makes it *material*. (3) As only one member of the body is affected its effects are *minimal*. (4) It is restricted to men, *males* only. (5) It is *mechanical* in that it is ceremonial and often is carried out in a perfunctory manner with little interest in its meaning. By contrast the circumcision mentioned in these verses partakes of none of these five features. It is spiritual and entire. There is no need for the Colossians to suffer the incision of a sharp knife when they are already enjoying the results of a spiritual circumcision through their living union with Christ. Paul further describes the Christian's circumcision by saying that it is "not made with hands" (RV), meaning that man has no part in it for it is not an outward but an inward circumcision. This circumcision is not "human" but "divine"; it comes from Christ, not Moses; it achieves spiritual results for it frees man from the flesh. Spiritual circumcision is not entirely a new concept for often in the OT it appears in various forms (cf. Deut 10:16; 30:6; Jer 4:4; 6:10; 9:26; Ezek 44:7,9). Stephen borrows from this terminology when lie calls his audience "uncircumcised in heart and ears" (Acts 7:51 RV). Paul's significant reference in Rom 2:29 shows that the language can be most explicit. Any performance of circumcision as a ceremonial rite is of no moral or spiritual consequence for it has been rendered obsolete by the death of Christ. Paul casts an intended disparagement when he reduces it to the low level of "concision" (*katatomē*) (Phil 3:2). A kindred word *katatemnō* is found in the LXX for the forbidden "cutting in the flesh" (Lev 21:5) practised by the priests of Baal (1 Kings 18:28) and the idolaters. He expands the character of the new circumcision in a threefold description: "who worship by the Spirit of God, and boast in Christ Jesus, and do not trust in the flesh" (Phil 3:3 JND).

From the AV rendering, "in putting off the body of the sins of the flesh", both the RV and JND, in common with the vast majority of translations, omit the words "of the sins" and render the expression as "in the putting off of the body of the flesh". This strongly-supported reading makes the new circumcision a more complete thing. It is not the question of sins, but rather of the whole carnal and evil propensity in the human self. "Sins", says W. Kelly, "would hardly be in keeping with the scope of the passage or phrase". The double compound noun *apekdusis* ("putting off") occurs only here in the NT. It stands for a dual action: a divesting and a discarding. That of which Paul is speaking is not only stripped off, but it is also cast away, as an old, filthy garment is thrown aside never to be worn again (cf. 2:15; 3:9 for the verb form).

Various ideas have been expressed regarding the phrase "the body of the flesh", confessedly a difficult expression. Eadie stresses that *sōma* ("body") must retain its usual signification. The interpretation propounded on this premise as Vaughan rightly observes, "... understands 'body' to be a reference to the physical body, 'flesh' to be a descriptive genitive marking the body as *conditioned by* our fallen nature" (*A Study Guide - Colossians*, 1974, p.74). Lenski suggests the term refers to "the physical body as belonging to and dominated by sinful flesh". "The Christian", he adds, "no longer has such a body". Others, however, take "body" as representing "wholeness", "totality" or "entirety". Then the question arises: what does *sarx* ("flesh") represent? Paul uses the word ninety-one times in his epistles (excluding Hebrews). These references fall into three categories, namely, those that refer to: (1) the physical body, (2) that which is human or humanity, and (3) inherent evil in human nature. It is with the third category that we are concerned. The more accurate way to interpret the recurring use of any word or phrase under the guidance of the Holy Spirit is to compare carefully all its occurrences and textual settings. Under component (3) there are some twenty-six references which are as follows:- Rom 7:5,18,25; 8:5,5,6,7,8,9,12,13; 13:14; Gal 4:23,29; 5:13,16,17,17,19,24; 6:8,8; Eph 2:3,3; Col 2:11,18. The reader, after pondering all of Paul's ninety-one usages, can best decide whether this list can be extended or reduced. Returning now to the full term, "the body of the flesh", it denotes the totality of carnal and evil propensity in self. This, says Paul, has been put off in circumcision, a circumcision not of men, but of Christ. This is the ground of holiness positionally as before God and the power of it conditionally in living experience. The moment we exercise faith in the Lord Jesus, all the value of His death is made good to us. It is in association with His death that we part with our evil state as man in the flesh. God has stripped off and has thrown it away, as one would cast aside unwanted garments. So that in the light of this it can be said *of* us, "But ye are not in the flesh, but in the Spirit..." (Rom 8:9). And to us it is said, "and make not provision for the flesh, to fulfil the lusts thereof" (Rom 13:14).

"By the circumcision of Christ", - that is,

1. not the circumcision Christ underwent in infancy, nor
2. the circumcision which is in its nature "of Christ" either as the agent who performs or as the author who provides, but
3. the circumcision which is Christ's own, that is, His death.

This rich, yet difficult verse establishes the *fact* of a new circumcision, different in many aspects from that of the OT. That rite is experienced by a surgical act, whereas the new circumcision is the result of a spiritual association with Christ in His death. The mark of the knife attested nationality, but the cast-off body of the flesh is the index of liberty, freedom from the legal and tyrannical power of the flesh. It is in this the intent of the new circumcision is implied. The means of this new circumcision is the crucifixion of Christ when He was "cut off out of the land of the living" (Isa 53:8). Finally, the verse presents the *message* of the new circumcision, a message which proclaims the glory of the work of Christ, in that it deals not only with what we have done - our sins - but it also deals with what we are. We see, as in the trespass-offering aspects of the death of Christ, that our sins are removed in His blood. By contrast the sin-offering teaches that we as sinners are released in the cross.

12 "Buried with Him in baptism" is a reference to christian baptism and its spiritual significance. Baptism forms a part, and a very sizeable part of the commission given by the risen Lord to His disciples in Matt 28:19. All who believed the gospel were to be baptised in the name of the Father, the Son and the Holy Spirit. It was practised by the apostles right from the commencement of their ministry in Acts 2:41 as other references in the book will show. The place it finds in apostolic writings indicates that baptism is not only the commandment of the Lord, but that it is also He who reveals by the Spirit its meaning (Rom 6:1-4; Gal 3:27; Col 2:12; 1 Pet 3:21). There is something new associated with baptism in these verses; in Rom 6 it is newness of life or, shall we say, *conduct*. In Gal 3, it is the newness of *character*: we put on Christ. In Col 2:12 it is the new *circumcision* and in 1 Pet 3:21, a new *creation* appears. The Colossian passage bears out two important factors about baptism: (1) it is only for those who have exercised faith in the Lord Jesus, because baptism always follows faith; it never precedes it, and (2) baptism is by immersion, as the meaning of the word implies - *baptō* ("to dip"). In v.11 identification with Christ in death precedes union or association with Him in burial. In the natural realm, only dead people are buried, and all dead people are buried in the normal course of events. Thus it is in baptism. The NT never envisages an unbaptised believer since Christ died. Several expositors disclaim that water-baptism is referred to in this expression, rather they suggest that it must be Spirit-baptism. The baptism in the Spirit is always associated with life and not with death; it is linked with Pentecost, not with Calvary. The baptism in the Spirit brings us into a living organism - the one body (1 Cor 12:13). What a tremendous death has taken place in v.11, the death of the self principle, described in all its totality as "the body of the flesh". Now there is burial, which evinces the reality of that death. Our cutting off is in His cutting off; our burial is in His burial; so also in His resurrection, we are raised, which Paul now brings in more forcibly than in Rom 6.

"Wherein" raises a question: Is this the correct rendering? Eadie, with Nicholson and others read, "in whom" referring not to baptism as do the AV, RV, JND, etc, but to Christ, which follows the similar expression at the beginning of v.11. Paul continues the symbolism of baptism for in the word itself three symbolic acts are seen, (1) immersion, (2) submersion and (3) emergence. The individual being baptised does not remain under the water into which he has been immersed. He emerges from the waters like as Christ rose from out of the tomb. So jointly we are entombed with Him in the baptism *in which* also we are jointly raised with Him.

Sunegeirō ("rise with") occurs again in 3:1 and also in Eph 2:6. It is a resurrection actually enjoyed by believers now in union with Christ, as we enter on a new state not in respect of our bodies as yet, but our souls. The Ephesian passage goes on beyond the point reached here by the apostle. He does not pursue the ultimate or highest results of the work of Christ. It is characteristic of this epistle that nowhere does it say that we are seated in the heavenly places. We are raised together with Christ, and it pleases the Holy Spirit to stop there. Paul always uses the passive when speaking of the resurrection of Christ, except in 1 Thess 4:4 (the reading of 2 Cor 5:5 is "was raised"). So unmentioned, God is the One who acts. It is He who has wrought the circumcision. He buries us with Christ and it is He who raises us up together with Him. This prepares us for Paul's concluding thought in the verse.

"Through the faith of the operation of God, who hath raised him from the dead" sets before us the revelation of God's power in the resurrection of His Son. It produces faith. Faith is the light of God in the soul. Abraham believed God because of the revelation God gave of Himself to him. This is presented in the gospel - Christ died, Christ was raised - and we believed. Faith here must be taken in the objective sense. The mighty working of God fully demonstrated in the resurrection of Christ is the object of the believer's faith and trust (Rom 10:9).

13 By the phrase "and you, being dead in your sins and the uncircumcision of your flesh" Paul describes the unregenerate state of the Colossians. He speaks of their former state before God in two ways: (a) in trespasses (RV), for their lives were lived in disobedience to God, for they were sinners from a fallen stock, and (b) in the uncircumcision of their flesh, which can mean two things: (i) They were Gentiles without the law and as such alienated from the covenant of God (Eph 2:11-12). (ii) There was a life of unrestrained sin, fulfilling every fleshly lust and passion (cf. Rom 6:20). This second view not only suits the passage but also conforms with the fact that Jews and Gentiles, physically circumcised or not, are alike dead due to their trespasses and their carnal human nature.

In the words "hath he quickened together with him", God is the subject. But the question arises: Is God the subject right through to verse 15? Again, authorities differ. Alford (Vol. III 1958, p.221) regards God as the subject throughout. Ellicott propounds the view that Christ is the subject (*Paul's Epistles to the Philippians, the Colossians and Philemon*, 1875, pp.162-163). Lightfoot says, "... it seems necessary to assume a change of subject". He takes God as the subject of the verb "hath quickened" and supposes that a new subject, Christ, is introduced with the verb "took" (v.14) and the verbs that follow (*Paul's Epistles to the Colossians and to Philemon*, 1892, p.183). It would appear that the transition of subject is in harmony with Paul's general usage of the terms. God has granted us new life in His Son. We have, in the language of the Lord Jesus, "passed from death unto life" (John 5:24). Now we are alive unto God in His Son. Our co-quickening with Christ means that His life is our life, our fulness and our all.

For "having forgiven you all trespasses", the RV reads "having forgiven us all our trespasses", showing that Paul hastens to include himself and all other believers in this rich experience of divine grace. This is the forgiveness that is preached in His Name (Acts 13:38), procured in His blood (Eph 1:7), provided in His grace (Col 1:13) and possessed by faith (Acts 10:42). The "all" has found its way through these great sections and its significance cannot be overlooked. In the RV there are twenty-three of them, including the "alway" of 1:3. As in this verse, so with every occurrence there is a comprehensiveness that is in keeping with the character of the epistle. Earlier statements of this epistle have reminded us of what has been called into existence - the whole creation in its magnitude and majesty. This verse tells of what has been put out of existence - all our trespasses. Hezekiah wrote, "For thou has cast all my sins behind thy back" (Isa 38:17), that is *out of sight*. Micah, in assuring confidence put it, "And thou wilt cast all their sins into the depths of the sea" (Micah 7:19), that is *out of reach*, while Jehovah Himself said, "For I will forgive their iniquity, and I will remember their sin no more" (Jer 31:34), that is *out of mind*. And here, the forgiveness is so complete and decisive - our trespasses are *out of existence* - all of them, forever! How important this little word "all" is in this verse, as it is in each of its twenty-three occurrences. It would be helpful to list each appearance. However, those which we have chosen may lead the reader to ponder further so that their full message may be enjoyed.

1. The "all" in connection with His fulness (2:9) comprehends the Godhead.
2. The "all" in connection with His treasury (2:3) comprehends all wisdom and knowledge.
3. The "all" in connection with His pre-eminence (1:18) comprehends all things.
4. The "all" in connection with His cross-work (1:20) comprehends the universe.
5. The "all" in connection with His forgiveness (2:13) comprehends all trespasses.
6. The "all" in connection with His mystery (1:26 RV) comprehends all ages.
7. The "all" in connection with His gospel (1:6) comprehends the world.

This magnifical bounty of gracious forgiveness touches Jew as well as Gentile. Paul's change from "you" Colossians to "us" indicates others besides the Colossians. God has also wrought for them what Paul says He has done for his readers. It is just the inclusion of the Jew which makes it possible for the apostle to continue as he does. Then, too, the matter of forgiveness is of such importance as to cause Paul by the Spirit to give it a more extended treatment which follows in vv.14 and 15. Going back to v. 13 for connection, we observe that through the quickening power of God the believer knows freedom from spiritual death. This is followed by (though simultaneous in experience) forgiveness which proclaims freedom from sins and their consequences. Bound up with these gracious actions of God in salvation is the consequent freedom from law. How that freedom came about in the operation of God and of Christ is shown ever so clearly in these verses. In order that we may see at a glance the titanic value of the work of Calvary, we shall list what was accomplished there as contained in vv.14 and 15.

In respect of the Law:

v.14 Annulment -	The blotting out (*exaleipsas*) of ordinances.
Banishment -	He took it out of the way (*ērken*).
Attachment -	Nailing (*prosēlōsas*) it to His cross.

In respect of the principalities and powers:

v.15 Divestment -	And having spoiled (*apekdusamenos*) them.
Disparagement -	He made a show (*edeigmatisen*) of them openly.
Achievement -	Triumphing over (*thriambeusas*) them in it.

In anticipation of what follows in the succeeding verses, it may be helpful to point out that the details of v.14 certainly provide the basis for the imperative advice of vv.16 and 17, while the statements of v.15 lead to the similar imperative of vv.18 and 19.

14 The translation of the RV "bond" is no improvement on the foregoing "handwriting" of the AV. Some see *cheirographon* ("handwriting") as an IOU, a statement of indebtedness personally signed (Moule op.cit.). "The word", says Vine, "was used for the autograph signature to a promissory note. It frequently occurs in Roman law". Such a signature must be found, so Lightfoot writes, "The bond is the moral assent of the conscience, which (as it were) signs and seals the obligation". That such a signature is to be found in Exod 24:3 when Israel obligated herself to the keeping of the law, and for the Gentile, a corresponding recognition of obligation in Rom 2:15, appears to answer the case. It is a question as to whether any signature of ours is even remotely thought of. The law of God bears His signature and seal, and stands as God's statement against our indebtedness. The demands of the Law found all mankind hopelessly in debt and totally guilty before God (Rom 3:19). Not only is the Law down on us due to our inability to meet its stern claims, it is also "contrary to us" inasmuch as it demands the penalty due to guilt. It was at Calvary God cancelled the "handwriting", He erased the awful indictment which stood hostile to us. The verse assures us that all our obligations which we can never meet are cancelled by the death of Christ. The penal claims of the Law have been fully met in a Saviour crucified.

In "and took it out of the way", the perfect tense of the verb *airō* ("took") lays stress on the abiding significance of what was done on the cross. This means that not only has the writing been erased, but also the very document which bore the writing has itself been taken away forever. The phrase "out of the way" emphasises the completeness of the Law's removal. Johnston thoughtfully notes, "the expression is found in 1 Cor 5:2 (*anarthrous*) of the excommunication of sinning brethren from the assembly's fellowship. The law has been excommunicated from Christian fellowship!"

By "nailing it to his cross" the "bond" has been taken away. The vivid language brings the verse to the climax of the cross in no uncertain way. There must be some connection between the superscription and Paul's thought here, for there is no such idea of nailing a document in such a manner to be found elsewhere. It is an act which never needs to be repeated as the tense clearly implies. The Law was put to death once and for all when Christ died. This is a glorious truth and one in which every believer in Christ can rejoice and respond to the hymn writer's appeal.

> Let us love and sing and wonder!
> Let us praise the Saviour's name!
> He has hushed the law's loud thunder,
> He has quenched mount Sinai's flame;
> He has washed us in His blood,
> He has brought us nigh to God.
>
> John Newton

This verse has taught three things about the Law, namely: (1) Its *Demands*: "handwriting of ordinances"; compare "writing *in* ordinances" (Eph 2:15). The word *dogma* ("regulations" NIV) includes both the moral and ceremonial enactments. This must be maintained in view of vv.16-17. (2) Its *Designs*: "by the law is the knowledge of sin" and in this verse it was "against us". It revealed our total indebtedness. (3) Its *Determination*: if its claims are not met our doom under its penalty is certain. So it "was contrary to us". But through the accomplishment of Calvary, the commands, claims and voices of the Law have been silenced once and for all. In this the Law has been (1) cancelled, (2) taken out of the way, never to return again, and (3) it has been nailed to the cross, the cross being the record of a permanently removed Law.

The next verse continues the theme of the cross and we should decide the subject of v.15 before proceeding any further. From a grammatical point of view, "God" is the subject in v.13; it is He who has quickened us together with Him. But from that point forward there is no name or pronoun that will help us determine the subject of the verbs that follow. We have already observed that some continue right through vv.13-15 with "God" as the subject (see JND). Others at various points change to "Christ", eg. Lightfoot changes to "Christ" with the verb "took it out of the way" (p.187). Moule makes the change earlier at "blotting out". The present writer proposes to make the change now at v.15 and suggests that "Christ" is the subject of the three verbs in this verse.

15 The participle *apekdusamenos* creates considerable difficulty in assessing its meaning. The word suggests "to put off" and is connected with the idea of "putting off an unwanted garment" (cf 2:11, where the noun occurs). Those who interpret the word as such arrive at a conclusion similar to Johnston when he says, "Christ divested Himself at the cross of the evil powers which had struggled with Him so strongly throughout His ministry in attempts to force Him to abandon the pathway of the cross (cf Luke 4:13; Matt 16:22-23; Luke 25:53 etc)". There are slight variations to this view, one being that the "principalities and powers" are not evil but good, and are reckoned to be those angels through whom God mediated the Law. But these will not meet the subject matter of the verse. On examination of the objects in each of the three passages where the word in either form is found there will be grounds given for a different sense of the word here, as for example, in 2:11, here the participle has "the body of the flesh" as something clinging like a garment, so it is cast off! Likewise in 3:9 it is "the old man" which must also be cast off. In the passage before us it is persons or personal powers who are stripped, so the AV is correct - "having spoiled" conveys the right sense. Then what about the middle voice? It is argued that the middle voice does not mean "having disarmed someone" (Kent) but if Christ did this *on His own behalf* for *His own glory*, then it will. It is a clear explanation of Luke 11:22; Matt 12:29; Heb 2:14. The conflict at Calvary far transcends our thoughts; we are only able to measure the intensity of the battle by the absolute victory accomplished. No angels of the class mentioned in 2:10 would solicit worship, indeed they would refuse it (Rev 22:8-9). Any angel that would invite worship to himself could only belong to those of this verse and has neither right nor worth nor honour to receive it (2:18).

Edeigmatisen ("he made a shew of them openly") means to be exhibited in public spectacle, to expose. The complete subjugation of the forces of evil is their public disgrace. This is emphasised by the word -openly (see John 7:4). The victory of Christ should nerve us in our conflict with the powers of evil (Eph 6:12). We should never be brought into subjection by a defeated foe nor fear its power. The practical value of His cross should be more and more experienced in daily living.

"Triumphing over them in it" refers to the cross, not the "bond". The picture must agree with that of Paul's other use of the word in 2 Cor 2:14. The subjugation is complete. They are a defeated foe. He leads them in His triumphal procession proclaiming His sovereign superiority over them. This was accomplished on the cross. The scene of His deepest humiliation is the place of His wondrous victory; His suffering, their subjugation; His death, their defeat; His cross, their car of shame.

> He subdued the powers of hell;
> In the fight He stood alone;
> All His foes before Him fell,
> By His single arm o'erthrown.
> They have fall'n to rise no more;
> Final is the foe's defeat;
> Jesus triumphed by His power,

And His triumph is complete.
His the fight, the arduous toil,
His the honours of the day,
His the glory and the spoil,
Jesus bears them all away.
Now proclaim His deeds afar,
Fill the world with His renown;
His alone the Victor's car,
His the everlasting crown.
Thomas Kelly

2. The Falsity of the Practice, the Headship of Christ 2:16-19

v.16 "Let no man therefore judge you in meat, or in drink, or in respect of an holyday, or of the new moon, or of the sabbath days:
v.17 Which are a shadow of things to come; but the body is of Christ.
v.18 Let no man beguile you of your reward in a voluntary humility and worshipping of angels, intruding into those things which he hath not seen, vainly puffed up by his fleshly mind.
v.19 And not holding the Head, from which all the body by joints and bands having nourishment ministered, and knit together, increaseth with the increase of God."

Paul has established beyond all doubt that the teaching of those who are troubling the saints at Colossae, by whatever name we denominate them, are entirely false. The strong admonition on their teaching in 2:8 cannot be easily forgotten. It is an inevitable corollary that if the teaching is false, the resultant practice derived from that teaching will likewise be false. In these vv.16-19, which both the RV and JND class as a paragraph, Paul raises warnings regarding the ritualistic observances advanced by the errorists. He exposes the groundlessness of their insistence upon observances which are mere shadows, transitory and external. No spiritual progress can be gained from these ascetic habits. Anyway they lead to the worship of the wrong object, though the present writer has no doubt that their asceticism fitted them for any encounter they proposed to have with angels or spirits.

From a positive standpoint the paragraph expresses the close and necessary connection between doctrine and practice. Those great verses of the foregoing section with all their rich presentation of the Person and work of Christ are now followed by careful application of the truth to a given situation. Too often mere theorising leaves the saints of God cold and unblessed. Truth must be expounded clearly and decisively, then its message must be brought to bear upon the spiritual needs of God's people.

16 The "therefore" links the reader's mind with the truth presented in vv.14 and 15. There has already been pointed out a suggestion that this imperative appeal of the apostle finds its basis in the words of v.14, and that of v.18 in the language of v.15. Generally speaking, however, the force of the "therefore" is to draw attention to the decisive victory won at the cross, so there is no need to be brought into bondage of fear that failure to adhere to the ordinances will bring displeasure and perhaps reprisals from spirit forces. Nor need there be any fear of criticism on a human level. Paul's words are firm yet comforting: "let no man therefore judge you". The word *krinō* means "to judge" (see in a similar context Rom 14:3). The sense here is "take you to task" or "call you to account". Paul assures the Colossians that there is no ground for judgment. The cross has put an end to all the compulsions of Law. When light is refused, how great the darkness! Once the truth of the cross reaches the soul in the power of the Holy Spirit, then there is light and liberty. The Colossians had experienced this, but were being threatened by men who did not experience the emancipating power of the cross.

"In meat, or in drink, or in respect of an holyday, or the new moon, or of the sabbath days" identifies five items representing the system of religion advanced by the false teachers, nothing spiritual, but plenty of the natural and sensual. Where eating and drinking became an issue in the NT, there is an unhappy gradation toward apostate evil. The question arises in Rom 14, as noted already, where it is a matter of *weakness*, a condition not to be lightly overlooked, though consideration toward those weak in the faith Paul thoughtfully advises. The occasion before us now reveals men who have refused divine light, such as comes through the preceding verses, so it is not merely weakness now, but *wilfulness*, a refusal to obey and to receive divine illumination. This, of course, on the part of the false teachers, whereas in 1 Tim 4:2-3 eating again arises this time as part of the doctrine of demons, so it is now fully manifested as *wickedness*, apostate wickedness inspired by demons. The believer knows that "the kingdom of God is not meat and drink; but righteousness, and peace, and joy in the Holy Ghost" (Rom 14:17), and so he should not be brought into bondage in matters of *eating or drinking*. The three items that follow reveal the adoption of the Jewish religious calendar was another feature of these false teachers. "Holy day", which the RV renders as "feast day", is one of the annual feasts such as Passover; "new moon" one of the monthly festivals, while "sabbath" the weekly holyday. These various appointed days served a distinct purpose under the old economy, but have nothing whatever to do with this present economy of God. Gal 4:10 provides a useful parallel, and there, as here, the apostle discredits such religious observances of days as inconsistent with their spirit of grace and of the gospel. It is of particular interest to observe that the sabbath is included with such items as are not binding on the believer today. Out of twenty-one epistles in the NT this is the only reference to the sabbath, and its observance is obviously unapproved. This provides cold comfort for those who impose its observance today. Once people put themselves under the Law, they became debtors to do *all* the law enjoined. The Colossians are to see to it that no one judges them in respect of these things.

Since the judge is not prompted by the truth of the gospel but by his inspired philosophy and empty deceit, the Colossians are not only to avoid what he forbids, but they are also not to do what such a judge approves. The liberty which is the portion of all who believe the gospel is best asserted in absolute terms, with no quarters given. Hence the imperative call of the apostle can read "let no man judge you either way".

17 *Skia* ("shadow") classifies the five items Paul has listed in the previous verse, not that they are the shadow but they are *a* shadow. Then they are nothing more than a shadow as they belong, one and all, to the age of preparation. Now in this period when the purpose of God is fully revealed in Christ, all this shadow is banished for good. There is a striking correspondence between Paul's terms employed here and those in Heb 8:5 which speaks of those "who serve" with "a copy and shadow (*skia*) of the heavenly things". The "heavenly things" in that verse compare more or less with "the things to come" here. Likewise, Heb 10:1 has the terms standing in close connection the one to the other: "For the law having a shadow (*skia*) of the good *things* to come, not the very image of the things".

In "but the body is of Christ", *sōma* ("body") is not an allusion to the physical body of Christ or to His body, the church: it stands here in opposition and contrast to *skia* ("shadow"). Therefore, it has the idea of substance. The RV by its rendering, "but the body (substance) is Christ", conveys that the substance belongs to Christ in that it *consists* of Him. Apart from Him and all that He is and has accomplished, the shadow is meaningless. He is the fulfilment of all that the law and its ceremonial observances foreshadowed. Since He came and revealed Himself, there is no longer any need for the shadow, So why submit to regulations, rites and rituals that have been stripped of their typical significance? The godly Jew was to learn from these ordinances of the coming One; they pointed to Christ. The Lord Jesus said, "Moses wrote of me" (John 5:46), others would say, "We have found him of whom Moses in the law and the prophets did write" (John 1:45). But the spurious teachers in Colossae prefer the shadow instead of the reality. How empty their philosophy. How deceptive their creed. It is therefore essential that believers today understand where they now are in relation to the purpose of God. In vv.16 and 17, Paul, by the guidance of the Spirit of God, shows how the fulness of Christ may be practically denied by going back to shadows. The warning is very much needed in these days. The religious systems patterned after the Judaistic order and ritual are not satisfied with the substance alone, they desire an overwhelming mixture of the shadow, as though Christ were not enough.

18 "Let no man beguile you of your reward" begins the second part of Paul's warning which is concerned not so much with ritualism as in vv.16 and 17, but with mysticism. The passage is fraught with difficulties, both textual and conceptual. Happily, the gist of Paul's thought is clear. It is expressed as a strongly-termed warning lest the Colossians should succumb to the adverse condemnation of the false teachers who hold out in place of the gospel their own brand of teaching, a product of their vain speculative imaginings. The apostle identifies these men as being victims of a sensuous system because they reject divine revelation and glory in their natural wisdom. The consummate judgment is that they have no relationship whatever to Christ. There is no link between them and the living Head, so they do not possess His life nor are they nurtured by His supply of power and grace. The danger threatening the Colossians is of such moment that Paul comes to close grips with the error and its abettors.

There is great diversity of opinion as to how the verb *katabrabeuetō* is to be translated and understood. The perplexity lies in the rareness of the word. A variety of renderings exist; RV, "rob you of your prize"; JND, "fraudulently deprive you of your prize", NIV; "disqualify you for the prize", etc. Arndt and Gingrich give the meaning as: "decide against (as umpire), rob of a prize, condemn" (p.410). Vine, *Expository Dictionary*, Vol. 3, p.301, suggests, "Another rendering closer to the proper meaning ... is 'let no man decide for or against you' (ie, without any notion of a prize); this suitably follows the word 'judge' in verse 16, that is, 'do not give yourselves up to the judgement and decision of any man' (AV marg. 'judge against')". There appears to be justifiable ground for regarding the word we are considering as a stronger synonym for "judge" in v.16, and accepting the AV marginal reading. Paul's imperative appeal shows his concern that the Colossians will not in any way be affected by the adverse judgment pronounced against them by these sophists because they refuse the imposing dogmas of the errorists. Paul's kind of Christianity would never gain the plaudits of these "arbiters". The false teachers wanted to be arbiters of the believer's conscience; causing him to approve what they approve and refuse what they refuse. Paul's ministry, in the power of the Spirit, places the believer in the rich possession and knowledge of a liberty only Christ can give. It was this liberty Paul would have the Colossians cherish - a liberty enjoyed in Christ, endorsed by divine revelation and experienced in the power of the Spirit of God.

The "in" (*en*) of "in a voluntary humility" is to be understood as instrumental, being the means by which the person assays to make such adverse judgment. The action of the preposition is of vital interest to the understanding of the phrase. It qualifies "humility" and "worshipping of angels", thus revealing the means by which the false teacher seeks to affect his judgment upon those who refuse to recognise his piety. There is again a plethora of views as to the meaning of these terms. Many expositors take *thelōn* to mean "delighting in" and quote LXX usages to confirm this sense. While the view is opposed by as many again, it comes within the drift of the context the more smoothly. Were these errorists not hoping to gain advantage over the Colossians by a spurious humility in which they took great pride? They were glorying in their self-abnegation. It was all show, a show in the flesh, a piety in a self-inflicted poverty and privation. This now brings us to face the change that only here and in v.23 becomes the word "humility" in the NT. In its other occurrences, humility is a christian virtue patterned after the One who Himself says, "I am meek and lowly of heart" (Matt 11:29), Paul sees it as false humility and warns the saints accordingly. When men become proud of their humility it ceases to be a virtue; rather it is a vice. The heart is so deceitful we cannot be careful enough lest our pretensions to piety become the display of our pride. It is a subtle snare that the treacherous teacher has laid in the path of the Colossian believers. The parade of his avowed humility was calculated to seduce the unwary. When the Lord Jesus spoke of giving, praying and fasting (Matt 6), He gave clear warnings against doing these things merely to be seen of men and having their praise. The Colossian Christian would allow his conscience to be guided by such principles and subsequently his actions. That is how it should be, Paul is saying; so do not allow any man to be arbiter of your conscience, who takes pleasure in a false humility which is contrary to every principle of the kingdom into which, by divine power and grace, you have been translated.

The -worshipping of angels" is another instrument by which the errorist would reduce the faithful. If the genitive is taken to be the subject then the meaning is as propounded by Lenski: "worship which angels perform" (p.130). The genitive, we believe, is that of object, which Vine does too as the following quotation indicates when he notes *"thrēskeia is used ... of the 'worshipping' of angels, Col 2:18 *which they themselves repudiate (Rev 22:8,9)"* (op.cit., Vol. 3, p.272). Eadie observes, "How angels came to be worshipped we may not precisely know, though, certainly it might not be difficult to account for it, when one sees how saintworship has spread itself so extensively in one section of Christendom" (p.185). There are post-apostolic records which confirm that the worship of angels was widespread. There was a temple built to the honour of the archangel Michael who, incidentally, was worshipped in Colossae for a miracle allegedly wrought by him. It would act as a bulwark to the testimony of the saints in Colossae to have received Paul's ministry in v.15, even if the seeds of these reprobate practices were being sown. The fulness of Christ and His work always answers every inroad of evil, whether it is moral, as in 1 Corinthians, or doctrinal, as here.

"Intruding into those things" is an element of the verse wrapped in obscurity. The reader is advised that the range of meaning given to this expression is such that it is not practical to record it all here. A recourse to the lexicon of Arndt and Gingrich will pose useful, where under *embateuō* (p.253) there are listed four possible meanings for this word. (See also Vine, Vol. 1, p.345.) The participle can be taken as "penetrating into". It forms part of the false system, one of a series that forms the pretentious claims of the false teachers. Not satisfied with divine

---

*T.B.'s italics.

revelation, nor possessing any holy respect for the sacred reservations of God in His communications to man (Deut 29:29), they rashly intrude with an unholy foot into those things which are the prerogative of the divine.

"Which he hath not seen" raises another debatable point, as to the presence of *mē* (not). The RV omits the word "not" while JND retains it. The meaning is not affected either way. Without the disputed negative the sense will be visions which he professes or imagines to have seen. On the other hand, if "not" is retained in the reading, it is the apostle's denial that this is their experience. It appeals to the present writer that the weight of evidence favours the RV rendering, for it seems natural to the passage that the visionaries would claim their whole physical, mental and religious state is conducive to acquiring sights and insights the ordinary Christian in Colossae knows nothing of.

"Vainly puffed up by his fleshly mind" contains the third participle in the series, of which another awaits us in the following verse. All that this envisaged preacher-philosopher has experienced is bound to have had effect upon him. What with assuming the role of a conscience guardian, and possessing the very elements of "humility", with power to penetrate the impenetrable, exercising the freedom of adorative worship to angels, surely the end result must be imaginably great! The wheel, shall we say, turns full circle in Paul's opinion so clearly expressed in the verse. Whereas the teacher appears as the very essence of humility, he is actually full-blown with his own conceit. He is being constantly puffed up by the special knowledge he claims to possess. The man, even in this particular frame of mind, is a denial of all that is bound up in the divine nature, and fully revealed in Christ, viz., love (1 Cor 13:4). The inflation is the result of a mind untouched by the power of God. The work of regeneration has never taken place for the "mind of the flesh" is the controlling power in the soul. It must ever be remembered that the "reason of the flesh" is wholly unable to cope with the "deep things" of the Spirit.

To sum up, Paul regards such people as dangerous, as deceived, as led astray by a vain deceit that is based on spurious fanciful knowledge. They are occupied with idle shadows and are visionaries, Christ is not a reality to them. He says, never allow such people to condemn you.

We append the paraphrase in summation of the intricate matters of this verse: "You see to it that no man affects your judgment, who, for all his pretended humility, worships angels and not the Lord. He is penetrating spheres beyond his range of vision treading on air because of what he thinks he sees; he is inflated with conceit through his unillumined reasonings. Furthermore, he does not hold the Head ..."

19 "And not holding the Head" supplies us with the fourth participle and shows that the person or persons considered in v.18 are not the Lord's. This verse recalls at once the parallel of Eph 4:15-16. The word *krateō* describes a firm grasp, a tenacious hold (Mark 1:31; 9:27) and is used metaphorically of holding fast a tradition or teaching in (1) an evil sense (Mark 7:3,8; Rev 2:14,15); in (2) a good sense (2 Thess 2:15; Rev 3:11). The active participle form suggests the errorists were resisting every effort and rejecting every expression of truth that would make them otherwise. The revelation of the Mystery and the fullness of the word of God meant nothing to them. All that Christ has become in resurrection glory, to them was meaningless. There was no apprehension of Christ and His glory as Head. The very heart of Paul's ministry was spurned. It is not as some translations say that they *lost* connection with Head. That is weak. They never had connection and actively repulse any appeal that they should have a connection. Whatever He was to them, He was not Head. Any such profession is worthless, for "What think ye of Christ?" is still the test. God is not awaiting man's opinion of His Son when He places this question before them. He is expecting a heart recognition that He is all that the word of God reveals Him to be.

The prepositional phrase "from which" should be rendered as in the masculine, hence RV "from whom". All that Christ is personally is very much the theme of the epistle. He is the primal source of all fruitful development. He alone is the source of the body's growth.

In the phrase "all the body by joints and bands", the body refers to the church as in 1:18. Paul does not identify the "joints and bands" apart from noting their function. Nor is it necessary, though some suggest the imagery can be explained as follows: (a) "*the Head*", Christ, (b) "*the joints*" are the apostles and (c) "*the bands*" are the teachers. This suggestion follows from a comparison with the parallel passage of Eph 4:1-16. If the "joints and bands" are to be representative of something more than their function, they could speak of the inter-relationship of the members of the body, showing their mutual dependence one upon another.

"Having nourishment ministered, and knit together" translates two participles *epichorēgoumenon* ("having nourishment ministered") and *sumbibazomenon* ("knit together"). In the previous expressions two elements of unity are stressed: (1) the relation of contiguous surfaces, and (2) the attachment of several parts. In this expression Paul advances two conditions necessary for the body's life and growth, namely, (a) nutrition and (b) organic unity. In order that these two participles may be shown to have immediate dependence upon "from whom", it is necessary to place "by the joints and bands" in parenthesis, or at least follow the RV which has "from whom all the body being supplied and knit together through the joints and bands ..." The source of nourishment is in Christ. It flows from Him continually and in abundance. The joints and bands perform their part in making the body, in keeping it together.

Indeed it "increaseth with the increase of God", that is, it groweth the growth of God. It is the growth which God intends. Everything that Christ accomplishes complies with the divine purpose. The nourishment He provides will bring to fruition the mind of God for the church.

There is to be no room given in the assembly at Colossae to those not holding the Head, for the assembly, as gathered to Christ Himself, is a company where Christ's headship is held and acted upon. These verses show that everything centres around Christ, all resources are concentrated in Him, as He is sufficient for the enrichment of the saints. How may an assembly be edified today? Certainly not by the innovative practices that abound, from which no spiritual establishment can be desired. The answer lies not in legalistic strictures either, of which this whole passage is conclusive proof. This enlargement, according to what God requires, is experienced as Christ is given His rightful place amongst His people.

V. Mystical (2:20-3:4)

1. The Meaning of their Death with Christ
2:20-23

> v.20 "Wherefore if ye be dead with Christ from the rudiments of the world, why, as though living in the world, are ye subject to ordinances,
> v.21 (Touch not; taste not; handle not;
> v.22 Which all are to perish with the using;) after the commandments and doctrines of men?
> v.23 Which things have indeed a shew of wisdom in will worship, and humility, and neglecting of the body; not in any honour to the satisfying of the flesh."

When Sarah, Abraham's wife died, he buried her in the cave of Machpelah. The suggestive meaning of Machpelah provides a useful illustration of this paragraph and that which follows. Machpelah was the place of two openings. There was a place in and a place out. Abraham buried his dead out of his sight, yet not without assurance of resurrection. If we may apply the picture, then that is what is suggested by the two paragraphs. The section opens with 2:20, "if ye died with Christ" (RV), there we have the way in. The next paragraph opens with these words, "If then ye were raised together with Christ," that (thank God) is the way out. The paragraphs combine to give the moral, spiritual and practical application of the believer's co-death and co-resurrection with Christ.

20   In "Wherefore if ye be dead with Christ" *ei* ("if") does not imply any doubt. Its force is argumentative; it is a way of stating the unquestionable, from which certain conclusions are drawn. The conditional clause may be rendered, "seeing ye died with Christ". The reference to the believer's mystical death reproduces the well known teaching already put forth in Romans, Galatians and in other letters. This mystical death is past, therefore it is properly expressed in the aorist: "If ye died with Christ" (RV). The truth simply stated is: "When Christ died, ye also died". It is an absolute, an accomplished fact which is to be accepted and recognised because God says it. Those who would bring the Colossian believers into bondage to ascetic practices were either ignorant of the fact or simply chose to ignore it. However, the question Paul is formulating is directed to those who have put their trust in Christ who had died for them, and now they are being reminded of the fact that they died with Christ.

For "from the rudiments of the world" see 2:8. The term continues to imply a rudimentary form of religion consisting mainly in external rites. Death always denotes separation, so this identification with Christ in His death separates them "from the rudiments of the world". Whatever the origin or nature of these ordinances is, they have no claim upon a dead person. This is what the world of religion has failed to perceive, that having died with Christ the believer has nothing more to do with nature or the world. When the believer died with Christ he died to sin (Rom 6:2), and also to the Law (Gal 2:19).

For *kosmos* ("world") see 1:6. The believer as such has nothing to do with this world system. He is in it, but not of it (John 17:14-16). He belongs to another sphere and his *living* is empowered by and conformed to that new spiritual realm.

"(Why) are ye subject to ordinances" translates *ti dogmatizesthe*. The verb is made up from *dogma* and indicates that "rules or decrees" were being imposed upon the Colossian believers. The question is: Were the saints at Colossae simply listening to the teaching or were they accepting the dogmas of these proponents of evil? The verb is to be taken as passive. This being the case it implies not their submission, but that their resistance may be more energetic. The word recalls the ordinances (*dogmata*) of God's divine law (v.14). It is also the term for a "decree", the edict of the Roman emperor (Luke 2:1) (see Arndt and Gingrich, p.200). It may be implied by Paul's fittingly chosen word that these doctrinaires esteemed their rules and regulations as being of no less compelling force than that of imperial, yea, divine decrees. This is always the spirit that marks legalism.

21 The three negative commands of this verse, "touch not; taste not; handle not", are not exhortations for believers to follow; rather they are a summary of the false decrees from which believers are delivered, having died with Christ. The RV alters the translation to "handle not; nor taste, nor touch" due to the assumption that *hapsē* ("handle" RV) is stronger than *thigēs* ("touch" RV). But the familiar rendering of the AV can remain as the difference is slight. With the order as in the RV, many see in the prohibitions a descending series. Since, however, in whatever order they are taken, "taste not" stands between handling and touching, the gradation is not apparent. The words have an inevitable meaning; they stand for what is physical, earthly and material couched in a negativism characteristic of legalism. It may well be the case that when the apostle penned the words he had in mind the well known teaching of the Lord Jesus contained in Mark 7:1-23. Questioned because His disciples eat their bread with unwashed hands, He quotes the words of Isa 29:13, "This people honoureth me with their lips, but their heart is far from me. But in vain do they worship me, teaching as their doctrines the precepts of men" (RV). He proceeds to denounce their use of the solemn word *corban*, which, by their legal invention, cancelled filial responsibility. It was by the sham giving up of his property that the most conniving son freed himself from the duty of supporting his parents. Of this most flagrant act of unjust behaviour the Lord Jesus declares, "You make void the word of God by your tradition", which draws attention primarily to the fifth commandment. There is then appended to this incident the parable concerning "the things which proceed out of man are those that defile the man" (Mark 7:15 RV). In the Lord's own interpretation of the parable, He says (about the thing which passes into the man), "it cannot defile him; because it goeth not into his heart, but into his belly, and goeth out into the draught", to which is added the terse comment by the inspired writer, "This He said, making all meats clean". The statement prepares us for a similar one by Paul in the next verse.

22 "Which all are to perish with the using", a relative clause, is parenthetical (see RV); it is inserted to expose the folly of the decrees which concern perishable things such as meat and drink. Seven times out of its nine occurrences *phthora* is translated "corruption" leaving us in no doubt but that the objects unspecified in the previous verse are material. The preposition *eis* ("with a view to") marks their destination or what they are intended for. The word "using" means more than mere use, but the using up of the thing. The clause may now read, "which things exist with a view to corruption by being used up". The statement corresponds with the reference made above to Mark 7:15. Paul therefore takes up these objects of the decrees that he may show their nature and purpose and thereby remove entirely the ground upon which they seek to stand. The observant Colossian will have been made to see at least two things: (1) that the asceticism of the deceivers is a slight upon the wisdom and design of a faithful Creator who has provided both meat and drink for man's strengthening and satisfaction; (2) that no genuine piety depends on abstinence from them. It becomes obvious then that spirituality does not depend on external and ceremonial forms.

"After the commandments and doctrines of men" continues from "ordinances" in v.20 according to the AV, or from the final "not" of v.21 according to the RV. The AV is to be preferred. The expression shows the origin of the dogmas. They are of men, thus supplying another reason why the Colossians should not submit. The main reason is: they died with Christ; but the subordinate one is: these edicts emanate from men. The believer in Christ has been delivered from all that is of man into a sphere where Christ is everything. When men intrude upon the sovereign territory of the Spirit of God, bondage ensues. Though His province is not the burden of the epistle His purpose is, for it is the Spirit's purpose to give effectual utterance to the glory of Christ as the all-sufficient One. Where this is questioned amongst the saints, the Spirit is not free to manifest His power and presence.

23 "Which things have indeed a show of wisdom" is literally "which very things", referring to precepts such as those Paul mentions in the previous verse. *Logos*, translated "show" (AV), "appearance" (JND), has the idea of reputation, appearance or report. It also means "talk". Two examples occur in Paul of *logos* in a deprecatory sense, 1 Cor 4:19; 1 Thess 1:5. It is noticeable that in both places, *logos* ("mere talk") is opposed to *dunamis* ("effective power"). These precepts, with their prohibitions, carry with them a semblance of wisdom, but in experience there is really nothing in them. They sound like wisdom, but wisdom they are not, for in reality they constitute will-worship.

"Will worship" (*ethelothrēskeia*), coined by the Holy Spirit to emphasise the source as well as the nature of these precepts, means a self-denial or self-imposed religiousness. There can be no doubt that some idea of pretence or unreality is to be gathered from the apostle's word. Then too, the compound *ethelothrēskeia* has the same meaning as *thelōn* in v.18, where both *thrēskeia* (the other part of the compound) and *tapeinophrosunē* "humility" occur.

For "humility" see v.18. Maybe the *thelō* should be affixed to *tapeinophrosunē*, so that the whole expression would suggest "self-devised austerities and *self-chosen* humiliations". There can be no doubt but that the pretended lowliness matches the self-chosen worship.

"Neglecting the body" (*apheidia*) is better rendered by "severity" or "hard treatment". Ascetics are known for their disciplinary self-denial, often involving flagellations and other hardness to the body. It is all of self, which brings in pride and sets aside the will of God and the work of Christ. The Colossian believers must be aware of the danger to which the testimony is exposed when man after the flesh imposes his self-made worship, and a matching self-abasement in a show of self-discipline.

"Not in any honour to the satisfying of the flesh" is possibly one of the most difficult expressions of the epistle. Many translators and commentators have attempted changes and interpretations, so the diversity of opinion is great. This exposition follows the sense as conveyed in the RV translation: "not of any value against the indulgence of the flesh". It appears from this rendering that *timē* (AV "honour") has the meaning of "value", a meaning which best suits that context. There is a difficulty in translating *pros* as "against", though Lightfoot presents significant support for this usage. The next word that receives a variety of treatment is *plēsmonē* ("satiety" or "indulgence") used only here. The expression is to be seen as revealing the futility of man's endeavour to curb the flesh. Paul is saying that no precepts, prohibitions and practices of asceticism will bring that sense of self-mastery which their advocates desiderate.

Paul has reminded the Colossians that they died with Christ. In the remembrance of what that death means it will put an end to all these carnal restrictions of man. He has outlined five reasons why they should not place themselves in bondage to these rigid ascetic austerities. Such restrictions are:

1. *rudimentary*. The Colossians died to this rudimentary discipline when they died with Christ.
2. *worldly*. The Colossians are no longer *of* this world, though they live in it. They are in the world, but the world is not *in* them.

3. *trivial*, for "handle not, nor taste, nor touch" refer to things which are perishable and are hence non-important.
4. *of human origin*, as Isaiah the prophet forewarns in language which the Lord Jesus repeats and which Paul endorses by the Spirit.
5. *futile*, for even the good they lay claim to in:
    (a) the pretentious parade of devotion,
    (b) the affectation of humility, and
    (c) the harsh treatment of the body,
is a *show* of wisdom, and of no real value in checking the indulgence of the flesh.

WORDS PECULIAR TO COLOSSIANS 2 ARE:

Apekduō	: having spoiled	2:15 and 3:9
Apekdusis	: putting off	2:11
Apochrēsis	: using	2:22
Apheidia	: neglecting	2:23
Deigmatizō	: made a show	2:15
Dogmatizō	: subject to ordinances	2:20
Ethelothrēskeia	: will-worship	2:23
Embateuō	: intruding into	2:18
Theotēs	: Godhead	2:9
Katabrabeuō	: beguile	2:18
Neomēnia	: new moon	2:16
Pithanologia	: enticing words	2:4
Plēsmone	: satisfying	2:23
Prosēloō	: nail to	2:14
Stereōma	: steadfastness	2:5
Sulagōgeō	: spoil	2:8
Sōmatikōs	: bodily	2:9
Philosophia	: philosophy	2:8
Cheirographon	: handwriting	2:14

WORDS COMMON TO COLOSSIANS AND EPHESIANS IN COLOSSIANS 2 ARE:

Auxanō:	increaseth	2:19;	Eph 2:21
Auxēsis:	increase	2:19;	Eph 4:16
Haphē:	joint	2:19;	Eph 4:16
Rhizoō:	rooted	2:7;	Eph 3:17
Sunzōopoieō:	quickened together	2:13;	Eph 2:5
Sumbibazō:	knit together	2:2,19;	Eph 4:16
Sunegeiro:	are risen with	2:12	Eph 2:6

2.   The Manifestation of their Resurrection with Christ
   3:1-4

v.1   "If ye then be risen with Christ, seek those things which are above, where Christ
        sitteth on the right hand of God.
v.2   Set your affection on things above, not on things on the earth.
v.3   For ye are dead, and your life is hid with Christ in God.
v.4   When Christ, who is our life, shall appear, then shall ye also appear with him in
        glory".

1   Having thus assured his readers concerning their complete freedom from
any obligation to the rudiments of the world and man's ordinances and
precepts through their co-death with Christ, the apostle proceeds to deal
with the complementary truth: the implications of their co-resurrection with
Christ. The cross not only involves death, it includes resurrection. It severs
connections with the past life of the believer and it introduces him to a new
life in union with Christ. The previous paragraph reveals some of the
ramifications of what death with Christ means. Now in this paragraph (3:1-4),
the apostle is desirous that we recognise the requirements resulting from
our identification with Christ in His resurrection. The particle "then" (RV) is
illative and also retrospective. There is an inference as well as a continuation
in that "if then ye were raised with Christ" is the counterpart of "if ye died
with Christ"; an inference, thus forming the ground upon which Paul gives
the exhortation which centres in two present imperatives. As in 2:20, so here,
the *ei* ("if") is one of reality and in no way does it betoken uncertainty.
Compare Phil 1:22, where instead of diminishing the certainty of the fact
stated the "if" enhances the probability of the truth. The word translated "be
risen", or as RV "were raised", is in the aorist tense in the Creek and looks at
what happened once for all in the past. By this resurrection a new spiritual
life is created within the believer. The moment he believes by incorporation
he becomes a sharer in His death and in His life. Those who were troubling
the saints at Colossae had not experienced such a spiritual resurrection. Their
religious life consisted of the rudiments of the world, in decrees and
ordinances about material, perishable things (2:16,20,21); their worship,
humility and severity to the body was merely a show of wisdom and vaunted
philosophy which was totally powerless and utterly worthless. What Satan
wished to corrupt was the glorious liberty and vitality that those who
possessed this spiritual life enjoyed and displayed. He would link them with
a system which was dissolved when the veil was rent in twain.

   This is the fifth occurrence of the preposition *sun* ("with"), by which the apostle
sets forth our position of identification with our Lord Jesus Christ. A notable
change takes place in Paul's terms at 2:12, which the reader must readily observe.
Prior to this the familiar preposition *en* ("in") has been frequently used. It would
be profitable to enumerate these usages as they appear in ch. 2.

(1) "In Whom"	- all the treasures of wisdom and knowledge are hid	2:3
(2) "In Christ"	- the stedfastness of your faith	2:5
(3) "In Him"	- walk even as ye have received Him as Lord	2:6
(4) "In Him"	- having been rooted, and being built up	2:7
(5) "In Him"	- dwelleth all the fulness of the Godhead bodily	2:9
(6) "In Him"	- ye are complete	2:10
(7) "In Whom"	- also ye are circumcised	2:11

The preservation of the Colossian believers depends very largely upon their acceptance and acknowledgement of this objective presentation of their position "in Christ". Such truth, held in an adoring spirit of love and appreciation, preserves from the inroads of pestiferous teaching, the type of which was being spread by the errorists in Colossae. The value of sound doctrine cannot be underestimated in these days when error and specious teachings abound.

From 2:12, as noted above, the theme changes and the language conforms to the truth enunciated by the apostle. In order that the saints may apprehend the richness of their mystical union in association with Christ, Paul uses the expression seven times in these two paragraphs (2:20-23; 3:1-4). The identification of the believer with Christ is shown to indicate that what Christ did, we are regarded by God the Father as having done also. A further enumeration is necessary.

(1) "With Him"	- buried in baptism	2:12
(2) "With Him"	- risen through faith of the operation of God	2:12
(3) "With Him"	- quickened, having received forgiveness	2:13
(4) "With Christ"	- ye died from the rudiments of the world	2:20
(5) "With Christ"	- ye were raised	3:1
(6) "With Christ"	- your life is hid in God	3:3
(7) "With Christ"	- ye shall be made manifest in glory	3:4

The form of the verb *zēteite* ("seek") carries the imperative in the present tense and can be rightly translated "keep seeking". The believer is to exert every effort to develop the characteristics of those things which are above in his life, service and testimony. There is to be an emulation of all that features the Christ in glory and all that His presence in glory has established. Such an exercise will deliver from any pre-occupation with the precepts and orders of man. They are only material, ritualistic and elementary; they are utterly futile in bringing any good to men and glory to God.

"Those things which are above" (1) are in sharp contrast to the rudiments of the world, the ordinances and precepts of men, (2) have been brought into display through the death and resurrection of the Lord Jesus, and (3) in the NT epistles are established as marking the form of the testimony in this period of grace. These things affect our lives spiritually and morally for they are heavenly and essentially holy. They also affect our corporate testimony as believers separated from all that came to an end when Christ died and rose again. Jewish forms once held a lawful place, but now they are no longer in force. They are of no account nor do they retain any value. In his judaizing work among the Colossians Satan's purpose was to link the assembly with a system which was totally dissolved when Christ died and rose again. Christendom has taken up the things that are proper for a Jew under Law, but are now termed "the rudiments of the world", since Christ died. Paul exhorts that saints "keep seeking- the things which belong to another world altogether. No need now for the ornate consecrated building, and the ceremonies that accord with such a place. The imposition of ritual involves the officiating priest which is all part of the rudiments and not after Christ. The "things above" involve us in a testimony free from every feature of legalism.

In the clause "where Christ sitteth on the right hand of God" or as the RV puts it "where Christ is, seated on the right hand of God", the great comparison between the Ephesian letter and this to the Colossians emerges clearly. When Paul alludes to this high point of glory in Ephesians, he states that we are seated with Christ in the heavenly places (2:6). Resurrection is the theme of the apostle and this he urges as the ground for our seeking the things above. Here in Colossians it is what we may call aspiration, the seeking of those things in the region where Christ is seated, whereas in the Ephesian letter it is the realisation of our position with Christ in the heavenlies according to divine purpose. The expression "on the right hand" recalls the Messianic interpretation of Ps 110:1, "The Lord said unto my Lord, Sit thou at my right hand, until I make thine enemies thy footstool", words which the Lord Jesus applied to Himself when confronted by the Sanhedrim in Jerusalem (Matt 26:64; Mark 14:62; Luke 20:41). Peter quotes the words as he proclaims the exaltation of Christ (Acts 2:34). To affirm the Lord's superiority over angels the writer to the Hebrews makes telling use of the quotation (Heb 1:13). Then on four occasions throughout the epistle, the same writer speaks of the Saviour's exalted glory and uses the word in the active voice implying His sovereign right to take that place of honour, power and dignity (Heb 1:3; 8:1; 10:12; 12:2). In the three remaining passages where Paul speaks of the "right hand of God" something of a practical touch emerges from the fact of the Lord's enthronement. With the exaltation of Christ there is assurance ministered to the heart knowing that He is interceding for us in that region of unsullied bliss (Rom 8:34). He is engaged on our behalf. We are to be engaged with Him and those things His ascension and exaltation have initiated; it is heart occupation with Christ that propels the believer (Col 3:1). The passage in Eph 1:21 forms part of Paul's prayer for the believer's empowerment, that the power that raised Him up from the dead diffuse its energy in all who believe. Another reference is found in 1 Pet 3:22. The heart filled with a spiritual apprehension of Christ risen and glorified is the secret of peace and contentment. When Jacob heard of Joseph's exaltation and beheld some evidence of its reality, he exclaimed: "It is enough". Elisha moved in the power of an ascended man, on having seen Elijah being caught up. The double portion was fully displayed in his service.

Stephen can plead forgiveness for those who hasten his death on seeing the "Son of man standing on the right hand of God".

2 "Set your affection on things above" translates the imperative verb *phroneite*, the present imperative of *phroneō*. Therefore the more accurate translation is: "Set your mind" (RV). The phrase is reminiscent of the familiar saying of Christ in the Gospel incident, "thou savourest not the things that be of God, but those that be of men" (Matt 16:23). Similar usages are found in Rom 8:5, "for they that are after the flesh do mind the things of the flesh", and Phil 3:19, etc. The believer is not to be controlled by emotion, whether of dread or desire, but by the mind as enlightened and instructed by the revelation of the mind of God in the Holy Scriptures. Paul's exhortation is centred in these two imperatives which, if we may assay to distinguish them, suggests in the one the outward aspiration (seek) and in the other inward attitude or disposition (set). As the mind is enlightened in respect of the glory of Christ in the region of the things above, those things will become the ardent pursuit of the believer in his life and testimony down here.

The "things on the earth" are those mentioned in the preceding chapter though Eadie (p.215) supposes otherwise. The apostle is not here speaking of those things that legitimately concern the believer in his pathway through life; he is referring to the earth-bound religiousness of men which he has faithfully repudiated in terms already considered in ch. 2.

3 "For ye are dead, and your life is hid with Christ in God" provides a summary of the complementary truths taught in 2:20 and 3:1 respectively, that is, the believer's union with Christ in death and in resurrection. Through this death with Christ the saint of God is viewed as a dead man, dead as far as religious response to human tradition and decrees about perishable, material things are concerned. Therefore the religious world and its systems should have no appeal to the Christian who lives in the spiritual good of this truth. But this very death brought life and so the apostle speaks of life which comes through our resurrection with Christ. Eadie puts it clearly when he says, "The death is past and over, but the life has been hid, and still is in that hidden state" (p.216). The perfect form of the verb which Paul uses is translated "hid" in our text, while in Matt 13:35 it is translated as "kept secret". Three ideas are suggested by this word "hid". (1) It gives the full *significance* of the life which we have in union with Christ: it is a life which belongs to the spiritual and to the eternal. It cannot be otherwise when it is a life that is hid together with Christ in God. (2) It denotes the *security* or *safety* of the life. It is beyond the reach of any alien force neither can it be defiled by any evil thing. The double bulwark secures it eternally *with Christ* in God. (3) It suggests the *secrecy* of the life. Only resources of divine origin can nourish it. Nothing of earth can minister to its growth and enrichment, which caused the Psalmist to confess, "All my springs are in thee" (Ps. 87:7).

The expression "in God" is found in Paul's other epistles only in 1 Thess 1:1 and 2 Thess 1:1, where the local assembly at Thessalonica is spoken of as finding its spiritual location "in God the Father". This denotes a spiritual relationship with God and suggests that the life of the assembly is sustained by all that God is, for He is the sphere in which that life exists. The thought in our passage is that the believer's risen life is identified with Christ's present hiddenness in union with God.

Paul's motivations in urging the Colossians to keep on minding and seeking those things in the sphere of heavenly glory where Christ is, have been clearly stated and thoughtfully applied. Now the climax is reached in an expectancy of glory.

4   For the fourth time in four verses Paul speaks again of Christ. It is Christ with whom we know co-resurrection. It is Christ whose exaltation to the right hand of God engages us with the things that take character from His sphere of glory. It is Christ with whom our new life finds its signification. It is Christ whose moment of manifestation will see us manifested with Him. The "highest" in the errorists' system are angels. Paul transcends far above all by engaging our minds and hearts with Christ. Only elementary things anyway, things of earth, form the core of the false teaching assailing the Colossians; Paul reaches out to things in the region where Christ sits. The former will perish with the using, for they are fruitless and futile; Paul touches on a life that never can be affected by decay - a life hid with Christ. A feature absent from the specious dictum is hope; Paul consummates his appeal with assurance that Christ's manifestation will be ours.

"Who is our life" - the statement is to be understood in light of the undeniable fact that Christ is the source, sustenance and summation of the christian life. It is not merely because He gives that life, neither that we share in His life, the meaning is: He is our life - He in us and we in Him.

"Shall appear" (*phanerōthēsesthe* "shall be manifested" RV), is used of:

1. the advent of the Saviour when
   He became Man   1 Tim 3:16; 1 John 1:2
2. the display of His glory in the
   sign wrought by Him   John 2:11
3. His appearance to put away sin   Heb 9:26
4. His appearance in resurrection   John 21:1,14
5. the second advent of the Saviour   1 Pet 5:4; Col 1:4; 1 John
                                                        2:28; 3:2

It is the second advent of the Lord Jesus that Paul has in mind here when he speaks of Christ's appearing. Other words associated with this event merit attention: *parousia* (usually rendered "coming") refers to a period beginning with the descent of the Lord from heaven into the air (1 Thess 4:16,17) and ending with His revelation and manifestation to the world (Vine: *The Epistles to the Thessalonians*, p.88); *epiphaneia* ("manifestation") translated "brightness" in 2 Thess 2:8, stresses the outshining of the glory of the Lord Jesus; *apokalupsis* ("revelation") declares the purpose of the event as unveiling the Person of the Lord Jesus. The moment of manifestation of which Paul speaks takes place when Christ manifests Himself to the world and sets up His kingdom.

"Then shall ye also appear with him in glory" shows the association is climaxed in glory. We are with Him in death, in resurrection, present hiddenness, so shall we be with Him in public display. Then men shall see the significance of the life that is ours in union with Him. They will see the hidden source from which that life is sustained. The world today cannot apprehend the nature of our life, for they know Him not. In that day when He appears we shall appear with Him in glory, a glory that will never fade, for it is eternal. Our bodies will be suited to it, for by then they will have been fashioned like unto His body of glory (Phil 3:21). Then the purpose of God will be realised and we shall be conformed to the image of His Son (Rom 8:29). That every moral defect will have gone everlastingly from us is assured us for "we shall be like him; for we shall see him as he is" (1 John 3:2).

VI Ethical (3:5-4:6)

1. *Individual Responsibilities in Putting off the Old*
3:5-11

v.5   "Mortify therefore your members which are upon the earth; fornication, uncleanness, inordinate affection, evil concupiscence, and covetousness, which is idolatry:

v.6   For which things' sake the wrath of God cometh on the children of disobedience:

v.7   In the which ye also walked some time, when ye lived in them.

v.8   But now ye also put off all these; anger, wrath, malice, blasphemy, filthy communication out of your mouth.

v.9   Lie not one to another, seeing that ye have put off the old man with his deeds;

v.10 And have put on the new man, which is renewed in knowledge after the image of him that created him:

v.11 Where there is neither Greek nor Jew, circumcision nor uncircumcision, Barbarian. Scythian, bond nor free: but Christ is all, and in all."

The apostle has stated three fundamental facts in the preceding sections:

1. We have *died* with Christ   2:20
2. We have been *raised* with Christ   3:1
3. We shall be *manifested* with Christ   3:4

Paul would desire that the Colossian saints give practical expression to these doctrinal facts in their life and testimony. The balance between doctrine and practice is scrupulously maintained in Paul's epistles. So it is here. Paul's endeavour is to have the saints in full possession of the mind of God. But he does not stop there. He is insistent that it should have practical effect upon christian experience and that truth is lived out in godly behaviour and conduct.

5 The use of the illative particle oun ("therefore") provides a clear connection with the foregoing doctrinal section. The inference is apparent. Because the Colossian believers possess such an exalted standing before God in the risen Christ, there must be a corresponding conformity with it in holy living. The revelation of God's truth makes known what God has done for us; it also unfolds what God wishes to do in us. Some put it: position and practice must agree, which reminds us that objective truth has its complementary subjective responsibilities. Nothing can be more disastrous to the testimony than for the Christian to be an open condemnation of what he professes to be. The admonition begins with the imperative *nekrōsate* ("mortify"). Paul employs the perfect passive participle to describe the condition of Abraham at the time when he believed God's promise of a son (Rom 4:19; Heb 11:12). Apart from those usages the verb is found only here. The exhortation to "slay", to "do to death", is clear enough; and is not to be construed as having a literal connotation. Similar truth finds expression in Rom 8:13 where *thanatoute* ("make to die", RV marg.) occurs, and is in Gal 5:24 where *estaurosan* ("crucified") appears. The continuity of the process appears to be the point Paul wishes us to observe by his use of the present form of the verb in Rom 8:13. In Gal 5:24 the aorist signifies the *intensity* and decisiveness of the act which crucifies the flesh violently, painfully, that, having died the death it deserves, it may cease its pursuit of sin once for all. In our passage where the aorist is also used, the figure appears to convey the sense of totality. This accords with the completeness of our death and our resurrection with Christ. But what are we to do to death? Paul says, "your members which are upon the earth". What are we to understand by the term *ta melē* ("your members")? In his *Figures of Speech*, Dr E.W. Bullinger offers the simplest explanation. "The members which commit the sins are put by a forcible *catachresis* for the sins themselves. For the sins are immediately enumerated, not the members". "*Catachresis*", he explains "is a figure by which one word is changed for another, and this against or contrary to the ordinary usage and meaning of it. The word that is changed is transferred from its strict and usual signification to another that is only remotely connected with it" (op.cit., p.674). For a clear summary of other views, the reader is referred to W. Hendriksen, *Colossians* pp.144-145, who also reaches practically the same conclusion when he quotes Ridderbos (p.207) as stating, "The members are here identified with the sins committed by these members, which in a similar connection in Rom 8:13 are called "the deeds of the body". The earth is the sphere in which these "members" function. The relation to v.2 is clear, and endorses the need for "minding things which are above". The more the mind is occupied with those things in the region where Christ sits, the less gratification will be paid to these desires that will endeavour to bring the members into unwholesome, unholy and unhealthy activities, with usually unhappy results.

"Fornication, uncleanness" begin the sombre list as in Gal 5:19 RV where Paul lists the "works of the flesh". Perhaps the reason why Paul heads this fivefold grouping of sins in this way is that these are the sins which set a man in defiance of the fundamental laws of God which govern the continuation and preservation of the human race (see Gal 2:23,24; Mark 10:6-9). Fornication, which covers every form of illicit sexual conduct, is put first by the apostle in at least three catalogues of sins (1 Cor 6:9-10; Gal 5:19-21; Eph 5:3-5). It constitutes a great threat to sanctification (1 Thess 4:3); it is the subject of special warning from the Jerusalem council (Acts 15:29); it is the grievous form of wickedness which the Corinthians failed to judge by excommunication of the person concerned (1 Cor 5). Its partner -uncleanness- adds the idea of perversion and is more general. While it denotes impurity in any form, it is usually associated with the sin of immorality, with which it is joined in Rom 1:24; 2 Cor 12:21; Gal 5:19; Eph 5:3; 1 Thess 4:7.

"Inordinate affection, evil concupiscence" are not easily distinguished, though Lightfoot helpfully suggests that the former views the same vice more from its passive, the latter more from its active side (op.cit., p.209). The three occurrences of *pathos* ("passion" RV) refer to erotic desire which leads to immorality (Rom 1:26; 1 Thess 4:5). Eadie observes, "It seems here to denote the state of mind that urges and excites to impurity, that condition in which man is mastered by unchastity, and the imagination being defiled, is wholly at the mercy of obscene associations" (op.cit., p.222). "Evil desire" (RV) is to be interpreted as evil lusts in terms of sex relations, hence it is joined with the preceding three expressions. The word *epithumia* ("desire" RV) can be of itself morally neutral, or even good, so the qualifying adjective "evil" is added. This can still express itself in numerous ways, but the subject of the context is sexual vices.

Pleonexia ("covetousness", literally "overreaching") is here linked with sexual immorality as in Eph 4:19; 5:3-5, while in 1 Thess 4:6 the cognate verb, translated "defraud", is definitely in connection with adultery, which is not surprising in light of Exod 20:17. It is therefore clear that pleonexia in this passage represents some distinctly fleshly sin, though Lightfoot and Eadie disagree with this opinion. They both deny it conceives of any form of sensuality. Carson is worth quoting in his excellent treatment of the view stated above, "This sin is idolatrous, for it concentrates the whole being upon something other than God. It is characteristic of sexual indulgence that it leads to an unhealthy, and ultimately perverted obsession ... when godliness is rejected, and the lust of the flesh encouraged it is not long before sex is worshipped instead of God" (p. 82).

6   *Orgē* ("wrath") occurs 36 times in the NT in relation to:

the wrath of man,	Eph 4:31; Col 3:8; 1 Tim 2:8; James 1:19,20;
the retribution of earthly authority	Rom 13:4,5;
the sufferings of the Jews during the tribulation,	Luke 21:23;
the judgments of the law,	Rom 4:15;
the anger of the Lord Jesus,	Mark 3:5;
the anger of God with Israel in the wilderness	Heb 3:11; 4:3;
the present judicial government of God upon Israel	Rom 9:22 (twice); 1 Thess 2:16;
the prevailing attitude of God towards those who do not believe in His Son	John 3:36;
the Sovereign right of God in judgment	Matt 3:7; Luke 3:7; Rom 1:18; 2:5 (twice), 8; 3:5; 5:9; 12:19; Eph 2:3; 5:6; here and 1 Thess 1:10; 5:9.

The six occurrences in Revelation relate to tribulational wrath and disclose that the earth is the theatre of God's judgments: 6:16,17; 11:18; 14:10; 16:19; 19:15.

The word "cometh" (*erchetai*) may refer to the present life or to the future or to both. If God did not punish sin, the moral stability of His throne would be disturbed, but because of His moral rectitude, the wrongdoer must be punished (Rom 1:18). The wrath issues forth from God's displeasure. He hates sin. The wrath is governmental rather than temperamental. The verse before us has an eschatological sense which makes the present form of "cometh" a futuristic present. The verse provides a doctrinal explanation of the outpouring of divine wrath as detailed in Rev 4-19. We know that very often in the NT the "wrath of God" refers to the coming tribulation period, e.g., 1 Thess 1:10; 5:9.

The expression, "on the children of disobedience", is omitted in the NIV and other versions but it is retained by the RV and JND. *Huioi* ("sons") is often used in a metaphorical sense of certain moral features as:

1. sons of this world	Luke 16:8 RV;
2. sons of disobedience	here and Eph 2:2 RV
3. sons of the evil one	Matt 13:38 RV; cf Acts 13:10 RV;
4. sons of perdition	John 17:12; 2 Thess 2:3.

These are descriptive of those who have not experienced the new birth and are still in unbelief. Those who have been born again are described as:

1. sons of God   Matt 5:9,45; Luke 6:35 (RV); Rom 8:19;
2. sons of the light   Luke 16:8 (RV);
3. sons of the day   1 Thess 5:5 (RV);
4. sons of peace   Luke 10:6.

7   Eph 2:3 has a similar relative clause where the pronoun "whom" is masculine. Here it is neuter, thus referring to the vices of v.5 which so thoroughly characterised their former manner of life. Paul is not inferring that the converted Colossians are practising these grim and grievous forms of evil.

Edzēte ("lived") is the imperfect active indicative of *zaō* ("to live"). The distinction in tense between the verb "walked" and "lived" is instructive. The former, being an aorist, denotes the state of sin in which the Colossians formerly lived, and views all the ungodly acts as a whole. The latter, an imperfect, shows the ungodly life in its continuance and leads us to expect in the next statement how the former conduct in these vices is to cease.

8   *Apotithēmi* ("put off") occurs seven times in a figurative sense. Compare Rom 13:12; Eph 4:22,25; Heb 12:1; James 1:21; 1 Pet 2:1. Luke uses the word in the literal sense in Acts 7:58 where it is translated "laid down". The verb is an aorist middle imperative, so it literally means "cast aside from yourselves once and for all". Its strength is: rid yourselves completely of all these things. Garments often denote character, so these awful practices must be cast off. If a person were to be characterised by these habits, either of v.5 or of what follows in this verse, he would still be a son of disobedience, irrespective of what he may profess to be. For the idea of behaviour and character being represented as a garment, compare Job 29:14; Ps 132:9; Isa 11:5; 61:10 in relation to good, and Ps 73:6 in relation to evil. See Pss 35:26; 109:29 also.

For "anger", see *orgē* ("wrath") above.

"Wrath" (*thumos*) denotes the explosive outburst of passion, while its synonym, with which it is often found (Rom 2:8; Eph 4:31; here and in Rev 19:15), suggests what is lasting, settling into a permanent state.

"Malice" (*kakia*) denotes the temper which makes a person want to do wrong, the source and origin of injustice and of cruelty and of every hurtful usage of others. It marks the unregenerate, those untouched by the kindness and love of God (Rom 1:29; Titus 3:3), a state in which we once were. Here it can be compared to a filthy rag to be forever discarded, while in 1 Cor 5:8, Paul likens it to the subtle corruptive working of leaven in the christian community. Malice breeds animosity, which, under the slightest pretext displays its ugly malignity. It was this that put Joseph in the pit, Jeremiah in the dungeon and Daniel in the den, and many more of God's people into endless grief. No wonder then that the apostle urges: put it away once and for all, because, in consort with its two partners on either side, it breaches spiritual fellowship.

"Blasphemy" (*blasphēmia*) within the context must refer to harmful speech which even believers can hurl at one another. It will be noted that the word often describes defiant speech against God (Rev 16:9, etc). Abusive speech or slander is the idea (1 Cor 10:30; Eph 4:31). Mephibosheth experienced the hurt of the slanderous tongue (2 Sam 19:27), as did our Lord Jesus, both on the pavement in Gabbatha and on the cross at Golgotha (Luke 22:65; 23:39).

> Yet no ungentle, murmuring word
> Escaped Thy silent tongue.

George Goodman's lines might well have been inspired by Ps 141:3, when he wrote:

> Jesus, Lord, Thy love so tender
> Is my greatest need of all,
> For without Thee pride and anger
> From unguarded lips will fall;
> But if Thou Thy love impart
> I shall have a gracious heart.

"Filthy communication" (*aischrologia*, here only) can be described as "vile speaking" and connotes "unseemly language". The close parallel is found in Eph 5:4. It covers obscenity, of which the Christian ought never to be guilty, the purveying of defiling stories which may cause lingering laughter but results in dishonour. The expression "out of your mouth" carries us back to the verb "put off", so these evil forms of speech must be put out of the lips entirely. The word *stoma* ("mouth") occurs six times in the Roman epistle where it is viewed as full of cursing (3:14); the verdict of condemnation causes every mouth to be stopped (3:19) which suggests *conviction*. When the gospel is preached and the word of faith understood, the mouth denotes *comprehension* (10:8). Then in 10:9,10 *confession* is made unto salvation by confessing Jesus as Lord. The final usage (15:6) suggests the *communication* of praise and glory to God.

9   The Ephesian counterpart to this admonition, "lie not one to another", states the reason why they should adhere to honesty: "we are members one of another" (Eph 4:25). Someone puts it succinctly: "Falsehood violates brotherhood". The point of the exhortation is clear, they are not to have the habit of lying. Truth is an instinct of the new life in Christ. Those who profess to be followers of Him who is the Truth (John 14:6) should guard against deceit either by life or lip. Understatement and overstatement are to be equally avoided at all costs. Lying, no doubt, is a sin of the tongue, but actions can equally deceive. Joseph's brethren unsympathetically allowed their father to believe his son was dead by presenting the blood-stained coat.

"Seeing that ye have put off the old man with his deeds", Paul advances, is the reason why no such habit of lying should be allowed to exist. The new association formed, we are members one of another, is Paul's basis for the exhortation in Eph 4:25, but here it is a dissociation that has taken place, the "old man" has been "put off" once and for all. There can be no doubt in our minds but that Paul understands lying, and indeed all the preceding evil practices he has listed, to be features of the old man. And so they are, undoubtedly. Old manhood is incompatible with new manhood!

The verb "put off" (*apekduomai*) engaged our thoughts in 2:15, and its cognate noun in 2:11. The action here must be considered as decisive as the action there (2:15). Those who weaken the strength of the vivid expression, do so because they interpret the "old man" as being what they call the *old nature*. It cannot be a radical, life-changing experience if what has been "put off" is still very much "on". There are three passages where the term "old man" occurs, namely, Rom 6:6; Eph 4:22 and here. Not one of these passages exhorts believers either to crucify or to put off the old man, not even Eph 4:22, though the AV puts it so. JND gives the sense: "(namely) your having put off ... the old man", which renders the aorist clearly. Paul's palaios always bears a deprecatory sense. In 1 Cor 5 there is "the old leaven"; in 2 Cor 3 "the old covenant" and "the old man" in Rom 6:6; Eph 4:22 and here. The word "man" (*anthrōpos*), occurring some 546 times in the NT, is always translated "man" in AV, RV and JND, apart from three insignificant changes. Adhering to these principles there can be no justification for interpreting the "old man" as being the "old nature" or as referring to something inside the individual. The point must be made that the "old man" is all that we have by connection with Adamic humanity. The cross judged all that we are by position and relation in Adam, once and for all, so that in the judicial reckoning of God we are no longer in *legal* bondage through *judicial* guilt. We profess this the moment we believe and publicly avow it in baptism, so the *act* is attributed to us: "ye have put off the old man".

10 In the phrase "have put on the new man", *endusamenoi* is the aorist participle of the verb *enduō* ("to clothe oneself with"). It is the root of the English "endue" by which it is translated in Luke 24:29 where the Lord Jesus speaks of the relationship between the promised Holy Spirit and those who are to receive Him. Noticeably, the word appears in the LXX with a similar connotation (Jud 5:34 RV marg.). The believer is viewed as having put on Christ at his baptism (Gal 3:27). He is said to have put on the new man (Eph 4:24, and here), and below, he is exhorted to put on bowels of mercies. Paul expresses the same ideas in Rom 13:14, "put ye on the Lord Jesus Christ". As the believer has enrolled as a soldier (2 Tim 2:4), suitable armour has been provided, which, once he has put it on, he must wear constantly (Rom 13:12; 2 Cor 6:7; Eph 6:11; 1 Thess 5:8). When the Lord comes for His own, the living will put on immortality and the dead will put on incorruptibility (1 Cor 15:53,54; 2 Cor 5:3). As prodigals repentant and pardoned, the Father has certainly put on us the best robe.

The Colossian text does not have the word "man" (*anthrōpos*), so JND "having put on the new"; "man" is, however, understood and is rightly added as above in the AV. A comparative study of this whole passage and its parallel in Eph 4 will yield many useful resemblances. Differences too will appear, among them the different Greek word used in each passage for "new". Here in Colossians we have *neos*, new in relation to itself; while in Eph 4 the word *kainos*, new in relation to other things. The distinction does not really hold, for the meanings of *neos* and *kainos* are determined by the antonym *palaios* ("old"). Furthermore, the renewal spoken of in the Ephesian passage precedes the mention of the new man, whereas here the renewal follows. But look again at the text and observe that the word for renewal in Eph 4:23 is the verbal form of *neos*, where it is followed by the adjective *kainos*, while in our passage the adjective *neos* is followed by the verbal form of *kainos*. However else we may determine the significance, Paul clearly intends the same general meaning to obtain.

To have put on the new man signifies that the believer has been severed from all connection with what he was in Adam, the federal head of the old creation, and has been made part of a new humanity, the Head of which is the last Adam, Christ. He is a new creation as Paul expresses it in 2 Cor 5:17, which rightly interpreted is the best exposition of our present passage.

In "which is renewed in knowledge", the relative "which" has its antecedent in "the new man", so the renewal here spoken of is not something which is taking place in the believer personally, so much as it is an operation performed by God bringing the whole of the new humanity into full knowledge. The end result far transcends what was seen in the pristine glory of Eden. There, however wonderful the scene was, knowledge in its fulness was not possessed. When Adam sought to reach out for it in defiance of God's command, he fell, resulting in a fallen race, his posterity. Now, the last Adam characterises a new humanity which is being brought into full knowledge in God's purpose. The process is continual, as the tense of the verse suggests; the subject is not the believer but the new man, and the pattern as stated below is the "image of him that created him". In Titus 3:5 Paul speaks of "the renewing of the Holy Ghost", the initial operation. It begins at conversion, at regeneration. The renewal is spiritual. This is clear from the contrasts in 2 Cor 4:16 between the "outward man", that which is physical, and the "inward man", that which is spiritual. The added "day by day" emphasises the renewal is continual. Personal renewal touches the "mind" (Rom 12:2) as Paul explains in the words of Eph 4:23, "and that ye be renewed in the spirit of your mind" (RV).

"After the image of him that created him" is an allusion to Gen 1:26,27, not likely to be the deciding factor in a sound exegesis of the expression. If the epistle did not contain the words of 1:15, we might justifiably allow the Genesis passage to determine the interpretation, but with the statement of 1:15 casting its light upon these words, it is clear that the continual renewal of the new man is according to the likeness of Christ who is the image of God. By a divine act of power God has brought into being a new creation, a new humanity. He also affects its constant renewal according to its Head - Christ. Paul shows in Eph 4:7-16 that the ultimate corporately is Christ.

11 With "where there is neither Greek nor Jew", compare Gal 3:28,29. The grandeur of the new creation fills the apostle's heart, so much so that it seems to interrupt the passage of practical admonitions and counsels. The word "where" places us in a sphere where the impossibility of divergence exists, that is, in the new man. There can be no human prerogative nor human handicap on any grounds in the new humanity of God's creation. Paul is not speaking here of the oneness of the body in which all differences are wiped out, as indeed he speaks of elsewhere. Here he says that as far as the new man is concerned, Christ is everything. There are Greeks and Jews in the new man, thank God for that, but Paul is saying that they are not in it because they are either Greeks or Jews. Whatever standing such distinctions provided in that day or even in this, it has no place; rather, it cannot have any place in the new creation.

"Greek and Jew" represent opposites in race. The Jews accepted such a term as an exhaustive analysis of humanity. Every one who was not a Jew was a Greek. National prerogatives disappear before the transcendent glory of the new creation. Entrance into this new order of humanity is by the new birth, so whatever race the natural birth brings a person into is of no consequence in the spiritual sphere.

"Circumcision nor uncircumcision" is in reality the same analysis as the preceding, though the cleavage is plainer in terms of the rite, which rite is the seal of the covenant people who are distinguished with theocratic privileges, while the "uncircumcision" stands for all the world beyond the pale of the Jewish covenant and its religious prerogatives. There is every likelihood that Paul mentions this pair to show that the new circumcision in Christ belongs not merely to the Jew (2:11). There is no spiritual advantage to be gained by the one or the other, for both, upon believing, will come under the effects of a new circumcision in Christ.

And of "Barbarian, Scythian"? The word "Barbarian" literally denotes one who speaks an unintelligible language (cf. 1 Cor 14:11). The Scythian's savagery was proverbial. He was looked upon as the lowest type of barbarian. Neither of these deficiencies deprives any man of entrance into the kingdom. The offer of divine grace goes out to all mankind. Herein lies the significant difference between the passage in Gal 3 and here. The truth of the gospel, and indeed more specifically, that of the Mystery is for all, irrespective of status or the lack of it.

"Bond" and "free" are social distinctions which, with the others, are obliterated in the new creation. Paul quickly breaks away from all order and classification, and hurries on to the great pronouncement that settles the matter once and for all, that Christ is all and in all.

"But Christ is all and in all". This positive statement, in contrast to the negatives Paul uses, above, declares the true position of the believer relative to Christ. The only standing that matters is the standing in Christ. In no conceivable form can the truth be more strongly expressed. It re-echoes the truth of the NT concerning the all-sufficiency of Christ and supplies the motif of the epistle. Paul presents this fact in an impressive way: "but everything and in everyone - Christ". The emphatic position of "Christ" makes clear the absoluteness of Christ in the new man. This would mean so much to the Colossians who were exposed to the assailants of the truth and it means the same to believers today, for Christ is all still. He is everything in *revelation*; hence no further mysteries or communications from whatever source are required (cf. 1:15, 2:2,3). He is everything in *redemption*; hence no agency is needed to make our release from sin's captivity more absolute than it is in Him (cf. 1:13,14). He is everything in *reconciliation*; making any intermediaries of whatever source totally unnecessary. His death removed the enmity and reconciled us to God (cf. 1:20-22). He is everything in resource; hence the foolishness of vaunted philosophy and the futility of man's decrees which gender to bondage (cf. 2:9,10; 2:20). He is everything in realisation; the entire life of the believer is filled by Christ. The three tenses of the believer's union with Christ confirm this: the past - "If then ye were raised with Christ"; the present - "your life is *hid* with Christ in God"; the future - "when Christ, who is our life, shall appear, then *shall* ye also *appear with Him* in glory".

2.   The Putting on of the New
   3:12-17

v.12 "Put on therefore, as the elect of God, holy and beloved, bowels of mercies, kindness, humbleness of mind, meekness, long-suffering;

v.13 Forbearing one another, and forgiving one another, if any man have a quarrel against any; even as Christ forgave you, so also do ye.

v.14 And above all these things put on charity, which is the bond of perfectness.

v.15 And let the peace of God rule in your hearts, to the which also ye are called in one body; and be ye thankful.

v.16 Let the word of Christ dwell in you richly in all wisdom; teaching and admonishing one another in psalms and hymns and spiritual songs, singing with grace in your hearts to the Lord.

v.17 And whatsoever ye do in word or deed, do all in the name of the Lord Jesus, giving thanks to God and the Father by him."

12   See above for the verb *enduō* ("put on"). The connection with the preceding paragraph is confirmed by the "therefore" and by the language of clothing used to convey the teaching. The divestiture has been suggested in what has gone before in the old being put off. Paul has exhorted the Colossians to have nothing to do with all that pertains to the old man, for like him they are corrupt and corrupting. The new man has features to be displayed, things that will be characteristic of all that Christ has introduced in the new creation. These are to be put on as a garment which no moth can destroy. Neither is it the patched up garment of Judaism; it is entirely new raiment fresh from the wardrobe of heaven.

"As the elect of God, holy and beloved" provides the reason why this best robe of heaven should be the attire of its citizens. As the "elect of God" we are the *subjects* of His choice; as "holy" we display the *effects* of His power and as "beloved" we are the *objects* of His love. The new garment which becomes the new man shows whose we are, what we are and why we are.

> How helpless and hopeless we sinners had been
> If He never had loved us till washed from our sin.

"Bowels of mercies" means "a heart of compassion" (RV), certainly not the passion of v.5 above. *Splanchna* by itself carries the sense of "tenderness". Zacharias sings of God's tenderness in forgiveness (Luke 1:78). Paul uses the word in Phil 1:8 in relation to the Lord Jesus when he speaks of the "bowels of Jesus Christ". The betrayer had lost all tenderness long before the event described in Acts 1:18. The whole expression suggests *sympathetic* feeling.

"Kindness" (*chrēstotēs*) is goodness (Rom 2:4; 11:22). God Himself is called by the Lord Jesus *chrēstos* ("kind") in the Gospel (Luke 6:35). God is rich in goodness which He dispenses toward men in beneficent acts that they may be led to repentance (Rom 2:4). Paul uses the word to describe the highest and holiest expression of divine kindness in the gift of salvation in His Son (Eph 2:7; Titus 3:4). The Spirit of God produces this kindness in the believer. He is the One who imparts the energy to display a kindness which expresses itself in acts of goodness. It speaks of sympathetic action. These two portions of the Christian's attire go well together as seen in the Lord Jesus. When the leper came to view, Mark wrote, "Jesus, moved with compassion (*splanchnizomai*), put forth His hand, and touched him" (Mark 1:41). First, sympathetic feeling welled up in the heart of the Saviour, then came the deed of kindness which brought such relief to the stricken soul. The need for such grace is beyond measure, but so is the grace that can meet that need. The question is: Are we characterised by these features of the new man?

"Humbleness of mind" in 2:18 and 2:23 was forced and false; here it is real and right. The Lord Jesus spoke of Himself as being "lowly" (*tapeinos*) and Paul may have had this claim in mind when he wrote to the Philippians to act in "all lowliness of mind" (Phil 2:3). It signifies a *sympathetic disposition*.

"Meekness" has the idea of harnessed power. The meaning is derived from the taming of a wild horse. The meek believer is one who lays no claim to his rights. Twice in the Gospel of the King is the Saviour spoken of as meek. Once by Himself (Matt 11:29) and the other in a quotation from Zech 9:2 (Matt 21:5). It symbolises *sympathetic behaviour*. Like the first pair, one is the inward grace; the other is that grace in display. A person who is not humble will certainly not display meekness. The words of Num 12:3 are divinely chosen, "Now the man Moses was very meek, above all the men which were upon the face of the earth". Moses is spoken of as a "man". If some other epithet had been used we might have despaired. His meekness was displayed under severe provocation in that he allowed God to arbitrate. It was manifest the more when, after the disease fell upon his erring sister, the only time he speaks in the chapter is to seek her early and complete release from the divinely imposed malady.

"Longsuffering", literally "long-mindedness", is a refusal to retaliate in the face of provocation. The word always stands in for patience by which it is translated in Heb 6:12 and James 5:10. It is listed among the fruit of the Spirit as several of this present catalogue are, and we judge it stresses the need for *sympathetic patience*.

13 "Forbearing one another" A.T. Robertson represents as meaning "holding yourselves back from one another" (op.cit. p.504). Each of these qualities finds its fullest display in the One to whose image we are being conformed. This One is no exception for He exercised the grace of forbearance too (Matt 17:17; Mark 9:19; Luke 9:41). So also did the one who here by the Spirit exhorts the saints to endure the actions of others (1 Cor 4:12). The action urged by the pastoral heart of Paul upon all those in Christ shows *sympathetic understanding*. Its partner, "longsuffering", discloses the duration of the patience, often extending far beyond human reasoning, but never beyond divine resources, while "forbearing" gives an insight to the intensity of the patience, hence the reason that it appears in several passages as "suffer" (Matt 17:17, etc).

The verb "forgiving" occurs in 2:13 where Paul speaks of God's forgiveness of all our trespasses. This is the seventh portion of the christian apparel. It suggests the outcome of the previous six, hence they are not seven distinct garments, but seven features of the one robe of righteousness. Any believer thus garbed is well dressed. This feature of the attire spells *sympathetic grace*.

Momphē ("quarrel") occurs only here in the NT. The cognate verb "find fault with" (*memphomai*) is used in Mark 7:2; Rom 9:19; Heb 8:8. It is not likely that Paul has in mind a concrete situation in the Colossian assembly. If such had been the case, he would probably have been more explicit in censure (Gal 5:15) and in consideration (Phil 4:2). The peace of God's assembly is often disturbed by trivial complaints of the one against the other. In many cases they are imagined; in other instances seldom justified. But whatever, the Christian is obligated to forbear and forgive gratuitously. It is not a matter either of saying, "I forgive but I cannot forget" , such is not the forgiveness Paul envisages. The participle carries the action on to its goal, where the wrong is cancelled completely.

"Even as Christ forgave you, so also do ye" finds its first example in Luke 7:42. Several versions have "the Lord" as the RV. Yet whether "Lord" or "Christ", it is Christ who is referred to here, while in the comparative verse in Eph 4:32 forgiveness is rooted in God. The ascription of the power to forgive attests Christ's deity. Forgiveness is a divine prerogative, which He Himself claimed in the days of His flesh when He said, "The Son of man hath power on earth to forgive sins" (Mark 2:10). The Ephesian counterpart reflects the grace of God; here in Colossians the right to forgive reflects the glory of Christ. This is in perfect harmony with the tenor of the epistle - Christ is all.

14 In "And above all these things *put on* charity", the prepositional phrase has no verb in the text, but one is supplied, that of v.12. The preposition *epi* sustains a varied range of meaning; (1) local, "upon" or "over" which follows closely the figure of the "clothing" in v.12; (2) "in addition to" as Moule suggests (p.123); (3) elative and means "above all else" as Mft, NEB and the RSV appear to suggest. The thought in the mind of the apostle seems to be that love (RV) is the virtue which holds all the other virtues together and completes them. Often people find it almost impossible to get things to match when it comes to clothing. That difficulty does not arise here: love matches the sevenfold apparel of the believer perfectly. Love is never out of fashion!

For *sundesmos* ("bond") see 2:19. It is used as a "fetter" which holds in bondage (Acts 8:23). In Eph 4:3, the word occurs as denoting the means by which the oneness is to be maintained. We have it in 2:19 in a surgical figure. Here it is viewed as something without which the christian attire will be incomplete. Some have espoused the idea of a girdle, binding the graces together. It is the "bond" which betokens *maturity* or perfectness and therefore it should always be in evidence in those who are going on to this goal.

Love begets love. The appeal began on the basis of our being loved of God; the exhortation ends on our love being expressed toward others in full and free forgiveness.

15 For "the peace of God" the RV has "the peace of Christ" which is in line with the Christo-centric emphasis of the epistle. However the term "peace of God" appears in Phil 4:7. It is the peace of Christ because He gives it (John 14:27) and because He Himself is it (Eph 2:14). The word *brabeueto* ("rule", "arbitrate" RV marg.) is one of four imperatives that mark out the precepts the Colossian believers are to observe. They are exhorted here to let the peace of Christ arbitrate when matters arise among them that will cause dissension. Mutual accord can be realised only as we let the peace of Christ decide the matter. Such a matter here must be one upon which the word of God gives no specific direction. It will be in the absence of "Thus saith the Lord" that such a situation will prevail, where the peace of Christ will arbitrate. The same principle applies in the life of the individual believer when faced with the affairs of life which can raise tension and uncertainty. The context guides the thinking and the main point with the apostle is not so much inner peace in personal affairs, but inner peace in one's attitude of mind and will towards others.

"To which also ye are called in one body" confirms that it is the attitude of the

believers one to another that is under consideration. The body comes readily to
Paul's mind when corporate unity is in view. The absence of the definite article in
connection with the word "body" may suggest that Paul has the local company
in view. Whether this is so or not, the main point is this: "if the members are
subject to Him, the peace which He imparts must regulate their relations one
with another" (Bruce p.282).

The company that knows the rule of Christ's peace, thus preserving mutual
relationships in godly order, knows something of what it means to have grace
enthroned. The same can be said of the individual believer.

"Be ye thankful" is the second imperative which Paul administers in this
section. The present imperative represents Paul as saying, "Keep on becoming
thankful". He views it as a continuous obligation, and he inculcates the
exercise at every opportunity. It is he who reminds us that ungratefulness is
an evidence of man's alienation from God, that in spite of God's providential
goodness, there is no return of thanks. The cause for thanksgiving here can
be the peace which Christ provides in all circumstances. There certainly is
every cause for thanksgiving that we have come into the possession of
such peace. Does not the thanksgiving arise however from a realisation
of the privilege of being called into the membership of the one body?
Judging this to be the case, is Paul not inferring that a consciousness of
God's grace in this particular will cause the saints to live worthy of such
a calling?

Six times in the epistle the theme of thanksgiving appears. This passage is the
only use of the adjective "thankful" in the NT. Three times the verb occurs, 1:3;
1: 12; 3:17, and the noun appears twice as "thanksgiving" in 2:7; 4:2. Under the
motif of "the hope" it may be enumerated as:

1. Thanksgiving in relation to the Hope   : Consummation: 1:3;

2. Thanksgiving that the believer is fitted
   for the Hope   : Condition: 1:12;

3. Thanksgiving for that which qualifies
   for the Hope   : Consolidation: 2:7;

4. Thanksgiving for the fellowship of the
   Hope   : Communion: 3:15;

5. Thanksgiving for the confidence of the
   Hope   : Confession: 3:17;

6. Thanksgiving for the anticipation of the
   Hope   : Contemplation: 4:2.

16   With "let the word of Christ dwell in you richly", the apostle now reaches his third imperative and urges that the saints give ample room to the "word of Christ", the ministry which comes from the risen Head and which receives Him. He is both its source and its subject, its origin and its theme. The "word" is variously described as:

the word of God	Acts 13:5; 2 Cor 4:2; Col 1:25; Heb 4:12;
the word of the message of God	1 Thess 2:13 RV;
the word of the Lord	Acts8:25; 13:48; 19:10; 1 Thess 1:8;
the word of His grace	Acts 14:3; 20:32;
the word of the cross	1 Cor 1:18 RV;
the word of truth	2 Cor 6:7; Eph 1: 13; 2 Tim 2:15;
the word of the truth of the gospel	Col 1:5;
the word of the gospel	Acts 15:7;
the word of this salvation	Acts 13:26;
the word of reconciliation	2 Cor 5:19;
the word of life	Phil 2:16;
the word of righteousness	Heb 5:13.

For believers to let the "word of Christ" dwell richly in them means to let it be at home in their hearts individually, and to let the ministry have full sway in every aspect of life. Paul uses the word of (a) the indwelling of God in believers (2 Cor 6:16); (b) the indwelling of the Holy Spirit (Rom 8:11; 2 Tim 1:14); (c) the indwelling of faith (2 Tim 1:5); (d) the indwelling of sin in the believer (Rom 7:17 RV); see also *oikeō en*, of the indwelling of the Holy Spirit in the believer (Rom 8:9,11); or in the local assembly (1 Cor 3:16); of the indwelling of sin (Rom 7:20); of the absence of any good thing in the flesh of a believer (Rom 7:18); of the dwelling together of the married (1 Cor 7:12,13); of God as dwelling in light (1 Tim 6:16). There is a close link between *dwell* and the Lord's own desire that His words should *abide (menō)* in His disciples (John 15:7), likewise with the word *katoikeō* which Paul uses in what must be a comparable text in Eph 3:17 when he speaks of the indwelling of Christ in the hearts of believers.

The word "richly" infers that the ministry of Christ must be appropriated in its completeness, fully understood and the soul be fully under its sway. If this is the experience of each believer in assembly fellowship then the corporate testimony will be enriched as the word of Christ finds its home with large and liberal occupancy.

"Wisdom" (*sophia*), is the fifth of six occurrences in the epistle (1:9,28; 2:3,23). Does the expression indicate the manner in which the "word of Christ" is to dwell in the saints, or does it describe how it is to be used in teaching? Both the AV and Mft for example adhere to the first proposal, that is, "let it inhabit you as if you were the house and home of this Word, let it do this in a rich way by filling every nook and corner of your being with its blessed, spiritual wisdom" (Lenski p.177).

Most, however, link the propositional phrase with the following clause, which refers to mutual teaching. The balance of the verse is best maintained by a correct punctuation thus clearly displaying the three subjects with suitable emphasis as follows: "Let the word of Christ dwell in you richly, as you teach one another in all wisdom, and as you sing psalms and hymns and spiritual songs with thankfulness in your hearts to God" (RSV).

The Colossians are encouraged to teach and admonish one another and thus follow the apostolic example (1:28) and bring others into the good of what they have already experienced (2:7). "Teaching" has to do with the impartation of positive truth; it is the positive aspect of instruction. "Admonishing" has mainly in view the negative aspect; the things that are wrong and call for warning. Paul expects the Colossians to rise to their mutual responsibility and as the saints in Rome, exercise themselves to these forms of instruction (Rom 15:14). He would have the saints understand that unless the word of Christ dwells richly within them, they could not fulfil this privilege; for they could not teach and admonish if they were not aware of the lessons to impart, and in what spirit to convey them. Both the lessons and the spirit alike are to be found in the word of Christ. Limited acquaintance with Holy Scriptures leads to meagre counsel and inadequate teaching. There falls to the responsible task of those who exercise care in the assembly the general ministry of admonition (1 Thess 5:12), as well as the more specific occasions as Paul urges in the words "admonish the disorderly" (1 Thess 5:14 RV).

"Psalms and hymns and spiritual songs" are not to be understood as the medium of the "teaching and admonishing", for it is particularly difficult to see how admonition would be conveyed through these channels, which are more commonly thought of as involving praise. Doubtless a separate activity is in view, that of singing as distinct from teaching, yet both activities flow from a rich possession of the word of Christ.

Few commentators offer any strict line of demarcation for these three terms which occur also in Eph 5:19. The word "psalms" (*psalmois*) denotes songs born out of experience and may very well link up with the idea of affliction. One has said, "If David's heart has ne'er been wrung, David's psalms had ne'er been sung". The Word welcomed to the heart and obeyed has often brought the saints of God into circumstances that have given rise to heartfelt songs that reflect the depth of their experience. The next term "hymns" (*humnois*) suggests songs which arise as result of divine revelation, and may convey a more objective note of praise to God and to Christ the Lord. Hymns of this nature suggest appreciation, adoration and worship. The third term "spiritual songs" (*ōdais pneumatikais*) could specify songs of aspiration. Whatever the distinction it is clear from the context that these sacred songs are rooted in the Word, and can be sung in the right spirit only when the indwelling Word gives rise to thankful adoration and praise.

For "singing with grace in your hearts to the Lord", the RV has "to God" (compare Eph 5:19, "to the Lord"). The singing must be rendered "with grace". Some interpret this as simply meaning "graciously" or "acceptably", while others suggest "gratefully singing" or "with thankfulness". The presence of the definite article (*en tē chariti*) seems to denote that the grace of God is in view. The grace will be the realm in which the praise ascends. The singing will be "in the grace", giving outward expression to an inner experience of divine grace. It will be the overflow of the heart which has recognised the wonders of God's truth and a desire to praise Him for it. As the word of Christ dwells richly in the heart, so the Christ of the word will be the object of praise. The praise in our present verse is the result of a deep assimilation of the word of Christ, while in Eph 5:18-20, it is the out-growth of the filling of the Spirit. A Word-filled Christian is a Spirit-filled Christian.

17 The apostle adds, "and whatsoever ye do in word or deed, do all in the name of the Lord Jesus," - the imperative *poieite* ("do") is understood although it is not actually expressed in the text, but is clearly implied from the opening clause "whatsoever ye do". This is the great practical lesson which flows from the doctrinal teaching of the epistle: the Lordship, the sovereignty and authority of Christ should be predominant in the life of every believer. Thus the main theme of the epistle is maintained, that in all things He might have the pre-eminence (1:18). "Whatsoever ye do" occurs three times in the NT (see v.23; 1 Cor 10:31) and embraces every aspect of life. Hence the expression has to do with the "name" of the Lord Jesus Christ, and means that all that we say and do must be in relation to His authority, and in keeping with the revelation of Himself in His Word.

In v.15 the believer is to know the arbitration of the "peace of Christ". Then in v.16 there is to be an adequate accommodation given to the word of Christ which will result in grateful acclamation to the Person of Christ, and promote his every action to be in the name of Christ.

In "giving thanks to God and the Father by him" the participle stresses the continuity of the thanksgiving which is rendered to God the Father for all that He has bestowed upon us in His Son. It is as we do everything in the Lord's name that we shall be constantly expressing gratitude to God the Father, all this thanksgiving and gratitude being mediated by our Lord Jesus Christ (Rom 1:8; 7:25; 16:27; Eph 5:20).

The chapter begins with our identification *with* Christ; then it speaks of our conformation *to* Christ as we put on the new man. Also, it shows the results of the appropriation *of* Christ in His peace and His Word. The summation arrives in all that we are in representation *for* Christ as acknowledging His Lordship in our every word and work. There is therefore adequate attestation to the fact that "Christ is all".

3. Natural Relationships: Wives and Husbands, Children and Parents, Masters and Servants 3:18-4:1

v.18 "Wives, submit yourselves unto your own husbands, as it is fit in the Lord.
v.19 Husbands, love your wives and be not bitter against them.
v.20 Children, obey your parents in all things; for this is well pleasing unto the Lord.
v.21 Fathers, provoke not your children to anger, lest they be discouraged.
v.22 Servants, obey in all things your masters according to the flesh; not with eyeservice as menpleasers; but in singleness of heart, fearing God:
v.23 And whatsoever ye do, do it heartily, as to the Lord, and not unto men;
v.24 Knowing that of the Lord ye shall receive the reward of the inheritance: for ye serve the Lord Christ.
v.25 But he that doeth wrong shall receive for the wrong which he hath done; and there is no respect of persons.
4:1   Masters, give unto your servants that which is just and equal; knowing that ye also have a Master in heaven."

18   Paul has already said, "Do all in the name of the Lord Jesus". He now shows the Colossians how to carry out this principle into the various relationships of life, namely, those of (a) wife and husband, (b) child and parent, (c) slave and lord. The passage should be carefully compared with its corresponding section of Ephesians (5:22-6:9) which presents a very instructive parallel. There is an obvious difference, however, in respect of the amount of space devoted to the various groups in the epistles. In Colossians,

1. the duties of wife and husband are much more tersely set forth, and the duties of child and parent somewhat more briefly than in Ephesians. The Colossians would be able to supplement the advice given in their own epistle from that given in the Ephesian letter.

2. the duties of the slave are very fully given. The case of Onesimus weighing heavily upon the apostle's mind would probably be the reason for the extended treatment he gives to the slave-master relationship.

There are three places in the NT where the duties of wife and husband are set forth; once by Peter (1 Pet 3:1-6), and twice by Paul (here and in Eph 5:22-23). In all three, the call upon the wife is one of *subjection*, but the reason given varies, and the change is instructive.

1. In Ephesians the wife is exhorted to be in subjection to her husband, as the church is subject to Christ.
2. In 1 Pet 3 subjection is urged that even the unbelieving husband may be won to Christ by the loyal submission of the wife.
3. In Colossians (the epistle which has as its theme Christ is all and in all) the demand is made because "it is fit in the Lord".

Christian women know what is involved in christian womanhood. In 1 Cor 11:2-16 the honour of christian womanhood is seen in a subjection displayed by the veiled head of the woman in assembly gatherings. Her subjection is further evidenced by the silence she is exhorted to maintain (1 Cor 14:34). Paul states clear reasons why the woman must be subject and in deference to the man is not permitted to teach (1 Tim 2:12). The women of Phil 4:3 are noted for their service, those in Titus 2:3,4, for their sobriety, while 1 Pet 3:2 stresses their sanctity.

The six classes of Christians addressed are paired into three different groups governed by their respective relationships. The first of each pair mentioned is called upon to evidence submission: wives (v.18), children (v.20), servants (v.22). There is a corresponding responsibility set before the other party in each couplet - husbands (not to be bitter), fathers (not to discourage their children) and masters (not to overlook righteousness).

The word Paul uses to counsel *the* wife, (note the various persons in these verses are prefixed by the definite article, denoting a compelling force), *hupotassomai* ("submit yourselves") is a term employed to denote a subordinate's relationship to his superior. It has military overtones. It is used of the Lord's subjection in His childhood (Luke 2:51), of a wife's relationship to her husband (Eph 5:22; Titus 2:5; 1 Pet 3:1), of servants to masters (Titus 2:9; 1 Pet 2:13), of people to state government (Rom 13:1; Titus 3:1) and of believers to God (James 4:7). The idea of subordination is clearly implied, for it means "to be subject to, obey, or be ruled by". This submission required from the wife is prompted by regard for God's order. Her heart, having given accommodating occupancy to the word of Christ will bring her into that voluntary desire to express the will of God in her home life. The middle voice (if retained) indicates that it best serves her own interests to give godly credence to the place given of God to her husband. Several authorities omit "own" but it is retained clearly in Eph 5:22 and Titus 2:5.

Anēkō ("fit") occurs three times, here, in Eph 5:4 where it is translated "convenient" and in Philem 8. It has a useful synonym in the word "becoming". Bruce beautifully expounds: "This phrase ('as is fitting', RV) has a thoroughly Stoic ring about it; but the injunction ceases to be Stoic when Paul baptises it into Christ by adding the words, 'in the Lord'. By treating the relation between the sexes in this context, Paul (contrary to popular opinion) places the essential dignity of women in general and of wives in particular, on an unshakeable foundation" (pp.289-290).

The expression "in the Lord" appears four times in Colossians (3:18,20; 4:7,17) and occurs some forty times in Paul's epistles. Our basic position in relation to God is conveyed by the term "in Christ", whereas "in the Lord" emphasises the believer's obligation in this divinely formed relationship. That it involves the recognition of the Lordship of Christ is undeniably clear, hence its significance throughout Paul's usage. There is a sevenfold mention of Christ as Lord within the section before us (3:18-4:1), following the RV. The believer's obligation to divine Lordship extends beyond mere ecclesiastical responsibilities. While the obligation of the wife may not be a popular practice in these times, it has always been God's purpose for mankind. Godly women who are "in the Lord" will be marked by this kind of behaviour and conduct thus acknowledging in the home what they avow in the assembly, that "Jesus Christ is Lord".

19 In "husbands, love your wives", *agapate* ("love") is to be taken as an imperative. It is a love that goes beyond natural affection and is best seen in the actions it prompts. The word denotes a caring love marked by sacrifice (John 15:13) and unselfishness (1 Cor 13) and has Christ as its fullest expression, who as the bridegroom loved the church without limit (Eph 5:25). The duty of the husband in 1 Pet 3:7 is *honour*; in Ephesians and Colossians it is love. In Ephesians it is love because (a) Christ loved the church, (b) man and wife are one flesh. In Colossians it is love, yet no reason is given, though the governing expression in the preceding verse is equally applicable, "it is fit in the Lord". Love, then, will require the husband to be all that he should be, in which is to be found the true secret of married bliss. If the love is to be qualitative, it is also to be quantitative, for the present imperative calls for a continual expression of love.

"Be bitter" translates the verb *pikrainō* ("to make bitter"), used literally in Rev 8:11; 10:9,10. Its adjectival form occurs in James 3:11,14; in v.11 in its natural sense with reference to water; in v.14 metaphorically of envying. As a noun it appears in Acts 8:23, denoting a condition of extreme wickedness; in Rom 3:14 of evil speaking; in Eph 4:31 of a bitter disposition; in Heb 12:15 of bitter hatred. The adverbial form gives poignancy to Peter's grief (Matt 26:75; Luke 22:62). This added injunction advises the husband against ill temper, inconsiderateness and harshness. The parallel passage in Eph 5:25-33 provides proper guidelines for the husband as illustrated in the relation of Christ to the church. Dr. J. Boyd has a suggestion worth considering which is very likely true in these groupings, he writes: "he (the husband) must never be bitter against her even though, *if not born again*, she may have given him occasion to retaliate, because of her constant nagging, and lack of submission to his wishes" (pp. 18,19 *Assembly Testimony*, No. 159). The "husbands" of v.18 may well be unsaved as possibly the wives of this verse before us. It is clear that the apostle's desire is to see the marriage tie preserved and honoured by both parties being activated by true deference and devotion to the other. The word of God never requires to be up-dated or sub-edited, for it meets the need of the present hour.

20 In "children, obey your parents in all things", the present tense of the verb *hupakouō* ("to obey") denotes the action is to be continual. The word implies a readiness to listen and a willingness to carry out the instructions given. Paul sets the exhortation in a christian perspective. A christian home is in view where christian principles prevail. If, however, the parents are not believers the obedience of the children must be to the utmost limit of christian principles. Often in heathen homes parents who are not born again use this and such texts to demand obedience in matters hostile to the faith of believing offspring. Many are slighted by these words because in obeying the Lord they desist from idol worship and relevant practices. Obedience to parents is to be encouraged but not at the expense of allegiance to Christ and His truth. The more obedient the believing children can be in such homes where Christ is not named, the richer the testimony to that name which God must own and honour. Let all believing children be careful to fulfil this duty for which the filial relation affords so many opportunities. Paul also infers that children are not the final arbiters of what they should or should not obey in matters of parental authority. No exception is stated; the words are "in all things".

"Well pleasing unto the Lord", or as in the RV "well-pleasing in the Lord", is the standard expected of those believing children who seek to acknowledge Christ's Lordship. Eadie thoughtfully remarks: "The construction is similar to that of v. 19, the specific difference of thought being that, in the former case, submission is an appropriate thing in the Lord; while in this case filial obedience is marked with special approbation, as being well-pleasing in the Lord" (p.260). In Eph 6:1 Paul says it is "right", and then quotes the fifth commandment which endorses the obedience as being a principle in Scripture, but here he regards it as a matter of spiritual significance as having the Lord's commendation. The point just mentioned gives rise to an observation perhaps not out of place at this stage, that is, the quotations from the OT that so frequently appear in the Ephesian letter are absent in this epistle. This probably indicates the assembly was largely composed of Gentile believers whose knowledge of the OT Scripture was scant. There are references to passages in the OT which are as follows:

2:3   "In whom are hid all the treasures of wisdom".
      Isa 45:3 "I will give thee the treasures of darkness and the hidden riches of secret places".
2:22 "Commandments and doctrines of men".
      Isa 29:13 RV "Their fear of Me is a commandment of men which hath been taught them" (cf Matt 15:9; Mark 7:7).
3:10 "After the image of him that created him".
      Gen 1:26 "Let us make man in our image".
      Gen 1:27 "God created man in his own image".
3:25 "And there is no respect of persons".
      Deut 10:17 "The great God ... which regardeth not persons".

21   The change from the term *goneusin* ("parents", v.20) to *pateres* ("fathers") is deliberate as it is the fathers who are singled out as the recipients of this exhortation. He is not to use his authority unreasonably, because it may lead to discouragement on the part of the children. The apostle uses *erethizō* in a good sense in 2 Cor 9:2, translated "hath stirred up" (RV). But here it is employed in the context of what is evil and of what should not be, that is, stirring up improperly by inconsiderate or even unjust treatment. The constant unjustified correction and reprimand for every little wrong or imagined wrong is what appears to be envisaged by the apostle. Yet he is not contradicting the added advice he gives in Eph 6:4: "bring them up in the chastening and admonition of the Lord" (RV).

Athumeō ("to be disheartened, dispirited, discouraged") occurs here only. When a child feels that he can never do anything right, he gives up trying, a danger that must be strenuously avoided by every believing father. The alienation of children from the truth of God through overseverity is what concerns the apostle and adherence to his appeal will certainly circumvent the experience.

22   The responsibility of slaves to their masters is akin to that of the children to their parents - obedience. The duties of the slave are more fully presented than those of the parent and child, likely due to

1. the case of Onesimus being in the apostle's mind,
2. the greater number of Christians in the Colossian assembly being slaves,
3. the testimony's being seriously threatened if believing slaves had misunderstood the freedom the gospel gave.

With these suggestions in mind, observe how that both here and in Ephesians the injunctions to slaves are more expansive and expressive than those to masters.

While the servant's obligations led him to a complete obedience, he is not at all obliged to carry out orders contrary to the principles of truth and righteousness. His desistence from such commands where unchristian behaviour would embroil the believer may indeed cause him suffering. This would of course be commendable if it were for righteousness' sake.

The term "according to the flesh" denotes human masters because believers in Christ have a "Master in heaven". The gospel never cancels earthly relationships but enriches them in that it enables the believer to bring all the resources of grace to bear upon his responsibilities in such circumstances as he is found.

The noun *ophthalmodouliea* ("eyeservice") is found only here and in Eph 6:6 and denotes service diligently performed while being watched, but neglected when he turns his eye away. The christian servant is called upon to render genuine service, whether or not the master according to the flesh is watching, for the Master in heaven is always watching. He is not to be governed by either the fear or favour of the master whom he serves, but by reverence of the Lord Christ. There is a slight yet observable difference between the Ephesian passage which has the preposition *kata* ("with") and here where the apostle uses *en* ("in"). The former denotes the attitude or style of eyeservice, while the latter suggests the atmosphere or spirit of it.

"Men-pleasers" is used only here and in Eph 6:6. Performance with such a motive would simply be perfunctory, and would fall far short of the diligence which the testimony of Christ requires.

Haplotēs ("singleness") occurs also in Rom 12:8; 2 Cor 1:12 (in some MSS only); 8:2; 9:11,13; 11:3; Eph 6:5. It designates a state of heart which is unaffected by lesser motive, referring to what is simple, unambiguous and sincere. It is the opposite of duplicity and hypocrisy. This is something that only the gospel can bring and such is to be expected of those who are disciples of the Lord, who says to His followers, "If therefore thine eye be single (*haplous*), thy whole body shall be full of light" (Matt 6:22; Luke 11:34). Compare 1 Chron 29:17, as revealing a service which can bear the scrutiny of God.

For "fearing God" the RV and most translations have "fearing the Lord". As we have already observed, the Lordship of Christ pervades this section, so it is in keeping with the context to follow the altered reading of the RV. Nothing transforms secular service more than realising that the work wrought is not merely out of respect and of obedience to earthly masters, but of due reverence to the Lord, our Master in heaven. It is just here the apostle would urge the believing slave to remember that the Lord's eye is constantly upon him. The change in the reading reminds the reader that he is Christ's bondslave (1 Cor 7:22 RV), a bondservice of an infinitely higher relationship than that "according to the flesh".

23 In the sentence, "and whatsoever ye do, do it heartily, as to the Lord, and not unto men", two different words are used here by the apostle: *poiēte* ("do") and *ergazesthe* ("do it"). The first covers any human activity that would become the responsibility of the slave to perform, while the second denotes the way the task was to be performed - putting all of one's energy into it. The word "heartily" which translates the Greek *ek psuchēs* (from the soul) suggests that whatever the nature of the service is, pleasant or distasteful, menial or honourable, it must be carried out cheerfully. The secret being that it is to the Lord as though He were the one employer. Paul is constantly focussing the eye of the believing servant upon his Lord who, in the first instance, must be satisfied with every effort performed by the strength He graciously imparts.

24 "Knowing that of the Lord ye shall receive the reward of the inheritance" properly continues the previous verse as it further reinforces the inspired admonition to christian slaves to give genuine service to their earthly masters. The participle "knowing" suggests that these instructions formed part of a body of teaching already familiar to them. Paul infers that they have already reached that point of knowledge and is simply asking them to bear it in mind continually as they serve. Perhaps the earthly master may not pay at all for labour faithfully rendered, not to speak of renumeration commensurate with the energy expended, but the christian servant of the past and the christian employee of today has this assurance that a full and an abundant reward awaits him. Paul uses the future middle of the verb *apolambanō* ("shall receive") showing that it is not only still ahead of the recipient but that it will be in his own interests to obtain such a recompense. During the days of Paul, he knew that there was little

hope of the earthly master sharing his inheritance with the slave, but because
the believing slave served well even in unkind and inconsiderate circumstances
and in his toil honoured his Master in heaven, there was reserved for him a share
in the inheritance of glory. Ample compensation awaits the diligent servant.

In "for ye serve the Lord Christ", most translators treat "for" as a gloss which
transforms the remaining words into a possible imperative - "Serve ye the Lord
Christ". The idea behind the apostle's appeal is: because such a reward, so rich
and so blessed, awaits the servant from the Master in heaven, then serve Him
fully. Paul also endeavours to heighten every lowly service to the lofty degree of
service to Christ. His purpose is clear: to give encouragement and incentive to
faithful service, and even more, if note is made of Titus 2:10.

25 "But he that doeth wrong shall receive for the wrong that he hath done- is
a warning which corresponds to the promise of Eph 6:7, and relates to the
judgment seat of Christ (2 Cor 5:10; cf Rom 14:10-12; 1 Cor 3:12ff; 4:4ff). The
solemn reminder is directed to the slaves, though some take it as being said for
the benefit of servants who endured harsh treatment from their masters. Masters
as such are addressed in 4:1. Injurious and unjust behaviour on the part of the
slave in respect of his master must be met with impartial judgment. This might
well invoke the chastening hand of God upon the believing yet dishonest servant
in that he becomes an object of divine judgment. While this is true, the context
points to the Bema of Christ. Here the apostle uses the word he employs in
describing what Onesimus may have done to Philemon, *adikeō* ("to commit an
unrighteous act, to wrong"). To be repaid for the wrong done would involve
suffering loss in the day of reward. The verb "shall receive" occurs in connection
with the judgment seat of Christ in 2 Cor 5:10, and being in the middle voice
shows how personally involved the servant will be in the day of recompense.

For *prosōpolēptēs* ("respect of persons") see Rom 2:11; Eph 6:9; James 2:1
and the noun form in Acts 10:34. The impartiality of God assures equity in
judgment, either now or hereafter. God performs in absolute rectitude what He
enjoins on others (Lev 19:15).

The passage directed to the slaves can in principle find a ready application to
all God's people who would have us to know singleness of heart (v.22); sincerity
of heart (v.23); satisfaction of heart (v.24) and sobriety of heart (v.25).

WORDS PECULIAR TO COLOSSIANS 3 ARE:

Athumeō	: discouraged	3:21
Aischrologia	: evil, obscene speech	3:8
Antapodosis	: recompense	3:24
Apekduomai	: strip off, disarm	3:9
Brabeuō	: direct, rule	3:15
Eucharistos	: thankful	3:15

| *Momphē* | : blame, complaint | 3:13 |
| *Skuthēs* | : Scythian | 3:11 |

WORDS COMMON TO COLOSSIANS AND EPHESIANS
IN COLOSSIANS 3 ARE:

Anthrōpareskos	: menpleasers	3:22;	Eph 6:6
Ophthalmodouleia	: eyeservice	3:22;	Eph 6:6
Sunegeirō	: raised together	3:1;	Eph 2:6
Humnos	: hymn	3:16;	Eph 5:19

4:1 The verse belongs more properly to the previous chapter as it concludes the paragraph begun at 3:18 (see RV). The christian slave-owners are now addressed and are instructed, as are the slaves, to demonstrate the highest christian principles in their treatment of those that serve them. If the slave is exhorted to do what is right, so the master is admonished to render in return what is right. Their personal duty is carried to their hearts by Paul's use of the word *parechesthe*, the present middle imperative of the verb *parechō* ("to give, provide, supply, show oneself to be something"); here it has the sense "supply on your part fairness to the slaves". The expression "that which is just and equal" has given rise to a variety of interpretations too numerous to mention. In these words Paul is seeking an amelioration of the slaves' lot. He requires of the masters that they render fair treatment and honest distribution to their slaves. The word *dikaion* ("just") suggests equality. If faithful service has been rendered, then give the slave all to which he is entitled, and thereby honour the Lord your Master. In *isotēta* ("equal") used elsewhere only in 2 Cor 8:13,14, there lies the idea of gratuitous distribution, hence adequate remuneration. To give what is equal may well involve sharing out the profits; if such had been done, there would have been little need for trade union guilds to plead on the behalf of those from whom due remuneration is withheld. Two voices blend harmoniously with Paul's in this connection, that of Job in 31:13-15 and that of James in 5:1-5. The master is to be gracious in his supervision and gratuitous in his remuneration. The final note is reached in the words which follow and it should create a conscious realisation that he himself is a servant to a Master in heaven.

For a useful treatment of *kurios* ("Lord", here translated "Master") as referring to the Lord Jesus, see *The Epistles of Paul the Apostle to the Thessalonians* by C.F. Hogg and W.E. Vine, Pickering & Inglis, London, 2nd edition, 1929, pp.22-25. As in v.24 above, "knowing" signifies "bear in mind" or "keep continually in mind". The reminder serves to make the master realise that they have to give account to the Lord Christ whom they also serve. Paul once again acknowledges the sovereignty of Christ as the exalted glorified Lord in heaven, which in so doing continues the theme of the epistle - the pre-eminence of Christ.

4. *Spiritual Requirements in Prayer and in Walk*
4:2-6

v.2 "Continue in prayer, and watch in the same with thanksgiving;
v.3 Withal praying also for us, that God would open unto us a door of utterance, to speak the mystery of Christ, for which I am also in bonds;
v.4 That I may make it manifest, as I ought to speak.
v.5 Walk in wisdom toward them that are without, redeeming the time.
v.6 Let your speech be alway with grace, seasoned with salt, that ye may know how ye ought to answer every man."

From the realms of the household and its needs, the apostle turns to the family of faith in general and considers themes of the christian life that apply to all of God's people, irrespective of marital, parental or social distinction. There are several elements in this short hortatory section which call forth our consideration. The paragraph may be summarised as follows:

1. Be constant in your speaking to God   v. 2a Our Asking
   Be careful in your speaking to man   v.6a Our Answering

2. Let your asking be mixed with the grace
   of gratefulness   v.2b
   Let your answering be seasoned with
   the grace of considerateness   v.6b

3. prayer for open doors for the Word   v.3
   A plea for opportunities for the work   v.5b

4. That I may know how to witness   v.4
   That you may know how to walk   v.5a

2 "Continue in prayer" (*proskartereite*) is the present active imperative of the verb *proskartereō* ("to adhere to", "to persist in"). Its ten occurrences in the NT are: Mark 3:9; Acts 1:34; 2:42,46; 6:4; 8:13; 10:7; Rom 12:12; 13:6 and here. The compound imperative used here by Paul has its root meaning "to endure" (*kartereō*, Heb 11:27), and is strengthened by the prefix *pros* ("towards"). What Paul is urging is perseverance in prayer. Nothing is to deflect them from this diligence and persistence in prayer. Paul was himself an example of this fervour and faithfulness in prayer (1:3,9), as was Epaphras (4:12).

"And watch in the same" shows Paul is appealing not only for diligence in prayer but also for vigilance as the word *grēgorountes* ("watch") implies. The RV translates the participle "watching", meaning to attend constantly upon and to be wide awake. It involves the Christian in an aroused conscience and a keen attention to the task, that should characterise him as he prays. Dullness of soul and distraction of mind much reduce fervency and effectiveness in prayer. Such dangers can be avoided only by a spiritual alertness to both the need for and the opportunity to pray with steadfast continuance. Sleep caused king Saul to lose his source of defence; the virgins to lose their distinctiveness; the church at Sardis its dynamism and the husbandmen their discernment.

As joy is to the Philippian epistle, so thanksgiving is to the Colossian epistle (see 3:17 for an outline of thanksgiving in Colossians). Not only is thanksgiving a characteristic element in prayer, but it also adds a spiritual vitality to prayer which acts as a panacea for the ill Paul is seeking to remedy, sluggishness of soul in prayer.

3   *Hama* ("withal") is an adverb denoting "at the same time", as in 1 Tim 5:13; Philem 22. Paul encourages a mutuality in prayer; he would pray for the Colossians generally (1:3) and specifically (1:9-14), now he urges that they in return pray for both him and his fellow-workers. He sensed the need for prayer; even though he had an honoured calling, he knew it could not be discharged in the energy of his own ability. He valued the prayerful support of the saints. "Praying also for us" may be taken as a plea for general remembrance in prayer, but Paul always desires to be specific, hence his specialised items follow.

Anoigō ("to open") is used here in the aorist and subjunctive active. For the figurative use of "opening a door" see 1 Cor 16:9; 2 Cor 2:12. The apostle is desirous that God in His providential dealings with him may open the door of opportunity to serve further in the proclamation of the message He has given him to preach. The movements of the apostle are restricted due to his imprisonment, yet he is conscious that all this lies in the hands of a sovereign God. Thus his request for release is not inconsistent with his submission to the will of God. It is not a selfish interest, nor even a need of a personal nature; it is that opportunity may be granted him to pursue the holy tasks his high calling involves. "The opening of the door of his prison would be the opening of a door of discourse" (Eadie, p.276). The rendering "a door for the word" clearly distinguishes between the request of Eph 6:19 where "utterance" is the proper reading.

For "Mystery" see 1:26-27; 2:3. Paul is no less attached to the mystery because of the persecution he suffered due to his preaching of it. He loves it the more and longs to be freed from his cage that he may circulate its glorious truth in an ever-widening location. And yet, as Paul remains bound, he is ever in such liberty, a liberty in the Spirit which has brought forth the exposition of the Mystery in this epistle as well as in Ephesians and Philippians, which reveal the features of those who have come to know the Mystery. God granted Paul much opportunity even in his bonds as Phil 1:13, etc. indicate.

Paul clearly identified the special cause of his imprisonment: it was his proclamation of the Mystery. The Colossians, having now been brought into the good and riches of Paul's ministry, had every reason to remember him in their prayers. It is still true: there is a line of teaching that will be permitted and for which no price must be paid. So long as Saul of Tarsus preached Judaism he was the favourite of priests and people (Acts 9:14); immediately he began to preach the gospel, the Jews sought to kill him (Acts 9:23-24). Ultimately it was his "proclaiming of the mystery of Christ" which led to his imprisonment.

4 Paul is anxious that not only will the Lord grant him liberty of movement, but that he may give him clarity in ministry. If the opportunity is provided, Paul is desirous that he may be given grace to take full advantage of it. To make the Mystery of Christ *manifest (phaneroso)* means to state it clearly and to preach it boldly. Even though he is a man of outstanding ability, yet he feels the need for prayer for the enablement of God in the ministry, that the "excellency of the power may be of God ..." (2 Cor 4:7). The high and holy nature of the ministry committed to Paul demands of him all he possesses in himself. All his fervour, all his power, all his ability, and more, must be utilised in the power of the Spirit to do what he *ought* to do.

5 In "Walk in wisdom toward them that are without", *peripateite* the present active imperative of *peripateo* ("to walk about") denotes conduct and behaviour (1:10; 2:6;3:7). What the Colossians are to help on by constant prayer must not be hindered by inconsistent conduct in daily life. Their walk is to be characterised by wisdom, not by the wisdom of man's philosophy but by that which is found in Christ (2:3). It simply means that the saints are to order their whole conduct in the world in the regulating power of the teaching they have now received in the epistle. Paul would have the saints in Colossae to be living exponents of the truth he has imparted to them. The imperative makes this obligatory. "Them that are without" is an expression that denotes all those outside the fellowship of the assembly at Colossae, similar to its meaning in 1 Cor 5:12-13; 1 Thess 4:12 and 1 Tim 3:7. The "without" is composed of two classes: (1) the unbeliever, that is, one who does not partake of divine life and is not a believer in the Lord Jesus Christ, (2) the unlearned of 1 Cor 14:24, that is, one who is not instructed as to his place in relation to the assembly. Not all believers are gathered to the name of the Lord Jesus, though indeed they should be. They are therefore classed in this distinctive group "them that are without".

"Redeeming the time" (*exagorazomenoi*) is the present middle participle of the verb *exagorazo* ("to redeem"); here and in Eph 5:16 it is used in the sense of "making good use of". It enjoins upon the Colossians to use every opportunity that comes their way of witnessing their faith to the society in which they live. There is a sense in which Paul may be speaking of the need to buy time out of alien possession. Time can be wasted with little accomplished for God. The word *kairos* translated "season" can mean an opportune or seasonable time, e.g. Rom 5:6 RV "season"; Gal 6:10 "opportunity". Taking the context as a whole the thought of making one's market fully from the occasion, so buying up every opportunity seems to predominate.

6   The previous exhortation relates to disposition and demeanour, while here "let your speech be always with grace" embraces discourse. The expression *en chariti* signifies a sweetness and courtesy which is to mark every word spoken in witness of the truth. This marked the Son of God in His every word (Ps 45:2; Luke 4:22; John 7:46) and Paul desires that it characterise every effort to discourse the gospel and all its relevant truth. The tongue must be ruled and only God and His grace can affect such control and make the teaching it utters stem an onrush to collision (the bridle); avert a wreckage (the helm); quench a conflagration (the fire); effect a restraint (the beasts, etc) and remove a duplicity (the fountain); see James 3:1-12.

Ertumenos is the perfect passive participle of *artuō* ("to season"). The sense seems to surround the thought of a well-ordered mode of conversation, for the word "seasoned", literally "fitly prepared", suggests a guided intercourse free from mere platitudes, foolish talking, jesting (Eph 5:3) and falsehood (Col 3:8-9). There is much trivial, flippant and unhelpful conversation which allows the opportunity for effective witness to be lost. The preacher is to search out acceptable words (Eccl 12:10). This is done in the secret place with god (Isa 50:4) as was the experience of the perfect Servant of Jehovah. Inward satisfaction abounds in his heart that he has spoken the word in season (Prov 15:23). No believer is excluded from this requirement; it is to be the experience of all the children of God.

"That ye may know how ye ought to answer every man" echoes the language of Peter when he mentions what makes for a readiness "to give answer to every man that asketh you a reason of the hope that is in you with meekness and fear" (1 Pet 3:15). Paul urges a suitability of language that will give the appropriate answer to every question raised by the interested enquirer. The power of the gospel is adequate. It can meet every need of man in his spiritual departure from God. The presentation of the gospel should flow in a language comprehensible to the hearer, and without compromising its truth; the discourse should be in terms with which the sinner is naturally acquainted. Paul excels in this. Observe his language to the farmers in Galatia (Acts 14:8-18) and to the idolaters of Athens (Acts 17:22-31). "Each single one" translates *heni hekastō*, reminding us that people cannot be dealt with by wholesale methods. Each must be treated as his peculiar requirements demand. Paul shows himself a master in the art of adaptability (1 Cor 9:22).

VII. Personal (4:7-18)

1.   *The Servants that Convey the Letter will Report my Affairs 4:7-9*

v.7   "All my state shall Tychicus declare unto you, who is a beloved brother, and a faithful minister and fellowservant in the Lord:

v.8   Whom I have sent unto you for the same purpose, that he might know your estate, and comfort your hearts;

v.9   With Onesimus, a faithful and beloved brother, who is one of you. They shall make known unto you all things which are done here."

What remains of the epistle may be rightly summarised under titles such as "Items of Interest" or "Echoes of Service". They are intensely practical passages and typically Pauline. He values every servant with whom it is his privilege to serve. He never over-rates them nor under-estimates them either. He delights to commend them, as all are in the concluding verses of this epistle; yet if by defection they come short of the demands of the testimony, he will clearly indicate their true relation to him and the work. Paul seems to be concerned that the saints should know who the faithful servants of God are. This is clear from the word concerning John Mark (v.10) and from the comments of v.11b.

7 "All my state" or "all my affairs" (RV) are items omitted from the page but which must have been eagerly received by the recipients of the epistle. Such personal items as his health, the happenings surrounding his period of restriction and his hopes, all draw forth the passionate prayerful interest of those who have him in their hearts (Phil 1:7 RV marg.).

The bearer Tychicus is mentioned five times in close association with Paul:

1. In association with Paul at the close of his third missionary journey (Acts 20:41).
2. In association with Paul in Rome during the first imprisonment from where, as Paul's messenger, he carries the two letters, Ephesians and Colossians (Eph 6:21; Col 4:7).
3. In association with Paul during his last imprisonment in Rome, from where he sends him to Ephesus (2 Tim 4:12) possibly instead of going to Crete (Titus 3:12).

Paul often addresses the gathered company of the saints as he gives report of the Lord's work (Acts 14:27-28). Now the church at Colossae will gather to hear another speak on his behalf, and Tychicus will report on Paul's affairs.

"Who is a beloved brother, and a faithful minister and fellowservant in the Lord" gives three beautiful designations of Tychicus which must endear him to the heart of every believer in the assembly at Colossae. The threefold description is similar to that found of him in Eph 6:21 and to that of Epaphras (1:7). In relation to the family he is a "beloved brother", denoting Paul's affection for him. In relation to the fellowship he is termed a "faithful minister", describing his fidelity to the apostle and his endorsement of the truth concerning Christ in the letter. This is Paul's approbation of him in the Spirit. In relation to the field Paul esteems him as a "fellowservant". This bespeaks Paul's appreciation of him. Again we meet this now familiar phrase, "in the Lord". Tychicus acknowledges that Lordship and thus is to be commended for his faithfulness to Christ in testimony.

8 In "whom I have sent unto you for the same purpose", the epistolary aorist is rendered by some translations as "I am sending". Paul intends that Tychicus will travel from Rome to Colossae with this epistle and the one to Philemon.

"That he might know your estate" is altered in favour of the context and other MSS to read "that ye might know our estate" (RV). This is preferred in view of his stated purpose in v. 7 above.

By reporting on the circumstances of both Paul and Timothy the saints will be cheered as they hear how God has overruled in the imprisonment of His servant. It is to be noted with due care that the reporting is restricted to Tychicus. Onesimus is not a *diakonos* ("minister") in relation to public ministry of the truth, not a *sundoulos* in relation to Paul. As Onesimus has yet to make things right with Philemon, no public place is given to him. He is not accredited for a responsible part in the service of God. Paul sets guidelines that should be strictly observed before a man is placed in public service. If outstanding issues in a brother's life are not settled, he should not be accorded a place in responsibility amongst God's people.

9 Onesimus is the converted runaway slave of whom Paul speaks affectionately in his personal letter to Philemon. He is the fruit of Paul's prison testimony (Philem 10). There is no mention of his offence in this epistle; any consequences are a private matter between Philemon and him. He returns now with an exquisite letter containing Paul's plea on his behalf.

"A faithful and beloved brother who is one of you" reveals Paul's tenderness toward him when he speaks of Onesimus as (1) a brother, (2) faithful and (3) beloved. The reality of saving grace in the man's experience is seen in the fact that he is a brother. He is in the family of God and enjoys its liberty and life. Paul observes his fidelity in the term "faithful", in contrast to what he proved to be before grace saved him in Rome. Endearment fills Paul's heart as he describes Onesimus as "beloved", all very precious as the convert returns to the scene of his former notoriety. Paul's words here prudently disclose his expectations that the Colossians will receive him as he likewise anticipates in his letter to Philemon that he will not only forgive him but will also give him his freedom (Philem 16-17). The returned slave is as much a part of the testimony as is the respected servant for Paul. "Who is one of you" describes Onesimus as it does Epaphras (v.12).

In saying *"They* shall make known unto you all things which are done here-, the cautious plural does not affect the firm singular of v.8. Among many things, the report will consist of the story of Onesimus' conversion. Certainly this he will be free to give publicly. What a story he has to tell! It will be the moving account of how he met Paul's Saviour under the clear tones of Paul's gospel. Events concerning the church at Rome may also figure in the joint report.

2. *The Servants that Confirm the Ministry Remain my Fellow-workers* 4:10-17

> v.10 "Aristarchus my fellowprisoner saluteth you, and Marcus, sister's son to Barnabas, (touching whom ye received commandments: if he come unto you, receive him;)

> v.11 And Jesus, which is called Justus, who are of the circumcision. These only are my fellowworkers unto the kingdom of God, which have been a comfort unto me.
> v.12 Epaphras, who is one of you, a servant of Christ, saluteth you, always labouring fervently for you in prayers, that ye may stand perfect and complete in all the will of God.
> v.13 For I bear him record, that he hath a great zeal for you, and them that are in Laodicea, and them in Hierapolis.
> v.14 Luke, the beloved physician, and Demas, greet you.
> v.15 Salute the brethren which are in Laodicea, and Nymphas, and the church which is in his house.
> v.16 And when this epistle is read among you, cause that it be read also in the church of the Laodiceans; and that ye likewise read the epistle from Laodicea.
> v.17 And say to Archippus, Take heed to the ministry which thou hast received in the Lord, that thou fulfil it."

There now follow salutations from Paul's friends who, either personally or at least by name, are known to the saints at Colossae. Paul sends salutations from six brethren; so together with Timothy (1:1) there must have been seven with him at Rome, Epaphras having recently arrived from Colossae. These salutations are more than a mere formal courteous gesture. Be sending their salutations they reveal their concern for the spiritual welfare of the Colossians. Above and beyond this their names give endorsement to Paul's ministry with which they obviously and heartily concur.

10 Aristarchus the Thessalonian was involved with Paul in Ephesus (Acts 19:29) and travelled with him on his mission of relief to Jerusalem (Acts 20:4). Later, he accompanied Paul to Rome (Acts 27:2).

Sunaichmalōtos ("fellowprisoner") denoted properly "a prisoner of war", or as Vine says, "fellow captives in war (from *aichmē*, a spear and *haliskomai*, to be taken)". Paul uses the term also regarding Andronicus and Junias (Rom 16:7); of Epaphras (Philem 23). What Paul intends to convey is difficult to understand for the term can hardly be understood in a literal sense. There are those who explain it as a reference to a voluntary sharing of Paul's imprisonment. His companions, some suggest, took their turn at different times to be with Paul. The fact that Epaphras is called a fellow-prisoner in Philem 23 while Aristarchus is named among others as a fellow-servant does not give credence to this view. The term is used metaphorically of a spiritual captivity to Christ, the sense in which it is to be understood here. It complies with Paul's use of military terms (Eph 3:1; 6:11; Phil 2:25; 2 Tim 2:3; Philem 1,2,9). *Aspazetai* is the present middle indicative of *aspazomai* which signifies "to greet", "welcome" or "salute". The verb really means "to draw one to oneself", "to embrace" and is used to indicate a salutation on arrival and on departing, and then in letters to specify the sending of salutation from a person that others may be saluted.

"And Marcus" refers without doubt to John Mark the writer of the Gospel, who is also named in Philem 24 as being among Paul's fellowworkers. He joined Barnabas and Paul on their first missionary journey, but later left them and returned to Jerusalem, which resulted in Paul refusing to take him on his second missionary enterprise (Acts 12:12,25; 13:5; 13:13; 15:36-40). He is now with Paul in Rome and has obviously regained the apostle's full confidence. His presence with Paul and his name in this letter show that he endorses the ministry and has fully grasped the nature of the Mystery, and is in accord with the truth Paul teaches.

Anepsios ("cousin") is used only here, so Mark is introduced as "the cousin of Barnabas". If the estrangement between Paul and Mark is at an end, it is evident it is so between Paul and Barnabas. Paul's subsequent references to Barnabas seem to indicate this (1 Cor 9:6; Gal 2:1,9 and here). Doubtless Paul mentions Barnabas here to give Mark acceptance among the saints in Colossae. Is Paul now acknowledging the substantial soundness of the judgment of Barnabas in respect of Mark? Anyway, Paul's studious recommendation of Mark removes the shadow of the past forever.

The parenthetical portion raises unanswerable questions. Communications had been received concerning Mark, but what they were or what they contained or when they were sent, we do not know. Lenski, however, indicates, "This is another epistolary aorist like the one used in v.8. Paul is now sending directions regarding Mark through Tychicus; an English writer would say, 'concerning whom you are receiving directions... (pp.199-200)' ". But Eadie remarks that the tense of the verb will not warrant such a supposition (see p.290). What we are certain about is, Mark is to be welcomed by the saints at Colossae and if by then he carried his portrait of Christ as the unfailing Servant, would it not have been to their spiritual benefit to be thus received?

11 Both the name Jesus and the surname Justus were common among Jews. Some translations render the name as Joshua. This is the only notice of this disciple in the NT. In the epistle to Philemon the concluding salutations include greetings from all those mentioned in the present passage with the exception of Jesus called Justus. He is with the apostle sharing in his exercise which reveals the man's spiritual maturity. He possessed an affection for the Lord's people in that he sends them greetings. Above all he has confessed the Lord Jesus as his Lord and Saviour, and bears testimony to His supremacy and grace by endorsing the letter Paul has written to fellowbelievers in Colossae. "Who are of the circumcision" refers to those of Jewish stock who had believed the gospel and were members of the one body. The "who" includes Aristarchus, Mark and Jesus Justus. Lenski strongly avers Aristarchus is not included, whom he claims is a Gentile pagan converted to Christianity (p.39, p.306).

For "kingdom of God" see note on 1:13. It is clear that these three brethren whom Paul names were aware of the present phase of the kingdom (Rom 14:17) and understood the truth of the Mystery as expressing that phase in this period of God's administration in grace. That they enthusiastically cooperated with Paul showed their "understanding of the Mystery". They were obviously not included amongst those whom Paul spoke of in Phil 1:15-18. It would appear there were many Jews in Rome who were not favourably disposed towards Paul's ministry. If these men proved so faithful in Rome it was clear that they would be so in Colossae and would therefore withstand all the efforts the false teachers were making to ensnare the saints there.

In "which have been a comfort to me" *parēgoria* ("comfort") is a medical term which occurs only here and denotes a soothing or relief from pain. The words "have been" are translated by some as "proved". *Egenēthēsan* being in the aorist may refer to a particular occasion when they ministered encouragement to the imprisoned apostle. Paul appreciates their presence, service and devotion, and gives them eternal renown for their fidelity.

12   Epaphras is one of the three Gentile believers Paul has with him at the time of writing. There is a significant balance in the company surrounding Paul; three Jewish believers and three Gentile believers, all endorsing the ministry. These stand together as a testimony to the truth of the pre-eminent Christ Paul has espoused in the epistle which should be a voice to the saints who receive the letter, irrespective of their ethnic origin. That Epaphras heads the list of this second group bespeaks the affection with which he is held in the heart of both Paul and the Colossians. Epaphras is likely indigenous to Colossae or at least he resided there. He not only heads the list, but most remarks are paid to this Colossian preacher.

Paul esteems Epaphras "a servant of Christ" - "a servant of Christ Jesus" (RV) - only used by Paul of himself (Rom 1:1) and of Timothy (Phil 1:1). The high commendation accorded this faithful servant shows us something of his spiritual greatness. Paul has more to say about him. The Colossians may know him as a preacher as the references in the first chapter of the epistle indicate, but Paul knows him to be a pleader as the next words of the verse disclose.

Agōnizomenos is the present middle participle of *agōnizomai* ("to struggle", "to agonise"). Paul reminds the Colossians that Epaphras is, as himself, continually striving in prayer on their behalf (1:29). The fact of Epaphras' prayer-exercise is in itself a real insight to the spirituality of the man. He can preach and does so, but it becomes the nature of the man, this servant of Christ, that he knows the holy art of intercession before God on behalf of the saints. The term Paul uses establishes the fervency of his partner's prayer-exercise. He agonises in prayer, an earnestness derived from acquaintance with his Master (Luke 22:44). The feature of his prayer appears in what Paul now adds, for he must have often heard the ardent supplicant peal out his intense longings at the throne of grace.

Three words are to be noted which convey the objective of Epaphras' prayer on behalf of the Colossians whom he loved. The idea of stability is indicated in the word *stathēte* (*stēte* TR), the aorist passive subjunctive of *histēmi* ("to place", in the passive "to be made to stand"). There was a great need for strength to resist the error of the false teachers that were assaulting the testimony in Colossae. Prayer was needed that through the ministry the epistle would bring, the Colossians would be made to stand firm upon the truth and thus repel the incursions of error in their character and in their company. Epaphras prayed not only for stability but also for maturity as the word *teleios* ("perfect") denotes. The spiritual growth of the saints under his pastoral care was his utmost concern. Paul's ministry was calculated to give them spiritual perception, an ability to recognise the truth presented in Christ and the Mystery and thus to realise that the fulness of God's purpose could never be matched by the faltering promises of error. Certainty is the third item in the servant's appeal. The word *plērophoreō* (*peplērōmenoi*, TR) is translated in the RV as "fully assured". The errorists could varnish their teaching to give the impression that they represented the expression of the divine will but Paul's letter removes that veneer. It unmasks the superficiality of their vain teachings. The truth Epaphras taught and all that Paul taught represented the will of God for the Colossian saints. The purpose of the prayer-exercise of Epaphras is that the saints may know stability, maturity and certainty in the truth they believed and in which they must make spiritual progress.

13   With "I bear him record", the apostle subjoins a further testimony to this faithful servant of Christ. It is something he has seen through personal acquaintance with Epaphras that enables Paul to use the word *martureō* ("to witness", "to testify").

For *zēlos* ("zeal") the RV has *ponos* ("labour") used in Rev 16:10,11; 20:4 (see Trench *Synonyms* p.378 for a useful treatment of *ponos*). It suggests a labour that demands all that a man can give; his strength is expended to the utmost in accomplishing the task set before him. Paul rightly discerned no mere professionalism in his servant, but prostration through untiring labour.

Laodicea and Hierapolis were the two neighbouring cities with which Epaphras occupied himself effectively in the spread of the truth of the gospel. He carried them all in his heart and sought earnestly that not one member was ensnared by the stratagem of the errorists. It is very possible that he was responsible under God for seeing the testimony raised to the name of Christ in these cities.

14   "Luke, the beloved physician" indicates Paul's dependence upon the medical care and skill of this faithful companion. The Lord never removed the thorn in the flesh (2 Cor 12:7-9) but He gave Paul a beloved physician to attend him right to the end (2 Tim 4:11). It is impossible to conceive how rich the meditations of these men must have been as they communed together on the person of Christ, His work, His church, His purpose and His present and future glory. Paul, Luke and Mark are the human instruments the Holy Spirit of God used to bring into existence approximately sixty-three percent of our NT. It bows our hearts in grateful thanks that God should use mortals to achieve such an eternal task.

Demas is a shortened form of Demetrius. It is possible that he may have been the Demetrius who opposed Paul in Acts 19 and the Demetrius mentioned in 2 John. It is good that at this stage of his life he is with Paul, in concord with the ministry, and endorsing the recovery of Onesimus (Philem 24). It is true that he is not given detailed mention in either this epistle or in the letter to Philemon, but at least he is mentioned and still worthy of due recognition. It is when Paul writes his last letter that notice is given of Demas' defection from the side of Paul and his company.

Both Luke and Demas send their greetings to the saints at Colossae. Kent suggests that perhaps Demas is the amanuensis who penned the letter, and so mentions himself last and without praise (p.146). The decision on such a matter will surely rest with the Spirit of God and not with Demas. Others suggest that Tychicus may have been Paul's amanuensis for this epistle.

15   The imperative form of the word "to greet" is used as Paul asks the Colossian saints to convey their greetings to the saints in Laodicea. The mention of "brethren" opens out the concept of fellowship and such must have existed between the two assemblies. Such a link is what the NT endorses. The confederation of assemblies under any name is foreign to the Spirit of the NT. Paul's concern for the saints at Laodicea has already been expressed in 2:1, and that of Epaphras in 4:13.

The manuscript evidence leaves the question unsolved, whether the name Nymphas refers to a man or a woman. The AV treats the name as masculine and follows with the expression "in his house". The *UBS Greek New Testament* takes the name to be Nympha, and hence a woman, and so gives the pronoun as "her". The RV following other manuscript evidence gives the pronoun as "their", indicating that Nymphas was a man's name, the head of the house in which the church met. Where was the house located? Some suggest Laodicea, and it certainly could be the case, but as no salutations have been sent to Hierapolis, would it be like Paul to miss out in this matter? Seeing Epaphras had such interest in both Laodicea and Hierapolis, it was likely that Paul would not pass them by unnoticed. Hierapolis might very well have been the location of the house in which the church met. It is an epistle of headship and to have Nymphas mentioned in this way seems to confirm his masculinity.

16   The instruction, "when this epistle is read among you, cause it to be read also in the church of the Laodiceans", makes it evident that it would be both the privilege and responsibility of the whole assembly to be gathered to hear the word from the Lord. That all the epistle would be read would be Paul's expectation, remembering that he himself was given to declare the whole counsel of God. Not only would greetings be sent from one assembly to the other, but there would also be the response to Paul's request that the letter to the Colossians would be sent to the assembly at Laodicea. Paul had a deep concern for the church in Laodicea for it too appeared to be assailed by the same false teachers as Colossae faced.

"The epistle from Laodicea" in all probability is referring to the Ephesian epistle (see Introduction). This assumption rests upon sufficient evidence that disposes of the many counter suggestions, the strongest and perhaps the most popular of which being that Paul is referring to a letter he wrote to the Laodiceans now lost (see Eadie, Lenski, Bruce, Kent, Martin and Vaughan for the "lost" theory, and Garrod, Westcott, Rutherfurd, Carson, Boyd, Harrison on The Epistle to the Ephesians conclusion). Lightfoot has some fourteen proposals and gives an expert treatment of the spurious letter to Laodicea (see his Colossians). Here is a quotation from Ellicott: "*Tēn ek Laodikeias* (that from Laodicea) ... two prepositions being really involved in the clause, 'the epistle sent to and to be received from or out of Laodicea', but the latter, by a very intelligible and not uncommon attraction, alone expressed. The real difficulty is to determine what letter is here referred to. Setting aside attempts to identify it with 1 Timothy, 1 John (Lightfoot), the epistle to Philemon - an essentially private letter, two opinions deserve consideration: (a) that it is the epistle to the Ephesians; (b) that it is a lost epistle. For (a) we have the similarity of the contents, and the probability, from the absence of greetings and local allusions that the epistle to the Ephesians was designed for other readers than those to whom it was primarily addressed. Against it, the improbability, that the apostle should know that his epistle to the Ephesians would have reached Laodicea at or near the time of the delivery of his epistle to the Colossians. For (b) we may urge the probable circumstances that Tychicus might have been the bearer of the two letters to the two neighbouring cities, leaving that to Laodicea first, with orders for the interchange and then continuing his journey. Against it there is the a priori improbability that a letter, which from the present direction given by the apostle stood apparently in some degree of parallelism to that to the Colossians (we have no right to assume that it was 'of a merely temporary or local nature', Eadie; see contra Meyer) should have been lost to the church. The fact that the orthodox early church does not seem to have ever acquiesced in (b) makes the decision very difficult; as however the epistle to the Colossians does appear to have been written first - as the title *Tois en Ephesō* (Eph 1:1) does seem to preclude our assigning to that epistle a farther destination than to the churches dependent on Ephesus - as there does seem a trace of another lost epistle (1 Cor 5:9) - as the close neighbourhood of Colossae and Laodicea might prepare us to admit a great similarity in contents, and consequently a very partial loss to the church, - and lastly, as a priori arguments on such subjects are always to be received with some suspicion, we decide in favour of (b) and believe that an actual epistle to the Laodiceans is here alluded to, which, possibly from its close similarity to its sister epistle, it has not pleased God to preserve to us. It may be added in conclusion that the above reasoning rests on the assumption that the epistle to the Ephesians was written to that church, and that the words *en Epheso* are genuine. It is right, however, to add that the newly discovered Sinaticus rejects them, and that thus an important authority has been added to the side of those who deem that a blank was left for the name of the church, and that the epistle was purely encyclical. If this view (which still seems doubtful) be adopted, the balance will probably, lean more to (a)" (pp.206- 208).

17   In Philemon, written at the same time, the name Archippus appears linked with those of Philemon and Apphia (Philem 2), giving evidence to the assumption that he is their son. He is called a fellow-soldier in the verse just mentioned. It was evidently the responsibility of those who had the care of the assembly at heart to speak very definitely to this servant of Christ and to place before him Paul's injunction. The way Paul advised the church would suggest that Archippus was in some other location, for would he himself not have heard Paul's exhortation on its first reading to the church?

"Take heed" (*blepe*) is the present active imperative of "to see", "to take heed", "to keep an eye on". A notable use of this word is to be found in Mark 13:5,9,23,33. When used in this connection, it warns of dangers; and such certainly appear against the background of this epistle, which alerts its readers to the perils of false teaching that will detract from the glory of Christ, the efficacy of His work and the completeness of every believer in Him. It may be that Archippus is growing slack in his vigilance and neglecting his service in the Lord. The form of service that was his is not specified; there is, however, notice to be given to the fact that another of Paul's famous associates is bidden in almost identical terms "to make full proof of thy ministry" (*tēn diakonian sou plērophorēson*, 2 Tim 4:5). A close parallel may be safely drawn that Timothy and Archippus have a ministry that is alike in many respects.

The expression "in the Lord" indicates that it is because he is living in close union with the Lord that Archippus is entrusted with this ministry. It is a ministry that displays his recognition of Christ's Lordship, because of which, he must *take heed*. The apostolic injunction to watchfulness and thoroughness in any ministry received from the Lord merits attention on the part of all who serve.

Plērois ("fulfil") in the present tense points to a continual action, Paul's motive for the appeal is sincere that Archippus may complete or bring to fulfilment the work entrusted to him by the Lord. When Archippus would read the letter or hear it read, he would be able to assess the measure of his responsibility by Paul's use of the word in 1:9,25; 2:10; 4:12.

3. *The Salutation that Closes the Epistle will Remind you of my Bonds*
4:18

> v.18 "The salutation by the hand of me Paul. Remember my bonds. Grace be with you. Amen."

18 "The salutation by the hand of me Paul" - the apostolic signature authenticates the letter written by an amanuensis (2 Thess 3:17; 1 Cor 16:21). What associations and feelings that handwritten signature would excite!

With "Remember my bonds" compare Philem 9, "Yet for love's sake I rather beseech thee, being such a one as Paul the aged, and now a prisoner also of Christ Jesus" (RV); and Eph 4:1, "I, therefore, the prisoner in the Lord, beseech you" (RV). Paul is not asking for their pity, but his imprisonment does constitute an additional claim on their obedience. They may be called upon to suffer for the truth now imparted to them. If so, they can be assured that he also is suffering for the same cause. Their obligation is to heed his apostolic instruction and to stand firm in unflinching loyalty to his Lord and theirs.

Having begun by drawing upon the resources of divine grace, he concludes by desiring them the grace which in its power and sufficiency will accomplish in them his deepest longings, God's highest purpose and Christ's chiefest joy.

"Amen" is omitted in RV.

WORDS PECULIAR TO COLOSSIANS 4 ARE:

Anepsios	: cousin comfort	4:10
Parēgoria	: comfort	4:11

APPENDIX
Subjects deserving special attention

1. Concerning God
a His Fatherhood. He is the Father 1:12; 2:2; 3:17; He is the Father of our Lord Jesus Christ 1:3; He is our Father 1:2;

b His mode of existence as being invisible 1:15;

c His sovereign choice of men 3:12;

d He is to be reverentially feared 3:22;

e His revelation 1:25;

f He has pleasure in making known His truth 1:27;

g He administers His truth according to what He has been pleased to make known in this period of grace 1:25; 2:2;

h His work in the resurrection of His Son 2:12;

i His grace as revealed in the gospel 1:6;

j   His saints can come into an experimental knowledge of Him 1:10;
k   His life infers vitality to the Body of Christ 2:19;
l   His Son is at His own right hand 3:1;
m   He is the security, source and supply of the life of His own 3:3;
n   He is the object of thanksgiving 1:3; 3:17 (RV "the Lord");
o   His peace is enjoyed by His saints 3:15 (RV "peace of Christ");
p   His will can be realised 1:1; 4:12;
q   His wrath will fall upon all unrighteousness and ungodliness 3:6;
r   He rules in and over a kingdom 4:11;
s   He has sovereign control in the affairs of men 4:3.

2. Concerning the Lord Jesus Christ
a   He is the Son of the Father's love 1: 13;
b   He is supreme 3:11;
c   He is Lord 1: 2,3, 10; 2:6; 3:16; 3:17,18,20,23,24,24; 4:1,7,17;
d   He died 2: 11 (and we died with Him) 2:20;
e   He rose from among the dead and we were raised with Him 3:1;
f   He is exalted 3:1; (and in Him we find our life);
g   He will be manifested and we with Him 3:4;
h   His Body, the Church 2:17;
i   He is in His own 1:27;
j   His Mystery 4:3;
k   His forgiveness 3:13;
l   His Word 3:16;
m   His servants 1:7; 4:12;
n   He is the object and the sphere of faith 1:4; 2:5; 2:8;
o   He is the sphere of spiritual life 1:2;
p   His afflictions (non-sacrificial) 1:24;
q   He is the perfection of His saints 1:28;
r   He is the Image of the invisible God 1:15;
s   He is the Firstborn of all creation 1:15;
t   He is the Creator of the universe 1:16;
u   He is Firstborn from among the dead 1:18;
v   He is Head of the Body 1:18;
w   He is the Beginning of the new Creation 1:18.

3. Concerning the Holy Spirit
There is only one reference in the epistle, 1:8.

4. Concerning the Church
a   Christ is its Head 1:18;
b   As the Body of Christ 1:24; 2:17; 2:19; 3:15;
c   It has a local connotation in this epistle 4:15,16.

5. Concerning the Work of Christ
a His Cross 2:14;
b Redemption 1:14;
c Reconciliation 1:20,21;
d Forgiveness 1:14; 2:13; 3:13;
e Ordinances of law blotted out 2:14;
f Principalities and powers made a show of 2:15.

6. Concerning the Gospel
a It is associated with truth 1:15; and with hope 1:23;
b It is the only message for mankind everywhere 1:6; and is capable of producing fruit in the souls of men 1:6;
c To believe the gospel is to receive Christ Jesus as Lord 2:6;
d It embraces the vast truth of the Mystery 4:3; and only God can impart the grace and ability to proclaim it as it ought to be spoken 4:3.

7. Concerning Faith
a The presence of faith in the heart causes thanksgiving 1:3-4;
b Continuance in it is a proof of reality 1:23;
c Steadfastness in it affords joy 2:5;
d Stability in it is the expectation of all teaching 2:7;
e Resurrection power realised through faith 2:12;
f Faithfulness 1:2,7; 4:7,9.

Other Subjects

Flesh	1:22,24; 2:1,5,11,13,18,23; 3:22
Heart	2:2; 3:15,16,22; 4:8
Knowledge	2:1; 3:24; 4:1,6; 1:9,10; 2:2; 3:10; 1:6
Life	3:3,4
Light	1:12
Love	1:4,8,13; 12; 3:14
Man	1: 28; 18,8,22; 3:23 (old man 3:9; new man 3: 10)
Peace	1:2; 3:15 (having made peace 1:20)
Prayer	1:3,9; 4:3 (see also "conflict" 2:3; "desire" 1:9)
Sin	1:14; 2:11
Thanksgiving	1:3,12; 2:7; 3:15,17; 4:2
Will of God	1:1,9; 4:12
Wisdom	1:9,28; 2:3,23; 3:16; 4:5
World	1:6; 2:8,20,20.

PHILEMON
A. McShane

PHILEMON

THE EPISTLE TO PHILEMON
Introduction

1. Characteristics of the Epistle
2. Occasion and Purpose of Writing
3. Links with other Scriptures
4. Outline of the Epistle
5. Bibliography

1. Characteristics of the Epistle

We are liable to judge the importance of the books of the Bible by their size, and, because of this, to pay less attention to the one-chapter books such as the prophecy of Obadiah, the second and third epistles of John, and the epistle to Philemon. Some have even questioned why such a short and merely private letter as the latter, even though written by Paul, should have found a place in the Canon of Scripture. Whoever arranged the books in our Bibles saw fit to place it at the end of the Pastoral epistles and possible intended it should be included among them. It was written at Rome about AD 62 at a time when God was pleased to use the imprisonment of the apostle to enrich His people by guiding him to write what are commonly called the "Prison Epistles". Obviously it was a kind of supplement to the epistle to the Colossians, for it was not only sent to the same place, and at the same time, but carried by the same men. Because the matter dealt with in it was of personal and private nature, it was not included in the letter to the church.

While the great doctrines common to other epistles are noticeably absent in Philemon, yet in it we are shown a striking example of how these can be worked out in a practical way, even in that most difficult relationship, i.e. between master and servant. Had this epistle been wanting in the NT we would have been the poorer, for doctrines demonstrated and applied are often more impressive than when expressed as facts. Here we are shown that the gospel turned the world upside down, not in a dramatic way, but by penetrating the ordinary mode of life, and changing it in a manner which none of the leaders of men in former ages could have imagined. As we ponder its verses we are made to feel that the apostle has put into the background all thought of his special honour as the custodian of the mysteries of God, and instead adopts the role of the intercessor. He does so with such politeness and courtesy that this short letter is unique in literature as an example of true gentlemanliness. The domestic difficulty in the home of Philemon may have been painful for him to bear, but, through the grace of God and through His providence, it has brought to us much help on the question of how to treat one another with due respect.

Textually the epistle presents few problems, for although some slight changes from the AV will be made in our exposition, basically the common version gives us an accurate translation.

2. The Occasion and Purpose of Writing

It would appear that Philemon had his home in Colossae, where he, his wife Apphia, and their son or servant, Archippus, occupied a large house - one sufficiently commodious to be the meeting place of the local church. Attached to this family and sharing their home was a bondman called Onesimus. This slave, apparently having tired of his master, fled from his post and took with him some valuables from the house. In those days any slave who acted like this was deemed worthy of death, so his only hope was to reach some place where he could expect to escape detection. Like most in such a strait he sought refuge amongst the crowds, and so fled to Rome where he could reasonably assume that all would be well. While there, he either fell into trouble or obtained employment in the prison service, for in some way or other he was brought into contact with Paul, who was in bonds at this time, and through his preaching was led to Christ and saved. Associated with Paul in his bonds was a man named Epaphras who was from the same city as Philemon and Onesimus. He, being a servant of the Lord, was fully aware of all that had befallen his fellow-believer, Philemon, and would doubtless communicate the facts to the apostle.

The time came when Tychicus was being sent to Colossae from Rome with the epistle addressed to the assembly there. Paul, though deeply attached to Onesimus, decided to send him also, but not without this letter we are considering, for it was intended to be the means used by God to end the estrangement existing between the runaway slave and his master. Likely, from that day to this, there never has been a more valuable treasure carried by mortal men than was entrusted to these two, for not only did they bring the two letters mentioned, but also that wonderful epistle directed to the Ephesian church.

The arrival of Tychicus, along with the once disloyal, but now converted slave, must have been a moving sight to behold, and one which displayed the power of the gospel to alter the lives of men. Nothing but joy could have been the outcome. The church at Colossae must have rejoiced to receive a letter from Paul; Philemon must have rejoiced at having a letter from his father in the faith, and that his slave was back a much better man than when he departed; and not least, that the day could be near when the apostle, too, would be lodging under his roof.

3. Links with other Scriptures

It is always helpful, as well as interesting, to compare Scripture with

Scripture. Even in this short epistle we would expect to find thoughts expressed which would call to mind other passages in our Bibles, especially in the epistles of Paul. Some of these we will attempt to point out. The Colossian epistle, which, as we have seen, was written at the same time, contains the same list of names as are mentioned in Philemon except that Philemon is not in Colossians, nor is Justus, who is linked with Marcus in Colossians, found in Philemon. The commendation of Onesimus to the Colossian saints (Col 4:9) and the fact that he belonged to their city are the chief reasons for believing that Philemon also belonged to the same place. The introduction of Paul as "prisoner of Jesus Christ" (Philem 1) recalls his words in Colossians, "Remember my bonds" (4:18). Both epistles are in response to what Paul had heard. In Colossians we read, "Since we heard of your faith in Christ Jesus, and of the love which ye have to all the saints" (1:4), and in Philemon the words are, "Hearing of thy love and faith, which thou hast toward the Lord Jesus, and toward all saints" (v.5). Likewise in both letters Paul prays for the readers. In Colossians he writes, "We give thanks... praying always for you" (1:3), and in Philemon "I thank you God, making mention of thee always in my prayers" (v.4). In Colossians he instructs slaves to obey and serve their masters, and also enjoins masters that they reward their servants righteously (3:22-4:1). In Philemon, as all are aware, the chief subject dealt with is a plea for the re-establishment of proper relations between a servant and his master.

Many of the links connecting Philemon with Colossians link it also with Ephesians. While the truth of "the one body", so prominent in these two epistles, is not introduced into Philemon, yet in it we are shown a vivid example of how that great "mystery" affected the everyday practices of the saints. The apostle, the slave, and his master are viewed as brethren in Christ and as members of the same body. When Philemon would receive and forgive Onesimus he would be doing what is enjoined in Ephesians, "Be ye kind one to another, tenderhearted, forgiving one another, even as God for Christ's sake hath forgiven you" (4:32) in his case not only for Christ's sake but for Paul's sake as well (v.17).

Onesimus had proved to Paul's satisfaction that he had put off the old man and put on the new and so was an example of the truth taught in Ephesians (4:22) and also in Colossians (3:9-10). He was no longer the man who had run away, but a completely new man, one who would be a joy to know. He had stolen his master's goods, but now he would "steal no more", and the once useless servant would now "work with his hands that which was good" (see Eph 4:28).

The teaching of the Philippian epistle also appears here, for the humble mind, so forcefully set forth in the example of Christ (Phil 2:5-8), is evidenced in the humble attitude adopted by the apostle. Had Paul been looking at his "own things" he would have retained Onesimus with him at Rome, but in so doing he would have failed to give proper consideration to the mind of Philemon in this matter (Philem 14). In Philippians Paul shows us that he had seen the most adverse circumstances turned to the furtherance of the gospel (1:12-18), so likewise he shows Philemon that what seemed to be for him a disaster, had under God brought about a sinner's conversion. Another link with Philippians can be seen in comparing the service rendered to Paul by Onesimus, who was from Colossae, and that rendered by Epaphroditus, who was from Philippi. Both were a comfort to him at Rome; both were sent by him to their native place; and their respective assemblies were enjoined to welcome them at their return (Phil 2:25-30). There is one more link between Philippians and Philemon to which we will draw attention. In both epistles Paul appears to be confident that he would soon be released from prison, and in both he purposes visiting the readers. His words to the Philippians are, "I trust in the Lord that I also myself shall come shortly" (2:24); and his message to Philemon is, "prepare me also a lodging: for I trust... I shall be given unto you" (v.22).

A feature of a number of Paul's epistles is that in them he views his converts as his children. The personal letters to both Timothy and Titus come to mind in this respect. Likewise in the two church epistles of Corinthians and Galatians the same close relationship is claimed by him. In Philemon Onesimus is of deep concern to him, chiefly because he was begotten by him while in bonds. Indeed the relationship was so close between them that Philemon was expected to receive the son as though he were receiving his father (vv.12-17).

A key thought in Philemon is "love". The word is used in vv.5,7 and 9 together with its kindred word "beloved" found in vv.1,16. These five references indicate to us that love is the healing balm for the estrangements that may exist amongst brethren. As we think of this we recall, not only the words, "The love of God is shed abroad in our hearts" (Rom 5:5), but especially the outstanding chapter on the subject, 1 Cor 13. Amongst the qualities of love described in its verses are the words, "Love ... seeketh not its own, is not provoked, and taketh not account of evil" (v.5 RV) - the virtues expected to be manifest in Philemon.

The word "receive" used in vv.12,17 of our epistle gives us another link with Romans. Neither here, nor in Rom 14 and 15 where it occurs, does it refer to assembly reception. Here it has to do with the reception of Onesimus into the household of his master, while in Romans it has to do with reception into social life of those who may have scruples about certain foods. Onesimus was warmly commended to the Colossian assembly (Col 4:9), so that aspect of the case does not arise in our epistle. When we look at vv.15,16 of Philemon and note how the defection of a wayward slave was overruled by God for blessing, our thoughts turn to the words in Romans, "All things work together for good to them that love God" (8:28).

The grace expected to be shown to Onesimus, in spite of what he was and what he had done, is not unlike the grace shown to Mephibosheth by David (2

Sam 9). Just as Onesimus was to be received for Paul's sake, so Mephibosheth was received for Jonathan's sake. In both cases the reception was to be for ever, and that into a new relationship - in the former as a brother beloved, in the latter as one of the king's sons.

There is one more book in the OT which we might notice as having some slight connection with Philemon, viz. Proverbs. Solomon says, "The poor useth entreaties" (Prov 18:23). Here Paul adopts the attitude of the poor man and entreats Philemon instead of commanding him. In Proverbs we read, "A soft answer turneth away wrath" (15:1), so Paul uses softness to assuage the righteous anger which might still have remained in Philemon's heart. Another statement in Proverbs comes to mind while reading Philemon, "The king's favour is toward a wise servant: but his wrath is toward him that causeth shame" (14:35). Poor Onesimus had caused shame to his master and incurred his wrath, but now that he was converted he would return and prove to be a wise servant who would obtain the favour of his master.

4. Outline of the Epistle

The epistle to Philemon divides into three main parts. First, the introduction (vv.1-7); secondly, its main topic which is an entreaty that Onesimus be received (vv.8-21); and thirdly, the intimation that Paul hopes to visit him soon. To this news is added parting greetings from fellow saints at Rome (vv.22-25).

I.	*Introduction*	vv.1-7
	1. The salutation to the reader	vv.1-3
	2. The prayer and thanksgiving for the reader	vv.4-6
	3. The reader's virtues	v.7
II.	*The Purpose of the Epistle*	vv.8-21
	1. Receive him as mine own bowels	vv.8-12
	2. Receive him as myself	vv.13-17
	3. Refresh my bowels	vv.18-21
III.	*Paul's Hopes*	vv.22-25
IV.	*Appendix*	

The first seven verses which comprise the introduction of the epistle might again be divided into three parts; (1) The salutation to the reader (vv.1-3), (2) the prayer and thanksgiving for him (vv.4-6), and (3) the virtues in him that caused the thanksgiving and joy (v.7).

5. Bibliography
See Epistle to Colossians.

1. Introduction (vv.1-7)

1. *The Salutation to the Reader*
vv.1-3

v.1   "Paul, a prisoner of Jesus Christ, and Timothy our brother, unto Philemon our
       dearly beloved, and fellowlabourer,
v.2   And to our beloved Apphia, and Archippus our fellowsoldier, and to the church
       in thy house:
v.3   Grace to you, and peace, from God our Father and the Lord Jesus Christ."

1   This is the only epistle where Paul introduces himself as the "prisoner of
Christ Jesus" (RV). At its outset he would touch the heart of Philemon with a
reminder of the cost of his service, and also of the control of his Master in all
his circumstances. There is a slight difference between the expression here,
"prisoner of Jesus Christ", and that of Eph 4:1 RV "prisoner in the Lord".
Here his imprisonment is referred to as originating directly from Christ Jesus,
while in the latter it is viewed as being in association with the Lord and in
fellowship with Him. In keeping with the character of the epistle he makes
no mention of his apostleship nor of his special stewardship of the "mystery".
He draws attention rather to his humble circumstances with the end in view
no doubt of softening Philemon's heart. What child would not be moved by a
letter from his imprisoned father? By so introducing himself, Paul, although
fully aware of his position, adopts a lowly attitude toward his son in the faith.
He goes further, for by referring to him as his "fellowlabourer" he put him on
the same plane as himself. Both men were engaged in the same task in which
they toiled together in the bonds of love. He associates Timothy with this
introduction, not that he shared in the writing of the epistle, but because his
fellowship accompanied it. His name is mentioned at the opening of eight
out of fourteen of Paul's epistles, and he is mentioned in all of them except
Ephesians and Galatians.

2   Apphia is included in the address (v.2) because most probably she was
the wife of Philemon and as such shared in the grief of her husband at the
flight of Onesimus. Archippus is also named as one of the household (but
whether he was their son or their servant we cannot tell) and likewise would
be concerned about the family trial. He is called a "fellowsoldier". The apostle
seems to be adept in the use of compound words beginning with "fellow".
He writes of "fellowcitizens" (Eph 2:19), of "fellowsoldier" here and in Phil
2:25, of "fellowlabourer" here and in 1 Thess 3:2, of "fellowheirs" in Eph 3:6,
of "fellowprisoner" in v.23 and in Col 4:10, and of "fellowhelper" in 2 Cor
8:23.
     Like Priscilla and Aquila before him, Philemon had accommodated the church
in his house. These saints would be fully aware of the trouble that had befallen
their host as a result of the defection of his servant and so they too are included
in the address. While the letter is a personal one to Philemon, yet we can see

how it broadens out from him to his family and now to the company which assembled in his house. Obviously, the early disciples had no buildings, such as our "halls", for their exclusive use as meeting-places. This, however, was no disadvantage, for it was overcome by using the large houses of the more wealthy believers for this purpose. Some of them may have been engaged in business or trade that required spacious premises (as was the case with tentmakers) and these, with a little effort, could have been accommodated to provide a suitable venue for church meetings.

Some have thought that "the church in thy house" is another way of referring to those saved people who lived with Philemon, but the other references to this expression would show us that this idea is untenable, for as here, the "church" is mentioned as distinct from the family (see Rom 16:5, 1 Cor 16:19 and Col 4:15). We would be tempted to think that the church in the house of Philemon was the Colossian church; that the church in the house of Priscilla and Aquila was first the Ephesian church and later the Roman church; and that the church in the house of Nymphas was the Laodicean church, but again for this proof is lacking. It was no small honour to have a company of saints under one's roof, but it was at the same time a great responsibility, for any misdemeanour that might appear in the home would be a reflection on the testimony attached to it.

The word "church" is derived from two words *ek*, out of, and *kaleō*, to call, yet in its use in the NT it has always the meaning "called out together" and can be best translated "assembly". It occurs in only one of the Gospels, Matthew (16:18, 18:17), and is used in all Paul's epistles except 2 Timothy, but is not found either in Peter's epistles or in 1 and 2 John. On the other hand, the English word "church" is derived from the word *kuriakos* and means "belonging to the Lord". Its primary use is for the building in which the company meets for religious purposes, and it is used in a secondary sense for those who meet in it.

3 The form of the greeting in v.3, "grace to you, and peace", seems to be a normal mode of address in letters in early days, for it was used by both Paul and Peter. The former word reminds us of divine favour and the latter of its result. It would appear that throughout Scripture "peace" includes all that is blessed and good and not merely an absence of disquiet. The grand source of these two mercies is "God our Father and the Lord Jesus Christ". By linking together in this way the two Persons of the Godhead the apostle gives us a clear implication of their co-equality.

2. *The Prayer and Thanksgiving for the Reader*
   vv.4-6

v.4   "I thank my God, making mention of thee always in my prayers,

v.5   Hearing of thy love and faith, which thou hast toward the Lord Jesus, and toward
      all saints;
v.6   That the communication of thy faith may become effectual by the acknowledging
      of every good thing which is in you in Christ Jesus."

4   In common with most of Paul's epistles (Galatians and Hebrews are the exceptions) he reminds Philemon of his constant thanksgiving and prayers on his behalf (vv.4-6). Doubtless it was a great comfort for him to learn that, in spite of the apostle's many commitments and in spite of being cut off from his convert for so long, he took time to mention him continually before God.

5   The basis of his gratitude was that he had heard concerning him, for news of his love and faith had travelled as far as Rome. We might have expected the order of these words "love" and "faith" to be different, for in our experience faith precedes love. Here, however, first place is given to love for it is a prominent feature of this epistle. A second difficulty arises in the verse, for while we can clearly understand "faith ... toward the Lord Jesus", yet "faith toward all saints" is much less obvious. Had the statements been reversed and the verse read, "love toward all saints and faith toward the Lord", all would be simple. Although some have taught this to be the meaning, yet v.6, where "faith" again is used, shows that this cannot be so. The Received Text has two different words translated "toward" in v.5, but some editors make both the same. It is interesting to compare the three statements, "toward (*pros*) the Lord Jesus", "toward (*eis*) all saints" (v.5) and "in (*eis*) Christ Jesus" (v.6). Perhaps the difference between *pros* and *eis* is that in the former the stress is on setting out to reach an objective, while in the latter the stress is on arriving at it. We might compare another passage where we have the same prepositions used as here, "for (*pros*) the perfecting of the saints, for (*eis*) the work of the ministry, for (*eis*) the edifying of the body of Christ" (Eph 4:12). It is clear that there is a distinction between "faith toward the Lord" and "faith toward all saints". When faith is operative toward Him it is in a spiritual sense, but when exercised toward the saints it is more practical. The meaning of the verse seems to be that Philemon had a rule or principle of faith which affected his conduct toward the Lord and toward His people. Thus his faith was at once both practical and motivating.

6   The special object of the prayer was that Philemon's faith would be shared by the saints so that they, as well as he, might have a full knowledge of the good that was in them, and in all of us, and thus his faith communicated would become effectual, or efficient, toward (*eis*) Christ (v.6). We cannot help contrasting "the good that is in us" (RV) with the words "in me (that is, in my flesh) there dwelleth no good thing" (Rom 7:18). Where faith is present there must also be good, but no good can be found in that evil principle, the flesh, which still remains within us.

3. *The Reader's Virtues*
   v.7

> v.7 "For we have great joy and consolation in thy love, because the bowels of the
> saints are refreshed by thee, brother."

7 The one feature of Philemon that caused Paul to mingle his prayers with
thanksgiving for him was the love for which he had become famed. It not
only brought joy and comfort to the apostle but relieved the burdens of the
saints. This virtue is mentioned intentionally, for it will be tested specially by
the request that is to follow. The word "bowels" (heart RV) appears ten times
in the NT: twice in Luke's writings, once in John and the remainder in Paul's
epistles. Only in Acts 1:18 is it used literally. Its figurative meaning appears to
have arisen from the ancient belief that the intestines were the seat of tender
affections, just as in the same way the spleen was thought to be the seat of
anger. The latter word is still used with this meaning. The word "refreshed"
is translated "rest" in Matt 11:28 and refers to that relief from labour which
allows for a renewal of strength. It occurs again in v.20 where, as here, it is
joined with "bowels".

II. The Purpose of the Epistle (vv.8-21)

In v.8 we come to the main purpose of the letter which is that Philemon
would heartily receive Onesimus into his house again. This paragraph, which
extends to v.21, divides into three parts, each of which terminates with a
special plea by Paul to Philemon: "receive him as mine own bowels" (v.12);
"receive him as myself" (v.17); and "refresh my bowels... thou wilt do more
than I say" (vv.20-21). The levers exerted upon Philemon's mind in these
verses are so powerful, that for him to refuse the request was well nigh
impossible.

1. *"Receive him as mine own bowels"*
   vv.8-12

> v.8   "Wherefore, though I might be much bold in Christ to enjoin thee that which is
> convenient,
> v.9   Yet for love's sake I rather beseech thee, being such as one as Paul the aged,
> and now also a prisoner of Jesus Christ.
> v.10 I beseech thee for my son Onesimus, whom I have begotten in my bonds:
> v.11 Which in time past was to thee unprofitable, but now profitable to thee and to
> me:
> v.12 Whom I have sent again: thou therefore receive him, that is, mine own bowels:"

8 Although the apostle was well within his rights to demand that Philemon
receive his converted slave, yet he discards his authority in this case and adopts
the attitude of a supplicant. In view of the reputation Philemon had for his love,

it was becoming that he should be "besought", for when mild measures are likely to be effective, there is no point in using stronger ones. The word "bold" literally means "freedom of speech", but in this instance it is used for "authority to command". Only here does Paul use the word "enjoin", but it occurs several times in the NT and means "to charge".

9   There are seven reasons put forth in vv.9-12 as to why Philemon should accede to Paul's request to receive back Onesimus. (1) It was asked for love's sake; (2) the plea is from an old man; (3) it was from a prisoner; (4) it was for a child; (5) it was for one begotten in bonds; (6) it was for one drastically changed; (7) it would be like receiving the apostle himself.

Some put a comma after "such an one" connecting these words with the "one" of v.8, and link "as Paul etc." with "exhort" (v.10). Whether this is more correct than the common versions is difficult to determine. "Paul the aged" has created some difficulty, because as far as is known, he could be only in his early sixties at this time. Still, when we consider all the afflictions he had borne we need not be surprised that he was already manifesting signs of old age. The word translated "aged" could be translated "ambassador", but when this is its meaning it is normal to use *presbeuō*. In this case, however as in Luke 1:18; and Titus 2:2 it is spelt *presbutēs* therefore the weight of opinion leans toward the AV. Men of the world expect to find life easier in their old days, but with God's servants the latter years of life are often the most trying. Peter was forewarned of his lot when he would become old; John was banished in his latter days to Patmos; and here Paul is a prisoner in bonds at almost the end of his life. Like Abraham of old he had the joy, even though aged, of begetting a son, but in his case it was not a natural but a spiritual child that was born.

10   Onesimus was specially dear to his father because of the circumstances in which he had been begotten. We might compare Joseph's experience in Egypt where he too was made fruitful in trying conditions. Note specially what he said when naming his second son, "God hath caused me to be fruitful in the land of my affliction".

11   It is evident that there is a play upon words in v.11, for the meaning of Onesimus is "profitable", but alas, like many others with a good name, he had failed to fulfil the hopes of those who named him. Indeed he had proved to be the direct opposite. However, now that he was converted, he could be relied upon to be a blessing wherever he might be. He was a monument to the power of the gospel, for it alone can change "wasters" into useful men and women.

Paul might well have had before him not only that "Onesimus" means "serviceable" or "useful", but, when he instructs Philemon to receive his slave for "love's sake", he might well be thinking of the fact that "Philemon" means "loving one", and so he is asking him to live up to his good name. Admittedly, throughout this epistle Paul uses a different but kindred word for "love", but nevertheless expects this quality to be manifest in Philemon, the loving one. Other occasions in Scripture where there is a play upon the meaning of names will readily come to mind , such as in the case of Jacob, whose name means "supplanter", being described by his brother as acting true to his name in that he has supplanted him twice (Gen 27:36). In contrast to this is the case of Jabez, whose name means "sorrow", when he prayed that he might be kept from the evil that it be not to his sorrow (1 Chron 4:10 RV). Perhaps the most outstanding example of the importance of names and their meanings concerns the Seven Churches in Asia (Rev 2-3). Most are agreed that there is a link between the meaning of their respective names and the messages addressed to each.

Peter, whose name means "a stone", proved very unlike stone when he fell in the presence of the maid and denied his Lord. In the same way we see John, whose name means "dove", showing nothing of the dove-like character when he asked the Lord to allow him and James to call down fire from heaven (Luke 9:54). Joseph's brethren denied the family relationship when they sold him into Egypt, and Job's friends proved very unfriendly when they explained his troubles as being the outcome of sin in his life. The church at Corinth was addressed as saints, but much that was practised in it was a far cry from saintliness, and the Galatian believers were taught that they were "sons of God through faith" (Gal 3:6), but their going back to law-keeping made them more like slaves than sons. The application to ourselves is plain and simple. Though we attach no great significance to the meaning of the name given to us by our parents, yet we ought to live in keeping with those names which God has been pleased to put upon us.

If we look at the names God has bestowed upon His own, we must be satisfied that in them He implies certain truths. For example, they are called "sons of God", which surely suggests that they should reproduce the features of their Father; they are called "saints" and so should be holy in their lives; they are named "Christians" and therefore ought to wear the image of Christ; and they are called "brethren" and should treat one another as brothers. Quite often we fail to live up to these great names, for we act very unlike our Father, fail to live holy lives, exhibit little of Christ-likeness and treat one another as though we were enemies.

12 At length we learn, after these many statements, what exactly was Paul's request to Philemon. It was simply that Onesimus, who was being sent back with his letter, should be received by him with the same welcome that would have been extended to Paul if he himself had arrived at his door (v.12). This close association between the two at once displays the humility of the one and the grace lavished upon the other. Here we see an end to the barriers which divided mankind in those days, and to some extent still divide: (1) the religious barrier was removed, for the once proud Pharisee now spoke of a Gentile as his son; (2) the social barrier was also gone, for the Roman citizen and free-born scholar now claimed relationship with a poor slave.

It is not revealed how Paul contacted Onesimus in prison. If he had been put there for evil doing, he had managed to gain his freedom before his father in the faith. There is no hint that Paul was in any way envious of his son's freedom, nor do we hear a murmur from him because of his hard lot.

2. *"Receive him as Myself"*
   vv.13-17

> v.13 "Whom I would have retained with me, that in thy stead he might have ministered unto me in the bonds of the gospel:
> v.14 But without thy mind would I do nothing; that thy benefit should not be as it were of necessity, but willingly.
> v.15 For perhaps he therefore departed for a season, that thou shouldest receive him for ever;
> v.16 Not now as a servant, but above a servant, a brother beloved, specially to me, but how much more unto thee, both in the flesh and in the Lord?
> v.17 If thou count me therefore a partner, receive him as myself."

13-14   After asking Philemon to receive back his slave, Paul in v.13 proceeds to reason that the cost to himself was much greater than the cost of what he was seeking from Philemon. Every friend at Rome was dear to the lonely prisoner, so to part with one so useful as Onesimus was like cutting off a member of his body. Not that Paul desired to have a servant dancing attendance upon him, but rather because the part played by the now-free slave was a help in the furtherance of the gospel, on account of which he was not only in prison but also in bonds. To retain him in these circumstances would have been the most natural thing to do, but out of consideration for Philemon's claims Paul was willing to forego this pleasure. No pressure was exerted upon Philemon to obey the request, but rather, in view of his known character, it was expected he would willingly respond. Another thought is introduced in v.13 which we must not pass over. It is that Onesimus, while remaining at Rome, was in fact representing his absent master, so the services which he rendered to Paul were really those which should have been done by Philemon. "In thy stead" is literally "for (*huper*) thee", and is, therefore, one of the occasions in the NT where *huper* comes very close to *anti* which means "instead of". Nevertheless, even here the normal idea behind *huper* is not wholly absent, for the slave not merely took the place of his master, but was at Rome "for him" i.e. to his benefit. This in much the same way as a soldier at the battle front not only takes the place of those at home but wars on their behalf.

15-16 Having shown Philemon why he was sending back Onesimus and the sacrifice that this entailed (vv. 13-14), Paul points out in v. 15 that the slave's departure had proved under God to be a blessing in disguise, for it had ended any further possibility of such trouble and had brought about a new relationship which would last for ever. He had gone away a disgruntled bondsman, but was returning as a devoted brother. The fleshly ties which his going away had severed would hopefully be reformed; yea, much stronger ones had already been forged in the Lord, and these being eternal could never be broken. The word translated "receive" in v. 15 is not to be confused with the word "receive" in v. 17, but means not so much "to welcome", but rather "to have as one's own". After his return the outward relationship between the slave and his master would be as it was before he went away, but an inward and spiritual relationship hitherto unknown now had come into existence.

17 In light of what had been said in vv. 13-16, Paul in v. 17 again appeals to Philemon to receive back his servant. This reception is to be in keeping with his esteem for the apostle and performed in the same manner which he would adopt if his spiritual father were to appear before him. It was to be warm and hearty and in no way marred by either malice or spite.

3. *"Refresh my Bowels"*
   ## vv. 18-21

> v.18 "If he hath wronged thee, or oweth thee ought, put that on mine account;
> v.19 I Paul have written it with mine own hand, I will repay it: albeit I do not say to thee how thou owest unto me even thine own self besides.
> v.20 Yea, brother, let me have joy of thee in the Lord: refresh my bowels in the Lord.
> v.21 Having confidence in thy obedience I wrote unto thee, knowing that thou wilt also do more than I say."

18-19 At the close of this main part of the epistle, Paul seeks to remove another obstacle that may well have been the most difficult for Philemon to overcome (vv. 18-21). It would appear that when Onesimus fled, he took with him some of his master's belongings. In the interest of righteousness it was only fitting that this side of things should also be cleared up. It was bad enough to run off and deprive his master of his services, but it was much worse to steal when doing so. Perhaps this was the most aggravating side of the sad case, and for this reason Paul tactfully leaves it to the last. He handles the problem like an auditor by showing Philemon that there are two accounts in his books, one under the name of Onesimus and the other under the name of Paul. What was owed by the former, however great the sum, was to be transferred to the account of the latter, who now signs, as it were, a promissory note taking full responsibility for the debt. How will a prisoner pay this debt? The answer is simple, for Philemon was so much indebted to him that the balance lay on his side even with the addition of Onesimus' share. In this way Paul skilfully leaves the account clear. When he says he has written this with his own hand, he may be referring only to this statement about payment, but it could be that the whole epistle was written without the aid of an amanuensis.

20-21 In vv.20-21 the last tender appeal is made to Philemon. Addressing him as brother, Paul sums up his plea by asking three things: (1) "let me have joy (profit) of thee"; (2) "refresh my heart"; and (3) obey my request. Possibly the word "profit" is another hint at the name "Onesimus mentioned above, but whether this is so or not, the profit would be "in the Lord", i.e. in His power and fellowship. When asking him to refresh his heart, he is simply expecting him to do for him what he was famed for doing for others (v.7). Although Paul used so many arguments to secure the slave's reception, yet he is in no doubt about the issue; yea, he even expects the kindness that will be shown to Onesimus to exceed anything that has been requested.

III. Paul's Hopes (vv.22-25)

> v.22 "But withal prepare me also a lodging: for I trust that through your prayers I shall be given unto you.
> v.23 There salute thee Epaphras, my fellowprisoner in Christ Jesus;
> v.24 Marcus, Aristarchus, Demas, Lucas, my fellowlabourers.
> v.25 The grace of our Lord Jesus Christ be with your spirit. Amen."

22 Before closing the letter, Paul makes one more request of his friend. "Prepare me also a lodging", he writes. Though a prisoner in bonds, yet he had confidence that he would soon be released and that the earnest prayers of the household at Colossae would be answered in the not-too distant future. At the commencement of the epistle he mentions his own prayers; now he refers to theirs. When the time comes that he will be with them in their house they then will have proof that God had heard their supplications. With this we might compare the visit of Peter to Cornelius, who also had prayed.

23-24 As already mentioned, the persons who sent greetings to Philemon are all named in Colossians except Justus. It is encouraging to see that Mark is back in full favour with the apostle after his earlier lapse, and no less significant to note that Demas is apparently in step at this time, but as we learn from 2 Tim 4: 10, he later turned aside to the world.

Is it not interesting to note here the variety of men who become attached to Paul? For example, Mark was the only one of his kindred and the only one converted before him, Luke was from Troas, Epaphras from Colossae, Aristarchus from Thessalonica and Demas may also have been a Macedonian, yet their different backgrounds and cultures did not hinder them serving together.

By including Mark amongst the rest we learn that Paul, though a strong minded man, knew how to acknowledge the grace of restoration. Great men are often slow to reinstate those who have fallen by the way, especially if they have caused them suffering and grief. None can deny that Mark was at the centre of the row that divided Paul and Barnabas, yet in spite of this, the apostle now values his fellowship and service.

The mention of Demas reminds us that a man may go on for years in devoted service, and keep the best possible company, yet be turned aside by the allurements of the world. We can scarcely imagine the sad feelings in the heart of the aged apostle at the desertion of his close friend and companion (see 2 Tim. 4:10). The world has still its attractions so we need to walk humbly with God, for this alone will preserve us.

25   In common with all Paul's epistles, Philemon closes with a reference to "grace". He expresses the wish that "The grace of the Lord Jesus Christ be with your spirit", using almost the same words as he does at the close of Galatians, except that there he adds the word "brethren". The expression, "with your spirit", not simply "to you" as in v.3, implies that the grace when granted will influence the spirit, the judging faculty and the highest part of man's tripartite being. The plural "your" includes Philemon, his household and possibly the church in his house as well. All alike were in need of grace with their spirits.

IV. Appendix

Practical Lessons in the Epistle

It would be a pity to dismiss this short, but beautiful, epistle without attempting to see in it practical teaching that would benefit our souls. The very fact that it has been given a place in the word of God implies that it has a message for all time, and that its instructions were intended for a much wider circle than the few who first read it. Teachers and expositors of Scripture often take for granted that those who listen to them or read their writings will have the spiritual wisdom to make the needful application, but alas, this is a false assumption. The Lord's preaching was well received (Luke 4:22), but when He applied it to His hearers they were ready to throw Him headlong over the brow of the hill (v.29).

1. Assembly and domestic problems
The first, and to some extent one of the most important lessons written as it were across this letter, is that private and domestic problems arising amongst the saints should be kept, if at all possible, in their own sphere, and not be introduced into the assembly. Nothing could have been easier than for Paul to have included the substance of this epistle in the larger one sent to the Colossian church, but he was too wise to expose to the entire company a personal matter, which really concerned Philemon alone. Later they, no doubt, learned of the apostle's letter to him, but by that time the whole affair would have been settled. Even the church which met in his house had no authority to direct him as to how he should treat his runaway slave.

It is of supreme importance that saints in assembly fellowship be able to distinguish between what are private and what are church matters, for if these be confused there will of necessity be sad results. Take for example the playfulness of children. It is quite lawful for parents to allow and even help their children to play in the home, but the assembly has no mandate to provide playing facilities for them. Again there are families which excel in music, but such talented people, even though they are in fellowship, must not press for the meeting-place to become a music centre. Paul writes to the Corinthians, "Have ye not houses to eat and drink in? or despise ye the church of God" (1 Cor 11:22). We must eat and drink to survive, but even such an essential matter was out of place in the church. What would he say to the demands of some of our young people who would virtually turn God's assembly into little more than a social club? Often these demands are reinforced with the threat, "If we cannot have what we want in the assembly, we will go to where we will obtain it". The example of the religious world is often cited, but we should not be influenced by its practices.

On the other hand, much trouble has resulted from bringing into the home matters pertaining to the church. While, as our epistle makes clear, a church may meet in a house, there are church functions which are essentially separate from home life and these should not be mixed with it. For example, "the breaking of bread" is an assembly, not a family, act. Even if the weather be ever so inclement, this does not warrant a saved household setting a table and attempting to remember the Lord. It is not unknown for some, who could not have their own way in the assembly Bible-reading, to commence one in their own home. Others attempt to conduct gospel meetings on their own premises, apart altogether from assembly responsibility, even at times in opposition to established efforts. One would not decry the study of the Scriptures nor the spread of the gospel but where there is a testimony already in existence, it should be the centre from which all spiritual work radiates.

2. The grace of beseeching

Another obvious lesson we can learn from this epistle is how to deal with our brethren when we desire them to do something which they ought to do but which they naturally resent. We all know enough about human nature to realise that it is much easier to rouse the passions of the flesh than to subdue them. How courteously Paul approaches the matter and musters every argument to support his claim. Not only so, even though he is an apostle he writes as though Philemon were his equal. Nothing is lost by humbly beseeching someone to do what is right. When arrogant demands are made, even if they are obeyed, the result is never satisfactory. Often brethren have been forced to make up their differences and shake hands but time has proved that there was little change, for their hearts were still estranged. The household of Philemon would have been a miserable place, not only for himself but also for his servant, if they had been brought together only by pressure from an apostle. We still need to learn the power of gentleness and grace. While courtesy and politeness characterise the epistle, yet this did not prevent Paul from facing the seriousness of the wrongs done by Onesimus. He neither exposed them, nor ignored them but sought to show Philemon a new way to view them.

3. Respect for the opinions of others

A similar lesson to the one we have just considered is the important matter of respect for the mind of others. This we can also learn from this epistle. "Without thy mind would I do nothing" (v.14) are words that not only suit the theme of the epistle, but can well be applied to many situations arising amongst saints. To plow on in self-will and disregard the views of others involved may be very convenient, but can at the same time be damaging to fellowship. Paul could have retained Onesimus at Rome where he had proved so useful to him, and could even have made his usefulness the sole reason for so doing, but instead he considered the "mind" of Philemon on the matter. An aged apostle respecting the judgment of an ordinary Christian may seem strange to our thinking, for we are prone to consider the views of our superiors or at best of our equals, but pay little heed to the thoughts of those whom we think are our inferiors, even when these are deeply involved in the case. Matters often arise in oversight meetings where oneness of mind is not easily reached. If some strong-willed brother attempts to carry through his view without allowing his fellow-elders to express theirs, this can be divisive and harmful, but if due consideration is given to those who differ, so that they are free to express their minds, then the desired harmony may at length be secured. Even at the very worst, if differences still exist, no one can say that his "mind" was ignored by his brethren.

4. The practical effects of doctrine

It is one thing to believe in the doctrine of "the one body", but quite another to put its implications into practice. Our epistle shows us, as we have already pointed out, the effect it had on the saints in apostolic days. Because we are more impressed by its achievement in the religious sphere, in that it brought together into one organism Jew and Gentile, we may be less appreciative of its effect in the social domain, but we should remember that it united "bond and free" as well (1 Cor 12:13). Due to the absence, to a large extent, of slavery in our times, we perhaps are unable to measure the distance which separated the bondman from his master and so cannot fully appreciate the wonder that in Christ both were united together. The same Spirit indwelt both and the risen Head was just as much linked to the one as to the other. The same principle should still operate amongst the saints, even though in the minds of most social distinctions die slowly. All are one in Christ, irrespective of social status in the world. The same ransom price was paid for all, whether at the bottom or at the top, and both are equally precious to the Redeemer. Well might we note the way the apostle speaks of the slave - "brother beloved", "my child", and "the faithful and beloved brother". There is not a mention of his birth nor of his mean upbringing. Does it not grieve the Lord when He hears slighting references being made regarding some of His trophies of grace? At times words are used about them which imply that too much cannot be expected from those who have such a poor background. Specially when one has fallen by the way, others remark that this is due to the poor natural stock from which he has sprung. The sad fact is that some have fallen whose parents, even before they were converted, were the most respectable in the land. We should believe in universal depravity as well as total depravity, for the Scripture says "there is no difference". In saying this we are not to overlook the sombre fact that distinctive weaknesses are more pronounced in some families than in others, but these are not determined by social status.

5. The sovereignty of God

This epistle teaches us another lesson. Throughout its verses we cannot fail to trace the powerful hand of God demonstrating His sovereign working in the events amongst men. Philemon and Apphia must have lost all hope of ever seeing their runaway slave, Onesimus, in the kingdom of Christ. We, as well as they, are amazed that God overruled for his blessing and their joy. Even if their prospects of winning him to Christianity had vanished when he left their home, yet eventually they learned that he was no further from God, even in Rome, than if he had remained under their roof. Stories can still be told not only of slaves but of sons, who, having fled from home leaving behind broken-hearted loved ones, also discovered that God's arm was long enough to reach them, even in distant lands. Paul was careful to point out to Philemon that God could turn evil into good. "Ill that God blesses is our good, and unblessed good is ill, but all is right that seems most wrong, if it be His sweet will." Many tears we shed are due to the fact that we fail to see the end of God's dealings. Jacob's grief at the loss of his choicest son, Joseph, was suddenly ended when he heard that he had been exalted to the throne in Egypt. It is wrong to judge events until they are complete, for unexpectedly they may be turned to be much more favourable than we at first thought.

6. The value of a testimony

The testimony established by Onesimus at Rome in what appears to be a rather short time has also a lesson for our souls. It proved that he had "put off the old man" and that he had "put on the new man". His profession was no shallow device aimed at delivering him from some present difficulty, but an experience which had changed his whole character and made him not only fit to serve his earthly master but fit to be a help in the church in his house. What an advertisement for the power of the gospel! There was no need to fear that he would run off again even if he had opportunity to do so. He was not being sent back in order that the saints at Rome might be rid of him. Rather, he had become so useful there that the apostle could ill afford to release him. There was no place on earth so full of temptations as was Rome at that time, so if he could live for God there he could do so anywhere. The "new man", reproducing the features of his Creator, is not destroyed by the darkness that surrounds him; indeed, the abounding evils make his holy life all the more conspicuous. No Christian can blame his environment for his lack of progress.

7. The power of example

We are slow to learn that those who put demands upon others cannot expect them to respond, unless they themselves are an example of self-sacrifice. Paul in this epistle is asking Philemon to do something which obviously was not easy, but in doing this he is careful to point out to him that he too is suffering no small loss in parting with the services of Onesimus. No matter how costly the reinstating of the slave might be, it would pale into insignificance when viewed in the light of the sufferings being endured by the aged apostle in bonds at Rome. At times we become irritated when pressed to fulfil our responsibilities, but if we could view these in light of the sacrifice which Christ has made to enrich us (2 Cor 8:9), then their fulfilment would be considered as a privilege rather than a burden. In keeping with the supreme example of Christ and his servant Paul, all who exhort the saints should not only practise what they teach, but should have paid a price for their convictions, so that those who hear them will be compelled to respect their ministry.

8. The impact of change

There is another practical lesson written across this little epistle. It is the changes that can come into our lives in a reasonably short space of time. It took less than eight years to bring about those implied in this letter. During this time great changes came into the life of Paul. He was engaged in his greatest work in Asia when Philemon was saved through his efforts. Now he is chained, not in Asia, but in far off Europe, even in its capital. Perhaps more than half of this time had been spent in prisons. He has experienced a deeper understanding of the "mystery" and been guided to put his knowledge of this subject into writing for the edification of the church. Though curtailed in his preaching, and doubtless feeling the absence of the evidence of the power of the gospel, yet he has had the joy of winning a wayward slave for Christ. His fruitfulness has flourished again and this must have brought joy to his heart. He has been spared to see John Mark back in service and now one of his best friends. In the near future he hopes to be sleeping in the homes of the saints instead of the cold hard bed in prison.

Philemon too has had his share of changes. His house has been disturbed by the eloping of his servant but now his heart has been cheered by the news of this same individual being converted. Over and above this, he knows that soon he will be returned under his roof. He is even more thrilled to learn that his prayers are soon to be answered in the expected visit of the apostle. How wonderful for him to think that the day is approaching when he, his wife Apphia, his son

Archippus, his servant Onesimus and even Paul will all be sleeping under the same roof all in full harmony of Christ.

Onesimus has experienced changes as well as his master. Little did he think when he left Colossae that he would ever return to it. Nor did he envisage the time when he would be part of the church in the house of his master. Likely he thought that by going away he would escape the claims of the gospel. Far less did he imagine that his father in the faith would be a prisoner in bonds. He had known nothing but bondage all his life, and could scarcely, even in his dreams, conceive what it would be like to be a beloved brother of his master.

Surely all this has a message for our souls. We too can look back but a short time and trace in our lives the unexpected. Scarcely one saint could have foreseen his future. What seemed fixed and routine has been upset to a degree unimagined. How foolish we are to plan, for we cannot fulfil our purposes. It is equally foolish to think that all will remain unchanged, for one of God's ways with His own is to empty them from vessel to vessel. Often we resent the disturbances of our nest as did Job of old, but God had a purpose in his trials, and though he was unaware of it, yet it did at the end prove him to be "fine gold". While heaven will be without either trial or pain yet it will be free from monotony, for the great Shepherd will lead His flock from fountain to fountain (Rev 7:17).

9. The distraction of social problems

The supreme social problem amongst men in past ages was slavery. All are agreed that it was not only degrading for a man to become the sole property of his fellow, but it was also abnormal. Our souls revolt at the thought of human suffering involved in the slave trade, and are thankful that in our time it has all but vanished. Only by payment of the ransom price could any slave be freed, so unless someone paid it for him, he was condemned to his thraldom until the day of his death. Strange to our way of thinking is the fact that throughout the epistles no instructions were given for masters to free their bondmen, not even in cases where both were converted. Whatever was the ultimate outcome of the spread of the gospel, there was nothing in its message that would have started revolutions in society, nor was its primary aim to bring about social reform. "Let every man, wherein he is called, therein abide with God" (1 Cor 7:24) are Paul's words to the Corinthians. While the spiritual relationship between the saved slave and his believing master was as close as the bonds of love and grace could produce, yet the physical relationship between them remained unchanged. If ever there was an occasion when he might have pressed for the release of a bondman, it was in the case of Onesimus, but no such demands are to be found in our epistle. Herein is another lesson for our learning. Those who imagine that the work of the evangelist or the missionary is to end the social miseries of this world have not as yet understood the Scriptures. Conversion changed the hearts of men and did end the cruelties and hardships of bondage, but it left the respective positions of master and servant unaltered. Because the Christian's heart is tender and he groans at the sight of the miseries amongst men, there is ever the danger of becoming so swamped in world reformation that he misses his true calling to spread the gospel and through it to meet the supreme need of humanity.

10. The value of hospitality

Another practical issue arises at the close of our epistle. It is the subject of hospitality. Possibly Epaphras conveyed the news to Paul of the prayerful exercise of Philemon regarding his release from prison and very specially regarding a visit to Colossae. Conscious that these prayers would be heard and answered, the apostle's faith was strengthened to believe that his freedom was near at hand, and that soon he would be lodging with his son in the faith. No greater honour could have been conferred upon Philemon than to have as guest the aged warrior of the cross. We have reason to believe that this visit was granted, for though no history of Paul's movements between his two imprisonments at Rome is recorded in Scripture, yet from his epistles we learn that he visited Ephesus, Crete, Troas, Macedonia and Miletum during this interval, so there are no grounds for thinking that he failed to reach Colossae. While assuming that Philemon had a large house, yet we judge some preparation was necessary ere Paul could be accommodated. Of this we are sure, whatever the state of this house, it would be vastly more comfortable than the dark, damp Roman cell. God's servants are not expected to be either fastidious or squeamish, but humble men, who value the kindness and friendliness shown to them in the homes of the saints. We might wonder why so much stress is put upon hospitality in the NT, but the facts are that the common inns and lodging houses in those days were so filthy and morally impure that no saint would have dared to shelter in them. It may seem strange to us, that when it comes to hospitality in the Scriptures , men seem to have preference over women. Whether we think of Abraham entertaining the heavenly visitors (Gen 18:1-8), Mnason (Acts 21:16), Publius (Acts 28:7), Gaius (3 John 5,6), or Philemon, all are credited with this service. In the qualifications demanded for oversight, "given to hospitality" is included (1 Tim 3:2), but in the same epistle when mention is made of the widows who were entitled to support from the church, they too, are expected to have shown the same feature, as clearly implied by the words, "if she have lodged strangers" (1 Tim 5:10). The needs of the Lord Himself were met by women (Luke 8:2,3), and Paul accepted the invitation of Lydia to come into her house, so we must not exclude women from this important work (Acts 16:15).

There is ever the possibility of confusing the entertainment in the homes of the saints in our day with the hospitality mentioned in the Bible. The merits of the former are diminished by the fact that, when it is offered, there is often the hope in view that the guests will requite their hosts by inviting them to their home. In NT times the travelling strangers, who were to be sheltered, were often without either means or homes and could never repay their debt for kindness shown to them. Like Paul, some of them had "suffered the loss of all things", and would never have a fixed abode until heaven would be their portion.